TRAVAIL   FAMILLE   PATRIE

Bad Faith

A Forgotten History of
Family and Fatherland

Bad Faith

A Forgotten History of Family
and Fatherland

Carmen Callil

JONATHAN CAPE
LONDON

Published by Jonathan Cape 2006

10 9 8 7 6 5 4 3 2 1

Copyright © Carmen Callil 2006

First published in Great Britain in 2006 by
Jonathan Cape
Random House, 20 Vauxhall Bridge Road,
London SW1V 2SA

Random House Australia (Pty) Limited
20 Alfred Street, Milsons Point, Sydney,
New South Wales 2061, Australia

Random House New Zealand Limited
18 Poland Road, Glenfield,
Auckland 10, New Zealand

Random House (Pty) Limited
Isle of Houghton, Corner of Boundary Road & Carse O'Gowrie,
Houghton 2198, South Africa

The Random House Group Limited Reg. No. 954009
www.randomhouse.co.uk

A CIP catalogue record for this book is available from the British Library

ISBN 9780224078100 (from Jan 2007)
ISBN 0224078100

Papers used by Random House are natural, recyclable products made
from wood grown in sustainable forests; the manufacturing processes conform
to the environmental regulations of the country of origin

Designed by Peter Ward
Maps by ML Design
Typeset in Garamond by Palimpsest Book Production Limited, Polmont, Stirlingshire
Printed and bound in Germany by
GGP Media GmbH, Poessneck

For PBH

Contents

PART I
COBBLERS & CONVICTS

PART II
COCK & BULL

PART III
HITLER'S PARROT

List of Illustrations

ILLUSTRATIONS IN PLATES

1. The Darquier family in Cahors, *c.* 1906–7 (courtesy of Paulette Aupoix).

2. Postcard of the sons of the Mayor of Cahors, 1907 (© *Le Lot 1900–1902 Memoir d'hier* – De Boué).

3. Edouard Drumont, 1901 (© Collection Roger-Viollet).

4. Charles Maurras and Léon Daudet (© Collection Roger-Viollet).

5. The Marquis de Morès, 1896 (© Collection Roger-Viollet).

6. Anatole de Monzie, *c.* 1920.

7. Henry de Jouvenal, with his wife Colette and their daughter, *c.* 1920 (© Collection Roger-Viollet).

8. Louis Louis-Dreyfus, 1938 (© Archives du CDJC – Mémorial de la Shoah).

9. The Jones family, *c.* 1911 (© Queen Victoria Museum & Art Gallery, Launceston).

10. Australia as *Terre Napoléon*, 1811.

11. Cahors, Boulevard Gambetta, early twentieth century.

12. Launceston, Brisbane Street, early twentieth century (from *Launceston* © M. Simco and P. Jermy, 1997)

13. Jean, Pierre and Louis Darquier, *c.* 1915 (courtesy of Yvonne Lacaze).

14. An unidentified soldier from the same battalion as William Robert Jones (© Australian War Memorial).

15. Statement of a witness at the Court of Inquiry into the death of William Robert Jones (© National Archives of Australia).

16. Charles Workman, with his son Roy, *c.* 1905 (© V&A Images/ Victoria and Albert Museum).

17. Charles Workman as Ben Hashbaz in Gilbert and Sullivan's *The Grand Duke*, 1896 (© V&A Images/ Victoria and Albert Museum).

18. Louis and Myrtle, court case 32 at Marylebone Magistrates Court, 1930 (© The City of London, London Metropolitan Archives).

19. Anne, *c.* 1933 (courtesy of Alistair Rapley).

20. Anne with May Brice, *c.* 1936 (courtesy of Alistair Rapley).

21. Louis and Myrtle, London, 1931 (from *l'Express*, 14–20 February 1972).

22. The riots of 6 February 1934 (© Collection Roger-Viollet).

Shoah), SS Hauptsturmführer Dannecker (© Archives du CDJC – Mémorial de la Shoah), Otto Abetz (© Photos12.com/ Oasis).

42. Franco and Pétain, Montpelier, 1941 (© LAPI/ Roger-Viollet).

43. General Maxime Weygand, Paul Baudouin, Paul Reynaud and Marshal Pétain, May/June 1940 (© Sigma, London).

44. Cardinal Emmanuel Célestin Suhard, Cardinal Pierre-Marie Gerlier, with Marshal Pétain and Pierre Laval, 1942 (© LAPI/ Roger-Viollet).

45. The *2ème Régiment d'Infanterie Coloniale* marches past Marshal Pétain, Admiral Darlan, Pierre Laval and Louis Darquier, 1942 (© Médiathèque Municipale Valéry Larbaud/ Ville de Vichy).

46. The men of the second Vichy government, 1940 (© Getty Images/Hulton Archive).

47. General Charles de Gaulle 1940 (© AFP/Getty Images).

48. Jacques Doriot, 1944 (© Snark Archives/ Photos12.com/ Oasis).

49. Léon Degrelle with Pope John Paul II, 11 December 1991.

50. The *Métro* advertises Louis' l'Institut d'Etude des Questions Juives, *c.* 1942–43 (© Klarsfeld Collection).

51. Louis with Reinhard Heydrich and Helmut Knochen, 1942 (© Klarsfeld Collection).

52. Louis Darquier on his appointment as Commissioner for Jewish Affairs, 1942 (© Collection Roger-Viollet).

53. Xavier Vallat, 1941 (© Archives du CDJC – Mémorial de la Shoah).

54. Joseph Antignac (© Klarsfeld Collection).

55. Monseigneur Mayol de Lupé, 1944 (© LAPI/ Roger-Viollet).

56. René Bousquet with Karl-Albrecht Oberg, SS chief Helmut Knochen and Herbert-Martin Hagen (© Klarsfeld Collection).

57. François Mitterrand, dining with René Bousquet in 1974 (© M. Bidermanas/ ANA).

58. The Schloss Collection (© A. Vernay).

59. Nazi and French services oversee Jewish arrests (© Klarsfeld Collection).

60. Jewish men, women and children in Drancy concentration camp, 1942 (© Klarsfeld Collection).

61. Jewish women and children at Drancy on the same day (© Klarsfeld Collection).

62. Louis and Myrtle dining (© Archives du CDJC – Mémorial de la Shoah).

Every effort has been made to trace and contact copyright holders. The publishers will be pleased to correct any mistakes or omissions in future editions.

Abbreviations

———◄O►———

AF: Action Française, the movement. Newspaper: *Action française*

AJA: Association des Journalistes Antijuifs, Association of Anti-Jewish Journalists

CATC: Coopérative d'Approvisionnement, de Transport et de Crédit, Cooperative for Supply, Transport and Credit

CDP: Centre de Documentation et de Propagande, Centre for Information and Propaganda

CGQJ: Commissariat Général aux Questions Juives, the Commissariat for Jewish Affairs

ERR: Einsatzstab Reichsleiter Rosenberg, untranslatable, always called ERR. Alfred Rosenberg's plundering office. One of Rosenberg's official titles was Custodian of the Entire Intellectual, Spiritual, Training and Education of the Party and of all Coordinated Associations

Gestapo: Geheime Staatspolizei, secret state police or political police

LICA: Ligue Internationale Contre l'Antisémitisme, the International League Against Anti-Semitism, now called LICRA (Race has been added). Newspaper: *Le Droit de vivre, The Right to Live*

LVF: Légion des Volontaires Français, an idea of Jacques Doriot's but founded August 1941 by Marcel Déat with Deloncle as president. These were French units, wearing German uniforms, who fought for the Germans on the Russian front. Integrated into the SS Waffen Charlemagne in August 1944

MBF: Militärbefehlshaber in Frankreich, the military command of France, provided by the German army, the Wehrmacht

MSR: Mouvement Social Révolutionnaire, a Pétainist group founded by Eugène Deloncle, which provided most of the troops for the LVF

OAS: Organisation de l'Armée Secrète

PPF: Parti Populaire Français, fascist party of Jacques Doriot

PQJ: Police aux Questions Juives, Police for Jewish Affairs, of the CGQJ

RHSA: Reichssicherheitshauptamt, the Reich Central Security Office

SCAP: Service de Contrôle des Administrateurs Provisoires, Department of Provisional Administrators or Trustees (for Jewish enterprises)

SD: Sicherheitsdienst, intelligence service of the SS

SEC: Service d'Enquête et de Contrôle, Investigation and Inspection Service, and 'police' service of the CGQJ

SOL: Service d'Ordre Légionnaire, created by Joseph Darnand in 1941, a paramilitary elite devoted to the service of Pétain, later to become the Milice

SS: Sicherheitspolizei, SiPo, Security Police, which had various subsections, one of which was the Gestapo

STO: Service du Travail Obligatoire, Compulsory Labour Service

UGIF: Union Générale des Israélites de France, General Union of French Jews

Louis Darquier's Associations and Newspapers

Association des Blessés et Victimes du 6 Février: Association of the Wounded and the Victims of 6 February
Club National: National Club
Club Sportif des Ternes: Les Ternes Sports Club
Rassemblement Antijuif de France: Anti-Jewish Union of France
l'Antijuif: the Anti-Jew, sequel to the *Bulletin* of his Club National
La France enchaînée: *France in Chains*
Union Française: French Union
Cahiers Jaunes: the Yellow Notebooks
Les Vieilles Souches: Ancient Roots
UFDR: Union Française pour la Défense de la Race, French Union for the Defence of the Race
Chaire d'Ethnologie: Chair in Ethnology, at the Sorbonne
Chaire d'Histoire du Judaïsme: Chair in Jewish History, at the Sorbonne
Commission Scientifique pour l'Étude des Questions de Biologie Raciale: Scientific Commission for the Study of Racial Biology
IAS: Institut d'Anthropo-Sociologie, Institute of Anthropo-Sociology
IEQJ: Institut d'Étude des Questions Juives, Institute for the Study of Jewish Questions
IEQJER: Institut d'Étude des Questions Juives et Ethno-Raciales, Institute for the Study of Jewish and Ethno-Racial Questions

Historical Note

FRENCH REPUBLICS

Before the Occupation:
First Republic: 1792 to 1804, when Napoleon declared himself Emperor
Second Republic: 1848 to 1852
Third Republic: 4 September 1870 to 10 July 1940

After the Occupation:
Provisional Republican Government: 1944 to 1947
Fourth Republic: 1947 to 1959
Fifth Republic: 1959 to present

The Third Republic, brought to an end by parliamentary vote on 10 July 1940, was a two-chamber parliament with a president and a prime minister, called the Président du Conseil des Ministres.

The Chambre des Députés, today the Assemblée Nationale, equivalent to the British House of Commons, is the lower house of the French Parliament. Under the Third Republic it consisted of six hundred members elected by universal male suffrage every four years. Its official seat is the Palais Bourbon. The three hundred Sénateurs, the upper house of the French Parliament, were elected by mayors and councillors in *départements* throughout France. The Sénat sits in the Palais du Luxembourg.

Marshal Henri-Philippe Pétain, installed as head of l'État Français with full governing powers, was authorised to produce a new constitution. This was never done; instead, for the first time since the Revolution of 1789, France had no representative national body in the Vichy state. Pétain ruled through his personal entourage and his Council of Ministers until April 1942, when much of his authority, though not his position, passed to Pierre Laval.

French regions and departments have changed over the years. As of 2005, France is divided into twenty-six *régions* – twenty-two metropolitan and four overseas – and the *régions* are divided into a hundred *départements*. The state's representative in a *région* or *département* is called the *préfet*, his office the *préfecture*.

GERMAN OFFICES IN FRANCE

Heinrich Himmler was in charge of all police and security services for the Third Reich, including death camps. In 1943 he also became Minister of the Interior. The Geheime Staatspolizei (Gestapo) was the secret state police, founded in 1933 by Goering, then controlled by Heinrich Himmler and his deputy Reinhard Heydrich. The Reichssicherheitshauptamt (RHSA), the Reich Central Security Office, controlled by the Nazi Party, was created in 1939 through a merger of the Sicherheitsdienst, the SD, the Gestapo and the Kriminalpolizei. Himmler placed Reinhard Heydrich in charge of the RHSA. After Heydrich's death in May 1942 Ernst Kaltenbrunner replaced him. The RHSA comprised the Sicherheitsdienst (SD), the intelligence service of the SS; the Sicherheitspolizei (SS, SiPo), the security police, which had various subsections, one of which was the Geheime Staatspolizei (Gestapo), the secret state police or political police.[*] Within the RHSA was Eichmann's Office Section IV B4, which ran the Judenreferat, the Jewish Section of the SD. Later, the Abwehr, the intelligence service of the army, also came under the RHSA.

---

[*] In France – and elsewhere – most people used the word 'Gestapo' for all these branches of the RHSA, except for the Judenreferat. I have used 'SS' to include the Gestapo, but have often used the general word 'Gestapo'.

'To keep good and bad faith distinct costs a lot; it requires a decent sincerity and truthfulness with oneself, it demands a continuous intellectual and moral effort. How can such an effort be expected from men like Darquier?'

PRIMO LEVI, *The Drowned and the Saved*

The Darquier Family

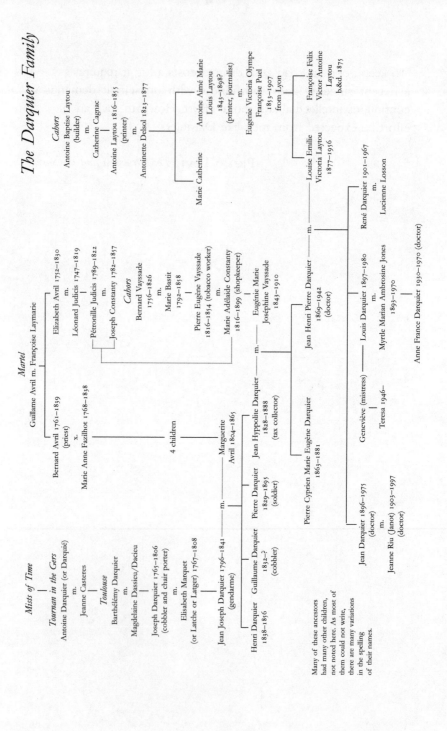

The Jones Family

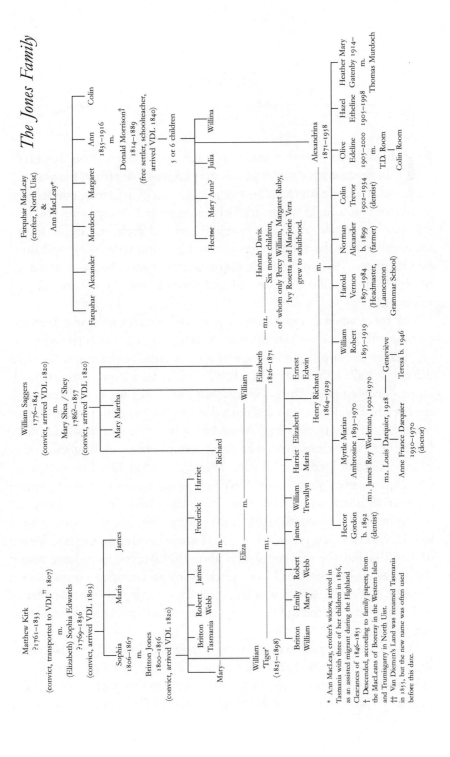

* Ann MacLeay, crofter's widow, arrived in Tasmania with three of her children in 1856, as an assisted migrant during the Highland Clearances of 1846–1855.

† Descended, according to family papers, from the MacLeans of Boreray in the Western Isles and Trumisgarry in North Uist.

†† Van Diemen's Land was renamed Tasmania in 1855, but the new name was often used before this date.

Prologue

———◁◦▷———

THERE ARE MANY THINGS to make one wretched on this earth. In my case my childhood was my purgatory, or rather, I saw myself as the Little Mermaid in Hans Andersen's fairy story, condemned to eternal suffering in return for becoming mortal. 'Every step you take will cause you pain all but unbearable – it will seem to you as if you were walking on the sharp edges of swords – and your blood will flow,' says the witch. And so the Little Mermaid, 'her heart filled with thoughts of death and annihilation, smiled and danced with the others, till past midnight'.

In 1960, when I was twenty-one, my adventures took me from the place where I was born, Melbourne, Australia, by way of ships and boats and planes to Europe, and then, a year or so later, to the day at the Villa d'Este on Lake Como, in Italy, when I swallowed a large bottle of inadequate sleeping pills. The good man who was with me at the time took me back to London and found me a doctor. The person carefully chosen for me, because she was half-Australian – not that you would know it, for all her thirty-three years had been spent entirely in England – was called Dr Anne Darquier, and she lived in London W1. For three days a week, for seven years, from 8 o'clock in the morning I would spend an hour with her, and I started to live in the world, like other people.

Anne Darquier was a doctor and a psychiatrist. She was born in 1930 in Old Windsor, just outside London. I knew her during the last decade of her life, and she told me stories about her Australian mother whom she never really knew, and her father, living in Europe – sometimes I thought in France, sometimes in Spain. Once she said matter-of-factly while speaking of them: 'There are some things and some people you can never forgive.'

One Monday, 7 September 1970, I rang the doorbell of Flat 38, 59 Weymouth Street. She had arranged the time, but there was no answer. Later that day, someone rang to tell me that Anne Darquier was dead. Ten days later I went to her funeral at Golders Green Crematorium, and there

I found that she had another name: she was to be buried as Anne Darquier de Pellepoix. This was odd, but it would have remained only an oddity had I not, by chance, watched a documentary on television a year or so later: Marcel Ophuls' *Le Chagrin et la pitié* – *The Sorrow and the Pity: The Story of a French Town in the Occupation*. As I read the English subtitles I saw Anne's full surname again, attached to one of the officials of the Vichy government, trotting up to Reinhard Heydrich, the head of the Reich Central Security Office, to shake his hand respectfully.

Who was this man? Eventually, Anne's birth certificate told me. The Vichy official, Louis Darquier de Pellepoix, was her father. Everything I had learned about Anne in the years I knew her – little, but enough – seemed to be shrouded in silence, buried beneath injustices to her which I sensed but could not comprehend. I had thought she was a child of the war, motherless and fatherless, like millions of others of her generation. In the decades that followed Anne's death, delving into archives and documents and bothering people in France, Spain, Germany, Australia, England, I became an expert on the lies and secrecy and the silence to which Anne felt condemned.

Louis Darquier and Myrtle Jones, Anne's mother, were both arch-confabulators, and those who knew them, or met them, often wished that they had not, and for good reason were wary of my interest. So it would not be true to say that everything I have discovered is the only truth, or that I have not speculated; but when I have, my speculation stems from extensive research and considered analysis. I started with Anne's story, which as the years went by became that of her parents, and of Europe at war.

I searched for Louis Darquier in histories of France of the Second World War. And I found him – always given his entirely fictitious name of Darquier de Pellepoix. He had been Commissaire Général aux Questions Juives, Commissioner for Jewish Affairs, in Vichy France, and was known as the French Eichmann.[1] When I began this quest Darquier was still alive, living in Madrid, happily ensconced in Franco's Spain, though I did not know this.

Anne's story began on 19 April 1928 when Louis Darquier, the second child of a provincial doctor and his wife in Cahors, in south-west France, married Myrtle Marian Ambrosine Jones, second child of an Australian grazier and his wife from the township of Carrick, eleven miles outside Launceston, in the north of Tasmania.

Louis Darquier was often described as a handsome fellow. By 1928 he had acquired the English uniform immortalised by P.G. Wodehouse: a monocle and cane, the former worn ostensibly for his far-sightedness, and never left at home even when his clothes were in tatters. He was five foot ten, but seemed taller. He had a huge head, and in photographs he always looks solid and juts his jaw forward or stands erect, flourishing himself at the camera. His eyes were browny green, and his other distinguishing marks were those of a boy and man used to punch-ups: a scar above his left eyebrow and a slightly flattened nose.

Louis resembled his father, and passed on to Anne the Darquier shape of face, his pale skin and straight hair. As is so often the case with married couples, Myrtle slightly resembled her husband, so that when you looked at Anne, the eyes and mouth of her mother, shared by Myrtle's three sisters and five brothers, stared out of her Darquier face. Myrtle Jones was not a beautiful woman. When Louis first met her the best he could say of her was that 'she is not ugly'. But what he added revealed that he had met his soulmate. Myrtle Jones, as formidable a fantasist as Louis himself, was, he told his brother René, 'that kind of agreeable woman who has a keen sense of reality'.

On their marriage certificate, Louis Darquier gave his age as thirty years, as indeed he was. Myrtle gave hers as twenty-six, whereas she was in fact thirty-five, and described herself as a spinster, which indeed she was not. In Sydney in 1923 she had married for the first time under the name of Sandra Lindsay. It is a national Australian characteristic to abbreviate names. Had Louis Darquier himself lived in Australia for any length of time – as he so often, and so falsely, claimed to have done – he would certainly have been known as Lew. Myrtle carried this habit for life. In Australia she was Aunty Myrt, in public she was Sandra, but in private, throughout the multifarious reincarnations of her life in Europe, she called herself 'San' except when someone was after her – creditors, passport officials, functionaries of that kind. On those occasions she had to use her given name, Myrtle Jones, Myrtle Marian Ambrosine Jones. In this book she is Myrtle.

During the years I knew Anne, from 1963 until 1970, she often mentioned that she had been abandoned by her parents when she was a baby and had been brought up by a nanny in an English village, in considerable poverty. In 1963 Anne was in her thirties, eight years older than I. She had a gentle, round face, her skin was very white, very English, and her voice was very English too. But nothing else about her was. Her body in particular seemed to belong nowhere; she had a sense of imminent departure about her, even when she gave you her closest attention, which she always did. She stooped, and her straight brown hair stooped with her – she was always pushing it back with one hand. Her shoulders were rounded, bowed almost, and her very French legs went all over the place. She could not sit on a chair without tucking them up underneath her as though she was packing them away. Her face was not happy, but it was not sad either: it was wary and alert and concentrated. She laughed, and she could be angry. She told me secrets she should have kept to herself, but had she not, I could never have begun the search for the truth about her. She sent me on my way with many clues.

I discovered that her story was not her own, but a keyhole into the dark years of civil war in France and of the victory of one faction during the Vichy years. Anne's story spread over continents, from France, the land of her father, to Australia, the land of her mother, to Germany and Spain, and to Britain – which gave her, as it gave so many at that time, what luck in life she had.

As Commissioner for Jewish Affairs, Anne's father was the longest-serving official of the Vichy state appointed to deal with the elimination and despoliation of the Jews of France. Before the war, Louis Darquier had been a leading French anti-Semite, funded by the Nazi Party. From 1935 to 1944 he held public appointments and ran private organisations through which he campaigned for the expulsion or massacre of the Jews of France. Both the French police and the Nazis considered him as a top man in his field. He was a professional who used Jews as a way of making a living. More than that, he was a con man, one who was in his turn used by the Vichy state and the German occupiers as their puppet.

For Vichy, as Commissioner for Jewish Affairs from May 1942 to February 1944, Louis Darquier controlled a staff of over a thousand and a police force which terrorised both Jew and Gentile. In July 1942 he was placed in charge of the notorious Vel' d'Hiv' round-up in Paris, which despatched nearly thirteen thousand Jews to death camps – almost a third of them were children. Though an idle man, he worked tirelessly to provide more Jews for deportation. He introduced the yellow star and took life-and-death decisions over the fate of the Jews of France. Most of those who died in Auschwitz were sent there during Louis Darquier's tenure. Almost all of the 11,400 children were sent there in his time. Most of them did not survive. Above all, he used the persecution of Jews to make money for himself and his cronies – through corruption, despoliation, looting and bribery. What energy remained to a man who loved high living was expended on propaganda efforts to achieve more of the same.

After the end of the German occupation of France in 1944, in the *épuration*, the purge, which followed, a man was lynched by a mob in Limoges or Brive – reports differ – in the belief that he was 'Darquier de Pellepoix'. But they got the wrong man.

In a letter in 1975, a Madame Laurens, a native of Cahors who had known the Darquier family when Louis and his brothers were children, wrote: 'What is interesting to us is the name he added himself – "De Pellepoix" – God knows why, out of pride I suppose. As a young man he was, they say, troubled and unstable, a spendthrift, always at odds with his parents.'

But where did he come from? What made him what he was?

I

COBBLERS
&
CONVICTS

1

The Priest's Children

CAHORS, IN SOUTH-WEST FRANCE, the Darquiers' native town, is built on a loop in the River Lot, and boasts monuments and buildings, bridges and churches of great beauty, strong red wine, plump geese and famous sons, one of whom was the great hero of the Third Republic, Léon Gambetta, after whom the main boulevard and the ancient school of Cahors are named. It is an amiable, sturdy, provincial place, with the windy beauty of so many southern French towns, dominated by its perfect medieval Pont Valentré and its Romanesque fortress of a cathedral, the massive Cathédrale de St-Étienne. Cahors was the capital of the ancient region of Quercy, whose many rivers cut through great valleys and hills, patched with limestone plateaux, grottos and cascades. In medieval times Cahors was a flourishing city of great bankers who funded the popes and kings, but up to the Wars of Religion in the sixteenth century Quercy was also an explosive region of great violence, one explanation perhaps for the cautious politics of its citizens – *Cadurciens* – in the centuries that followed.

Quercy reflected an important fissure in the French body politic, in the rivalry that existed between Cahors – fiercely Catholic during the Wars of Religion, when its leaders massacred the Protestants of the town – and its southern neighbour, the more prosperous town of Montauban, a Protestant stronghold. But under Napoleon Cahors became the administrative centre of the new department of the Lot, Montauban of the Tarn-et-Garonne. (The rivalry continued: when the Vichy state came to power in 1940, and wanted to work with the Nazis to control its Jewish population, the two Frenchmen who managed much of this process were Louis Darquier of Cahors, Commissioner for Jewish Affairs, and René Bousquet of Montauban, Secretary-General for the Police.)

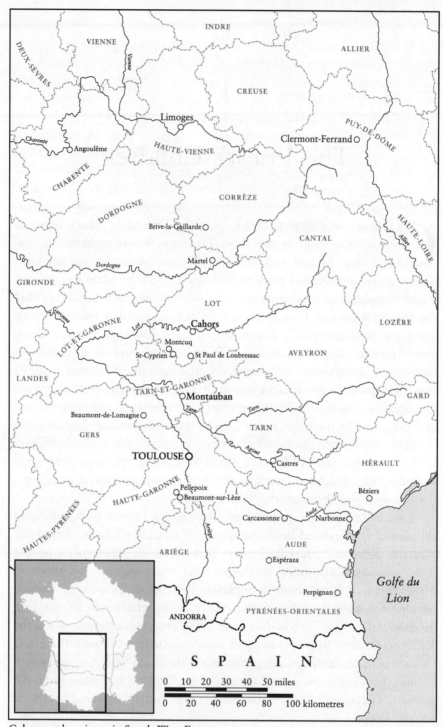

Cahors and environs in South-West France

In the late nineteenth century the Lot was a poor agricultural department, covered with vineyards large and small, a place where 'notables' – the elite bourgeoisie – reigned supreme, looking after a rural community who worked a hard land. The Lot was modestly revolutionary after 1789, restively Napoleonic under Napoleon, imperially Bonapartiste in the time of Louis Napoleon, warily republican after 1870. By 1890 the department had become solidly republican, and remained thus ever afterwards. Isolated from the political sophistications and turmoils of Paris, the Lot turned its face towards Toulouse, a hundred kilometres or so to the south.

The *Lotois* were conformists, but they were individualists and pragmatists. The scandalised clergy of the Lot watched as their congregations went to Mass on Sundays and holidays, while regularly voting for the godless republic and indulging in the 'murderous practice' of birth control for the rest of the week. The Lot stood out in the south-west for this singularity: nearby Aveyron remained fervently Catholic; other neighbouring regions veered to the left and distanced themselves from the Church. In Cahors '*On allait à l'église mais on votait à gauche*';[1] they went to church but they voted for the left – piety on Sundays and holy days, anticlerical the rest of the week. The Lot remained faithful to both republic and Church, on its own terms. But in 1877 the vineyards which provided so much of its prosperity were destroyed by phylloxera, and so began a long decline, as the *Lotois* left to find work in the cities.

———————————— ❧ ————————————

For the first half of his life Louis Darquier's father, Pierre, was a fortunate man. He was born at a propitious time, he married a wealthy wife who loved him, and he had three handsome and intelligent sons, and at least one other child born out of wedlock. He was a good doctor, and almost everyone who knew him spoke well of him and remembered him fondly. Born in 1869, he was only a year old when the last of the French emperors, Louis Napoleon, Napoleon III, made the mistake of attacking Prussia in 1870. The Franco-Prussian war ended in the defeat of France and the bloody suppression of the Paris Commune in 1871, and it was also the end of all kings and emperors in France. The Third Republic, proclaimed in 1870, was to last until 1940, almost the entire lifetime of Pierre Darquier.

The origins of the Darquier family were extremely modest. Louis

Darquier always varied his claims to nobility, adding and subtracting claims to aristocratic, Gascon or French Celtic blood as the whim took him. His obsession with pure French blood flowing from French soil is genuine, however: most of his ancestors, the dregs of the earth for centuries, are buried in the small towns of the Lot. They were poor, and many were both illegitimate and illiterate.

Pierre Darquier was born on 23 January 1869 at number 10, rue du Tapis Vert, the street of the green carpet, one of the medieval *ruelles* which cluster around the Cathédrale de St-Étienne. This was the house of his maternal great-grandmother, and generations of his family had been born and lived there. Pierre's grandfather, Pierre Eugène Vayssade, a tobacco worker in Cahors, had died there at the age of thirty-eight. His widow, Marie Adélaide Constanty, supported herself and their only child Eugénie, born in 1843, by working with her mother-in-law in the family's grocery shop, which served the clergy of the cathedral nearby; it is still there on the angle of rue Nationale and place Chapou, and was worked by the family until 1907.[2]

Pierre's father Jean often helped his wife Eugénie and his mother-in-law at the counter, and Pierre grew up between shop and home, with his parents and grandmother, fluent in the local *patois*, a variant of Occitan, *la langue d'Oc*, the language of the Languedoc. After a lifetime's work, Louis' great-grandmother, when she died, had nothing to leave.

About ninety kilometres to the north of Cahors lies the medieval town of Martel, where a large number of Pierre's paternal ancestors were born, all carefully chronicled in the records of Church and state. His great-grandfather, Bernard Avril, was a priest working in the Dordogne when he authorised the marriage of his daughter Marguerite in 1827, and agreed to provide her with an annual dowry of 'wheat, half a pig, two pairs of conserved geese and twelve kilograms of nut oil'.[3] Marguerite was twenty-three when she married Jean Joseph Darquier, a policeman from Toulouse, where his father Joseph was a cobbler and chair porter. It is necessary to be precise about these persons and dates, because it is this unfortunate Marguerite Avril who was used to give Louis Darquier his erroneous claims to nobility. Marguerite had four children, all boys, all born in Martel, before her husband Jean died at his barracks at the age of forty-five. Their first son, Jean the younger, was born in 1828, and it was he who initiated the social rise of the Darquier clan when he took up the lucrative post of tax collector.

On 25 August 1862, when he was thirty-four, Jean the tax collector married his relative Eugénie Vayssade by special dispensation, for Eugénie was also related to the fecund Father Avril. The nineteen-year-old Eugénie took her husband to live in her mother's house in rue du Tapis Vert. There were two sons of this marriage, both called Pierre, but only the second, christened Jean Henri Pierre, survived to inherit all the considerable worldly goods garnered by his father, who died when Pierre was nineteen. Louis' paternal grandfather the tax collector left shops in Cahors earning rent, other houses, furniture worth over twenty thousand francs, as well as letters of credit, savings, buildings, land and vineyards at Montcuq and St-Cyprien, near Cahors.

Pierre was now a wealthy young man. He turned twenty-one just as the *belle époque* ushered in the joys, both frivolous and practical, of those legendary pre-war decades. As a medical student in Paris from 1888 to 1893 he and his elder brother, who died there at the age of eighteen, were the first Darquiers to savour the full glories of the Parisian *vie bohème*. Three years later, in 1896, he married an even wealthier young woman.

Louis Darquier's mother, Louise, was a class above Pierre Darquier, but in fact her family's prosperity was only one generation older than that of her husband. The Laytou family had lived in Cahors for generations, and Louise's grandfather made their fortune with his printing works and the newspaper he founded in 1861, the *Journal du Lot*. His son inherited the business, and his daughter Louise Emilie Victoria was born on 11 April 1877. Like Pierre Darquier her only sibling, a brother, also died, so she alone inherited all the wealth and property of her printing family.

Cahors was a bustling provincial city of some twenty thousand persons in January 1896, when Pierre and Louise married. He was almost twenty-seven, she eighteen; they honeymooned in Paris, Nice and Marseille. By then he had completed his medical studies in Paris at the time of the great French medical teacher and neurologist Jean-Martin Charcot.[4] Pierre's thesis, which qualified him as a doctor, was on the subject of one of Charcot's neurological discoveries. Pierre seems to have taken the best from Charcot, unaffected by the latter's theories of racial inheritance, and he was often described as a gifted practician, always as a kindly one. Louise Laytou brought wealth to her marriage, and was thought to have married beneath her, but in return Pierre Darquier's profession qualified him to become one of the leading notables of Cahors and the Lot.

Pierre was blue-eyed and not tall – Louise was taller than he – and had inherited the tendency to corpulence of his mother and grandmother. When young he was a handsome fellow with brown curls and a round, cheerful face, the shape of which, if not the temperament it expressed, was passed on to his second son Louis, his granddaughter Anne and many of his other grandchildren. He had a rather feminine voice, wore the formal clothes of the time – bowler hat in winter, frock-coat, necktie, a boater in summer – and a handsome handlebar moustache at all times. His personal appearance, however, does not explain his success with the opposite sex.

Pierre cherished his wife, but he was a creature of his time, as addicted to dalliance as was Marshal Pétain, thirteen years his senior but a product of the same sexual mores. Pierre was a jolly man, self-indulgent, a typical 'hearty bourgeois of the period, a woman-chaser, and a doctor in his spare time'. He was 'big and solid, cordial and joyous, much loved in Cahors', and was often spotted, braces flying, returning home at the crack of dawn. One early morning a worker called after him, 'Hey, Doctor, do you take your trousers off to examine your patients?' But this shocked no one in those days, least of all Louise. Her 'real Don Juan . . . has the charm of a Marquis', she would say with pride. 'One must know when to shut one's eyes.'[5]

Louise Darquier was beautiful when young, and remained so all her life. She was attended by the consideration such women are accustomed to receive, but this was not, in her case, always accompanied by much affection. Louise was 'impeccable', with *l'air presque aristocratique* – an almost aristocratic air. To some she seemed warm and lovable, to others she gushed and fluttered. Some who worked for her loved her for her kindness and affection, others regarded it as mannered patronage. Family recollections describe her as remarkably stupid, and acquaintances are not much kinder – she was 'very proud', 'very spoiled, very old France, very beautiful', 'with a high, studied voice, given to little exclamations'.[6] Everything about her was exquisite, her clothes, her hats, her considerable collection of jewellery, her carefully coiffed fair hair. Even her handkerchiefs, delicately embroidered by herself, were the envy of the women of Cahors.

Louise enjoyed ill health, feminine maladies and exercising Christian charity towards the unfortunate. She took the waters at Vichy, read poetry, wrote to her women friends, stitched and embroidered beautifully – for herself, for the church, for family and friends – and trained her maids and poor relations to look after her properly. Her letters – outpourings of domestic fuss and bother, alternating wheedling requests with woes plaintively enumerated – throb with her anxious hold on social position. She bequeathed her habitual note of lamentation to Louis, together with her pretension to social grandeur. Louis spent much of his adult life complaining that his parents did not support him, did not help him financially as they did his brothers, and when the time came, during the Occupation, that he could support himself, he made the same complaints about Pétain and the mandarins of Vichy.

Louise was what they called '*une punaise de sacristie*', a churchy woman. The French Church had been in a state of recurrent war with the anti-clerical republic since the Revolution – it was Gambetta who had said in 1877 that '*Le cléricalisme, c'est l'ennemi!*'[7] The Darquier marriage perfectly encapsulated this French duality. Educated at the convent of Les Dames de Nevers in Cahors, Louise went to Mass every Sunday and often during the week, while Pierre confined his attendances to weddings and funerals. Louise Darquier embodied every reason why French women were not to receive the vote until 1944.

In the early years of the Darquier marriage the struggle between the French Church and the republican government reached its climax over the Dreyfus affair and the control of education.[8] The outcome was the separation of Church and state in 1905, the removal of education from clerical hands and the expulsion from France of a number of religious orders. The republic, ruled by governments of the Radical Party, formed in 1901 and representative of the politics of the provinces and the *petite bourgeoisie*, thus won its major victory over the Catholic Church in France.

The men who represented the Lot politically, at both national and local level, were almost always lawyers and doctors, rarely the nobility, and of these doctors were always the most numerous. Pierre Darquier had wealth, the right profession, family connections and a family newspaper. He joined the Radical Party and proceeded in the classic manner: first mayor, then councillor for the department – after that would follow Paris, and national politics.

His party, which would be dominant in French politics until the Second

World War, was by no means radical in the British sense of the word. It was a centrist party, republican, anti-clerical, but moderate – like the Whigs in England. The Radical Party was an umbrella group of many different opinions and cliques, tolerant of considerable dissent. In the Lot, Radicals often belonged to the Radical-Socialist wing of the party, the use of the word 'socialist' being even more baffling to Anglo-Saxon ears, for these politicians ran the Lot like a private business. The ruling Radicals were progressive but fatherly, almost feudal men of position and profession, manipulators of influence and patronage and accustomed to being obeyed.

To its numerous enemies on the right, being a member of the Radical Party was synonymous with being a Freemason, and thus hostile to the power of the Catholic Church. However, while there were two Masonic lodges in Cahors at that time, mysterious and fearful places to the local Catholic children, in the rural world of the Lot its notables were neither markedly anticlerical, nor Masonic. 'They believe in man, I believe in God,' was a typical *Lotois* attitude towards Masonic practices. Pierre Darquier had been raised by pious Catholic women – his wife described him as 'a Christian, but not a martyr' – and was neither a Mason nor a man of the left. 'In the Lot, everyone was Radical Socialist . . . It was a party which veered more to the right than the left,' a party that 'respected a certain hierarchy, at any rate a hierarchy which favoured themselves'.[9] When France fell in 1940, all the deputies of the Lot, socialist, Radical Socialist, Radical republican and otherwise, brought an end to the Third Republic by voting full autocratic powers to Marshal Pétain.

The Darquiers' first child, Jean, was born eleven months after their marriage, on 12 December 1896. Twelve months later, Pierre Darquier had moved his family into the handsome Laytou family house at 34, rue du Lycée in Cahors (now 394, rue Président Wilson). Pierre and Louise raised their three sons in the house, linked by a beautiful garden to the massive Laytou family printing works behind it. Here, on 19 December 1897, Louis Darquier was born.

Louise Darquier had greeted the news that she was pregnant again while still weaning her firstborn with the usual gloom of women under these circumstances. Louis leapt out of his mother's womb at six and a half months, almost a miscarriage. 'I cried the very first day I knew of his existence and I will weep for him until the last day of my life,' she would bemoan in later years, as she listed the troubles he had caused her mother's heart.[10]

Louis grew up securely entrenched in the fortunate classes of the town; not for him the labour in the vineyards and fields of tobacco, or the shops and barracks of his ancestors. Of the three Darquier sons – the baby, René, was born in 1901 – Louis turned out to be the classic middle child, always scrabbling for attention, a problem from the day he was born. Physically, Jean and René resembled their mother, while Louis, though taller, strongly resembled his father. Pierre was as authoritarian a father as were all Galsworthian men of property of his time. Children did not speak until spoken to, never before the *plat principal* at meals, and did as they were told. Louise loved her namesake son, but he was permanently at odds with his father.

In 1906 when Louis was eight and his father thirty-seven, Pierre was elected mayor of Cahors, the only mayor ever to be elected on the first ballot. His acceptance speech gives the flavour of the man: 'All my actions will be inspired by the fine ideal of liberty, equality and fraternity, and of the social solidarity which constitutes the strength, the honour and the glory of our Republic.' The family newspaper, the *Journal du Lot*, described him then as 'a steadfast friend, devoted, selfless', a man to whom 'hatred, rancour, jealousy' were unknown. 'His openness and loyalty are as well known as his great goodness.'

Louise now became the first lady of Cahors. She entertained a great deal and in considerable style, maintained two maids, a cook and a German chambermaid, and the family holidayed each year by the sea and in the mountains. Pierre Darquier had a good practice, but the Lot was poor and Pierre kind: his patients often paid him with 'skinny chickens and old eggs'. As the years went on, a German and an English governess were added to educate the boys, and a chauffeur to drive Pierre's motorcar, acquired by 1910, which he used to visit his patients, to the astonishment and joy of the inhabitants of Cahors and its environs. Both Louis and René spoke English and German exceptionally well.

The boys were sent to school across the road, to the Lycée Gambetta, where Pierre himself had been educated more than twenty years before. Like all French schools after the Separation Law of 1905, the Lycée was not religious. Children of political antagonists, right and left – the *noirs* and the *rouges* – were taught together. Catholic children, like Louis Darquier, were instructed in their catechism by a chaplain; the children of socialists, Freemasons, atheists and others were left in peace. All of them marched and sang the '*Marseillaise*' together. The curriculum of the time was a preparation for war. Young men were raised in the spirit of *Revanche*, revenge for the Prussian defeat of 1870 and the German appropriation of Alsace-Lorraine. Throughout their childhood, German family employees notwithstanding, Louis and his brothers were brought up under the shadow and the threat of Germany.

At school the boys were securely uniformed in cap or beret, stiff collar and flowing tie, learned shooting and fencing, were rigorously educated in patriotism, high culture and sport, and trained to be good sons of France. Their teachers matched their formality in dress coats, starched collars, top hats or bowler hats, and often sported the monocles and canes Louis was to adopt as his adult insignia in the 1920s. There is a photograph of the three Darquier boys fencing at school in 1907. René, only six, is heroically feinting his elder brother, while Louis' arrogant little face stares proudly at the camera. All three were handsome, intelligent and self-confident, and were dressed elegantly; their schoolmates, by contrast, look like Richmal Crompton's William, a *Cadurcien* collection of rapscallions.

In Cahors those who knew Louise Darquier were unanimous that she was excessively ambitious for her sons. Jean had the fine physique of his mother, but Louis was a '*fort cailloux*', a hard nut, 'no Gary Cooper', but he grew into 'a good-looking man, strong, broad-shouldered like a good rugger player'.[11] The more delicate, more sophisticated Jean was to become an elegant man, artistic, poetic, and musical. René was unlike his elder brothers, shorter than both, as spirited, but more reserved and serious. Though the youngest, he seems very early to have become the father of the family.

Jean and Louis started school together when they were seven and six respectively, and were immediately the best pupils in their class. When René joined them in 1905, only four years old, he performed equally well: until 1914 the brothers jostled to bring home the most honours and prizes. Their parents rewarded them with five francs for achieving first place in class, three francs for second; but the boys had to pay back five francs if they came third, or worse.

Louis was baptised at the cathedral in Cahors when he was a month old. His fabrications about his life begin here. He always claimed that his godfather was Pierre's close friend, the crippled advocate, dubious parliamentarian and future quasi-collaborator Anatole de Monzie, whereas in fact Louise's uncle filled this role. In 1909 Pierre wanted to stand for election as deputy for the Lot, but gave way so that de Monzie could stand as the sole republican candidate. The department became de Monzie's fiefdom for more than thirty years. Mayor of Cahors from 1919 to 1942, between 1909 and 1942 he also reigned variously as councillor, president of council, deputy and senator for the department. De Monzie was a wheeler and dealer, a power-broker with a finger in every pie of social and political life in the Third Republic. He was, tenuously, a Radical Socialist, but his political ideas and practices were his own. He was either a man without principle or an independent spirit, a pontificating fixer who conquered the world with his charm and intelligence.

After a pushchair accident as a baby, de Monzie limped all his life; he was physically deformed and formidably ugly. His vast bald head, with a protuberance which he covered with a Basque beret, was compared by Colette to 'an unassuming Japanese volcano'; nevertheless, 'you could not be in his presence without falling under his charm: he was very brilliant, very gentle, he talked so well. He was also absolutely immoral.'[12]

De Monzie mixed enthusiastically in the Parisian intellectual salons of the time; he wrote and published voluminously, and was in charge of the committee of the French Encyclopaedia, '*l'Encyclopédie Monzie*'. Closely linked to the world of big business, industry and banking, he wove all these threads into a political life which was above all apolitical. He seems scarcely to have believed in the republic he served for so many years. He dealt with Mussolini, corresponded with Trotsky, but in his involvement in European politics, particularly with Russia and Italy, neither communism nor fascism mattered to him. The British assessed him, correctly, as a 'scintillating but corrupt figure'.[13]

If Pierre Darquier was an enthusiastic woman-chaser, de Monzie, described as 'one of France's greatest *cocottes*',[14] was more than enthusiastic. Half a century later people in Cahors still talk about his *baisodrome*, a special little house he is said to have kept on the outskirts of the village for his sexual encounters with the local girls. 'He kept nude women in his château,' one gossip recalled. 'The priest couldn't say anything because de Monzie gave him money not to.'[15]

Louis' later habit of equally indiscriminate copulation perhaps contributed to de Monzie's fondness for him, and they also shared the instability noted mildly in de Monzie, rampant in his protégé. De Monzie liked to be surrounded by handsome youths, and he was much in evidence as guide and protector to the young men of the Lot. For Louis Darquier he became *éminence grise* and alternative father, and as patron, role model and saviour he provided dangerous tolerance of Louis' singularities.

Louis' troubles with his father never ceased. 'He is not my father,' Louis used to say of Pierre, 'he is a wolf.' Pierre Darquier was a strong man, given to violent tempers, a trait he passed on to his second son. Because of the tension between them, in 1909 Louis was sent across the street to board at the Lycée, but he was home again the following year, for at school his vehement personality and unpredictable temper, and his inability to fit in with teachers or fellow pupils, were all too obvious. In his last year at school, 1913–14, Louis was doing his baccalaureate in mathematics, but also won a prize for English, in the form of a visit to England. The outbreak of war in August 1914 seems to have put paid to this, as it ended most things for the Darquier family.

The photographs of Louis as a child show the man he was to become: he stares straight ahead, reckless, with a bold and impudent eye. The descriptions given by those who knew him as a young man are much the same as those of his Vichy colleagues: 'You must understand that Louis Darquier was a phenomenon ... proud, pretentious ... a swelled head, a gambler, a gadabout, an idler.'[16] Although his mother's fluttering influence was obvious, no *Cadurciens* blamed his parents or his education for the man Louis Darquier became. 'It was rather the atmosphere of the time, when anti-Semitism was normal and in no way shocking ... it was the norm, the result of the anti-Semitism of reaction'[17] – reaction to the republic and its values.

<hr />

Louis Darquier's anti-Semitism flowered under the influence of a particular French tradition, imbedded in a dark side of the Catholic Church. The anti-Semitism of the Catholic Church is still a touchy subject, but in recent years the taboo surrounding its consequences has been broken and apologised for, by both the late Pope John Paul II, in uneasily vague terms, and by the prelates of France most specifically.

Anti-Semitism has always been an integral part of Catholic instruction, based on the view that the Jews murdered Christ, always ignoring, and in some extreme cases denying, that Christ himself was a Jew. France, the eldest daughter of the Church, has sometimes distinguished itself by

a tentatively independent, rational, not to say occasionally snappish, attitude towards its Vatican parent; indeed by 1914 only a quarter of French
Catholics practised their religion.

The Lot had no more than fifteen Jewish families before 1940, and
Cahors was not openly anti-Semitic, at least until the decades of the
Dreyfus affair. 'I am not what you would call an anti-Semite "by tradition",' wrote Louis in 1938. 'To tell the truth, I knew absolutely nothing
about Jews until I became an adult. My father, a Dreyfusard and Radical
mayor of a small provincial capital, was imbued with egalitarian and
humanitarian ideals, and as we only had one Jew in the entire town (he
was a little haberdasher who wore a fur hat in winter), he could not cause
any trouble.'[18] In 1978 however, he contradicted himself: 'In Cahors we
have never liked Jews . . . An ancient tradition.'[19]

The Dreyfus case was the dominant event in French public life during
Louis' childhood, a bitter crisis which polarised further a country of
intransigent political and religious differences. The affair erupted in 1894,
when an obscure Jewish army officer, Alfred Dreyfus, was wrongly
accused of selling national secrets to Germany, and after a secret court
martial was shipped by the army to life imprisonment on Devil's Island,
in French Guyana. The case almost led to civil war, as those who rightly
defended his innocence – Dreyfus was framed – fought the army and
the Church. The furore dragged on for twelve years, and the acrimony
for much longer, pervading the atmosphere in which Louis Darquier and
his Vichy compatriots grew up.

After Dreyfus, anti-Semitism became a 'known thing' amongst the
Catholic bourgeoisie. The Jew was created by God to act the traitor everywhere, 'to fight the religion of Jesus Christ and to dominate the world
by the power of money.'[20] Abuse like this was unceasing in the violently
un-Christian polemics of certain Catholic newspapers, such as the popular
Le Pèlerin and the daily paper of the Assumptionist order, *La Croix*, which
happily claimed to be 'the most anti-Jewish newspaper in France'. In the
years of Louis' childhood these papers, with vast circulations, issued
instructions in language of vitriolic hatred to 'Black France' – the Catholic
faithful – many of them, like Louise Darquier, members of the upper
bourgeoisie. In the catechism used by the chaplain at the Lycée Gambetta
– and in Catholic institutions worldwide throughout the centuries –
Catholic propaganda shaped 'the Conversion of the Jews' into a subject
for childhood prayer. '*Oremus*' – 'Let us pray for the perfidious Jew.'

In Cahors, the priests at the cathedral were so bitterly divided during those years that 'in the courtyard of the seminary, there was one part of it called "The Royal Walk", frequented by those who were rather Action Française, and the democrats had another section of the courtyard, but they never mixed'.[21] After the Dreyfus case, however, 'The Church in Cahors was anti-Semitic.'[22] The practising Catholics of Cahors usually went to 11 o'clock Mass on Sundays at the cathedral. While *hoi polloi* gathered in the body of the church, the wealthy Catholic notables of the town, Louise Darquier among them, in descending order of importance, paid for pews near the stalls of the clergy.

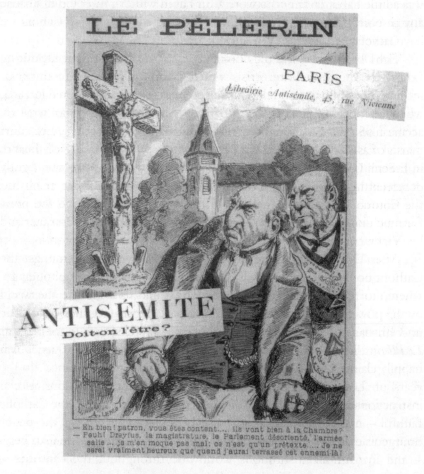

The Catholic journal, *Le Pèlerin*, 3 January 1898 (© Archives du CDJC – Mémorial de la Shoah).

Every week from 1897, the year of Louis' birth, the Catholic weekly of the Lot, *La Défense*, as virulent as *La Croix* and *Le Pèlerin*, was sold to devout parishioners after Mass, delivering the Church's instructions both political and spiritual. This was a successful weekly newspaper, its circulation, thirteen thousand, equal to that of the thrice-weekly paper of Louis' grandfather, the *Journal du Lot*. The faithful were directed to oppose the republic and all its institutions, to disapprove of socialism, and to be tolerant of parties and leagues of the extreme right. Strikes were the 'insupportable tyranny of a group of irresponsibles',[23] irreligious school textbooks were denounced as 'abominably doctored and distorted'.[24] These messages continued through the decades. 'We must bring an end to the corruption of the race,' *La Défense* announced in August 1940.

Catholic France was by no means the only source of the anti-Semitism of Vichy France, or of Louis Darquier; it had its own, French, philosophers. The Catholic Count Joseph Arthur de Gobineau in the mid-nineteenth century, friend of Wagner and a potent influence on Nietzsche and Hitler, was one such. Maurice Barrès, nationalist and populist orator at the turn of the century, who bequeathed to his followers a profound sense of decadence and decay, was another. But the father of French anti-Semitism was Édouard Drumont,[25] who, with the help of the famous nineteenth-century novelist and republican Alphonse Daudet, published his notorious book *La France Juive* in 1886, and whose *La Libre parole* became one of the most influential daily newspapers of the 1890s.[26]

Drumont was a representative of Catholic anti-Semitism at its most un-Christian. He divided his Catholic world into pure and heroic Aryans, and impure and scheming Talmudic Semites. His bestseller popularised the notion that Jews controlled French banks, property, universities, letters, theatre, press, media, prostitution – that in fact they controlled everything, and that France was now an enslaved nation in their thrall. Drumont linked Jews and Freemasons together, and his influence was at its apogee during the Dreyfus affair in the 1890s.

Temperamentally, however, Darquier's true model was Drumont's contemporary and fellow anti-Semite the Marquis de Morès, the first French 'national socialist'.[27] This sombrero-hatted, red-shirted young aristocrat married an American heiress and spent some formative years in the North Dakota badlands, cattle-rustling and bringing ill fortune to the town of Medora, which he founded and named after his wife. After various disasters in the USA – for which, like Darquier in similar circumstances, he blamed the Jews – he consigned America to his personal mythology as Darquier would do later with Australia, and returned to France in 1887. Morès was fond of forming associations; he was a brawler and a ruffian who careered around with groups of bully boys and killed people himself rather than leaving it to others, as Darquier was to do. Both Morès and Darquier were self-publicists and sought money from Jew and Gentile alike. Darquier constantly made reference to Morès, and imitated both his aristocracy and his violence.

But since the end of the nineteenth century the most important ally of the French Church – one it could often have well done without – was Action Française. If the Church gave Vichy France its belief system and language, Action Française, born of the Dreyfus affair, provided its rhetoric and its political blueprint. Action Française the movement, and *Action française* its newspaper, derived their character from the fanatical teachings of the classicist and intellectual Charles Maurras, and its journalistic genius from Léon Daudet, son of Alphonse. Léon Daudet was an erudite man of noisy charm, merciless yet given to occasional kindnesses, while Maurras, almost deaf from childhood, was the isolated – and thus revered – intellectual giant of the movement.

Philosopher and poet, Maurras was also, crucially, a talented propagandist and, through *Action française*, published daily in Paris from 1908, he and Daudet incited the nationalist right to action. But despite the fact that Maurras considered the idea of a 'Jewish Christ' unpalatable, and despite being an atheist himself, he nevertheless saw in the hierarchical arrangements of the Catholic Church the key organising force for those who would not accept the Revolution of 1789 and the republic which it established. So firm was his belief that everything engendered in 1789 was an aberration, an outcome of English and German influences with Jewish overtones, that he refused to call the Revolution 'French'.

Maurras' political philosophy (known as 'Integral Nationalism') called for the return of royalty, for a king who would bring about the return of the 'real France' and banish 'legal France', the verminous republic and its democratic practices. He rejected parliamentary democracy and those he considered to be its rulers – Jews, Protestants, Freemasons and *métèques*, a word Maurras invented and which was speedily absorbed into the French language to describe all foreigners who lived in France.[28]

This political stance Maurras adopted 'like a religion'. He shared the views of the Church on authority, an alliance appreciated by the French

Church for many years. The Catholic hierarchy printed articles from *Action française* for dissemination to its flock, used its arguments in sermons, and gave Maurras, his movement and his newspaper active and loyal support in public and in private. As Pope Pius X told Maurras' mother: 'I bless his work.'[29]

Both Maurras and Drumont became Louis Darquier's demigods, all the more so because Drumont insisted that Gambetta, Cahors' great hero of the republic, was in truth a Jew, and worse, a German Jew. The immense contemporary importance of Maurras is difficult to appreciate today, as is the reverence in which he was held as an intellectual. This was a man who attacked the 1926 film of *Ben Hur* for being pro-Jewish, and who was 'struck, moved, almost hurt' on his first arrival in Paris to find street names which he considered to be foreign and Jewish because they included a 'K', a 'W' or a 'Z'.[30]

In the years in which the Darquier boys grew to manhood, Maurras was the leading nationalist figure. Action Française came to south-west France in 1904, when a branch opened in Toulouse, and later in Cahors and Montauban. By the time Louis was thirteen and Jean fourteen, the movement was holding badly attended meetings in the rue du Château du Roi in Cahors, though its influence was negligible. In Cahors its work was done by the Church and in the pages of *La Défense*.

However, the Holy See was not always happy with its unruly ally, and with the advent of Pope Pius XI, in 1922, the Vatican tardily moved against its rival. Action Française was banned in December 1926, dismaying the thousands of priests, the hierarchy and the faithful who were its fervent followers – including eleven of France's seventeen cardinals and archbishops. But by then it was too late; the language of Action Française had entered the Church Militant, and given a certain kind of Catholic their marching song.

With his colleague Maurice Pujo,[31] Maurras composed the battle hymn for his movement:

> *The Jew having taken all,*
> *Having robbed Paris of all she owns,*
> *Now says to France:*
> *'You belong to us alone:*
> *Obey! Down on your knees, all of you!'*

Insolent Jew, hold your tongue . . .
Back to where you belong, Jew . . . [32]

Insistence on purity of blood was only one of the doctrines Louis Darquier borrowed from Action Française. He also adopted their fixation on genealogy; in their attachment to the principle of monarchy, many members of Action Française assumed nobility, and bought, begged or lied about ancestors who would permit them to add a particule to their names. Denunciations of such assumed aristocracy by the *vraie* nobility were frequent, but Louis Darquier got away with it. [33]

Gascony is the region to the south and west of Quercy, whose inhabitants are noted for their panache. Two of the most popular stories of Louis' childhood were Edmond Rostand's *Cyrano de Bergerac* and Alexandre Dumas' *The Three Musketeers*, tales of daring Gascons, younger sons unfavoured by the gods, misunderstood, courageous, outspoken and heroically belligerent.

When he appropriated his noble title – Baron Darquier de Pellepoix – Louis took it from the Darquier nobility in Gers, Gascony, and so claimed to be a Gascon. Anatole de Monzie was a true Gascon, but Louis Darquier's only fragile link to the region was provided by two of his great-great-great-grandparents, a baker and his wife of the name of Darquié or Darquier who lived in the little Gascon town of Tournan in the early eighteenth century. The name Darquier, and its variants Darquié, Darcher, Darqué, Arquier and d'Arquier, is found in state and parish registers in Toulouse and throughout many of the south-western departments which surround it, including the department of Gers, ancient Gascony. In documents and records, many hundreds of these Darquiers rise from the past as servants, cooks, carpenters, chair porters, plasterers, hosiers, tinsmiths, tailors, second-hand clothes dealers, hat-makers and candle-makers.

There was a noble family of Darquier/d'Arquié in south-west France, and it was two of its bachelor members whom Louis purloined for himself. One was the famous astronomer Antoine Darquier de Pellepoix of Toulouse, who discovered the first planetary nebula in 1779 – Darquier's Nebula. [34] Antoine derived his name from his estate of Pellepoix, south of Toulouse. Louis' great-great-grandfather was a cobbler and street porter at the time the noble Darquiers flourished in that city, but a claim to being a mere by-blow was not on Louis' agenda.

He appropriated the entire clan, and proudly added links to the bachelor Baron François Isidore Darquier, a *Baron d'Empire*, a Napoleonic title.

Louis would work at his noble Gascon persona as he worked at nothing else, and to the end continued to claim absolute proof of his noble blood. Gascons were known for their boastfulness, bragging and unreliability, so that to *'faire une offre de Gascon'* in French means to raise false hopes. Louis Darquier was thus a spiritual Gascon, if nothing else.

2

◇

The Convicts' Kin

AFTER PIERRE DARQUIER BECAME acquainted with his daughter-in-law Myrtle Jones, he would explain the provenance of his son's bride as 'the pendant that hangs on the bottom of Australia'.[1] This jewel began its European life as 'that island between heaven and hell',[2] a place where Britain sent its criminals – men, women, children – politically suspect persons, Irish rebels, and the impoverished dregs of its rich earth. The colony was named Van Diemen's Land by the Dutch navigator Abel Tasman, after the governor-general of the Dutch East India Company, which sent Tasman to explore the South Pacific in 1642.

By the eighteenth century the shores of *Terra Australis Incognita* were another battleground in the continuing contests of strength between France and Britain. The French connection is most obvious in Tasmania, where exploratory French vessels complete with artists, zoologists and scientists preceded British settlement and carried out so much exploration and research. Marion Bay, for instance, is named after the French explorer Marion Dufresne, the first European to reach the island after Tasman. Myrtle Jones grew up on an island studded with French names: Cape Tourville, Freycinet Peninsula, Cape Baudin, D'Entrecasteaux Channel, Bruny Island, Huon River.

In 1769 the British despatched Captain Cook to the South Pacific. He entered Botany Bay on the Australian mainland in April 1770; later, when Britain was no longer able to send its convicts to its former colonies in America, over a thousand of them were sent to establish a new penal colony there.[3] The First Fleet reached Botany Bay in January 1788. Six days later the French explorer Jean-François la Pérouse arrived. Though their countries fought five wars between 1701 and 1815, the French and the British passed an equable six weeks together on Australia's east coast before la Pérouse sailed off, never to be seen again.

Hobart, the capital of Van Diemen's Land, became Britain's third antipodean penal setttlement in 1803, and in 1804 the settlement around Launceston became a fourth. By 1825, when Van Diemen's Land became a separate colony ruled directly from Britain, the island had become perhaps the most barbarous penal establishment of the British Empire, and expressed its objection to this by renaming itself Tasmania two years after it received its last convict from the Mother Country in 1853.

Australia was to develop as a nation divided in three, not two as in France: Anglo-Australians, devoted to King, Queen and Country, and others – workers, republicans, dreamers of different freedoms for their New World. Overarching this division were, and are, the original inhabitants of Australia. Their suffering and centuries of mistreatment became something every white Australian lives with, with varying degrees of shame.

About three or four thousand Tasmanian Aboriginals – slightly different physically from those on the mainland, being darker of skin and curlier of hair – were on the island when the first convict ships came to land. The island became a British gulag of starvation and punishment: dark cells and solitary confinement, chains and leg irons, diabolic instruments of torture, horrific wounds and the stench of men flogged almost to death time and time again. For the Aboriginals it was even worse. Though admonished by their betters that it was 'absurd to call the Tasmanian aborigine an upright-walking monkey, a talking brute',[4] the brutalised convicts and early settlers, victims themselves, demonised and hunted down the Aboriginal Tasmanians, already ravaged by imported European diseases. The savagery and brutality of Van Diemen's Land was so great that its name still has a sulphurous odour about it, like Devil's Island.

Carrick, the little town near Launceston where Myrtle Jones was raised, has a ghostly, faintly eerie atmosphere. By 1853 Tasmania's Aboriginals were all but exterminated, but the white communities flourished: when Queen Victoria died in 1901 and Myrtle was eight years old, Australia had become a federated nation with a population of nearly four million. Myrtle's island was always a special place. Divided by Bass Strait from Melbourne on the mainland's southern coast, facing the Antarctic below, everything about Tasmania is slightly different from the vast continent above. Its winters are mild, its summers generous, and it has a limpid southern light, and naked-nose wombats and Tasmanian Devils which it shares with nowhere else.

By Myrtle's time free settlers, the discovery of gold and the wealth of its pastures meant that the major settlements of Australia were proud and prosperous cities of the British Empire. Before 1900, eighty per cent of the white inhabitants came from the British Isles, with a sizeable proportion of Irish convicts and immigrants to provide a permanent irritant to the British status quo. Tasmania, isolated from the mainland, became the most English of the Australian states. The mountains and valleys, lakes and uninhabitable wildernesses of most of the island are not conducive to this ambition, but the north-west is different. Launceston's polite parks and squares, its colonial buildings and the rolling hills and pasturelands which surround it, tell the visitor: 'This is Australia, but we – and you – really wish it were England.'5

Mainland Australians tease the islanders about their undiluted Anglo-Saxon population, about inbreeding and the similarity of the island's outline to the female pudenda, but most of all for their enduring desire to hide their convict past. The Tasmanian proverb 'Here, men are men, women are knocked up and sheep watch their backsides', and its convict days, when the island was known as the 'Isle of Sodom', seem to have given birth to nostalgia for a past and a country which were never theirs.

The convicts who survived mixed with indigent settlers to provide a collection of eccentric rogues and bolters, reformed felons of questionable virtue, lecherous prelates, ranting non-conformists, remittance men, political firebrands, Scottish evangelicals and personifications of English gentility. This latter species became the Tasmanian elite of which Myrtle was an arch-representative, 'so English, they wish that England could go to war so they could fight for her again'.

Something like half of all woman convicts transported to Australia were sent to Van Diemen's land, where men outnumbered women seven to one. About four hundred had survived the long voyage by the 1820s, and two of them were Myrtle's ancestors – Sophia Edwards, transported in 1800 'for feloniously stealing a silver mug', and Mary Shea, convicted in County Cork in August 1816 for stealing muslin. After earning her Free Certificate on 28 January 1825 Mary Shea married William Saggers, sentenced to transportation at Middlesex in 1798; their fifth child, Myrtle's grandmother Elizabeth, was born in 1826.

Pardoned at the same time as Mary Shea and William Saggers was the ebullient Britton Jones, who arrived in Van Diemen's Land in 1820. A waterman by trade, he was sentenced to seven years at Bristol Quarter

Sessions on 14 July 1817 for stealing a piece of lead.[6] In 1822, still serving his sentence, Jones married Sophia Kirk, the daughter of Sophia Edwards and another convict, Matthew Kirk. Sophia Kirk was the thirteenth white girl born on the island. This collection of former 'incorrigibles' was, like Louis Darquier's ancestors, mostly illiterate.

The island became infamous as the 'dust-hole' of Britain. 'Drunkenness, especially, was all but universal.' By 1825, when Britton Jones became a free man, there was only one church in Launceston, where the clanking of convicts' chains disturbed the Anglican congregation, but thirty taverns – the Cat and Fiddle, the Jolly Sailor, the Help Me Through the World: names of jollity and hope. This was where Jones was to make his money; he became one of the earliest brewers and innkeepers in Launceston. A fine swearer, boozer and adventurer, in 1833 he called his public house the Sir William Wallace, a good rebellious Scots name, even though Jones claimed to be Welsh and proud of it. These early Tasmanian pothouses, exuding fumes of tobacco and erupting with 'shrieks of passion', oaths and laughter, in which prostitutes like Fat Catherine and Carroty Kate earned their keep, meant that prelates of every persuasion descended upon Van Diemen's Land to inject the word of God or sprinkle holy water upon the sinful.

Apart from depravity and rum, whaling and sealing were the staffs of island life; but Britton Jones looked to property and the land, and became a prosperous farmer and livestock breeder. In 1838 he built for himself what was to become one of Tasmania's stately homes, Franklin House, a confident Georgian construction now open to the public. A few years later he sealed the status of his progeny by bestowing land for the erection of a church and school.

Sophia Jones meanwhile had eight children, and many of these had even more. Three of the Jones children married children of William Saggers, and one of these couples, Elizabeth Saggers and Britton's eldest son William 'Tiger' Jones, were Myrtle's grandparents. Elizabeth had nine children, in twenty years, and died at the age of forty-five. A year later William Jones, a farming man, propertied and well-to-do like his father, married again. This second marriage produced a further six children, and the vast brood settled around Launceston, so that even now Joneses are thick on the ground.

In 1864, five years before the birth of Pierre Darquier in Cahors, Myrtle's father Henry was born. Many of the family lives have been recorded in a booklet, *Keeping up with the Joneses*, written by one of Britton's descendants. The genteel aspirations of Anglo-Australia, later immortalised by Barry Humphries, flourish in this whitewashed account in which Britton Jones, their *onlie begetter* and a man not to be ashamed of, is described as the son of a Bristol portrait painter to George III, who once had a letter from Queen Victoria.[7]

Today, for most Australians a convict ancestor is the equivalent of royal blood, but in this family history all Myrtle's convict ancestors are portrayed as adventurous pioneers who 'came ashore' or 'landed' or 'settled' in Van Diemen's Land. There is not a word about convict ship or chain gang. Myrtle grew up at a time when fantasy was already well in the air, and many incriminating records of convict ancestry were removed from state archives and destroyed. The price paid for such pretensions in Launceston, as in Cahors, was an anxious silence about anything that might damage a family name so recently acquired.

The Jones family encountered a more severe form of gentility when Henry Jones – Harry – married Myrtle's mother, Alexandrina – Lexie – Morrison in 1891 according to the rites and ceremonies of the Free Church of Scotland, later known as the 'Wee Frees'.[8] Lexie's maternal grandmother Ann MacLeay, an indigent crofter's widow, brought this harsh fundamentalist faith from the remote island of North Uist in the Western Isles of Scotland in 1855, and she also brought three of her six children with her – Colin (farm labourer), Murdoch (ploughman) and Ann (housemaid). The following year Ann the housemaid married another hardy Scot from the Western Isles, Donald Morrison, a schoolteacher and small farmer, who arrived in Launceston with his violin in 1840.

The Wee Frees are zealous Calvinistic Christians, fiery preachers, often in the Gaelic, and their flock keep themselves to themselves, upright folk, careful, dedicated to the professions and to teaching in particular. Ann MacLeay Morrison, her Wee Free grandmother, lived until Myrtle was twenty-three. The fortress against sin constructed by followers of the Wee Free persuasion, made up of strict opinions about the Sabbath, Popery, gambling, alcohol and dancing, together with a grim view of women's lot, was certainly shaken when Lexie married Harry.[9] The Joneses' world of brewers, hoteliers and graziers extended to the Turf and Racing Club in Harry's case, because he was a fine horseman, a noted judge and breeder of horses who trained and raced his own thoroughbreds and was an avid racing man. According to Myrtle, in her family 'the Mother is always Sacred', and Lexie seems to have won the day with most of their progeny, who, at least outwardly, became pillars of respectability.

Myrtle, who did not, was born on 26 November 1893, as summer began, at Freshwater Point, on the Tamar River eight miles north of Launceston, just as Pierre Darquier was graduating as a doctor in Paris. This lovely old colonial homestead, encircled by verandahs, with lawns sloping down to the banks of the river, is a place of beauty exceeding anything offered by the rue du Tapis Vert or the rue du Lycée. In the following year Harry purchased his first property at Carrick, eleven miles from Launceston, and later bought again, calling his house and estate Armidale.

Carrick is a rural township – of about three hundred people in Myrtle's time – set on the River Liffey. There was a great deal of wealth amongst the 'Families of Launceston'; the rich grazing land produced some of the best merino wool in Australia in those days. To wool and wheat Harry added stockbreeding. Like Pierre Darquier he became a notable of his district, and his business dealings and positions were so numerous that by 1927, when Louis Darquier met Myrtle, his 'Yankee style' heiress, he was easily able to check on Harry's wealth by consulting the Launceston directory.

Harry and the tall and handsome Lexie had nine children: Myrtle was the second. As a child Myrtle was neither pretty nor otherwise, just a female version of her many siblings, with good wide eyes and dark hair. Her personality made up for any physical inadequacies, and her warmth and vivacity were qualities she was never to lose, just as Lexie, however far she moved into the Anglican establishment, always remained the daughter of her careful Scots parents.

'I was brought up,' Myrtle's younger sister Olive wrote in 1991, 'in the early part of this century when values and principles were high . . . That seldom heard word "self-discipline" was encouraged and expected. Bad language and vulgarity were not permitted in our house.'[10] Discipline, rectitude, duty and concern for education and social position seem to have formed the circumference of Lexie's life. She made her children's clothes, taught them music, gave them their lessons; they were raised to be 'true believers in Christian principles'. As the 'children of the big house' they were kept away from the township and, like the

Darquier boys, each Jones child was encouraged always to be top of their form.

By the time Harry moved his family into the house he built at Armidale, Carrick's heyday as an important grain town had given way, along with the bushrangers, poachers and riff-raff of earlier days, to graziers and pastoralists who lived with the inhabitants of Carrick in the English way – they employed them, but did not mix with them socially. On Sundays Lexie combined hymns around the piano with attendance at St Andrew's Anglican church, taking her children there on a route which avoided the township. Here too the Jones children went to Sunday school, sang in the choir, or played on the small organ, transported from the crypt of St Paul's Cathedral in London, encased in English oak, a relic of 'Home'.

Except for the mill-owning Monds family, the other pastoralists of the district and the rectory, there was little company, although there were plenty of children the Jones clan could have played with had vulgarity not been an issue. Carrick still had all the usual requirements of a small Australian country town: wide gravel roads, gum trees, wattles, neat little cottages of brick and weatherboard, hotels lining the main street, a police station, a school, two churches, a Public Hall and Monds Roller Mills, which dominated and gave work to the town. Myrtle's incapacity to earn her living may well have come from seeing the motto of this enterprise on the factory flourbags every day of her young life – 'Work Conquers All'.

Even today there are horses everywhere in Carrick. Then, the big race days on Boxing Day and Queen Victoria's birthday were highlights of the Carrick year. There was a Carrick Hunt, complete with pink coats, bugles and tally-hos, a Turf Club and a racecourse. Harry Jones was treasurer, clerk of the scales and secretary of the West Tamar Race Club, and his horses won more races at Carrick and throughout northern Tasmania than those of any other owner. All the Jones children were taught to ride, but Myrtle particularly seems to have been her father's child. She insisted that one of her numerous uncles teach her showjumping, and she raced one of her father's horses at the annual Launceston Show, and won.

Armidale was in its way the manor of Carrick, a large wooden Federation house, set amongst trees and reached by an imposing avenue of poplars and pines. The River Liffey bordered the property, and the house, complete with running water and one of the first telephones in the district, had a charming landscaped garden rolling down from its handsome verandah to a wandering picket fence. There were climbing roses and lilac trees, shamrocks and daffodils, orchards and stables. Weeping willows lined the banks of the Liffey, where the children paddled and swam. Lexie looked after the *basse cour* and dairy, and until 1912, when Harry acquired one of the first motorcars in the district, drove a horse and buggy into Launceston to do her shopping.

As the daughter of a Scots dominie, above all Lexie was ambitious for her children, whose outdoor life and access to the racetrack were balanced by her passion for education and for music. The Jones children were taught to play and to sing, and to forge useful social contacts; they were not permitted to attend the village school, but they were allowed to encounter the townspeople at Carrick penny concerts, where Myrtle and her brothers would play and sing the songs of the day, poetic – 'Believe Me, if All Those Endearing Young Charms', 'Come into the Garden, Maud' – and music hall – 'My Grandfather's Clock', 'Two Little Girls in Blue', and of course 'Soldiers of the Queen'. In the town there were shows and competitions, concert artistes in the Public Hall, and dances where Myrtle could play for the matrons of Carrick, 'in long flowing gowns gliding gracefully to the strains of a waltz or Pride of Erin'. Otherwise, the Jones children grew up behind the picket fence of Armidale. Olive remembered: 'My wonderful mother gave us our lessons every morning and for the rest of the day we were free as the fresh air we breathed. We wandered and walked all over the place, visiting our make-believe friends. We rarely played with other children, and at the table we spoke when we were spoken to.'[11]

Not opening one's mouth seems to have been as important at Lexie's Armidale as it was in Louise Darquier's rue du Lycée. Myrtle's world of fantasy was nurtured here. While the larrikin children of Carrick enjoyed real Australian childhoods of bush and river, birds like flying jewellery in the skies above, the Jones children were placed in the best schools: the boys in the Anglican Launceston Church Grammar School, and the girls in Methodist Ladies' College, which sent them on the way to university and propertied gentility. Except for Myrtle and her brother Will, the next-born. Myrtle boarded at Miss Windeatt's modest little private school in Launceston, where manners and deportment were the order of the day. For Will, the First World War was to be his education. All the Jones girls were musical, but Myrtle was exceptional. At the piano she could captivate the world; the instrument came alive under her flying fingers as she played and sang.

From the earliest days of European settlement white Australians loved music, loved to sing and play it, thronged to touring opera and theatre companies. Launceston in Myrtle's time was more populous than Cahors, but still a small country town. By the turn of the century its vast Victorian Albert Hall held audiences of a thousand or more for its Patriotic Concerts and those of 'the Tasmanian Nightingale' Amy Sherwin, and especially Nellie Melba. Melba, Australia's national heroine, toured the country twice during Myrtle's childhood, in 1902 and 1909, mobbed wherever she went.

This was the age of operetta, especially of Gilbert and Sullivan's Savoy operas, which first came Myrtle's way with Launceston Operatic Society's enthusiastic performances of *HMS Pinafore* and *The Pirates of Penzance*. Myrtle was an exception in her family in many ways: she was theatrical and outgoing, quite untouched by Presbyterian habits of thrift, industry and temperance.

By 1912 Lexie was spending her weeks in a Launceston house so that the younger children could attend their schools more easily. Perhaps Myrtle left home then. By 1916 her older brothers, Hector and Vernon, were both working on the mainland; the boat trip from Launceston to Melbourne is short, and it seems that Myrtle took it before Harry Jones sold Armidale and moved what was left of his family into Launceston.

How Myrtle became an actress and singer, and why and when she left home, remain mysteries, but by 1916 she was gone across the water. She was twenty-two. When she married in 1923 she signed herself as 'Sandra Lindsay, Actress'. Anne Darquier told me her mother was a singer, and next to his bed Louis Darquier always kept a cheeky Edwardian photo of 'Sandra' in a bathing suit, posing with her stockings rolled down her thighs in the postcard manner of the time. It seems a fair guess that when Myrtle left home she perhaps took some classes – in piano, acting or performing – and tried her luck on the stage.

Myrtle was never abandoned by her parents: quite the opposite – they never ceased to fret about her. Louis would cause the death of many thousands, but these deeds seem never to have been acknowledged by the Jones siblings in Australia. For them, Myrtle achieved undreamed-of heights, and their horror of anyone investigating her life intimates that some of them, at least, knew what Louis Darquier did, and what Myrtle Jones accepted and approved.

The youngest of Myrtle's sisters, Heather, wrote a record of Myrtle and Louis' lives. That Myrtle called herself an actress, that she drank – was in fact an alcoholic, most probably from her twenties – and that she almost certainly had a drug habit too, are glossed over in family accounts of her wonderful later life as a real European baroness, living in the fabled land of 'abroad'. Their Myrtle was a creature whose vibrant personality was little suited to their small island, a sister who could only flourish on a larger stage, and who happily found this in a great, aristocratic European love affair. The convict Britton Jones offered his descendants much to be proud of, instead it was Myrtle's life that was the fairy tale for the Jones family.

In fact Myrtle knew more of the constancy of love, physical comfort and financial security in her Tasmanian years than she was ever to know again. The Darquiers of Cahors were by no means as blind or as loving as the Jones family of Launceston. Otherwise the two families had much in common. Their unsteady hold on social respectability and professional achievement demanded silence, the forgetting of disturbing facts, and gave birth to children who escaped into fantasy worlds, and there wrought havoc.

3

Soldier's Heart

THE GREAT WAR OF 1914–18 began with a roar of patriotism as France and Great Britain, with their empires and their allies Russia and Belgium, confronted Germany and its allies, the Austro-Hungarian and the Ottoman Empires. Many other nations were sucked into its maw, and by its end nearly nine million men were dead, millions more were missing, twenty million more wounded, disfigured, mutilated, gassed. Most were young men of Louis Darquier's generation. When war broke out in August 1914, all French men aged between twenty and forty-eight were called up and marched away to the glorious adventure, 'the purifying war'.[1] Even the extremist Catholic press, and Charles Maurras – rejoicing because the object of his unremitting vituperation, the French socialist leader Jean Jaurès, had been assassinated by a fanatic on the eve of war – united behind the republic in a *Union Sacrée*, a sacred union.

Louise wanted both her elder sons to become doctors. Louis was a sturdy fellow by now, the tallest of the Darquier men. Jean graduated from the Lycée Gambetta in the summer of 1913, bedecked with honours in philosophy. In September 1914 Louis' equal success in Latin, sciences and maths took him to Toulouse to join his brother as a student in the Faculté des Sciences.

In the years before the war, Action Française had spread throughout France with its rituals and meetings, its groups, sections and student branches. Its young royalists, the Camelots du Roi, went on the streets to sell the movement's newspaper and, as wandering bands armed with bludgeons and lead-tipped canes, did the movement's dirty work, creating incidents and administering beatings – actions described as just 'fooling about' by *La Défense*. They were also much given to surprising their enemies by slapping their faces in public.

Neither Jean nor Louis belonged to Action Française at this point, though they would certainly have heard of the noisy activities of its Camelots, many of them fellow students in the faculties of science and medicine. Both brothers studied for the *Certificat de Licence ès Sciences*, the PCN – Physics, Chemistry, Natural Sciences – the entrance examination required to study medicine in France. Jean passed. Louis failed his chemistry examination, giving Louise 'sleepless nights of worrying about him'.

Pierre Darquier, forty-five in 1914, was mobilised immediately as a major and chief medical officer. Posted to an ambulance service, he was attached to those first armies sent to war by cheering crowds, to the singing of the *'Marseillaise'* and cries of *'Vive la France!'* Inspired by the fervent wish to avenge the defeat of 1870, they believed the war would be over in a few weeks. Within a month Pierre witnessed the near victory of the German army as it made for Paris and the French and British armies fought to push it back. From August to November 1914 he followed the battles of the Guise, the Marne, the Aisne and the Yser in Belgium, treating the wounded and the columns of exhausted men in fields and towns which were to be fought over again and again – Ypres, Passchendaele, Messines, the ridge of the Chemin des Dames.[2]

As the hope of early victory disappeared, the scale of suffering became clear. Arms, legs, heads and bodies cut or blown to pieces were strewn over the fields and along the roads, often dwarfed by teams of bloated dead horses. Soldiers fought alongside, on top of and surrounded by corpses and fragments of corpses. Thunderous offensive confronted counter-offensive, and furious fighting alternated with stalemate. Trench warfare began, and with it the intensity of sound which marks all the descriptions of this war – the moans and cries of men wounded and dying, the stuttering and thunder of rifles and whizzbangs, machine guns and howitzers. Worse, past human imagining, was the destruction of human flesh which Pierre Darquier saw – the hideous wounds of the soldiers in this first mechanised war, and the carnage of battle on a scale hitherto unknown. In 1916 Henri Barbusse, the French writer called 'the Zola of the trenches', wrote in his bestseller *Le Feu* (*Under Fire*): 'This war means dreadful, superhuman exhaustion, water up to your belly, and mud, and grime and unspeakable filth. It means rotting faces and flesh in tatters, and corpses that no longer even look like bodies floating on the surface of the voracious earth.'[3]

Pierre Darquier had not qualified as a surgeon, but in war he became one; his experience of the suffering of the troops at the front was to end with the first battle for Ypres. He had left Cahors in August 1914 a prosperous and jolly doctor-mayor; on 18 November he was evacuated to Dunkirk, prosaically with sciatica, but he had seen enough of this new kind of warfare to turn him into the 'coward' his son Louis considered him to be. 'The French Army, with a mobilised strength of two million, had suffered by far the worst. Its losses in September, killed, wounded, missing and prisoners, exceeded 200,000, in October eighty thousand and in November seventy thousand; the August losses, never officially revealed, may have exceeded 160,000. Fatalities reached the extraordinary total of 306,000 . . .'[4]

As winter set in Pierre was posted to Tours, where, attached to a military nursing home, he was in charge of deciding whether wounded soldiers were fit enough to return to the front. Something vaguely shameful about his attitude to the war, murmured about in Cahors, muttered about more forcefully by Louis later, could well have been his over-generosity in diagnosis. In January 1915, Louise joined him. In Tours she socialised, visited the châteaux of the Loire, embroidered, and summoned pears, eggs, truffles and services from those who did her bidding in Cahors. Louis and Jean joined their parents in Tours, and in July 1915 both enlisted at the Hôtel de Ville. The seventeen-year-old Louis belonged to the class of 1917 – that is, he would have been called up for military service in that year – but instead he volunteered two years early. The French army accepted underage volunteers, but they had to be eighteen before they could fight. Young men who knew their way about sometimes volunteered early in order to avoid being sent directly to the infantry, where casualties were atrocious in the trenches. Joining as an underage volunteer also meant training courses and better preparation to become an officer.

All this worked for Louis. By February 1916 his brother Jean was serving as a gunner in the 18th Artillery Regiment under General Pétain, in the first months of the battle for Verdun, 'on the front line in the battery, crouched at the bottom of a hole'. Louise was beside herself. Jean was 'in a regiment where we know no one'; she did not want her sons to be common soldiers – *poilus*. She wrote: 'Pierre has heard details from injured soldiers coming back from Verdun and they all agree that since the beginning they have never seen such scenes. The ground in the trenches trembles constantly and the soldiers say it is like a train rushing by right next to them with sudden jolts and tremors. You can imagine . . .'[5]

A million men were killed or wounded at Verdun. Jean exacerbated the state of Louise's nerves with letters from mid-battle, as did Pierre, who horrified her by applying to serve again at the front. Anatole de Monzie visited the Darquiers in Tours and caused more pessimism and gloom, reducing Louise to 'a state of madness'. She was almost as concerned that her boys should join the best regiments as that they should survive. She wanted Louis to go into the artillery, but found it impossible to arrange. The First World War was, in its first years, a war of men and horses. Though tanks and dismounted action took over as the war progressed, horses pulled the field guns and heavy cavalry was still used. France fielded over 100,000 cavalry, still accoutred in the magnificent costumes of Napoleon's time, still trained for mounted combat. 'The idea of Louis in the cavalry fills me with dread,' Louise wrote, but Louis, always in love with uniforms, joined the 5th Cavalry Regiment as a Cuirassier Second Class.

Louise delivered him personally, 'very nervous', to the instruction centre for officer cadets at St-Cyr. By December 1915 he had completed his initial training and had advanced to Cuirassier First Class. He applied to train as an officer, but this was to be a second disappointment: he came eighty-eighth out of an intake of 128, not a position any Darquier boy was used to. His superiors admired his strength, energy, stamina and intelligence, judged him to be 'more energetic than punctual, but should go far if he is well guided', but found his character 'slightly weak'.[6] A year after enlisting, he had not yet engaged in battle. In July 1916 he was appointed first corporal, then sergeant in the 3rd Cavalry Regiment, as handsomely costumed as the 5th, and he finally became a cadet officer on 1 August. He was now ready for war. The first battle of the Somme had already begun.

———————— ⁂ ————————

In September 1915, two months after Jean and Louis had enlisted in Tours, Will Jones went from Carrick to the town of Claremont, near Hobart – he was twenty, eighteen months younger than Myrtle – and, with the approval of Henry and Lexie, enlisted in the Australian Imperial Force, the AIF. Nearly half a million Australians volunteered to fight for

Britain and the Empire, and most of them made the long journey over the seas to fight for 'Home'. Australian soldiers of the Great War came to be known as Anzacs, the initials of the Australian and New Zealand Army Corps who fought on the Gallipoli peninsula alongside men from India, France and Britain in early 1915.

Gallipoli dominates popular Australian memory of the First World War, although almost three times as many British, and more French than Australian soldiers were slaughtered there. But their real graveyard is in France and Flanders, where Australian soldiers – called 'diggers' because so many former gold-diggers were in the early army units – dug, fought and died in the horrific trenches of the Western Front.

Gunner Jones, soldier number 8911, Howitzer Brigade of the Ammunition Column, 2nd Division of the AIF, stood five feet seven inches tall, had green eyes, was a member of the Church of England and set sail from Melbourne two weeks before his sister Myrtle's twenty-second birthday. Before he left for the front, Will popped into Miss Windeatt's school in Launceston, to say goodbye to his younger sisters. The school rose to farewell him by singing the national anthem.

Two months later his ship reached Suez, then, after three months' training in Egypt, the Australian soldiers joined the British Expeditionary Force at Alexandria. In March 1916 they were shipped to Marseille and sent on by train to the battlefields. Will joined the 4th Field Artillery Brigade just in time for the first battle of the Somme, which had begun on 1 July, the day on which the British army walked steadily into barrages of German machine-gun fire, with the loss of some sixty thousand men.

When Pierre Darquier served as a doctor at the front, the only horror he did not witness was poison gas, first used by the Germans in April 1915. Otherwise he knew perfectly well what his sons might endure, Jean at Verdun, Louis in the trenches. As it turned out, it was Will Jones who got the worst of it. The first battle of the Somme lasted for a little over four months, and over a million men were killed, went missing or were wounded. Into this inferno Will Jones's division and the 2nd AIF descended in the last week of July 1916. Louis Darquier was a fine horseman, Will Jones a better one, but this was a skill Will could use only in pulling the howitzers and mobile guns of field artillery. He was a gunner, subject to the barrage of fire that often drove men mad. He had two weeks of normal life left to him.

Will fought at the battle of Pozières in the department of the Somme.

The little village of Pozières was razed to the ground in July and August 1916. Twenty-three thousand Australian officers and men were killed or wounded there within five weeks. As one Australian soldier wrote: 'One feels on a battlefield like this that one can never survive, or that if the body holds, the brain must go forever.'[7] Will was gassed on his twenty-first birthday – 13 August 1916 – but was back at the front four days later. He was gassed again on 29 October in the assault on the Transloy Line and admitted to hospital. The number of times he had been gassed now qualified him as wounded and won him a trip in a hospital ship to Blighty.

At this time, Louis' cavalry regiment was near the front, but in reserve, helping with the harvest near Beauvais. Cavalry divisions were of little use in the exploding world of flying bombs and earth, smoke and shrapnel of the Somme, and Louis' youth still protected him. As Will left for England, Louis' regiment moved from behind the lines to take its turn in the trenches at Vailly, along the Chemin des Dames, the ridge above the Aisne originally built by Louis XV as a pleasure path, now the sector of the front which stretched from Rheims to Soissons. As a cadet officer, only eighteen years old, Louis was back at base camp doing stable guard service. Misbehaviour began immediately – 'eight days of "open arrest"' for 'kicking a horse'.

The United States declared war on Germany as the French 3rd Cavalry moved towards the front as part of General Nivelle's new offensive of April 1917, along the Chemin des Dames. In May, Louis' regiment was in the trenches near Rheims, and saw violent action. Nineteen of the 3rd Cavalry's 'officers and men who displayed brilliant conduct during the Hun's offensive of 30 July against the Prunay trenches' received the Croix de Guerre in July. Louis was not among them, but he shattered his mother by reporting that his best friend in the regiment had been killed. Although there were fewer horses at the front now, and cavalrymen were being sent to fight in the trenches or moved to tank or artillery brigades, his cavalry regiment was still a place of relative safety.

In 1917 the French army was losing thirteen thousand men a month. In eight months of fierce warfare, Louis' regiment suffered ten deaths and forty wounded. Well before then, Louis had had enough of horses and uniforms and stables behind the lines. During the worst days of the battle for Verdun in 1916, General Pétain had provided the French people with their great symbolic victory of the Great War, and its patriotic cry: 'They shall not pass!' Following the disastrous failure of General Nivelle's April offensive, Pétain replaced him as commander-in-chief of the French army. But that month French soldiers, enraged by decreasing success, poor food, no rest, and the endless mud, rain and cold, rats and lice, coupled with the overpowering tedium of waiting for almost certain death and their distrust of the generals who sent them to it, began to mutiny.

Few soldiers were unaffected by the violence and disobedience, although it was mostly the infantry, entrenched in appalling conditions along the front, who raised their voices against their leaders. In August 1917 Louis refused to carry out an order and gave a ridiculous excuse, resulting in four more days of single arrest. While he was having a wretched war inactive behind the lines, his father was promoted and moved to Paris, to the army discharge centre at Clignancourt, still certifying the wounded as unfit for service.

Everyone who worked with Pierre Darquier in the army during these war years gave a good report of him – 'sweet tempered, highly intelligent' was a typical comment – and in September he was appointed chief medical officer to the Garde Républicaine, the elite corps of defenders of the president of the republic and the French state.[8] Louise did not regret leaving Tours for Paris and a rented apartment in the avenue de Clichy. 'There are not even any victories to speak of,' she wrote from Tours. She was 'reading books about Byzantium . . . making myself two muffs with some old fur'.

The mutinies continued. The fears of the French high command, including Pétain, of Bolshevik anarchy were exacerbated by the revolution in Russia of November 1917. Pétain restored order by improving conditions in the trenches for his *poilus*, but some soldiers were arrested and tried, a few were sent to Devil's Island, and fewer were shot. Louis made his escape. He applied for transfer to the artillery in October, and by the time he turned twenty on 19 December 1917, his commanding officer had sent him off for training with the following assessment: 'excellent background, good military mind, excellent behaviour, intelligent and well educated. Should be highly suitable for a position of command although still shows signs of a slightly weak character for his young age.'[9]

⁓

When Will Jones's hospital ship arrived in England in November 1916 he was diagnosed as suffering from 'debility', a word to be used over and again about him, sometimes interspersed with 'sick in field' – the latter often caused by the stench and sight of unburied, mutilated or decomposing corpses, bones and human parts. During the Great War 'debility' was 'often the result of repeated acute states of exhaustion', which sometimes led to D.A.H. (disordered action of the heart), effort syndrome, stress, panic attacks caused by fear – 'soldier's heart'.[10] For the next eight months Will was treated in hospitals, convalescent homes and Australian retraining centres. He managed to add mumps to his debility, but by June 1917 he had been set sufficiently upright to be sent back to the front.

This time he fought in Belgium, in the sea of mud which was the third battle of Ypres, or Passchendaele. While Louis was kicking horses behind the lines, Will was transferred to the 2nd Division Signal Company as a sapper. From September to October his division fought through the battle of the Menin Road, at Broodseinde Ridge and Passchendaele. As the pelting October rains came down, in these hopeless encounters, fought up to the waist in the deep swamp of the flooded landscape, small victories brought vast losses: there were thirty-eight thousand casualties in the Australian divisions alone, many of them drowned in submerged shellholes.

Will was arrested for drunkenness: he spent seven days in the clink, and on the day he was released he was gassed again, and again the day after. A fellow soldier recorded: 'The poor creatures were blind ... suffering great pain in their throats and stomach,' as 'helpless as babies'.[11] On 31 October, as his division was withdrawn for rest, Will was invalided once more to England. Again he spent nearly eight months there being reconstructed for the front.[12]

Louis Darquier was luckier. Until 1918 he had spent most of his time in training or behind the lines. In his month of preparation for the artillery at Fontainebleau, just outside Paris, Louis did well. He was appointed corporal, then sergeant: 'calm and thoughtful', the reports said, 'energetic and full of drive', and he came twenty-ninth out of 159 young cadets. Now he was to fight as Will Jones had, in the thick of it. In February 1918 he was posted as an officer to the 49ème Régiment d'Artillerie de Campagne, the 49th Field Artillery Regiment, and the following month he reached the front at last. By this time artillery was more accurate, of better quality, in better supply. The German army was almost exhausted, and now it faced a unified enemy.

General Ferdinand Foch was appointed commander-in-chief of all Allied forces in April 1918. The Allies were helped by improved resources, technological advances in communications and weaponry, tanks and aeroplanes, and, at long last, troops from the USA. Pétain was not happy with the idea of a unified command. He resented Foch's appointment and wanted to retain American troops under his control. Vain and pessimistic, he saw the US Commander-in-Chief General John J. Pershing as inexperienced, and himself as 'a great man'.[13]

In Paris, Louise stood at the windows of her apartment, watched the first air bombardments and agonised. Both her sons were at the front. Louis joined his unit, the 6th Battery of the 49th, at Toul near Nancy on 10 March, and two days later General Pétain arrived to review the regiment, to present the men with souvenirs of his visit, and formally to promise its officers the honorary insignia of the *Fourragère* after the war.[14]

Louis' regiment fought in the second battle of the Somme throughout April 1918, at Moreuil to the east of Hangard Wood, alongside Will's division, part of the Australian corps which halted the German advance at Villers-Bretonneux. Will, meanwhile, was convalescing in Weymouth. This was a combined French and British attack; French posts next to British, Australians, Canadians and New Zealanders, fighting close to the enemy. The second Somme battle was no longer only stalemate trench warfare, but also hand-to-hand fighting under continuous heavy fire and shelling, in copses, woods and gullies, using bayonets, revolvers and bombs.

There were heavy losses and hideous shrapnel wounds, and 'the whole countryside was literally drenched with gas'.[15] It was mustard gas now, and Louis was in the mêlée of death and mutilation, fighting among the first German and British confrontations by tank attack. He was mentioned in despatches for his bravery in combat at Hangard-en-Santerre on 9 April, although the wrist wound he later added to his career details was too slight to be mentioned in his regiment's daily journal.[16]

Louis had performed well, and in July was promoted to second lieutenant. A month earlier his regiment had moved on to take part in the second battle of the Marne, around the Montagne de Rheims where the last German offensive was to begin. Fighting in support of Allied troops along the Somme, Louis reached the Rheims sector, where Corporal Adolf Hitler's regiment was part of the massive German assault. Will Jones rejoined his unit on the Somme in July, as it prepared to take part in the battle of Amiens.

Louis fought on until the end of August, when his unit was pulled from the front, and in September he went on leave to stay with his parents in Paris. In her letters written to Cahors throughout the war, though she is always concerned about Jean, a medical auxiliary now – often at the front line, often under fire, often ill – it is Louis, 'my second lieutenant', about whom Louise frets the most. She loved all her boys, but 'Louis made himself noticed and felt more than the other two'. Still, for her, 'all that matters is that my children survive!'[17]

After two days at home in Paris Louis wrote to the War Office requesting release from the army. He was still a boy: the handwriting of the letter is childish and hesitant. He sent it off on 4 September 1918, and five stamps, many addresses and over a year later it arrived at the War Office on 12 September 1919. 'I have been engaged as a volunteer for the duration of the war since 5 July 1915 . . . I beg to request a transfer to the reserve,' Louis wrote to the Minister of War.[18] He had been at the front for six months, and had written his letter knowing that on his return from leave he was to be reassigned to the 8th Battery and his artillery regiment was to be placed with the 2nd French Colonial Corps, under the command of the US army and General Pershing.

This first solo attack by the American forces, part of the huge Champagne offensive, began on 12 September 1918 at St-Mihiel, southwest of Verdun. Here Louis fought in soaking rain and deep muddy trenches. The American onslaught was only one of the Allied offensives orchestrated by General Foch. Another was the battle of Amiens, which had begun on 8 August. This time Will was lucky. His division's successful attack on Mont St-Quentin in August, followed by the last Australian attack of the war at Montbrehein in early October, was the end of his war. Peace was declared on 11 November 1918; he had survived.

While his request for release from the army winged its way from military office to office, Louis had to fight on in the quagmire of the Meuse-Argonne offensive. Where he fought – at Souain-Perthes-les-Hurlus – is today a necropolis for many thousands of the dead – French, American and German. By the end of October 1918 Louis' Colonel Cambuzat commended him again: 'Perfect behaviour. Remarkable drive, good conduct under fire. Good sense of command. Will make an excellent battery officer.'[19]

As Louis' regiment was preparing for the last great offensive in November, the armistice was declared; a few days later the 49th Artillery made a triumphal entry through small French villages in the Moselle. Nearby, Louis' hero Pétain led the triumphal march into Metz, and Louis and his regiment attended when the president of the republic, Raymond Poincaré, arrived to decorate Pétain with his marshal's baton. General Pétain, now an exalted *Maréchal de France*, immediately fulfilled his promise and honoured the 49th Regiment with the *Fourragère*.

For the next twelve months, as other soldiers were gradually demobilised, Louis was based at or near Metz in barracks. The year was passed in recovering ammunition and taking part in reviews and parades. Louis might have distinguished himself at hand-to-hand combat, but acting under orders remained impossible. In May 1919 he was cited for 'unshakeable bravery' and 'superb disregard for danger' under enemy attack at Hangard-en-Santerre on 9 April 1918, but his new squadron leader reported of him: 'better in combat than during rest and instruction periods', lacking 'sufficient understanding of the role of the officer during the post-armistice period'.[20]

Will Jones, meanwhile, was on his way back to Tasmania. After the armistice and three weeks' leave in Paris he set sail in the troopship SS *Ypiranga* in March 1919, heading for Cape Town, then Australia. He was just coming up to his twenty-fourth birthday. On 7 June, with two other diggers, he went into Cape Town to have several drinks at the Grand Hotel. At another hotel, the Fountain, they did likewise, went back to the Grand and had a few more, then went upstairs to dinner where they each had another couple of double whiskies. Dead drunk, the Australians were put out on the hotel balcony. Will fell to the pavement below and fractured the base of his skull. He was heaved into a taxi and taken to hospital, where he died an hour later. He left a kitbag and a wallet with £28.10s, souvenirs of battle in the shape of two German watches, seven pence, a German belt and a French calendar.

At the Court of Enquiry proceedings in Cape Town, the finding was that the deceased 'met his death by falling from a balcony of the Grand Hotel, Strand Street, Cape Town, on the evening of the seventh June 1919, about 9.45 p.m.: that there is no evidence showing any reasons for the deceased climbing or falling over the balcony fence – which stands some three feet six inches high ... in the opinion of the court the deceased soldier was intoxicated at the time of the accident.'[21]

Two-thirds of the Australian soldiers who served overseas became casualties of the Great War; over forty thousand of them are buried in the towns and fields of northern France, in known and unknown graves. Will Jones was given a military funeral.

On 12 September 1919 the Ministry of War replied to Darquier's request of a year earlier and he was appointed to the reserve. He was demobilised on 1 October in Metz, and sent off from the 49th Artillery Regiment with this final report:

> In peacetime has not lived up to the hopes founded on his wartime behaviour. Has carried out no noteworthy service. Took advantage of his achievements as a group commander to make no further effort. Poorly carried out subsequent missions he was entrusted with. Ended his career with an act of indiscipline which entailed a punishment of 15 days' arrest.
>
> Judging himself to be demobilised, [Darquier] discharged himself from the regiment in the morning of 1 October, without waiting for the arrival of ministerial orders concerning his demobilisation – orders received in the evening of 1 October.[22]

And so, in 1919 Louis Darquier left the army in disgrace.

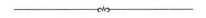

Pierre Darquier remained nominally mayor of Cahors until 1919 – thirteen years of service which earned him the decoration of chevalier of the

Légion d'honneur in 1913. Towards the end of 1918 the old family home in Cahors was rented out and he and Louise moved to an apartment in Neuilly, the leafy and elegant Parisian suburb near the Bois de Boulogne. The wide avenues and substantial private houses of Neuilly exude careful affluence, and Louise's choice was large enough for all the family, for Pierre's surgery and for the one or two domestics they always retained.

Unlike the men of so many French families, the three Darquiers who served throughout the war survived, and by 1920 Pierre and Louise had their sons with them in Neuilly. While Jean ended up as a medical captain and was awarded the Croix de Guerre for heroism at Verdun, Louis left the army in disgrace, despite the fact that he had fought well. His army citation entitled him to a minor decoration – a Bronze Palm on his Croix de Guerre, but as, most unusually for him, he never mentioned this in his voluminous *curricula vitae*, it may well be that it was removed from him at this time. He spent the following decade loathing France.

Later Louis transformed his hatred for France and his ignominious departure from the army into vehement patriotism. He remembered only the glorious victory of *la patrie* and his relish for battle, and bewailed the fate of French soldiers such as he, who had shed their blood for France while Jews and financiers had remained at home, making personal fortunes out of the war.

Before the Great War, pacifism had little appeal in France to generations brought up in the shadow of the German enemy. After it, 1,400,000 had died, and more than a million disabled French soldiers returned home – the crippled, the disfigured, the gassed, the traumatised. There were the 600,000 widows, and many more thousands of fatherless children. Pacifism was to permeate an entire generation, as was its shadow, fascism.

The rise of Hitler and the Nazis is always linked to the First World War and the humiliation inflicted upon Germany by the Treaty of Versailles, signed in June 1919. As firmly linked to the aftermath of that war is the rise of nationalism and fascism in France, which pounced upon the old divisive issues and weakened the republic, already enfeebled by the nation's terrible losses, both human and economic. To veterans who shared Louis Darquier's convictions, their hatred of the parliamentary government of the republic was based on their belief that it was now in the hands of parasites who used the sacrifice of the French soldier for their own ends.

Action française had a good war, its jingoistic support for the royalist and nationalist cause expressed in witch-hunts against Germans, traitors, spies and foreigners. Omnipresent in hospitals, barracks and at the front, the newspaper loved to mythologise the immortal glory of the military heroes of France, one of whom was General Pétain, the supreme commander of the French army and the 'Victor of Verdun'.[23]

Many men prominent on the Catholic right and in Action Française after the war had been leaders during it: Pétain himself, General Maxime Weygand[24] – Foch's chief of staff – and the Catholic General Édouard de Castelnau,[25] who went on to found the Féderation Nationale Catholique, the fraternal partner of Action Française within the right wing of the Catholic laity. These were only a few of the vast army of shaky survivors who, like Adolf Hitler in Germany, extracted a poisoned sense of destiny from the Great War. By 1939, nothing could make the people of France, who had paid the highest price in the First World War, feel enthusiastic about repeating one month of it.

II

COCK
&
BULL

4

◄◦►

Scandal and Caprice

EVERY TIME WILL WAS wounded, or invalided out of France, the Jones family received a telegram. When they received the telegram announcing his death in Cape Town, the Premier of Tasmania helped them find out almost immediately the true reason for it. Thereafter alcohol was never mentioned: Will was a casualty of the Great War, or had been 'killed in an accident'. His kitbag and wallet were restored to his family, and his medals followed. In the same year, 1919, the old wooden homestead at Armidale burnt down. Harry moved his family into a comfortable house in Launceston.

He was still a wealthy man, but seems to have become less so with each passing year, as the family homes became increasingly modest. In 1921 they moved into the last of these, 'Glenholme' at 3 Cypress Street, Launceston, a small and typically Australian suburban house, prettily gabled but unassuming, its kitchen mantelpiece decorated with the painted words: 'Jesus is Lord'. Cypress Street is as gloomy as its name. In family accounts of those years in Launceston, Will is never forgotten, Myrtle never mentioned. By 1915 her older brothers were teaching and studying, in Queensland and New South Wales. Myrtle may have followed them; there is no way of knowing for certain where she was until her marriage in Sydney in 1923.

Louis in the meantime, after two weeks under military arrest, returned to Neuilly in October 1919. The war had devastated the population of the Lot, and like many of his fellow *Lotois* Pierre Darquier did not return to Cahors after the war. As he had done before, he made way for Anatole de Monzie, who added to his portfolio of political activities by taking over as mayor of Cahors. Pierre took a position as a doctor for an insurance company in Paris, La Préservatrice. He continued to have a surgery at home, but something had happened to his spirit during the war. He

49

had seen too much. His eldest son Jean had been gassed, and returned home in 1919 to succumb to the worldwide influenza epidemic. He survived to follow his father into that field of medicine in which Pierre had become interested as a medical student, neurology. René, who was now eighteen, was studying law, which to Louise's delight he 'passed with flying colours'.[1]

Louis, the only brother with no academic qualification, had to begin his working life more humbly. In 1920 he took a job at 53, rue Lafayette, selling advertising for the Société Fermière des Annuaires, agents of Bottins, producers of telephone directories for France and abroad. France was exhausted economically and emotionally. Post-war disenchantment – galloping inflation, strikes, unemployment, national debt, national mourning – was compounded by the sight of so many *mutilés de guerre*, war wounded, in the streets. Louis Darquier, however undistinguished his war career, was a product of the disillusion which followed victory. Others, like him, drank from a well of anger and grief, fuelled by a sense of decline and decadence, a sense of the passing of an empire, of all the old values gone.

But in 1920 Colette published *Chéri*, Scott Fitzgerald *This Side of Paradise*. The jazz age and the age of the flapper were on the horizon. The Paris Peace Conference of 1919 concluded with the signing of the Treaty of Versailles which in turn, in 1920, set up the League of Nations to arbitrate international peace and cooperation. The harsh revenge France exacted on defeated Germany led to twenty years of diplomatic failures as France struggled to keep Germany to its treaty commitments. The heartbreaking monuments to the war dead which sprang up in villages, towns and cities in France and in most of the belligerent countries – used again in 1945 to record deaths in the Second World War, often in the same families – witnessed the futility of war, not its glory.

Louis' academic failure before the war was not to condemn him to selling advertising in phone books forever. He was only twenty-two, and his 'godfather' was to hand. De Monzie, too disabled for war service, had more time on his hands: he was defeated in the 1919 elections for the Chamber of Deputies, the lower chamber of the French Parliament, though he quickly moved on to become senator of the Lot. He was not an anti-Semite, had no political animosities and was a prolific entertainer. The great and the good sat at the dinner tables of his estates in the Lot and his apartment in Paris. The person he loved most in the world was his school friend Henry de Jouvenel,[2] man of letters, charm and politics, now one of the editors-in-chief of *Le Matin*.

By 1920 de Jouvenel had been with Colette, married or unmarried, for a dozen years; his previous wife, and his next one, were both Jewish.[3] De Monzie was ambitious for de Jouvenel's political career – politicians, editors, thinkers, writers, industrialists and businessmen were part of his salon, and outside his salon his acquaintance and influence were even larger. Action Française was now at the height of its power. Proust, Rodin and Gide took its newspaper regularly, and in Britain T.S. Eliot gave it his imprimatur in the *Criterion*.[4] De Monzie first met Charles Maurras in 1920. They argued about everything, but their admiration was mutual.

Anatole de Monzie placed both Louis and René Darquier in the wheat trade.[5] One of his key affiliations was to Jewish wheat families, many of them living in Alsace, which with the department of the Lorraine bordered France and Germany. Revolutionary France had been the first western European country to emancipate its Jews in 1789 and 1791, and in Alsace-Lorraine a small Jewish community prospered – Alfred Dreyfus of the *affaire Dreyfus* was one of them, though his family were in textiles, not wheat. These wealthy families valued the freedom granted them by the French republic, and were patriots, leading local politicians and councillors. By the time Louis Darquier went to live in Strasbourg, in 1922, the Jews of Alsace were particularly conspicuous in trade and commerce, and omnipresent in the grain trade.

After the war French farmers, prodigious wheat producers, found themselves threatened on all fronts. The wheat of France had to compete with cheap varieties from foreign parts, countries reached by the great ships which sailed the 'wheat run' and fed Europe in peace and war – Argentina, Canada, the USA and Australia. Most Australian farmers, like Harry Jones, unlike their European counterparts, produced both wool and wheat for export; but their markets were oceans away. Into this vacuum stepped the wheat barons and their steamships. These vast fleets were owned by a new class of magnate, powerful men with global reach whose companies became international giants. The sons of the Jewish wheat merchants of Alsace profited too.

It was the visibility of the immense wealth these men amassed during the Great War that fuelled so much anti-Semitism during the twenties and thirties, and that became a running sore to some, like Louis Darquier.

Following Mussolini and his Italian *battaglia de grano* in July 1925, and Goebbels' demand for 'freedom and bread' for every German, they saw the apparent Jewish control of wheat, the staff of life, as poisoning the staple food of the French nation, ruining the revered French peasant, and weakening the race. In Australia, at the other end of the wheat run, anti-Semitism was fuelled by similar myths and conspiracy theories.

By this time de Monzie was a national figure. He became a minister, variously, of the Merchant Marine, of Finance, of Public Works, of Education and of Justice, fourteen times in all, in the many inter-war French governments. He was also a barrister, with a good practice at the Paris bar. De Monzie had twice been Secretary of State for the Merchant Marine during the First World War, when the purchase of wheat was under state control. He knew all the wheat barons, Jewish or not, and with one of them, Ernest Vilgrain, he paid his dues to Pierre Darquier.

Three men from Alsace-Lorraine directed the fates of Louis and René Darquier over the next decade. Ernest Vilgrain was one; the others were Henry Lévy of the Grands Moulins de Strasbourg, and Louis Louis-Dreyfus – often known as King Two Louis, a pun on the highest gold coin of the *ancien régime* – of the immense grain merchant company Louis Dreyfus & Co.[6] The Louis-Dreyfus family were Jews from Alsace, modest traders in grain with a modest bank in Paris. By the early twentieth century Louis Louis-Dreyfus had transformed the family firm into an international empire: he added a flotilla of ships, expanded his banking interests and opened offices all over the world. He specialised in buying surplus wheat in bulk, and shipping and selling it to countries without it, taking the profit of every part of the procedure for himself. He did this for nation states on a vast scale, and became monarch of his commodity world, King Two Louis, the 'King of Wheat'.

Louis Louis-Dreyfus was a man of many attributes, a millionaire who was careful about money and a deputy, then senator of the French republic, a Freemason, leftish – he and his brother Charles were share-holders in *l'Humanité*, the newspaper of the French Communist Party – and he entered Parliament as a Radical Socialist, like Pierre Darquier. He prospered during the First World War by adding maritime arma-ments to his portfolio, and was denounced in several government reports for profiteering from state wheat contracts. King Two Louis, reputed to be the richest man in France, came to be considered the quintes-sential enemy of the small man – in this case the small French wheat farmer – who blamed him for the collapse of farm prices in the 1930s Depression.

Ernest Vilgrain, of an old Lorraine milling family, worked for the French Ministry of Trade during the First World War. While still in government he began to build up his Grands Moulins de Paris, transposing the supplies system he had learned as Under-Secretary of State for Supplies into his own private business. He left the government on 19 January 1920, and the next day started his own company, the Coopérative d'Approvisionnement, de Transport et de Crédit (CATC), to operate as a purchase and finance office for his firm.[7] Vilgrain made vast profits by importing Australian wheat via CATC, using the services of an English cohort, Sanday & Co., commodity brokers on the Baltic Exchange, and selling it at vastly inflated prices to the French state. This wheat, well named 'exotic', was often paid for, but never delivered. The Australian wheat scandal of 1920, as it came to be known in France, brought about a parliamentary investigation, a report and a court case. De Monzie defended Vilgrain, whose name so perfectly encapsulated his activities, and his relations with the Louis-Dreyfus family were almost familial. In this fevered world Vilgrain and King Two Louis were old enemies.[8]

In 1921, de Monzie placed Louis Darquier in Vilgrain's firm. Louis worked in 'different services'[9] at Vilgrain's Paris headquarters at 150, boulevard Haussmann until June 1922, when he was sent to Strasbourg to open a subsidiary there. Strasbourg's port on the Rhine was a conduit to the huge corn and grain exchange in Antwerp, where wheat was shipped in from all over the world. Louis Darquier, grain merchant, of 15, avenue des Vosges, Strasbourg, was now a managing director earning three thousand francs a month (roughly £2,000 in today's values) 'and percentages'. Soon his brother René, after obtaining his law degree, joined Vilgrain's CATC in Paris.

In Strasbourg from 1921, and then in Antwerp from 1922 to 1926, Louis was close to a part of Europe which was prey to tumultuous political events. Alsace itself was a battleground of conflicting national identities, and a nursery for activists of one kind or another – Action Française worked hard to stimulate paranoia there, as elsewhere, during these years. Support for the Communist Party was strong, while hard by the occupied Rhineland was a running sore, scratched at by separatists, dissidents, the burgeoning Nazi Party and Germans generally.

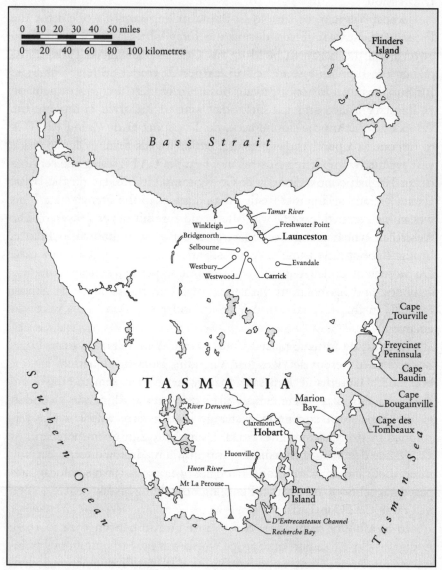

0   10 20 30 40   50 miles
0   20 40 60 80   100 kilometres

Flinders
Island

Bass Strait

Winkleigh
Bridgenorth
Selbourne

Westbury
Westwood

Tamar River
Freshwater Point
Launceston

Evandale
Carrick

Cape
Tourville

Freycinet
Peninsula

Cape
Baudin

Southern Ocean

T A S M A N I A

Cape
Bougainville

Marion
Bay

Cape des
Tombeaux

River Derwent

Claremont
Hobart

Huonville

Huon River

Mt La Perouse

Bruny
Island

D'Entrecasteaux Channel
Recherche Bay

Tasman Sea

Tasmania

In Italy, Mussolini and his Blackshirts marched on Rome in October 1922, one of the first signs of the rise of fascism in Europe. A year later Hitler was leader of the Nazi Party in Germany. France battled and failed to extract war reparations from Germany; as a result, in 1923 the French and Belgian armies invaded the Ruhr. Meanwhile, the Nazi Party had grown from a thousand members in 1920 to over fifty thousand by June 1923; that November Hitler was imprisoned after his failed Beer Hall Putsch in Munich, and *Mein Kampf* was published in 1925 and 1926.

For intellectuals, artists, musicians and writers, Paris in the 1920s was to become a legendary hotbed of activity and incident, both political and artistic. These were *les années folles*, the years of Josephine Baker and *Ulysses*, of impoverished and drunken bohemians of genius living *la vie en rose*. Work took Louis Darquier away from this for most of the decade, but in his years in the wheat business the rebellious young war veteran nevertheless managed to become a perfect, if somewhat sinister, bounder of the Roaring Twenties.

In Sydney and Melbourne, Myrtle was moving in a similar direction, albeit with Edwardian overtones. At some point in these years she abandoned her name, Myrtle Marian Ambrosine Jones, for her new persona of 'Sandra Lindsay'. The 'Sandra' she appropriated from the middle of her mother's name, Alexandrina; the Lindsay remains a mystery, although possibly she took it from the Australian poet so dear to Queen Victoria, Adam Lindsay Gordon. Everything about him and his poetry seems to fit the Tasmanian descendants of Britton Jones. He came from a branch of an old Scottish family, and his chief interest in life was horses. He was despatched to Australia for stealing one. There he fell into debt from gambling, drinking and over-borrowing, and shot himself at Brighton Beach in Melbourne in 1870. Not before he had become, however, the national poet of Australia, and its 'laureate of the horse', though his most famous lines have nothing equine about them. To this day, generations of Australians write rude versions of the lines for which he is best remembered:

> Life is mostly froth and bubble
> Two things stand like stone

Kindness in another's trouble
Courage in your own.[10]

Everyone who met Myrtle, sober or otherwise, throughout her life as Sandra, described her as the kind of woman given to utterances of this kind.

It is not difficult to imagine what a comfortable and churchgoing Launceston family thought of a daughter who went on the stage in Sydney in the 1920s. P.L. Travers, author of *Mary Poppins*, an Australian only a few years younger than Myrtle Jones, toured New South Wales as an actress and dancer in the 1920s: 'It was a very shocking thing to do in those days.'[11] By 1922 Myrtle had certainly done something to shock her parents. When Harry Jones made his will that year, it was almost entirely constructed to protect the errant Myrtle from the consequences of her follies. All the other children are swiftly and generously dealt with, but special arrangements are made for Myrtle: the threnody 'other than my said daughter Myrtle Marian Ambrosine Jones' runs through her father's will like a fretful cry.

Myrtle's escapades are kept hidden behind the net curtains of Launceston to this day, but Harry's will suggests what might have been the problem. The will is dated 17 July 1922. Three weeks later Myrtle's future husband, James Roy Workman, always known as Roy, sailed off on a steamer with his parents in a Gilbert and Sullivan touring company to perform in India and the Far East. Myrtle had met Roy before that, while he and his family were touring Australia. It seems likely that she sailed with them, and that this led to her father's new testamentary arrangements. Not that Myrtle was cut off without a penny: quite the opposite. While her family had money, she was provided with it for many years, but after July 1922 she alone of the Jones children was not permitted to touch her capital.

Family descriptions of Myrtle's years on the mainland imply little professional activity. This seems to have been the case, because no mention of a Sandra Lindsay or Myrtle Jones surfaces in Australian theatrical archives. Myrtle lacked application, and she liked to gallivant. She was probably one of the Idas or Ivys, Ethels or Berthas, Minnies or Maudes so fetchingly exhibited in theatre programmes of the time, which in those days merely listed '13 in the chorus'. Audiences for musicals were phenomenal, for the 1920s were the years when the success of 'Australia's Queen of Musical Comedy', Gladys Moncrieff, in operettas such as *The Maid of the Mountains*, made her as famous in Australia as Nellie Melba. On the other hand, photographs Myrtle left behind suggest that she may have posed for saucy postcards – 'Dark-eyed beauty in swimsuit revealing thighs and stocking tops and holding a Parasol' with captions such as 'The Glad Eye', 'Lady Disdain' or 'Miss Caprice'.[12]

By 1922, when the Workmans' theatrical entourage departed on tour, Australia, like Europe and America, had begun to froth with the spirit of the jazz age, its heroines very often being young persons like Myrtle, scallywag daughters of middle-class families. Short skirts and cigarettes, bobbed hair and bandaged bosoms were all the rage. Perhaps the personality and charm Myrtle added to her musical talent led her to try her hand at the piano in one of the numerous all-night dances of the time. If she did indeed race through 'Let's Misbehave' and 'Yes, We Have No Bananas' – not to mention ragtime, jazztime, swing – she remained a musical child of the 1890s, and her repertoire could easily have extended to performing as a maid or nymphet in a Gilbert and Sullivan opera.

Roy Workman was the only child of a Belfast soprano, Bessel Adams, and C.H. Workman, the celebrated Savoyard and principal comedian of the D'Oyly Carte Opera Company in London from 1898 to 1909. Charles Workman appeared in every Gilbert and Sullivan operetta except *Ruddigore*, playing Bunthorne in *Patience*, the Duke of Plaza Toro in *The Gondoliers*, Ko-Ko in *The Mikado*; but his greatest claim to fame was his Jack Point in *The Yeomen of the Guard*, a role which he established and made his own.[13] He managed the Savoy Theatre in London for one unfortunate year from 1909, when he came to legal blows with W.S. Gilbert, having made the mistake of inserting a song of his own choice – 'Oh Love, that Rulest in Our Land' – into a Gilbert libretto.[14] They also quarrelled about leading ladies, and Gilbert banned Workman from performing his works in England.

A Savoyard remittance family, in 1914 the Workman *ménage* embarked for Australia, where they spent many successful years touring the Savoy operas. Charles Workman was fêted throughout Australia for this, and for his Bumerli in *The Chocolate Soldier*. They loved him too as Ali Baba in *Chu Chin Chow*, famous for its on-stage camels and horses and its Cobbler's Song. The Workmans worked for the great Australian impresario of the time, J.C. Williamson, and travelled with his D'Oyly Carte Gilbert and Sullivan touring companies, which did as much as the game of cricket to maintain affection within the British Empire. This alliance could have been of tremendous importance to Myrtle's theatrical aspirations had the Workmans survived their 1922 tour. Alas, Bessel Adams died of a heart attack in the Grand Hotel, Calcutta, in February 1923, and Charles died at sea off Hong Kong three months later. They left their underage son an orphan. Back in Sydney, three weeks before his twenty-first birthday, Myrtle married him.

When Myrtle married Roy Workman at the office of Sydney's registrar general on 1 August 1923, both gave their address as Her Majesty's Hotel, Sydney, he giving his profession as actor, she as actress. Myrtle's inventions at this time were wide-ranging. She lied about her name, her age, and her parents – she called her father Harry Lindsay – and claimed to have been born in Weymouth, England, where her brother Will had convalesced during the First World War.[15] But she could admit her marriage and a month after the event it was suitably announced in the *Launceston Examiner*.

The only account we have of Myrtle in the years after her marriage comes from Louis Darquier, who told his younger brother in 1927 that 'these two phenomenons [Roy and Myrtle] have been travelling for three and a half years! China, Japan, America, Honolulu: they have been everywhere...'[16] If this was true – did Louis Darquier ever tell the truth about anything? – it could be that Myrtle and Roy joined a J.C. Williamson touring company (perhaps replacing his defunct parents) which left for the Far East at the end of 1923.

Louis described Roy as 'a kind of fool, charming I might add . . . He is twenty-six years old: he drinks like a lord and is completely impotent.' Myrtle's drinking, learned perhaps in her bohemian years in Sydney or perhaps during her four years with Roy – whom she later complimented for hitting her but *'once'*, and then 'only when maddened by drink'[17] – was something henceforth never abandoned, but something she always struggled to hide.

In France, by 1924, Louise Darquier was a happy woman. 'Pierre is still working. Jean is a brilliant intern, Louis is going to set up another branch in Antwerp, and René has joined the same firm as Louis . . .'[18] That January Louis went to Antwerp as one of two directors – he was Vilgrain's representative – to manage a new General Grain Company, a joint Anglo-French venture set up by Vilgrain and British firms with which he had been involved in the Australian wheat scandal. This began Louis Darquier's long involvement with England – he was paid in sterling, £1,500 a year plus percentages, about £53,000 today. A year later Vilgrain's partners were gone, the company was renamed the Grain Union Company, and it was said to handle 'monetary operations and illegal transactions'.[19]

Louis was now a wheat broker, and he had a share in the company. His mandate included, fatally, permission 'to sign, endorse and discharge cheques and money orders'.[20] And he signed the accounts. He had a fiancée called Line, whose expensive ring he used in later years to raise money when down and out. Nearby, in Munich, Hitler's trial following his Beer Hall Putsch was making headlines. In July 1924 Louis visited his parents, to go to the Olympic Games at Colombes in the western suburbs of Paris. He used his excellent English during numerous trips to London, where he stayed in comfort at Brown's Hotel in Mayfair near Piccadilly, an elegant place beloved of the smaller kind of European royalty and 'but a stroll away from Buckingham Palace'.

The high point of Louis' life as a working man was 1924, the last year of peace for all members of the Darquier family, and the last year of any continuing relationship with his father. At the same time, the elections of that year were won by an alliance of parties on the left, and France's political fissures were deepened by terror of communism and hatred of fascism. Louis' handsome prospects began to ebb away in the following year, when the country was in the midst of economic depression.

In Strasbourg Louis had already acquired the reputation of a rake, but now mention of debts began too. It is also said that he was arrested in London for being drunk and disorderly.[21] It seems that he was often intoxicated, for one day at the Antwerp stock exchange – a magnificent Moorish Gothic building with an immense colonnaded and arcaded hall – he galloped in 'on a horse, and tried to take it into the central enclosure'. But his real crime was his use of company money 'for his own purposes'. Other reports suggest that he used the money to speculate against the franc, which seems likely. 'At the same time he also began his swindles: he used the business information he found on the Stock Exchange for his own purposes if an interesting opportunity arose, and passed the bad deals on to the company. Management discovered this at the end of six months: these manoeuvres and his characteristic abuse of trust cost the company nearly 500,000 francs!'[22] Louis traded in futures: good ones for himself, bad ones for his company. On 29 November 1925 his fellow director called an extraordinary general meeting and demanded Louis' dismissal. It took two months to get rid of him.

Louis wrote to an old friend and political colleague of his father's in Cahors, telling him he was returning to the town for Carnival – he now had plenty of free time on his hands – and that he wanted to go into the political life which 'Papa has unfortunately abandoned'.[23] Louis' reconstitution of recent events included a claim to have made a fortune of about two million francs on the Antwerp Bourse; but only his family and their connections now saved him from his embarrassments. When Louis' fraud was discovered, René was in Antwerp too, as director of Vilgrain's CATC office there, and presumably he pacified Vilgrain.

Henry Lévy had set up Grands Moulins de Strasbourg with Achille Baumann in 1899. By 1924 Baumann had resigned and by 1927, when René went to work for him, Henry Lévy had become 'The Miller King', in sole charge of the vast Baumann-Lévy empire. Vilgrain and his companies had encountered financial problems: whether these were due to the court cases, or investigations into the Australian wheat scandal, or were brought about solely by the depredations of Louis Darquier is unknown. Lévy bought out Vilgrain's company. All reports agree that René rescued Louis with the help of Lévy, but this would have been only one of a thousand of his generosities, for Lévy was known as a 'man with great heart', a benefactor to Jew and Gentile, whose greatest qualities were his boundless generosity and his 'understanding and kindness to those in distress'.[24]

The years 1925 and 1926 were the peak of de Monzie's ministerial power, and Louis was not sent to prison. Scandals much larger than his were chronic in France in the 1920s and 1930s anyway. His honour was restored to him, inasmuch as his reinstatement was announced on 31 December 1926, and his 'resignation' accepted the following day. Louis' anti-Semitism was always to be linked to these Jewish wheat barons, and he chose King Two Louis, who added insult to injury by using Louis' good French Christian name twice, as representative of them all. So, whilst it was Henry Lévy who bought out Vilgrain, Louis hid his ignominious dismissal and its resolution by transforming these events into a principled resignation because Vilgrain's company had been 'sold to the Jew Louis-Dreyfus'.[25]

Louis Darquier now led an existence that was the despair of his father, never ceasing to complain that his parents would not help him as they helped Jean and René. His fiancée Line had committed suicide. He had already seen his older brother become a doctor, which he had failed to do, and now he had to bear the further indignity of watching his younger brother prosper where he had come to grief. René's good fortune and Henry Lévy's generosity were to support him for the next ten years: 'crippled with debts, with creditors at his throat, his back against the wall . . . each time he knocked at the door of his brother and Henry Lévy, each time they got him out of his fix, though obviously not for very long'.[26]

Before the 1960s all Australians had British citizenship, but now, as the wife of the Northern Irish Roy Workman, Myrtle had a British passport, of which she was immensely proud and which she treasured until the end of her days. This devotion to the 'Mother Country' nevertheless seems to have caused interminable problems, because Myrtle's grizzles about passports flicker through the following decades. Perhaps she obtained her passport as Sandra Lindsay or Sandra Workman, but whatever the original problem she compounded it, for although Roy Workman was a singer who only appeared in musicals and Gilbert and Sullivan, they presented themselves to Europe in late 1926 or early 1927 as Lord and Lady Workman-Macnaghten, of Belfast.

There are many explanations as to how Louis Darquier met Myrtle. Some say she met him in France where her husband was singing, others that it was in a military convalescent hospital where Roy was performing, while Louis once claimed that they met at the casino in Monte Carlo. Gambling is a distinct possibility, but the favourite of the medley on offer is that they met in Germany, where Roy's company was entertaining the troops.

After the Great War, as a protective buffer between France and Germany, the Rhineland was occupied for eleven years by the armies of the *Entente*. The British left in 1929. Until 1926 their headquarters were in Cologne, thereafter in Wiesbaden. The occupying troops were provided with every British comfort: cricket, marmalade, Scouts and Guides, theatre and cinema. In the Walhalla Theatre in Wiesbaden, the Rhine Army Dramatic Company put on productions of plays by John Galsworthy and, of course, the operettas of Gilbert and Sullivan. In Strasbourg in 1922–23 and in Antwerp from 1924 to 1926, Louis Darquier was a whisper away from Cologne and Wiesbaden, and, with the Rhineland virtually a French protectorate, the latter had become almost a border town.

Around these troops hovered a number of prostitutes so excessive – an estimated thirty thousand in Cologne alone – that it was proposed that a team of British policewomen should patrol the streets. Louis was known to be partial to this kind of sexual opportunity, and his good English enabled him to move around where he liked. Finally there was a casino, the Casino Wiesbaden, an old and famous place of entertainment, dripping with chandeliers and fantastical neoclassical grandeur. Today it has blackjack and roulette and stud poker, but it was closed for gambling from 1873 to 1949; then, as now, it had a concert hall, and here the troops were entertained. This gingerbread palace would have been a perfect setting for the meeting of Louis Darquier and Myrtle Jones.

By 1927, however much René and Henry Lévy had helped him, Louis could no longer actually earn money. He now looked to other quarters for financial rewards, and he wrote happily to René in 1927 – 'not without some cynicism' – about his new arrangements. He was living 'as man and wife' with Sandra in her guise as Lady Workman-Macnaghten, with Roy in tow, at the Hôtel Bristol on the Canebière in Marseille. This port city of strangers and travellers was another perfect setting for the three adventurers to arrange reincarnation. Myrtle, Louis told René, was 'an Australian woman, married to an Englishman, nephew and heir of Lord Macnaghten but who has not a sou. She is the daughter of a *grain and wool producer of Tasmania* [Louis writes the latter words in English]. Family with Yankee style – 9 children –

unquestionably lots of money ... In any case the directory indicates several of her father's firms. But she is fed up with her husband.'[27] Roy Workman drank so much he was 'completely helpless', wrote Louis; all three of them drank. Louis would become violent, but he was not an alcoholic. Myrtle was.

When 'Lady Workman-Macnaghten' met Louis she presented herself to him as an Australian version of those American heiresses much dreamed of by indigent Europeans in the 1920s. In photographs she stands about five inches shorter than Louis; sometimes she looks ample, sometimes thin and distrait. But whatever she may have lacked in beauty Myrtle made up with glamour; she had a tireless sense of humour, was always anxious to please, and she decorated herself like a child at play. Myrtle had style. In 1927 she was still in regular receipt of funds from Tasmania – '£40 a week without taking into account gifts on every occasion', wrote Louis, with the expectation of a substantial inheritance of 'as much as £130,000 at the age of 28'.[28] Myrtle was already thirty-four when she assured Louis of these handsome prospects, unaware of the special arrangements Harry had made for her in his will.

Roy Workman's adoption of a Northern Irish peer as his uncle was the kind of fabrication Myrtle dreamed up for all the men in her life.[29] Her habit of claiming aristocratic relations seems to have come from an anxious aspiration to belong to England and 'Home', as Australians of English descent liked to call the country which despatched their convict ancestors in the eighteenth and nineteenth centuries. Such aspirations were thoroughly removed from the facts of Myrtle's existence as noted in her birth and marriage certificates. These circumstances made divorce difficult. Nevertheless Myrtle offered to divorce Roy, to marry Louis and take him to Australia. Louis equivocated, then settled the matter by marrying Myrtle, divorced or not. Family tradition reports that Roy remained devoted to Myrtle to the end, but his loss did not prevent him from returning to Egypt and living with another woman older than himself.

Myrtle was to learn the truth about her inheritance two years after she assured Louis of her millions, just at the moment when, in the personae of Baron and Baroness Louis Darquier de Pellepoix, they descended upon Brown's Hotel in Mayfair to begin four years of life in London (save for Louis' constant dashes to Paris in pursuit of funds). Louis never showed any sign of fury when Myrtle proved yet again to be parsimonious with the truth – he could not afford to. Their mutual inventions were one of the strongest cords that held them together.

5

Baby

'IT WOULD BE BEAUTIFUL to have little ones around me,' wrote Louise to a faithful minion in Cahors in 1924. 'I feel I am getting old.'[1] When Louis and Myrtle married in St Giles Register Office in London on 19 April 1928, they were staying at the St Kilda Hotel in Torrington Square, in the heart of Bloomsbury. This hotel, obliterated by German bombs in the Second World War, was advertised in the *Daily Telegraph* as 'Overlooking Gardens. Excellent Cuisine. Billiards. Full or part board. Most convenient for business and pleasure. Comfortable. Terms moderate.'[2] Such terms were necessary, for by 1928 Louis was no longer speaking to his father. The couple was living on Myrtle's money. As Louis compounded his early differences with his father with constant imbroglios and demands for money, matters between them never improved. Though sorely tried by Louis' marriage to Myrtle, Louise continued to defend her 'lame duck' son.

The help Louis insistently demanded was sometimes given to him by his mother (who in 1934 sold the Laytou family home in Cahors to pay Louis' debts), and always by his brother René, but in 1928 his parents had other expenses. All three of Louise's sons married in that year, Jean and René in Paris, René's marriage properly taking place at Louise's local church of Saint-Pierre de Neuilly. Louise dreamed of great marriages for her sons. In Jean's case she had succeeded in parting him from a girl-friend in Cahors, explaining that she was a Protestant and 'too modest in origins and not sufficiently rich'.[3] She had no opportunity to inter-fere in Louis' choice. His London nuptials were unattended by any of his family, but at least he married first, always an important position for the Darquier brothers.

'As you can see, my two beloved boys are so alike,' said Louise of Jean and Louis, maternal wishful thinking of a high order.[4] Jean was a medical man but also an artistic *touche-à-tout*, a Jack-of-all-trades, while Louis was Poor-Johnny-One-Note:[5] once he chose Jews as his trade, he rarely moved off the subject for a moment. René, the youngest, was the businessman, the one with his feet on the ground. Jean qualified as a neurologist at the Faculty of Medicine of Paris in 1927, worked as an intern at the famous Salpêtrière Hospital and lived with his parents in Neuilly until he married Jeanne Riu – 'Janot' – in July 1928. Four months later René married Lucienne Losson, who lived in another of the flats in the Neuilly apartment block: 'Lucienne was a girl whom the three brothers used to meet on the stairs, and pull her plaits . . . she fell in love with Jean but that did not work out so she married René.' Pierre is reported to have said that she chose 'the best of the bunch'.[6] Louis missed the marriages of both his brothers. René was now living in Strasbourg, where Henry Lévy had acquired a shareholding in Les Minoteries Alsaciennes – Flour Mills of Alsace. René was appointed its operations manager, one of about forty top managers within the empire of Lévy's Grands Moulins de Strasbourg.

It would be hard to pinpoint which of her daughters-in-law disappointed Louise the most. Jean's wife Janot was the most formidable of the three – 'she was a fascinating woman, not beautiful at all, which was astonishing because Jean was elegant, handsome and a sweet talker'.[7] Janot was 'a little brown thing, ugly, with prominent teeth', but she had a brain – she too became a doctor, in 1943. Lucienne disliked Louise and *vice versa*, while Myrtle was simply beyond the pale. It is unlikely that Louis explained the bigamous nature of his marriage to his adored mother. In the 1920s divorce was a lengthy, costly and scandalous procedure, and it would have been impossible to complete it in the short period between the encounter of Lord and Lady Workman-Macnaghten and Louis Darquier in Marseille in 1927, and the marriage of Louis and Myrtle in London in April 1928. If Myrtle did divorce Roy Workman, there are no records of it in the registers of Australia, France or Britain.[8] Perhaps they divorced in Egypt, although it seems unlikely. Possibly Myrtle convinced herself that she had not been married before, because she had not used her real name. The Tasmanian family seems to have known the truth of it: that Myrtle did not have a divorce when she and Louis married. Bigamy was transmuted into elopement, a romantic French love story, as the years went by.

Whether or not Myrtle and Roy were later divorced, for a Catholic like Louise, Myrtle's previous marriage was unacceptable. What is more she was a Protestant, also unacceptable. Louis' marriage meant he now had problems with both his parents, and he dealt with them at this point by staying away from France. In a sense he became a French remittance man, because, as a wedding gift, René Darquier gave Louis and Myrtle a first-class ticket to Australia. On the passenger list of the elegant steamship the *Principe di Udine*, which sailed from Genoa in mid-June 1928, both of them stated that their 'intended future permanent residence' was to be Australia. They listed themselves as plain Mr and Mrs Louis Darquier, he a grain merchant, she a housewife, heading for 3 Cypress Street, Launceston. It seems that the appurtenances of nobility descended upon them during the voyage, because on arrival the entire Tasmanian family appears to have sincerely believed that their daughter and sister had married a baron.

Louis Darquier made grand claims for this wedding trip. The inventions are rich and various, swerving from accounts of a year spent raising sheep and cattle, to the running of a 'sheep-farm', to the management of a large agricultural concern. He obliterated the years 1926 to 1933 from his memory under a mountain of faradiddles in his *curriculum vitae*, ranging through: 'From 1925 to 1928 having made a fortune of about 2.000.000 Darquier worked for himself and travelled particularly in Australia, the United States and in England,'[9] to 'Went to Australia in 1927 to manage a livestock and agricultural farm,'[10] to 'In 1927 he failed at sheep-farming in Australia having previously married an heiress.'[11] He was nowhere near Australia in 1927, and he did no work of any kind there. Tasmania was unknown to 1930s Europe, so the story of Myrtle's fortune was a safe claim which could never be investigated.

The couple reached Melbourne in July 1928, and by the end of the month they were in Launceston. As they were steaming towards Australia, Harry Jones ensured that Louis could not get his hands on any Jones money. On 6 July he added a codicil to the effect that no one could inherit until Lexie's death. As Louis and Myrtle approached Launceston, she ceased to be an heiress.

If Louis and Myrtle had serious intentions of living in Australia, they were quickly dispelled. They did not stay at Cypress Street; indeed its suburban proportions probably gave Louis his first indication of disappointments to come. These were to be many. Launceston was a small antipodean rural town, and Louis and Myrtle were night birds, creatures of the city. Myrtle had told Louis that one of her brothers was a student at Heidelberg, another at Oxford, and a third a doctor. All this was untrue, though her brothers were accomplished and educated young men, and Louis now met the dentists, teachers and farmers they actually were.

The Baron and Baroness are said to have enjoyed a riotous time in Tasmania, but ten days in Launceston, housed in the grandiose Australian pub known as the Hotel Launceston, was all they could tolerate. Though divorce and remarriage – to a Catholic – were as unacceptable to Lexie and Harry Jones as they were to the French Darquiers, when Myrtle's family met Louis Darquier in 1928, her sisters Olive, Hazel and Heather all became besotted with him. Louis sat at the piano with his wife and entertained the family with English and French songs. With his enchanting French accent he was the stuff of dreams: 'Louis was romantic, French, wore a monocle, was handsome. All the Jones sisters were in love with him.'[12]

After Launceston Myrtle and Louis stopped off in Melbourne – where Myrtle's sister Hazel was studying at Melbourne University and where Louis Dreyfus & Co. had substantial headquarters – then went on to Queensland, where her brother Hector was a dentist in Toowoomba, a visit remembered by a relative: 'Louis was a very well-dressed, handsome man who impressed us with his European manners and travellers' tales. Aunty Myrt was a beautiful lady, always well dressed with a very outgoing personality.'[13] Floating around the world in a first-class cabin was much more to the Darquiers' taste than driving along the unmade roads of the Darling Downs in Hector's little Austin. They visited Sydney in early 1929, when Louis renewed his passport at the French consulate.[14]

Louis noticed none of the joys Australia can offer. True, when he visited the country in 1928, before the influx of immigrants who have transformed the country into a gourmet's paradise, it had the worst cooking in the world. Overdone steak and overboiled cabbage, and several thousand different kinds of cake or sponge finger, accompanied by strong tea, could not tempt a European palate. Louis and Myrtle were avid gamblers, but Australian pursuits – horse-tracks and two-up – provided none of the glamour of European casinos. Louis hated hot weather, and he failed to notice the light in the vast skies of many blues, the miraculous calls and colours of the birds, the bush of such a particular and hypnotising green. What he did notice he used in another fantastical *curriculum vitae* in which he asserted: 'In Australia, in particular, he learned, to his own cost, of the catastrophic effect of Marxist doctrine and the system of state control on large farming enterprises.'[15] Harry Jones still owned three estates outside Launceston. There was a huge wheat surplus in 1928, a slump in prices and talk of re-establishing state control of the sale of Australian wheat – rejected by farmers as a socialist concept. Louis might have purloined Harry's opinions, or he might have seen for himself that 1920s Australia was as jittery and riven as any European country after the Great War and the birth of communism.

The Darquiers' arrival coincided with an extended 'wharfies' (water-side workers) strike which, apart from inconveniencing them, would have been an eye-opener as to the suitability of Australia as a domicile. There were riots on the docks, and sympathy strikes in key industries. Particularly in Sydney, always a Labor stronghold, King-and-Empire Australians – the establishment – confronted the trade unions and the Communist Menace. Newspaper headlines such as 'Police Fire on Strikers', 'Red Rule', 'Unionism Declares War' were daily fare.[16] Then, having been governed by conservatives since the war, in October 1929 Australians voted the Labor Party into power.

Louis and Myrtle had left by then, but they sailed into the Great Depression, landing in the USA as the New York stock market was preparing to collapse, and in London just as the slump was to reach its worst there. As the first signs of recovery were appearing in Britain, they moved on to France when the world economic disaster had just begun to bite. Louis' reported words of farewell were to promise Harry Jones that he would always look after Myrtle, and in his own way he did. When Harry died on 10 February 1929, the terms of his will, revealed a month later, put paid to all Louis' hopes of immediate wealth. At his death Harry, whose assets would have made him a modest millionaire at today's values, left all his money to Lexie.[17] A month later there were disastrous floods in northern Tasmania, and the land around Launceston was devastated, then, in October 1929, Wall Street crashed and so did the Jones fortune.

'The more I go on,' wrote Louis to René in 1927, 'the more I think that one must stretch one's field of action as far as possible.' Now a citizen of the world, he later described his and Myrtle's 'series of voyages in Australia, the United States and New Zealand' (in fact it is unlikely that they ever travelled in the USA or New Zealand – at the most the ship they travelled on from Australia called in at ports there on the way) as an invaluable opportunity to 'study the constantly worsening state of the world economy'.

Money, preferably unearned, was a god to Myrtle and Louis; the gods did not reciprocate in kind. Within a few months of their taking up residence in Louis' favourite Mayfair hostelry, Brown's Hotel, in December 1929, the Great Slump had hit Australia, the price of wool and wheat fell and the value of the Australian mining shares in Broken Hill collapsed. Myrtle's £40 a week, a handsome sum in the 1920s, was whittled down to £10, and then £3. The disappearance of her crock of gold coincided with the news that she was pregnant.

But at first nothing changed for Myrtle and Louis. The part of London they inhabited – Piccadilly, Mayfair – was the centre of life for the bright young things of the day. Brown's has two entrances, one in Dover Street, the other in Albemarle Street, an excellent thing if one needed to avoid creditors, which was very soon to be the case, but in the meantime they were near every part of London they most loved. They fell in with the Jimmy Rutlands and other lesser Wodehousian honourables, with denizens of Buck's club in Clifford Street and adventurers and adulterers on long golfing weekends at Le Touquet. Nightlife, gambling and music were at the door. Hutch, the black pianist and singer so beloved by Lady Edwina Mountbatten,[18] sang and played exactly to Myrtle's taste – 'Ain't Misbehavin', 'What is this Thing Called Love?' The haunting songs of the time were played at the Café Royal in Regent Street, the Café de Paris and the Berkeley. Nearby were the theatres and cinemas of Shaftesbury Avenue and Covent Garden, Rosa Lewis's legendary haunt of Bohemia the Cavendish Hotel, and Fortnum and Mason for tea and goodies. The Baron and Baroness, dressed to the nines, could hear Noël Coward, Jessie Matthews and the Cochran revues, with songs Myrtle would have played in a trice had they been able to afford a piano. There were cabarets and nightclubs galore – the Gargoyle in Soho, haunt of the decadent upper crust, the Blue Train, the Silver Slipper, the Not.

By the middle of 1930 there were two million unemployed in Britain, despite all the promises of Ramsay MacDonald's Labour government.

Louis could not get a position. Very soon, despite his winnings at poker, there was no money left. Louis turned to René. It soon became his habit to telegraph René in Strasbourg first, letters of explanation following. All his telegrams are similarly breathless. In the spring of 1930 he cabled:

FOUND POSITION 1000 POUNDS PLUS SIX PERCENTAGE BASE
LAST BALANCE SHEET NEED TO HOLD ON TILL AFTER
EASTER CAN YOU ADVANCE 150 POUNDS VITAL URGENT AND
SECRET KISSES LOUIS THOS. COOKS BERKELEY STREET[19]

'I have been entirely ruined for a long time – I've lived any old how for some months and feel the end approaching,' he then explained by letter. The 'cow of a hotelkeeper' at Brown's was threatening to throw them out. Would René buy his ex-fiancée Line's ring, his tiepin or 'Sandra's diamond brooch' and send him £150 immediately so he could pay the bill? He was about to become the manager of a car sales company, 'Automobiles, new and second hand, garage, accessories etc.', in which, he assured René, his role would be 'above all to talk to the distinguished people who do not like, in England, as you know, to do business with a professional mechanic'.[20] He begged René, when he sent the money, to remember that he was now Darquier de Pellepoix.[21] René never did remember.

Louis earned his keep by pursuing anyone with a title or a position: the 1930 candidate was 'the manager' of Lloyds Bank, a Yorkshireman named Robinson, who promised him '3 or 4 consultancies' worth '400 or 500 pounds a year'.[22] Myrtle's family were dunned too, but unfortunately Hector, applied to for £100, was too far away to provide immediate relief. By the time Myrtle was five months pregnant, in April 1930, Brown's Hotel refused to accommodate them any longer, and the Baron and Baroness appeared in Marlborough Street Magistrates' Court, in company with the beggars and indigents of the time, because of Louis' failure to register as an alien. As such he was required to demonstrate, under clause 1a of the Aliens Act, that he was 'in a position to support himself and his dependants', so he scarcely had a leg to stand on. Preceded into court by Albert Gabb, aged fifty-six, accused of begging, Louis, 'aged thirty-two . . . grain merchant', 'tall and distinguished-looking' in 'a smart speckled-grey overcoat' was fined £100, not the usual £50. 'What! A Baron and a Baroness?' remarked the magistrate. 'I should be insulting if I were to suggest such a small sum to them.'

The *Evening Standard* of 17 April reported the case: 'MONOCLED BARON CHARGED'.[23] For her appearance at court Myrtle wore the uniform of her aspirations. 'Baroness Darquier', aged thirty-seven, was described as 'aged twenty-eight ... an attractive-looking woman' wearing 'a dark blue coat with a fur collar and a close-fitting black hat'. By the time this account reached Tasmania, these events had been transformed into a glamorous peccadillo, a small misunderstanding which could in no way mar the image of the aristocratic Baron and his beautiful young wife. More realistically, Father Robert Steuart of Farm Street, London's most exclusive Catholic Church, 'stood surety for each'.

After this Louis was entirely on his uppers. Their Mayfair life was quite over. Hotel managers, men whom Louis liked to describe as 'taverners', objected to not being paid. After their ejection by Brown's, Louis and Myrtle's descent was rapid: they flitted through the Curzon Hotel, followed by a swift descent to the Hotel Rubens in Buckingham Palace Road, a street less grand than its royal name might imply. Their energies were now devoted to extracting money from their respective families to pay the weekly bills. René and Lucienne were also expecting their first child, but this did not prevent Louis from ringing Strasbourg at midnight, or ticking his brother off if money did not arrive in time, or if René suggested investigating the reasons for Robinson's failure to come forth with anything sound. Louis' nerves became 'frazzled', while Myrtle grew 'enormous'. She was due to give birth in August, and by June they moved out of London for her confinement.

It is likely that they chose Old Windsor because of its propinquity to the royal castle and Eton College – Louis hoped for a boy, and wanted him educated at Eton. In fact Old Windsor was not the Windsor of the British kings and queens but a more ancient nearby parish with some four hundred houses in 1930, none of them meaner than Treen Cottage, where the Darquiers lodged for £4 a week, 'everything included', in the summer of 1930.[24] In July Louis had a 'violent discussion' with Robinson which ended all hopes of money from that quarter, and immediately car sales companies became a thing of the past. Louise Darquier was the daughter and granddaughter of printers and journalists; Louis decided to earn his living by becoming a writer.

The Jones family sent Louis and Myrtle £100 to pay for the birth of their child, and Louis found himself a literary agent and tossed off some travel articles and four short stories in a matter of weeks. 'I hope he will sell them,' Louis told René, and every time he wrote asking for more money, he informed his brother that he hoped it would be his 'last begging'. Louis wrote his fictions in English and sometimes in French, and Myrtle said they appeared 'in the French papers at intervals'. Nothing is left to inform us of their quality or flavour, or even their existence, the records of his dealings with literary agents and putative publishers having been either lost in the mists of time, discarded as unimportant, or destroyed by bombing during the war. Louis could write a novel, in English, in a few months; this may be one reason they were never published.

Anne Darquier was born in Treen Cottage, Old Windsor, on 3 September 1930, the certificate recording this event being a fabrication from beginning to end, except for the date. Giving Anne the middle name of 'France', as was the habit of patriotic Frenchmen, Louis now officially signed himself as Baron Louis Darquier de Pellepoix. Despite the fact that he and Myrtle were to live in hotel rooms of considerable seediness for most of their lives, he described himself as a 'Landowner and French Baron'. Myrtle, as ferocious a fibber as Louis, gave her name as 'Myrtle Marion Ambrosene Darquier de Pellepoix, formerly Lindsay-Jones'. A week later, Adolf Hitler's Nazi Party was elected in sufficient numbers to make it the second-largest political party in Germany.

Myrtle, presumably because of her incoherent marital status, was always anguished by any demand to see her passport, or any other official documentation. Possibly for this reason, or perhaps because she and Louis were so often pursued by angry creditors, her use of aliases continued throughout her life. Sometimes she is Myrtle Darquier de Pellepoix, formerly Lindsay-Jones – later she changed the spelling to the more aristocratic Lyndsay; sometimes she is Morrison-Jones, sometimes Sandra Lyndsay-Darquier. On the run after the war she was Cynthia de Pelle Poix. Sometimes she is English, sometimes Irish, sometimes American; often she is a wealthy heiress, the proprietor of vast 'ranches' in Australia. Always she liked people to address her as 'Baroness', '*Baronne*', '*Baronesa*'.

Elsie Lightfoot of Duns Tew in Oxfordshire called herself a children's nurse. It is unlikely she had any training, but it seems certain that in 1930 she answered an advertisement placed by Myrtle in *The Lady*, the English weekly magazine which has matched nannies, maids and menials with those in need of them since 1885. In those days *The Lady* carried advertisements requesting 'thoroughly experienced cake makers', 'companion-helps' and 'strong, willing and early rising' persons of all kinds to come to the assistance of ladies and gentlewomen of the leisured classes.

Elsie was thirty-seven years old when she went to work for a couple whom she believed to be Baron and Baroness Louis Darquier de Pellepoix. Anne always implied that Elsie was paid to take her in almost immediately after she was born. Six weeks later her parents registered her birth in Windsor; three months later they were gone, back to London, and then to Paris. These three months constitute more or less the entire time Myrtle, Louis and Anne Darquier were to spend together. Anne was given away for a fee of £1 a week.

In later life Louis explained this away as normal behaviour for the time; if he had indeed possessed the lands and estates he claimed, Anne would have lived apart from her parents with her nanny in the standard English upper-class mode. Louis and Myrtle called Elsie 'Nurse' in the accepted way, and gave Anne to her to take away to live in Duns Tew. Neither Myrtle nor Louis ever referred to their daughter by her name: for Myrtle she was always 'Baby', for Louis '*la gosse*', the kid.

There are three Tews in Oxfordshire: Duns Tew, Little Tew and Great Tew, nestling north of Oxford and bypassed by the road from Chipping Norton to Banbury. These were still Domesday feudal villages in the 1930s, with tied cottages, lords of the manor of the hunting, shooting, fishing and absentee kind, and ancient and charming parish churches. There was no sewerage, no gas, electricity or mains water, and only an occasional public telephone.

Elsie Lightfoot was born in the village of Cumnor, very near Oxford, on 4 July 1893 – four months before Myrtle Jones. Her parents, Reuben and Emma Hall Lightfoot, were the class of person whose ancestral role was to serve as nannies, grooms and gardeners, or, as in Reuben's case, as a blacksmith. Oxfordshire, near the Cotswolds – described by Sylvia

Plath as 'a county on a nursery plate' – is wealthy, both because of its rich farming land and its proximity to London. But in the 1930s 'everybody was poor'. 'It wasn't all rising fields of poppies and blue skies. A large part of it was lashing rain; chaps walking round dressed in bits of soaking sacking, and children dying of quite ordinary diseases like whooping cough.'[25] That is how Anne remembered her country childhood.

When they were not 'working away', as domestic service was called at the time, Elsie and her sisters lived with their mother Emma in Duns Tew. Anne always called Elsie 'Nanny', and her sisters became Aunty Violet, Aunty Maud and Aunty Annie. By 1930 John Brice, Annie's husband, had died, and her daughter May was living with her grandmother. Almost immediately Emma Lightfoot died, the tied cottage returned to the estate of the Dashwoods, owners of Duns Tew Manor, and Elsie and Maud rented a little thatched cottage, two-up two-down, next door to Daisy Pym the village schoolmistress.

This cottage, much improved, is still there in the main street of Duns Tew, opposite the post office, next to the church. Anne was three months old, and Annie's daughter May, thirteen, was never taken back by her mother. Maud and Elsie, May and Anne were to live together, one way or another, for most of the next fifteen years. May became an older sister to Anne, sharing the particular bond of maternal rejection. One of her friends remembered: 'May never forgave her mother – Anne didn't either.'[26]

Until she took Anne, Elsie was used to working away, but she could do so no longer, at least while Anne was a baby. If she had hoped to live on the money Louis and Myrtle had promised her for Anne's upkeep, she was soon severely disabused. Though she continued to believe that Anne's parents were the Baron and Baroness she liked them to be – Elsie was as partial to royalty and titles as Myrtle – she soon gave up any hope of noble behaviour from either of them.

The Darquier family had almost written Louis off by this time. For ten years he had failed at everything: everywhere he was well known for 'his extravagances and his follies'. The birth of Baby, though, mended fences, so after they left Anne with Elsie, Louis took Myrtle to Paris to meet his family, probably for the first time. Myrtle's accounts, always chaotic, are not specific on this point, but they make it perfectly clear that the Darquiers made it obvious that she would not do. The visit was a disaster. Myrtle wrote to René: 'You will never know how it hurt me to find you all hated me. I liked you too and somehow I fondly imagined you did me.'[27]

They did not, and Louise in particular. Louis worshipped his mother, and Myrtle was 'particularly grieved over Madame's attitude'. 'Australians sound terrible to us and we both look and sound terrible to them.'[28] This was not the reception Myrtle expected. She belonged firmly to that class of Australians who hankered after Europe. When she was sober she assumed a very British accent; when drunk she became Australian. Whether drunk or sober, she had no command of any foreign languages, and her French was at best vestigial. There are fleeting references to something which went terribly wrong during their stay at Neuilly: the chances are that enough became apparent about the drinking habits of both Myrtle and Louis to horrify the Darquier family.[29]

Horrified they certainly were. After the couple's ignominious departure from Neuilly, Louise opened a letter from Roy, addressed to Myrtle. This may be how she discovered that Myrtle was at best a divorced woman, at worst a bigamous one. The despatch of Louise's first grandchild to a nurse in the English counties was unacceptable, though Myrtle maintained that 'it costs far less to have her there than with us as we would have to pay board here for her – it is healthy there for her'.[30] Louis' lack of employment was a major source of displeasure, as were his and Myrtle's nightlife and their spendthrift days. The family called Myrtle '*une Anglaise*', '*la Tasmanienne*', and longed to return her to the strange place from whence she came. Just as important, it seems, was the absence of the anticipated inheritance.

Myrtle struggled to please. Louise Darquier was always beautifully and expensively dressed, with exquisite jewellery, and was most particular about her hats, made for her by her personal '*modiste*' (milliner). Henceforth Myrtle attempted to flatter – or compete with – her mother-in-law by appropriating a passion for hats that always caused comment wherever she went. A vain attempt, because the Darquier family spent most of the next three years trying to force Louis to get a position, and to get rid of Myrtle.

The couple stayed on in Paris while Louis tried to find the money to return to London. Both he and Myrtle thought he could do so by writing a book. Myrtle was sure he could. Closeted together in their hotel room Louis worked on his first novel – *False Gods* was its title – while

Myrtle took up the task of dealing with René. Louis' hatred for his family's 'profoundly cruel attitude' and 'inhumane solutions' meant that the only contact he now had with them were 'fire-eating letters' to René, whose growing impatience was expressed only in a modest request that Louis could perhaps cease wounding him every time he tried to help.

Myrtle's letters tell us everything about her, except for those matters she could not face or would not talk about. Her spelling was shaky in English; as for French, she spelt the language as she heard it, and her inventive attempts to spell the names of her Darquier relations changed in each begging letter. Sometimes there is only a day or so between letters, some of them fourteen pages long, imploring, beseeching René:

> 'Could you let us have 500 francs to get things necessary for Baby and ourselves and collect the book and send it away . . .'
>
> 'Louis or not I will have any more children – we cannot keep ourselves and the poor little one. I have been very queer myself for the last fortnight . . .'
>
> 'My dear René we are again in a very difficult situation. We have had, so to speak, nothing to eat since Saturday . . .'[31]

The word 'grateful' counterpoints 'please send' and 'as soon as possible' in all Myrtle's letters. René sent her the money, with admonitions she accepted with humility, apologies, abasement: 'please Renè [sic] try to forget personal feelings about me . . . My people are not any more pleased with the match than yours . . . I am not material . . .'[32] Louis, meanwhile, made matters worse by applying to family friends and colleagues for money, with calamitous results. He approached one of René's former colleagues, Jean Ostermeyer, who worked for the Grands Moulins in Paris, and followed up his initial success with further demands, writing: 'be careful in what you say to René – he is a little boy, very pretentious and quite stupid despite his commercial sense about practical matters'.[33] Ostermeyer sent the letter on to René. 'I suppose,' wrote Ostermeyer, 'that similar letters have been sent in many directions – As for me, I shall not be taken in twice. His last furore was not worthy of him, he lied and spoke badly about his parents.'[34]

Anatole de Monzie's office told Louis he would assist him later – 'they were helping a banker at present'.[35] When Louis applied to Jean's medical teacher, Dr Clovis Vincent of the Salpêtrière Hospital, Vincent replied that Pierre Darquier had already warned him off, accompanying this instruction with richly descriptive comments about his second son. 'I want you to realise,' roared Louis to René, 'the hate that I have held for the last twenty years for the bastard whose name I regret to say I bear (and who always conducted himself, in war and in peace, in politics as in the family, physically and morally as the worst of cowards) . . . There are many personal elements in my failure, but also many profound causes for which I am not responsible – a heavy family inheritance, combined with intellectual poverty on one side and congenital cowardice on the other – a dreadful education, low in all points of view – the war above all – Two or three years of attempts are not too many, believe me, to get rid of this dross.'[36]

Myrtle's work became even harder, her letters longer. Baby, she wrote, 'has wonderful health and is a very good and obedient child. She needs so many things.'[37] So did Louis, who had ordered a new suit, but who was to pay for it? 'To find a job is a terrible problem,' wrote Louis. 'I wrote a big novel which I did in a desperate effort to be published as quickly as possible – the reader of one of the biggest publishers in London . . . wrote to me yesterday . . . "I have read the beginning of it with considerable interest."'[38] Louis wrote his novels under the name of Louis de Pellepoix; he wrote in longhand, and could not afford to get his manuscript typed; he knew nothing at all about British, or any other, publishing habits.

Myrtle never returned to Australia after 1928, but the threnody of her Tasmanian family and the money she would one day inherit trills through all her letters like the sound of a piccolo. She was prone to use Australian idioms, and René did not take kindly to being told he was not 'fair and sporting', or was hitting 'below the belt' when he occasionally did not send the money demanded. Myrtle herself knew how to get a blow in: 'you know René all these men who went through the war are not as strong and able as you are . . . [Louis'] nerves were completely shot to pieces.'[39] She insisted, again and again, that her prospects had been ruined only temporarily by the Depression in Australia, that the family land would boom again, wheat would recover, and 'a good price for wool would greatly alter their position'.[40]

Myrtle's mother Lexie was only fifty-two when Myrtle used her anticipated death in such letters to assure the Darquier family that when she died Myrtle's share of the estate would be 'considerable and will provide a happy future for us'. Until that day (which was not to come for nearly thirty years, and which would provide no fortune then) she implored them to imitate the generosity of her own family, who continued, with difficulty, to send what they could. Myrtle's tactless comparison of Tasmanian generosity with the parsimony of the French family was the last straw. Louis' family offered bribes for Myrtle to go away. Myrtle fought back:

> Despite all the difficulties in England [Louis] was so much better there . . . It is very silly of you to imagine that by me going to England Louis would be better . . . I realise Madame wants me to leave Louis but I venture to say she does not realise what would happen . . . every day I say I will not stand any more but despite a heavy black eye etc, numerous bruises, many dreadful insults and locked doors and disturbances I cannot leave him . . . I have nothing to gain by staying but hunger and more difficulties and the dread of something even more frightening.[41]

After six months of this, Louis caved in and went to see René in Strasbourg. He now had 'nothing, nothing, nothing'. Before his final submission he tried once more:

> For a long time Maman set out two assumptions, which despite all appearances are false, i.e.
> 1. Sandra is responsible for everything that has happened, happens or will happen 2. Louis is ready to leave her in one way or another.
> On this basis, on my first return to Paris, I had to listen to inhumane solutions that the greatest wretches would not be able to accept . . . and you . . . asked me yesterday; 'Has Sandra left?' forgetting, no doubt, that having nothing to pay for her shoes, it would be difficult for me to pay for her passage to London.
> But that is not the point –
> The essential fact is that all these difficulties that I have undergone, undergo and will undergo are due to me, to my ideas, to my need to escape from the principles of a country where I cannot live – whatever have been the difficulties (for a long time so stressed by poverty together) that I have found in my marriage – it remains

that I have found in it the only satisfactions that I have known in my life. There is nothing of a genital nature in this – (another of the stupid and gratuitous hypotheses of Maman) – it is of the most profound spiritual nature – so much so that if I sacrificed it I would lose my reason for living . . . [42]

Louis refused to give up Sandra; returning to live in France would be moral suicide. If his family declined to finance his literary career, he preferred to live in the gutter in London. This was his last sally. The family promised Myrtle £2 a week – over £100 a week today – to stay away from Louis.

Myrtle was 'really very worried about him – he is so nervy and tired and bursts into tears at the slightest provocation. I cannot help but be frightened at his violence and I dread the thought of scandal and really Louis is completely impossible at present. He is quite broken and when I think and speak of leaving him he goes to pieces – I am really afraid how all this is going to end – hitting people in restaurants . . . It would be far from cricket to leave him when he is poor and miserable.'[43]

But she went. Louis wrote to René: 'Sandra left yesterday – Do not forget her – and above all the blonde child who must be beginning to cry famine.'[44]

6

Shreds and Patches

AWARE THAT THE DARQUIER family 'cordially dislike even the mention of my name', Myrtle nevertheless told them that she knew 'in her heart' that Louis would be a lost person without her, and he was.[1] The rue la Boétie, in the 8th arrondissement, is home to a long corridor of hotels – the Rochester, Excelsior, d'Artois, La Boétie, d'Angleterre. Suitably near the Champs-Élysées for Louis, as dismal today as they were then, with cheap rooms mouldering beneath the dull glare of angry flock wallpaper, these dubious hotels were home to Louis and Myrtle for most of the next decade.[2]

Louis spent much time in the bar of Le Select, around the corner on the Champs-Élysées, where he wrote despondent letters to René. Within weeks of Myrtle's departure for London he fell sick in his 'vile room' at the Hôtel Excelsior: 'all is truly awful – you have separated me from the only being in the world who matters to me'.[3] He did not care whether he lived or died. In that part of London which Myrtle could no longer frequent except to pick up her post, Noël Coward and Gertrude Lawrence were enchanting the world in *Private Lives*, and Al Bowlly was singing 'Goodnight Sweetheart' at the Monseigneur. Within months, Myrtle's bank manager gave her the fare back to Paris to 'see what René and Louis' friends could do'. Back with Louis, she dared not approach the Darquier parents, and so began to plead with René again, her letters lengthening as her shame grew: 'Louis received your cheque for 300 francs – you will perhaps wonder why I am answering this letter considering I already know your intense dislike of me and all appertaining to me.' Their luggage had been seized by the hotel, they owed money in London, Louis could not pay the hotel bill in Paris and had only two shirts left. Myrtle complained that she had to 'wash my lingerie and put it on next morning – also my stockings – I may tell you I have never before been used to that'.[4]

Myrtle wanted to take Louis back to England to write his novels, 'not the career I would have chosen for him but if he makes even a moderate success we will all be so proud and happy'.[5] Also, a Major Lawrence was presenting an opportunity, offering a cottage for Louis to write in, and was waiting for them in London.[6] The Darquier family seems to have decided that Louis could not function without Myrtle; another start together in London was therefore to be financed. René provided the funds, but this time the money came not as a gift, but as an authorised loan. Myrtle insisted that Louis needed to be suitably dressed to meet his great new opportunity: 'unfortunately Louis cannot emulate Ghandi [sic]' – Gandhi was in England in the autumn of 1931 – 'in clothing – such a pity as it would be so much more easy'.[7] Louis felt the same:

As soon as I arrive in London I race to the tailor who there can
deliver in three or four days – I prefer to buy everything there
because it is better made and cheaper, I know it – However I look
at it the total is the same
   5000f or thereabouts for the hotel
   3000f for Sandra (already committed!)
   5000f – clothes, shirts, shoes etc for me
   5000f – travel, pocket money for the future.
   18.000[8]

Baby cost him, or rather should have cost him, five hundred francs – £175 in today's values – a month, half the average industrial wage in Britain at the time.

In October 1931, back in London, Myrtle thanked René profusely: 'All I ask,' she wrote, 'is for Louis to be a successful writer.' Louis promised nothing would be spent on anything else, and gave René his 'word of honour . . . never to ask anything of you again'.[9]

In Oxfordshire, Elsie's sister Maud was working as a weekend cook for Sir George Schuster, a prominent company director, economist and government adviser. The first photos of Anne are as a bonneted baby sitting in the palatial grounds of the Schuster estate at Nether Worton, near Duns Tew. Initially Louis erroneously assessed Elsie as 'not very demanding usually as to the regularity of her payments'.[10] Elsie was more intelligent. She knew early on that, aristocrat or not, he was no better than he should be. Between themselves Elsie and Maud 'always thought he was a wrong'un and a swine for abandoning Anne: a swine AND a Baron'.[11]

But for them, as for Louise Darquier, it was Myrtle who was really beyond the pale. Myrtle's view of Elsie as 'a good honest woman' who 'does not bother me till she cannot go on any longer'[12] did not fit in at all with Elsie's view of herself. As a children's nurse, she had lived in the aristocratic world to which Myrtle and Louis only aspired. Though Myrtle considered Elsie to be 'only a poor working woman', those she lived amongst considered her 'a superior person', 'upper class', and she was treated as such by the country folk she knew. 'She liked being above herself,'[13] just as Myrtle did.

In the Tews, those who knew Elsie in those days loved her. 'She was a fine person' and 'could see the funny side of things'. She amused them with her sense of humour, her sharp tongue and her anecdotes. Elsie was a goer, a positive person with a mind of her own – 'Anne could not have had a better person to look after her'[14] – and what she wanted for Anne, she would get. Elsie loved her Baby, but she wanted the money too.

Myrtle saw Elsie as a woman of the lower classes who 'adores Baby and nobody else would look after her as she does and for little more than the milk bill',[15] but Myrtle's tactlessness, as with the Parisian Darquiers, seems to have enabled Elsie to see through her immediately. As Anne was just beginning to walk, Myrtle was buying herself clothes in London; no matter how often France and Tasmania sent money 'for Baby', Myrtle's allowance seldom made its way to Duns Tew, and came to Elsie, if at all, months in arrears.

The kind of hotel the Baron and Baroness returned to in London in 1931 had no stationery of its own, and no telephones either. Thomas Cook in Berkeley Street and American Express in Haymarket were their post offices, while in their room Louis wrote on and on, from 9 a.m. to two in the morning, or so he said. Fuelled by his great belief that he possessed 'the sacred fire',[16] Louis longed for recognition: 'I follow a hard road, perhaps a long one, but which is the only possibility for me, and in which I am practically sure of success.'[17] 'I am tired of this existence but I feel sure he will forge ahead slowly,' said Myrtle, adding, 'I know he would make a success as a writer. He was born to be one.'[18]

Louis was happier with this new book than he had been with *False Gods* – rejected and so now forgotten. In addition he produced some 'soldiers' stories' which he fired off for publication in Australia. This time he was writing only for the public; he was trying to produce a best-seller. Until his new clothes became 'too shabby to go and see people',[19] he pursued publishers and titled persons – the Comte de Castellan (sic),[20] a Mr Magnus, Major Lawrence. All of them drifted into thin air. Louis and Myrtle gave up lunching; sometimes they had nothing to eat for days.

In 1931 Spain ejected its monarch, the Second Spanish Republic was declared and the Great Depression reached France. But nothing impinged much upon the Darquiers' closed world. In 1930, when Louis had been battling with Robinson to become a glorified car salesman, Oswald Mosley had left the Labour cabinet. In March 1931 he founded his New Party, and in August Ramsay MacDonald abandoned the Labour Party and formed a national government. The pound was devalued in September, and in October, just as Louis returned to London, MacDonald's national government won a landslide election and Mosley formally launched his British Union of Fascists.

Louis Darquier and Oswald Mosley were near-contemporaries; despite the resemblances between them – the strutting and fretting, the speechifying and fisticuffs, unquestioning, loyal and adoring wives – Louis Darquier made no contact with Mosley and his British fascists when living in London. He appears never to have mentioned Jews in these Depression years, though Myrtle often did. Comments such as 'A Jew named Lang sent [Louis] to the film people and he has to go back there on Friday' (Louis was now attempting a film script); 'that Jew told him last week he would do something he would regret if he were not more careful'; 'even that Jew told him it was impossible and had quite a lot to say',[21] while unexceptional for the time, nevertheless make it clear why Myrtle had no trouble tolerating Louis' future activities.

After 'the most terrible Nöel imaginable', in 1932 they were back in Paris for New Year, on the scrounge again. In these quick flits to Paris in search of funds, Louis would visit Anatole de Monzie. Always in awe of de Monzie himself, or wanting his good opinion too much to ask him for help, Louis often mentioned applying to Ramy, de Monzie's amanuensis, for this and that.[22] De Monzie, his eyes 'glittering with malice' in his bald, round head, was not an easy man to face up to; Louis never could do so.

'We have experienced the greatest difficulty in "hanging on",' wrote Myrtle to René. 'Louis has written his book in record time' – this one took him three months – as well as some short stories about French soldiers in the trenches and his film script. Now, she added, 'comes the difficult part – we cannot possibly go three days longer without help'. *Le tout* London 'prophesy a success' – but Louis could not pay to get his work typed, they had nothing to eat, and Baby had to have 'a high chair, blankets, coverlet, warm woolies [sic], pram and now she requires a new bed'. Myrtle had the wit to add, 'You must be thoroughly sick and tired of the sight of our handwriting.'[23]

René paid again, but this time the money for Anne went directly to Elsie, and the authorised loan was increased by fifteen thousand francs; it now totalled ninety-six thousand francs in all – the equivalent of almost £40,000 today. Both Louis and Myrtle had to sign for it legally, Myrtle promising repayment within ten years at the latest, against her future inheritance. She hesitated a week before signing – further trips to Paris were necessary. Despite Louis' insistence to René that 'I use, as you know, the full name Darquier de Pellepoix which I intend to legalise as soon as possible', the loan was signed without any pseudonyms or false baronetcies.[24]

On receipt of René's money, Louis' book was typed, Myrtle was sent back to London; further help from the Darquier family would be forthcoming only on condition that she accepted a fare back to Australia. Louis let fly. This was his mother's doing, he knew; he raged that for many years they had helped Jean become a doctor, but for him, nothing. 'When you speak to me of idleness, you make me want to laugh. To write in these conditions, within a year, two books, one of which was three hundred pages long, twenty-five short stories without counting many other things ... is a small *tour de force*, when you do not know if you will eat the next day or if the hotel manager is going to throw you out.'[25]

Louis to and fro-ed between London and Paris until August 1932, when they upped their legal debt to René by a further thirty thousand francs and he returned to London to start again.[26] De Monzie's office promised free crossing tickets – Louis was infuriated to be obliged to travel third class – but otherwise his cup was full: 'I cannot tell you how happy we are . . . I have come back to London with profound pleasure – the kindness of the people is a habit you cannot give up after experiencing it.'[27]

They had not seen Anne for twelve months, and Louis was 'excited as a child at the thought of seeing her again'. This visit in the summer of 1932 seems to have been the last time Louis saw Anne as a child. It is hard to say accurately how often Myrtle managed it, if she did at all. Anne's medical contemporaries report that she met her mother only a few times in her life. No one who knew Elsie and Anne in any of the Oxfordshire villages in which they lived before the Second World War ever saw Myrtle or Louis. In her letters Myrtle occasionally writes as though she has actually seen her daughter: 'Anne France is well and just trying to walk'; 'she is a pretty girl with deep blue eyes and a wonderful head of red hair!'; 'she has such a lot of red gold wavy hair and is really very pretty . . . and knows some French'. As she also describes Anne as luxuriating on a farm with horses – 'She lives in the fresh air – such a healthy life for her on the farm' – whereas she was actually living in a tiny village house in Duns Tew with Elsie, May, and often Maud – and is mistaken about Anne's hair, which was neither red nor luxuriant, it seems probable that Anne's version of events is the truthful one.[28]

The Tasmanians continued to send the little they could afford to Myrtle, and to Anne they sent blankets, coats and bonnets; Myrtle made use of their generosity in letters of complaint to France. Elsie was required to get photographs taken of Anne, and Myrtle posted them off with requests for funds. Anne was a pretty baby, blonde and pale, and as time passes, in Elsie's photos for Myrtle she turns into a charming little girl, with a podgy tummy, stringy legs and a sweet smile. One photo followed another – on the beach at Bournemouth with Maud, Elsie and May; grinning toothlessly at the camera surrounded by dolls; cuddling the Lightfoot dog of the day – Patch, Ruby, Spot, Rover; posing outside a rented caravan smiling like a good little girl for Mummy and Daddy.

The acute financial antennae of the Darquier family meant that they had seen through Myrtle, as had Elsie. It was only the Jones family in Tasmania who maintained that Elsie turned Anne against her mother. Everyone else became aware of Myrtle's 'sentimental blackmail', that she wrote words of love from afar, but that she was never with her 'Baby', and rarely paid Elsie.

From her weeks with them in Old Windsor, Elsie knew how the Baron and Baroness lived; she knew about the alcohol and she knew what it led to. She used to threaten to put Anne into care if Louis and Myrtle did not pay up, but she soon realised that her only hope was the hapless René. She now had to master the despatch of international dunning telegrams and correspondence, signed 'Yours respectfully', to René in Strasbourg.

Elsie was nobody's fool. While the Schusters called their cook Maud 'Waddy', Elsie was always 'Miss Lightfoot' or 'Nanny Lightfoot', and she had carefully replaced her Oxfordshire country burr with the accent of her betters. Both Maud and Elsie were small of stature but had large personalities. Elsie was bony and sharp, with a stoop – which Anne was to copy – and wore tweeds and sensible skirts and brogues. As she got older she dyed her hair ginger, that particular shade of red so poisonously available during the war. Maud was quite different, big-busted and jolly, a friend to everyone.

'The most courageous and most profitable thing I will have done will have been this change of countries, customs and principles,' Louis assured his family as he left France, forever, in 1932. He did not want to return to his own country 'at any price': 'it is only in England that I can find my way'.[29]

By 1932 there were three million unemployed in Britain, with hunger marches to London and demonstrations in Trafalgar Square. The Baron and Baroness lived amidst this in blindfolded hope. Within months, however, their money had gone again. Their chosen aristocrat for this year was Sir James Erskine, who had been Conservative MP for the St George's Division of Westminster from 1921 to 1929, and who wrote a 'warm letter' to Lord Beaverbrook, the owner of the *Daily Express*, on Louis' behalf, and also put him in touch with the *Daily Mail*.[30] Louis went to see the foreign editor at the *Express* twice in an attempt to work as a journalist on the paper. Nothing came of his visits.

Within three months he finished another novel, 'considerably superior' to his previous work, and had become 'intimately acquainted' with Lady Kathleen Skinner, whose son Edgar was managing director of Allen & Unwin, 'one of the best English publishers'. But, but,

but ... nothing seemed to work, and in December Louis had to write to René: 'I am reduced to asking you for help again ... I am going to take my book to the typist this afternoon – that will cost me 6 or 7 pounds – at the moment I owe my hotel about 2000 francs and their faces are beginning to get longer ... There are so many writers here (and of all nationalities) who earn a great deal but are worth nothing.'[31]

Louis' literary competition ranged from Evelyn Waugh, whose *Vile Bodies* was published in 1930, to Shaw, Woolf, Maugham, Aldous Huxley, Rosamond Lehmann, T.S. Eliot, Auden and Isherwood, Elizabeth Bowen, Graham Greene and Henry Green. As for bestsellers, Wells, Galsworthy and Buchan were still going strong.

Thanking René for money in early 1933, Myrtle made the mistake of telling him that their months in London had not been spent entirely toiling over a hot typewriter, but had included 'a trip down to Italy', where 'Louis had a month's swimming and it did him the world of good'. But now that was over, and 'sometimes for days he will not speak a decent word to me and he often hits me unmercifully – violent blows to my head ... sneers at my family and my virtue – there have been several times when people have had to intervene to stop him ... In Paris two workpeople came to my aid when he knocked me down and when remonstrated with that no Frenchman ever hit a woman Louis said "She's been used to it for the last five years."' Louis thrashed Myrtle repeatedly when she was pregnant with Baby: three weeks after her birth Elsie had to intervene and stop him. 'On July 16 last year there was not one place on my back or arms you could put a pin on – it was all black with bruises.' Every time Louis wrote a begging letter to René he took it out on Myrtle: 'everything I say is wrong, if I don't speak that is wrong – Waiters, servants or people nothing stops him – two days ago he was shouting at the top of his voice "Rotten dirty prostitute – come from low bitches" etc then he flings me from the room.'

Alcohol is never mentioned in this extraordinary epistle, but every word reeks of it, as do Louis' rants: 'Dirty prostitute go and find another man to keep you – you have separated me from my people.' Louis would put Myrtle in a corner and bang her about, then send her out in the streets black and blue, saying, 'My mother would never have stayed where she was not wanted.'[32] Myrtle's vivid catalogue raises the question as to how

Louis could have found time to write amidst such unrelieved physical activity. It also finally closed the door in France; silence fell from Strasbourg and Paris.

In Germany, on 30 January 1933, Hitler became Chancellor of Germany. 'I am less mad than ever,' Louis sometimes told René. By madness he was referring not to anything clinical, but to the habits he had exhibited since infancy, the incoherent rages of a thwarted child. He and Myrtle were now holed up in their hotel room 'without any money, the bills have to be paid weekly',[33] with no clothes, no food, rowing and drinking. Louis, unaware of the tale Myrtle had told, wrote and cabled for money to pay to get his book typed, but nothing came. Worse, he had to register as an alien again, and with no visible means of support he was terrified – he had already had two police encounters, and they had recently warned him again.

Myrtle was beside herself: a German had been deported the previous week for becoming a public charge, and 'the newspaper publicity was terrible'. The hotel was about to throw them out, she was terrified of the scandal, and the manuscript, now typed, could not be collected without payment. Louis had an appointment to show Edgar Skinner the new novel on Tuesday at 11 a.m., so if René would send the cheque for £5.16s.9d directly to Prompt Service, Conduit Street, London . . . ? Prompt Service received no money. 'We have waited all week to hear from you,'[34] Myrtle wailed; the appointment with Mr Skinner had passed. Using a scratchy pen at American Express she beseeched, she begged, implored. In London Louis broke his last monocle and could not afford to replace it. It became obvious to him that René had called a halt to paying for monocles or anything else.

In March Louis went back to Paris and knocked on the family door. They took him in and Myrtle was left in London, darting in and out of the Piccadilly Hotel, stealing their writing paper: 'the hotel has stopped credit and that means I cannot get anything to eat – I have 2/9 left and I must wire Louis – I am literally on the street and I am really ill . . .' She drifts away at the end of this agonised appeal:

I would be glad of anything
You cannot see what misery I am in
Give us one more chance please . . .
It is easy to be hard when one is sure of a living

She wrote this on 23 March 1933, as Hitler was granted sweeping powers by the Reichstag, the beginning of his dictatorship of Germany, two weeks after Franklin Delano Roosevelt was inaugurated as president of the United States, and as *The Times* was publishing one of its first reports of attacks on Jews in Berlin. Meanwhile the world was spinning away from Myrtle, who was left sitting in 'churches and railway stations until both closed' for three days and nights in the cold and rain. Interviewed by the hotel manager and detectives, she was threatened with gaol and deportation: 'even my passport is wrong'. 'I *cannot* have scandal – I will be branded thief.' She met every train hoping Louis would return to save her. She did not know where Louis was, but he sent her a telegram: 'Can do nothing miserable love.'[35]

———————————— ⬥ ————————————

In Paris, Louis was with Jean and Janot Darquier in their apartment at 92, rue Jouffroy. One of the reasons for René's silence had been the birth of his son in March; René thus having other things to do, Louise and Janot took Louis over. They extracted him from his hotel room in Paris, paid the bill, fed him, gave him bed and board, but nothing else. Louis knew his credit was exhausted. Jean was never one to lend Louis and Myrtle money, though he was a well-considered neurologist, head of the Neurology Clinic at the Faculty of Medicine of Paris. But they were fond of Louis, and Janot maintained contact with him throughout his life.

They took Louis in, and it was Janot who wrote to René with the family instructions as to what they were now going to do with him, but most of all with Myrtle. It was all her fault. No Frenchwoman would have behaved as Myrtle had done, purloining for herself – for her addictions? – money that was meant for Baby. Louis was trying to extricate himself from her, but he was weak, and Myrtle was a blackmailer. 'When one is *Sandra* on a bench in Piccadilly without a sou, one's feet in the water, *one does not give up.*'

Swan & Edgar
RESTAURANT
PICCADILLY. W.1.

Monday 3 p.m

Dear René,

I am very grateful for the money you so kindly sent me – I am too ill to stand and my feet are bleeding – I cried when I received the money. Nothing will ever wipe out of my mind the sheer horror of the last days particularly yesterday – I have sat in churches and stations till lost – closed – I had nowhere to go and no lunch and my friends were away. I have a racking

Myrtle on the streets in London, 1933.

The Darquier contacts were now put into action to get Louis a job, to get his book published, place his stories in *Le Petit Parisien* and generally set him on his feet again. But René must 'not send a sou to Sandra . . . we have vast expenses here and we cannot manage to maintain the two of them . . . And I think, very sincerely, that she is bad for Louis.' Janot was without question the most intelligent woman in the Darquier family.

The Darquiers in Paris knew what they were up against: 'Sandra . . . represents for him the opposite of all that his family tried to teach him. Today, exhausted with their terrible adventures, he is trying to re-establish himself and to extricate himself from the situations in which his wife has placed him – this is not easy.' Louis was 'perfectly capable of saying one day "she must stay in London" and the next day running off to find her again'.[36]

René had sent Myrtle £5 before Janot's letter arrived, but after that he obeyed instructions. On 27 March, sitting in the restaurant of Swan and Edgar, crying, Myrtle scrawled a note of thanks; her feet were bleeding, she was ill, she was grateful, but where was Louis?

By April 1933 she and Louis were in touch again, but secretly. Louis, forbidden by his family, could do nothing for her. Sir James Erskine, who built and owned the Eccleston Hotel in Victoria, tried to help again. Myrtle, very shaky on her feet, longing for her impounded suitcases, wrote and wrote and wrote to René. 'It is not for myself I ask it is for Baby ... Surely you will not let her starve ... I will promise to stay away from Louis ... I am unable to understand why you do not answer?'[37]

Elsie had not been paid. After the disappearance of René, Maud helped out for as long as she could, but when she went to work full time as the Schusters' housekeeper, Elsie was 'threatened with being turned out of her cottage as she cannot pay her rent, and the grocer and the milkman will not give her any further credit'.[38] 'At the extremity of her means', she moved to meaner quarters in Kidlington, a much larger village than Duns Tew, on the doorstep of Oxford itself. The Baron and Baroness owed her £30 by now, more than six months in arrears.

In the following years Myrtle rarely raised her head above the parapet. The early months of 1933 seem to have been a watershed for her, just as they were for Louis. 'Elsie never talked about Anne's mother, but she talked about her father,'[39] and Anne followed suit. As she grew up, Anne would often say to her friend Beryl Clifton that she was the daughter of a count. About her mother she said nothing, and she seems never to have written to her, after the odd little notes of a very young child, enclosed with photographs of 'Baby' before she was four.

Louis' time with Jean and Janot was to change his life, and to provide his final transformation. In his new incarnation, the man who had insisted that he must be a writer and must live in England dismissed his literary career, such as it was. His novels and short stories were never mentioned, and were replaced by mythical years in Australia running sheep farms and battling with Marxism. He managed this so well that even the French security services, who kept a permanent eye on him after 1934, believed his assertion that he had spent the years between 1929 and 1933 living at number 5, cité du Retiro, in the 8th arrondissement of Paris.

In his years in England, Louis often mentioned his hatred of France,

the land of his father: France to him was 'the straitjacket of family autoc-
racy'. But to France he returned, while Myrtle descended into a sea of
silence and, presumably, alcohol. 'One thing is certain,' Myrtle mourned,
'I will never bring Baby to see this misery.'[40]

III

---◇---

HITLER'S PARROT

7

The Street

IN 1933, LIKE MANY OF the European powers scarred by the First World War, France was moving towards civil war. Mussolini in Italy and Hitler in Germany had already overcome such opposition as existed in those countries, but France and Spain were a different matter. One of the key figures in the Franco-French confrontation was Charles Maurras, a potent influence in Louis' political conversion.

Louis had moved into Jean's apartment by the end of March, and seems to have remained there for some months. As Myrtle wept onto her letters to René, promising to stay away from Louis if he would only send money for Baby, Louis, back in the bosom of his family, was once again under the influence of his mother, and God had begun to feature in his thoughts. At this point in his spiritual rebirth Louis Darquier was dismissive of Maurras, as he was of all the other leaders of the leagues he was to dally with, for lacking 'the spiritual'. His language and aspirations took on an elevated quality, in keeping with his mother's thoughts – 'What is to be done? We must always think of others first.' This change of mood was sensible, because Louise was now supporting him with an allowance of between twelve and fifteen hundred francs a month (£500 to £600 at today's values). When in this mode Louis would write to René: 'The will of the Almighty is accomplished above our heads and very often, it is from worries, sadness, sufferings and depths that you find the source of happiness and of so many other things.'[1] This is the language a Catholic child learns at its mother's knee.

As an institution the record of the Catholic Church in Europe towards fascism was, generally speaking, a wretched one. Freemasonry, the older enemy of the Church, had already been proscribed, but after the Russian Revolution of 1917 the Vatican confronted another godless, world-wide, authoritarian rival, communism, which was also closely associated with the Jews who contributed so much to it – Marx, Trotsky, Rosa Luxemburg. The words 'communist' and 'Jew' became synonymous. As it had done before, the Vatican reacted to this new threat by turning to European dictators as Defenders of the Faith. It was in this context that Louis Darquier began his new career.

Charles Maurras was not physically gifted by the gods. He was a short man with a goatee and a stutter, and his deafness made him squint. He was stern, authoritarian, and though a man of violent words, never took action himself. Others did his dirty work. His young activists, the Camelots du Roi, were past-masters at riots, disturbance and physical battering, and it was in their company that Louis Darquier took his first step towards the recognition for which he longed.[2]

At the time that Louis returned to Paris in March 1933, Charles Maurras addressed a large banquet for Action Française organised by the medical fraternity, including Dr Jean Darquier, by now a member of Action Française.[3] In France there was a long tradition of medical involvement in politics, locally and nationally. Léon Daudet was a failed medical student; Maurras' eulogised younger brother was a doctor. There was an Action Française medical review, *Le Médecin*, and the movement held banquets all over France, those in Paris sometimes attended by over a thousand medical men. Most French doctors traditionally belonged to the Radical Party, but in the 1930s, following the rise of Hitler, many students from other European countries came to the great French medical schools to study, and remained to take clinical appointments. French doctors, resentful of this new competition, became fertile ground for Action Française.

Cadurcien contemporaries admit that Jean Darquier was 'openly anti-Semitic. He accused the Jews of blocking his advancement in the hospitals of Paris. He truly believed this.'[4] His mother agreed, and claimed to have heard Jewish doctors openly plotting about medical appointments and promotions, favouring Jews and letting in only the odd Christian. Louise thus contributed to the belief of two of her sons that the prospects of true Frenchmen were being ruined by encroaching hordes of foreigners.

In April 1933, beautifully printed copies of Maurras' speech were made available to the doctors present at the March banquet. Jean Darquier was a carefree fellow, an *'antisémite de salon'*. It was what Louis read – Maurras' words – however, that was perfectly attuned to his needs. Now that his England of aristocrats and peers had failed him, Maurras' call for France to be ruled by 'the natural hierarchy of talent or birth' transformed Louis' hatred for his native land into a passionate attachment to it.

Le Corps médical français et la Restauration nationale

DISCOURS
aux Médecins d'*Action française*

PAR

CHARLES MAURRAS

Maurras' March speech to the medical fraternity of Action Française. Published April 1933. (Paris: Presses de Guillemot et de Lamothe pour 'Les Amis des Beaux Livres'.)

Soon it was not his mother or God whom Louis invoked, but Maurras; he borrowed his nationalism, his insistence that France was being 'betrayed, occupied, exploited by an internal enemy'; the disgusting republic, '*la gueuse*', ruled by 'British, Jewish, Bolshevik and German' foreigners – many of whom were Freemasons, or Protestants, or crooks.

For nationalists, parliamentary democracy was the '*république des camarades*' – the republic of Masonic cronies, each of them scratching one another's backs. What Myrtle made of Maurras' hit list of groups, to so many of which she or her family belonged, is unknown – her father and her brother Vernon were prominent Freemasons.

Throughout the summer of 1933 Louis, wilting at the rue Jouffroy, and Myrtle, living from hand to mouth in London, began to crawl surreptitiously back towards each other; in June they met in Belgium. Myrtle nagged plaintively from London, and Louis whimpered, 'I have Sandra on my back all day.' In August they went together to see René. He had been heroic before; he now achieved sainthood: a weekly stipend was agreed upon for each of them. It seems that René took on the responsibility for Myrtle and Baby in England, and the Darquier parents took on Louis in Paris; they were not permitted to live together.

In 1933 France was about to join the rest of the world in economic crisis and decline. It began its descent into the Depression later than other countries, but also continued it for much longer. Succeeding French governments refused to devalue the franc, weakening the nation economically while troubles multiplied at home and abroad. Louis, ever the victim of fate, fell in love with his native land just as its governments, its economy and its ancient political schisms erupted in turmoil.

While Louis had been in London, conservatives, including Pierre Laval, a former socialist and pacifist, had dominated French governments, but neither right nor left could rule without the Radical Party in coalition. The Radicals were, in a sense, the government of the Third Republic. Then, in 1932, with the Socialist Party, the Radicals won a handsome majority – which brought Anatole de Monzie back to cabinet office as Minister of Education.

Periodic crises and scandals were endemic in the Third Republic, but the 1930s was its sorriest decade, and were to end in its demise. Fear of Russia and the spread of communist revolution was as strong in France as it was in all the established governments of Europe. This concern moved the parties of the right, and their supporters in the press, to frenzied attack. Terrified too by the advent of Hitler, conservatives feared a German population with a birth rate twice that of France, blossoming under a fascist leader, while France withered under an unstable parliamentary republic. The nation was united in fury that Germany was not paying its war reparations, while France was required to pay its own war debts to the United States.

Unsupported by Britain and America – which then, as now, made their own political and financial arrangements – France struggled to keep Germany to its treaty commitments. It feared German rearmament, feared fascism, feared communism, feared war. The Radical and Socialist Parties could not agree on economic policies. There were nine government ministries from 1932 to 1934, and while unemployment never reached the depths seen elsewhere, there were beggars in the streets, protest meetings and disturbances throughout the country. A quarter of a million people were out of work, and Louis Darquier was once again to join their number.

On his return, however, Louis found others more unfortunate than himself. By 1930 there were three million foreigners living in France, three times as many as before the First World War. Many immigrants came as labourers, to make up the shortages that followed the war – Polish, Spanish, African, dozens of different nationalities. The Lambert law of 1927 significantly relaxed French naturalisation procedures.[5] This provided men like Maurras and Louis Darquier with their *métèques* – foreigners and undesirables. First among these were Jews, particularly those claiming to be French, then refugees from fascist Italy. And when Hitler instigated his first Jewish boycott in April 1933, followed in May by Goebbels' ceremonial burning of books, and in June by the opening of Dachau concentration camp, German refugees – political, Jewish, communist, socialist – began to seek safety in France too.[6] One of them was the great Austrian writer Joseph Roth, a Catholic and a Jew, the most feared *métèque* of all.

Action Française was the first to raise its voice against these hated immigrants. Others followed. Although Jews comprised only fifty-five thousand of the influx, Maurras and his followers magnified this small number into swarming Jewish millions bent on destroying France. When de Monzie arranged to offer Albert Einstein a Chair at the Collège de France, the perfume magnate François Coty, legendary financier of numerous fascist groups and movements in the twenties and thirties, accused de Monzie of being a communist, a Soviet agent, a Jew-lover, a Marxist, and a militant Bolshevik. This did not affect the relationship between de Monzie and Maurras: in 1935, when Maurras published the names of – and threatened with death – over a hundred deputies alleged to favour sanctions against Italy over its invasion of Abyssinia, it is said that de Monzie prepared the list for him.

In the ten years since Anatole de Monzie had become a friend and admirer of Charles Maurras, the latter had entered into his personal kingdom. The front page of *Action française* was now required reading. The two columns on the left, written by '*le gros Léon*' (big Léon), Léon Daudet, were the most popular. Daudet was a man with a big appetite and a murderous pen, ebullient, vicious, inventive and scurrilous – and poisonously anti-Semitic. So was Maurras, who issued forth his *credo* daily in his large column in the centre of the page, '*Politique*'. Despite the fact that he was a repetitive monologist, Maurras' violence and certainty seem to have cast a spell over his readers. The paper also concentrated on the activities, deaths and funerals of the kings and queens of Europe, and the *duc de* this and the *duchesse de* that.

In October 1933 the French government, led by the Radical Édouard Daladier,[7] was brought down by the socialists' refusal to accept salary cuts in the public services. From that date demonstrations began in the streets of Paris. By November Louis had moved into another hotel in rue la Boétie, the Élysées, only a five-minute walk from the offices of Action Française in rue du Boccador. Here he wrote that he was 'living a very terrible existence . . . but I have a very firm hope and that suits me perfectly'.[8]

Louis found himself in the middle of Paris with nothing to do. The headquarters of the Camelots were on the second floor of an old town house at 33, rue St-André-des-Arts, near place St-Michel, off the boul' Mich' and boulevard St-Germain. There Louis attended Action Française meetings with other young militants and the many literary figures of the time who wrote for the paper. At the cafés nearby they would discuss into the night the contents of the daily newspaper and the books of Daudet, Maurras and Jacques Bainville, the deluded but illustrious historian of the royalist cause. Louis was now thirty-five, but the appearance, optimism and absolute self-assurance of these younger men of Action Française were exactly the qualities to which he aspired. As was their love of banquets. The Camelots with whom he dined and drank in the Latin Quarter had an air of the Household Cavalry about them, sporting canes, wearing gaiters and decorations.

Louis often denied being a member of Action Française – and they agree. After the war Maurras' movement changed its name, tarred by

1. The Darquier family in Cahors,
c. 1906-7. Louise, Pierre, and in front,
left to right, René, Jean, Louis.

CAHORS. - Lycée Gambetta (1907) - Escrime

2. Postcard of the sons of the Mayor of Cahors, at fencing class at the Lycée Gambetta, 1907.
René is fencing with Jean; Louis, immediately to the right behind the fencing master, adopts
what was to become a typical pose.

3. Edouard Drumont and his anti-Semitic newspaper, *Libre Parole*, 1901. He was the father of twentieth-century French anti-Semitism, of 'France for the French'.

4. Charles Maurras and Léon Daudet, the two founders of the nationalist movement and newspaper, Action Française.

5. The Marquis de Morès, Antoine Amédée Marie Vincent Monca de Vallombrosa, 1896. Aristocratic adventurer, anti-Semitic bully boy and Louis' preferred model.

6. Louis' 'godfather', Anatole de Monzie, Republican politician, lawyer, writer, wheeler-dealer, at his desk in Cahors, *c*. 1920.

7. Henry de Jouvenal, de Monzie's closest friend, with his wife Colette and their daughter, 'Bel-Gazou', *c*. 1920.

8. Louis Louis-Dreyfus, 1938. 'King Two Louis', the 'King of Wheat', nominated by Louis Darquier as king of a world Jewish conspiracy.

9. The Jones family, *c.* 1911. Left to right, back row: Myrtle, Hector, William, Vernon; middle row: Colin (?), Henry, Alexandrina, Norman (?); front row: Olive, Hazel.

ORBIS AUSTRALIS DULCES EXUVIÆ

Carte Générale
de la
TERRE NAPOLÉON
(À LA NOUVELLE HOLLANDE.)
Rédigée

10. Australia as *Terre Napoléon* in Louis-Charles de Saulces de Freycinet's *Voyage de Découvertes aux Terres Australes*, 1811.

11. Cahors, Boulevard Gambetta, early twentieth century.

12. Launceston, Brisbane Street, early twentieth century.

13. Jean, Pierre and Louis Darquier, in uniform, First World War, *c.* 1915. Louis, again, in a typical pose and as distant as he can get from his father.

14. The National Archives of Australia have no photographs of no. 8911 Gunner William Robert Jones of the Second Australian Divisional Signal Company. This is a photo of Gunner Harold George Cope who enlisted three months before Will Jones and who was killed in action in France in September 1917. Will Jones would have looked just like this on his enlistment in September 1915.

Report, Death of W.R.Jones.

I, Johannes Knorhus van Oostugen Duminy, am a House Surgeon at the New Somerset Hospital.

At about 10.30 p.m. on the 7th inst., an Australian soldier named W.R.Jones, was admitted to hospital in a dying condition. He was unconscious and was bleeding from the left ear, and showed other signs of the fracture of the base of his skull, with injury to the brain. Over the postiner aspect of the skull on the left side was a large haematoma. He died about half an hour after admission from shock due to the injuries described.

On admission his breath smelt strongly of alcohol.

15. Statement of a witness at the Court of Inquiry into the death of William Robert Jones, June 1919.

16. The famous Savoyard Charles Workman, Myrtle's father-in-law, with his son Roy, *c.* 1905. Myrtle Jones married Roy in Sydney in 1923.

17. Charles Workman as Ben Hashbaz in Gilbert and Sullivan's *The Grand Duke*. He was in the original cast which opened at the Savoy Theatre, London, 7 March 1896.

IN THE METROPOLITAN POLICE DISTRICT.

Register of the Court of Summary Jurisdiction sitting at _Marlborough Street_ Police Court.

Thursday The _17th_ day of _April_ 1930

Number.	Name of Informant or Complainant.	Name of Defendant. Age, if known.	Nature of Offence or of Matter of Complaint.	Date of Offence.	Time when Charged. Bailed. (if any).	Doctor's Fee, (if any).	Plea.	Minute of Adjudication.	Time allowed for Payments and Instalments.
29	219 C	Peter Leonard Hale (whites?) 49	Placing himself to beg	16/4/30 4.0 pm			G	1 day	
30	327 D	Albert Ellis (colours) 56	Begging	" 1.15 pm		NG	Remanded 14 April	
31	225 D	Jessey Berry (boat sellers) 46 Patrick Rogers (colours) 33	"	7/4/30 2a.m.		NG	NG 1 month H.L.	
			"			NG	NG 1 month H.L.	
32	Mann Louis Bargues de Bellpois 6 (marchand) 32 Myrtle Bargues de Bellpois (married) 28	Being aliens did fail to furnish to the Registration Officer particulars as to the matter set out in the first Schedule of the aliens order	16/4/30 5pm					Remanded to 24th April in £50 each	
			"					Adj'n £1.0.0 continued	

R. McLeod
Magistrate Adjudicating.

18. Louis and Myrtle, court case 32 at Marylebone Magistrates Court, 17 April 1930.

association with Vichy, to Restauration Nationale. Today, with dark and dusty offices at 10, rue Croix des Petits-Champs in the 1st arrondissement, its website opens to the accompaniment of a medieval French jingle. The current director, Pierre, son of Maurice Pujo, one of the leading figures of Action Française, is categorical that no one of Louis Darquier's tenor could have been a member of the movement. 'We thought of him as a lunatic, a dropout,' says Pierre Pujo;[9] by 'we' he means his father and Charles Maurras.

Like many of Maurras' followers, Louis had no longing for the return of a king, but he 'was unquestionably an Action Française man'. It may be that he did not pay his annual subscription, but despite his later denials – and theirs – he remained an active and public supporter of Action Française until 1939. Amongst the Camelots he met in 1934 was the swaggering young Henry Charbonneau. In 1999 Charbonneau's former wife Jeanne, by that time widow of the leader of the Belgian fascists Léon Degrelle, insisted that Louis Darquier had been cradled by Action Française. 'My first husband knew him very well, because they were in Action Française together. They used to meet on evenings, to talk in a café on the place St-André-des-Arts, because the headquarters of Action Française was in that street. They used to talk, to read the newspaper, to discuss the news for hours . . . they were young, and had ideas and values.'[10]

Maurras ensured the survival of his movement by refusing to permit it to change, or to move beyond incitement to revolution. Action Française did not become a political party; its power was intellectual, its ethos entirely anti-parliamentary.[11] A number of Maurras' followers demanded direct political action. After 1926, when Action Française came under papal interdiction, many Catholics had left it for the Fédération Nationale Catholique, the FNC, whose numbers swelled to two million members. Even earlier, in 1924, as a reaction to the leftist government elected in that year, the Cartel des Gauches, others had fled the nest to form parties and leagues of their own. A paramilitary right grew up, of dissident nationalists obsessed with what they saw as the decadence of France and the paralysis of its parliamentary democracy. Their leagues fought for national renewal and an authoritarian government which would end class warfare and prevent the growth of international communism.

The most important of these new groups was Croix-de-feu,

launched in 1928 and funded by François Coty. By 1931 its president was the Action Française dissident Colonel François de la Roque.[12] A decorated soldier, la Roque turned Croix-de-feu, originally only a veterans' group, into a paramilitary organisation. Though supposedly neutral on the subject of religion it was marked by rigorous Catholicism, military discipline, impressive public rallies and parades. In their black leather jackets, wearing the medals so many of them had gained in war, Croix-de-feu became immensely popular: in 1937, by then a political party, it had three-quarters of a million members, more than the French Communist and Socialist Parties together.

One of the earliest leagues to follow in the footsteps of Action Française was the Jeunesses Patriotes, founded in 1924 by Pierre-Charles Taittinger, a right-wing entrepreneur of considerable wealth who bought the champagne company which bears his name in 1931, and also a newspaper editor and owner with aristocratic and business associates of the kind Louis Darquier most favoured. Taittinger was a war veteran too, a cavalryman who like Louis had fought in the Champagne area during the First World War. Under him the Jeunesses Patriotes became a Catholic league, noted for violent skirmishes with communists, sometimes with fatal results. Taittinger's son Claude, who heads the champagne firm today, considers his father to be *un homme politique unanimement estimé*, 'a universally admired politician'.[13]

A deputy since 1919, Taittinger belonged to the right-wing parliamentary group Fédération Républicaine, many of whose deputies were members of the paramilitary leagues. Taittinger was thus an anti-parliamentary parliamentarian, an admirer of Mussolini and Hitler, if not of Germany. He praised Hitler in 1932 for 'the constant development of racism in all classes of Germans, and the enthusiasm of [his] troops for a leader who makes their heart beat under their brown shirts'.[14] In 1936 Taittinger was elected to the Paris city council, based in the Hôtel de Ville, the town hall, which became a centre of power for the extreme right. At its peak, membership of the Jeunesses Patriotes numbered about a quarter of a million, mostly young men derided at the time as 'dandies in gaiters and monocles, grouped together to defend their daddies' dividends'.[15]

Action Française, Croix-de-feu and Jeunesses Patriotes cover the political passage of Louis Darquier, though he also joined the Union Nationale des Combattants – the National Union of War Veterans. Initially Jeunesses Patriotes was as important to him as Action Française.

The latter satisfied his aristocratic aspirations, provided the words he would use and the enemy he would fight for the rest of his life, but the former gave him a political platform and a political career, and its Catholicism was more in tune with his 'spiritual' vision of France.[16] Also Taittinger was a dynamic, expansive fellow, with a certain charisma and a fine oratorical talent, more attractive to Louis than the insignificant Maurras, or the Olympian chilliness of la Roque.

Many of the ultra-conservative leaders of these groups were bankers or industrialists, and a surprisingly large number of them made their money out of perfume, cosmetics or wine. The talcum powder and scent of the omnipresent financier François Coty eventually enabled him to pay for his own league, the aggressively anti-Semitic Solidarité Française, and his own right-wing newspapers, including *Le Figaro*. Eugène Schueller,[17] founder of the l'Oréal beauty empire, and Jean Hennessy and his brandy were other sources of funds. These men could buy followers, and they provided Louis with his first inspiration as to how he could make his way, and make money in doing so.[18]

There is endless quibbling about the fine-tuning of these nationalist leagues, including Action Française. Were they fascist? In the 1930s France was surrounded by fascist dictatorships, but they were by no means fascisms of the same kind. In France, what emerges from a cloud of over-analysis is what each organisation had in common. The words used to describe the leagues at the time still seem accurate – they were called fascists, or nationalists, and their multifarious movements were known as the French 'fascist leagues', the parties of 'the Street'.

Not all French fascists were anti-Semites, and many Catholic fascists – Pierre Taittinger and Colonel de la Roque, for instance – chose communists and Freemasons as their preferred demons. But however much these 'semi-fascists' averred before, during and after the Occupation that they were not anti-Semitic, they worked, marched, congregated and voted with a revolutionary right of leagues which were dominated by that sentiment.

Many men of the Street passed happily from one league to another, but their leaders were rivals, and their followers often followed suit. These turbulent factions could never submit to a Mussolini or a Hitler, and they failed later to unite under one of their own, Marshal Pétain. Among them were many who used the word 'socialism' in their rhetoric, and who had their roots in the socialist and communist left. For both the left and right, it is somewhere in their shared fear of the Bolshevik terror that the binding threads of French fascism can be found. The close bonds with Catholicism which shaped French fascism saved Vichy from the worst excesses of Hitler's version, but also cast a veil of authoritarian and religious approval over terrible deeds.

By the end of 1933, however wretched Louis was in the Élysées Hôtel, events had begun to move in his favour. After the fall of Daladier's government in October, and a three-week interregnum when yet another government fell, the Radical politician Camille Chautemps, a Freemason particularly loathed by Léon Daudet, was asked to form a cabinet. Chautemps' crisis-ridden government was soon floored by a scandal insubstantial in itself, but which acted like a match to paraffin. Just after Christmas, Serge Alexandre Stavisky, a small-time swindler with good connections, was revealed to have defrauded the public of two hundred million francs by issuing fake bonds on the municipal pawnshop and loan office in Bayonne.

Action française leapt onto the revelation. Stavisky was a Ukrainian Jew, though a naturalised Frenchman, but better, his involvement with prominent members of the Radical government, many of them Freemasons, including Chautemps, meant that his previous imbroglios had never come to court; attempts to bring cases against him had been adjourned nineteen times in the previous six years. The rage of the public, suffering all the miseries of the Depression – unemployment, high taxes, reduced incomes – and now presented with a government which not only could not govern, but which also seemed thoroughly corrupt, hardly needed incitement by the press to come to boiling point.

First, the Comédie-Française staged Shakespeare's *Coriolanus*; its passionate denunciation of political leaders was interpreted as antiparliamentary. This brought Action Française members to the theatre in force to cheer every word. In early January 1934 the defamations of Léon Daudet and Charles Maurras reached their apogee. In *Action française* Shakespeare was invoked in every revelation about the Stavisky scandal. His words were used to attack democracy and to hurl accusations of villainy, corruption and decay at the republic and its parliament. The circulation shot up – as did that of all the right-wing press of the time which took up the story and ran with it. *Action française* urged 'the people of Paris to come in large numbers before the Chamber of Deputies, to cry "DOWN WITH THE THIEVES"' – adding, 'Instructions will be sent in due course.'[19]

Then, on 8 January, the police came for Stavisky in Chamonix, where he had fled, and found him dead. The press accused the police of murder and cover-up; the Radical Party, Freemasons, the government, cabinet ministers, judges, newspaper magnates and bankers were all implicated. Stavisky, it was alleged, had been 'suicided'. Throughout January, led by *Action française*, the scandal raged in the press, on the streets, outside the Chamber of Deputies and inside, within the government.

Anatole de Monzie's tentacles were by now even more firmly entwined in French affairs. He had just begun his work on the *Enclyopédie française*, and his friend Henry de Jouvenel – who acquired fabulous wealth in 1933 by marrying the widow of Charles Louis-Dreyfus, the brother of King Two Louis – had become French ambassador to Rome. That year de Jouvenel, and so of course de Monzie, had been deeply engaged in negotiations with Mussolini to sign a Four Power pact between Germany, Britain, France and Italy which would act as a deterrent, outside the League of Nations, to another European war. De Monzie was caught up in the Stavisky affair as lawyer to two of the directors involved. Then another deputy, Philippe Henriot,[20] a cohort of Taittinger's, let loose in the Chamber of Deputies and accused de Monzie of consorting with Stavisky's mistress before she became his wife. De Monzie retaliated by threatening a duel, and fainting. The Chamber of Deputies was in uproar, while outside de Monzie's 'godson' Louis Darquier, so meek in his presence, was preparing to bring the house down.

Tension mounted throughout January. While the Palais Bourbon and the deputies within were firmly guarded, nearby and on the place de la Concorde malcontents were tearing up iron railings and benches and smashing cafés and kiosks night after night. This culminated in a dress rehearsal for what was to come, when Action Française demonstrated in force on Saturday, 27 January. The police recorded Louis Darquier's participation. There were hundreds of arrests, which came to nothing under the benevolent eye of the powerful police chief Jean Chiappe,[21] who was anyway implicated in the Stavisky scandal. Chiappe was a man of the right, a member of Croix-de-feu – he liked his police to beat up communists, but to tread softly on Action Française.

In the turmoil, the government fell again. Daladier returned with yet another Radical cabinet, including a former socialist, Eugène Frot, as Minister of the Interior. Chiappe was asked to resign. He refused. This was Sunday, 4 February, and on the following day the leagues and

newspapers of the right called their troops to action: 'Socialist anarchy
. . . Masonic crooks . . . enough of this putrid regime'.[22] Ministers
received death threats. There was talk of tanks in the street.

On the afternoon of Tuesday, 6 February, while the investiture of
Daladier's new ministry was taking place, the opponents of the Third
Republic took to the streets. Louis Darquier was at the head of the fray.
The riots continued with growing frenzy until midnight.[23] By 8 p.m. the
Palais Bourbon was surrounded by ex-servicemen's organisations of both
right and left. All converged on the place de la Concorde, while nearby
la Roque kept his Croix-de-feu in hand, singing the '*Marseillaise*'.[24] Many
of the rioters were young men; many infuriated citizens of Paris joined
them. The police and mounted guards barricaded the pont de la
Concorde; there were reinforcements. The mounted guards charged the
crowd, buses and kiosks burnt.

The rioters used everything they could lay their hands on: iron railings, stones and bits of asphalt, barricades, fires, guns; they slashed the
horses' legs or disembowelled them with razor blades attached to walking
sticks, and threw marbles under their hooves. The Concorde was alight,
the air full of the smell of burning rubber and the cries of forty thousand angry citizens. The police charged, using batons and fire hoses;
firing started from the mob, and the police responded; blood flowed,
and the rioters howled 'Assassins! Assassins!' Some deputies and many
members of the Paris city council were on the Concorde with the rioters,
attacking their own Parliament. It was rumoured that Pierre Taittinger,
who also took part in the riots, was to announce the formation of a
dictatorial government from the Hôtel de Ville.

That day, 6 February, seventeen people were killed and nearly fifteen
hundred wounded, three hundred of them hospitalised. Among them
was Louis Darquier, who had been on the Concorde alongside his fellow
Camelots.[25] Another was Pierre Gérard, only nineteen but already a
veteran of Jeunesses Patriotes and an *habitué* of the cafés of the boulevard St-Germain. He was an insignificant-looking little fellow, short and
dark and one-eyed, but like Louis he had been active in the January
disturbances. On 6 February he went to the boulevard St-Germain, found
nothing going on there, and took the metro to the Concorde. By 7.30
p.m., with 150 others, he was about to break through the police vans
barricading the pont de la Concorde and to storm the Chamber of
Deputies, 'to shout under its windows' – though worse than shouting

was feared. Gérard was shot in the groin and taken to hospital, where he was operated on by Robert, the brother of Marcel Proust. He was to join Action Française immediately after 6 February, and to spend much of the 1930s as Louis Darquier's closest sidekick. It was with men like Gérard that Louis stormed the barricades. Louis himself was shot in the thigh and, a wounded hero, was at last catapulted towards the fame he craved.

The riots of 6 February 1934 were the decisive event of Louis' gener-ation, that of the 'comrades of the trenches' of the First World War. At the time Louis said that his part in it happened by chance: 'No wonder the Greeks put the God of Chance above all others. After many years about which the least we can say is that luck has not been on my side . . . I go to demonstrate with some fifty thousand others . . . I'm among the first thirty of those fifty thousand. It's like having a winning ticket in the lottery.' As for his injury: 'I was lucky to find two AF guys who took me away and helped me towards a car.' He was taken to the Hôpital Bichat on boulevard des Maréchaux on the inner *périphérique* of Paris, and there he stayed for the next three months.

Louis had a bullet in his thighbone, and the wound was deep and suppurating. He was very pleased with himself, and two weeks later he was writing to René in Strasbourg. He was a changed man; gone forever was the entreating tone of his London years. He was now cock of the walk. He had almost brought down the government, 'but we're not there yet. My feelings on that evening of the 6 February were overwhelming. For five minutes, I thought that we'd sweep everything away – and those bastards thought so too, hence what happened!'

Louis was looking for a new way, under the guidance of God. His path was to be 'Nationalist, racial and more or less aristocratic.' Nationalism was the superior philosophy in every way, but the govern-ment might need 'a series of kicks in the arse' to trigger off the final revolt against the republic. God would find a way. 'I'm becoming more and more a mystic! How can it be otherwise? Difficult times, more than any others, bring us closer to God . . .'[26]

In all these months, and for some time afterwards, there is no sign or mention of Myrtle, though she seems to have been sufficiently upright to let Tasmania know that, while patriotically marching along the Champs-Élysées, Louis had been shot in the leg by communists. It was in 1933 and 1934, her last years in London, during which she was a remittance woman of the Darquier family, that Myrtle lost to Elsie in the grim tug-of-war over the body of Baby. Elsie loathed Myrtle with the honest distrust of a labourer never paid for her hire, and with the particular vitriol women reserve for inadequate mothers. By the time Anne was four she was aware of the battles about money which marked the lives of the two women responsible for her.

In Paris, Pierre Darquier would not visit his son in hospital, but Louise and Janot were in attendance; presumably Myrtle's banishment was more acceptable to Louis in his new religious phase. Three days after Louis was wounded on the place de la Concorde, Myrtle's sister Olive married in Tasmania, an elegant wedding complete with 'richly hued' gladioli and Hazel a bridesmaid in rose-pink chiffon velvet. The widowed Lexie wore black georgette and French lace, and the Jones tribe gathered at her brother's home for the event, dining on the sunny verandah. How Myrtle coped during this period is hard to imagine. On occasion Louis would say that alcoholism was a disease, not a vice, though he always saw it as the latter if Jews were involved. He took Myrtle to doctors for her alcoholism. Perhaps treatment, and not Louis' new belief in religious principles, explains her disappearance until mid-1934.

In the days following the riots, the parties of the left reacted, and republican and nationalist France began to line up for their final, epic struggle. February the sixth was a victory for the fascist leagues of 'the Street', but as a political coup it failed. Daladier resigned, civil war was avoided and the republic held on under a conservative–centre government of national unity, brought in to restore order. This was headed by a former president, Gaston Doumergue, a Radical Protestant Freemason, but a most conservative one, with Marshal Pétain as Minister of War.[27]

Louis missed nothing in hospital; he followed each succeeding scandal and disturbance, and pontificated in letters to René of extraordinary length. His wound would not heal, and a month later he had to be operated on again, with Jean at his side giving him the necessary anaesthetic. Perhaps it was the quantity of the ethers that affected his prose: '. . . they've taken out a serious bit of femur . . . I now have a hole as big as a fist in my thigh . . . When it was over, [the doctor] asked me: "is it painful?" "No," I said, "but I thought you were about to come up with two doves as well!"' Louis was disgusted with the aftermath of the riots: 'And they all forget about the spiritual! That it's not Mussolini, Hitler, Frot, or Whoever who make revolutions, but the ascendance of the spiritual in each of us – And we must not delude ourselves, we don't have a great spiritual movement here in France at the moment, we have people who worry about money . . .' Money made him think of Baby: 'I have good news from my kid whom I haven't seen for nearly two years. When you get this letter, can you send 10 or 12 pounds to the nurse?'

On the night of 6 February, Charles Maurras had been at the office of Action Française, writing Provençal poetry. Many young men besides Louis Darquier were disillusioned by his cerebral reaction to political events: 'What is terrible to see,' wrote Louis, 'is most of the young men joining lots of Leagues, thinking that the achievement of power by force is the height of ambition and that when they put at the head a guy of their choice, this guy will automatically be virtuous . . . the League chiefs, they slither along. Maurras with his atheism and his breathless intellectualism, Daudet with all his denunciations and premonitions which make you feel he knows too much about things, Colonel de la Roque, an elegant leader of a regular army, and I won't talk to you about the others! A revolution with that? It would be much worse than the status quo and at the moment I am absolutely with Machiavelli who said that it's better to keep a bad Prince than to change him.' Bolshevik troubles, bastard German barons – Louis spared René nothing of his new concept of the sacred, except to add a postscript: 'Don't forget my kid.'[28]

Despite his spiritual outpourings, on 9 February the wives of both Daudet and Maurice Pujo were at Louis' bedside, and on the following day *Action française* listed him as one of 'Our Wounded'. Louis was a very happy fellow during these months. The more serious his wound became, the more he could make of it. He had his board and keep for the first time in years, he was coddled by the nurses, had cigarettes and wine and books to read. Janot brought him food, Jean looked after him, the family paid all expenses.

Since 1933 the Lightfoot *ménage* had been living in a tiny bungalow in Kidlington, mystifyingly named 'Esquimault'. Kidlington was a jolly village, with a railway station and a cinema and a lot going on. Children could hear the Kidlington Silver Band play every Sunday evening in the Orchard Tea Gardens Restaurant, have a ride on Rosie the elephant or gaze at the red kangaroo and the flamingos and pelicans in Kidlington's Gosford Zoo – strange animals to find in any English village.

Few of these pleasures lingered in Anne Darquier's memory of her years with Elsie. Elsie barely subsisted: she had no paid employment, yet she was not officially unemployed. She could get no Public Assistance and could never submit to the Means Test, introduced in 1934; she could not apply for the dole. She was not Anne's legal guardian, and though there was no state system to investigate why Anne lived with her nanny, Elsie knew enough about the dubious Darquier parents to be obsessive about snoopers, and obsessively protective of Anne. Until 1943 Anne lived in Kidlington with Elsie and May, with Aunts Violet and Maud coming and going, supported by underpaid women for whom rural poverty was as bitter as it had ever been.

The disappearance of Myrtle from the Lightfoot family scene was underlined by the telegrams – 'GRATEFUL HEAR BY RETURN LIGHTFOOT' – Elsie had to send to the Hôpital Bichat or Strasbourg to get enough money for Baby to survive. Louis' leg did not improve, though his circumstances did. On 10 May he received an official visit in hospital from the directors of Action Française, Léon Daudet and Maurice Pujo, and its president, Admiral Schwerer. They brought him best wishes for his recovery from the Duc and Duchesse de Guise, the Bourbon Pretender and Maurras' chosen leader. The length of Louis' stay in hospital made him one of the select few, the seriously wounded. Action Française now gave him an entrée everywhere. He had been reported to the police for his unpaid bill at the Élysées Hôtel, but his parents paid up and he returned there on 20 May, limping but in tremendous spirits. The visit of Daudet and his comrades was only a beginning; God flew out the window: Louis at last saw how to make his way in the world. 'I think I'm going to find influential friends now, as I'm a unique example (the others who were severely wounded are cooks, drivers and shop employees). I believe that I'm going to profit from the accident – I've decided to play this card for all it's worth and get in touch with all the heavyweight patriotic pimps. The republic really owes me that!'[29]

He wrote to Marshal Lyautey,[30] the great colonial administrator, who had grown more and more reactionary in his old age, and in March 1934 had been elected honorary head of Jeunesses Patriotes. Lyautey replied with 'a charming letter'. He also wrote to Charles des Isnards, vice-president of Croix-de-feu and a conservative Paris city councillor. Des Isnards replied immediately, and Louis met him and joined Croix-de-feu.

As to Action Française, the police recorded his membership in their files, and kept an eye on him.

While pursuing these avenues Louis, like Myrtle, constantly dunned René for money for Baby. But by June 1934 Elsie was owed £44, and telegrams continued to come from Kidlington throughout the year. Louis was still wary of his parents, but his requests for money from René had almost become orders. His approaches had brought him 'a lot of support' on the Paris city council. 'I promise you that I'm on the move and if those chaps do not get me out of this mess I will play "the hero of 6 February" with noisy dignity,' he wrote to René.[31]

In June 1934 Myrtle, 'in a terrible physical and psychological state', finally rejoined Louis in the Élysées Hôtel. They wanted money to go and visit Anne in Oxfordshire, but now that Myrtle was back, the Darquier family conferred on every move. In Tasmania the Jones family believed Myrtle was enjoying Paris to the hilt, fitting in without effort, blossoming amidst the joys of Parisian society. That was not how the Darquiers saw it; Louis was allowed to dine *en famille*, but not Myrtle. 'With normal people . . . there is no doubt that a convalescence like this would do him the most good . . . On the other hand when he has his baggage it is possible for them to escape – to go to other hotels – charge up credit etc . . . you know the programme better than anyone else!' wrote Janot to René.[32]

With Myrtle back, Louis' parents refused further help. He did not go to Oxford; his leg collapsed again and he had a third operation on his thigh, but not before, in the middle of July 1934, he launched the first of the many organisations he was to create, the wonderfully titled Association des Blessés et Victimes du 6 Février, the Association of the Wounded and the Victims of 6 February. It was a perfect idea for making money, for now he met 'everybody and this is how I'll get a job and in no other way . . . because the general situation is *lamentable*'.[33]

Announced in *Action française* on 8 July, and noted by the police at 11 a.m. on 14 July 1934, Bastille Day, Louis collected his first twelve members in the square in front of the church of the Madeleine. There he placed a wreath at the foot of a statue of St Geneviève dedicated to the victims of 6 February. Three weeks later, he had a job.

8

◦

Fame

IN 1931 LOUIS LOUIS-DREYFUS had bought into the conservative Parisian evening newspaper *l'Intransigeant*, run by Léon Bailby,[1] a highly successful proprietor of the period. Bailby managed to stay with his paper for another year, but Louis Louis-Dreyfus wanted to stand as a deputy for the Radical Party in the 1932 elections, and political differences sent Bailby off to found *Le Jour*, a daily morning paper which in October 1933 joined *Gringoire*, *Candide*, *Je Suis partout* and *Action française* as one of a quintet of newspapers of the extreme right.[2]

The office of *Le Jour* was in the Champs-Élysées, at number 91, opposite Louis Darquier's favourite bar, Le Select, around the corner from his hotel. Bailby flirted with all the leagues, but particularly with Action Française, and was a firm supporter of Mussolini and Franco. So when Louis founded his Association des Blessés, Bailby, he reported, 'backed me up totally. They took up a small subscription among their readers and asked me – O! irony! to distribute the money – But it will be very very difficult for them to drop me after the summer. I'm very close to the secretary-general of *Le Jour* and there's a chance there I'll pursue when Bailby gets back.'[3] Bailby was a wheeler dealer, subsidised by various questionable organisations, who mixed with all who were fashionable and dubious in Paris society. He hired Louis on the platform of the Gare du Nord in August 1934, as he was about to go off with the Duc d'Abrantes to summer in his villa on the Côte d'Azur. Louis was left with a newspaper to run as deputy to the secretary-general, with a salary of two thousand francs a month (about £850 today).

Over the next month he poured out orders to René, demanding first '<u>Silence</u>. As you know I have quite a lot of enemies, a large number of talkative friends, and a huge number of debtors of all kinds . . . I've said

114

nothing to Jean and Janot and I don't intend to say anything to the parents. You know how terribly they gossip, a sickness no amount of entreaty can stop . . . It's absolutely <u>necessary</u> that they continue to give me what they give me at the moment.' Secondly, money: 'I cannot for one second . . . live on my 2000 francs a month.' He must look the part. All his baggage was still in hock to the Hôtel Majestic, his bill unpaid from the previous year. 'My only jacket is very frayed at the cuffs but with a clean collar and a monocle . . . it will pass.'[4] He needed a new suit, and René was to pay Elsie for the foreseeable future, while Louis attended to matters of state and the acquiring of members for his association. He would charge:

> Members 10 francs a year
> Patrons 50 francs
> Honorary 100 francs
> Benefactors 500 francs.

Within weeks, pursued for payment of their bill by the Hôtel Élysées, Louis and Myrtle had moved into the more salubrious Hôtel California in the rue de Berri. Using all the services of *Le Jour*, Louis started recruiting:

ASSOCIATION DU 6 FEVRIER 1934
91 Champs-Élysées Paris
Sir,
    The Association of 6 February 1934 has been constituted with the aim of forming a group of the Frenchmen wounded in the course of the patriotic manifestation of 6 February 1934 into a single Front, without distinction of party, league, opinions or beliefs.

His programme was lengthy, but only its first point was relevant:

1. To obtain from the powers that be, with the shortest possible delay, indemnities, reparations and due sanctions for the wounded of 6 February, and also for the families of the dead.

So passed the summer of 1934. In Germany, Hitler became Führer and banned all political parties except his own; in France, re-suited at

René's expense, Louis began to attend functions: 'I made a speech in front of almost a hundred guests with much success, may I say with modesty.'[5]

Louis' next opportunity arose in November, when two young men wounded on 6 February died from their injuries. One was a sixteen-year-old apprentice butcher, Lucien Garniel. In the centre of Paris, everyone from the Street turned out for his funeral, waving their flags and pennants: Croix-de-feu, veterans' associations, Jeunesses Patriotes, Solidarité Française, Action Française, over two thousand men displaying their passion for uniforms – coloured shirts, berets and boots, coats with insignias, medals, badges, armbands. Deputies and Paris city councillors and leaders of the leagues were there. Chiappe, Maurras and Taittinger attended, with Louis holding high his own flag and pennant. The procession stretched from rue la Boétie and continued down the boulevard Haussmann up to place Lafayette in the 9th arrondissement. There the hearse lay, surrounded by Louis and his men, the councillors from the Hôtel de Ville and the family of the dead boy. The leagues filed past, each laying a wreath on the coffin, only the occasional cry to be heard – 'Maurras!' and 'Front National!'

As deputy secretary-general of Le Jour Louis had now met anyone who was anyone; every newspaper, particularly those of the right, covered the funerals. Bailby organised lecture courses at Le Jour on public speaking – François Mitterrand trained there at the time – and very soon Darquier took up public performance. Five days after Lucien Garniel's funeral the government of Gaston Doumergue fell, and the conservative Pierre-Étienne Flandin took over, but not for long.[6] Louis' association announced the next funeral, which took place in December, this time a Catholic funeral at Saint-Pierre de Neuilly, the local church of Louise Darquier and of the dead boy, Jean Mopin, an engineering student from Neuilly. For the Catholic hierarchy the dead of 6 February had 'paid for the fatherland's salvation with their lives'.[7] An even more distinguished gathering attended this funeral, including Xavier Vallat, who was to become the first Commissioner for Jewish Affairs in the Vichy government.

Louis used Catholics and nationalists of every hue. In addition to his commitment to AF, he had already placed 'his pen and his courage at the service of Croix-de-feu, Volontaires Nationaux [its youth movement] and the Front National'. The young François Mitterrand[8] was an

activist in Croix-de-feu's youth movement. Crying *'France aux Français'* –
'France for the French', the catchphrase of Édouard Drumont and his
followers – on 2 February 1935 Mitterrand demonstrated against the
'envahissement des métèques' – the invasion of foreigners, in this case foreign
medical students. Within two months of Louis founding his association,
the men of 6 February 1934 had become a legend, heroes of the fatherland, *'la fleur de la race'*, unarmed and patriotic citizens fighting for 'national
regeneration' who had been slaughtered by the police under orders of
the government of the Third Republic. All the most important national
leagues joined Louis' association, and day after day *Action française*
published the many letters Louis wrote to the paper; usually they appeared
on the front page.

It was by no means unusual for a man like Louis Darquier to join
both Action Française and its rivals, which it appears he had managed
to do by the beginning of 1935. As Louis was leaving hospital in May
1934, setting aside their differences, Jeunesses Patriotes, Solidarité
Française and about eighteen other conservative veterans' associations
and smaller leagues had united to form the Front National – the name
used today by Jean-Marie le Pen. While Action Française worked
closely with the Front National, la Roque did not permit Croix-de-feu
to join it. Croix-de-feu had now become the largest and most important opponent of the republic, eyed jealously by Taittinger and
Maurras.

Throughout his life Louis kept a favourite photograph of eight men
in raincoats and jackboots. It is most likely that they were wearing the
blue trenchcoat, blue shirt, jodhpurs and Basque beret of Jeunesses
Patriotes.[9] Dressing up was only one of the attractions of Taittinger's
group: while Action Française refused to participate in parliamentary
politics, by 1935 Jeunesses Patriotes had amongst its members seventy-
six deputies and many Paris councillors. Taittinger and his cohorts took
Louis up politically, for, as Louis wrote to René, 'it is very difficult at
the moment to do anything without me'.[10]

One veteran of Jeunesses Patriotes – although a year younger than
Louis Darquier – was Charles Trochu,[11] who was also close to Action
Française, and who for the last three years had been chosen by Jeunesses
Patriotes as a candidate for the city council of Paris. A businessman in
the import and export of cod, he had much in common with Louis: like
him he had enlisted in the army at the age of seventeen, and had been

wounded and decorated. He was fond of organisations, a member of many, and was a boastful and inventive man, much given to the sort of ancestral claims Louis himself favoured. Trochu, who had fought on the place de la Concorde during the riots of 6 February, described Jews as 'the scum from the Orient'. In January 1935 he was appointed secretary-general of the Front National.

As dignitaries of his association, Louis acquired militant members of the leagues, a general, and, as his first members, widows of the fallen. The president of the Paris city council accepted the honorary presidency, and Louis was invited to speak in public. His first public performance took place on 28 January 1935 at an Action Française student meeting, in the company of Charles Trochu, Maurice Pujo and Admiral Schwerer of Action Française, and others. Louis distinguished himself. As he read out the names of the dead of 6 February, 'thousands of men stood up, and at each name, with one voice, they responded "Died for France!"' Ovations and prolonged bravos greeted the speech that followed: 'We are French. Certain people, mostly *métèques* or Jews of the lowest kind, want to prevent us from raising our heads in our own country. Our roots in this country go back for thousands of years. We will not be tyrannised by such people.' *Action française* praised to the skies his 'sober and direct eloquence, his natural way of speaking, the energy of his approach, the sincerity of his words'.

Louis wrote copiously in *Le Jour* about the widows and children of his association: 'The loss of her husband has ruined her; she lives in a cold little apartment, where the only light is that of the gaze of her child. But she does not give in.' The hyperbole of his prose, then and later, gives some insight into the quality of Darquier's missing novels.[12]

Brushing aside accusations that he had filched the association's membership funds, when the first anniversary of the great day came round on 6 February 1935, Louis instituted an annual day of commemoration with the support and approval of the Paris council, Action Française and the Front National. To obtain government permission for this he spent an hour and a half with the prime minister of France, Pierre-Étienne Flandin, outlining his plans. A compromise was agreed upon – the widows would be allowed to pay their respects on the place de la Concorde, but not the leagues. A memorial service followed at Notre Dame on the morning of 6 February, attended by Flandin himself, despite considerable parliamentary objections.

After these encouraging events, Trochu invited Louis to stand as a Front National candidate for the Paris council elections to be held in May. At the end of April his candidature was announced for the Ternes quarter in the 17th arrondissement, on the north-western edge of Paris, adjacent to Neuilly and his family home. He was thirty-seven years old. He hoped to represent the district stretching from the avenue de la Grande Armée, leading off the Arc de Triomphe and l'Étoile, to the boulevards de Courcelles and de Clichy, crisscrossed by the broad thoroughfares of the avenue Wagram and avenue des Ternes. This was the chic side of the 17ème.

Earlier that year Elsie had moved from the bungalow to a gloomy semi-detached house nearby, the ill-named 'Sunny Bank' in Kidlington High Street. Elsie always moved house or village in pursuit of Anne's education, and she first sent Anne to Kidlington Infants' and Junior School, in nearby School Road. The school had been set up in the nineteenth century as a Church of England establishment to educate the children of 'the Labouring, Manufacturing and other poorer classes in the Parish'. When Anne went there, in addition to the descendants of those commoners, the pupils included children of unemployed men from depressed areas outside the county who had been recruited by Morris Motors in Oxford.

Anne's education was standard fare for English girls who were expected to have few ambitions: the three 'R's, cooking, gardening and needlework. There was corporal punishment for boys, but only one light stroke on the hand for girls. Schools were always to be a problem for Anne and Elsie: they had so many aspirations, and they had so much to hide. In January 1935, while Louis was using his salary to produce leaflets and banners for his association, and was having a fourth operation on his leg, Myrtle, prostrate over the death of her younger brother Colin and his family – all killed when the *Miss Hobart* crashed into the sea on a flight from Launceston to Melbourne – was forced to extract a further £12 for Nurse from René.[13] Myrtle's tone in her begging letters, like that of Louis, had now become peremptory.

In the five years between 1930 and 1935, René had given Louis 150,000 francs – worth about £60,000 today. Now Louis needed a further ten thousand francs to finance his candidacy for the Front National. On 1 April, on the stationery of the Hôtel California, he scrawled a note to René, accepting his debt: 'I acknowledge very willingly that in the course of the last years you have lent me at different times a sum of about a hundred and fifty thousand francs, which I promise to repay you in instalments as and when and in proportion to the amelioration of my situation.' He signed with his baronial name in full, very grandly, twice. René did not appreciate this approach. Four weeks later, on 29 April, by which time he must have been desperate for the money, Louis presented his brother with a more official version, stamped 'République Française', in which he agreed to repay René's 150,000-franc loan at his 'first demand', adding: 'p.s. The acknowledgements of former debts up till now are annulled.' The next day Trochu guaranteed a similar note for the necessary extra ten thousand francs.

None of these miserably typed documents was satisfactory, so René placed the matter in the hands of an unfortunate director of the Banque Cotonnière in Paris, a M. Habault, who spent an unhappy week of it. René insisted that Myrtle sign the authorised loan for 150,000 francs, and that Louis repay the extra ten thousand by the end of the year – or as soon as he received his state reimbursement for his wounded leg. 'I have received a visit from [Louis] this morning,' Habault wrote to René on 1 May. 'Certain modifications have been brought in . . . Your brother repeated once again that his wife will refuse to sign this acknowledgement . . .' Trochu made himself unavailable, Myrtle refused to sign, but Louis extracted the further ten thousands francs anyway, Habault complaining that the unsigned note was 'typed by a machine which makes the guarantee non-existent'.[14]

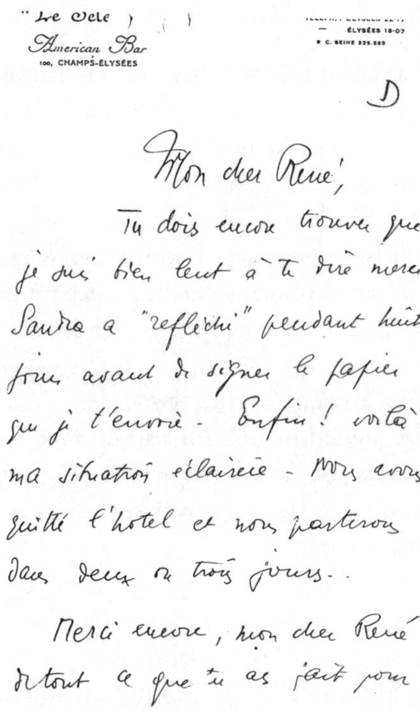

[handwritten letterhead: "Le Select" American Bar, 100, Champs-Élysées — ÉLYSÉES 18-07]

[handwritten letter in French:]

Mon cher René,

Tu dois encore trouver que je suis bien lent à te dire merci. Sautra a "réfléchi" pendant huit jours avant de signer le papier que je t'envoie. Enfin! voilà ma situation éclaircie. Nous avons quitté l'hôtel et nous partirons dans deux ou trois jours...

Merci encore, mon cher René, et tout ce que tu as fait pour

Louis wrote many of his begging letters from his favourite bar in Paris, Le Select.

In 1936 relations between Louis and René seem to have deteriorated further. During the six years Elsie had spent fighting the Darquiers for payment, René had been the last resort for all of them, but by May it seems he was attempting to pass the financial responsibility for Anne and Elsie back to his brother, and that he told Louis and Elsie so. Myrtle surfaced again, but in disordered form, feebly scrawling one last attempt to make her case to the Darquier family who found her so intolerable. Her handwriting is enlarged and wandering, much of it undecipherable. She dated her letter 1926, but it was written in 1936, on 22 May, from the Hôtel Windsor Étoile in the Ternes. Whatever René had said to Louis and Elsie had offended Myrtle:

> in my own family I have never even thought of daring to speak
> [about?] how my brother's children were cared for – it is a religion
> for us not to interfere. The Mother is always sacred. Somehow I
> have always trusted you René and was more than surprized by
> your letter. Our baby is not as yours, she is internadiorial [sic.
> international?]. I suppose I will have to seperate [sic] from

Louis and years ago you told me that one day I would have
to go.

But it really was 'below the belt' to write against me – after all
René, I am the Mother . . . My family paid for her to be born into
the world and have borne a lot of the expense since – certainly all
her clothes? etc. It is not sporting of you to write against my back
about her – Louis can have many children – I have this one and
every day my thoughts are not away from her for five minutes.[15]

This seems to have been Myrtle's last letter to René Darquier, and
it is the only one she signed in full flourish – 'Sandra Lyndsay Darquier
de Pellepoix'. Her last words as she slips into obscurity for most of the
following decade were: '. . . sleeping, waking my first and last thoughts
are for Louis and my Baby'.

───────────── ✧ ─────────────

Presumably, in 1935 Louis needed René's money to pay for the expenses
of his election campaign, but he was also supported by Bailby and his
newspaper and a twenty-six-man committee, of whom Jean Darquier
was one. Jean even raised ten thousand francs for his brother by
borrowing from medical colleagues, who also joined Louis' electoral
committee. The campaign leaflet Louis produced was the first public
statement of his political life, and he began as he intended to continue.
Under the banner of the Comité d'Union et de Rénovation Nationale
(Committee for National Union and Renewal) he presented himself to
the public as secretary-general of *Le Jour* and president of the Association
of the Wounded of 6 February. His photograph is rigid with aristocratic
hauteur. In Napoleonic mode, jaw jutting forward, pose patriotic, it takes
up more than half the front of the four-page leaflet, giving physical presence to the fantasies which absorbed Louis' days. Its text delivers, for
the first time, some of the vast number of lies he was to continue to
tell about his past life.

Mr. L. DARQUIER DE PELLEPOIX was born on 19 December 1897.
He comes from a family from the South-west which has given
France many soldiers and scientists (the astronomer Darquier de
Pellepoix, member of the Academy of Sciences, Colonel Darquier

of the Grenadier Guards, Commandant Darquier of the 51 Infantry etc.). Mr. DARQUIER DE PELLEPOIX is a Catholic, married and a father.

His academic and military failures glossed over, his 'good humour and courage' described, he transmutes his sticky end in the wheat business into a resignation on the grounds that during the recession his company 'had come under the control of international finance'. The two latter words meant Jewish ownership in the *patois* of the Front National. Louis also attributed Myrtle's lost Tasmanian inheritance to the influence of the Bolshevik Revolution on the Australian wheat industry.

Claiming for himself 'superior administrative qualities . . . vitality, independence and idealism . . . fearless patriotism, strong intelligence', his years in London were turned into a period of international travel. His previous hatred of France disappeared into a misty spray of heroic prose about 'the renaissance of France' as 'an inviolable Credo and the only reason for living'. The demands he issued included stronger authoritarian government, a more aggressive foreign policy, national defence as agreed by Marshal Pétain, the reduction of taxes, electricity, gas and water rates, the revision of naturalisation laws, reorganisation of everything to do with foreigners, repatriation of unemployed foreigners living on public relief, the suppression of trade unions, Freemasonry, monopolies, class warfare, parasitic organisations, and the defence of the birth rate and the family.[16]

The Salle Wagram in the avenue of that name in the 17th arrondissement is a vast meeting place, a Second Empire Parisian version of the Albert Hall in London. This was the venue for Louis' next success, a resounding speech about the glory of France and the men of 6 February. Jews were rarely mentioned in his discourse during this election campaign; he fought solely as a nationalist and a 'man of 6 February'. It was Parliament, the left, socialism and communism that were the enemies in May 1935; this antagonism was exacerbated when, just as Louis was standing for election, Pierre Laval, then Foreign Secretary, was required to sign a pact of mutual assistance between France and Russia, a fearful coupling to anti-communists, of whom Laval was one.

In the council elections throughout the country the Radical Party

lost heavily, while the left made great gains, as did some of the nationalists of the extreme right, Louis among them. In the first round of
voting, held on 5 May 1935, Louis led the list, and in the second round,
though only three hundred ahead of the republican candidate of the
left, he won with 2,803 votes. He was now a councillor of the Paris city
council and a councillor-general of the Department of the Seine, which
in turn had a vote in the election of the upper house of French government, the Senate.[17] How long he maintained his position at *Le Jour* is
not known – Louis never referred to the reasons for his departure,
although gossip had it that Bailby got rid of him for putting his hand
in the till and offending female visitors. It was said that no woman was
safe in his presence.

In May, Louis, with Maurras, Pujo and the devout Catholic writer
Henri Massis,[18] addressed a banquet for the Students of Action Française,
and the trio appeared together again in June before over four thousand
supporters at the Salle Bullier, this time joined by Charles Trochu instead
of Massis. *Action française* celebrated with *brio* Louis' success and that of
the extreme right in its pages, and continued to do so regularly, day after
day, reporting all Louis' interjections, objections and speeches at the town
hall, the Hôtel de Ville.

The elaborate Hôtel de Ville of Paris was built by the Third
Republic to replace the original, burnt down in 1871 during the Paris
Commune. Louis spent much of the next seven years in this ornate,
turreted and curlicued edifice. The handsome council chamber was
now his playground, and he soon acquired a secretary, Paule Fichot,[19]
who was to remain with him throughout his Vichy years. Today the
council chamber has a plaque in honour of the Paris city councillors
who were executed in the Resistance, but no testament to the men of
the right who so dominated the chamber until the end of the Second
World War.[20] Jean Chiappe was its president in Louis' first year there,
and Taittinger and Trochu controlled it throughout the German
Occupation.

Of how Myrtle lived, and how she was, during these great changes
in Louis' life, there is only a police record of a time in a Paris hospital,
where she was treated by Jewish doctors whom Louis, only beginning
his career as a professional anti-Semite, thanked for their care of her.
The two continued to move from one hotel to another. The police
followed Louis first to 1, rue du Four, in the 6th arrondissement, on the

Left Bank, very near the stamping ground of Action Française. Jeanne Degrelle, married to Henry Charbonneau for many years, remembered: 'Darquier at that time loved drinking, eating, laughing and partying . . . But he was always broke. He never had any money . . . [Charbonneau] told me this anecdote at least ten times: one night, Darquier could not pay for his drinks, at the end of one of these big discussions in the café. He had to pay by leaving his coat to the barman.'[21] Later, others recorded Myrtle taking part in such jollities, but not in these early years. By now Louis and Myrtle had moved to the Hôtel Windsor Étoile at 14, rue Beaujon in the 8th arrondissement. From here Myrtle wrote her last letter to René. This was a cut above their usual abodes, but by now Louis had met the professional anti-Semite Henry Coston, and was also pursuing other financial sources of support.

If by night Louis was living high, by day he made himself felt immediately in the council chamber, giving voice to '*Bravos*' and his opinions. He liked to display himself as a citizen of the world, informing the council about circumstances in Australia or England, pretending to have lived in the former, though never the latter – the opposite of the truth. He had a rather piping voice, blustering but insistent, and he loved to hear it; public speaking, as much as journalism, became his chosen *métier*. Uncompromising, intransigent, vulgar, long-winded, he would interject, play the jester, cause a stir whenever he could; but until 1936 it was always the money which he needed so desperately – the compensation he demanded for the widows and wounded of 6 February – that was his prime concern.

Throughout 1935, both sides of a divided France were gathering strength, facing each other across a widening chasm, made worse in October when Mussolini invaded Abyssinia and, by demonstrating the impotence of the League of Nations, sent Europe into disarray. The slump and unemployment now affected the living standards of all. Earlier, in 1934, as the threatening shadow of Hitler grew longer, Stalin had permitted the French Communist Party to make an about-turn from revolutionary and anti-militarist isolation and to join with the socialists in defence of the republic against fascism. By June 1935 the French Socialist and Communist Parties had agreed on a closer working union. Vast rallies were held. Writers and intellectuals – André Gide, Louis Aragon, André Breton, Georges Bataille, André Malraux – publicly entered the fray against fascism and in support of the republic. On

14 July 500,000 marchers rallied at the stadium of Buffalo de Montrouge in a mass parade from place de la Bastille to place de la Nation. This was a turning point in the birth of the Front Populaire, the Popular Front, because the Radical Party joined with socialists and communists. The political structure of a new parliamentary group began to take shape, and this was their pledge:

> ... to remain united to defend democracy, to disarm and dissolve seditious leagues, to place our freedoms out of reach of fascism. We swear, on this day which reincarnates the first victory of the Republic, to defend the democratic freedoms conquered by the people of France, to give bread to the workers, work to the young, and to the world a great and human peace.[22]

In the latter part of this year Louis busied himself in public with the pursuit of Eugène Frot, the Minister of the Interior, whom he and Action Française considered to be the government's executioner on 6 February. Wherever Frot went throughout France, speaking on behalf of the Popular Front, he was pursued by Camelots who would leap upon him and slap his face. Rows, arrests and disturbances were recorded daily, as were letters of congratulation and gratitude from Louis Darquier – 'courageous gesture ... moving act of justice ... health of the fatherland'.[23]

Since the riots of 6 February the previous year the dissolution of the anti-parliamentary leagues had been much discussed, inside and outside the Chamber of Deputies. On 5 December the Basque deputy Jean Ybarnégaray, speaking in the chamber on behalf of la Roque, offered to comply, and to disarm his paramilitary troops. Louis Darquier, outraged by this act of submission, ended the year in a blaze of glory by resigning from Croix-de-feu with a much-quoted diatribe in which he called la Roque a 'rosewater dictator'. La Roque always counselled moderation by saying, 'Dogs bark, but the caravan passes by.' Louis' riposte was: 'Yes, but if the leader of the caravan gets diarrhoea he is dropped in the first watering hole.' Maurras, envious of la Roque, loudly praised Louis for these outbursts, while la Roque dismissed Louis as a 'snob and lounge lizard'.[24]

Rural France had now begun to match the near civil war in Paris as its 'time of hatred' too set in.[25] Henri Dorgères' Chemises Vertes (Greenshirts), a peasant militia he founded in 1935, never missed an opportunity to blame peasants' sufferings on Louis Louis-Dreyfus. All these strands began to come together for Louis Darquier in early 1936, moving him from the extreme right to its outer fringes.

After he left Croix-de-feu in high dudgeon, Louis decided upon a new strategy. Most of his new bedfellows were veterans of the First World War, but Henry Coston, another significant figure in Louis' life, was thirteen years younger. He had been active in Action Française for years by 1934, when Louis Darquier probably first met him. Coston was above all a professional anti-Semite: 'The number one enemy of France is not the French communist, it is the JEW.'[26] Like Louis he was a journalist, and had been an activist against Jews and Masons since 1928, in which year he rescued and republished the famous nineteenth-century anti-Semitic newspaper of Édouard Drumont, *La Libre parole*. 'Darquier de Pellepoix!' he said, in the 1970s: 'I taught him all he knew. When he came to see us after the riots of 1934 he knew nothing about anti-Semitism. It was I who gave him all the necessary books and pamphlets.'[27] Coston visited Germany in 1934, and made contact with the Nazi Party and other anti-Semitic sources which enabled him, in January 1936, to set up a Centre de Documentation et de Propagande (CDP), a Centre for Information and Propaganda, in rue Guersant, in the 17th arrondissement, a street away from Louis' office at 20, avenue Mac Mahon.

After meeting Coston, Louis Darquier the novelist, journalist and defender of widows and the wounded disappeared in a puff of smoke, and turned his energy solely towards Maurras' and Coston's most loathed *métèques*, Jews. Not that Maurras and Coston agreed on the subject. Maurras insisted on the *French* quality of his anti-Semitism, based upon reasons of state, half nationalist, half Catholic, and accepting of old, French, 'well-born Israelites'. Coston's anti-Semitism was more in the style of a French Nazi – he accepted no qualifications. For Louis Darquier, all species of French anti-Semitism were acceptable.

Louis had been showing signs of restlessness before he parted from Croix-de-feu. His perpetual problem was his debts: his bar bill alone was fifty thousand francs, an enormous sum (almost £22,000 today), most of it owed to the Brasserie Lorraine in the place des Ternes. The Darquiers loved nightspots, gambling and clothes. These pleasures, and eating every meal in a restaurant, could account for Louis' permanent state of near bankruptcy. But there is one other possibility, which is that Myrtle used drugs. When Anne Darquier was sixteen, she met her mother and dismissed her as a hopeless washout from both drink and drugs. If this was the case, it could account for the enormous sums they needed. Drugs would have been easily available, because Henry Coston's cohort at the CDP, Henri-Robert Petit, was a known trafficker in cocaine. Cocaine was the drug Anne mentioned.

Louis was a conspicuous figure now, and strangely enough, perhaps because he was rarely seen with Myrtle, but perhaps also because he had worked for Bailby – known to be homosexual – the first of many such accusations came his way. *Voltaire*, a satirical magazine, called the Association for the Wounded of *'Pellepoix en monocle'* 'the Recovery League for the Arse-Kicked', hailed him as the great 'Hunter of the Circumcised', referred to him by every French word for homosexual and suggested he adopted the habit 'while shearing sheep in Australia'. The magazine laughed at everything he did and said; when a friend of Frot's slapped Darquier, *Voltaire* published a delighted cartoon of the monocled, red-cheeked councillor.

Conseiller Municipal Baron et Madame Baronesse Darquier de Pellepoix were to be found in the phone book of 1936, and by the time he had been on the Paris council for six months Louis had mouthed enough pomposities for the magazine to swoop upon him. *Le Canard enchaîné* and others soon followed suit. Jokes about his sexual habits and 'strange friendships' proliferated, as did those about his name and the dubious origins of his title. He was often referred to as *'Darquier sans Pellepoix'*. Most of the rest of his nicknames were untranslatable, and most of them rude: *'Darquier de Bellenoix'* and his *'Ligue des Dix Sous'*, *'Darquier de CarQuoi'*, *'Barbier de Pellepoix'*, *'Darquier de Pelleharicots'*, *'Darquier de Pelle Pouah'*, *'Darquier von Pellepoix'*, *'Darquoi de Quel Pied'*, *'Carquois de Quelpied'*, *'Cartier de Petitpois'*, *'Darquoy de Pelletier'*, *'Darquier de Montcuq'*. Despite these splendid inventions, widely disseminated, Louis Darquier has maintained his assumed baronial name in the indexes of French history to this day.

The councillor for the Ternes was everywhere, busy as a bee, looked upon benignly in the council chamber for a rather humorous kind of eccentricity and vigour. Louis demanded that the name of the avenue des Ternes should be renamed after Queen Astrid of Belgium, killed in a motor accident in 1935, and he celebrated the second anniversary of the riots of 6 February with Taittinger in tow. Events like these meant he was beginning to enjoy the publicity he was itching for, but up to June 1936, by which time he had been in the council for a year, he had made no anti-Semitic interventions of any kind.

On 9 February 1936 the great Action Française historian Jacques Bainville died, and four days later Action Française staged a vast funeral, which Louis attended. Léon Blum, the leader of the Socialist Party, was driving down the boulevard St-Germain when he came across the procession. He was recognised by the Camelots du Roi, dragged out of the car and severely beaten. Later, Louis Darquier was quoted as saying, 'Well done, what the hell was he doing there?' but later rephrased this into 'Yes, I publicly slapped Léon Blum, and I don't regret it.' This was another of his lies. It was the murderous Camelot Jean Filliol who beat up Léon Blum.[28]

When Maurras' office was raided after the attack on Blum, apart from Blum's hat and tie the police found a cup on Maurras' desk filled with coins and bearing the inscription 'Product of the sale of Baron Blum's glasses'. An outraged government dissolved Action Française; only its newspaper survived. This blocked one of Louis' outlets, but anyway he had already almost squeezed dry the events of 6 February 1934. He was looking to extend his range, and Jews were only one of a number of options. The attack on Blum provided an early opportunity when socialist militants took their revenge on an AF party office in rue Asseline, and seriously wounded a royalist doctor. Blum's blood was Jewish, one of these socialists was Jewish – and the blood of the doctor was French. When rewriting his history later on, Louis dated the beginning of his anti-Semitic career to the Asseline affair of February 1936.

The next day Louis was a star speaker at Coston's first public meeting, attacking Parliament and the Jews, while his letter about the events in rue Asseline was published in *Le Jour*. His words of abuse were more to the point now, directed against the 'autocratic oligarchy swarming with newly naturalised Frenchmen, international Jews, cynical financiers, crooked *métèques* and all their clique of parasites'. The key words here are 'international Jews' and 'parasites'. This is the language of the world Jewish conspiracy and of Hitler's anti-Semitism, to which Louis added the French Catholic anti-Semitism with which he was already familiar: he referred to the Bishop of Lyon, Agobardus, who in 820 complained of 'Jews practising usury, fraud, and white slave trading with Saracens'. It is also the language of a man who had now read – and believed every word of – the fantastical anti-Semitic hoax *The Protocols of the Elders of Sion*, Henry Coston's bible and handbook for war against the Jews.

After appearing with Coston for the first time Louis came to the attention of the Ligue Internationale Contre l'Antisémitisme (LICA), the International League Against Anti-Semitism, and its paper *Le Droit de vivre*, *The Right to Live*. Jewish war veterans protested; Louis replied in *Action française*, and the story spread throughout sympathetic Paris circles. At this point, however, Louis was also testing other waters. In February 1936 the ratification of the Franco-Soviet pact caused further uproar – 'The enemy isn't Hitlerism, it's communism.' A month later a paralysed French government glumly resigned itself to German reoccupation of the Rhineland.

National elections loomed, and with the Popular Front increasing its support, some of the intellectuals and student militants of the now

Action française publicising Louis' 'Association of the Wounded and the Victims of the 6th of February' next to Maurras' column, *Politique*, 22 January 1936.

dissolved Action Française – Thierry Maulnier, Robert Castille, a legal colleague of Xavier Vallat and leader of the Camelots – formed the Comité National de Vigilance de la Jeunesse, the National Youth Vigilance Committee.

Comité National de Vigilance de la Jeunesse

29, AVENUE MAC-MAHON, PARIS (17°)

A CEUX
QUI SE FERONT CASSER LA GUEULE

Depuis 1918 tous les gouvernements qui se sont succédés au pouvoir, qu'ils fussent de droite ou de gauche, se sont trompés et ont trompé les Français.

D'abandon en abandon, leurs fautes criminelles nous ramènent aujourd'hui au seuil de la guerre.

La dernière en date, le Pacte franco-soviétique, exigé par le Front Populaire et voté pour des raisons électorales, a servi de prétexte à Hitler, pour un n⟨...⟩el attentat contre la paix.

Les politiciens, qui se sont toujours trompés, réclament aujourd'hui l'union de tous les Français autour d'eux.

NOUS NE MARCHONS PLUS

Nous savons que l'"union sacrée" se fait, pour les Français dans les tranchées, pour les Parlementaires à Bordeaux

La guerre est voulue par l'Internationale des financiers, par l'Internationale de Moscou et par les parlementaires, leurs valets et complices.

A BAS LES POLITICIENS, qui pour la S.N.D. nous ont désarmés

A BAS LA S.D.N., génératrice de guerre

A BAS «LEUR» GUERRE

Grande Réunion Privée à Magic-City

180, rue de l'Université — SAMEDI 14 MARS à 16 heures

Le Comité National de Vigilance :

DARQUIER DE PELLEPOIX, Conseiller Municipal.	ROBERT CASTILLE.
HENRI DORGERES.	M. DESSELLIER.
J.-P. MAXENCE.	RAYMOND PRINCE.
THIERRY MAULNIER.	HENRI CHARBONEAU.
HENRI LAURIDAN.	JACQUES REYSS.

TOUS MOBILISABLES

Renseignements : Comité de Vigilance, 29, avenue Mac Mahon, Paris (17°)

PARTICIPATION AUX FRAIS 0.95

Intellectuals, nationalists and fascists joined the National Youth Vigilance Committee, March 1936 – its headquarters, Louis' office (© Archives Nationales, Paris).

131

The purpose of the Vigilance Committee was to enlist young activists from the leagues to 'rid France of parliamentary government', and to prevent the war currently being arranged by international financiers, Moscow and Members of Parliament. The intellectual Jean-Pierre Maxence, a journalist on *Gringoire*, and other members of Coty's Solidarité Française were also on the committee, as was Henry Charbonneau. Louis immediately offered them his services and his office in the avenue Mac Mahon. Like Louis, Castille was the son of a doctor. He was a clever lawyer, fond of the table and a man who loved a fight. A close friend of Henry Charbonneau, he became one of Louis' most stalwart supporters. Louis moved further into the limelight when he chaired the Vigilance Committee's first meeting, alongside Maulnier, Castille and Henri Dorgères of the Greenshirts, on 14 March.[29]

Over a thousand people at the vast dance hall Magic-City applauded Louis' speech, in which he praised 'the great figure, the great man of France, Charles Maurras', and told them: 'We do not want to go to war for Freemasons, for financiers, for the Soviets ... the future is yours and your youth will save the country.' He attacked the Socialist Party, his name was blazoned on posters, and the legislative elections beckoned. At their next meeting Louis Louis-Dreyfus was not forgotten – Maxence accused him of destroying the French peasant, of buying government votes to import foreign wheat and of subsidising the Popular Front.[30]

In 1935 Taittinger declared that a majority of the Paris city council were friends of Jeunesses Patriotes, which also exercised a serious influence in the Senate. Louis had always hoped to take up at national level the political life his father had abandoned. Action Française suggested him as parliamentary candidate for Neuilly in the elections of April–May 1936, but instead Bailby, Taittinger, Chiappe, Trochu and his other nationalist cronies gave their support to the maverick conservative Henri de Kérillis.[31] This was a crossroads for Louis Darquier.

Discipline, obedience and a somewhat austere manliness of purpose were favoured by the nationalist leagues; Louis shared their views, their furies, their enemies, their attitude to women (for personal use, and best kept within the home) and their passion for purity of race. He could bring them the violence and the martial qualities they demanded, but his indiscipline and self-indulgence and his gadfly contributions to the council discussions blocked his path to national politics. He also drank, and his wife drank more, he gambled if he could, he lived in nightclubs and bars and used other people's money to pay for everything. Even his friends described him as 'always drunk and always broke . . . vain and self-satisfied'.[32]

For Taittinger and la Roque it was communists, not Jews, who were the prime enemy. All the more so because in the 1930s, their leagues were funded by powerful French industrialists and by some rich Jewish banks and bankers – Rothschild, Dreyfus, Lazard, Worms.[33] Mussolini, also uninterested in anti-Semitism until the end of his reign, was their model, soon to be joined by Franco.

Louis Darquier's lack of administrative skills did not prevent him being an instinctive strategist who manipulated men much more able than himself. After this political rejection by his nationalist colleagues, Henry Coston provided Louis with the stage and income he was looking for. By March 1936, with the national elections approaching, Louis was attacking the Popular Front and all its candidates – socialists, Radicals, communists – as members of a Jewish conspiracy of financiers, stockbrokers and Bolsheviks who wished to place France under the power of international Jewry. By this time he was already fingered as being among the Parisian friends of Hitler for saying that 'Any man who, like Hitler, has given his country such great demonstrations of spirit, faith and honour, is worthy of our esteem.' A month later, on 5 April, he received messages of gratitude from Nazi Germany.[34]

In the two months leading up to the election of the Popular Front government in May 1936, the last elections in France for almost a decade, and the last elections of the Third Republic, Louis moved away from national politics into the Parisian anti-Semitic underworld which, together with the anti-republican right, greeted the arrival of the 'Jewish-infested "*Front Popu*"' with incredulity and horror. Over five and a half million men voted for the left and centre, the Popular Front, and just over four million for the right (women could not vote in France until 1944).[35] Of the three parties which formed the Front, the socialists gained the most seats, and so the socialist leader Léon Blum, a Jew, became prime minister of France.[36]

A few months before, in February, the people of Spain had preceded the French by electing a Popular Front government of their own. France and Spain were thus left and centre coalitions, surrounded on almost all sides by fascist dictatorships – Mussolini in Italy, Hitler in Germany, Salazar in Portugal. Britain would shortly be occupied with the abdication of Edward VIII, Stanley Baldwin was prime minister and Winston Churchill was in the wilderness, watching his government appease the European dictators. Both Spain and France, however, had vociferous minorities who preferred Hitler to Blum and Franco to socialism. In Cahors in 1934, Canon Viguié, the editor of *La Défense*, described Léon Blum as a 'sinister Jew . . . hideous *métèque* who is preparing new massacres to establish his tyranny on our corpses'.[37]

The first round of the elections took place on 26 April, the final round on 3 May, but Blum would not form his government until 6 June. In that intervening month, tension in Europe mounted as Mussolini finally defeated Abyssinia, while in France workers all over the country celebrated their new dawn. On one particular day, 24 May, there was a Popular Front parade to commemorate the Paris Commune of 1870, and hundreds of thousands of supporters marched. It was a Camelot tradition to attack Jews in cafés and brasseries, and on that day Louis, drunk, went berserk on the terrace of Chez Doucette, a restaurant in rue Paul Baudry, and attacked three Jews, two of whom were called Blum, Max and Jules, though how Louis discovered this is unknown. He began by making the remarks which were *de rigueur* in extremist French circles: 'I can smell Jews here,' or 'Get out! We'll teach you a lesson!' He then stood up and threw a cup, saucer and mustard pot, tried to punch one of the Jews and, brandishing his cane, shouted, 'I am Darquier de Pellepoix, city councillor. If I want to, ten thousand men will take to the streets tomorrow and kill a hundred thousand Jews. I can arrange for the assassination of Léon Blum. Hitler was right to throw them out of Germany.'[38]

On 1 June Louis received a telegram from Germany inviting him to Berlin to meet 'friends and politicians'. In those days Paris councillors were not confined to discussion of municipal matters: they contributed to Assembly debates and could give free rein to their political opinions about national affairs.[39] On 4 June, two days before Léon Blum's government took power, in the council chamber Louis, sober now, put down a motion for 'a debate against Jewish tyranny and the invasion of foreigners', proposing the annulment of naturalisations granted since the Armistice of 1918 and, for Jews, withdrawal of their right to vote or to occupy public office.[40] These ambitions were borrowed, almost word for word, from Henry Coston's instructions,[41] and covered every point Louis was to repeat many hundreds of times over the coming years: 'time to put an end to the destruction of France ... men of destiny ... heritage of France today in Jewish hands ... Socialist Party ... Communist Party ... product of foreign and Jewish powers ...'

Louis' way of rousing the interest of his male colleagues was to refer regularly to the male sexual organ – impotence, emasculation, and the circumcision of Jewish penises were not spared. Nor was anyone named Dreyfus, 'belonging to that privileged race', nor Jewish 'grain merchants and flour milling trusts'. Though he bowed to his nationalist colleagues by acknowledging that exceptions could be made for Jewish war veterans – a position he was to maintain for scarcely another week – this was the beginning of Louis' rejection of Catholic and nationalist anti-Semitism in favour of the French version of the Nazi racist variety.

Closing his speech, he demanded the discussion of his proposal at the next sitting. Some councillors tittered, but generally the response was angry; insults flew. Amongst the ripostes was a request to know 'exactly what epoch gave birth to the ancient nobility of M. Darquier de Pellepoix', as well as jokes about his monocle.[42]

Louis was to be prosecuted for his attack at Chez Doucette, and his imbroglios – and more – were reported daily in the newspapers. On 5 June the headlines of *Action française* read '*La France sous le Juif*'; this issue covered in full Louis' performance and 'bristled with provocation to murder, gross anti-Semitism, calumnies and lies'.[43] But there was one reader unimpressed by Louis' speech:

Strasbourg, 15 June 1936
My dear Louis,
    I have given myself time for reflection before deciding upon my attitude towards you following the motion that you have put down at the General Council, which has been published in toto by *Action française*. I did not want you to think that I have yielded to a bad-tempered moment, and so here is what I want to tell you calmly and with moderation.
    For nearly eight years I have played the role of 'providence' for

you. This unrewarding role has never brought me anything but rebuffs; the last is of such an order that I have decided to change my attitude.

I venture first to remind you in case you have forgotten, that I belong to the trust of the mill, which controls (!) eight per cent of French production. I belong to it financially because it gives me my living and also thus permitted me to advance to you more than 150,000 francs to get you out of unpleasant situations and to pay for the larger part of your election costs.

But I also belong to them morally and with all my heart, and for those who run it I feel an affection which far exceeds that of an employee towards an employer.

In these circumstances I consider that you have attacked me personally, in an absolutely unwarranted and gratuitous manner. I would have hoped for a different attitude on your part.

It's up to you to treat with disdain the most elementary feelings of gratitude. I ask for nothing: you doubtless reckon that this justifies every liberty as far as I am concerned.

As this is the case, I inform you that I have made over your debts to a specialist Company, that is to say:

1– a bill guaranteed by Monsieur TROCHU for 10.000 francs

2– an acknowledgement of debt of 5000 francs

3– an acknowledgement of debt of 150.000 francs payment due on demand

This Society having acquired the said debts, for a consideration, you should not expect any consideration on their part.

With all my regrets

[René Darquier]*

Some member of the Darquier family has written on this letter, in red ink, 'ENFIN!!!' – AT LAST!!!

---

* Each French anti-Semitic group seems to have published its own version of the *Protocols*. Louis' edition, published by his own newspaper, *La France enchaînée*, in August 1938, and lavishly footnoted and annotated by himself, was obviously subsidised and came cheaper than Coston's at two francs a copy. In his preface, he wrote – of René?: 'Every government in the world is consciously, or unconsciously under the yoke of the great "super-government" of Sion, because all the money is in its hands, since every country is in the debt of the Jews, for sums that they can never repay.'

9

Pot of Gold

I N 1936 LOUIS WAS NEARING his forties, and he was to live for over forty years more. He did not have to bother with an original thought or speech in his new *milieu*: he was the inheritor of a rich tradition of French anti-Semitism, absorbed from Charles Maurras and Henry Coston, but stretching back to centuries past. The mainstream left had renounced the anti-Semitism of the right during the Dreyfus Affair. But in the 1930s there were traces of anti-Semitism in a section of the left which concentrated its vigour on the financial domination of Jewish banking families such as the Rothschilds, and extended this sentiment to Jews generally. All bankers were Jews, all Jews were bankers. Capitalism was the enemy of the worker; all capitalists were Jews.

On a more ludicrous level, these connections extended, in ways mysterious to most minds, into a nether world of French anti-Semitic extremists, and often drifted into secret worlds of Masonic and Jewish rituals and societies, spiritualism and revolutionary plots, druidic and occult practices, apocalyptic utterances and visions, the Templars, the Illuminati,[1] Rosicrucians and the Holy Grail. Satanic/Jewish plots were often invoked. Édouard Drumont, the father of French anti-Semitism, carried a mandrake root on his person, while Louis' newspaper patron Léon Bailby was a lifelong devotee of the occult sciences. The rantings of Drumont, like those of Darquier, sound like the outpourings of a lunatic, but then, often so did those of Hitler. Like Hitler, Drumont was respected by his vast readership. Words and thoughts which appear in his twelve-hundred-page diatribe against the 'Jewish Conquest' of France appear again in Maurras and Darquier and le Pen, most particularly his catchphrase 'France for the French'. Jews could never become part of France, they were inassimilable.

Louis Darquier's intense anti-Semitism was a product of various sources and conflicting attitudes, and for some years he worked within all its different arenas. Once he was given power no Jew was safe from him, because every Jew was a criminal, part of a world conspiracy. At this level of contemplation, Jews were not human beings like the rest of us. In the minds of men like Louis Darquier they became mysterious bodies, another species altogether, creatures of enormous power controlling ordinary mortals through international finance and international communism. The idea of blood was central to this hatred and fear, rather like the fear of menstrual blood exhibited by certain men of religion over the centuries. Anti-Semites hated the physical appearance of persons they decided were Jewish, and caricatured them relentlessly – curly hair, balding, large round faces, curving long noses, long-nailed hands like octopus tentacles grasping every part of the world – but it was the blood inside they concentrated on the most. The book which fired Louis' words, words he mixed with those of Maurras into his signature tune, was *The Protocols of the Elders of Sion*. This book and its fate would also lead to Louis' first links with Germany, and his personal pot of gold.

Louis Darquier said the *Protocols* first came his way in 1935; probably Coston gave him his own edition of it when both men were standing for the Paris city council in that year. There were, and are, many versions and thousands of different editions of this forgery, probably the invention of the Tsarist secret police in 1903. The *Protocols* is, in fact, a cut-and-paste job from various sources and countries mixing medieval anti-Semitic mythology with more recent political and Catholic tracts from strange abbés and disappointed activists, plagiarising all of them into a patchwork which sold more copies in the twentieth century than any other book except the Bible. Published originally in French, in Russia, the *Protocols* appeared in Germany in 1919, and in Britain and France in 1920.[2] Millions of sane and insane people believed its convoluted message. In the USA Henry Ford promoted it for years. Hitler used the *Protocols* extensively in *Mein Kampf*, and made it a set text in all German schools of the Third Reich. Its message, decorated and elaborated within a tapestry of paranoia, was that there was a world Jewish conspiracy and a secret Jewish government with plans, enunciated in these *Protocols*, to control the world.

The anti-Semites who believed in the *Protocols* were often obsessed with numbers, with identification. Many of them, like Coston, were fanatical archivists, eternally collecting, filing and annotating proof of the satanic Judaeo-Masonic forces arrayed against Western civilisation. The obsession with blood permeates the *Protocols* too – Jews using the blood of Christian children for Passover, Jews poisoning wells, spreading the plague through Gentile blood, encouraging drunkenness and prostitution and thus polluting the seed of future generations.

Louis liked to quote *The Times* in the council chamber, his command of English being part of his monocled Wodehousian persona. The paper had exposed the forgery of the *Protocols* in detail in August 1921, but in this case Louis did not believe *The Times*,[3] he believed in satanic Jews; though he ignored the *Protocols'* advice that drunkenness and prostitution were Jewish weapons for world destruction. As the *Protocols* spread around the world in the 1920s and 1930s, each country adapted its message to suit itself, so that it could be marshalled to suit any current hatred. Christianity itself could be considered Jewish, and the governments of Britain or France also, if such an opinion was useful.

The trial of the *Protocols* in a Swiss court from 1934 to 1935 also brought the book to Louis' attention. Since the 1920s the Nazi Party had disseminated the *Protocols* everywhere, and in Berne Swiss Jews brought a court case against Swiss and German Nazis for 'publishing and distributing improper literature'.[4] This was one of those cases which drew into court a multitude of mysterious Russian spies, pseudo-mystics and table-rapping eccentrics, to the amusement of the public at large, and it became internationally notorious. As the trial progressed in fits and starts, the Swiss defenders of the *Protocols* turned to Nazi Germany for financial and philosophical support: both were supplied by the star witness, a German, Colonel Ulrich Fleischhauer, who was to intervene assiduously in French affairs over the next few years.

Coston had met Fleischhauer in 1934, and went to Berne to serve as a witness on his behalf in 1935. Like all Fleischhauer's supporting witnesses, Coston was not called because Fleischhauer submitted evidence running to nearly five hundred pages, and defended the *Protocols* himself for five days, without drawing breath. Fleischhauer had begun his work in 1919, with his own publishing house; after 1933, when he moved to Erfurt, he launched his Weltdienst – World Service – a non-profit-making anti-Jewish press agency for 'International

Correspondence for Enlightenment on the Jewish Question'. But it was the Berne trial, which he lost, that made Fleischhauer's name forever afterwards entwined with the *Protocols*, which the Swiss judge had dismissed as 'ridiculous nonsense'.[5]

The Nazi Party used Fleischhauer for foreign dealings while it suited them, which was until 1939, when Goebbels got rid of him and Alfred Rosenberg, chief ideologue of the party, took over his Weltdienst. With it came Fleischhauer's 'flawless' library of apocryphal literature, much of it pornographic, with such precious volumes about Jewish ritual murder that in 1943 Rosenberg began to construct a rock cellar below ground to protect it.

Until then, Erfurt became *la Mecque de l'Antisémitisme*, the Mecca of anti-Semitism. Fleischhauer had agents – spies? – all over the world, and information poured in: 'Greyshirts of South Africa are with you, if not in person, in spirit and our hand of cooperation is stretched out to your Assembly in Erfurt.'[6] By 1936 Fleischhauer was dealing with Himmler's SS, and was supported by Hitler's propaganda ministry, run by Goebbels, and by Rosenberg's foreign policy office.

The documentation of the Nazi Party's relationship with its French postulants is complex, but all of its warring departments seem to have used the services of Julius Streicher in their dealings with foreign countries. Streicher, Hitler's most favoured journalist and the most brutal of all Jew-baiters, was the founder and editor of *Der Stürmer*. Henry Coston met him in Germany in 1934, and other French anti-Semites followed him. Streicher also had a vast library of pornographic *anti-Semitica* and, as Hitler said, 'had only one disease, and that was nympholepsy'.[7]

Streicher was considered a maniac by many prominent Nazis – as indeed were Rosenberg and Fleischhauer – but under Hitler's favour he flourished. *Der Stürmer* was a scandal sheet full of cartoons and photographs, sex and crime, rape and plunder – all Jewish – presented in words of one syllable. It was the most verminous of all Nazi anti-Semitic publications, and after 1935, at its most successful, sold well over 600,000 copies a week. Louis Darquier and his comrades got their personification of the Jew from *Der Stürmer*: 'short, fat, ugly, unshaven, drooling, sexually perverted, bent-nosed, with pig-like eyes'.[8] And they learned about promotion from Streicher: copies of *Der Stürmer* were sold at bus stops, in the street, outside factories.

Fleischhauer told Rosenberg that all other French anti-Semites were too chauvinistic or reactionary; only Coston could be of any use to Hitler. From 1934, through his Weltdienst, Fleischhauer gave enthusiastic publicity to the activities of Coston and his comrades-in-arms, such as the ferocious anti-Semites Jean Boissel and Pierre Clémenti.[9] Though precariously funded himself, in the early days of the Nazi Party Fleischhauer was a conduit for these men, and for Louis. They copied his style, too. A typical Fleischhauer news story, headed 'Jews in Hollywood', read: 'Eddie Cantor = Issy Iskowitz, Charles Chaplin = Tonstein, Bert Lahr = Isador Barrheim, Ethel Merman = Ethel Zimmerman . . .' and so on.[10]

On 5 April 1936 Louis Darquier received a telegram from Fleischhauer's secretary Emilie Vasticar offering him a subscription to the Weltdienst, telling him about certain other anti-Semitic contacts, and giving their opinion on la Roque and Julius Streicher. Louis replied, and at the end of April there is a reference to a meeting in Paris. On 1 June 1936 Emilie invited him to Berlin. Did they meet? Did he go? We do not know.[11] What is certain is that by early June 1936 Louis had acquired sufficient money, and confidence about more to come, to take his revenge on René and to expand his activities on many fronts.

On the day he received René's letter, 17 June 1936, he stood up in the council chamber to demand 'the withdrawal of civil and political rights from Jews', using the words of the *Protocols* and the Weltdienst to create an unprecedented scene. Every sentence he uttered was greeted with raised voices, interruptions, sarcasm, protests, abuse, raillery or fury. The row went on and on, a perfect microcosm of the continuing war between republican and nationalist France, as councillor after councillor stood up to defend the right of Jews, established by the French Revolution, to live in France like other Frenchmen. 'The Unknown Soldier could be Jewish,' Jewish 'writers, artists, thinkers . . . have added to the glorious heritage' of France. Jews belonged to the great family of France: 'There is no difference. They are as French as we are!' 'Go and make this speech to Hitler!' they cried. The words 'Hitler' and 'Jew' ricocheted around the chamber like a hail of bullets.

Within this maelstrom Louis quoted, as proof of the decline of France under the Jewish Peril, the opinion of the *Daily Telegraph* in London that France was now a second-class power. The riposte flew back: 'If the *Daily Telegraph* said that, it's because they know you.' Louis maintained an injured dignity as he explained, again and again, that Jews were 'not only a religion, but a race, and above all a nation', which had spread through France and taken it over. The health of France was at stake! The life of France was at stake! 'We, whose roots have been buried in the soil of France for millions of years', were now ruled by 'a foreign race, a nation of wanderers' who 'have taken over everything, even the government of the country! When we take in a guest who behaves properly, we treat him with honour, but when he puts his feet on the table and pisses on the curtains, we show him the door!'[12]

Georges Hirsch, a socialist, then raised the name of Louis Louis-Dreyfus, 'that grain speculator and enemy of the people', whose Jewish money Louis had been so happy to accept in taking a salary from Bailby. Louis went berserk. He demanded satisfaction outside the chamber for any calumny that associated his name with that 'appalling man', and called Hirsch 'a dirty little Jew'. Later, in the cloakroom, Louis attacked Hirsch, and the scuffle continued until other councillors pulled them apart.[13]

But this was all as Darquier wished, because he had been, for hour after hour, the absolute centre of attention. More important for him financially, the uproar had been so great that, as one councillor intuitively remarked, every newspaper would report on the astounding scenes, and such reports would, of course, be picked up in Germany. In one manoeuvre Louis had placed himself at the front of the queue of French anti-Semites waiting for attention from the Reich.

Outside the council chamber another immensely influential man had already spoken out. Xavier Vallat, deputy for the Ardèche since 1919, had always been noted for his hostility to Masonry rather than for his anti-Semitism. After the First World War there was hardly a league, group or movement of the extreme right that Vallat did not join. His transformation into an anti-Semite came about with the election of Léon Blum. In the Chamber of Deputies, at the inauguration of Blum's Popular Front government on 6 June, Vallat became both notorious on the left and celebrated by the right when he stood up to deplore the fact that for the first time 'this old Gallo-Roman country will be governed by a Jew'.[14] Vallat's speech encouraged Louis to speak even more violently in the Hôtel de Ville ten days later. There were only three Jews in the Popular Front government, but for the next two years a good part of the French right insisted that it consisted entirely of Jews.

Sixty-four years old when he became prime minister of France, Léon Blum was a well-to-do intellectual, a lawyer, an elegant writer, a literary and dramatic critic and an able civil servant. Physically, he had a Proustian kind of beauty – floppy straight hair, straight nose, thick round-rimmed spectacles, a dignified moustache. His feet, in spats, turned outward, his hat was black and large and his voice was light, 'flute-like'. He was much caricatured. Blum was a parliamentary democrat hostile to communist and fascist dictatorships, a clever, witty, cultured man, not a great orator nor a man of the people. But he was the first socialist and the first Jewish prime minister of France, the successor and friend of the great socialist Jean Jaurès, and his compelling honesty commanded attention and loyalty. His Popular Front government was always an uneasy coalition, a very shaky threat to the right even in the best of times. The Spanish Civil War broke out a month after Blum came to power, posing him insoluble problems abroad and for his coalition at home, where he was always dependent on the support of the Radical Party. In addition, the Depression had not yet lifted. But to French conservatives the Bolsheviks had taken over, and they were now ruled by the industrial working class and/or by Moscow. Indeed Stalin kept a firm eye on the policy of his international adherents, but his French communists, who numbered seventy-two deputies, the largest figure they had ever achieved, did not participate in the government, merely gave it support inside the chamber.

This meant nothing to Blum's opponents, because after the victory of the Popular Front, and to its great detriment, spontaneous sit-down strikes, the largest in French history, broke out and continued throughout May and June. Workers occupied the premises of heavy industries, factories, department stores, mines, hotels and restaurants, waving red flags or the tricolour, and dancing to accordions. The social reforms the Popular Front introduced, despite furious opposition, offered a forty-hour week, pay rises, two weeks' paid holiday a year, and raised the school leaving age to fourteen.

Later in 1936, a quarter of a million workers were on strike and Blum was forced to devalue the franc. All this caused terror amongst business leaders and on the right. 'A man to shoot, but in the back,' said Maurras. One of Daudet's contributions was to call Blum a 'circumcised hermaphrodite'.[15] If the Vichy years played out the Franco-French civil war, the excessive fear of revolution – to be wrought by communists for one side, by fascists for the other – began here. In a way the strikes were victory festivals, but 'the great fear of June 1936' stretched the divide between left and right to breaking point.

As Hitler increased his persecution of Jews and the world refugee crisis escalated, the Jewish population of France changed, but they were always a tiny minority. The history of persecution and containment meant that most 'old French Jews' lived in big cities – Paris, Bordeaux, Lyon, Marseille – and that their occupations were often noticeable, or distinguished – banking and the commodities, the professions, politics. Many Jews still lived in Alsace, while a large number of Alsatian Jews, French patriots, had moved to France after the defeat by Germany in 1871 – the families of Louis Louis-Dreyfus and Léon Blum being two examples.[16] Many, like Blum again, no longer practised their religion.

By 1939 France was home to about 330,000 Jews, of whom some thirty per cent were refugees.[17] About these the French Jewish community itself was divided. As is ever the way, many 'French Israelites', the 'polite' name by which long-established French Jews were known, were unhappy about the influx of these poorer Jews. Even so, whether old citizens or new refugees, Jews remained less than one per cent of the population of France; but they did not seem so to those who magnified this small number into an invading horde. The result was xenophobia and resentment, by no means confined to men such as Louis Darquier.

When he began his anti-Semitic career, Louis did not concentrate wholly upon Jews. In the short term he added the Popular Front, communism, Masonry and all foreigners to his list of mortal enemies, and he used these hatreds to make his living. His relationship with Maurras was now at its zenith, and he was a regular visitor at the headquarters in rue Boccador. *Action française* followed his every word, and when he arrived at the Salle Wagram on 20 June 1936 to make another speech on behalf of the Vigilance Committee, he entered to a standing ovation. He lauded Maurras, attacked Blum, socialists, communists and Jews, and left to cries of '*Vive Darquier!* . . . Down with Jews! . . . Death to Blum!'

Louis needed the Nazis all the more because René had called in the bailiffs, and his salary from the Hôtel de Ville was already sequestered by a monthly payment to the Hôtel California – the Darquiers had not paid their bill before departing, and the California had seized their luggage, again.[18] That he got financial help is demonstrated by the fact that despite all these debts, by June 1936 Louis had acquired sufficient funds to found the next of his associations, the Club National.

In that month, in the midst of the flurry of telegrams and letters to and from Émilie Vasticar, Louis rented two buildings, numbers 8 and 12 in the drab and insalubrious rue Laugier in the 18th arrondissement. Number 12, a large but unimposing building, was to be the headquarters of his new National Club for 'selfless Frenchmen' devoted to 'the grandeur and prosperity of the fatherland by devoting themselves to the practice of sport'.[19] This was an ambitious project: the building was three storeys high and included a meeting hall for about a hundred people, as well as a sitting room and bar. Number 8 was his Club Sportif – the Sporting Club of Ternes, where men could engage in physical culture and bodybuilding and take water treatments in the form of hot showers and water jets. According to Louis it was 'a magnificent two-storey building which comprises offices, meeting rooms, a large gymnasium where members can practise PT, boxing, fencing, table tennis, pistol shooting etc., with first-rate instructors. The locker rooms, shower rooms and a brightly decorated private bar also make this one of the finest private clubs in Paris.' According to the police it was a club for 'fervent right-wing elements who could well serve as leaders in time of trouble'.[20]

Louis had always been good at sport, an able horseman and fencer, and for those with eyes turned to Germany this was important. The Berlin Olympic Games, Hitler's theatrical masterstroke, were only six weeks away. Louis loved the characteristics of fascism: the violence of language and action; the uniforms and impedimenta, the passion for propaganda. However, one contemporary said that he never set foot in the gym, and it is hard to see how the physical exercise of which fascists were in principle so fond could be combined, on a daily basis, with drinking and nights on the town and the furious concentration required by his new role.

From 12, rue Laugier Louis published a shoddy four-page roneoed weekly *Bulletin*, combining his hatred of Blum and Jews with his love of journalism.[21] It is likely that the entire endeavour was made possible by various Nazi subsidies. In his first *Bulletin*, which also presented a photograph of the club's president, looking chubby and in need of the services provided by no. 8, he asked the public: 'What is the National Club?' And he replied:

The National Club takes a firm stand
Against Jewish and Foreign domination
Against the anonymous power of money
Against Soviet enslavery
Against the trickery of international Socialism
And For
National Renewal

There was a section for 'Young Nationalists' – these were Louis' 'biff boys', the thugs who now accompanied him, a product perhaps of training received at no. 8.[22] There would be a women's section, and 'Sons of France' for those between twelve and eighteen years of age. There were to be no exceptions to the membership rules:

> The National Club refuses to admit Jews, Freemasons or anyone belonging to, or believing in, international organisations. Each member has to swear the following: 'I declare upon my honour to have been born French and to be neither of Jewish nor Masonic origin, nor attached to any international organisation.'[23]

Myrtle could not have joined its women's section.

Maurras, unaware of Louis' contacts with Fleischhauer – Louis lied about his German money for years – heralded the National Club in *Action française* as a place where 'all Nationalists will find indispensable information for the battle against Jews and wogs who pillage and dishonour our country'.[24]

A characteristic of all the French nationalist groups was a constant process of rechristening. This was forced upon them just as Louis opened his club when the Popular Front government followed the earlier closure of Action Française with the dissolution of all the paramilitary nationalist leagues. Some immediately re-formed into political parties, ready to participate in the election process. Taittinger's Jeunesses Patriotes became the Parti National Populaire (PNP); la Roque toyed with rebellion and considered an approach which would make General Weygand head of state, but Croix-de-feu too peacefully reshaped itself into a parliamentary party as the Parti Social Français (PSF). On the fringe both of these newly named nationalist parties and of the Paris intellectuals, more ridiculous, wildly less intelligent than those often brilliant men whose activities he aped and whose words he borrowed, Louis founded his club to pick up the residue and the membership fees of the disbanded leagues.

Launched at the same time was Jacques Doriot's fascist Parti Populaire Français (PPF), another beneficiary, and a far more successful one. Because Doriot had been a passionate communist himself, and because, like Taittinger and la Roque, he received money from wealthy Jewish sources, the target of the PPF was, initially, communism. For the Nazi bankers of anti-Semitism in the mid-thirties, Louis therefore had much of the field to himself.

In early July 1936, Louis held the first large meeting of his club. Many of his speakers were Action Française comrades – Robert Castille, Henry Charbonneau. Jean-Pierre Maxence took part too, but Louis' most important coup was the contribution of the celebrated writer Lucien Rebatet, and of the devoted disciple of Maurras, Henri Massis, who presided. Both of these men brought Louis' club and his anti-Semitic movement intellectual endorsement. He could now mix with some of the most gifted writers of the time. His hero was Louis-Ferdinand Céline, but he came to know Rebatet and Robert Brasillach, both products of Action Française, Brasillach's brother-in-law Maurice Bardèche and Georges Blond – who married a neighbour and friend of the Darquier family in the Lot – as well as Thierry Maulnier and many others of the French intellectual world. All of them gave a literary gloss to the fight against the *Youpin*, the Yid.[25]

For men like Louis Darquier, and those to the left and right of him in anti-republican France, Franco's revolt against the Spanish republic was a national revolution, a patriotic uprising against communism. Throughout 1936 Darquier addressed tumultuous public meetings in the Salle Wagram and elsewhere, gave rousing anti-war speeches – the Spanish republicans were communists, the coming world war was a Jewish conspiracy – and worked closely with, and on behalf of, Action Française. He continued to posture in the city council, where he interjected constantly, sometimes spoke from the rostrum, but rarely strayed from jokes, innuendos and lectures about Jews, communists, Masons and foreigners.

Maurras went to jail in October, and held court there until July the following year, sentenced for his articles in *Action française* demanding the death of over a hundred deputies, including Léon Blum (not forgetting previous articles demanding that Blum be lynched, shot in the back, or have his throat slit 'with a kitchen knife').[26] With Charles Trochu, Louis arranged for forty city councillors to make a statement of public homage to Maurras on his incarceration. He held meetings of his club in the rue Laugier: Léon Degrelle, the Belgian fascist leader, was turned back at the frontier on his way to one of them. Louis was permanently under police surveillance, and reports on the bumping and grinding and bellowing which issued from his Sports Club added further to his reputation as a homosexual. Louis also ran off tracts and leaflets modelled on the anti-Semitic propaganda of Fleischhauer's Weltdienst, and wrote for Coston's *Libre parole*, favouring the kind of nationalist fascism advocated by Maurras.

Nevertheless, for the next few years Louis' success in Nazi-funded French anti-Semitic circles was seriously limited by his connection to Maurras. Within the walled encampments of Parisian anti-Semitism, one of the most bitter enmities had always been between Maurras and Léon Daudet and other veteran anti-Semites – the followers of Drumont such as Urbain Gohier, to whose camp younger fellows such as Coston belonged. 'Bandits', Gohier called the men of Action Française, demanding that they be 'defenestrated by the righteous anger of the people'. This mutual loathing, based on some anti-Semitic inadequacy invisible to the naked eye, simmered on despite court actions for defamation.

Coston and Gohier and their clique – some of them rivals or disillusioned followers of Maurras – particularly abhorred the royalism of the AF and Louis' continued support for the movement in Paris and in other provincial cities. Like squabbling soldiers ignoring the enemy and turning upon each other in the trenches, they argued and disagreed and fought each other with words and fists and through their little newspapers and journals. They swapped wives and mistresses, shouted their ideas to small audiences of like-minded people, aped the rituals of their fascist neighbours, and congregated in the meeting halls, cafés and gathering points of their agitated *milieu*. Many of these men were editors or journalists. Some of their groups or newspapers barely lasted a few weeks: each rose again in different form to join or create another, each given names of considerable length and ambitious grandeur.[27]

By 1938 Louis had come to the conclusion that 'every nationalist party is full of Jews'.[28] He put men such as Pierre Taittinger behind him, except in the council chamber, where Trochu remained an unfailing supporter. However, he convinced Charles Maurras, if few others, of his independence from Germany and so, uniquely, managed to straddle both nationalist French and Nazi-French anti-Semitic circles until 1939.

***

As a frequenter of Louis' club, Jean Darquier saw the papers from René's bailiff inscribed 'Darquier vs. Darquier', announcing the seizure of Louis' assets. Jean found the reading of this so painful that he wrote to René:

> for [Louis], the seizure means he will have nothing to live on, at little profit to you, and at the risk of a frightful scandal – which the political and police scum will exploit to the full.
> ... I attach no importance to Louis' belief that you are deliberately doing as Jews do. I know too much what you think of those people to believe such a fact.
> ... I cannot believe that the very vague notions in Louis' phrases could really have offended those people [Jews] who are only a part of your Mill's trusts.
> ... I am certain that Louis will pay you back when he can ... the sight of the bailiff's papers has forced me to talk to you as an older brother who has always loved all his family ... [29]

In the middle of all this, Louis still looked to his earlier patrons. Anatole de Monzie was older now, his infirmities increased by a bad car accident, but he remained a powerful figure, and though he held no ministerial position in the Popular Front, he became the centre of a 'kind of phantom cabinet for peace within the government'. An expert on Russian affairs and a known acquaintance of Mussolini, he wanted an *entente* with fascist Italy and communist Russia against the German threat. His unusual position in this as in so many other matters meant that he could not take Louis Darquier's anti-Semitism seriously, and as long as Louis still paid court to Maurras, who remained one of de Monzie's esteemed intellectual companions, he continued to consider Louis' endeavours as nothing more than the activities of a raffish bohemian. And so, after Louis' frenzy in the city council in

June 1936 and the subsequent rupture between the Darquier brothers, de Monzie intervened. Louis was instructed to behave less wildly. On 10 November René withdrew his action. Louis was asked to visit the bailiffs in order to come up with a different arrangement. He answered no letters, made no visits, and a year later René himself closed the affair by paying the bailiff an honorarium. Louis and Myrtle never repaid René.

Throughout 1936 Louis was occupied with other legal matters. In June he refused to attend court 'in a most incorrect manner'[30] to answer charges brought against him for his attack at Chez Doucette, and only agreed to appear before the judge in October after receiving a personal letter of invitation from the commissioner of police – he was eventually fined a thousand francs. As soon as he had dealt with that request, one night with Myrtle in the Bar Marlène in the elegant 1st arrondissement he attacked and incapacitated a Romanian barman, Dino Banatzeano (though Louis called him 'the Jew Simon Botzananeano' in the protracted lawsuit which followed).

Hitler had numerous organisations with overlapping responsibilities and initials, all of them dependent upon his favour, each cordially loathing the other: he ruled by division. When Louis applied to the German embassy in Paris for money, Ambassador Johannes von Welczek was cautious, but wrote to the German Foreign Ministry: 'Yesterday a young lawyer called Robert Castille . . . came to see me. He said he belonged to the National Club. He intended to write a thesis on the question of the Jews in universities and wanted information as to how the German universities had rid themselves of Jews . . . Then he came out with the actual purpose of his visit . . .' This was to ask for money for Louis' club: 'not actually a club but a big association with 3000 members [sic] in Paris who are mainly anti-Semitic lawyers [sic] . . . an explicitly nationalist and anti-Semitic organisation, actually the only one which openly confesses anti-Semitism'.[31]

Louis' first cheque, for 2,500 marks (worth about £27,000 today), came on 4 January 1937 by way of Elizabeth Büttner, a resident of Berlin who, as a *demi-mondaine* woman of mystery, worked as a Nazi spy in the years before the war.[32] The British Foreign office believed she worked for Otto Abetz, a former art teacher who had joined Ribbentrop's Foreign Bureau, the Dienststelle Ribbentrop, in 1934. Abetz was a francophile, a blond and charming fellow and a close friend of the Radical journalist

Jean Luchair – whose journal *Les Nouveau temps* was one of the many Abetz was later to 'subsidise'. In 1932 he had married Luchaire's French secretary, Suzanne de Bruycker. Two years later he was introducing Hitler to French veteran leaders, and by 1935 he was head of the French section of Ribbentrop's office. His great success was the Comité France–Allemagne – the Franco-German Committee – in 1935. This committee, in which his French counterpart was the journalist Fernand de Brinon, included notables such as the writer Drieu la Rochelle, the mad Catholic chaplain Monseigneur Jean Mayol de Lupé and Jean Luchaire.[33]

Although he did not become a member of the Nazi Party until 1937, on Ribbentrop's orders Abetz's job was to 'reconciliate' French artistic, intellectual and journalist circles with Nazi Germany. Nominally working at the French embassy, he used the inducements of free visits to Germany and abundant entertainment, in a combination of wine, women and song which brought him great success in the salons of Paris. Through the fashionable Champs-Élysées club Le Grand Pavois, where de Brinon held court, French Nazis mixed with an elite of intellectuals and high society. The British Foreign Office reported that Abetz spent £2,000 a month on bribing the French press, with Elizabeth Büttner as his assistant.[34]

Abetz has always been presented as among the more affable German presences during the Occupation, but his connections to the seamier side of French anti-Semitism were long-established, and they continued, although its denizens were, and remained, persons not at all to his taste. Though some of Elizabeth Büttner's cheque stubs, discovered by the French police in 1939, are unreadable, quite clear are those for cheques made out to Fleischhauer's French followers, amongst them Darquier, Coston and de Brinon.[35]

Many of Louis' Reichsmarks seem to have been spent on drink. At the end of January 1937 the police were called to throw him out of the Lord Byron Cinema in the Champs-Élysées because, with a woman – Myrtle? – he took over some already-occupied seats, refused to show any tickets, and refused to move: 'I'm here and I'm staying here.'

With his German cheque Louis' *Bulletin* became simultaneously lower and louder, and he began to spread his wings.

Bulletin of the National Club

No. 52, 17 April 1937

THE MOSES-EUM

... It has also come to our notice that n° 57, rue de Varenne [the office of the French Prime Minister] ... has been used since June 1936 as the home-lair of the entire Jewish clique which gravitates around Blum, the Blumels, Blumschens, Mochleins who now are solidly installed there and encrusted en famille with grandfather Abraham, old mother Sarah, uncle Laban, cousin Isaac and cousin Rebecca and all the little brothers, sons and nephews, Simon, Levey, Mordecai etc. etc.

All these come and go, bustle about, fly hither and thither, raise their fists, yell, chirp and swarm about from morning to night and from night to morning. Number 57, rue de la Varenne has become a Polish Jew-house, a Leghorn ghetto, a Moroccan *mellha*. To keep up the neighbourhood tone, the nearby Rodin Museum may as well be renamed a 'Moses-eum'. Its façade could then be painted deep blue just like the homes in North Africa of the innumerable and disastrous posterity of Jacob-Israel; 'The Deceiver' and worthy forebear of Léon Blum.

And:

A few weeks ago, a Miss World Fair was elected. She was called Mademoiselle Jacoview. Then Miss Cinema. A 'Goy' was elected, protests were made and, under a fabricated pretext, the election was cancelled. Mademoiselle Joel was elected instead.

Yesterday *Ce Soir*, the Jewish-Soviet journal, published an interview with Miss Venus. She is called Yvonne Heymann, and she has a nose, but what a nose![36]

Each of the *Bulletin*'s fifty-five issues was more or less exactly the same.

The third German financial source Louis used was the Geneva office of l'Internationale Antisémite, a nineteenth-century organisation which by this time seems to have been working with Julius Streicher. Later Louis added the Gestapo, and many strange figures on the occult fringes of the Nazi world were also to surface, bearing gifts, in the coming years. This flow of German money into the lower reaches of French anti-Semitism resulted in a flurry of activity in March 1937. Coston's *Libre parole* proposed a National Anti-Semitic Congress in the style of Fleischhauer's annual Erfurt Congress, held each September.

A month later a Comité Antijuif de France (Anti-Jewish Committee of France) was constituted, with Louis Darquier as president and Henri-Robert Petit as secretary.[37] On 11 May, in full flourish, the first meeting was held in the Salle Wagram, and the anti-Semitic brotherhood turned out in force. 'Subjects discussed: History of the Jews in France, from the Talmud to Marxism, Jewish capitalism, Jews and Freemasonry, the Jewish invasion.'[38] Louis spoke last, and it was on this occasion that he uttered his most quoted sentence: 'We must, with all urgency, resolve the Jewish problem, whether by expulsion, or massacre.'[39]

'It is already well known,' Louis wrote in 1938, after being in receipt of Nazi money for nearly two years, 'that through the intervention of organisations like the Franco-German Committee (Vice-President Fernand de Brinon, married to a Jew) there are men who sympathise with Jews, Masons and democrats, in a word, scum, who are *persona grata* with the top Germans, and in particular with His Excellency Herr Ribbentrop.'[40]

This kind of lie was inspired by Louis' exclusion from de Brinon's aristocratic circle in Le Grand Pavois, doubly irritating as 'Comte' de Brinon was another French journalist said to have bestowed nobility upon himself. Though Louis used 'Baron Darquier de Pellepoix' without pause, and though he received money from Elizabeth Büttner, the elite club of Abetz's pro-Nazis had little to do with his rabble fringe. None of this fooled the French security service, who recorded most of Louis' German contacts, but until 1939 such words satisfied Charles Maurras, a happier man that year because Pope Pius XII revoked the interdiction of Action Française; Catholics could now join it again.

Louis Darquier's court cases and his financial connections with Nazi Germany were referred to regularly in the press, yet Charles Maurras, to whom all contact with Germany remained anathema, chose to ignore them. The explanation for this, and for Darquier's fealty to Maurras, lies perhaps somewhere in the relationship between Anatole de Monzie and Maurras. While de Monzie relieved him of his fraternal problems, *Action française* gave front-page coverage to Louis' anti-Semitic speeches, lectures, fights and court cases, published his letters and shared platforms with him. Until 1939 Maurras gave Louis Darquier fame as a Jew-hater, fame sufficient to satisfy the Germans that Louis Darquier would be prepared to murder them.

10

―◄◦►―

On the Rampage

A s Louis became more successful in his chosen profession, and
as the Nazi money he was paid became more and more obvious,
Renseignements Généraux – the French equivalent of MI5 –
began to follow him around. Louis called them his 'guardian angels'.[1]
They followed Myrtle too, and it is only through police reports that she
surfaces after 1934, when she returned to Paris in such wretched shape.

By 1937 she seems to have been on the mend, dealing with matters
at the Sports Club, seeing workmen and paying the gas bill. She convinced
her family in Tasmania of the 'importance to him [Louis] of food, restaurants, dress and high standards in everything associated with the social
side of life'. Myrtle, the 'born entertainer' who sang with 'such wit and
verve', had lived for years now in one hotel room after another, without
a piano. She told her family her life was full of music, but no one who
came across them makes any mention of it.[2]

The Baron and Baroness had moved again, and by August were living
in the Hôtel Terminus, 108, rue St-Lazare in the 9th arrondissement.
Beyond the Hôtel Terminus and the dismal rue Laugier, Paris offered
extraordinary film, music and song – jazz, Piaf, Charles Trenet; its painters
were legendary. The Jones family sincerely believed that Myrtle 'learnt a
great deal from Louis, a fount of knowledge in so many spheres, and a
true scholar'.[3] But the names of Jean Gabin or Jean Renoir, Picasso or
Matisse were never heard on Louis' lips, and his rare references to the
cinema were always in character, as when he described the great director
Abel Gance as a 'filthy Jew'.

When the police began tracking Myrtle they called her 'Myrthe',
believed that she was childless, that she came from 'Launcestan', and
that her family name was Lindsay-Jones, or Morrison-Jones. They thought
she was an heiress, but that her fortune had been dissipated by her and

Louis' expensive lifestyle and the Depression. It seems, therefore, that Myrtle was still bemoaning the Australian wool prices and hoping for the inheritance removed a decade before.

Towards the end of 1937 extant bills, paid and unpaid, suggest that after over a year in the Hôtel Terminus Louis and Myrtle went to live in rue Laugier, though Louis seems to have kept a hotel room too from time to time. Two establishments were more suited, anyway, to his frenetic sexual arrangements. At other times he was seen with his buddies, mostly younger than he, a kind of rat pack of bully or homosexual boys, depending on who made the report. With them went Louis' dog Porthos, trained to chase Jews at the words '*Aux Juifs!*'[4] Money still ran through Louis' fingers. He had two clubs, his National and his Sports Club, was painting the town with Myrtle or his 'boys', and, the police noted, holding 'numerous reunions' and distributing 'a vast number of tracts protesting against the dictatorship of Jews and foreigners'.[5] At these meetings, year after year, sat plainclothes members of the Special Branch, taking down notes and misspelling names.

In the letters to which Myrtle was addicted she told the Jones family that she had fallen in love with Paris, and spent her days satisfying 'her love of museums, picture galleries, old buildings, history, theatre, ballet and music . . . with the best of the old and the new around her . . . she acquired a considerable knowledge'. To Myrtle, history was 'no string of dates, wars and treaties . . . No, it was warm, breathing people.'[6]

It is hard to believe that Myrtle did not shower letters upon Anne and Elsie in Kidlington, but there are no signs of such correspondence. Louis now had to deal directly with Elsie, and his occasional letters were noted, though the despatch of money was as ragged as it ever had been. René was still sending money to Elsie in May 1936, but *enfin* for Louis was also *enfin* for them. Anne was six when Louis quarrelled with his brother René. Paying Elsie was never first in his financial considerations, and Nanny Lightfoot and her charge survived until the outbreak of war assisted by the ever affectionate 'aunts', Maud and Violet, and in the mid-thirties by their niece May, who was earning too, as an assistant in the perfumery department of Babcock's store in Oxford. When Anne was seven, Neville Chamberlain became prime minister and the British appeasement of Hitler began. There was still fun to be had in these anxious years. May Brice would go to sixpenny hops and dances with her boyfriend Danny Puddefoot; Danny had a car, and he and May often took Anne on such jaunts, freeing her from the hovering Elsie.

Everyone commented upon Nanny Lightfoot's fiercely protective attitude towards her charge. Anne was not allowed to mix with all and sundry, and Elsie – how she learned it we will never know – spoke French with her at home.[7] She told the world that Anne came from an aristocratic French family, but in public the additional 'de Pellepoix' was never used; Anne entered schools simply as Anne Darquier. Anne's 'Dear Daddy' letters to her father attest to her dreams of a fabulous French family of aristocrats and doctors; it was her father the baron who was the linchpin of her fantasies about her missing parents during her childhood.

The magnificent International Exhibition of Art and Technology opened in Paris in May 1937, with the German Pavilion built by Albert Speer growling at the Soviet Pavilion which faced it, and on display everywhere in Paris were masterworks of art deco architecture and design. As the exhibition opened, Louis' *Bulletin* recorded what he thought to be the great success of the first meeting of the National Anti-Jewish Committee, and announced the birth of another association, his Rassemblement Antijuif de France (Anti-Jewish Union of France), and the launch of a new weekly newspaper, *l'Antijuif* (the Anti-Jew).[8]

THE ANTI-JEWISH UNION OF FRANCE

... Its aim is to bring together all people of French race, of whatever political opinions, to liberate France from Jewish tyranny. Its sole credo is that the renewal of France is not possible as long as Jews are not considered as foreigners and treated as such, and as long as they continue, behind more or less camouflaged labels and fronts, to stir up division, excite hatred and prepare with impunity revolution and wars of which they are the sole beneficiaries.

Lengthier explanations of 'our passionate propaganda movement' were also provided – honour, dignity, service to the nation 'strangled by Jews and Freemasons', love for the Fatherland, return of national wealth to true Frenchmen, protection of French patrimony both artistic and moral – as well as a requirement that all members must have four non-Jewish grandparents. All this came at twelve francs a year, half the charge for the National Club. For the insignia of his new union Louis chose a sword and shield, 'purely Aryan symbols in opposition to the six-pointed star of the Jews'. His colours: red and white – 'in politics the colours of extremes, because the solution of the Jewish problem demands an alliance of all opposed parties'.9 The National Anti-Jewish Committee collapsed immediately after its first meeting.

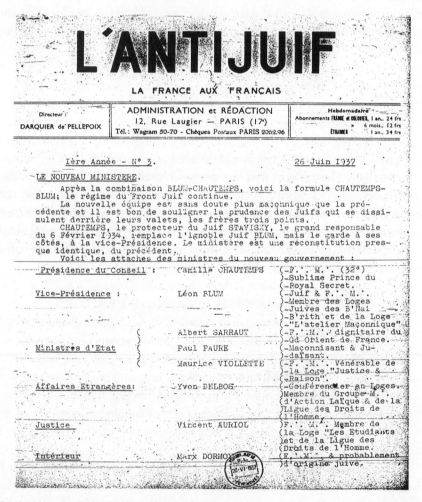

Louis' 'newspaper' before he received sufficient Nazi funding, *l'Antijuif* no. 3, 26 June 1937 (© Bibliothèque Nationale de France).

In Erfurt in 1937 Fleischhauer held his annual Weltdienst Congress. Adolf Eichmann, at that point in charge of the Nazi office for 'Jewish Emigration', was there, and he reported: 'Most of these Weltdienst members give the impression of being dubious characters who are obsessed with the idea of achieving recognition as leaders of parties and organisations in their own countries. They devote their entire attention to losing themselves in small details, to put it mildly, and this makes them incapable of working out or following any major strategy.'[10]

Coston had been leader of the pack. Now Louis had taken over the committee from Coston and made himself president, so all of Fleischhauer's French cohorts refused to join it, using one excuse or another. In the spring of 1937 Coston fell upon Henri-Robert Petit and accused him of mismanaging his library and archive. Petit extracted the *Bulletin* of the Centre for Information and Propaganda and fled with it to Louis.

This was the residue of the faithful with whom Louis launched his new organisation and paper, printed and distributed from the rue Laugier. There was nothing original about it; there had been various versions of *l'Antijuif* in France, using the same name, since the nineteenth century.[11] The first meeting of Louis' Anti-Jewish Union at the Salle Wagram on 4 June 1937 was a prototype. The gathering at which Robert Castille and other men of Action Française mixed with Louis' small band of brothers was disrupted by *provocateurs* with truncheons; many were injured.

This gang could have been sent by Bernard Lecache of LICA. Already an arch-enemy of established French fascists such as Coston, Lecache now pinpointed Louis, who called him 'the yid from LICA' or 'servant of Stalin'. Lecache's *Le Droit de vivre* made fun of Louis' rantings, clubs, associations, unions and grotty little newspapers. He also accurately denounced the 'sinister Darquier *sans* Pellepoix' as 'sold to the Nazis'.[12] Much the same age as Louis, a former communist, Jewish and a journalist, Lecache was a militant. A quick phone call to LICA could produce a car full of North African boxers who could clear a gathering of fascists in minutes. Communist fighters would do the same thing.[13]

In this case, however, it was not Lecache but the *Francistes* of Marcel Bucard, another man on Elizabeth Büttner's payroll, who invaded the Salle Wagram, given vociferous support by all those furious about Louis' invasion of their cabbage patch. To his rivals, Louis Darquier's intense narcissism was their greatest problem; also, as a councillor he was the only one of them with a public appointment and a civic platform from which to sell his wares. They never ceased to object to his vainglorious approach.

Coston joined Doriot's Parti Populaire Français in 1936. Apart from the greater success of the PPF, Louis competed with Doriot instinctively. Both were large, strong men, bruisers, greedy and self-indulgent, fond of brothels too. Doriot was a tough, independent fighter, a rousing orator, a bully and an authoritarian. He was a classic fascist leader, big, black-haired, spectacled and charismatic, while Louis bored people to death. Very few things united these fascists and anti-Semites of the 1930s; hatred of Jews and communists did, and also the habit of hunting in groups, journalism, speechifying and alcohol. All of them were desperate for money.

Léon Blum's Popular Front government fell in June 1937. Blum's attempts to be a '"loyal manager" of capitalism' failed, both because they were inadequate and because the hysterical opposition he faced was equalled in volume only by the hero-worship the German populace was offering to Hitler. 'With Hitler against Bolshevism' and 'Rather Hitler than Blum' were cries of the time, and not only from the right. Sections of Blum's own Socialist Party, and both the Communist and Radical Parties – purportedly supporters or partners – displayed rigorous and unchanging hostility to their Popular Front, and the French Senate consistently opposed Blum, while the fragility of the franc, the disastrous rise in the cost of living and the need for rearmament also contributed to his failure.

From 1934 French fascists were offered money by both Mussolini and Hitler, but for anti-Semites Germany was the most generous banker.[14] Paying agents to foster anti-Semitism in France was an essential item in Goebbels' Nazi propaganda budget, while the Spanish Civil War was the melting pot in which all European anxieties boiled and bubbled, particularly in France, already on the way to its own civil war.

One of the reasons Britain was finally left in lone resistance to Hitler in 1940 was that throughout the 1930s British governments sacrificed almost every other European country in pursuit of British foreign policy, always failing to support France in its attempts to hold Germany to at least some of the conditions of the Versailles Treaty. Nowhere was this more obvious than in the tragedy of the Spanish Civil War, or the long sequence of events which led to Munich, and which began with Hitler's *Anschluss*, his invasion of Austria in March 1938. After each submission to the will of Hitler, often forced upon them by their allies, and often by their own divisions, French republicans – even partisans of peace and the grandeur of Europe such as Anatole de Monzie – began to abandon hope. Nineteen thirty-eight was the year of democratic despair in France, the year in which nationalist France first began to scent victory.

Without British support Blum could not help the Spanish republic; nor was he permitted to by the Radical and pacifist socialist members of his own government. To men like Charles Maurras it was the Russians who had bombed Guernica, and for Louis Darquier 'the massacres of Christians in Spain are the work of the Jews'. The non-intervention pact signed by Britain, Portugal, Italy, Russia and Germany in September 1936, then enthusiastically promoted by Britain but ignored by Hitler, Mussolini and Stalin, doomed both the Spanish government and the impotent Blum and his Popular Front. The French government limped on until April 1938, but except for a brief return, Blum had been deposed.

On 6 July 1937 Louis stood outside the doors of the Santé prison to greet Charles Maurras on his discharge. Two days later an enormous meeting was organised to celebrate Maurras' release at the Vélodrome d'Hiver, the cycling stadium near the Eiffel Tower, then one of the largest places of assembly in Paris. Once again Louis stood beside Maurras, Léon Daudet, Jean Chiappe and the two Catholic militants Xavier Vallat and Philippe Henriot, and spoke to a crowd of thirty thousand, all of whom stood as he 'concluded his speech with the phrase that swept through the meeting ... "Charles Maurras, until today you were the Leader of Action Française. From this evening, you are the Leader of the French Union."' 'The only possible national solution,' Louis said, 'is to unite around Maurras, against the Jews.' Maurras continued to publicise Louis' activities, and permitted him to distribute his paper at provincial meetings of Action Française. 'More than ever France is divided in two, composed of the great majority of good people, surrounded by many cretins, and led by filthy scoundrels,' was the tenor of Louis' propaganda.

In *l'Antijuif* Louis reported on Jewish activity everywhere, always referring his readers to his bible, the *Protocols*: 'The Jewish Republic of the USSR ... *The Protocols of Sion* ... The Jewish Popular Front ... *The Protocols of Sion* ... The Jewish massacre of Catholic Priests in Spain by the Jewish Spanish Republic . . . *The Protocols of Sion* . . . The Jewish World War . . . *The Protocols of Sion* . . .'

Not one country was spared, but there were new themes. Louis seems to have given up paying any attention to Myrtle's sensitivities, because he now took up the public anglophobia Maurras had always preached but which Louis had hitherto eschewed. He inveighed against Britain in almost every issue:

THE ANTI-JEW

His Royal Highness and the Jews: 'It is whispered among well-informed English circles that George VI will be elevated in the ceremony of 30 June, to the dignity of Grand Master of English Masonry . . . Violent Anti-Jewish demonstrations in London under the leadership of Sir Oswald Mosley, who was wounded . . .

The Jewish Government in England

The British Empire, like the United States, like France, is currently governed by the Jews . . .

M. Neville Chamberlain, Prime Minister

His father, Joe Chamberlain owed his brilliant career to Jewish support . . . Chamberlain's aunt was Jewish . . . the Chamberlain family, like the Churchills, are in the service of Jews . . . Mr Anthony Eden . . . is the great-grandson of Frances Schaffalitsky a Polish Jewess . . . Duff Cooper's great-grandmother was called Stein . . . [15]

The tally goes on and on. Though the accusation of madness is most frequently directed at Louis Darquier and his extreme anti-Semitic brethren, it is also true that in November 1938 *Action française* was still peddling the idea that Hitler was a Jew, and that his persecution of Jews in some way exalted them.[16]

In *l'Antijuif* the influence of Henri-Robert Petit, Louis' new fellow-in-arms, is obvious: Masons were dug up from under every toadstool. Henry Coston's training is even more vividly felt: there are lists of doctors with Jewish names, lists of government ministers, all Masons or Jews, lists of kings and generals murdered by Masons and Jews, lists of the percentage of Jews in every profession: 'Dentists 37 per cent, Money lenders 96 per cent . . . Here are the names of the Jews in the Syndicate of Stockbrokers at the Paris Bourse.'[17] To these new tics were added two old ones. Louis never forgot the medical profession, and never ceased to ask his readers for money: 'send financial assistance to the Anti-Jewish Union of France and particularly to its President, Darquier de Pellepoix,' he wrote on 5 August.[18]

Three weeks later Elizabeth Büttner replied with another cheque for three thousand marks (worth about £35,000 today). Immediately *l'Antijuif* gave up the rickety office typewriter; Louis could now pay for typesetting. The issue of August 1937 shows the effects of German money from other sources too, as Louis 'distributed for the first time in France a grossly anti-Semitic brochure entitled "The Key to the Mystery". It was imported from Canada and propagated in Switzerland through the intermediary of Princess Karadja who used German funds to this end (World Service, Erfurt).'[19]

Princess Karadja was a remarkable table-rapping and Theosophist patron of the astral spheres who in earlier days, with Annie Besant and Mrs Pankhurst, pursued Krishnamurti, the Great World Teacher, Avatar of the Order of the Star of the East. She was a prolific writer of bad poetry and prose: 'Originally the dual souls are part of the same Divine Ego. They are golden fruits upon the great Tree of Life.' Now an elderly woman inhabiting the Villa Lux in Monti, near Locarno, Princess Karadja, who liked to be addressed as 'Your Highness', sent out mystic messages and money to anti-Semitic groups across Europe, in particular through her Anglo-American Aryan Protection League. 'I wish to create,' she said, 'a "façade", all white and bright and shining . . . I am "the left hand" and do not want to know what "the right hand" does . . .' In pursuit of a New World Order, her right hand was in constant touch with Fleischhauer in Erfurt.[20]

In his paper Louis wrote about Jewish incest, about Jewish men's lack of respect for virginity, abuse of Gentile women and general sexual habits. Jews 'return from a lover as naturally as they return from lessons or taking tea with a friend'.[21] In 1939 Pierre Gérard was sued for writing that Jews were responsible for the divorce law and the low French birth rate, and that foreign Jewish doctors performed most abortions: 'The Jew prevents us from having children.'[22]

Yet another addition to Louis' formulae in 1937 was one which, henceforward, was to mark his entire life: 'Here are the names of Jews and half-castes . . .' The explanation for the millions of words about Jews which Louis Darquier left behind lies in this obsession, an obsession with blood. The body of a half-Jew contains only 50 per cent Jewish blood, the rest of it is Aryan or whatever: how can you divide the blood? This impossibility tormented him: 'We should particularly distrust those half Jews who, under French surnames, are sometimes more harmful than whole Jews, if you can call any Jew that!'[23] In the Paris council chamber, where he continued as before to mix boyish interjections of questionable wit with anti-Semitic insults and diatribes, Louis lamented that 'most French people still only have a poor understanding of the Jewish question'. This, finally, was his greatest cause for distress. Louis Darquier came to feel that his people, his French people, were being prevented by Jews from understanding what divided France in two: 'the microbe of disintegration, of division, is the Jew'.

Louis saw himself as a militant prophet holding 'every evening, in all districts of Paris and in several suburban towns, propaganda meetings about the Jewish problem'.[24] He produced postcards with Joan of Arc saving France on one side, Jews destroying France on the other. Sometimes he used the hammer and sickle to disguise his tracts as communist leaflets. These were distributed outside factory gates. Various henchmen who did this sort of work now lived in the houses in the rue Laugier – Petit had moved in, Louis' secretary lived there, and also Pierre Gérard, providing Louis with articles and illustrations for his papers and writing his booklet *The Jew . . . Our Master*.

Even more tormenting than the ignorance of the French people about the Jewish threat was Louis' own lack of success. His meetings, often sparsely attended, ended up in brawls, arrests and general turmoil. But most of all: 'We need *money* and it is the duty of everyone to help us financially and to *invite all French people to help us* . . . for in THE ANTI-JEWISH UNION OF FRANCE there are neither sinecures, nor ways to make easy money. One works here for glory . . .' This was an obvious swipe at Henri Petit, the kind of anti-Semite who took great trouble proving that Jesus Christ was not a Jew, and that He was anti-Semitic to boot. Petit was no use at all as Louis struggled to compete with Jacques Doriot. By 1938 Doriot's PPF could claim a membership of nearly 300,000, while Louis sometimes addressed as few as thirty men at his meetings in the rue Laugier.

Despite his subservience to the sedentary intellectual Maurras, Louis had links to the most violent of all the enemies of the Popular Front: the underground revolutionary movement La Cagoule, literally 'The Cowl'.[25] Its members were the Cagoulards, the Hooded Men, who in

1936 formed a clandestine and ritualistic organisation. They were dissidents from the leagues, with the usual army officers – some close to Marshal Pétain and General Weygand.[26] Most important were the Action Française apostates, in particular the leader of the Cagoule, Eugène Deloncle.[27] Their terrorism was based on violent anti-communism, and in 1936 and 1937 Cagoulards devoted their energies to political assassinations and the stockpiling of arms for an attempted overthrow of the state. Their aim resembled Franco's – a civil war to get rid of the French republic. Louis Darquier knew many of them: Jean Filliol, the former Camelot leader who had attacked Léon Blum, was the Cagoule's assassin; other members included Darquier's old Action Française comrade Henry Charbonneau. On behalf of Mussolini, the Cagoule assassinated the anti-fascist Rosselli brothers in 1937.[28]

French Nazis and anti-Semites went en masse to the Nuremberg rally of 1937. The courts finally sentenced Louis to pay a thousand francs[29] for the incident in the Bar Marlène the year before, and he was months in arrears for his rent.[30] At this low point, Louis followed Charles Maurras to Geneva, where Maurras was to give a lecture on the poet Horace. In the course of the event Louis contributed a vehement diatribe against the French government and the League of Nations – 'Diplomacy is crawling with Jews.' He was publicly expelled from Switzerland the next day, and as the League of Nations was sitting in Geneva at the time, all the newspapers reported his outburst.

Results were instantaneous: within a month Louis could afford to expand on all fronts. By October 1937 he had paid the rent bill and improved the kitchen and plumbing. In November he presided over a large meeting of his Anti-Jewish Union with the Cagoulard Charbonneau as star speaker, to loud cheers of 'Bring on Maurras!' and 'Down with the Jews!' A thousand young men attended. Two weeks later the planned Cagoule insurrection was called off at the last moment and their conspiracy was announced in the Chamber of Deputies. By December its leaders were arrested, and *Voltaire* immediately published an article fingering a senior Cagoulard as Louis' banker.[31]

A more accurate assessment of the source of his new funds came from the Ministry of the Interior, which in December reported that Goebbels' Propaganda Office – probably by way of Julius Streicher and '"*l'Internationale Antisémite*" which is based in Geneva, under the directorship of Otto Grutzner . . . provided Darquier de Pellepoix with all the "means" he needed. This permitted him to publish the most violent tracts for distribution throughout the entire country. But it is in Alsace and North Africa that they are achieving the most success.'[32]

A year later a furniture salesman from Lyon was sent to Louis Darquier by the German consul-general for advice as to how to proceed in the anti-Semitic marketplace. Louis told the salesman 'take money from anyone, with the excuse that the movement which inspires you is fighting the enormous power of Judaeo-Marxist finance and they have no scruples of any kind'.[33] The consul-general considered Louis 'the national leader of the anti-Semitic movement' in France.

Production stepped up at the rue Laugier. One sticker, in vivid yellow, proclaimed, 'The breast of France is the last defence of the Jew. Join the Anti-Jewish Union of France'; posters were plastered all over Paris and provincial towns. The rue Laugier could also now afford to make merry at Christmas. Louis called 'all women sympathetic to our movement' to a meeting to form a women's section and its president, Madame Dehouve, celebrated Christmas 1937 with Louis by installing a Christmas tree in the club and requesting all to bring their children, for whom a party, games and presents were provided. Anne, seven by this time, was of course not there, but Myrtle would have heard Louis' Christmas message:

> The weak deserve to be massacred.
> We French are a strong people.
> We want to subdue the Jews and we shall subdue them . . . [34]

Towards the end of the 1930s the Parisian world of anti-Semites was wider than its cliché-ridden newspapers and ill-attended meetings might suggest. Many French writers – literary authors and editors, essayists, novelists and orators, poets and playwrights, but above all journalists – put their facility with words at its service and, in a great number of cases, at the service of Nazi Germany. Some of these men of letters were renowned, and many of them were former protégés of Maurras who gathered around the newspaper *Je Suis partout*, 'one of the intellectual melting pots of French fascism'. Articulate, voluble, over-educated, these included the paper's distinguished editors, first Pierre Gaxotte, then

Robert Brasillach, and a journalistic elite: Lucien Rebatet (who thought of Louis as 'a most sympathetic daredevil'), Pierre-Antoine Cousteau, elder brother of the famous oceanographer Jacques, Alain Laubreaux,[35] Georges Blond and, from time to time, Maurice Bardêche. Cousteau, Blond and Brasillach made the obligatory visits to Germany in 1936, 1938 and 1939. This clique produced a special edition of *Je Suis partout*, 'The Jews', a perfect French mirror of Streicher's *Der Stürmer*. As editor-in-chief, Brasillach used the same approach as Louis, calling the 'Jewish Question' the 'Monkey Question'.

All these writers admired their wildest representative, Louis-Ferdinand Céline, the outlaw genius – yet another man wounded and decorated in the First World War – whom Louis selected as his next hero. In December 1937 the author of the epic masterpieces of the 1930s *Voyage au bout de la nuit* (*Voyage to the End of Night*) and *Mort à crédit* (*Death on the Instalment Plan*) produced *Bagatelles pour un massacre* (*Trifles for a Massacre*). This was the first of his three books of venomous hatred of Jews – 'pamphlets' they were called at the time because they were works of propaganda, fragmented and bizarre, staccato streams of abuse making use of the 'insane statistics culled from the anti-Semitic den of Darquier de Pellepoix'.[36] These 'pamphlets' were also literary antidotes to the 'Jewish' Proust whom Céline so despised – '*Prout-Proust*', he called him, 'Fart-Proust' – and they caused a sensation: 'We welcomed with joy and unlimited admiration Céline's *Bagatelles pour un massacre*,' wrote Lucien Rebatet.[37] 'We knew pages of it and hundreds of its aphorisms by heart.' Céline followed *Bagatelles* with *L'École des cadavres* (*The School for Corpses*) in 1939 and *Les Beaux draps* (*A Fine Mess*) in 1941, each reprinted throughout the Occupation.

Céline was Louis' near-contemporary, and both were firm believers in the *Protocols*. Céline was a doctor, a specialist in children's diseases, and had worked since 1927 in the Parisian medical circuit before taking up a position at a municipal clinic in Clichy, not far from the Ternes and Neuilly. Both he and Louis had one child, a daughter despatched from sight, and both were sexually promiscuous. Like Louis, Céline spoke English fluently and knew England well, but early admiration of England, for both men, had been transformed into anglophobia. Céline declared, 'Jew or an Englishman, same thing,' and predicted that in the coming war, 'We'll all be maggots by the time the first Oxford queers disembark in Flanders.'[38]

It is tempting to imagine that Céline and Louis Darquier had met in London. Nineteen thirty was the year of Louis' agonised confrontation with the duplicitous bank manager named Robinson, and 'Robinson' is Céline's mysterious 'messenger of misery' in *Voyage to the End of Night*, published two years later. In *L'École des cadavres*, Céline hailed Darquier as essential reading for all anti-Semites, and for his 'pamphlets' he borrowed all the regurgitated prose of Petit, Coston, Darquier and Fleischhauer's Weltdienst, added a dash of Princess Karadja, and created his own language, using French speech rhythms to give French anti-Semitism his own foul-mouthed but magical style.

Like T.S. Eliot's anti-Semitism, Maurrassian and elitist, Céline's version – violent and hallucinatory – has been hard to accept for those who cannot couple great writers and intellectuals with gross inadequacies, as is so often necessary. Céline was a comic genius consumed by self-hatred, a combination of attributes which meant little to Louis Darquier, who demonstrated no appreciation of the innovative wonder or black humour of Céline's prose.

Céline was a shabby, scruffy, bright-eyed, ratty-looking man, as tall as Louis but with none of his brute force. But both were bullies, physically exhausting to all they encountered, and utterly committed to a belief that the coming world war was a Jewish conspiracy. 'A Jew in every turret, right from the start of mobilisation,' wrote Céline. '. . . I don't want to go to war for Hitler, I'll admit it, but I don't want to go against him, for the Jews . . . Hitler doesn't like the Jews, nor do I! . . . I'd prefer a dozen Hitlers to one all-powerful Blum. Hitler, at least, I could understand, while with Blum it's pointless, he'll always be the worst enemy, absolute hatred, to the death.'[39] In this one extract from *Bagatelles* – by no means the most remarkable example of Céline's crackling writing – the relation between French anti-Semitism and the use the Nazis made of it is perfectly explained.

Louis' entourage of outsiders was a natural habitat for Céline. They all courted him, fed him and published him in their newspapers. He came to their meetings, wrote about them in his books, and recommended their papers. In return Louis published lengthy extracts from his books, any article or letter Céline cared to send, and sold his books from rue Laugier. After one meeting, on 2 December 1938, Céline repaired with Louis and his cohorts to a café, where Céline's despair confronted Louis' optimism as to the inevitable triumph of French will and French blood.

'Understand,' said Céline, 'when gangrene has reached as far as the shoulder, you've had it. Before that you can cut the arm off. But at the shoulder it's too late. That's where we are. We've had it . . . We're rotten to the core with Jews.'[40] Louis, replying in the heightened tone he used when matters spiritual were involved, indignantly assured Céline that France would rise again; not from the seed of ordinary Frenchmen, though, but from that of 'a tiny elite'. It is hard to see how the Australian Myrtle and the half-caste Anne fitted in with Louis Darquier's constantly repeated ideas about 'French roots'. For he had now created a kingdom in which he could be monarch of all he surveyed, leading a chosen race of French saviours, with Céline as his muse.

Louis' National Club gradually disappeared under the weight of his Anti-Jewish Union. Because of the continuous riots at his meetings the government forbade any more public gatherings in the large Parisian meeting halls Louis could now afford to hire, so he held lavish meetings at his Sports Club. In February 1938, 'thanks to generous donors', he could also rent number ten next door when necessary.[41]

In October 1936, desperate to get René to call off the bailiffs, Jean Darquier had assured René that Louis 'always avoided any propaganda in Strasbourg, even though it is a stronghold of anti-Semitism . . . a sign of his desire not to harm you'.[42] Now, all concern for René abandoned, Louis sent Pierre Gérard to open an office in Strasbourg, to serve as a regional office for Alsace-Lorraine and the Franche-Comté. Soon he also had branches in Nancy, Marseille, and Orléans.

For the Nazis in 1938, Strasbourg and Alsace were the front line, a hotbed of conflicting French and German national loyalties, swarming with spies and secret groupings dedicated to returning Alsace and its German-speaking population to the Reich. Strasbourg also served as a centre for the distribution of German funds and propaganda to Parisian centres of anti-Semitism. The French *préfecture* in Strasbourg amply provided the Ministry of the Interior in Paris with information about the 'flagrant German propaganda'[43] rampant in the area, particularly the activities of Fleischhauer and his Weltdienst.

As war approached, the Nazis were pouring money into Strasbourg's fascist parties, and Gérard, now a young lawyer, was instructed to divert some of this towards Louis. Most important for Louis Darquier was the participation of 'M. Goebbels, Reich Minister of Propaganda, who has sent an important sum of money to acquire a building in Strasbourg, number 7 or 8 rue de la Douane, where [Darquier de Pellepoix] is to set up an Anti-Jewish Centre for Alsace and the eastern region'.[44]

After Gérard had placed the brass plate of the Anti-Jewish Union on the door of his Strasbourg office, police spies were sent to each meeting, and took notes on each generously distributed tract and on the monthly journal he began to publish, in German. 'The waters of the Rhine will be red with Blood of Israel'[45] was typical of his work, but mostly each leaflet posted through the letterboxes of Strasbourg was a request for money – 'Help us, send us donations, they will be well used and they will save your life.'[46] René Darquier would have recognised this sort of thing should one of these tracts have landed on his doorstep. Rue de la Douane, along the *quais* of Strasbourg, was not far from René's home, and he and Louis could have met in 1938 and 1939, because Louis often visited his subsidiaries; but a few years later Louis told the Germans that he had not spoken to his younger brother for some years, while he worked for those Jews.

Louis' list of demands was simple by this time: all Jews who had arrived in France since 1918 should be expelled; no Jews who remained should be entitled to hold public office; their activities in all spheres should be limited and their ill-gotten gains returned to the French state. Most important: all well-meaning people should give money to the Anti-Jewish Union of France to assist in this great cause. In Alsace Gérard was lucky if twenty people turned up to his meetings, but when Louis spoke about three hundred came to swell the coffers.

In Paris, Louis' presence had become so pervasive that he and his 'biff boys' were followed around not only by the police, but also by Lecache's LICA, for whom he was now public enemy number one. They hounded him for his 'Hitlerian staff' and Nazi money, and on one occasion Louis and Lecache fell to blows.[47] Lecache described Louis prancing up to him, hopping from one foot to the other like a dancing bear or a heavyweight learning to box. When Lecache called him a 'foreign agent, a traitor, a spy', Louis sued for defamation. As Louis had called Lecache 'excrement of the ghetto' and a 'circumcised swine', Lecache sued back for racist abuse. The trial began at the end of January 1938, and for the first and only time Louis, frenetically adjusting his monocle, was required to admit that his real name was Darquier, without any Pellepoix.

In March 1938, on the day Hitler took over Austria, Léon Blum returned to head the government for a brief three weeks before being replaced, finally, by Édouard Daladier, that other veteran of the 6 February riots. As the Popular Front died in France, Louis' insignificant *Antijuif* also disappeared, and on 24 February he launched his first real newspaper, a large broadsheet, *La France enchaînée (France in Chains)*.[48] This 'Organ of Defence against the Jewish Invasion' appeared twice a month and was decorated with monumental headlines, exclamation marks and the usual gross cartoons, interlaced with lengthy articles by Louis himself, mostly transcripts of his speeches in the city council. It is from this date, perhaps because Goebbels had now entered the picture and Louis was being paid for a specific purpose, that the objects of Louis' other animosities – communists, Masons, capitalists – disappeared from his rhetoric.

With so much going on in the early months of 1938 Louis had been absent from the council chamber, but in April he began to attend again, his focus narrowed to Jews, and only Jews. He insisted that the council debate the naturalisation of foreigners in France, and spoke for hours about the invasion of Jews into every nook and cranny of the French body politic. Obviously briefed by his brother Jean, he took medicine as an example: 'I will read you a list of names.' Beginning with A – 'Abdalian, Adda, Aïchenbaum, Amirian, Amir-Sikal, Anencov . . .' and ending with Z – 'Zarrabi, Zimmerlich, Zwahlen, Zyngerman', he listed every position in the medical profession occupied by a Jew, down to the last alphabetical obstetrician and rhinologist.[49]

The German inspiration for Louis' rhetoric is obvious in the vast flood of facts, figures and percentages, and his insistence that 'the essence of a Jew is not his religion, it is his race'. Mostly he read out long extracts from newspapers or obscure thinkers, with more lists of invaded professions – Jews in the theatre, in politics, at the bar: 'Schwartz, Guilevich, Bisbaum . . .' Stunned by this endurance test, his colleagues of right and left reacted with insults, mockery or silence, but as he continued '*violentes protestations . . . tumulte*' erupted. At this April sitting of the city council Louis fought another Jewish Councillor. When Louis objected to the 'insolence' of the 'Jew Hirshcovitz', Maurice Hirschovitz replied: 'A Jew who kicks your arse.'[50] Their confrontation led to the suspension of the sitting for two hours as glasses, water, sugar, ink, carafe and bell ricocheted around the chamber.

After the First World War, with so many men dead, so many injured, France had watched its birth rate dwindle as that of Germany grew.

Conservative France blamed the Third Republic for its empty cradles as well as for everything else. Louis moved on to this subject: 'There is no reason to believe,' he said, 'that a strong and virile race such as the French would be incapable of abundant procreation if they lived under a regime which gave them the chance ... but always, and everywhere, thanks to their genius for procreation we are surrounded by little Cahans, little Isaacs, little Jacobs.'[51]

By early 1938 Louis was paying particular attention to children in the rue Laugier. The Anti-Jewish Union offered child-care facilities every Thursday afternoon, from 3 to 6.30 p.m.: 'we look after children, we amuse them, we give them a nice snack. A renowned Professor teaches them to have a knowledge of, and taste for, music.'[52] The name of the music teacher is not mentioned, but it is unlikely that Louis would spend good money on hiring anyone when he had Myrtle to hand – but the children she taught had to be French.

11

War

UNTIL 1939, ANNE AND THE other subjects of Kidlington, like the rest of the British population and the French across the water, watched their country hiccup towards another world war. In France, through the dark glass of the *Protocols*, Louis Darquier and his like saw its approach as 'the Yids of the world' preparing for 'another massacre of Christians, pushing "the goyim" into wiping each other out . . . for the greater benefit of the so-called "chosen race"'.[1]

Though *La France enchaînée* had its own handsomely printed stationery, blazoning 'Director: Darquier de Pellepoix', Louis used his position on the Paris city council to add status to his associations, and purloined twenty thousand of their inscribed envelopes in which to distribute a particularly noxious leaflet and an invitation to his meetings at the rue Laugier.

Fleischhauer was receiving reports commending Louis' progress,[2] and his work was appreciated, for in July 1938 he was invited to go to Nuremberg to meet Alfred Rosenberg and Dr Ernst Bohle, head of the Auslandsorganisation (AO), the Nazi organisation for foreign countries. He did not go, for in July 1938 King George VI and Queen Elizabeth came to Paris. When Daladier became prime minister again in April 1938 he strengthened the Anglo-French alliance and fully endorsed Neville Chamberlain's policy of non-intervention in Spain and appeasement of Hitler. A four-day visit to Paris was arranged for the British King and Queen. The city council held a grand reception for them; as a councillor Louis attended with Myrtle. She wrote to her family about the occasion, and their version relates that 'The King and Louis stood by, nervously fingering their ties and finding little to say to each other, while their wives chatted together. Louis felt that the Queen was delighted to discover among the crowd of Frogs a woman of Scottish ancestry, who knew and loved Scotland. Knowing Myrtle I shouldn't be surprised if she didn't claim kinship!'[3] Louis would have found little to say because his anglophobia was well advanced; he now considered Britain, his former sanctuary from France, to be entirely controlled by Jews: 'No man with self-respect lives infested with lice. Nor does a country.'[4] Myrtle seems to have kept from her family in Tasmania a *volte face* which doubtless gave her many more bruises than those she had wept over in their London years.

In the summer of 1938 Anatole de Monzie was sitting in his garden in his country home in the Lot, writing a book about Savonarola, when Édouard Daladier rang to ask him to return to the cabinet as Minister of Public Works. De Monzie had not been in government since 1934, and after the *Anschluss* of March 1938 all that remained of his European ambitions was his 'Franco-Italian vocation'. The cabinet de Monzie joined descended immediately into crisis as Hitler mobilised his troops and ordered the dismemberment of Czechoslovakia. Chamberlain's Britain would not support France in her sworn commitment to Czechoslovakia, and the French government, particularly its pacifists and appeasers, would not fulfil its promises. On 30 September Chamberlain, Daladier, Mussolini and Hitler signed the Munich Agreement, giving Hitler what he wanted. The French people, like the British, reacted with a mixture of joy, relief and shame. Léon Daudet cheered. 'Israel and Moscow can go into mourning,' he wrote in *Action française*. 'We will not fight for "the Czechs".'[5] Chamberlain, whom Daladier described as a 'desiccated stick', returned to applauding crowds in London and declared 'peace with honour . . . peace for our time'; Daladier was welcomed by similar crowds in Paris – '*Les cons!*' he said. 'The idiots!'[6]

As Anne turned eight, the distribution of gas masks and preparations for evacuees (anticipated during the Munich crisis) gave Kidlington a good idea of what was to come. Just at this time, Elsie moved up in the world. Paying £25 down, she took out a mortgage on 98 Hazel Crescent – now number 12 – in a rural part of Kidlington which was meant to become Oxford Garden City, but failed to do so because of the war. Though in what was hailed as 'Oxford's Latest and Finest Estate', this redbrick house, brand new in 1938, is notable for its charmless and utilitarian ugliness, a desolation only increased by its duplicates which line Hazel Crescent. It did, however, promise, and deliver, a modern kitchen, bathroom and indoor lavatory. This was Elsie's home from 1938 until 1957, and Anne's too, with room for Aunty Violet and for May, before she went off in the early 1940s to become an ambulance driver. According to Elsie's friends the down-payment on the house was actually in Anne's name. Elsie varied her accounts of the purchase: sometimes she mentioned Anne's father, sometimes 'Anne's trustees'. If so, it is unimaginable that she had any notion as to the money's Nazi provenance – nor that some of it came from a tyre factory in Paris.

However unintelligent he found her, Louis was close to his mother, and like his brothers continued to visit her at Neuilly throughout the thirties, particularly when he wanted money. Pierre Darquier never came to terms with his middle son, and would not see him. When other guests were at Neuilly at family Sunday lunches, Louis was never there, never mentioned, and certainly neither was Myrtle. Pierre disliked Louis' political views, but more than politics was involved here. He tolerated similar, if more modest, opinions from his son Jean, but Louis 'had wasted all their money'.

At Neuilly in 1938 Louis met a neighbour and industrialist, Pierre Auguste Galien,[7] the owner of 'SUPER GOM', a tyre-retreading factory in La Plaine St-Denis, in the north of Paris. Galien was a wealthy man, and a more belligerent anti-Semite and more capacious liar than Louis Darquier. Only a year younger than Louis, shorter and brown-haired, he shared Louis' carousing tastes; together they became ruffians in arms, and Pierre Galien took over the role that René Darquier had filled until 1936: he lent Louis money.

Galien's first contact with Louis coincided exactly with the launch of *La France enchaînée*.[8] As director of propaganda for Louis' union, Galien was also in charge of distribution and publicity for the newspaper; he made sure it was in all the kiosks of Paris. A mixture of German money and Galien's wealth thus provided the down-payment on Elsie's new house in Kidlington.

At the end of October 1938 the Nazis forcibly expelled some fifteen thousand Jews to Poland, putting them into boxcars and dumping them at the Polish frontier town of Zbaszyn. They included the family of Herschel Grynspzan, who on 7 November in Paris attempted to assassinate the German ambassador von Welczek, the man to whom Louis had applied for money a year earlier. Instead Grynspzan shot and killed the Third Secretary at the embassy, Ernst vom Rath. Two days later Hitler ordered a massive coordinated attack on Jews throughout the Reich – *Kristallnacht*, the Night of Broken Glass – an attack so murderous that world outrage was immediate. Louis greeted these events with the words 'Bravo, Fritz!' and, bearing a large garland of chrysanthemums, took his boys to the Protestant funeral service of vom Rath to pay his respects. Surveillance of Louis Darquier by the French state and its police intensified. The government seized the September issue of *La France enchaînée*, which accused five French ministers of warmongering, and the security services made plans to suppress both Louis and his newspaper.

Meanwhile Lecache vs. Darquier came before the courts, and during its disorderly proceedings the amount of German money that Goebbels had placed at Louis' disposal was spelled out clearly. Distinguished professors appeared in court on Lecache's behalf. Marcel Bloch, Lecache's lawyer, outlined Louis' long commercial relations with Jews, as employee and debtor, and described him as a 'French Hitlerite'. But most noteworthy were the words he used, always borrowed thereafter, to describe Louis' brand of French nationalism – '*patriotisme alimentaire*': patriotism for money, patriotism for hire. The exchanges between the two sides reached such a pitch that the hearing was suspended. Louis wrote vainglorious appreciations of his own theatrics in *La France enchaînée*, and *Action française*, as ever, published daily encouragement. The court case ended the day before the signature of a Franco-German Declaration of Friendship, on 8 December. Darquier and Lecache were both fined two hundred francs and ordered to pay two thousand francs in damages. Louis, who could now afford to hold private dinners in restaurants such as La Chope Cardinale in boulevard St-Germain, could afford to appeal, and he did.

By the end of 1938 Louis announced that his 'Anti-Jewish sections have multiplied tenfold the number of members', and the police agreed that his union was now the most important anti-Semitic organisation in France.[9] On 13 December, speaking to his followers after dinner, Louis called upon them to celebrate the growing success of his Anti-Jewish Union, recalled its shaky start – now a thing of the past – and rendered homage to Hitler, 'not because he is a national socialist, but because he is the only statesman who understands the Jewish problem'.[10] Two days later, in the council chamber, he harangued his fellow councillors with a violent attack on republican, 'Jewish', France: 'They have invented another France, a kind of synthetic machine . . . their France . . . the product of their hysterical and neurasthenic brains . . .' Then he shouted at his old foe Maurice Hirschovitz, 'I despise you. Before the year is out you will be in a concentration camp.'[11]

According to Céline, all Jews were 'buggers'. In 1938 Louis was also denounced as such, and the vice squad was sent in to investigate rumours about his 'special tastes', but found the accusation unsubstantiated. With his Anti-Jewish Union permanently under attack, Louis advertised for a live-in guardian for the rue Laugier, and for volunteers to protect the members selling copies of *La France enchaînée* on the streets of Paris. There was already a lengthy police report on Louis; by July 1939 the police had prepared a second, more detailed analysis which covered all anti-Semitic organisations, with Louis the leader of the pack.[12] Until war broke out, he and his fellows spent most of their time fighting – at meetings, in the streets or in court. The months after Munich and the victory of Franco in Spain saw the clash of ideologies in France reach its bitter apogee. The streets of Paris were littered with leaflets shouting 'Down with the Jewish War', many of them emanating from the rue Laugier, many of them printed in Germany.

In January 1939 Pierre Galien was arrested after a brawl with LICA's troops selling their newspaper, *Le Droit de vivre*. Louis could print forty thousand copies of his own newspaper by this time, and though it was sold in Paris by his boys, it was also well distributed throughout France. He began to praise Hitler openly in its pages and amongst friends, thus preparing the way to put Maurras and Action Française behind him. He was now in receipt of German subsidies from many sources, while Maurras' hatred of Germany continued to express itself volubly – particularly in his insistence that the Nazis were Jews. Louis permitted Urbain Gohier to accuse both Maurras and Daudet of being Jews themselves in *La France enchaînée*. The publicity Lecache vs. Darquier gave to the complex sources of Louis' Nazi funding provided such detail that even Maurras could no longer ignore the truth. All this led to the final break: 'Our enemies cannot be our friends,' said Maurras in February 1939.

After his rupture with Maurras, Louis Darquier took on men of a more distinguished mien than the Costons and Petits of the anti-Semitic underworld. His new team looked upon the destruction of Jews as a financial and professional enterprise, and included doctors and men of business and the professions. Most of them were veterans, and each Croix de Guerre or Légion d'honneur was paraded with pride. Marcel Jouhandeau,[13] the respected novelist – and author of *Le Péril juif* – having flirted with Doriot's PPF, settled for Louis' Anti-Jewish Union. On the basis of Louis' belief that 'it is always better, in all cases, to be a stupid Frenchman than an intelligent Jew', another addition to his inner circle, madder than all the rest, was his 'right-hand man', a retired colonial officer, Captain Paul Sézille, a French version of Ulrich Fleischhauer, though more damaged by alcohol.

Many associates came Louis' way through Céline or Galien. Céline supplied Louis' first scientist in the sinister Swiss anthropologist, ethnologist and doctor of medicine Georges Montandon. By March 1939 Montandon was giving slide shows for Louis' union on 'The Jewish Race' in the Café St-Sulpice in rue du Vieux Colombier, with Céline in attendance. Montandon proposed a racial theory of anti-Semitism, a theory of hierarchy of civilisations and races, asserting that the yellow, black and white races each came from a different kind of ape – orangutans, or gorillas, or chimpanzees. He considered the Jewish people to be the most dangerous of all racial groups, and advocated their isolation within their own separate state. He hoped to improve them in other ways too: 'I am sure that I have read somewhere about the proposal, for example, to brand Jews with a hot iron and I am personally convinced of the efficiency of, in certain cases, cutting off the noses of female Jews since they are no less dangerous than the males. When I was a student doctor in Zurich I noticed the excellent effect of such an operation on an individual whose nose had been bitten off.'[14]

Céline wrote often of his affection for Montandon. He was particularly attracted to the obsessional nature of Montandon's research, often attended his lectures, and liked his proposition that France was really a Celtic, Germanic nation, not of the Latinate Catholic stock claimed by Maurras. Montandon also insisted that Maurras was Jewish on his mother's side. After his encounter with Montandon, Louis took to adding Celtic aristocratic roots to all the other bloodstock he had invented for himself.

In early 1939 *La France enchaînée* was in vibrant form, serialising the *Protocols*, with Louis announcing all kinds of new endeavours. The previous

May he had founded another association, a Union Française – much the same kind of thing as his Anti-Jewish Union, but concentrating on French racial purity rather than on its Jewish opposite, and this took over his Sports Club at 8, rue Laugier, replacing water jets and pistol practice with a space for large private meetings, necessary now that he was banned from most public halls.[15] Louis injected further energy into this second union, the manifesto of which differed from that of his Anti-Jewish Union in an unsurprising emphasis on delivering France from democracy, and the physical and spiritual training of an elite of young men, and a surprising insistence on the defence of the family and encouragement of an increase in the birth rate. The voice of Pierre Galien could be heard in Louis' unusual eloquence on the subject of a corporate economy and capital and the worker.

At the same time Louis announced the publication of a quality review, the *Cahiers jaunes*, the Yellow Notebooks. During his evening with Céline in December 1938, Louis had tried to convince that determined pessimist of the imminence of a pure-blooded French victory over the Jews. To that end he came up with yet another association, which he called Les Vieilles Souches, Ancient Roots, aiming 'to give back to the French people the family and racial pride . . . to gather together all French people of the white race, no crossbreeds with Jewish blood'.[16] To belong to Louis' Anti-Jewish Union, one had to prove four non-Jewish grandparents; to qualify for Ancient Roots one needed eight similarly pure great-grandparents.

Louis was becoming what he had laboured to be, the top man in his field, the baronial *capo* of an anti-Semitic industry, and an expert on human bloodlines. His two unions in rue Laugier, his newspaper and journals and his National Club all brought in contributions. He charged twelve francs a year for membership of the Anti-Jewish Union, twenty-five francs for an annual subscription to each of his newspapers, twenty francs for membership of his French Union, and a special rate of a hundred francs a year for the lot. He had never abandoned his widows and orphans of 6 February, and that association still brought in a little, particularly on the anniversary each year as he continued to celebrate the great day of the 1934 riots. Louis threw a banquet for his new team at the rue Laugier on 11 February 1939 to celebrate the first anniversary of the publication of *La France enchaînée*, and his comrades met regularly on the first Friday of every month in the large meeting room of 8, rue Laugier. The new team remained in close touch with Erfurt.

Fully under the influence of Nazi policies now, though never admitting it, monotonously praising Hitler but always trumpeting in the pages of *La France enchaînée* the essential Frenchness of his own theories, Louis had taken on the Nazi idea of corralling Jews together in some distant land. Most Nazi theorists and their French twins selected the island of Madagascar (whose inhabitants were never consulted) for this purpose, and occasionally Louis did too, but he also recommended Soviet Russia, the home of 'Jewish communism'.

In March, despite Goebbels' generosity, Pierre Gérard's lack of success in Strasbourg brought him back to the rue Laugier, and even with the reinforcing presence of men such as Céline and Jouhandeau, Louis' empire ceased to grow; it never exceeded about a thousand members. All his ideas for new clubs and journals and associations also came to naught, because from April 1939 he spent most of his time in court, and when not there, in fighting with anti-fascists and Jews, imaginary or otherwise, wherever possible.

But there were some changes. To earn his German keep Louis had to do as he was told, and in March 1939, in the council chamber he turned on Le Provost de Launay, president of the council, who had sent a message of congratulation to Isaïe Schwartz, Rabbi of Strasbourg, on his appointment as Grand Rabbi of France. Le Provost de Launay publicly reprimanded Louis. This was intolerable: de Launay was a 6 February man, and his family were linked to Édouard Drumont. This time the level of uproar brought to an end all tolerance from the right in the council chamber, even from Charles Trochu.[17] Louis took the Hitlerian line, as he was paid to do: 'Good Jews are perhaps more dangerous than the others . . . I fire on all of them!'[18]

Being on Hitler's payroll had lost Louis the approval of Action Française, and now his allies of the Front National and the old diehard nationalists of the former paramilitary leagues. All nationalists, as patriots, retained the notion of Germany as the ancient enemy, however much they approved of some of Hitler's methods. Louis' 'egotism' and his Nazi money were known things, but his association with Galien and other businessmen brought the new and accurate discovery that he was in it for the money. More important, he and his fellows were accused, rightly, of being 'under orders from Berlin' to use anti-

Semitism as a front for a German fifth column attempting to weaken France before the war all now saw coming. Isolated and boycotted by the right, Louis appealed to the readers of *La France enchaînée* for 'a war contribution': 'Faith can move mountains. She can also rid us of the Jews. HELP US.'

France and Britain were entering on their last months of the appeasement of Hitler. In March 1939 Hitler finally invaded Czechoslovakia and the Spanish Civil War ended with victory for Franco. Daladier, the seasoned Radical warrior, extracted almost dictatorial powers from Parliament, providing nationalists like Taittinger, Trochu and la Roque with the authoritarian government they had always wanted. Daladier was a suspicious, ill-tempered man, which most people attributed to the amount of alcohol he consumed and his dispiriting appearance 'of having had too few or too many'.[19] At this point the French republic, encircled by fascist dictatorships, finally took action against the enemies within. Naturalisation laws were tightened, and Daladier's government prepared the ground for later Vichy measures, with a series of restrictive decrees which brought forth internment camps and intense police surveillance for all foreigners. The Marchandeau Law, named after Daladier's Minister of Justice, was promulgated in April: limitations were placed on the freedom of the press – racial or religious attacks became crimes. Louis was a principal target, for in the March and April issues of *La France enchaînée* his campaign 'THE JEWS WANT WAR' had reached a hallucinatory level of delirium.

Louis had his favourite whipping boys. Medical matters always received attention in his newspaper, and in almost every issue he attacked the 'Judaised hypocrite' Henri de Kérillis, dubbing him a 'hack in the pay of Louis Louis-Dreyfus'.[20] De Kérillis, since December 1938, had been running an exposé in *l'Époque* of the hundreds of fascist agents in key positions in France. Louis was notorious for his attacks on President Roosevelt, his favourite enemy: American power was Jewish power. 'IS ROOSEVELT A JEW?' headlined long articles which Louis often illustrated with family trees going back to the seventeenth century, in which, with the assistance of the *Wichita Revealer* and its Reverend Winrod, he revealed all the SAMUELS and SYVERTS in Roosevelt's ancestry. 'Let us recall as well,' he would write, 'that the mother of the President bears the first name of Sarah and that the mother of his wife, who is also a ROOSEVELT, bears the first name of Rebecca . . .'[21]

Louis' newspaper after he received sufficient Nazi funding. *La France enchaînée*, June 1939 (© Institut d'histoire du temps présent, Paris).

By the time the Marchandeau Law came into being, Louis was already known by the soubriquet of 'Hitler's Parrot'.[22] Under the Marchandeau Law he was prosecuted for two articles, one on the Jewish 'invasion' of

France, the other asserting that 'The readers of this paper know the leading role that the Jew has played in corruption in general, and in drug trafficking in particular.'[23] His first court case of 1939 was, however, the appeal he had launched against the Lecache decision: this he both lost and won, inasmuch as the appeal was denied, but Lecache's fine was raised by a hundred francs because he had made the first attack. It was a pyrrhic victory, because within weeks Darquier was indicted and a search warrant issued; the police invaded rue Laugier and seized his papers.[24] 'What did they find?' complained de Monzie. 'Without doubt only unpaid rent bills.'[25] Two days later, on 19 June, Louis Darquier and Pierre Gérard were charged under the Marchandeau Law for disseminating propaganda on behalf of a foreign power.[26]

From this date Anne and Elsie could have known of Louis' activities in France, for the next day *The Times* reported: 'M. Darquier de Pellepoix, a member of the Paris city council, has been indicted on a charge of publishing libels against the Jews ... shopkeepers and insolvent merchants listen with approval to what he says, but his campaign as a whole falls on deaf ears.'[27] Scrambled reports such as this continued in *The Times* and the *Manchester Guardian* over the next six years, but no one who knew Elsie could imagine her reading those newspapers; it would have been the *Daily Mail*, or most likely the *Banbury Advertiser*.

In Paris, Louis Darquier, unknown to himself, had a distinguished ally in the shape of the former British King Edward VIII, now Duke of Windsor. On 12 May 1939 José de Lequerica, Franco's ambassador to France since March – 'a gigantic golden turkey-cock, pot-bellied like one of Charles V's galleons'[28] – sent a report to Madrid of a long conversation with the Duke at a dinner party at the Argentinian embassy. While admitting that the Duke's official standing in Britain was 'non-existent', and his personality 'somewhat worrying', Lequerica enthusiastically reported that 'the Duke, as can be discerned from his conversation, has political opinions which run contrary to those of the country he once ruled. He believes war to be a complete catastrophe, and the triumph of Moscow, but he does not see the way to avoid war as residing in the rearmament of the democracies. He attributes the policy of war and of alliance with Russia to the influence of the Jews, who are extremely powerful in his country.' The Duke of Windsor went on to attribute his loss of the British throne to the same influences.[29]

Before the outbreak of the Second World War, pacifists and defeatists of the right and the left staged a last-ditch stand, many of them gathering in de Monzie's ministry office in the boulevard St-Germain. This included morose encounters with Marshal Pétain, at this point French ambassador to Madrid, who informed de Monzie, 'They will need me in the second week of May.'[30] De Monzie engaged in secret diplomatic dealings with Italy and Spain. Then, in July, Henri de Kérillis denounced Otto Abetz as a spy and corrupter of French citizens.[31] Abetz brought a suit against de Kérillis for defamation. 'Never,' he declared, 'have I given any money to bribe newspapers.'[32]

The source of these revelations could not have been worse for Louis. De Kérillis was deputy for Neuilly, chosen for the seat by the nationalists in preference to himself in 1936. He was the parliamentary representative of Pierre and Louise, and politically everything that Louis failed to be. De Kérillis had a touch of Churchill about him: he was a fervent anti-communist, a patriot, but one who put resisting Hitler before any other consideration.

Abetz was expelled from France for subversive activities, and suspicion centred on Fernand de Brinon as Abetz's front man. Louis, who as recently as June had been receiving money by way of Nazi agents in Belgium, appeared in court to deny vehemently that he had ever received a foreign penny. 'TO BE ANTI-JEWISH,' he declaimed, 'IS TO BE ANTI-HITLERIAN. TO BE ANTI-JEWISH IS TO BE FRENCH.'[33] The minimum sentence under the Marchandeau Law was a month in prison and a five-hundred-franc fine. On 26 July Louis stood in court with Pierre Gérard and was sentenced to three months in jail, Gérard to one month, and both to a fine of five hundred francs, plus costs. 'I have done nothing except to follow the dictates of that true Christian ideal, the truth,' stated Louis. His defence counsel Pierre Leroy explained that while the Catholic Church instructed us to pray for the perfidious Jew, and to pardon him for the murder of Christ, we were not obliged to forget it, and 'the Jewish race can never efface that stain'.[34]

The following day Daladier prorogued Parliament, and trenches began to be dug all over Paris. There were air-raid shelters in the lawns of the Champs-Élysées, gas masks were distributed, street lights blacked out and the sirens tested every Thursday. In Britain Winston Churchill, as convinced an anti-communist as any French nationalist, presciently urged his government to ally itself with the USSR against Hitler.

La France enchaînée, into which Louis poured out his injured dignity,

Louis boasting about his performances in court, in his newspaper *La France enchaînée*, 1–15 April, 1939 (© Archives du CDJC – Mémorial de la Shoah).

was the only newspaper to be charged under the Marchandeau Law, and Louis and Pierre Gérard were its first victims. Louis appealed, but in the midst of his first trial he was arraigned again, for another article in *La*

France enchaînée, 'The Jews and the War'.[35] The new court case began a month later, in August, and with Abetz's departure the publication of *La France enchaînée* ceased, its thirty-third and last issue blazoning Louis' Pétainist anthem: 'We'll get them!'[36]

Throughout the hot summer months, Louis was not unhappy. His lawyer colleagues kept him out of prison, and his name was in every newspaper. Then, in late August, in Moscow, the German Foreign Minister von Ribbentrop and Stalin signed a non-aggression pact between Germany and the Soviet Union.[37] This came as a thunderbolt to Europe's democracies, the union of their two greatest fears: communism and fascism, Hitler and Stalin. Their alarm was mild in comparison with the bombshell the treaty presented to both communist and fascist activists, who had been trying to murder each other for over a decade.

The next day Britain signed a pact of mutual assistance with Poland. War was imminent, mobilisation began. Daladier immediately banned *l'Humanité*. Later in September, those communists faithful to Moscow were required to perform a monstrous about-turn and start mouthing support for Hitler, though rebellious members quit. Daladier reacted instantly by dissolving the French Communist Party. Thirty-five communist deputies were arrested, and other *'undésirables'* were rounded up and dumped in camps, where already interned by the French republic were 350,000 Spanish republican refugees who had fled from Franco's armies after his victory in March 1939.[38]

On 1 September Hitler attacked Poland. Two days later, France, Great Britain, Australia and New Zealand declared war on Germany and, twenty-one years after the end of the First World War, the same enemies resumed battle.

The Second World War broke out on Anne's ninth birthday, a Sunday, 3 September 1939. Kidlington went on full alert: it had its own small airport with anti-aircraft guns near the grain silo, and this became an RAF training ground, providing endless fascination for the children of the village. Evacuees from London flooded in, and every garden and allotment was turned over to Digging for Victory.

Myrtle's life in Paris in the years before the war is mysterious. She was glimpsed occasionally by the police who tracked Louis, and was noticed at restaurants on occasion; but mostly she was little seen and rarely mentioned. Louis' comrades gathered around him in court, but there was no sign of Myrtle. She was, however, always in touch with her family. Her letters home demonstrate that her fantasies were in full flood, for the Jones family's understanding of Louis' court cases, sentences, German funding and street brawls reached Tasmania in an unrecognisable portrait which transformed him into a patriotic Frenchman for whom France, 'the jewel of European civilisation', was under threat from the 'twin evils' of 'communism and international Jewry'. The Jones family accepted Myrtle's luscious embroideries. For them Louis was no 'Hitler's Parrot' but a baron of ancient lineage who, 'in common with most of the old French families', 'favoured right-wing politics and disliked the Jews'.[39]

Louis had a very good war. He was mobilised the day before war was declared, on 2 September, and took himself for a farewell evening to the Brasserie Lipp.[40] There he encountered Alain Laubreaux, an equally large and belligerent fellow anti-Semite, the theatre critic and polemicist of *Je Suis partout*. Louis announced to the restaurant what he thought of this 'Jewish War'; a woman slapped his face and Louis punched her two companions and set about them with his cane. A full-scale brawl ensued, with Louis and a 'big black man' yelling '*Mort aux Juifs*' together and taking on all comers.[41] Darquier, delighted to have found a black anti-Semite, left the next day to join his anti-tank unit as a lieutenant in the 66th Artillery Regiment. This came in the nick of time, as on 21 September he was tried, again *in absentia*, and sentenced again to a further two months' imprisonment and another fine of five hundred francs, for injuries inflicted on Jews two months earlier.[42] By October 1939 his regiment was still awaiting final orders. His disappearance into battle on 23 October was crucial for him as two days earlier he had been tried, again *in absentia*, and condemned again to a further two months' imprisonment and another fine of five hundred francs, this time for incitement to racial hatred. The court was told that Louis could not go to prison, he was fighting a war. But he was not at war until October and these were the months of the Phoney War, so until June 1940, Louis was often back in Paris.[43] The police noted his presence in the Café Weber in the rue Royale in February 1940, drunk again, and reported '*la violence de ses propos antisémites*' and his praise for Hitler, who, he claimed, had 'turned out to be the stronger man' while the French had been left 'fighting for the Jews of the entire world . . . now they are sending us to the slaughterhouse for them, while they find safe jobs and continue to run their businesses on our backs'.[44]

When not in Paris, Louis was serving 'his' France as lieutenant of the 10th Anti-Tank Battery and doing very well. 'He effectively communicates his faith and ardent patriotism to the men,' his superior officer reported. 'He is thorough and very tough.'[45] These were the static months of the *drôle de guerre*, the Phoney War, with Britain and France desperately building up their fighting strength for the onslaught to come. By February 1940, in the coldest winter for decades, the British and French were unsuccessfully attempting to prevent the Soviet invasion of Finland and quarrelling with each other about their willingness to do so.

When Finland capitulated on 19 March, Paul Reynaud[46] took over as prime minister of a flailing French government. Daladier remained as Minister of War, and de Monzie as Minister of Public Works because, as 'a known friend of Mussolini', it was hoped that he could use his wiles to detach the Italian dictator from Hitler. Reynaud was a conservative politician, a tiny man, but robust and spirited, and like de Kérillis a stalwart anti-Nazi. He quickly came to an agreement with Neville Chamberlain that France and Britain would make no separate peace with Germany.

On 9 April Denmark fell after the briefest of encounters and Germany invaded Norway, where the battle went so badly for the French and British that both countries turned on their war leaders. In Britain Chamberlain was brought down by British parliamentarians who turned, with much greater ease than the French, towards a new war leader, Winston Churchill.

———————————— ❧ ————————————

Elsie's house in Hazel Crescent had two large bedrooms and a smaller one, and she immediately took in evacuees, receiving five shillings a week for each child. Anne was still at the Old Church School, due to begin at the local Gosford Hill County School when she turned eleven. In September 1939 East Ham Grammar School was sent to Kidlington from the East End of London. Billeted on the Gosford Hill School, its three hundred pupils and staff survived only five months of sour cohabitation with their indignant hosts before appropriating the local zoo and setting up school across the road from Hazel Crescent.

Elsie took on one family, the Prissians, two of whose children, Mildred and Iris, lived at Hazel Crescent until the summer of 1943.[47] The distressed evacuee children, name tags around their necks, clutching a bag of food, a gas mask and a bundle of clothes, became the first victims of the war, and Anne's circumstances, motherless and fatherless, dreaming of absent parents, were now almost universal.

Nineteen forty saw the beginning of rationing in Britain, and in April Elsie received the last of her sporadic payments, this time probably from Myrtle, as the commanding officers of the 66th Regiment were informed of Louis' judicial record, and his appeal against his prison sentence was heard again, all of which entered his military file. But Louis' patriotism was never in question. He was a good soldier; he used his furies well.

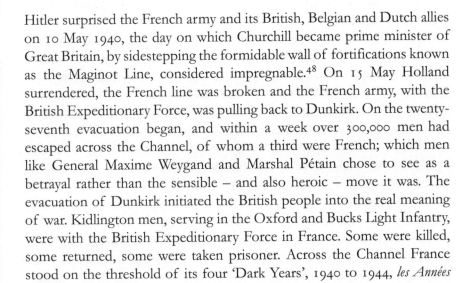

Hitler surprised the French army and its British, Belgian and Dutch allies on 10 May 1940, the day on which Churchill became prime minister of Great Britain, by sidestepping the formidable wall of fortifications known as the Maginot Line, considered impregnable.[48] On 15 May Holland surrendered, the French line was broken and the French army, with the British Expeditionary Force, was pulling back to Dunkirk. On the twenty-seventh evacuation began, and within a week over 300,000 men had escaped across the Channel, of whom a third were French; which men like General Maxime Weygand and Marshal Pétain chose to see as a betrayal rather than the sensible – and also heroic – move it was. The evacuation of Dunkirk initiated the British people into the real meaning of war. Kidlington men, serving in the Oxford and Bucks Light Infantry, were with the British Expeditionary Force in France. Some were killed, some returned, some were taken prisoner. Across the Channel France stood on the threshold of its four 'Dark Years', 1940 to 1944, *les Années Noires*.

As the Germans headed for the Channel, Reynaud, his army outflanked, recalled two old soldiers to the government. Of the long list of reasons given for the fall of France, the one which rings most true with the passing of time is that the country was grossly unfortunate in these new military leaders, both rigid with hostility to the republic they were called upon to serve. Reynaud appointed the eighty-four-year-old Pétain as deputy prime minister on 18 May, and on the next day replaced his supreme commander General Gamelin[49] with the seventy-five-year-old Weygand. These decisions were greeted with joy by the cabinet, but Reynaud was to rue them within a very few days. At Pétain's trial in 1945 Reynaud testified: 'I thought they would place patriotism before their political passions and ambitions. All France made this mistake, but I was the chief and I am therefore responsible.'[50]

Pétain and Weygand were by no means twin souls; their mutual antipathy stretched back to the First World War and continued after it. Though he served the republic as Minister of War after the riots of 6 February 1934, Pétain kept his political opinions and dealings to himself. He had allied himself to no leagues and no parties. Nevertheless, throughout the 1930s his name was brought up repeatedly by nationalists who wanted a strong leader and an authoritarian government. Both Pétain and Weygand received and rejected such offers, for both were patriots and, conditionally, loyal soldiers – but to 'their' France, not to the French republic.

On 4 June 1940 Churchill told the House of Commons and the British people: 'The British Empire and the French republic, linked together in their cause and their need, will defend to the death their native soils.'[51] Churchill flew to France five times between 16 May and 13 June for last-ditch talks with Reynaud, his cabinet and his military chiefs, but British parliamentarian that he was, he could never accurately assess men such as Pétain and Weygand, soldiers called upon to defend a government, a democracy, a republic and a large section of the French population which they both despised.

The British military command in France, understandably unconfident, began to withdraw on 23 May – this was seen by the French as another desertion – and on the twenty-eighth King Leopold ordered Belgium to surrender. By 3 June the Germans were bombing Paris, although three days later the courts were sufficiently in session to hear Louis' appeal against his prison sentence, which was again not upheld.

On 12 June and for the next two days, Louis took his men into battle at Le Cadran, Connantre, Voué and Bréviandes in the Champagne, in the hills and plateaux between Rheims and Troyes, and he was in the thick of action in the last days before the fall of France. His commanding officers commended his enthusiasm, his vigour, and his *foi*. On 15 June he was cited for bravery in covering his battery in retreat – 'He was the last officer to stay in position with a machine gun until all of his battery were out of enemy fire.'[52] On the same day he was taken prisoner, one of two million captured by the Germans in these last days of the war in France, and was sent off to prison camp in Poland.

In early June Reynaud sacked de Monzie and Daladier and other defeatists in the cabinet, and installed General Charles de Gaulle as under-secretary of state in the Ministry of War; but it was too late, for by 13 June Weygand had abandoned all military endeavour. Reynaud begged his supreme commander to offer Germany a military capitulation only, a settlement which would allow the French government to continue the war from France's overseas colonies. Weygand was intransigent. He would not continue with the battle. He would not resign. He wanted to end the war. Pétain, the more lugubrious, more pessimistic and more personally ambitious of this military duo was entirely in agreement with Weygand's approach.[53] Weygand reported that communists were about to take over Paris. Instead the German army reached the capital the next day, 14 June; over two million Parisians had already left, leaving an almost empty city for German occupation. Both Churchill and Reynaud had been bombarding Roosevelt with requests for American support; this Roosevelt could not publicly supply.

On 13 June Churchill came to France for the last time before it fell, to Tours, to which the French government had fled. De Gaulle, who flew to London to beg for help to move the French government to North Africa, had convinced Churchill to 'proclaim the indissoluble union of the French and British peoples'.[54] As the French government fled further south to Bordeaux, on 16 June the British cabinet authorised a 'declaration of union'. Reynaud was euphoric; Pétain said it would be 'a fusion with a corpse'.[55] The rejection of Churchill's offer for a union between France and Britain was the end for Reynaud. Pétain, supported by Weygand, formed a cabinet of national defence and prepared to sue for peace. Reynaud resigned; Pétain was declared prime minister and immediately ordered his armies to cease fighting.

Pétain had been in Spain when Reynaud summoned him to save France, as the first French ambassador to Franco's new government. From 5 June he had kept José Felix de Lequerica, Spanish ambassador to France – and by way of him Germany too – informed that he wanted an armistice.[56] Pétain sent de Lequerica – a Spanish, Catholic and monarchist version of de Monzie in almost every way, who became another figure of importance in the life of Louis Darquier – to open negotiations with Germany.

These were completed on 22 June, and the next day Hitler came to Rethondes in the forest of Compiègne to see the armistice signed in the same railway carriage in which Germany had accepted its defeat in 1918. Hitler gave a jig of triumph when it was done, and went on next day for a quick inspection of the wonders of Paris, now acquired for his Third Reich. Shortly afterwards he issued instructions to 'take into custody all objects of art, whether state-owned or in private Jewish hands'.[57]

Two days after the fall of France, on 17 June, the day he came to power, Pétain told the French people that in taking over their government he was bestowing upon them 'the gift of my own person'. Arthur Koestler, who heard his radio speech, thought he sounded like 'a skeleton with a chill', but Pétain's thin, reedy voice belied his appearance.[58] He was in fact a portly pouter pigeon of a man, with round cheeks, clear blue eyes and a careful grey moustache, his neat head held stiffly above a substantial stomach. This body requires description because, just as Churchill's speeches to the nation are woven into the fabric of British life, so is Pétain's first speech to the French people, who welcomed his assumption of power as the arrival of their Saviour.

Because of his age, eighty-four when he came to power, anecdotes about Pétain's dotage abound. Was he senile? He was prone to irrelevancies, and was known to fall asleep in public on occasion, and to prose on. But this was one of many myths sent forth into the world by himself and others, and judiciously fostered over many years. After the First World War, in which he had become established as a national hero, Pétain had achieved an almost godlike reputation as the compassionate general, the father figure of the republic. For this reason he was also a hero to socialists like Léon Blum. Pétain preserved this reputation effortlessly because he was a secretive, silent man who hid the fact that his concern for French soldiers during the 1917 mutinies in the First World War had compounded his conservative Catholic fear of communism and socialist ideas. Though not a practising Catholic, Pétain was a traditionalist who had absorbed the Church's apprehensions and fixed opinions, one of which was that the fall of France was due to its politicians and its teachers, all pacifists, godless communists or, worse, Freemasons. He always spoke about his beloved France and its people with paternal affection, and when he took command in June 1940 the people of France trusted him. They continued to do so almost without question for the first two years of his rule, many of them until the very end, deluded by a belief in secret strategies hidden behind his impassive face.

But Pétain's immaculate public persona sheltered an inflexible and touchy army man, who viewed a good portion of his countrymen and women as unworthy of defence, and Hitler as the lesser monster. Weygand, having determined not to fight, now proceeded to instruct Pétain as to what must be done next. 'The old order of things,' he stated, 'a political regime made up of Masonic, capitalist and internationalist deals, has brought us where we stand ... France's recovery through hard work cannot be achieved without the institution of a new social regime ... We must return to the cult and the practice of an ideal summed up in these few words: God, Country, Family ... Today a new team, made up of a small number of new men untainted and uncommitted, and animated solely by the desire to serve, must, under the direction of Marshal Pétain, the leader recognised by all, proclaim its programme and set to work.'[59]

As one of Weygand's 'new men', a member of this team from 1942 to 1944, Louis Darquier was indeed set to work. In 1973 Henry Coston said of him: 'From 1937 he demanded that they [the Jews] be expelled or executed ... and he achieved both these aims.'[60]

IV

VICHY FRANCE

12

Work, Family, Fatherland

BOTH PÉTAIN AND WEYGAND firmly believed that as France had fallen, Britain would shortly follow, and Hitler would be in England within a week. Instead, as Pétain was issuing his instructions to his subjects, General de Gaulle flew from Bordeaux to London, and on the next day, 18 June 1940, this unknown general broadcast on the BBC to the few in France in a position to hear him: 'Must all hope vanish? Is defeat final? No!'[1]

A vast number of those he addressed – a quarter of the stupefied population of France, accompanied by Belgians and Dutch who had fled before them, took to the road as the Germans advanced.[2] Hauling their possessions strapped to bicycles, carts and cars, lorries, hearses, prams, boxes on wheels, this slowly moving caravan of terrified humanity created the atmosphere in which the French people were to accept their defeat. After this exodus many families were never reunited, many homes never restored, and over ninety thousand children lost their parents in the mêlée. On the road, strafed by German Stukas as they huddled for protection with their families, the death of the children began here.

The towns and villages of southern France were swamped with refugees. Anatole de Monzie escaped Paris on 10 June 'in the packed car of a fellow Cadurcien'. Charles Maurras left on the same day. Pierre Darquier may have been de Monzie's driver, for he and Louise fled Neuilly in early June, taking René's wife and children with them. They took refuge in St-Paul-de-Loubressac, a village south of Cahors, in the holiday house of an old friend.[3] The village, like Cahors, was flush with refugees; within weeks the population of Cahors alone had grown from thirteen to sixty thousand. During his stay in St-Paul, Pierre comforted the villagers in the *patois* he had known since childhood, and treated them for nothing, or for a chicken or a duck, as he had decades before. Also in the village was Germaine, the wife of Georges Blond, noted journalist of the rabid *Je Suis partout*, known for fascist views well to the right of '*Pétain et Compagnie*', as the lower orders called the Vichy government. Germaine Blond was accepted with the rest.

Louis was in prison camp in Poland, and Jean, who had been mobilised in an ambulance brigade in 1939, had also been captured. Myrtle, back in Paris, 'alone in the wake of defeat, not knowing which way to turn', sent a last card to her family, which escaped the censors in the confusion of June 1940 – 'just a few lines, the old Myrtle shouting defiance at the enemy'.[4] After that, Tasmania heard nothing more from her until the war was over.

Hitler's orders for the occupation of France had the appearance of leniency at the time. In retrospect his instructions can be seen as a clever, but bloodsucking arrangement in which France was partitioned but given a sedative pretence of sovereignty. France was chopped into pieces. Sections to the north, east and west, and the Atlantic coast, were carved off and either annexed or appropriated. The rump that was left was divided in two. German-occupied France stretched through Rheims, Rouen and Paris, and down to Angoulême – Tours, Dijon and Bourges were all occupied, and wandering underneath these cities Germany drew a demarcation line. Below this, except for fifty kilometres which Italy took along its border, two-fifths of France was left to Marshal Pétain for so-called 'self-government'.[5]

This was the Non-Occupied Zone, the Vichy Zone, often called *Zone NonO*, the 'Free' or 'Southern' Zone. It began in the centre near Vichy and Clermont-Ferrand, and stretched south to Lyon and Marseille, and westwards to include Toulouse.[6] This remnant of France was permitted to retain control of its extensive overseas empire, a small army of 100,000 men, and its demobilised fleet. Apart from this surgery, the armistice had two scorpions' tails. A million and a half captured Frenchmen were transported to camps in Germany or its occupied territories and kept there. These servicemen, the same vast number as the French dead of the First World War, were Hitler's trump card, used to extort compliance from the Vichy state and the French people. And France had to pay the costs of occupation. Unspecified in the armistice agreement, these were to bleed the country dry.

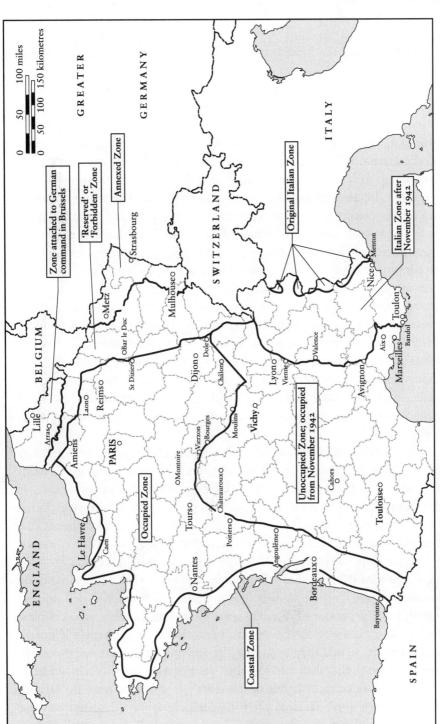

Occupied and Unoccupied (Vichy) France, 1940–1944

In June 1940 the French population was left with two rulers instead of one, each of them eager to harry the population into his own chosen shape. Five days after his return to Cahors, de Monzie was called to Bordeaux as the French government arrived in the city. There, the day before Reynaud resigned and Pétain took over, de Monzie sat in the office of José de Lequerica to 'plan the procedure and practical details of the armistice'[7] though he used a word which also means 'predict', an interpretation he was to need desperately after the Liberation.

When Pétain was asked to form a government on 16 June, he drew out of his pocket his list of ministers. By 1 July he had installed them in the spa town of Vichy in the Allier, a northern department in the Auvergne, long famous for its natural springs, its gambling casinos and its curative regimes. Vichy had large and numerous hotels and an up-to-date telephone system, blessings which turned into a curse as the name of the town became forever associated with the French puppet government that collaborated with Nazi Germany. Today Vichy labours hopelessly to lose the image bestowed upon it by the *'gouvernement du Maréchal Pétain'*, as its inhabitants insist on calling the regime everyone else calls Vichy France. A pretty town then, and a pretty town now, its gracious parks, imposing hotels and stately buildings with their pilasters, glass and wrought-iron balconies provided comfortable space for the new French state.

In Vichy's Grand Casino on 10 July 1940, 569 deputies and senators of the National Assembly voted full powers to Pétain and so brought an end to the Third Republic. De Monzie voted in favour of Pétain, as did Louis Louis-Dreyfus. The eighty men who voted against included Léon Blum; there were eighteen abstentions.[8] The next day Pétain became head of state and suspended Parliament indefinitely.

General de Gaulle never accepted that the Vichy government was a legal inheritor of republican France. But it was. On the other hand, de Gaulle asserted that Vichy was 'collaborating with murderers',[9] and he was right. The people of France, citizens no longer, were subjects now, and it was with the rituals of Action Française and the Catholic Church, and using the words they used, that Pétain was welcomed to power. He told the French that they had lost the 'spirit of sacrifice', which had been replaced by a decadent 'spirit of pleasure'. It was now time for 'atonement for their sins'. He told them that they had been defeated because of 'too few children, too few arms, too few allies . . .'[10] Immediately *'Papa'*

Pétain shepherded his children into his National Revolution, an idealised attempt to recreate old France – Catholic, agrarian, authoritarian, with an emphasis on order and obedience.

Maurras hailed Pétain's election as 'a divine surprise'; the Papal Nuncio described it as the 'Pétain miracle'. The *Pater Noster* was adapted for him:

> *Our Father who stands before us,*
> *thy name be glorified,*
> *thy kingdom come,*
> *thy will be done on earth so that we may live.*
> *Give us our daily bread, though we give nothing in return.*
> *Give once more life unto France.*
> *Lead us not into false hope nor into deceit,*
> *but deliver us from evil, O Marshal.*[11]

Pierre Laval negotiated the vote which gave Pétain his dictatorial authority. Fifty-seven years of age in 1940, during his long political career as both deputy and senator Laval had twice been prime minister of France and many times a cabinet minister. He began his public life as a lawyer and a socialist, then went on to become a wealthy and successful businessman, and in so doing solidified into one of those men who demonise excessively all those whose views they themselves once held but have since discarded. Anti-communism allied him with men such as Pétain, Taittinger, la Roque and traditionalists generally, but in a most uneasy fashion.[12] Catholic nationalists like General Weygand loathed him, and he reciprocated. Laval hated war, but for many years before 1939 he had worked towards the achievement of an authoritarian government, hopefully under the figurehead of Pétain. He was very much a republican in the mode of de Monzie, a committed European who had struggled to achieve a special relationship with Mussolini's Italy, quite oblivious to Mussolini's dislike for his brash persona.

Pétain was supposed to govern only the Non-Occupied Zone, but to administer both zones; French administrators, not valuable German bodies, were to manage what was left of France. In practice the Germans constantly intervened and never permitted Vichy to do this satisfactorily. In the four years of the Occupation Pétain visited Paris, only three hours from Vichy, but once. Pétain's Zone was left with France's wine industry, its better weather and a little over a third of its population, so that when he began to implement Drumont's catchphrase 'France for the French', he had lost most of France anyway.

Pétain rewarded Laval's kingmaking by naming him as his successor and deputy prime minister. Except for the first few weeks, theirs was a disastrous relationship. Pétain detested Laval, his ambition, his cunning, his pacifism, his non-military and parliamentary past, and his habit of blowing smoke into his face. Laval, for his part, misread Pétain, and continued to do so. He expected Pétain to be 'a statue on a pedestal . . . nothing more', while he, Laval, got on with running the country.[13]

Louis Darquier expressed a prevailing view when he described Laval: 'He was ugly. Good Lord that man was ugly!' With his nickname of 'Don Pedro', Laval's ugliness, coupled with a smouldering mistrust of him, is as often mentioned as the mindless devotion offered to Pétain. Laval was not prone to Pétain's moralising, but he was neither ugly nor merely a forthright and uncharismatic rough diamond. His bluntness sheltered a devious and ruthless intriguer, a fatal combination which brought him the hatred of his people.

Apart from Laval, Pétain surrounded himself with men who also had ambitions for power of their own, and with them he proceeded to construct his National Revolution. For his rebirth of France Pétain jettisoned the maxim of the French Revolution and its republic, *Liberté, Egalité, Fraternité*, and replaced it with la Roque's words of command for his Croix-de-feu: *Travail, Famille, Patrie* – Work, Family, Fatherland.

Laval matched Pétain in his view of Britain, *la perfide Albion*, as 'France's most implacable enemy',[14] a self-interested country that liked to fight its wars on French soil. This hostility was exacerbated a few days after Pétain signed the armistice, when the British government recognised de Gaulle as leader of the Free French forces, as those citizens of France who followed the general to London were called. Then on 3 July Churchill ordered the destruction of the French navy at Mers-el-Kebir in French Algeria. Over a thousand French seamen were killed. Pétain broke off relations with Britain, and in August tried de Gaulle in his absence and condemned him to death.

Unlike Laval, Pétain never extended his hatred for Britain to the United States, which maintained an embassy in Vichy until 1942. Prominent Americans around Roosevelt, re-elected president in November 1940, resisted involvement in the European war, adopting an ambiguous attitude which included seeing little difference between Pétain and de Gaulle, whose 'certain idea of France' Roosevelt resolutely loathed. In the early years of the war, for the USA 'such hope as there might be for the future was centred almost entirely on Marshal Pétain himself'.[15] The French people felt the same.

———————— ∽ ————————

In August 1940 Hitler was preparing Operation Sealion, the invasion of Britain. As Anne Darquier turned ten in September, still in junior school, German aircraft bombarded British airfields, factories, towns and cities, and the London Blitz began. Kidlington men went off to fight in the Middle and Far East. Many were pilots and sailors; others, men and women, were at work in factories, at the motor works or on the land. From Kidlington you could see the bombing of London and the reply of the anti-aircraft guns, lighting up the night sky. By the end of September the RAF had won the Battle of Britain; Hitler postponed the invasion and turned his attention to the Soviet Union, but the bombing did not cease. A German Junker bombed Kidlington airport in November 1940. Later the German planes came again, dropping a stick of bombs on the fields behind the cinema, destroying the cricket pitch and breaking the leg of a cow.

The citizens of Kidlington were Firewatchers, Air Raid Wardens, members of the Home Guard; mothers and spinsters were working in factories or offices or on the land, or busy being patriotic on the Kitchen Front. An untroubled local Kidlington builder advertised, 'We don't think Hitler can damage Oxford – but we know the weather will still take its toll.' The last letter Anne had received from her father had given an address in Poland. She believed him to be a prisoner of war.

French soldiers were sent to Stalags, others, including officers, to Offlags. As an officer, Louis Darquier was despatched to Offlag II D at Groß-Born, now called Borne Szczecinecki, in Poland. He arrived in June 1940, prisoner of war number 1294/9. Some of the men at Offlag II D – most of them remained prisoners until 1945 – have left vivid descriptions of the camp: men packed into wooden huts, burning hot in summer, freezing in winter, soup and dry bread to eat, lice and boredom to live with – the stuff of a thousand war films. Louis arrived rather plump, without his monocle, his reputation well known by his fellow prisoners. He gave lectures about the 'Jewish question', and other accounts tell of him boasting about his womanising.

Jean-Louis Crémieux-Brilhac was one of the few to escape Offlag II D. He became an officer of de Gaulle's Free French forces in London, and after 1945 he was an important French historian of the Second World War. During the war the BBC broadcast to France from 6.15 a.m. to midnight: news bulletins, discussions, reflections, messages, secret codes, and de Gaulle's own programme, '*Honneur et Patrie*'. The BBC's French broadcasters received voluminous fan mail from their French audience, who listened to them clandestinely. By 1941 the penalty for being caught listening to the broadcasts from London was a ten-thousand-franc fine or two years in prison; by the end of 1942 it was death.

One of the most famous evening magazine programmes of the BBC French service was '*Les Français parlent aux Français*' (The French talk to the French). It was on this programme that Crémieux-Brilhac broadcast his first attack on Louis Darquier, in May 1942:

> ... As one of eleven officers who escaped from Germany, we were, if not comrades, then at least neighbours of Darquier in Offlag II D. I knew this man and can state that he is a coward. Eleven officers will support my testimony: in a camp of six thousand officers, where comradeship was a duty and a rule, Darquier de Pellepoix was an object of scorn and disgust. He arrived at the Offlag wearing espadrilles and told his roommates that he 'put them on to flee from the invader as quickly as possible' ...
>
> He did not have the courage of his convictions. One day, after one of his speeches, a Jewish officer, respected by everyone, a hero of both wars and decorated captain for his actions during the battle of Rethel, challenged Darquier de Pellepoix to withdraw his remarks or he would settle the matter with his fists. Darquier de Pellepoix, who no longer had his thugs from the Foire du Trone [funfair] to protect him, retracted immediately. He went pale, stuttered, apologised with a stream of 'Dear friends' and finally made his way out under a hail of abuse ...
>
> Finally, after two months in captivity, towards 1 September 1940, the news broke that Darquier – and Darquier alone – was to be released. At first, no one believed it: the Germans had not set anyone free before ... but ... a German officer came to get him ...

By August 1940 Louis Darquier was back in Paris. As he departed, his cellmates begged him to send them the compass and civilian hat so essential for escape. Darquier did not say no, he promised everything – he would have promised the moon to get out the camp with the minimum of trouble.

Later Louis wrote to one of the few prisoners who would speak to him, reporting that

he had enjoyed an excellent trip, that he had stopped in Berlin where the Germans presented him with a civilian suit. He had returned to Paris on an express train where he had been delighted to find his apartment. As for his prisoner friends, he counselled patience.

Two months later Jean Darquier was liberated, also surprisingly early. Later Louis was heard making speeches about 'the happy life of prisoners'.[16]

When the Germans moved into their new French territory they immediately restored order, ruling Occupied France, *ZoneO*, directly from Paris, controlling three-quarters of the country's industrial wealth, most of its important agricultural land, and nearly seventy per cent of its population. Housed in Paris in the Hôtel Majestic in the avenue Kléber, the Wehrmacht provided the military command in France, the Militärbefehlshaber in Frankreich, the MBF,[17] which was responsible for administration, management of the economy and the maintenance of order. At the Majestic, Goebbels' Propaganda-Abteilung (Propaganda Division) started work at once, informing the defeated inhabitants: 'It's the English and the Jews who have brought you to this sorry pass.'[18]

In Paris the occupiers distributed food, cigarettes and posters of a benevolent Nazi soldier cheerfully holding a little boy munching a piece of bread, with two little girls attached to his other, outstretched hand, with the message: 'Abandoned peoples, put your trust in the German Soldier.' The presence of the conqueror was on every corner. Paris was transformed by German street signs and instructions, banners and posters, the latter becoming more malevolent with the passing of time, for the friendly German soldier vanished once resistance began, which it did very soon.

The Germans requisitioned many of the most historic and beautiful buildings of Paris. The blood banner, the *Blutfahne*, waved from the Hôtel de Ville. The Palais Bourbon, which had housed the National Assembly, was festooned with a vast banner proclaiming 'Germany is victorious on all fronts'. The flag of the swastika flew from public buildings, the best hotels were taken over, and German soldiers changed guard and stood to attention outside them. Within weeks of the Nazi arrival the French stock exchange opened again, as did the universities and schools. Industrialists and bankers turned their attention to doing business with their conquerors. Paris became a centre of high life for the German victors and those French who were happy to entertain them; together they filled the restaurants and cinemas, nightclubs and racecourses, and as the German soldiers goose-stepped to duty, the French people went back to work.

Hitler ruled France through numerous organisations with overlapping responsibilities, all of them dependent upon his favour. A number of Nazi offices operated in France under direct control from Berlin, while in Paris the MBF vied with the office of Ribbentrop's Ministry of Foreign Affairs, the German embassy. Ribbentrop returned Otto Abetz to Paris at the moment of victory, and on 8 August 1940 he was appointed German ambassador to France. From his headquarters in the rue de Lille Abetz soon became a more important agent than the military command; Céline called him 'King Otto I' with good reason. His role was to 'transmit the wishes of Hitler', and as early as 19 August 1940 he was circulating plans to dispossess and expel Jews.[19]

Charming francophile that he was, Abetz's personality soon made his embassy a magnet for Parisian social life during the war. Before this, Abetz included Louis Darquier on a list of pre-war sympathisers for immediate release from prison that he drew up after his first meeting with Pierre Laval in July, when he and Laval took to each other with mutual enthusiasm.[20] Laval barely knew Louis Darquier at this point; it was the Nazis who prepared this July list of pre-war mercenaries, which included Marcel Bucard, Robert Brasillach and many others.

On Louis' return the Germans had been *in situ* for only two months. France had fallen apart, and Paris was a dead city with its tongue cut out. Communication of all kinds was forbidden by the Nazis; no letters, no travel – even carrier pigeons were forbidden to fly. German soldiers settled into the towns and villages of Occupied France, greeted by a populace stunned into resignation or acceptance.

During this time and for many months to come, the office of General Charles Huntziger, who became Vichy Minister of War in September 1940, wrote a sequence of letters to several commandants of different regions asking where Darquier had been, was or would be. In fact the French War Office was writing such letters just as Louis was signing off from the army at the Paris mobilisation centre in the rue de Liège and applying for the *feuille de démobilisation* he needed to carry to demonstrate that he was neither a deserter nor an escaped prisoner of war. The police could have told them that Louis was living with Myrtle at 2, rue Chauchat, not, it seems, an apartment, but the usual hotel room.[21] On 27 August 1940 Vichy France abrogated the Marchandeau Law, but Louis Darquier was not yet a free man. His pre-war criminal convictions still held.

Louis was happy to take German money and lie about it, but he was also a rabid French patriot. He had alienated many recent comrades – Maurras, the nationalist right, the Paris city councillors; he needed to mend many fences. In the confusion of these early months no one knew how the balance of power would settle between Vichy and the Germans. For some months Louis bided his time, and avoided his anti-Semitic cronies. He was by no means unusual in keeping mum in the autumn of 1940; the entire population of France was doing much the same as they anxiously assessed the lie of the new land.

In Vichy, gathering around Pétain, were the men who formed his first government and his consultative council of ministers, many of whom shared with Louis Darquier the political inheritance of Maurras and the nationalist leagues, and of the Fédération Nationale Catholique and the Catholic Church. A disparate collection of machinators, rarely sharing each other's politics or ambitions for France, Pétain's followers were, however, usually entirely united by a demonisation of everything that the Popular Front had represented, a strong belief in authoritarian government, and anti-Bolshevism, 'the nearest thing to a Vichy common denominator'.[22]

Like that of Louis Darquier, the nationalism and anti-Semitism of Pétain's chosen disciples in Vichy was French, not Nazi. Very soon ranged against them and centred in Paris were the French intellectuals and journalists – the Rebatets and Brasillachs – and the politicians – Doriot and his rival Marcel Déat,[23] the most socialist of all the French fascists. On the fringes of these tribes was Céline's scruffy underworld of 'ideologues, adventurers and bandits'[24] – the Montandons and Deloncles, the Costons and Darquiers and their fellow muckrakers and crusaders, who in August 1940 were ready to pounce upon every opportunity the Germans might offer them. All of them energetically disagreed amongst themselves as to how much, how little or for what reason they welcomed Nazi rule. Whatever their differences, they now formed a pro-Nazi alternative to the Vichy state, with Occupied Paris as its capital city. Described as 'collaborationists' and often called 'Paris *collabos*' to distinguish them from 'collaborators' – the men of Vichy – some of these Parisian fascists adored Hitler, and many took to uniforms and marching and saluting. These Paris *collabos* passed the war years tormenting Vichy for its moderation and fighting amongst themselves for German favour and money.

If Paris was the Nazi capital of France and Vichy its French capital, both shared anti-Semitism and anti-communism, more rabid in Paris, more Catholic in Vichy. While Paris and Vichy vied with each other in their attempts to please the German victors, the Nazi occupiers dealt with Vichy as they wished, and treated the Paris *collabos* as gigolos to dine with and be diverted by. Even the affable Abetz, considered to be too much of a francophile by his German peers, rarely took them seriously.

Hitler's various representatives in France immediately took control of the media – all news agencies, the press, publishing, radio and the cinema. The injection of so much energy and money into propaganda was a boon to these fanatics. After Vichy repealed the Marchandeau Law, which had prohibited attacks on ethnic or religious groups, racist newspapers proliferated, most of them a *mélange* of fascist idealism, poetic imagery and incantatory patriotism, interwoven with vicious denunciations of Jews, Masons and the English. Vichy monitored everything, as did the Germans, but both also subsidised generously the collaborationist press in Paris, which flourished throughout the Occupation.[25]

Typical of the pre-war anti-Semites was Henry Coston, who, like all the old warriors of *The Protocols of the Elders of Sion*, glowered at the new arrivals invading his territory. With so much on offer, former colleagues became rivals. Coston wanted to start up his paper, *Libre parole*, again, but he had joined Jacques Doriot's fascist Parti Populaire Français in

1940, and Abetz and Laval were suspicious of anyone connected with Doriot. So Coston's considerable energies turned towards 'the Jews' auxiliaries', Freemasons. Vichy set him up in the former premises of the Grand Lodge, with a Centre d'Action et de Documentation (CAD) (Action and Documentation Centre) under the murderous Bernard Faÿ, the great friend and protector of Gertrude Stein and Alice B. Toklas, both of whom did so much to help him escape retribution after the war. Pétain placed all these efforts within his Ministry of Justice, for he shared the traditional Catholic view of Freemasonry: 'A Jew cannot help his origins, but a Freemason has chosen to become one.' He was particularly hostile to schoolteachers, whom he considered to be Freemasons, socialists or both, responsible for raising a generation unfit to fight and die for France: a thousand of these lost their jobs.[26]

Coston's passion for categorisation and identification was of the greatest use to Faÿ; he drew up a card index containing sixty thousand Masonic names. Many Catholic papers made use of these lists in order to boycott and publicly shame those listed. Nine hundred and ninety-nine Masons were sent to Germany, and 549 were executed by firing squad or died in concentration camps. A further fourteen thousand lost their jobs. Coston did this work as a French civil servant working for the Ministry of Justice, but he was also Gestapo spy number R12. He flourished like the green bay tree in a world of German-sponsored circles, groups and centres, pouring out pamphlets, brochures, leaflets, tracts, articles and essays which culminated in the 'pinnacle of his art', *'Je vous hais'* – 'I Hate You'. Produced for Doriot and his PPF by Coston and colleagues in 1944, this pamphlet was considered to be the most violently anti-Semitic publication of the period.

Louis Darquier's ideological position within the complexities of French support for Germany was driven first by his strategies for survival. After survival he wanted recognition, and both desires were tied up with his hunger for money and success. By early 1941 it became more than obvious that he could be paid by the Vichy state as well as the Germans to rid France of its Jews, and at the same time public recognition, power, honour and acclaim would be his; 1940 to 1941 was therefore the period of his most determined assault upon his final goal. Within twelve months every speech Louis Darquier made would reveal detailed and thorough briefings from German sources. But outwardly, the police reported, he was avoiding all public activities in order to demonstrate his disagreement with the ideas of the occupiers and his independence of spirit.

The ambition of both Pétain and Laval was to place France, powerful again, at the side of Germany in a new world order. In October 1940 first Laval and then Pétain met Hitler at Montoire, near Tours. Photographs of Pétain and the Führer shaking hands appeared in every French newspaper. Pétain told Hitler that de Gaulle was 'a blot on the honour of the French officer corps', and a week later he told his people that he was taking them 'on the path to collaboration'.[27]

The greatest obstacle to this fantasy was Hitler himself. He had no desire for any good to come to or be done to France, Germany's 'mortal enemy'. He permitted a Vichy state because it was cheaper; French civil servants and administrators ran the country. Hitler wanted France rendered powerless to obstruct his war plans for Europe, and to function as a source of wealth and labour for Germany. Unlike every other defeated European country, France had been permitted an armistice; now Vichy wanted a peace treaty. Hitler was not interested. Vichy would devote years of wasted effort to useless negotiations with Nazi Germany as it failed to come to terms with this humiliation.

Hitler turned France into a milking cow for Germany throughout the war years. Everything was sent to Germany, but money most of all. Reparation payments to the Reich, the cost to the French people of being occupied, were vast, and were used as blackmail. When Vichy behaved the sum was lowered, and *vice versa*. Most French food production went to Germany. There continued to be food for the occupying Germans and their French cohorts, but the people of France were among the worst-fed in Occupied Europe. Hunger and cold dominate every memoir of those who lived in France during the war, as do a pall of prohibitions and a forest of papers of permission required to live, to travel, to work. Between the Germans and Vichy, French subjects were tethered to the ground. From September 1940 everything good was rationed: from butter to clothes, from tobacco and wine to salt, from petrol to coffee. There was little meat. Family pets had to watch their backs, as did the pigeons in the parks.[28]

In 1940 however, sheltering under the grandfatherly protection of the Hero of Verdun, the French people believed in Pétain with the faith of the desperate. This was the period of *attentisme*, of 'wait and see', and Pétain was quickly sanctified. His face adorned a vast army of mugs, statues, magazine covers, stamps and postcards. There were Pétain streets, squares and buildings, most of them hastily renamed when Liberation came. There was even a Pétain suit. Mothers held up their children to receive his touch. He was showered with gifts – cigarettes and crystal, baby lambs decked out in pink ribbons. In his toy kingdom, the men who served him rose and fell with a frequency identical to that of the governments of the Third Republic. Group contended with group, squabbling courtiers came and went. The torment such men passed on to their scapegoats, the Jews, Masons, Gypsies, communists and socialists they had so long despised, was to be great, but under Pétain's National Revolution the suffering of his French subjects was not inconsiderable either.

Pétain courted the peasant, and extolled the wonders of the French soil, its beasts and its produce. The family and *its* produce – the young – came next. It is an eternal truth that when the word 'family' is uttered by a politician, women, and therefore men, have everything to fear. Pétain, a womaniser, was not himself a family man. This did not prevent him from holding firmly to Catholic sentiments about family life as the cornerstone of the ordered state, and the Catholic hierarchy welcomed the reforms of the National Revolution with enthusiasm.

Vichy authorised financial rewards for the birth of children. Fathers of a family of more than five children were given additional civic rights, while childless men had employment disadvantages. Pétain gave French women bronze medals for having five children, silver for eight, and gold for ten. In 1942 divorce was forbidden until a marriage had lasted for three years. After that time it was rarely permitted, and never in the case of adultery.[29] Pétain, who had married a divorcée in 1920, rearranged his own marital situation to suit the conditions he now imposed upon his people. The Vatican annulled his wife's first marriage, and the Archbishop of Paris secretly remarried the couple by proxy in church. Pétain did not attend.[30]

Actually women spent most of their lives during the Occupation queuing and working. Day after day and hour after hour, beginning in the dark, they queued for tiny amounts of food and for the basics of life, most of which very soon disappeared for good or were priced exorbitantly. In schools the children were taught to write: 'If your bread is grey and your piece of it smaller, it is not the fault of Marshal Pétain.'[31] Amidst air-raid warnings, hunger and mourning – almost every French family was touched by the permanent absence of a father, brother, husband or son – making do, not making children, was women's chief occupation. With their men away, not even the most willing wives could manage to produce fifteen legitimate children, which automatically qualified the last child to have Pétain as a godfather.

As to their children, they were indoctrinated with the principles of the National Revolution at school, and were encouraged to send Pétain little messages, cards and presents. As usual boys got the most attention, and thus came off worse. Vichy youth groups, clubs and organisations introduced them to outdoor life, hiking, camping, rural work and physical exercise, an approach matched and approved of by the Catholic Church. Singing around campfires and male purity and virility were much encouraged, but as the Germans needed more and more men to fuel their war machine, Church and state both lost their quarry as men and boys were summoned to serve in Germany.

A new anthem, '*Maréchal, nous voilà!*', 'Marshal, Here We Are!', replaced the irreplaceable '*Marseillaise*'. Apart from that, 'Thou shalt not' was perhaps the most noticeable aspect of Pétain's National Revolution. Hostility to the Germans was forbidden, listening to the BBC or Swiss radio was forbidden, helping Jews to escape, or helping escaped prisoners of war, was forbidden. It was forbidden to locate cafés near schools. Catholic women were instructed not to wear shorts, and the Church permitted no mixed sports meetings. To such prohibitions were added punishments for a myriad misdemeanours, ranging from 'transmission of information to the detriment of the German army', which covered a great deal of ground, to 'street gatherings, distribution of leaflets, public meetings and demonstrations, and any other activity hostile to Germany'.[32]

The most hated new control was the almost impassable frontier, the demarcation line which the Nazis used to control Vichy. Getting a permit, an *Ausweis* or *laissez-passer*, to cross the border between *ZoneO* and *Zone NonO*, policed by the Nazis and garlanded with prohibitive signs in French and German, was almost impossible. As this extended to members of the Vichy government, it made a joke of Vichy's supposed administrative control of both French zones, and strengthened the hostility between Paris and Vichy.

Letters were censored, and limited. Time changed too. The Occupied Zone kept Berlin time, two hours behind Britain, and by 1941 Vichy did

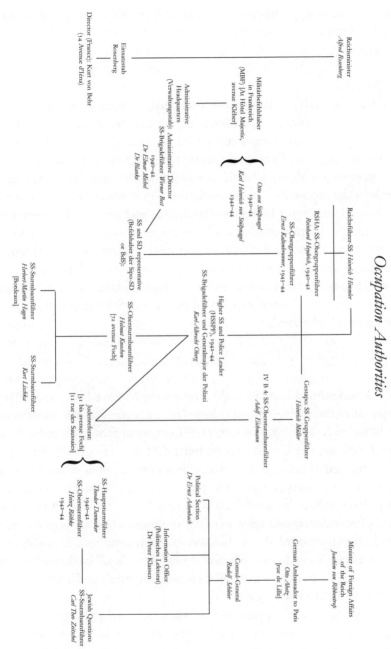

Principal authorities dealing with Jews, 1940–44 (adapted from p. 373 of *Principal Occupation Authorities Dealing With Jews 1940–1944* by Marrus and Paxton, published by Stanford University Press.)

too. The electricity supply was intermittent. Ill health, malnutrition, chilblains and eternal cold were among the first results of the National Revolution. So was the black market, known as *le système D*,[33] universally practised, although officially banned, as was dancing – but dance the people did.

After the early months came the most noticeable characteristic of the 'Dark Years': silence. The silence of the dark mornings and the black-outs at night, of the streets after curfew. The silence between people faced with the worst in human nature; the silence of a population doing what it was told, doing what it was safest to do, and the mirror image of this in the mountains of denunciatory letters which poured onto official desks. Faced with betrayals, disloyalties and greed, with trust gone, it was always dangerous to speak your mind.

But even though there was compliance, resignation, fear, despair, self-interest, betrayal and shame, a strong sense of sullen, hungry fury growls through these years. Matching it was an astute capacity to navigate the ocean of instructions doled out to every French subject in the new French Fatherland.

When Louis settled back into Paris he seems to have lived with Myrtle, at least until the spring of 1941; his silence for the first six months may well have been partly due to her. Her Tasmanian family describe Myrtle as always flying the Union Jack in her heart. In her cups, however, she was wont to make this public, and she was living now in a city draped with swastikas, German signs and proclamations. It wasn't until later, in Vichy, that she had any trouble, when other Vichy wives of consequence – one of whom was Madame Pétain – objected to her presence and her attitude, and, presumably, to her alcohol consumption. Louis claimed that an explanation to the Marshal himself – that Myrtle was entirely uninterested in politics – was all that was required, and that after that she was never troubled again.

But in these early years of the war, before Louis came into his kingdom, Myrtle's insistence that 'Britain must win!!!!'[34] was dangerous. It was also another cause for rows between them, for in Louis' circle the war was the fault of the Jews and the English. In these months of uncertainty he had no money. Physical violence always erupted between them when money was short, another of many reasons for Myrtle to leave Louis. By May 1941 the police recorded that they were living apart – she in the Hôtel Cousin in rue des Mathurins, he flitting from hotel to hotel, probably with another woman, because the hotels he passed through at this point were elegant and expensive.[35]

Throughout this period letters flew in all directions about Louis' pre-war criminal convictions. An outstanding case investigating the Büttner cheque stubs had been transferred to the military courts in September 1939, and a year later the War Office was considering imposing disciplinary sanctions on Louis. He knew his sentence was likely to be two months' imprisonment; instead, in November 1940 he received an official pardon, and for the first time could edge his nose above the parapet.

In the meantime Louis was keeping company with a few trusted disciples – the faithful Pierre Gérard was one, but in his pursuit of Vichy his old nationalist colleagues were the order of the day. He made his first public appearance since the Occupation on 6 February 1941, when he went on German-controlled Radio-Paris to ask, again, for contributions to his Association of Widows and Orphans, inviting listeners to its annual Mass in the church of the Madeleine. Following the ceremony, with Charles Trochu he led a delegation of twelve to lay a wreath at the foot of the fountain in place de la Concorde.

Some days later, questioned by the police when he crossed the square outside the Hôtel de Ville without using the pedestrian crossing, Louis took umbrage and the usual altercation ensued. This was his first eruption since his brawl in the Brasserie Lipp on the eve of war. A month later, back on form, his name appeared in the files of the occupiers for the first time.

Vichy was in disgrace in early 1941. In December 1940, after only five months in office, Pétain, supported by certain of his courtiers, dismissed and arrested Laval for, amongst other things, keeping his manoeuvres too close to his chest and too close to Otto Abetz in Paris. The results were disastrous for Pétain in both the short and the long term. The Germans were furious. The demarcation line was closed, and Abetz came to Vichy, brandished a pistol at Pétain and refused to deal with Pierre-Étienne Flandin, Pétain's first choice as Laval's replacement. After some months of crisis and negotiation Admiral Jean-François Darlan, commander of the French navy before the war and Pétain's Naval Minister from June 1940, was appointed Pétain's deputy, and Pétain raised up Fernand de Brinon, Abetz's crony, to be Vichy's delegate in Paris. Hitler finally accepted Darlan in February 1941. Darlan had something of Laval's matter-of-fact manner, but none of his occasional charm. He was another of those who thought the decadence, decline and thus defeat of France had been due to its Jews, to an international Jewish conspiracy, Anglo-Saxon warmongers and Freemasons (though Henry Coston spent a great deal of time asserting that Darlan was a Freemason himself).[36]

On 1 March Abetz submitted two lists to Vichy of names of suitable candidates to head a central Jewish agency the Germans wanted Pétain and Darlan to create. Both lists included Louis Darquier.[37] Amongst the other names were all those which had appeared on the Elizabeth Büttner cheque stubs, as well as Georges Montandon and Céline. This new agency was to control the 'Aryanisation' of the wealth of the Jews, and so to be the cornerstone of the Nazi–Vichy system for the elimination and despoliation of the Jews.

Although every piece of Vichy legislation had to be submitted to the German military command, the occupiers were particularly anxious that control of the Jews should be seen to be the responsibility of the French government. Pétain, under pressure from the Americans, who kept an ambassador at Vichy and an unhappy eye on the persecution of its Jews until November 1942, worried about an anti-Jewish agency. But Vichy was anxious to appear to be self-governing, and on 29 March Pétain signed legislation to create the Commissariat Générale aux Questions Juives, the Commissariat for Jewish Affairs – the CGQJ, the initials by which it was always known. This time, Louis did not get the job: Vichy's choice, Xavier Vallat, was appointed. Nevertheless, six months after his liberation from prison he knew that his name had been on the German list; now he set about convincing Vichy of his worth.

On 15 July Louis was mentioned in despatches and awarded the Croix de Guerre with Palm by General Huntziger, who was distributing honours liberally at the time.[38] Though Pétain had certainly seen Louis Darquier's name as a candidate for the CGQJ, Vichy's Ministry of War still could not locate him. Substantial correspondence about his whereabouts revealed nothing, and in July 1941 his Croix de Guerre was sent to the Paris city council on the assumption that Louis was still in Offlag II D.

Of Myrtle the ministry knew nothing, although as the wife of a prisoner of war, the medal should have been sent to her. But when Louis went to war he had given the city council as the address to be informed should anything happen to him. Myrtle's name never appears on Louis' civic documents, as is compulsory by French law, perhaps an indication that he was aware of the true state of his marital arrangements.[39] Charles Trochu pinned the Croix de Guerre on Louis' chest at the Hôtel de Ville, after which Louis ventured out to secure his essential identity card from the police.

The English education system in 1941, then as now, stratified its children. At the age of eleven the brighter children of Kidlington Junior School were bussed to Bicester Grammar School, five miles away. Those who did not pass the scholarship exam necessary to go there were sent to Gosford Hill County School in Kidlington. Elsie told everyone that Anne was 'brainy', but she failed the scholarship exam. This meant she must go to the County School. When she enrolled on 22 September she was the only child listed as having no parents and no legal guardian.

This school, already notorious for its treatment of the East Ham evacuees, was simply not good enough for the indomitable Elsie, who took immediate steps to move Anne elsewhere. First she tried to track down Louis Darquier. After the fall of France a number of charitable committees and clubs were set up under the aegis of de Gaulle and his Free French government, and one of them, the Maison des Ailes, was at Ditchley Park at Enstone, about ten miles from Kidlington.[40] Elsie started there. When Myrtle was down and out in London in 1933 she had asked the London Société Française de Bienfaisance (French Benevolent Society) for money. They always refused her, but ten years later they did not refuse Elsie. On 15 September 1941 the Comité d'Assistance aux Familles de Soldats Français (Committee for the Aid of the Families of French Soldiers) in Cullum Street, London EC3, wrote to the French consul-general in London asking him to find out the whereabouts of Louis from the Vichy War Ministry. It was more than a year since Anne had heard from her father, eighteen months since he had sent Elsie a penny. On receipt of the letter from London, the Vichy

Ministry of Foreign Affairs – Admiral Darlan's bailiwick at this time – applied in turn to General Huntziger.

It was Free French charities that gave Elsie the money for Anne, after one term at the County School, to go to East Ham Grammar, which, evacuated from the East End of London in 1939, had appropriated Kidlington Zoo. No one understood why she was the only local child allowed entry to this romantic school, since she was neither a resident of East Ham, nor had she passed the necessary scholarship exam. But Anne had earned the reputation of being very clever; Mildred Prissian and she talked French to each other and competed at lessons. This friendship may have helped gain her admission, but it was the fearless Nanny Lightfoot who managed it.

The old zoo provided a school hall in Rosie's former Elephant House, air-raid shelters in the pigsties, geography lessons around the walrus pond. This could have been the happiest time of Anne's school life, but her zoo school years convey the same sense of isolation. The girls at East Ham Grammar did not mix with the Kidlington children, which pleased Elsie. The grammar school girls noticed that Elsie guarded Anne like a mother hen, and brought her up to be different from the rest of them, though they suspected that Anne would have liked to make friends and to have a family of her own. Though Anne was not to learn much about Catholicism until later, it was generally known that she was meant to be a Catholic, and this too set her apart at her school in the zoo. Anne, one Kidlington neighbour remembered, 'wouldn't do things some of the other girls did'; she 'spoke almost like a Londoner, never like a foreigner, but she was a complete mystery to all of us. She tried hard to fit in, but she didn't, quite.'[41]

French authorities in London were assured by Vichy in October 1941 that Louis Darquier was still in prison camp, just as Louis contacted them in pursuit of more decorations, this time the supreme accolade, the Légion d'honneur, the decoration his father Pierre had received.[42] By that month Vichy had reconstituted the Paris city council: no Jew (by race or religion), no Freemason, no naturalised foreigner, no 'person of doubtful morality in both public and private life' need apply. Charles Trochu was nominated as its president, and Louis, described as 'journalist, liberated prisoner', was one of only forty-four councillors reappointed to their old jobs.[43] The charities in London seem to have been aware of this, because they insisted to General Huntziger and the Vichy

Ministry of Foreign Affairs, to no avail, that Louis Darquier had been spotted in Vichy, in Lyon, in Paris.

At the same time, Louis had inveigled the CGQJ to take him on the payroll. Vallat gave him a fictitious post, with a retainer of eight thousand francs, a substantial advance against 'travel costs' (which he later refused to return, despite three reminders) and two months' employment as a 'temporary agent . . . with a pass for the unoccupied zone'. He needed this to visit Cahors.

For a few years René Darquier had been uneasily reconciled with Louis, but his father still refused to see him. By now Pierre and Louise had moved into Cahors, renting an apartment at 7, rue St-Géry, very near their old home in rue du Lycée. Amongst old friends again, Pierre took up his practice but very soon he knew he was dying. He had phlebitis, blood clots for which he had no medicine, though Jean came down from Paris with injections on several occasions.

As befits a department which was a bastion of Radical republicanism, the *Lotois* combined an attitude of respect for the Marshal with a healthy dislike of his regime and the German Occupation. Many Jews were hidden by Cadurciens, but many were denounced, and the people who had hidden them shared their fate. Those who knew Louise and Pierre in these war years describe their attitude as *Pétainiste*, but they were not in any way collaborators. *Résistants* of Cahors who knew Pierre knew him as a good man who would denounce no one.

For Louise, a harder line was preached at the Cathédrale de St-Étienne. Paul Chevrier, appointed Bishop of Cahors in 1941, was a strong supporter of Pétain.[44] Chevrier came to Cahors from Vichy, where he had been curé of St-Louis, the parish church of Pétain and his ministers. His sermons and pastoral letters were refulgent with praise for the Marshal, and when Mass was celebrated in the open air in Cahors in front of the statue of Léon Gambetta – hero of the anticlerical republic – this act was seen as 'the revenge of the curés'.[45]

References to Louis Darquier's visit to Cahors in 1941 are fleeting, but he seems to have achieved some reconciliation with his father. The visit also enabled him to observe the flood of refugees, and to complain, 'Cahors, which before the war had only one Jew, now has the sad privilege of welcoming two to three thousand.'[46]

By the end of the summer of 1941, French resistance in Paris was mounting, as it was throughout France. Death notices began to appear,

Affiches Rouges, wanted posters, printed in red. Hitler ordered German reprisals of up to a hundred hostages for every German victim, and the execution of communists, anarchists, Gaullists and Jews began. Vichy, which liked to handle these reprisals itself, continually finagled to get communist hostages shot instead of 'good Frenchmen'.[47]

If there had been a honeymoon between the efficient German occupier and the defeated French, the autumn of 1941 saw the end of it. Pétain reacted to the 'evil wind' of discontent by issuing even more 'Thou shalt nots' to his refractory people. Darlan was wont to describe the British leader as 'the drunkard Churchill'.[48] But it was Churchill who described best these men of Vichy:

> They lie prostrate at the foot of the conqueror. They fawn upon him. And what have they got out of it? The fragment of France which was left to them is just as powerless, just as hungry, and even more miserable because divided, than the Occupied regions themselves. Hitler plays from day to day a cat-and-mouse game with these tormented men.[49]

13

———————◄○►———————

Tormenting Men

THE LAWS VICHY INSTITUTED against its Jewish population came about without German instruction: they were the creations of Pétain and his National Revolution, carefully designed to avoid any implication of alignment with the German approach.

Louis' efforts at ingratiation were about to pay off. To Vichy he said little about Jews. He had no need to. He now lived in a world which fulfilled almost every longing to rid France of them. The speed of Vichy's approach could not fail to please. Vichy made its first moves in the midsummer aftermath of the chaos of 1940, as demobilised soldiers were returning home and some of those who had fled south were making their way back to Paris and the Occupied Zone. Amongst their number were some thirty thousand Jews. On 17 August the Germans forbade the return of any more. 'The government of Marshal Pétain,' Vallat assured the German occupiers, 'is perfectly aware of the extent to which Jewish elements are responsible for the ills affecting France.'[1]

A week after Pétain was voted into power, on 17 July, employment in the civil service was closed to anyone without a French father. Five days later a commission was established to review the citizenship of all persons naturalised after 1927. Foreigners and refugees were put to work in 'foreign work units'.[2] In August all secret societies were forbidden, including Masonic lodges. In September restrictions which already applied to the medical profession were extended to the legal profession. These laws, which exceeded German demands, affected all refugees and foreigners – and automatically, a large number of Jews. As with all Vichy laws, they applied in theory to everyone in both *ZoneO* and *Zone NonO*, as long as they fitted in with German laws in the Occupied Zone. When Vichy set to work, the Germans in Paris were still involved in administrative and military matters. Only in September 1940 did the German occupiers catch up with Vichy and issue their first decree applying to Jews. This secured abandoned Jewish property and defined whom they considered to be Jewish. A sign, 'Jewish business', in German and French, was required on all Jewish shop windows. To the Germans, a Jew was a Jew if he practised or had practised the religion, or had more than two Jewish grandparents.

This German decree required the word '*Juif*' or '*Juive*' to be stamped on all Jewish identity cards, and for a census of such persons to be undertaken in the Occupied Zone. This became the infamous *fichier*, the 'Tulard file', named after the French police official who organised this meticulous information, colour-coded for deportation and death. The Jewish census began in Paris on 3 October 1940, and was carried out for the Germans by French civil servants; 150,000 Jews registered for the *fichier*. It had orders to list women and children, and it did. As he walked around Paris, Louis Darquier saw Jews labelled and segregated as he had always wished.

All this was the first shot in what was to become a battle royal between Vichy and the Germans for possession of the Jewish wealth of France. The Germans wanted the French to do the work, but to retain

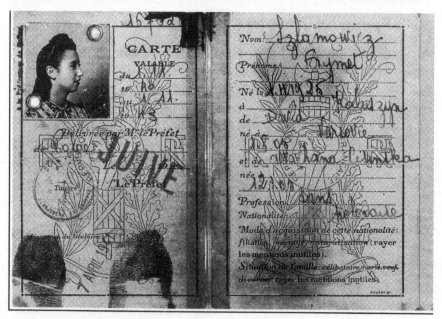

Jewish *carte d'identité*, introduced by Vichy in 1940 (© Klarsfeld Collection).

the proceeds for the German war effort; Vichy fought to keep the wealth in French hands.³ A complication was that German command in France proved to be as divided and contentious as its French counterparts. The third German authority in Paris, working alongside and often in conflict with the MBF and Abetz's embassy, was the kingdom of Reichsführer-SS Heinrich Himmler, Hitler's minion in charge of the Reichssicherheitshauptamt (RHSA), the Reich Central Security Office. All its divisions sounded like snakes hissing – the Sicherheitsdienst (SD), the Intelligence Service, the Sicherheitspolizei (SS, SiPo), the security police. The SS wore a death's head on their black caps, and their black uniforms made them as frightening as their secret state police, the Gestapo, the most frightening of them all. Perhaps because of this, all of Himmler's services, whether Gestapo, SD or SS, became known in popular parlance as the Gestapo.

Himmler's deputy, under whom all these organisations so terrifyingly flourished, was Reinhard Heydrich, also responsible for the RHSA's Judenreferat, its Jewish Office. For that office Heydrich's appointed authority in Berlin was Adolf Eichmann. Himmler's police service had offices everywhere in Paris. Its address, as well as that for other miscellaneous and proliferating German police bodies, was 11, rue des Saussaies, formerly the French Sûreté Nationale. Here the French police and the German Gestapo worked together, finally achieving 'twelve torture chambers . . . functioning twenty-four hours per day'.⁴ Also at their disposal were the cells of the rue Lauriston, where French gangsters aped the torture of their Gestapo masters. Hovering around these German and French police services was an army of informers, spies and crooks and members of the public recruited to spy, denounce and inform. For this spider's web of security services the Nazis almost took over the great avenue Foch in Paris, which stretches from the Arc de Triomphe to the Bois de Boulogne. In 1940 a young Nazi, Helmut Knochen, arrived in Paris as senior commander of the SD and SS.⁵ Only thirty years of age, an intellectual who spoke English and French, a journalist with a doctorate in literature, he ran his command from 72, avenue Foch, extending also into numbers 82 and 84. None of his qualifications fitted him to cope with Louis Darquier.

In a typical Nazi arrangement, reporting to Knochen, but also to Eichmann in Berlin was the SS Captain Theodor Dannecker, a young

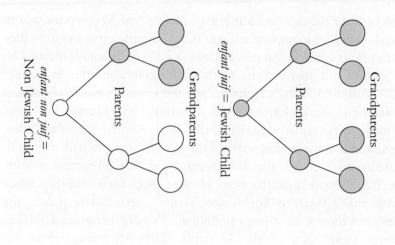

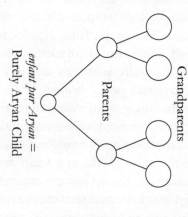

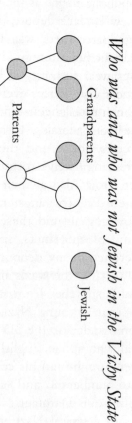

Who was and who was not Jewish in the Vichy State

protégé of Eichmann who had worked for him in Berlin, Vienna and Prague. Dannecker inhabited number 31, avenue Foch, a house which continues to exude a sinister air to this day. He was only twenty-seven when he was sent to Paris in the summer of 1940 to run the Judenreferat.[6] Vallat, in his post-war justifications, called Dannecker 'a mad sadist' deluded by 'frenzied fantasies'.[7] Darquier added to this: for him Theodor Dannecker was a 'raving idiot', and more, mentally ill. Dannecker was generally considered insane, but while he was certainly one of the most fearsome members of those complex and secret services, he was not without competitors.

On the day of the Paris census, 3 October 1940, Pétain signed Vichy's first *Statut des Juifs* (Statute on the Jews), more stringent than the September decree of the Nazis, and more extensive than they had asked for. It was drafted by Raphaël Alibert,[8] Pétain's first Minister of Justice, a Catholic convert and a fellow traveller of Action Française. He defined a Jew by race, not religion: three Jewish grandparents, or two Jewish grandparents if the spouse was also Jewish, were sufficient. Except for special cases – and such exemptions had to be laboriously applied for – Jews were banned from teaching, journalism, film, theatre, radio, the officer corps and the civil service: anywhere they could 'influence' the French race. A *numerus clausus*, a quota of Jews, was to be established in the liberal professions. The next day a second decree permitted the *préfets* of provincial France to round up all foreign Jews and put them into internment camps, or confine them to forced labour. This law made life dangerous for Jews everywhere, for the difference between foreign Jews and French Jews more or less disappeared at this level, and a local functionary could arrest a Jew for any reason whatever. Later that month General Huntziger removed all Jews, officers and men, from the army.

Only the Protestant leader Pastor Marc Boegner[9] made any objection to these laws, though he specified that his objections related only to 'French Israelites', that is to 'well-born' Jews who had been French for generations. The Catholic bishops of France remained silent. The defeated French population had other worries. In public Pétain talked about all his Vichy measures in the high-flown language of moral regeneration, the purification of the French *patrie*, and the establishment of order and authority.

Meanwhile Maurras had taken his newspaper *Action française* first to Limoges and then to Lyon, where he continued to publish throughout the Occupation. Léon Daudet died in July 1942, but a few acolytes remained. Age – he was now in his seventies – did not dim Maurras' capacity for idolatry. Pétain became his King, and though his intractable hostility to Germany remained, in practice it softened under the weight of his approval of what the Nazis, and Vichy, were doing to the Jews of France. Open collaboration with the Germans remained intolerable to him, but collaborate he did because of Pétain.

To his long list of enemies Maurras could now add de Gaulle, and more, any fellow Frenchman or woman who failed to agree with him; denunciation became his chief occupation during the war. His column 'La Politique' still appeared on the front page of Action française, hailing the 'rare and sublime'[10] Pétain or calling 'for hostages and for killing without mercy... that captured Gaullists might be shot out of hand... that if the death penalty is not sufficient to put a stop to the Gaullists, members of their families should be seized as hostages and executed'.[11] Though a number of Maurras' former followers were to join the Resistance, men of Action Française were ubiquitous at Vichy in the early years, writing Pétain's speeches, filling many secondary posts where they could enthusiastically interpret Vichy laws with Maurrassian vigour. Pétain made no objections to any anti-Semitic laws, and signed all of them. He was content as long as he was allowed to make odd exceptions for Jews his wife knew personally, for the occasional 'old French Jew', and in particular for war veterans or any in his entourage.

The men who governed under Pétain at Vichy in these early days were by no means all followers of Maurras, for in the contest between Vichy and the German occupiers over the transfer of Jewish enterprises and the despatch of Jews to Auschwitz, former republicans, socialists and Radicals accepted Vichy's edicts. But not in Paris. Within a month or two the Paris collabos had taken a quick look at Vichy and found it wanting. By September 1940 they were back in the capital, and these men of the extreme right – Jacques Doriot, Marcel Déat, Marcel Bucard, Eugène Deloncle – began to circle round each other, plotting the formation of a state National Socialist Party along Nazi lines.[12] Hitler had no interest in uniting these pro-Nazis into a unified French fascist party, and much German money was spent in fanning the flames of already fiery hostilities. Louis Darquier wanted to lead a national Vichy anti-Semitic movement; he wanted a purified Christian France, not a pagan Nazified patrie. In this manner he managed to alienate everyone.

Of the 330,000 Jews in France at this time, the larger number were in the Vichy Zone – they felt safer there. In their pursuit of Jewish assets, the Germans continued to dump Jews into the Non-Occupied Zone, to the fury of Vichy. For the Jews of France the demarcation line was closed in both directions. Vichy's anti-Semitic laws were for elimination, not death, but its method of ridding itself of undesirables – internment camps – was perfectly adapted to German requirements: they became concentration camps in all but name.

After the fall of the Popular Front, Daladier's government had set up internment camps to detain political refugees, criminals, foreigners in general and communists in particular.[13] By March 1940 nearly three and a half thousand communists had been interned, but the camps multiplied to contain the 350,000 Spanish republican refugees interned in 1938–39, after Franco's victory in the Civil War. German and Italian refugees from their fascist states were also sent to the camps, together with all suspicious persons collected at the outbreak of war in September 1939. So republican France had prepared the ground; the French were used to these camps before the war. They called the internees 'enemy aliens' or 'undesirables', and their internment camps 'centres d'hébergement', lodging centres. Many of the inmates were set to work in special labour groups.

Under Vichy the purpose of the camps changed. Vichy's internees were almost entirely the enemies listed by Maurras. There were fifty-two camps in all, perhaps more, in both zones. Most of them were along the Mediterranean or inland from it, carefully obliterated today to hide them from tourists – Récébédou, Noé, Le Vernet, St-Cyprien, Rivesaltes, Rivel, Argelès, Bram, Agde, Saliers, Langlade, Aubagne, Les Milles and many more. By the end of 1940 something between forty and fifty thousand prisoners were interned in the Vichy Zone.

The worst of the camps were in the Pyrénées. In the most notorious, at Gurs, thirty people died every day during the winter of 1940–41; in its cemetery you can see the graves of more than a thousand, some Spanish republicans, but most Jewish. Hannah Arendt was at Gurs, Arthur Koestler at Le Vernet, which he later described as 'below the level of Nazi concentration camps', Max Ernst at Les Milles. Equally notorious were Pithiviers, Beaune-la-Rolande and Compiègne in the Occupied Zone, and above all, in a north-eastern suburb of Paris, Drancy.

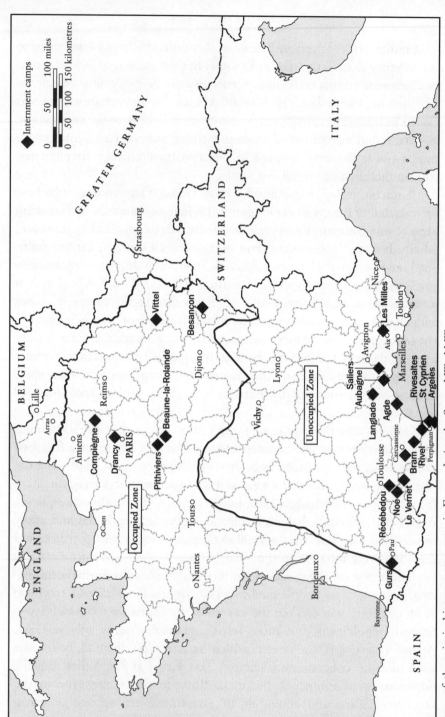

Some of the principal internment camps in France during the Second World War

Drancy, the final camp before transportation, filtered Jews from all over France, usually to Auschwitz. Opened in August 1941, administered by the French and guarded by French police until July 1943 when the Nazi Aloïs Brunner and his SS took over, Drancy today is a massive housing estate near the Drancy-Le Bourget and Bobigny railway stations. In 1941 it was unfinished. There was no electricity or water, and no toilets, but for its first prisoners latrines were dug in the yard and it was surrounded with barbed-wire fences and watchtowers.[14] Drancy was a working-class suburb, but not built-up as it is today. More open land surrounded it then, but there were sufficient members of the working class – subjects considered unimportant witnesses by Vichy – to know what was in their midst. And Drancy saw the worst of it. From 1942 to 1944, sixty-five of the seventy-four convoys that deported 73,853 Jews to German death camps passed through Drancy.[15]

The French camps were run by the Vichy Ministry of the Interior; French police or French military watched over them. Barbed wire, electrified wire, unfurnished and unheated huts, sometimes without windows, sometimes with sealed windows, with polluted drinking water, rotten food, lice, fleas, rats, no latrines; all the usual horrors afflicted these prisons, as did dysentery, pneumonia, tuberculosis, typhus, starvation and death. Malnutrition was the key to most of the diseases that caused such suffering. Corruption was rampant. Between 1939 and 1946 these camps imprisoned 600,000 men, women and children: 350,000 Spanish refugees, 40,000 other foreign nationals, 1,500 political prisoners, 3,000 Gypsies and 100,000 Jews. The Jews were not the only ones deported, though it was mostly the Jews who did not return.

The French concentration camps were not extermination camps, though thousands died in them. They became the source of forced labour for Vichy and for Germany, as slave labour was sucked into the Reich from all the defeated territories to feed the Nazi war effort. By the end of the war in Europe the millions who died 'at work' for Germany in Albert Speer's production programmes became a different, largely overlooked, holocaust. But most of all the French camps became the assembly points for the fulfilment of the Final Solution. Hitler could not spare Germans for this collection work; it was Vichy's CGQJ and its civil and administrative services, and most of all the French police, who carried out his orders. The photographs of the French police in their uniforms and *képis* organising the detention and concentration camps all over

France, rounding up Jews, communists and French dissidents, looking down on the wretched internees or herding them onto trains for the long journey to Auschwitz, are among the most vivid images of the Vichy years, as painful and desolate as all others.

As are the photographs of old women and men who can hardly stand up, the babies and the children and prisoners marked in so many ways. There were at least nine other badges beside the yellow star the Jews were forced to wear. Worn on the left, German political prisoners bore a red triangle, French political prisoners red and black. Jewish political prisoners wore red and yellow, anti-socials black, Gypsies brown, Jehovah's Witnesses purple, stateless persons blue, and ordinary prisoners green. In addition to this there was a red-and-white circular piece of material, exactly like a rifle target, which, worn on the back, signalled that a prisoner should be brought to the attention of the SS.

The stringency of Vichy's *Statut des Juifs* of October 1940, and its compliance with all German decrees freed the Nazis to set in motion the Final Solution for the Jews of France. On 21 January 1941, twelve months before its final formulation at the Wannsee conference, Theodor Dannecker wrote out his blueprint for the Jewish Office he wanted Vichy to create, and for the scope of its activities.[16]

> In accordance with the wishes of the Führer, the Jewish question in those parts of Europe administered or controlled by Germany must be settled definitively once the war is over. The chief of the SS and SD [Heydrich] has already been commanded by the Führer, after negotiations with the Reichsführer SS [Himmler] and the Marshal of the Reich [Goering], to submit a project for the 'final solution'. . . It has been submitted to the Führer and the Marshal of the Reich . . .
>
> For this reason, it is now extremely urgent to create a 'Central Jewish Agency' . . . [17]

At this point, the Final Solution was phrased as 'a carefully established colonisation plan in a territory that is still to be decided'. Thereafter, acting on instructions from Goering, the German authorities met every Tuesday in Dannecker's office. Joining Dannecker were representatives of the MBF; from the embassy came Abetz or his 'men of steel', notably Consul-General Rudolf Schleier, an 'uncompromising party man'.[18] Also in attendance was Baron Colonel Kurt von Behr, Alfred Rosenberg's

19. Anne, *c.* 1933, one of the photos which accompanied begging letters from Louis and Myrtle to René Darquier throughout the thirties.

20. Anne with May Brice, with whom she was brought up. May was the niece of Elsie and Maud Lightfoot, *c.* 1936.

21. Louis and Myrtle, 1931. Re-financed – and soon to be re-suited – by his brother René, Louis is ready to launch himself again upon literary and fashionable life in London.

22. Place de la Concorde, Paris, the riots of 6 February 1934. Louis was at the front of the fray.

23. The removal of the wounded, of whom Louis was one, from Place de la Concorde, 6 February 1934.

24. The funeral of Lucien Garniel, who died from his wounds after the riots. Members of the 'Association of the Wounded and the Victims of 6 February' amidst a crowd of 2500 persons, march towards Place Lafayette, where Louis, their founder and President, awaited them with the family of the dead boy.

25. Colonel François de la Roque, leader of Croix-de-feu at the Arc de Triomphe, 14 July 1935.

26. The nationalist leagues on the streets of Paris, 1934. Solidarité française, Croix-de-feu and the Camelots du Roi of Action Française.

(*Left*) 27. François Coty, the perfume and cosmetics baron, whose talcum powder funded numerous parties and newspapers of the far right, including his own nationalist league Solidarité française and newspapers, *Ami du peuple* and *Le Figaro*.
(*Right*) 28. Eugène Schueller, founder and proprietor of L'Oréal. He and his beauty empire found it worth it to finance the most extreme – and murderous – of the fascist leagues and movements before, during and after the Second World War. After the Liberation, L'Oréal became, and continued to be, a hiding place for many French war criminals.

29. Pierre Taittinger, 1942, right-wing politician, admirer of Mussolini and Hitler, a powerful Catholic whose champagne and newspaper wealth enabled him to found his own league, Jeunesses Patriotes, and to wield vast power in many spheres, notably from the Paris city council at the Hôtel de Ville.

30. Pierre Taittinger's league, Jeunesses Patriotes, at the Salle Wagram, 1928.

31. In the middle, Taittinger's colleague and Louis' patron and supporter, Charles Trochu, towering over his fellow councillors during his tenure as President of the Paris city council at the Hôtel de Ville, 1941–43.

32. Charles Trochu arranged for Louis' election to the Paris city council in 1935: Louis' campaign leaflet, a fantastical document full of fabrications about his past, present and hoped-for future.

33. One of many similar covers of the many French editions of *The Protocols of the Elders of Sion*. This one, published *c.* 1934 could be Henry Coston's.

M. Darquier de Pellepoix
a comparu en correctionnelle
pour un article diffamatoire

Il est condamné
à trois mois de prison

C'est la première application du décret-loi du 25 avril 1939

M. Darquier de Pellepoix, conseiller municipal du quartier des Ternes, était traduit hier devant la 12e chambre du tribunal correctionnel de la Seine, présidée par M. Roux, pour avoir publié dans son journal *la France enchaînée*, le 31 mai 1939, un violent article contre les israélites.

Cette poursuite constituait la première application du décret-loi du 25 avril 1939 qui réprime « les diffamations envers les groupes de personnes qui appartiennent par leur origine à une race ou à une religion déterminée, en vue d'exciter la haine entre les citoyens ou les habitants » et les punit de peines allant de cinq jours à six mois d'emprisonnement et d'une amende de 25 à 2.000 francs.

M. Darquier de Pellepoix fit une

M. Darquier de Pellepoix pendant son interrogatoire

34. Louis Darquier appearing in court July 1939, charged with disseminating propaganda on behalf of a foreign power. With him, most probably, is his side kick and fellow accused, Pierre Gérard. Louis' newspaper *La France enchaînée* 15–31 July 1939

35. José Felix de Lequerica, Spanish Catholic and fascist, ruthless anti-Republican, ambassador to France and Vichy, arch collaborator during the war; after it Spanish Minister of Foreign Affairs, then ambassador to the USA and the United Nations.

representative in Paris. Rosenberg was the official philosopher of the Nazi Party, but his Einsatzstab Reichsleiter Rosenberg (ERR) was given an extra duty – the sequestration of the art collections, archives and libraries of Jews and other enemies. Together these men determined upon action against the Jews, agreed on the need for a central agency and discussed how to achieve the compliance of Vichy. The 'Central Jewish Agency' became the Commissariat for Jewish Affairs, the CGQJ, which Vichy set up for Dannecker in March 1941. Unlike other Vichy departments, it was given power in both zones to ensure that the appropriation of Jewish assets would be diverted into French, not German hands. Vichy's specifications for this 'Ministry for Anti-Semitism' were quite simple:

> The CGQJ was responsible for the preparation of all laws relating to the removal of Jews from the French body politic, for the implementation of all the government decrees concerning Jews, for the encouragement of other government ministries to do likewise, for the liquidation of Jewish property, for the appointment of trustees to do this, for the supervision of these trustees, and for the initiation of police measures against Jews as dictated by the general interest.[19]

At much the same time, in the interests of divide and rule, the Germans moved swiftly to provide a gathering point for all the disputatious anti-Semites of Paris, who looked upon Vichy's considerable efforts as grossly inadequate. The German propaganda office for this purpose was the Institut d'Étude des Questions Juives (IEQJ), the Institute for the Study of Jewish Questions, which was provided with its own shock troops of rabble-rousers, and offices at 21, rue la Boétie in Paris.

During Louis' absence, Captain Paul Sézille, the strangest and most inebriated of all his pre-war brethren, had formed a Communauté Française and taken on Louis' Anti-Jewish Union, organising meetings, publishing brochures and nagging Vichy to do more about the Jews. Dannecker, after some months' experience of dealing with the over-enthusiasm of men such as Petit and Coston, placed Sézille in charge of the IEQJ and made it directly responsible to Baron von Behr of Rosenberg's office.

On 11 May 1941 the Germans allowed Sézille to inaugurate his new empire, an occasion marked by violent altercations when Sézille attacked one of the invitees whom he took for a Jewish spy. All the usual suspects attended, as well as their cultural patrons in the shape of Rebatet and Céline. Sézille and his fellows informed and spied and assisted the Gestapo in arresting Jews, searching their houses, appropriating their property. They were paid for such work. Many of Louis' old colleagues in his Anti-Jewish Union resurfaced in the IEQJ. Louis, who wanted the Vichy job, did not, for Vichy and Paris were already at war over the subject of Jews.

In Xavier Vallat,[20] Vichy's first Commissioner for Jewish Affairs, Dannecker had to accept considerable frustration. Vallat, a friend of Maurras, was Pétain's choice for the job, and in its first year his CGQJ was very much a Vichy/Action Française construct. Vallat's militant Catholicism, absorbed in his rural childhood in Provence, was also shaped by the rabidly anti-Semitic Catholic journal *Le Pèlerin*. He was only six years older than Louis Darquier, not as tall but equally hefty. In the First World War Vallat, wounded three times, won the Légion d'honneur but lost a leg and an eye, and wore a black eyepatch thereafter. In photographs this patch echoes Darquier's monocle, so that both Vichy's Commissioners for Jewish Affairs seem similarly one-eyed.

Vallat's anti-Semitism was carefully defined. He called his philosophy state anti-Semitism, '*antisémitisme de l'État français*', 'inspired by the doctrine of the Church',[21] and indeed at his trial after the war he used this as a defence. He repeatedly claimed the support of the Church, its teachers and its teaching, both historically and during the Vichy years. He would be governed, Vallat stated, by 'neither hatred nor reprisals', but by 'simply the strict defence of the national interest'.[22] The anti-Semitic regime he created and handed on to Louis Darquier was the most elaborate and the most severe in Europe. As a French patriot, Vallat wanted to eliminate Jews in a French, not a German, way. He insisted again and again that his, Alibert's and Vichy's anti-Semitic laws were of a piece – French, not German or Nazi, but Catholic, natural, established by precedent and by the views of St Thomas Aquinas. And so Vallat – and many of his punctilious Vichy comrades – proved themselves to be as compulsive in their way as Louis Darquier.

In a twenty-thousand-word essay he wrote in Fresnes prison after the war, Vallat traced the spiritual ancestry of Catholic anti-Semitism from St Paul and St Thomas Aquinas to Charles the Bald, and pointed to fifty-seven bulls issued by twenty-nine Popes between 1217 and 1755 to prevent 'Jewish saturation' of Catholic life. 'Let us understand this point clearly,' wrote Vallat. 'It is not a matter of taking Rome as a shield, and of finding in ancient pontifical texts some absolution for a political fault. We are not "pleading guilty with attenuating circumstances". It is simply a matter of proving, in intellectual honesty, against those who accuse the Marshal's government of having been a servile plagiarist of the Nazis, that this anti-Jewish legislation, as distinct from that across the Rhine, never went beyond the just limits established by the Church in accordance with the right of protecting the national community against the abuses and harmful influence of a foreign element.'[23] In practice Vallat's philosophy led to an investigation of French Jewishness which was morbid, pernickety and ridiculous.

The new Minister of Justice, the distinguished lawyer Joseph Barthélemy, prepared with Vallat the second Vichy *Statut des Juifs*, issued on 2 June 1941.[24] Vallat's new law, which widened and replaced the earlier Vichy decree, provided for a census of Jews, as newly defined, in the Vichy Zone and changed the reasons for which they could be dismissed from their jobs. It also broadened their removal from industrial, commercial and artisan sectors. It combined extended exclusion for Jews from most walks of life, totally forbidding them from others – markedly anything to do with money or the media – with a convoluted list of specific criteria to protect more carefully the 'old' French Jews. 'French Jews', 'Israelites', were defined by Pétain and Vallat as all Jews who had 'rendered exceptional service to the state, or whose families have been established in France for at least five generations or whose families have rendered meritorious service'.[25]

After this Vallat was still unhappy, for he discovered that 'since the publication of the last decree many Jews have converted to Catholicism, a move very much disapproved of by most Jews'.[26] The Germans knew that the exceptions applied to 'old' French Jews were a sticking point with both Pétain and Vallat, and attributed this to Pétain's desire not to alienate the United States.

During Darlan's fourteen months in power, Pétain's lofty visions for his National Revolution had fallen by the wayside as technocrats and civil servants took over. These were an efficient bunch of men, with a touch about them of Mussolini's railway-station fascism.[27] With no parliamentary impedimenta to slow down the execution of their plans, they had a free hand to instigate change from above. There was a barrage of new decrees: on 16 July 1941 the number of Jews permitted to practise law was limited to two per cent; on 22 July the confiscation of Jewish property and enterprises was authorised; on 13 August Jews were prohibited the possession of a radio; on 15 August Jewish doctors, chemists and midwives joined lawyers in the same two per cent limitation; on 24 September architects were added.

Charles Maurras applauded and praised everything, encouraged further improvements and objected to the 'inordinate fuss' that shortly began, particularly the murmurs of 'unpatriotic Christians' and prelates.[28] The French judiciary fully participated in applying Pétain's enormous raft of laws, as did its civil servants. Many of those involved in the fate of the Jews were men of the law. Laval and Vallat were lawyers, so was Dannecker and his successor, SS-Hauptsturmbannführer Heinz R. Röthke.

To complement the Paris *fichier*, Vallat's new *statut* instituted a census of Jews in the Vichy Zone. This resulted in a list of 180,000 Jews, though Vallat fretted that up to ten per cent more remained unaccounted for. Added to that of the Paris census, this provided 330,000 Jews, an efficient basis for the round-ups to come. The conscientious care with which the *préfets* and their officers carried out this census is revealed in a host of memos and instructions and in the final, tragic lists.

Both Vichy and the Nazis shared a view about the omnipotent wealth of the Jews. The results from the Aude revealed otherwise. The French official who took the census in this southern department first divided the 765 Jews he tracked down into French Jews and Foreign Jews (only 239 of the French Jews and 350 of the foreigners had actually filled in the census). He then categorised them by business or other identification. Then he looked for the others. There are many annotations and additions on this report in the handwriting of this diligent flunkey. 'Children are often left off the declarations,' he noted. Near the name of Cohen, Oscar, salesman, living in Carcassone, he annotated in his best script the names of six more Jews he discovered in nearby villages who had not filled in the census. One of them, Eliazar Davidovici of Esperaza, he presumed to be Jewish because of his name; another had no name, being recorded only as 'One (1) Jew, thatch merchant, rue du Pont'. 'In the department of the Aude,' he reported, 'there are few Jews, none of them very active, they arouse little sympathy.'[29] As to wealth, the occupations of the Jews on his list included: salesman, soldier, prisoner of war, hospital worker, shopkeeper, travelling hosier. Each department of France carried out similar investigations, and made similar reports, with widely varying degrees of enthusiasm.

At the end of this month of intense anti-Jewish activity in Vichy, on 22 June 1941 Hitler invaded Russia and laid the foundations for his own defeat. While the French Communist Party was always at war with the Vichy state, which imprisoned its members by the thousands, it continued to prevaricate over collaboration with the German occupiers as long as Hitler and Stalin's Nazi–Soviet pact endured.[30] Germany's declaration of war on Russia released loyal communists to fight both the Nazi and the Vichy state; henceforward the Communist Party was at the forefront of the Resistance. At the same time Hitler's plan for the destruction of Soviet Russia, Operation Barbarossa, also liberated the Paris *collabos*, who could now combine their pro-Nazi position with the defence of Christianity.

At the Majestic, the headquarters of the MBF, a unique gathering of all the fascist rivals took place – Doriot, Déat, Deloncle and others. With the priestly blessing of Cardinal Baudrillart of Paris and of their chaplain, the bellicose Monseigneur Mayol de Lupé, who liked to end Mass with the cry '*Heil Hitler!*', the Légion des Volontaires Français contre le Bolchevisme (LVF), the Legion of French Volunteers against Bolshevism, was born. Pétain's message, blown up beneath a vast poster of himself, was: 'IN JOINING THE CRUSADE LED BY GERMANY, THEREBY GAINING THE UNDENIABLE RIGHT TO WORLD GRATITUDE, YOU ARE PLAYING YOUR PART IN WARDING OFF THE BOLSHEVIK PERIL FROM OUR LAND.'[31] In a rare instance of unity, French fascists and their followers now donned German uniform, swore an oath of loyalty to Hitler and marched off to fight the Soviet army.

And so, in July 1941, when Louis Darquier felt confident enough to get his identity card from the authorities, Vichy had created a world in which he could happily flourish. The Nazis had already begun to exterminate communists and Jews in Eastern Europe. Dannecker received further instructions from Berlin:

Order from Hermann Goering to Reinhard Heydrich, Berlin, July 31, 1941
To Gruppenführer Heydrich:
Supplementing the task assigned to you by the decree of January

24, 1939, to solve the Jewish problem by means of emigration and evacuation in the best possible way according to present conditions, I hereby charge you to carry out preparations as regards organisational, financial, and material matters for a total solution [Gesamtlösung] of the Jewish question in all the territories of Europe under German occupation.

Where the competency of other central organisations touches on this matter, these organisations are to collaborate.

I charge you further to submit to me as soon as possible a general plan of the administrative material and financial measures necessary for carrying out the desired final solution [Endlösung] of the Jewish question.

Goering[32]

July 1941 was therefore the beginning of the end for French Jews. In preparing them for their future, Vallat regularly redefined who they were. German racial theory, dividing humankind into Aryan and non-Aryan, was much simpler than this tortured Vichy system which injected religion into its racial laws.* Vallat's achievements added up to the eighteen

---

* A person was a Jew if he or she had three Jewish grandparents, whether or not they had been baptised. So was anyone with two Jewish grandparents if they were married to someone half-Jewish. A person might also be considered Jewish if he or she had two grandparents and no baptismal certificate dated before 25 June 1940.

Miscellaneous sects took up a great deal of time. Were Mosaic Georgians, Karaites, Jugutis, Subbotniks, Ismaelites, Jewish or not? Mosaic Georgians, for instance, accepted the Torah but not the Talmud; all fifty of them living in France in 1941 came under intense scrutiny. Vichy considered them Jewish for religious reasons; the Nazis did not. The 270 Karaites in France were considered Jewish by the CGQJ, while the Catholic Church, when consulted, considered them as 'leaning more towards Islam than the Jewish religion'. The Germans did not consider Karaites to be Jewish. Vallat and Vichy agonised. An additional problem with Moslems and Armenians was that they could sometimes be Jewish. An Armenian Jew was a possibility. Muslims were often Semites and were sometimes circumcised, which complicated life for that rich inspector of this sexual organ Georges Montandon. Then there were illegitimate children to consider, and, most worrying, children of mixed race. Here, more than anything else, blood spurts out of the myriad papers, memos and instructions of the Vichy state. Two sets of racial blood flowing together: was it Jewish? Was it Christian? How can you trace the grandparents of illegitimate children who know not from whence they come? When first cousins married, with fewer than two Jewish grandparents each, such a marriage might well provide them with the necessary quota for imprisonment. Many preposterous and tragic circumstances surround the rows between the German occupying force, Vichy France and Vallat and Darquier on these subjects.

laws, eighteen executive orders, sixty-seven texts and 397 articles in all. The mountain of discussion Vichy's CGQJ left behind as to what exactly constitutes a Jewish human being is at once exhaustive, frenzied and ludicrous. Tortuous definitions added to the number of persons Vichy could arrest. It also meant that some Jews were Jewish in the Vichy Zone, but not Jewish in the German Zone, and placed an enormous burden on the Jews of France to find the necessary proof of ancestry or religious adherence. This led to corruption on a vast scale. Clerical records were tinkered with, documents were forged, blank forms and baptismal certificates paid for, as were the CGQJ's *Certificats de Non-Appartenance à la Race Juive* (certificates of non-adherence to the Jewish race), introduced in October 1941.

To keep an eye on all this, Vichy's Ministry of the Interior formed the Police aux Questions Juives (PQJ), Police for Jewish Affairs, in October 1941. Vallat and Dannecker tussled over the control of this force, but the Jewish people spied upon, pursued, arrested and interned by these French policemen of the PQJ would hardly have noticed any difference between Dannecker's grip on its Parisian office in the rue Greffulhe, or Vallat's firm control in the Vichy Zone.[33]

There were more Vichy decrees, and Vallat left behind a third *Statut des Juifs*, in many versions, each draft aimed at tightening the law, zealously striving for a perfect definition of the Jew, which he ultimately

The certificate of Aryan blood issued by Louis and Vichy's CGQJ.

achieved, for Dannecker accepted Vallat's definition: '. . . being broader [it] will now serve as a basis in all doubtful cases'.[34]

In the summer of 1941 Dannecker offered Louis Darquier the opportunity to set up an exhibition, financed by Otto Abetz, *Le Juif et la France*, The Jew and France. Darquier declined, though he made it perfectly clear that he was available for higher things. Paul Sézille took the exhibition on, and it opened at the Palais Berlitz in the boulevard des Italiens on 5 September. Over a quarter of a million Parisians went to see how the Jews had strangled France and now controlled the black market. Using Nazi and French material – slogans, cartoons, paintings, films, graphics, caricatures – Sézille presented an unending sequence of 'Jewish noses', curly hair and curling fingernails; Jews in the movies, Jews as journalists, writers, painters; rich Jews, famous Jews, Jews as whores, Jews as bankers. Vichy disliked such obvious racism, and Xavier Vallat refused to attend the official opening; in pursuit of Vallat's job, so did Louis Darquier. Otherwise *le tout Paris*, German and collaborationist, was there, and the exhibition went on to attract packed audiences in Bordeaux and Nancy.

After the Vichy internment law of October 1940, Protestants, Quakers and international relief agencies came to the aid of the internees. With many exceptions, throughout the Occupation, the French Catholic Church provided essential support for Pétain and Vichy, their difficulties exacerbated by required obedience to a most unfortunate Pope, the Italian Eugenio Pacelli, who in March 1939 became Pius XII. Obsessed with the fear of communism, from 1930 onwards Pacelli strove for, and achieved, alliances through diplomatic means with any state that could be considered as a bulwark against it.

Accommodating Hitler was only one of the terrible mistakes made by Pius XII in his attempts to destroy Bolshevism, perhaps one of the most bizarre being that though he condemned Nazism, German Catholics were never excommunicated for belonging to the Nazi Party or for voting for, or supporting, Hitler.[35] Catholics who became communists, on the other hand, of whom there were so many in France, were automatically excommunicated. Hitler, Stalin and Mussolini were irreligious, but Pétain, Franco and Salazar, unchristian certainly, were not, and paid lip service to the tenets of the Catholic Church. If the Pope had spoken out against the treatments of Jews, communists and dissidents, his influence would have been considerable.

Instead, throughout the war the Vatican remained silent on the fate of the Jews. On 31 October 1942, in the year which saw the implementation of the Final Solution throughout Europe, when seven hundred thousand Jews were murdered in Poland alone, the Pope consecrated the world to the Immaculate Heart of Mary. Despite worldwide pleading, including a request from President Roosevelt, Pius XII failed to condemn Nazi war crimes and Nazi Germany to the end. His culpability is much debated, and his good works during the war, of which there were many, are often enumerated in his defence. But no debate can mitigate the silence which ensured the collusion of the large community of German Catholics in Nazi persecution of the Jews.

In France this hobbled the Catholic hierarchy. The most virulent among them was Cardinal Baudrillart, eighty-one years old in 1940. He supported the Nazis 'as a priest and a Frenchman . . . should I refuse to approve this noble common enterprise, in which Germany is taking the lead?' His fellow cardinals, Cardinal Liénart of Lille, Cardinal Suhard of Paris and Cardinal Gerlier of Lyon, all greeted the arrival of Pétain with fervour, and regarded the fall of France and its occupation as a punishment. As the Bishop of Nantes put it: 'France has driven Christ from the law courts and schools. She has expelled the religious congregations. She has systematically and deliberately destroyed all faith in the souls of too many of its children. She has tolerated vice, immorality and wrong. She has undermined the family by divorce and suppressed the birth rate.'[36]

Gerlier twinned Pétain with Franco as '*un chef magnifique*', and 'speaking on behalf of the Church in France', said: 'France needed a leader to guide her towards her eternal destiny. God permitted that you should be there.'[37] In December 1940 Otto Abetz reported to Berlin: 'Cardinal Suhard, the Archbishop of Paris, assures me that the French clergy is ready to act in favour of French collaboration with Germany. The Church has given instructions in this direction to the French clergy . . . that the national interest of France today and in the future lies in close collaboration, and not in hostility to Germany.'[38]

Thousands of priests and their flock did not obey; more thousands did. Cardinal Suhard joined Pétain's council of ministers, while Gerlier and Liénart often changed their attitudes as the true nature of Pétain's Vichy state revealed itself over the coming years. Selective sympathy towards the plight of the Jews in France, and of the French people in general, often moved them to intervene with both the German occupiers and the Vichy government. Yet despite the exceptions they made,

both cardinals, like the others, condoned horrific acts by silent acqui-
escence.

Gerlier, asked to do so by a Jewish Catholic priest, was the only
cardinal to object to the camps, but he delegated the matter and Vichy
changed nothing. Gerlier also oversaw relief work and cooperated with
the Protestant Church to help refugees and Jews, but his humanity was
always drowned by obedience to the Vatican, which did not challenge
the legality of Vichy's anti-Semitic discrimination. Much of the population of France shared the Vatican's inaction only in the early years of
the German Occupation; after the deportations began, both the public
and Gerlier protested.

Discussing Vichy's anti-Semitic laws with Vallat, Gerlier said, 'No
one knows better than I the enormous harm the Jews have done to
France . . . No one supports more zealously than I the policies of Marshal
Pétain . . . it is in its application that justice and charity are lacking.'[39]
Pétain, disquieted, instructed his envoy at the Vatican to sound out the
papal position, and was reassured that there was nothing 'intrinsically
wrong' with Vichy's anti-Jewish statutes. Vallat was assured that the
papacy would not make trouble over the issue: 'The Holy Father does
not disapprove of the recent anti-Jewish measures.' When some Catholic
clergy asked for condemnation of the Jewish laws from the Assembly
of Cardinals and Archbishops, they were told to bow to the wishes of
their rulers. The position of the Catholic hierarchy was fatal for the Jews
of France, because now that Pétain ruled without Parliament, the Catholic
Church was the strongest institution left in France, and moreover it had
influence at Vichy.[40]

Theodor Dannecker had never been able to impose upon Vallat his
desire for an anti-Semitic propaganda machine, so he had made use of
what was to hand in Paris, Captain Sézille and the Paris *collabos*. They
hated Vallat, and he reciprocated; Vallat was too Catholic, too soft, a
'Jew-lover', to these men of the extreme right, and they attacked him
remorselessly in their venomous newspapers and journals, demanding
his replacement. Dannecker obtained 'unfavourable details' about Vallat's
private life.

Céline despised Pétain – 'Philip the Last', he called him – and Vichy's
approach to the Jewish question. He was also dissatisfied with the
continued animosities of his Parisian colleagues, who were well on the
way towards providing fifty-six anti-Semitic parties and associations,

squabbling angrily amongst themselves for Reichsmarks. 'Are you racists,' he bellowed, 'like Hitler, like all National Socialists? If not, what are you?' In December 1941 he organised a meeting with the anti-Semitic paper *Au Pilori*, with a view to forming one united anti-Semitic party. It was only two days after Pearl Harbor, and Germany had just declared war on the USA. Only nine of the twenty-six anti-Semitic notables he invited came to the meeting. Louis Darquier refused to attend because he considered *Au Pilori* to be 'in the pay of the Germans'.[41] Instead he shook out his old Anti-Jewish Union, and wrote to Georges Montandon and asked him to join him again. Montandon agreed. The round-ups of Jews in France had already begun – there had been one in May, another in August. A week after the third round-up, of 12 December 1941, the French police were asked to provide a full dossier of information about Louis Darquier.

Knowing that he was to replace Vallat, Louis felt secure enough to collaborate with Sézille and to express the 'independent views' which would not altogether alienate Vichy, but which would please his Germans too.[42] On 15 March 1942 he wrote a piece for the first issue of the IEQJ's publication *La Question juive en France et dans le monde* (The Jewish Question in France and in the World). After trawling through the history of the Jewish destruction of France and saluting his heroes from Drumont and the Marquis de Morès onwards, after attacking and repeatedly misspelling Dreyfuss (sic) and guardedly awarding Hitler honours in the anti-Semitic struggle, he concluded in full Célinian mode:

> Personally, I could not be less German. Born in the south-west of France I am a Celt or Celt Iberian with a solidly Roman culture.
>
> I can claim to know better than anyone what I owe to the soil of France. I have defended it twice to the best of my abilities, as did my father, brothers and my many forefathers before that . . .
>
> Today, the (not-so-well) hidden Jews continue their underground work while the government looks on indulgently.
>
> Today, as in the past, in the two Jewish poles of finance and revolution, in Washington and Moscow, a clever offensive is being prepared to deliver France to slavery . . . [43]

By the end of 1941 Dannecker had almost everything in place for the Final Solution. In November he had finally coerced Vichy and the

Jewish community to set up the 'enforced Jewish association' he wanted. After the usual tussles over power and principle, Vallat collaborated with Dannecker over the foundation of the Union Générale des Israélites de France – UGIF – and this too was placed under the control of the CGQJ.[44] All Jews had to pay a tithe to UGIF; all were forced to belong to it. With offices in Occupied and non-Occupied France, UGIF superseded all the various charitable Jewish associations which had catered to the relentlessly increasing needs of the Jewish community of France, both citizen and refugee.

Thus UGIF was forced to enact that most horrific of Hitler's methods: Jews now serviced, and paid for, their own persecution and death, for, to the horror of old French 'Israelites', they were now lumped together with their immigrant Jewish brethren. Worse, when the Resistance began to show its face, German military command insisted on reprisals. Communists and Jews became interchangeable, and hundreds were shot. A billion-franc fine was imposed on UGIF, paid in March 1942 as the first trains left Paris for Auschwitz. The money to pay it came from UGIF's assets, those of the old French Jews, for the immigrant Jewish population had hardly a sou to its name.

The German round-up of Jews in December had included many of the French Jews whom Pétain protested so often that he wanted to protect. These prominent French Jews were arrested at the end of a December week in which the Japanese bombed Pearl Harbor, the Allies declared war on Japan, Germany declared war on the United States, and the United States entered the war. Britain remained pugnacious and undefeated. Australia turned from tending the European war to fighting the Japanese in the Pacific; GIs flooded into Australia too. The famous magazine *l'Illustration*, by 1942 so firmly collaborationist that it was closed down forever at the Liberation, kept Myrtle unhappily informed. On the Eastern Front the German army had to abandon its attack on Moscow, and the Soviet counter-offensive had begun.

Pétain and Darlan had been convinced that the USA would never enter the war. That it did was the second nail in the coffin of Nazi Germany, and so of the Vichy state. Winds of hope began to rouse the French population from compliance in defeat. The relief and salvation expected from 'Papa' Pétain began to give way first to resignation, in time to resistance. The V (for victory) sign began to appear on walls, German ammunition was stolen, communications cut, and there were

L'AUSTRALIE
EN DANGER

■

ON avait déjà signalé avant la guerre le danger pour l'Empire britannique de l'attraction exercée par les Etats-Unis sur le Canada, l'Australie et la Nouvelle-Zélande. En 1924, un homme politique anglais, sir Auckland Geddes, n'avait pas craint de le proclamer dans un discours d'un certain retentissement.

« Les dominions britanniques qui ont une façade sur le Pacifique, avait-il dit, sentent bien qu'à Washington la compréhension de leurs difficultés est, en quelque sorte, instinctive. Lorsqu'ils viennent à Londres, au contraire, ils ne réussissent que laborieusement à faire saisir leur point de vue aux autorités de Downing Street... S'étant tournés vers la mère patrie et n'ayant pas trouvé toute la compréhension désirée, ils sont susceptibles de se retourner vers Washington, qui, sachant voir, saurait aussi leur répondre. »

Ces lignes, vieilles de dix-sept ans, sont d'une bien cruelle actualité ! Il ne faut donc pas s'étonner aujourd'hui quand on voit le Premier australien demander aux Etats-Unis plus encore qu'à l'Angleterre l'appui militaire dont il a besoin et que l'on entend M. Churchill annoncer aux Communes le partage de la zone de combat du Pacifique entre les hauts commandements anglais et américain, l'Australie et la Nouvelle-Zélande étant comprises dans la sphère des Etats-Unis.

Au point de vue des Australiens, la crise a été déterminée surtout par la rapide avance des Japonais dans la Nouvelle-Guinée, en particulier à Rabaul. Il s'agit là, en effet, de « colonies de la couronne britannique » confiées à la gestion du gouvernement australien (1901) et d'anciennes possessions allemandes placées par la Société des Nations sous la juridiction de Canberra.

Rabaul, principal centre des îles sous mandat et leur capitale administrative, est un point inté-

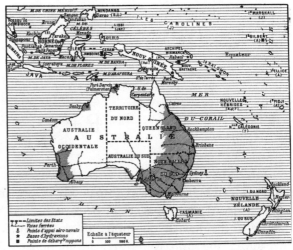

Le grisé indique les régions habitées.

fait qu'en temps normal le gouvernement fédéral n'avait pas de raison sérieuse de posséder un établissement militaire important. Après la crise de Munich, en effet, et la mainmise japonaise sur la Chine du Sud, le gouvernement de Canberra s'était décidé à un effort militaire assez sérieux. En trois mois, de décembre 1938 à mars 1939, l'armée permanente : 1.500 instructeurs seulement, fut portée à 10.000 hommes ; les réserves organisées, de 35.000 à 70.000 hommes, c'est-à-dire de quoi former 5 divisions d'infanterie et 2 de cavalerie, pour lesquelles le matériel existait. Bien que les Australiens soient légalement soumis à la

dant qui avait presque doublé de l'exercice 1938 à l'exercice 1939, année au cours de laquelle il avait pour la première fois dépassé le milliard. Cette marine comprenait au début de la guerre 2 croiseurs lourds, 4 croiseurs légers, dont 3 incorporés en 1938-1939, 5 destroyers, 2 escorteurs, une demi-douzaine de bâtiments divers. Elle avait sur cale 2 destroyers, 2 escorteurs, 12 vedettes rapides. On sait que, depuis, d'autres destroyers et de nombreux escorteurs ont été lancés. Une partie de ces bâtiments ont été construits par l'arsenal de la marine australienne, installé à Sydney, dans l'Ile Cockatoo.

Dès le premier jour de la guerre, l'Australie a

'Australia in Danger,' *l'Illustration*, 14 February 1942.

defections from Pétain, particularly amongst those on the left.

However much it pleased Myrtle, Louis did not like the growing disillusionment of the French people or the 'thunderous rounds of applause for England [he] witnessed in Parisian cinemas'. He told the German embassy how superior he would be as an alternative to Sézille and his team, whom he called a bunch of 'rogues, imbeciles and untrustworthy elements'.[45]

The German command was not happy with Vallat. Vichy had given him full powers to implement total Aryanisation, but economic rewards from the Vichy Zone were far inferior to those in the German Zone. They considered Vallat's French laws too lenient, and wanted them to include French Jews too. Vichy's police force, the PQJ, was, Dannecker felt, insufficiently robust under Vallat.

After Pearl Harbor the decision was taken. The MBF, Abetz, Dannecker and the SS initiated angry rows with Vallat; in March 1942 they sacked him, and gave Louis Darquier his job.[46]

14

Rats

LOUIS DARQUIER WAS CHOSEN by German command 'solely for reasons of propaganda', because he had 'the correct conception of the Jewish question'. In the months preceding his official investiture, the embassy buffed up his public persona with a round of publicity engagements. He was advised to proceed tactfully with Vichy, and to restrain his 'too energetic' manner until Vichy accepted his appointment. He gave his usual radio broadcast on 6 February 1942, various anti-Jewish conferences were arranged for him – and it appears that he was told to rid himself of encumbrances which Vichy would not tolerate, for he had rejoined Myrtle in January.[1]

At Vichy they knew about the 'complex activities' of Louis' tumultuous private life, which had given him such a bad reputation, and Myrtle so much to put up with. But her approach to his beatings, temper tantrums and infidelities remained fixed: 'Louis is Louis and there are a great many worse than he is.' During their separation in 1941 Myrtle had moved into the fleapit which was the Hôtel Fortuny at 35, rue de l'Arcade, a place of rabbit-warren rooms, with walls so thin that their rows and the blows they exchanged could leap from one room to another.

Myrtle needed comfort in early 1942, because in addition to her dismay over the plight of Britain, on the radio Lord Haw-Haw broadcast German propaganda on the progress of the war in North Africa, where for five months Australian soldiers – he called them 'Rats' – were holding out against Rommel at the siege of Tobruk. Then, on 15 February, Singapore fell. Four days later the Japanese bombed Darwin and the Pacific war was now on Australia's doorstep.

In the following months Louis was a busy man, although nothing could prepare him for the responsibilities he was about to be given. Now forty-four years old, he had lived on his wits all his life; he was now to take over 'a hybrid body whose multiple organs formed a complex and grotesque whole'.[2] By 1942 the CGQJ had acquired vast powers, and it was to be given more almost immediately. Louis began to entertain old cronies and various CGQJ employees in Parisian bars, promising them jobs or promotion. In January 1942 Sézille, ever vigilant, warned Vallat of the plots Louis was hatching. Carl Theo Zeitschel, the malevolently anti-Semitic former ship's doctor who was Abetz's specialist on Jewish affairs at the embassy and their liaison with the SS, noted in March that the Jewish round-ups could be put on hold to await Darquier's arrival. Louis discussed his plans with Dannecker. The security service continued to observe him, and on 12 March noted that he was to become the new commissioner as soon as the Vichy government could be cajoled into accepting him. This took nearly two months.

A number of Vichy ministers opposed Louis' appointment. Pétain's men of Vichy rejected the 'vulgar anti-Semitic elements' of the Paris *collabos*, of whom they considered Louis Darquier to be an extreme example. As far as money was concerned, Vallat was an honest man. He begged Darlan not to appoint Louis, 'quite simply because he had a reputation for being hard-up. (There is nothing wrong with being hard-up if you have no expensive habits; but a hard-up man with expensive habits is always dangerous in a position like this ...)' In private Vallat was much ruder: Darquier, with his manias and swindles, would be a catastrophe.[3]

During Darlan's time in charge of Vichy's government, neither he nor his ministers had managed to achieve the longed-for peace treaty with Germany. When Pétain moved to replace Darlan, he was again in disfavour. From February to April, Blum, Daladier, Reynaud, Gamelin and Georges Mandel were on trial at Riom, accused of a variety of seditions which included sending France to war, unprepared, at the behest of Britain and against the advice of Pétain and Weygand. The brilliant advocacy of Léon Blum made the trial such a fiasco of embarrassment for Pétain that German pressure and Vichy discomfort brought a stop to it.[4]

Anatole de Monzie kept in touch with Otto Abetz and the embassy in Paris. In these strange weeks *The Times* in London reported that de Monzie was heading a group of leading French politicians in an attempt to unseat Pétain, and that Laval had reported this to Pétain, as he 'cordially detests' de Monzie.[5] Whatever the truth of this, when on 18 April 1942 the Germans reinstalled Laval as head of government, he inherited the vacillation over the appointment of the new commissioner of the CGQJ.

The unanimous Vichy view of Darquier was expressed in a letter passed on to Pétain by General Émile Laure, who had been Pétain's aide for many years before the war and who became his faithful secretary-general in 1940.

Nîmes, 25 March 1942
Mon Général,

Please excuse an old Alsatian who has endured much over the years and who wishes to present his fears to you . . .

In Strasbourg, I knew M. [René] Darquier well . . . I learned from him . . . that his brother, who calls himself Darquier de Pellepoix, was not a commendable individual, that he had abandoned his wife and 3 children [sic], and that he (René) was forced to see to the needs of his brother's family.

As the Marshal is a fine supporter of the family, this being one of the principles of the new state, I believe that our honoured leader will be delighted to learn about [Darquier de Pellepoix] . . . currently a candidate, supported by the Germans, for the post . . . of Commissioner for Jewish Affairs.

This man will put himself at the service of the highest bidder.

After the war, in 1919, I know that he almost went to work for a Jewish company. And today he is against them. Tomorrow, who will he attack next? . . . [6]

This letter arrived in Vichy as the first convoy of Jews left Paris for Auschwitz. Less than a week later, on 31 March, Pierre Darquier died in Cahors. He was buried there on 4 April 1942, and his funeral Mass took place in the Cathédrale de St-Etienne. Anatole de Monzie gave the eulogy for his 'oldest friend in the Lot' before a considerable throng at Pierre's graveside, who heard him bury Louis' lifelong alienation from his father in a welter of mendacious praise. Louis, 'most outstandingly gifted', said de Monzie, had 'delighted his beloved father with his resolute and loyal understanding of his duties as a Frenchman. If I brought Pierre Darquier any joy in his retirement, it was in telling him of Louis' army citation and in conveying to him the growing esteem shown to this great young man by all patriots in our unhappy times.'[7]

For his appointment as commissioner, possibly for German use, Louis rewrote his family history in one of his longest and most fictitious *curricula vitae*, covering himself and all his family in full collaborationist garb. The typewriter he used was still rickety, but this time, as the stakes were higher the lies were more extravagant: 'From 1925–1928, having made a fortune of about two million francs, Darquier worked for himself and travelled, particularly in Australia, the United States and in England.' Next he addressed the 'Principal Calumnies' that persisted about his character: he was not a drunk, a pederast, a Mason, a member of Action Française, nor did he take his orders from Maurras.[8]

Then he took his revenge on René. The only legal promissory note Louis and Myrtle had signed was that of 23 April 1932, for ninety-six thousand francs, to be repaid 'no later than a delay of ten years being the 23 April 1942'. Henry Lévy, the 'Miller King', had died in April 1937 – René attended his funeral.[9] The Grands Moulins de Strasbourg had been burnt down by the Germans in 1940, and the business was moved to Paris under Lévy's right-hand man – happily an Aryan. Some of the Lévy and Baumann families escaped and made their way to the USA, others were in prison camps or in hiding, others were deported and murdered. Vichy grouped professions and businesses together in syndicates. By 1942 René had been appointed president of the Comité Général d'Organisation des Corps Gras (Organisation Committee for the Production of Fats) – that is, those industries which produced butter, margarine, soap and oil, all so scarce and precious during the war.[10]

On his appointment as commissioner, Louis presented his brothers to the world as follows: Jean was 'an ardent collaborationist and anti-Semite'. Of René, Louis wrote that he had refused to see him for three years 'because he was working for a Jewish group. Now that business is Aryanised and this brother, now president of the Organisation Committee for the Production of Fats, whom the Jews treated very badly before their departure, is equally anti-Semitic'. René's position took him into Louis' kingdom; but by now Louis hated René, who was known not to share the anti-Semitism of either of his brothers. Whatever the truth of it, Louis' statement made it impossible for René to return to work for the Lévy family, which after the Liberation he tried to do.

About himself Louis was much kinder: 'For all those who know him,' he wrote, 'Darquier is a man of total independence towards all powers, driven by one sentiment alone: the desire to serve his country, in the European and anti-Jewish sense. He is absolutely indifferent to money and has preferred to remain poor rather than lose his freedom of opinion . . . He has been accused of being in the pay of England . . . and of Germany. The best proof of the stupidity of these calumnies is that [he] owns nothing and has always lived modestly . . .'[11]

All these explanations and obeisances towards Vichy did Louis Darquier little good. Vichy did not want him, but was forced to accept him as part of a package of new appointments the Nazis insisted upon. Laval resigned himself to Darquier because 'the Germans are determined to have him'.[12] German command made inside arrangements for other controls of the new CGQJ, and passed Louis over to Laval to restrain his more extravagant characteristics.

Louis Darquier's predecessor Xavier Vallat had authority over acts and ordinances Louis was never to have, for on the day of his appointment Laval passed a decree taking back full control of the CGQJ. He allowed Louis Darquier into the Vichy government on the condition that he accepted a secretary-general, a supervisor. The man chosen, Georges Monier, a distinguished lawyer and civil servant, lasted a month. Laval had asked Monier to write a report on the CGQJ, with a view to ridding himself of it, but Monier 'did not have to prepare the report because in a very few days I learned enough to tell [Laval] immediately what the situation was, and in consequence to give him my oral resignation. M. Darquier de Pellepoix on his side, after the one and very stormy interview which I had with him, demanded that I should be immediately removed.'[13] So, from June 1942 until February 1944, Vichy and the Germans had to accept Darquier in undiluted form.

Laval now had much increased power; he was head of government, president of the council, and personally ran the Ministries of Information, Foreign Affairs and the Interior. Pétain remained only as head of state, his hopes for his National Revolution dashed for good. A little over two weeks after Laval's resurrection, Reinhard Heydrich and accompanying Nazi officials came to Paris to implement the rest of the changes they wanted: the despatch to Germany of a million French workers to serve in German war industries, and the implementation of the Final Solution in France. This could not work until they had an efficient puppet in control of the CGQJ to provide the Jews for this purpose, and another efficient puppet in charge of the police to gather them up for transportation.

One of Laval's first appointments was that of René Bousquet as his Secretary-General for the Police. Bousquet was only thirty-three years of age in 1942, a Radical republican from the south-west. Like Darquier he had studied at Toulouse University – law in his case – and like Darquier he failed and he lied about it.[14] Bousquet, who always insisted that everything he did, he did 'in the service of the French republic', was one of the most brilliant young men of his time. He became nationally famous for saving lives by braving the raging southern floods of 1930. Impelled into national politics, by 1940 he had become the youngest *préfet* in France. He was a classic example of a civil servant of the Third Republic, and by the time Laval appointed him chief of police, he was, and was known as, 'Laval's faithful assistant, using the same arguments and the same tactics'.[15] But Bousquet was more sophisticated and a far more careful manipulator than Laval, particularly about covering his own tracks.

Bousquet was an elegant and handsome man, a true Gascon, although he had none of the rumbustious attributes associated with that region; he was decisive and a hard worker and, unlike Louis Darquier, never made a fool of himself. More exceptional altogether, a self-controlled and determined man, he worked well with the Germans. He was a man who got things done; the Germans would have achieved little without him.

When, three weeks later, Laval was forced to accept Louis at the CGQJ, Bousquet, the charming republican, was put into harness with the pseudo-Gascon, pseudo-aristocrat Louis Darquier, two men doomed to disagreement. There were three rounds in their encounters: responsibility for the deportation of the Jews, the control of the special French police force needed to hunt down these Jews and to acquire Jewish assets, and the denaturalisation of French Jews to make available sufficient Jewish bodies for extermination. At the time, Bousquet seemed to be the victor on every front, although as a strategist Louis demonstrated near-genius in wriggling out of any instruction Bousquet gave him. After the Liberation, protected by François Mitterrand, Bousquet lived happily and richly until 1978, when Louis Darquier rose up to deliver the blow that was to kill him.

In Paris in 1941, Vallat had settled the CGQJ at 1, place des Petits-Pères, an operetta square near the Bourse and the Banque de France. The building he appropriated was the Dreyfus Bank, and had belonged to Louis

Louis-Dreyfus. Louis' delight at this was considerable, and often expressed. He invariably exhibited, too, another common human trait, hatred for one's benefactors – first René Darquier, then his brother's patron and employer Henry Lévy, who had saved Louis from debtors' prison or the equivalent in 1926, and whose money, through René, had supported Louis and Myrtle for ten years. None of them was to be forgiven now. One of Louis' first acts on taking up his office in the Dreyfus Bank was to forbid any Jew to set foot in the premises, and to instruct his staff:

> The Commissioner has noticed that in the correspondence of
> certain departments, Jews are referred to as 'Israélites'. The use of
> this term is due to Jewish influence which, by banishing the word
> 'Jew' has managed to achieve, finally, the first principle of Jewish
> defence, which is to pretend that the Jewish problem is only a
> religious problem. At the Commissariat for Jewish Affairs, a Jew
> must be called a Jew, and you must not write 'Monsieur Lévy' or
> 'Monsieur Dreyfus', but 'the Jew Lévy' and 'the Jew Dreyfus'.[16]

King Two Louis was not alive to know that Louis Darquier now occupied his premises; he died in a car crash in Cannes in November 1940.[17]

Louis' new Parisian office was a 'private townhouse like a financial fortress separated from its surrounding streets like a triangular island'. He now sat in King Two Louis' armchair in a large office on the ground floor, with a bay window looking out onto a leafy Parisian garden. Ensconced behind his large desk, wearing his monocle, he was much interviewed and photographed by the collaborationist Paris press. Today the place des Petits-Pères is as pretty as ever, but, unlike its Vichy counterpart, there is a bold plaque on the front of number 1:

> From 1941 to 1944 this building housed
> the Commissariat for Jewish Affairs
> instrument of the anti-Semitic policy
> of the French State of Vichy.
> This plaque is dedicated to the memory
> of the Jews of France.

Louis' appointment was greeted with a shower of publicity, articles in newspapers, agency reports and interviews. He was very fond of holding press conferences at the Nazi Propaganda Staffel, the Propaganda Office, and told journalists at his first one that the French government was to be instructed to punish severely any French person who made common cause with Jews; he would open the eyes of all Frenchmen to the evils of the Jewish race. Race, not religion, would be his criterion, and he would concentrate on the youth of the nation: for them he would create a Chair of Jewish History at the Sorbonne, and the subject would be taught in every school.

The German propaganda machine went into action in support. Elaborately fabricated press releases were sent about, always inventive and untruthful, many of them written by Louis himself. In these he claimed 'the astronomer and member of the Academy of Science Antoine Darquier de Pellepoix, 1730–1810' as his ancestor, added 'Colonel Baron Darquier, Grenadier of the Imperial Guard' as well, and congratulated himself on having resigned from 'a large Anglo-French Grain company. This company having sold one of its subsidiaries to the Jew Louis-Dreyfus . . .'[18] Aristocratic ancestors were cleverly interwoven with Pétainist evocations of himself as a son of the soil, with the blood of *la vraie France* running in his veins.

Louis wallowed in praise, and was inundated with letters from the public, denunciatory, pleading, oleaginous. One man wrote from Lyon:

> I have, for a long time, admired your intrepid courage in purging our unfortunate France of the horde which has dragged it into the mire and which continues to ruin our nation and drive the country to distraction . . . place all these filthy foreigners in a concentration camp . . . [19]

His anti-Semitic comrades from the 1930s hailed 'our old leader, who personified Hope for us through all the dark years'.[20] Many who had known him in the past, in Cahors, in prison camp, in Paris, and many who had discounted him, came out of the woodwork to ask for favours. Those who had not discounted him, such as Pierre Taittinger and Charles Trochu, were now in clover. One professional anti-Semite expressed his joy: 'There are those who sometimes say that our struggle against the Jews is only a pale copy of German racism. Fools! Don't they know that a true, pure Frenchman, and Darquier is one such, has nothing to learn from anyone in this respect.'[21]

The files of letters Louis received bear witness to the vociferous French minority who shared his beliefs. A former member of his Anti-Jewish Union of the 1930s asked him what had become of that 'good old dog of yours you used to make bark by siccing him to "get the Jews"'.[22] Sézille, ecstatic, wrote to Dannecker offering his total support and denying that he had ever said 'that M. Darquier de Pellepoix had been trepanned and did not possess all his mental faculties'.[23] 'All its anti-Semitic friends around the world join together to wish you our very best wishes in your new task,' wrote the Weltdienst.[24]

Denunciations too poured in, and never stopped. 'I write to inform you of the following facts,' wrote a member of Marcel Déat's Fascist Party: 'The black market is a continual Judaeo-Masonic machination. Shrewd and moneyed Jews have agents who run across the country on bicycles buying all they can...'[25] Lists of Jews and their whereabouts followed.

In Cahors, Louise Darquier, a widow for two months, still walking every day to visit Pierre's tomb, was showered with congratulations. Her apartment in the rue St-Géry was in receipt of 'more flowers than a cemetery', offerings from Cadurciens who hailed the mother of 'the youngest minister in France'. This was untrue – Louis was not a minister of state, and René Bousquet, to take only one instance, was his junior by eleven years. Louise never abandoned Louis; she would scold him, but she was, in her own way, proud of him. Her own way also involved considerable grief.

As a practising Catholic, after the death of Pierre, Louise was even more occupied with the activities of Catholic Action, helping the poor and sewing for the clergy. She had adored her husband, she was a Catholic anti-Semite, but she was hostile to the Germans, and was not a denouncer. Louis' words and cries for murder were not what she liked to hear. 'What mess has he got himself into this time? Since he was eighteen years old he has never obeyed me, never taken seriously a word I say.' That said, she was now a person of power in Cahors, solicited by all and sundry for everything from food coupons and passes to intercession at the *préfecture*. So muddled were the reactions of some in Cahors that Louise's maid Augusta recounted that Louis Darquier had married an Australian Jew.[26]

In England the reception was less complimentary. On 21 May at Balliol College in Oxford, the Foreign Research and Press Service prepared a briefing on Louis Darquier for the Foreign Office. While it is as precise as most documents based upon Louis' own fabrications, it accurately recorded his career to date, and described him as a dissipated rake and 'one of the most notorious anti-Semites in France'.[27] British newspapers continued to report Louis' activities in a sporadic fashion. The *Daily Herald* announced on 12 May 1942 that under Heydrich's orders he was to head a special anti-Jewish police force and the *Manchester Guardian* warned that 'the Jews are likely to suffer harsher treatment for a notorious anti-Semite Darquier de pellepoex [sic] was appointed Commissioner for Jewish Affairs in May'.[28] The British press reached Tasmania, so the Jones family knew that Louis had a position in the Vichy government, news the average patriotic Australian would have found difficulty in celebrating. The International Red Cross informed them that all was well with Myrtle.

The moment Louis' appointment as Commissioner for Jewish Affairs was announced, French officials in London were again in touch with Vichy, pointing out in an irritated tone that this was the man they had been seeking. They demanded that he begin paying Elsie the £80 or £100 a year needed to feed and educate Anne, and repay both Elsie and them all the sums owed. This time they requested an assurance of this from Vichy, because Louis Darquier 'when living in London twelve or thirteen years ago, after his return from Australia, incurred various debts of honour and borrowed from left and right from many different people in our French colony here, which since his return to France and despite his new and significantly improved circumstances, has never reimbursed any of the debts in question'. Louis sent £50 in due course, but despite more telegrams and letters he paid nothing else.[29]

After this, Elsie knew where Louis and Myrtle were and what Louis was doing, and she watched Anne like a hawk, for from 1940 onwards foreign nationals discovered in Britain were identified, classified and interned. She would walk with Anne to see that she crossed the road safely, and waited for her after school. Beneath the wings of the hovering Elsie, Anne, now twelve years old, held on to her dreams of her father the Baron, and of a heroic and superior France, undefeated, *résistant* and uncompromising, personified in the troublesome de Gaulle, who continued to be an unremitting thorn in the flesh of Roosevelt and Churchill. It was well known that de Gaulle had a beloved daughter named Anne, a Down's Syndrome child born two years before Anne Darquier.

When Elsie died in 1983, amongst her few belongings, preciously kept, were a few of Anne's books. One of them, *Daughter of France*, tells a morbid story of a French servant girl who flees to London to escape the Germans.[30] This fervent tale of a wistful and silent young girl, a foreigner alone in London as the bombs descend, misunderstood by the insensitive English yet like de Gaulle an embodiment of *la vraie France*, reveals some of Anne's fantasies about her French family, and about bearing a French surname in harsh times.

After swift appraisal by Reinhard Heydrich in Paris, within a week of his appointment Darquier was in Vichy, where the CGQJ had its head office. Pétain had his rooms on the third floor of the Hôtel du Parc, Laval on the floor below. The Parc, linked to the Hôtel Majestic – not to be confused with the Paris hotel of the same name – by a passageway, made these two palatial hotels the centre of the Vichy universe.[31] Inside, where the Office du Tourisme is now, was the Restaurant Chanteclair. Here the men of Vichy dined, mixed and mingled, and were conveyed to their masters above in the huge glass cage of the lift.

Vichy presented two faces to the world. There was the stern carapace of Pétain's ruled and regulated town, and the razzmatazz of the thirty thousand functionaries and the army of ambassadors, journalists, flunkeys and criminals who descended upon it in July 1940. For four years, sitting in their icy hotel rooms in winter – there was no fuel for heating – using bidets and bathrooms as filing cabinets and offices, their beds often serving as desks, the men of the Vichy state poured out paperwork and propaganda. All were within walking distance of the Hôtel du Parc, a proximity which encouraged the vicious rivalries and quarrels of all closed worlds. For Lucien Rebatet 'Vichy buzzed like Deauville in its heyday. From the railway station to the River Allier poured forth a flood of smart dresses, clever little beach robes, tailored jackets, elegant suits . . . together with the classiest whores on the boulevard de la Madeleine.'[32] But 'Vichy is ghastly' was the opinion of François Mitterrand, who worked in the office for prisoners of war in the Villa Castel Français.[33]

Above this mêlée, Pétain transformed Vichy into a place of ceremonies: of marches past – flags waving, veterans in berets, saluting to military music. A place too of a thousand photo opportunities. Homage hovers in the air in these photos. The results fill volumes in the libraries and newspaper files of France, and in those of Vichy itself. Pétain was photographed everywhere: surrounded by cardinals outside the church of St-Louis, waving from on high to vast crowds, with veterans and youth groups and officials, and most of all with small children, girls in particular. These photos of Pétain dandling little girls on his knee, chucking them under the chin, giving them a cuddle, are as hard to look at today as those of Hitler, equally ubiquitous, doing the same.

Most countries maintained embassies at Vichy, and the Hôtel des Ambassadeurs housed the forty-odd accredited foreign diplomats, one of the reasons its bar became so vivid a part of Vichy intrigues. De Monzie held court there in the early years, but despite the services with which he had provided Pétain, his time had passed. The pink art deco Villa Ica, the American embassy of Admiral William Leahy, had the most cachet until Roosevelt closed it down in November 1942. (Leahy's return to the US only increased Roosevelt's stubborn faith in Pétain, or rather anyone but de Gaulle; all the more surprising as Pétain, like Darquier, thought the United States was controlled by Jews.)

Vichy should have been the perfect spot for Louis Darquier. The spa town partied exactly as he and Myrtle liked to do. There were diplomatic receptions, dinner parties, and private carousing in the hotel rooms and villas, while behind the pomp and circumstance, tales of sexual abandon flourished. Vichy could also command the best of artistic France: Sacha Guitry performed, Yvonne Printemps sang; there was wonderful music and opera at the Grand Casino; there were cabarets and nightclubs and crowded cafés. Actors from Danielle Darrieux to Pierre Fresnay came to perform; five (heated) cinemas played to full houses.

On 14 May 1942 Jean-Louis Crémieux-Brilhac devoted his BBC programme '*Les Français parlent aux Français*' to his exposé of Louis Darquier in Offlag II D. He also deplored his appointment as commissioner:

> The annals of political infamy include examples of those who have sold themselves, those who prevaricate, crooks, cowards and traitors. Darquier de Pellepoix, an expert collector of titles and positions, can be proud to represent all these qualities. He was an enemy agent before the war and made little attempt to hide it. This shady

salesman and regular at the German embassy did not shrink from
making public speeches in praise of Hitler and he was supported in
his activities by German money . . . [34]

This was not a good beginning: the broadcast coincided with Louis'
arrival to take up his post in Vichy, and it was published by the
Resistance journal *France* immediately. On 16 May Henri Frenay, the
future leader of the Resistance group Combat, bumped into Louis in
the bar of the Majestic. Louis made a tremendous scene about the
BBC programme, which news, reported back to Crémieux-Brilhac,
prompted him to go further in a second radio jeremiad. All of France
listened avidly and secretly to the BBC, issuer of 'Anglo-Jewish lies',[35]
beamed on short wave. For obvious reasons, its German and Vichy
masters did likewise.

Nothing improved. Louis brought Myrtle to Vichy later that month.
Though entertainment of the kind which raised funds for food for
prisoners of war was not Myrtle's cup of tea, there was a great deal
in fashionable Vichy which could have suited her. With so much
rationed and unavailable, women who could afford it, or who had
access to state money, poured their coupons into monumental hats
which echoed the architecture of the town. In Vichy, most of the
social hum took place in the packed hotel bars, the only places in
which you could get a drink.

On 23 May Louis, in Vichy with Myrtle for a meeting with all the
regional directors of the CGQJ, met a journalist, Wanda Laparra, again
in the bar of the Majestic. She describes Myrtle as an 'Englishwoman
born in Tasmania . . . already celebrated for her eccentricities of dress'.
Myrtle was forty-eight, though admitting to only forty, when Wanda
spotted her sitting in the official corner on the left of the crowded bar,
wearing an enormous confection 'weighed down by multicoloured
bunches of flowers'. Wanda Laparra was one of the beauties of Vichy,
and thus had no mercy for Myrtle: 'Apart from a musical voice, she had
the indestructible charm of those Englishwomen who *have been* [my
italics] very pretty. Was she sincere when she pretended to total ignorance of her husband's professional activities? In any case, only one thing
mattered to her: rejoining her children [sic] who were in a school outside
London. I listened, incredulous. That the wife of the Commissioner for
Jewish Affairs should innocently avow that she had only one wish and

that was to get to London, was beyond belief! Darquier listened to her revealing all without intervening, directing an ironic smile at us as if to say: "You weren't expecting that!"'

Laparra thoroughly disliked Louis' 'square jaw, deep-set eyes, thick eyebrows and large, low forehead'. While Myrtle 'babbled', Wandra and Louis came to verbal blows, with the usual result – a lengthy diatribe about Jews and what to do with them. Myrtle's 'face had flushed, not because of the discussion – it's unlikely she could follow stormy conversation in French – but because of the second glass of whisky which she'd got someone to pour her'. Louis helped Myrtle roughly to her feet, looking irritated with everyone but most of all with Myrtle, 'because she'd given in to her little weakness, alcohol'.[36] This was only ten days after Myrtle and Louis had been reminded of Anne's existence by the French consul-general in London, and the BBC had beamed its first character assassination of him, which may explain both the irritation and the alcohol.

Wanda Laparra's account makes it clear that Myrtle's drinking habits were as well known as her hats. When she was drunk she would repeat her anglophile tally-hos, and though Louis safely withstood the complaints of Madame Pétain and other wives, for most of the war Myrtle remained in Paris. He was generally tolerant of Myrtle's addiction, which to some degree he shared, so perhaps a more important reason for her despatch to Paris was the chance of so much other sexual activity in Vichy.

Louis spent the summer of 1942 between Vichy and Paris, where the deportations to Auschwitz were just beginning. In Vichy he settled into the CGQJ's office in the seedy Hôtel Algeria. Vichy allotted hotels according to rank and status, and its uneasiness about its Ministry for Jews buried it in one of the town's least attractive hotels, more distant from Pétain's offices than most others. The Algeria is one of the few Vichy hotels to have changed its name after the war years; today it is called the Hôtel Carnot, though the almost obliterated words 'Algeria Hôtel' linger on one side of the building – boarded up now and empty for over a decade.[37]

You can still stay in many of the Vichy hotels of the time, and see the stretch of townhouses around the Hôtel du Portugal which housed the Gestapo after November 1942. At right angles to it the Germans built a wall three metres high with a bunker guarded by four surveillance boxes. The road was closed when prisoners were delivered to the Hôtel du Portugal; the screams emanating from it were so loud that the neighbours had to keep the radio on all day to drown out the noise.

Today the Hôtel du Portugal is open for business, as is the Hôtel Thermal which housed Darlan and many other Vichy dignitaries. Many of the more modest hotels are still functioning, names unchanged, but others have been shut down or converted into apartments. Whatever is left seems pickled in aspic or submerged in genteel dilapidation, and the only memento of Pétain's four-year government in Vichy is a plaque inside the old Hôtel du Parc in memory of the 6,500 Jews, including hundreds of children, sent from the Vichy Zone to the Occupied Zone and then to Auschwitz on 26 August 1942.[38]

Some of these were the Jews of Vichy itself. During his brief sojourn at the Hôtel Algeria Darquier passed by the Vichy synagogue on every walk to the Hôtel du Parc, but though Jews were officially banned from Vichy from June 1941, the synagogue was still open in May 1942 to scandalise him. There is a large board in the synagogue today listing the names of the 138 Jews deported from Vichy and its environs. Today the list of names – 'EBSTEIN: Monsieur, Madame et 2 enfants; FEINSTEIN: bijoutier, et Madame; FEIST, Philippe; FENSTER, Claire Fanny; FOGIELMAN, Esther: ses enfants Anna, Paulette, Marcel...' – hangs next to the sign instructing female worshippers as to which portion of the synagogue they are permitted to enter.

Vallat drafted his avalanche of laws against the Jews of France in the Commissariat at the Hôtel Algeria, often complaining about its inadequacies. His constantly expanding staff were jammed into its rooms, and he shared some of its four floors with its then proprietor, who much admired the pious Vallat, who went to Mass at 6.30 every morning, saying of him: 'Every time he makes a decision, he consults the Pope.'[39]

Louis Darquier liked to raise difficult matters by letter. Only two days after Myrtle's lapse at the Majestic, Laval received the first of many demands to supply 'without further delay, the necessary means to accomplish the mission that has been assigned to me'.[40] After the request for money followed his proposals for the tightening up and extending of Vallat's legal measures.

Pétain and Laval and the Vichy ministries could be convinced of the necessity of extreme measures against Jews, as long as someone they trusted and respected was running the CGQJ; the fervent Catholic Vallat was such a man. But once Darquier took over, matters were different. At loggerheads with him from the very beginning, well briefed by the BBC and the police, Vichy stalled on every aspect of the platform Darquier elucidated. Crémieux-Brilhac had already addressed Laval in his broadcast on 14 May:

> It was money from Colonel Fleischhauer, that is to say from Hitler, that financed Darquier's electoral funds and allowed him to recruit a whole crowd of thugs from a sideshow at a funfair to work as his security police during public meetings . . . M. Pierre Laval knows this better than anyone since he has, in his services, photographs of the counterfoils from the cheques sent to Darquier de Pellepoix . . . Now Darquier de Pellepoix is about to enjoy the ultimate gravy train: the Commissariat for Jewish Affairs . . . [41]

Despite this transmission, by 9 June Darquier had extracted five million francs from Laval for his CGQJ; but at the same time, to fill in any gaps that might be missing, a new police dossier was opened on Louis Darquier. Although it included the usual errors, the portrait of Louis and Myrtle presented to Laval and Bousquet did him little good. The Jones family in Tasmania were transposed into French: *'Mlle Morisson, Jones, Myrthe, Marione'* born in *'Lancaster (Tasmania)'*, daughter of *'Henri et Alexandre Lindsay Morisson, d'origine britannique'*. Louis and Myrtle were childless, Louis was Anatole de Monzie's godson, he had run a sheep station in Australia for several years, and before the war his particular brand of anti-Semitism had brought him the loathing of his fellow anti-Semites and those on the right who might have agreed with him, because he had no political programme but had whipped up a fierce hatred of Jews simply to draw attention to himself.

On 15 June Louis had a meeting with Dannecker in which he promised to place at the disposal of the Germans 'many thousands of Jews from the Non-Occupied Zone'.[42] This was no shock to Laval or Bousquet, as Bousquet himself had suggested to the Germans that they should make use of the foreign Jews languishing in French camps in the south for their deportation plans. But Louis Darquier took the German line: all Jews must go, French or foreign.

Crémieux-Brilhac launched his second attack on 1 July 1942. This time he gave the whole story of Louis Darquier, but also first reported the horrors unfolding in Poland, where the Nazis had just put 700,000 Jews to death. The method of exterminating them was fully described by Crémieux-Brilhac – gas. Louis was in Paris when this was broadcast, preparing, with René Bousquet and German command, for massive Jewish deportations. On 12 July Cardinal Hinsley, Archbishop of Westminster, solemnly protested on the BBC about the Nazi extermination of these Polish Jews, and added that Pope Pius XII was convinced of the truth of the report. On 17 December Anthony Eden, British Foreign Minister, told the House of Commons too.

Mostly however, the BBC's '*Les Français parlent aux Français*' of 1 July was devoted to Louis Darquier. 'Who is this man?' asked Crémieux-Brilhac.

> ... neither a big-time crook, nor the grand bohemian that de
> Monzie has called him, nor is there anything romantic about him;
> he is a common spiv who, pursued by his creditors, took refuge in
> treason. Every step in his so-called glittering career has only been
> camouflage to hide his most recent scandal. He threw himself into
> politics in 1934 because, having married for a vast British dowry,
> he squandered the lot and was reduced to living in hotel rooms
> from which he had to scarper every two weeks on the sly. 6
> February was his salvation: he made himself President of the
> Wounded and on this basis was taken on as secretary-general of *Le
> Jour*.

This was not a short programme; it was well researched and thorough. Crémieux-Brilhac told his listeners that Louis Darquier had lost his job at *Le Jour* for putting his hand in the till and up women's skirts, that he had only gone into Paris politics to wheel and deal, and that his career as a councillor was nothing but a sequence of debts and bar bills. And so, 'in a roundabout way, through politics and drunkenness, he became an enemy agent ... Naturally, he has always denied it. "Me? Touch German money? Never."' Then Crémieux-Brilhac read out the numbers on the stubs of the cheques which had found their way from Elizabeth Büttner into Louis' bank account. 'Darquier de Pellepoix,' he concluded, 'drink another cognac to German victory.'[43]

Four days later René Bousquet, calm and impressive, completed the process of removing Vallat's police force, the PQJ, from Louis' control.[44] As the Germans were about to test his mettle with the first massive deportations of Jews from France, the loss of his own police force began Darquier's war with Bousquet, a war ignited by envy. As Vichy's police chief, Bousquet had his headquarters there. He was close to Laval, and as Vichy's favourite son he seemed to possess everything Louis longed for, except perhaps money – though that was to come. In Paris the Germans praised him to the skies, while Louis Darquier had instantly become the functionary whose character was most thoroughly assassinated by all who met him.

In the torrent of memoirs and chronicles of Vichy France which mention Louis – though generally only in passing – it seems as though looking at him or hearing him for one second told the men of Vichy a truth they did not like to face. His 'constant preoccupation with money' is always noted. He is described as a 'street ruffian' and an 'outsider', 'indolent and pleasure-loving', 'a right-wing agitator', 'scatological', with a 'reputation for high living, recklessness and venality', 'bored by administration', 'obsequious', 'quarrelsome', 'hot-headed with an extravagant personal style'. Within a month of his arrival in Vichy a German spy, agent FR10, reported to the Gestapo that Louis Darquier was publicly wailing, 'I can do nothing against the Jews. I am a foreigner in this government. No one supports me.'[45]

Laval, an efficient man, found the unmethodical Darquier an agonising subordinate. Darquier had the habit of all bullies: he would only behave when bullied himself. Until the end he pestered Laval with new projects, new laws, bills for even tighter control of every Jew in France, as well as piercing complaints about the loss of his police force and monotonous applications for more money. He used methods most calculated to achieve failure. All his missives were lengthy. Timid in Laval's presence, he would listen meekly while Laval explained why such and such could not be permitted. Then, the meeting over, he would send Laval tedious memos and letters covering the same ground, making the same requests, complaining of ill usage, threatening, his rages fuelled by the praise and respect meted out to Bousquet by Vichy, and the ridicule he himself received. Within weeks Laval began to manoeuvre with German command to close down the CGQJ and get rid of Darquier.

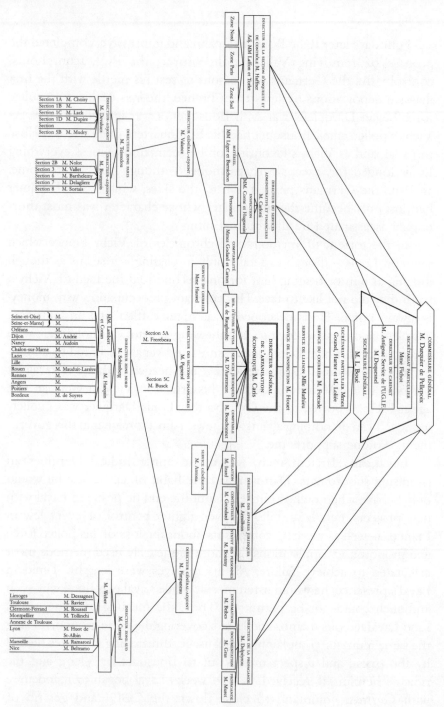

The CGQJ: Vichy's Commission for Jewish Affairs.

Louis shared the almost unanimous French admiration for Pétain, the Victor of Verdun. In fact Pétain's dislike of Louis Darquier was as well known as the intense irritation which throbs in every account of Louis' numerous approaches to Laval. Pétain nicknamed Darquier '*le tortionnaire*', 'the torturer', possibly because almost the first thing Louis did on arrival in Vichy was to ask him for more money, as the means at his disposal were 'absolutely insufficient for the heavy task the Marshal has placed upon him'.[46] Pétain had to listen to these pleas only a week after the BBC broadcast listed Louis' German cheques.

'They say everywhere,' said Louis in 1978, 'that Pétain opposed my actions, that he hated me. But, first, it was he who nominated me to the Commissariat, and secondly he never disapproved of me. Each time I went to see him, as soon as he saw me in the distance he would call out: "Look, here comes my torturer!" But that was a joke. What's more, he laughed. And that did not prevent him from shaking my hand.'[47] Louis behaved with Pétain exactly as he did with Laval. In his fight over the loss of his police force Louis went to Pétain – a dinner, a meeting at which little was said, followed by a long letter, a screech of anxious complaint.

At this time, July 1942, Louis was proving grossly inadequate in Paris, where the Jewish round-ups were underway. This had not gone unnoticed. As ever, he diverted attention by creating trouble elsewhere. He immediately told his *collabo* fellows in Paris, who already despised Vichy, that he was faced with the 'silent conspiracy of every existing organisation, indeed of the entire administration'.[48]

The SS knew of Louis' shortcomings too. De Brinon hosted a dinner party in Paris at the beginning of September 1942. Laval was there, as was Himmler's new representative, General Karl-Albrecht Oberg. Laval patronised Darquier as 'a good chap, but useless for regular administrative work',[49] and described his stream of impossible requests and accusations against various ministers; it was clear Laval wanted to see the back of him. Particularly amusing was his description of Louis' silence in his presence, and the accusatory letters he showered upon him as soon as he left the room. Otto Abetz was at the dinner, so were other German officials, and this account of Darquier as an object of ridicule was minuted and circulated.

Before his appointment as commissioner Darquier had assured the embassy that he was in 'such a combative mood' that 'he would resign quickly if the government did not accept the bills he was preparing'.[50]

Instead, on 15 September 1942, in the Berlin magazine *Die Judenfrage* (The Jewish Question), Louis took his revenge in a front-page article which he headlined 'The Current Position of the Jewish Problem in France'. The article was rushed and badly written, no more than a cut-and-paste job from his earlier journalism, but it was a detailed attack on the 'maudlin sentimentality' of the Vichy legislation against the Jews, and it had a sting in its tail.[51] After the usual reference to his French masters, the Marquis de Morès and Édouard Drumont, Louis launched into his familiar hymn of anti-Jewish clichés, all taken from the *Protocols*. He followed this with an all-out attack on Laval.

> When I took over the Commission for Jewish Affairs I envisaged a series of laws which would suit all of France and which would permit us to do without the German ordinances in the Occupied Zone. At the moment, I have been unable to achieve this aim. The French administration, which still includes many Jews in its ranks, opposes me with all its might . . .
> If we want to stop this sabotage of anti-Jewish laws, a purge of this administration is therefore the first task we have to undertake . . . the influence of a certain number of Jews reaches the highest levels.

In charge of the embassy's political section was Dr Ernst Achenbach, a blond and stylish young Nazi with an American wife. Louis managed to get his diatribe sent to Germany by the malleable Achenbach without Abetz's approval, after which he disappeared 'for a very long absence'.[52] Telegrams flew from the Foreign Office in Berlin; Abetz reprimanded Achenbach; systems were overhauled so such an outrage could not occur again.

After September 1942, contempt for and despair of Louis Darquier began to thrum in German circles too. Rejection by Vichy placed Louis in the dubious position of being a rabid French patriot who could only demonstrate his wares within the Nazi camp. German command, in choosing Louis Darquier, had ignored the personality disorders for which he was notorious. They estimated that he would react to their approval, a sentiment so rarely bestowed upon him, with docility. The embassy had even assured Berlin that 'We are much nearer a definite and clear-cut solution to the Jewish problem with the appointment of Darquier de Pellepoix to the post of Commissioner.'[53]

The Germans made numerous misjudgements in appointing Louis Darquier, Abetz being the chief culprit, because though he insisted on a commissioner who would be 'a French national of complete financial independence and undisputed authority', he chose Darquier with full knowledge of his financial history. The Germans were also aware that in Vichy there were two political camps, that of Pétain and that of Laval. They knew that the CGQJ was not a senior Vichy department, and had agreed to raise its status so that Louis could attend meetings of the council of ministers. From his first hour, therefore, Darquier made matters worse for his German masters, and brought relations between Vichy ministries and the German authorities to a new low.

Timing was against all of them. Darquier's appointment began only six weeks before Laval made the famous broadcast on 22 June 1942 which so shocked the French people, and which was to lead him to the firing squad: 'I hope for the victory of Germany because without it, communism would soon be established everywhere in Europe.'[54] He spoke just as the possibility of Germany losing the war was becoming obvious to even the most hardened Pétainist. American forces arrived in Great Britain as Darquier took up his appointment. With the German advance, on 9 July the battle of Stalingrad began.

After unpleasant encounters with men he revered, Louis always alternated outbursts of fury with descent into fantasy. Such was to be the case with the Vichy state. By 1978, he could speak well of Laval: 'We had words sometimes, that is true, but Laval was a splendid fellow, he did his job very well ... he was a good man, very hard-working, very competent. Unfortunately, one must be frank – he knew nothing about the Jewish question.'[55]

In November 1942, for different reasons, both Laval and Darquier began plans to close down the CGQJ's Vichy office completely, and from that time, although Louis had to divide his time between his two offices, he came to Vichy as rarely as possible. He told everyone that he hated working there. But then, he barely tolerated working in Paris. He did not like to work.

15

The Rat Pit

WHAT LOUIS LIKED TO do was to gallivant in Paris. There, as commissioner, he could do what he liked best, dining at Maxim's, drinking in nightclubs, casing the brothels and living the triumphal life of the German occupiers. Otto Abetz's embassy provided a patron absolutely to his taste, 'Waiter, more champagne' being words heard more than any others during Abetz's years in Paris.[1] The Paris office of the CGQJ, with its close contacts to the German occupiers, was in all ways a much more sophisticated *milieu* than the Hôtel Algeria.

In Paris Louis had set about creating his own commission immediately – his 'spring clean', he called it. His old secretary Paule Fichot joined him, and spent much of her time doing his office work: 'He often called and told me to sign his post as he couldn't come to the office.'[2] His first move was to get rid of almost everyone who had worked for Vallat and to install his own friends, arranging matters with them 'in cafés and especially in bars'.[3] Pierre Gérard, already employed by Vallat, was instantly promoted to assistant director of the Service de Contrôle des Administrateurs Provisoires (SCAP), the Department of Provisional Administrators or Trustees, responsible for the Aryanisation of Jewish enterprises. Next came revenge. Marcel Garnier, who worked in the Ministry of Finance at the CGQJ, had fought with Louis over money. Louis sacked Garnier 'from one day to the next', his wife was arrested by the PQJ, his mother's home was searched, the family ration cards taken and his home searched by the Gestapo.

Since René had ceased to support him, Louis had gathered together a collection of people who lent him money. Some he had milked by way of his anti-Semitic associations, others gave personal loans. The men he called his friends were in fact either an army of creditors, or biddable young fellows who would do as they were told. Throughout the years of the war, these were the men who were to benefit from the sale of Jewish possessions. Louis believed that he was rewarding his old friend and creditor Pierre Galien when he appointed him as his deputy.[4] In fact the Germans had chosen Galien to keep an eye on him.

The structure of the CGQJ looked imposing. At the top was Louis Darquier, and beneath him his *cabinet*, his management team, led by Galien. Under them fanned out various branches, each dedicated to a different aspect of anti-Jewish activity. The General Services department included an Administrative, Financial and Legal Section, and a Status of Persons[5] office which examined racial inheritance. Economic Aryanisation was devoted to acquiring and administering Jewish wealth. The CGQJ, and so Darquier, were also responsible for UGIF, the Jewish body Dannecker had constructed to organise Jews for their own despoliation and deportation. Finally Louis was to have his favourite toy, the Propaganda Department Dannecker had always wanted.

Into all this German military command tucked in a 'representative' to observe matters. Galien did the same job for the SS, while economic Aryanisation was supervised by Rosenberg's Colonel Behr. In fact, every department was under German control, another reason Louis Darquier spent so little time in the office. Out and about in Paris, he added his usual accompaniment, a younger man to act as general factotum, personal secretary and bodyguard who went everywhere with him. For this body-guard, Roland Lécuyer,[6] and for Galien and himself, Darquier demanded of Dannecker permission to carry guns, to cope with the 'anonymous threats' they were already receiving.

When he took over the CGQJ, Darquier inherited a department with a budget of nearly thirty million francs. He nearly doubled this during his time as commissioner. By 1944 it was raised to fifty million francs, over seventy per cent of which paid the staff, who under Darquier grew from nearly seven hundred to over a thousand. Darquier's CGQJ was described by his successor as 'a complete and utter shambles and an absolute free-for-all'. The chief reason for this was the 'ceaseless, useless personal quarrels',[7] and an overpowering atmosphere of financial skul-duggery. Sexual intrigue merged with the financial: Louis' private secre-tary often heard groans coming from his office – his habit of draping secretaries over the office desk was complained of in later life too – and he liked to have pretty secretaries at his disposal. He was the office bottom-pincher, and tried to seduce both the wife of one of his colleagues and her sister.

The vicious rows of the men in the Darquier rat pit, conducted in a haze of intoxication, were so extensive that the concierge at place des Petits-Pères was given a list of people who were to be thrown out if they tried to set foot in the building. Paule Fichot described Galien's behaviour: 'I remember asking him to intervene on behalf of a ten-month-old infant whose parents had been arrested. He replied, "It's a Jew child, let it die." I should add that he seemed to me to be in a state of inebriation.'[8]

Working for the CGQJ was viewed as a low occupation from the safe altitudes of other Vichy ministries. None of its staff had secure tenure, nor were they civil servants. As the qualifications required were to be 'a trustworthy, determined anti-Jew, anti-Freemason and racist', the work attracted a strange class of person.[9] They were paid less than and did not have the benefits of other Vichy personnel, perhaps because Vichy, though always unwilling to admit it, knew that the staff had access to Jewish money on such a large scale. For Vichy the Commissariat was temporary. Once the Jewish problem was solved it would cease to exist. Darquier and his appointees and successors, however, gave no sign of seeing their work as finite. Or shameful. They encouraged all their employees to act as informers, and automatically hired people who would be indifferent to the growing hostility of the French public.

German command had been waiting for Louis' investiture to force all Jews in France to wear a yellow star, so that it would appear to be a Vichy measure. This he achieved – in the Occupied Zone only – on 7 June 1942. French and foreign Jews over the age of six were ordered to wear the Star of David; on the yellow background '*JUIF*' or '*JUIVE*' was printed in bold black. Instructions were minutely detailed: the star must measure so and so, and it must be sewn on the top left side of outer garments. It was sold to Jews at police stations and cost one month's clothing rations.

For children the star was often the hardest to bear – it meant torment at school, exclusion from public places, no more ice creams in the park. The French began to commiserate: some who were not Jewish took to wearing the star, or sported yellow handkerchiefs. Some wore a star marked 'Papuan' or 'Buddhist', or shook hands with Jews in the street, or gave up their place in a queue so a marked Jew could go to the front

of it. Some of these 'Friends of Jews' were labelled as such and imprisoned, one young girl for tying the yellow star to the tail of her dog.
Cardinal Suhard of Paris requested that Jews converted to Catholicism
be exempted. Vichy refused. After the war, Knochen complained about
Dannecker's mismanagement of Vichy in the matter of the yellow star.
It had made the French public indignant, particularly on behalf of the
children; it created pity for the Jews and ridicule for the Germans. Apart
from anything else, he added, the star was a waste of precious material.

Once his star was seen upon Jewish breasts in Paris, Louis was rarely
to be found in either of his offices, in Paris or in Vichy. If an important meeting took place in the morning, as like as not he was not there.
He could often escape to his provincial empire, for the CGQJ was
instructed to have branches in both Zones, in the office of each regional
préfecture. These in turn were connected to a police section, and when
Louis got into full stride they were threatened with a propaganda department as well.

This network was an essential pillar for the chief activity of the
CGQJ – tracking down Jewish assets while its police arm assisted
Bousquet and the Germans in tracking down Jews for deportation. To
regional branches already in place when he took over, in Limoges, Lyon,
Clermont-Ferrand, Toulouse, Marseille and Nice, Darquier added new
ones in Bordeaux, Dijon, Nancy, Poitiers, Rennes and Rouen. He
enjoyed this; in particular he liked to visit the Nice office on the Côte
d'Azur.

Pierre Galien had probably had more to do with Louis' appointment
as Commissioner than anyone else. He was a German spy who, under
the code name of 'J11', worked for Knochen's Gestapo and Dannecker's
Jewish Office, the Judenreferat, in the avenue Foch. Dannecker and
Galien were friends, their shared pleasures extending to the Paris nightclubs and brothels which were to bring about Dannecker's downfall at
the end of July 1942, after which Galien continued to work seamlessly
with Dannecker's replacement, his former deputy Heinz Röthke.

As Galien spent as much time at avenue Foch as he did at rue des
Saussaies, it may well be that he had been in the pay of the Nazis from
1938, when he first funded Louis. Little is known of his activity before
the fall of France, except that he was one of the signatories to placards
that went up all over Paris denouncing the war as a Jewish plot. On
5 December 1944, after his arrest, Galien stated, 'I never displayed any

pro-German sentiments.' But Knochen described him as a man in whom they had 'full and entire confidence'.[10]

The PQJ had been set up as a separate body within the CGQJ, to work with but not under other police forces – the anti-Masonic police, the anti-communist police, economic brigades, not to mention the various arms and legs of many other German and Vichy bodies – to provide information about 'suspect Jewish activity'. Whatever its lines of responsibility, wherever it worked, Vichy had endowed it with considerable powers to 'pursue enquiries', 'confirm findings', 'detect violations'.[11] After Bousquet closed it down in July 1942, he permitted Darquier to form another investigatory force, but removed all its police powers. This was the Service d'Enquête et de Contrôle (SEC), the Investigation and Inspection Service, with no legal right to search or to arrest. It was this proposal which set off Darquier on his persecutory pursuit of both Pétain and Laval in July 1942. Five days later, on 10 July, overbriefed as to Louis Darquier's administrative inadequacies, the Germans placed the SEC under Galien's control. Galien ignored Bousquet's instructions and made the SEC an arm of the Gestapo, using them as 'a team of bodyguards . . . for petty police duties'.[12] More, because the men of the SEC were French, with ears and noses closer to the ground than the occupiers, they specialised in spotting Jews and communists, and passing them over to the Gestapo.

Darquier had wanted the SEC to be his very own Gestapo, 'a sort of *2ème bureau*' – a secret intelligence unit.[13] All the more irritating for him, under Galien, this was achieved. The SEC did what they liked and became looters, the private army Darquier had always wanted. These police concentrated on denunciations of Jews in hiding, and of those French who helped them; more, they checked on Aryanisation in other administrative services and ministries. Fear of denunciation and consequent internment meant that the SEC could make money from both Jew and Gentile.

By day Galien imposed German rule on the CGQJ, from which he embezzled money on a grand scale. By night he caroused with German officers in 'establishments of pleasure'. One of his most passionate statements in his post-war police testimonies was that his job at the CGQJ was 'purely fictitious', confined to greeting visitors and dealing with the rampant disorder of the office. He maintained that he had 'no authority' and took no decisions with any German officers, although he admitted that he felt that the 'Jewish problem' needed to be addressed, but with honesty and humanity. The secretaries observed matters differently. One testified that Galien 'did his utmost to tighten links with the Gestapo. There was a certain amount of ill feeling among the Germans during the Xavier Vallat period. He was accused of laxness and they ended up demanding his dismissal from the post. Galien did everything he could to win back their favour.'[14] Galien was highly paid for his 'fictitious' job as Darquier's chief of staff, and was even more interested in the cash profits than Darquier, who mostly wanted the money to dine at Maxim's, which he did. Louis' secretary, Paule Fichot, pinpointed the extent of his power: 'Galien worked directly with the German authorities for the massive arrests of Jews. He was renowned for his cruelty . . . I saw him as the blackest type of collaborator . . . he boasted of having good contacts with the Gestapo.'[15]

Galien had a personal doctor, Maurice Tussau, who claimed to be related to Madame Tussaud of waxworks fame. Galien sent him into the Rothschild Hospital, the Jewish hospital, to check if any healthy Jews were lurking there. Tussau decided that the nurse in charge was suspect, after which instructions were sent to the French police chief, François, to 'proceed with all urgency and have the Jewess ASSON arrested and interned at Drancy'.[16]

From the earliest days, it was clear that the management of the Commissariat left a great deal to be desired. Numbers of its agents had criminal records, made false declarations as to their civic status and were guilty of massive infringements against Vichy's regulatory procedures for the Aryanisation of Jewish assets. Typical of the men who found a home in the CGQJ was Jean Bouvyer, an extremist who had left Action Française for Deloncle's Cagoule. Xavier Vallat had been his defence lawyer when Bouvyer was tried for the Cagoulard murder of two anti-fascists, the Rosselli brothers – Bouvyer had witnessed the assassination. On his release from a two-year prison sentence Vallat gave Bouvyer a job at the CGQJ, and after Vallat's departure Galien placed him in charge of liaison between the SEC and the Gestapo. Bouvyer, a friend since childhood of François Mitterrand – who always maintained that he knew nothing of anti-Semitic activity during the Occupation – was Galien's most 'faithful assistant'. His mistress during these years was Mitterrand's sister Marie-Josèphe, 'Jo', a portrait painter in Paris. For Galien, and later for his successor Joseph Antignac, Bouvyer worked at spying on and denouncing Jews, tracking them down, sending them to camps and deportation, and then Aryanising their wealth.[17]

The CGQJ's leaders, first Xavier Vallat and then Darquier, were finicky men. For though Darquier was out of the office most of the time, when he was there he pestered his menials with instructions about discipline, use of the telephone, punctuality, what to do about half-Jews and about raising the number of Jewish Aryanisation cases. Letters went off in every direction on the finer points of anti-Semitism. Letters to Laval such as: 'The profession of bookseller is not forbidden to Jews. However, since the trustees of Messageries Hachette are likely to sell works published by the Hachette company, they fall under the remit of the laws of 2 June and 17 November 1941,' or pointing out that 'the profession of Algerian lottery ticket sellers [should] be forbidden to Jews', explain why Laval always coupled the word 'irritating' with Louis Darquier.[18]

A friend of the Darquier family in Cahors reported: 'one of my friends . . . was contacted by Louis Darquier when he was nominated. Louis explained to him that he was setting up a small team of about a dozen men from amongst his friends, to manage property within the CGQJ.'[19] This practice contributed greatly to the inefficiency of Darquier's CGQJ, and to resentment and rivalry between his employees, exacerbated by his choice of young men from his days at rue Laugier to staff various departments of the CGQJ.

One of a thousand reasons Laval had no time for Darquier and his CGQJ was that from the moment of his return to power in April 1942, all Laval's considerable energy had to be devoted to coping with increasing German war demands. In March 1942 Hitler had appointed one of his most perfectly formed monsters, Fritz Sauckel, to provide the Reich with workers – slave labour. Two months later, when Louis was appointed, Sauckel came to Paris, and demanded 250,000 men. Laval's bargaining 'victory', called the *Relève*, was that one French prisoner of war would be freed for every three 'volunteers' who went to work in Germany. The French people heard Laval announce this new collaboration on 22 June 1942 in the same speech in which he told them of his desire for a German victory. If France was to 'find her place in the New Europe', she could not 'remain passive and indifferent in the face of the immense sacrifices Germany is making'.

The French populace hated Laval already, and 22 June gave them reasons for hating him even more. Many thousands of workers had to go to Germany, and if not to Germany, they slaved for Albert Speer's construction office, Organisation Todt. From 1941 to 1944 French workers and prisoners from French camps were forced to build Hitler's massive line of concrete bunkers along the coast – the Atlantic Wall – their fate another lost story of the D-Day landings.

All the departments of the CGQJ had boundless opportunities. The Status of Persons section, which examined racial inheritance, issued certificates as to Jewishness and pursued forgeries, was a goldmine. This was the hounding department, sniffing out Jews or people whose 'attitude and actions seemed highly suspicious', snuffling out false baptismal certificates and complicit priests, and working with the police to pursue Jews for such assessment. Under Vichy many of the Catholic clergy, and some of the hierarchy, dared to differ from their bishops and speak out on behalf of their flock, the Jews, and resistance generally. Dissenting Catholics became a formidable *cadre* within the Resistance, reminding their parishioners 'that Christ was a Jew'. Such clergy often provided Jews with false baptismal certificates. Darquier's hatred for baptised Jews was particular and vivid: 'Baptism cannot change their livers, their spleens, their ovaries.'[20] To delve behind these documents he put another old friend into his Status of Persons section as its resident ethnologist: Georges Montandon.

Montandon, who claimed to be able to determine racial characteristics by the examination of blood, was already working for Vallat as his ethnic expert. Now Darquier gave him the job of looking at the bodies of Jewish persons, measuring their heads and inspecting their penises. Montandon had a monopoly in this business, and his examinations were exhaustive and very expensive. The bribes he took to declare a body non-Jewish and provide the necessary *Certificat de Non-Appartenance à la Race Juive* were to make him a very rich man. He took this money at all points of the persecution ladder. Applicants came to him willingly to be 'cleared' of suspicion; Darquier and his staff sent him cases, so did the police. He also carried out his work at Drancy concentration camp. If he decided a prisoner was Jewish, Auschwitz; if not, freedom.

All the CGQJ departments could venture into blood inspection. Typical was the man Darquier chose as director of the Legal Section, Jean Armilhon, the sort of person who, like Vallat, would continue to fuss about the Jewish blood count of Mosaic Georgians, and who thought that the defeat of France in 1940 was 'a miraculous turnaround of events', for 'defeat – which could have led to our ruin – has in fact enabled us to purify and regenerate the nation once again'.[21] Even the Administration and Finance Section could make money by passing on information or taking bribes.

Every department, in pursuit of Jewish wealth and Jewish blood, worked closely with the Commissariat's police force. For money, Louis would write letters like this:

> For the attention of Monsieur Röthke – SS – Obersturmführer
> Re: Messieurs André et Jean Boshorn [sic]
>   ... despite the fact that Messieurs André and Jean Boxhorn have
> both been issued with certificates declaring that they do not belong
> to the Jewish race, they have been detained in the Compiègne camp,
> in the section reserved for Jews. Furthermore, I have learned that
> they may be selected for deportation.
>   ... it would be extremely regrettable to see people deported who
> are not considered to be Jews either in terms of French or German
> law.
>   Signed: Darquier de Pellepoix

Mostly, Louis Darquier's CGQJ charged for help with property, and being an old friend of the commissioner helped:

> Monsieur le Baron von Behr
>   One of my comrades from the war, Monsieur Dehesdain ... was
> previously married to a Jewish woman but is now divorced ... His
> former wife, who ruined him, still has property that belongs to
> Monsieur Dehesdain, and he would like to try, with your help, to get
> this back. Could you please tell me when it would be convenient for
> him to come and see you ...
>   Signed: Darquier de Pellepoix[22]

Throughout France the CGQJ police, the SEC, investigated the behaviour of appointed trustees, enquired about the presence of Jews in prohibited positions, checked on Jewish property declarations and identity cards, and followed every Jew, watching for 'suspicious behaviour'. The connection between the Gestapo and the SEC gave the CGQJ the necessary muscle to plunder as it wished, and to sustain a financial section with a staff of twenty-five 'including accountants, insurance agents, clerks, attorneys, brokers, bank clerks, currency dealers . . . It was widely acknowledged that its inspectors exacted ransoms from Jews and mistreated them if they failed to deliver. This explains the legend of the "Torture Chamber" at rue Greffulhe, which was, no doubt, an ordinary interview room but one in which the agents perfected a special interview technique for the poor victims who were arrested in their homes.'[23]

Everything about the SEC infuriated Darquier: the fact that Bousquet had taken its police powers away in principle, and the fact that the Gestapo had given these powers back to Galien in practice. It also led to the end of Darquier's relationship with Galien, for the latter often used the SEC without consultation. One of Galien's largest lies after the war was his statement that he 'always refused to have the least contact' with the SEC. In its first five months, when it was under his control, the great round-ups of Jews began. Galien and his SEC methodically robbed the Jews in Drancy concentration camp as they awaited deportation. For Galien, money always came first. He was an oddball amongst extremist anti-Semites because he was a ruthless businessman and enormously energetic, which Louis Darquier was not. Thus the bonds of brotherhood between Galien and Darquier survived only six months, and when they broke, the Gestapo joined the embassy on the list of German authorities that found Darquier intolerable.

Galien always acted as though he, and not Darquier, was Commissioner, which was easy to do, as Darquier was so rarely there. He treated Darquier as 'his subaltern'.[24] What Galien and the Gestapo most disliked were the favours Louis distributed to French Jews, 'Israélites'. A witness testified in 1947: 'The Commissariat was notorious for its use of "fiddles" to get its hands on Jews' money. This was particularly so for the issuing of non-Jewish certificates. I heard that Darquier de Pellepoix himself was happy to do this.' Louis always left the actual work to others, but he insisted on signing the precious non-Jewish certificates himself.[25]

As the two camps developed within the office, and Louis' problems outside it multiplied, he started trying to cover his tracks. On 6 October 1942 he wrote to Röthke:

Today I received two letters from Aryan individuals requesting permission to accommodate or temporarily foster Jewish children whose parents have been interned.

One of these children is a boy of eight years old, currently still at Drancy; the other is a girl of twelve, living alone in Paris.

Before sending a reply to these people I would like to know if you consider that German ordinances allow such requests to be granted or whether it would be easier, for racial reasons, to issue a refusal.[26]

Darquier and his CGQJ had indeed become notorious for accepting vast bribes from rich Jews. He had often met these wealthy men through Anatole de Monzie. Later, Louis explained away such encounters: 'Good French Jews, whom I helped in difficult times. Between ourselves, a certain Worms. I will say no more.' For Louis, as for Pétain and indeed for most 'Israélites', there was a hierarchy of Jews. The Worms bank was a merchant bank with shipping interests, and amongst its vast portfolio was a chain of hotels which included the Crillon in Paris. The Worms group was said to belong to a mysterious international banking fraternity known as the Synarchie. Its director Gabriel le Roy Ladurie and his associates, one of whom was de Monzie's acolyte Hippolyte Worms, were perfect targets. For de Monzie Darquier would ignore the fact that Hippolyte Worms was half-Jewish, though his mother was a Catholic, as was Hippolyte himself.[27]

Darquier always quailed in the presence of powerful or rich men, English, French, German or Jewish. If such Jews paid him enough he would turn a blind eye. Later he boasted of the Jews he helped. One of his secretaries described his approach: 'He was married to an Englishwoman who had no qualms about speaking publicly of her Gaullist sympathies and he himself granted several substantial favours to Jews. I must add though, that his attitude was contradictory and I saw him issue both false papers and arrest warrants against Jews with the same ease.'[28]

At the end of October 1942 the Gestapo interrogated Darquier for an entire day, during which he doubtless learned about aspects of Galien's role which displeased him mightily. He returned from avenue Foch in a fury and dictated a letter demanding Galien's resignation; two weeks later, resignation not received, he sent a second letter, barring Galien the door.

Galien stormed into the CGQJ in place des Petits-Pères, knocking down the guards at the door. Darquier, summoned to the office – as usual he was not there – punched it out with Galien with all the staff watching; 'it was a nasty scene and very violent'.[29] Galien returned to avenue Foch, repeated again that Darquier was taking Jewish bribes, and came back the next day with an order from Knochen, insisting on his reinstatement.

Pierre Leroy, Louis' pre-war barrister, and René Darquier, who knew Galien as a Neuilly neighbour, now intervened. For excellent reasons Laval had no wish to see Louis Darquier replaced; he wanted to get rid of the CGQJ, but in the meantime Darquier's ineptitude remained an excellent excuse for any Vichy inaction on 'the Jewish Question'. This, in turn, infuriated German Command. First, in September, Darquier had alienated most of the embassy over his *Judenfrage* article. In October he added the Gestapo to the list. The embassy and the Gestapo both agreed that he had to go. He had been in the job for only seven months, but was to survive another fourteen.

An even worse punishment for the Germans responsible for his appointment was their discovery that Darquier was a pestiferous bore. As Knochen testified later: 'We didn't take him seriously, his behaviour was often contradictory, depending on the fluctuations of his private life and his financial position.' He nagged Knochen to put pressure on Vichy, arguing that 'the more money he had, the better he could serve us'. He complained to Abetz and the embassy about Vichy's cold shoulder; but they knew what Laval thought: 'However large the sum you give him today, he'll have nothing left by tomorrow.'[30] The SS, the MBF and the embassy discussed Darquier's dishonesty. But they knew that if he was unacceptable to Vichy, Pierre Galien was out of the question, for the excesses committed by his SEC, its 'arbitrary arrests, spoliations and beatings',[31] had such an effect that the Germans arrested fifteen of its agents in October 1942 and ordered its disbandment.

In this way, Darquier survived. Mostly it was the Allies who saved him, for in November 1942 Rommel was in trouble in North Africa and the Red Army was completing its encirclement of the German 6th Army at Stalingrad. The siege of that city and the fear that Germany, like Napoleon's France, would be defeated in Russia continued throughout the year. Then, in January 1943, the German army at Stalingrad surrendered. Those 'good old French Jews' who were not sent to Auschwitz

– and many were – were saved by Russia and the Allies, and by many French people, but not by the French state.[32]

By this time, bombing had become a part of life for Paris, as it was for London. Suspicion that the Allies might win was becoming a certainty, raising the decibels of anger amongst the *collabos* in Paris. Lucien Rebatet spoke for all of them in his famous bestseller *Les Décombres*, a memoir and a polemic published in the autumn of 1942, in which he called for 'Hate unto Death!'[33] and urged Vichy to join Germany to fight the Allies in '*my* war, our war'. Talk of a coup against Laval was in the air. Jacques Doriot was the most successful French fascist, the one Laval feared the most. In Paris, on 4 November, he held the annual congress for his fascist party, the PPF. Doriot spoke for eight hours to fifteen thousand or so of his delirious followers, uniformed in various shades of blue, shouting 'War with England' and 'Laval to the scaffold.'[34]

All this came to naught, for, on 8 November 1942, with Operation Torch, the Allies landed in North Africa. Two days later Hitler ordered the arrest of all Jews and other enemies of Germany in France, and on 11 November, Armistice Day, he ordered his troops to occupy the Vichy Zone. Otto Abetz was summoned back to Berlin, and remained there until December 1943.[35] After the German army took over the south, Mussolini extended his portion of France to include much of the Rhône Valley, so that Italy now controlled eight French departments which stretched from the Riviera to Switzerland.

Henceforth the grip of the Gestapo tightened. Coping with the German Occupation of the entire country and the increasing agitation of the Paris *collabos* became Vichy's priority. Pétain delegated more powers to Laval, but told his subjects: 'I remain your guide. You have only one duty: to obey. You have only one government: the one I have empowered to govern. You have only one country: the one I embody, France.'[36]

Laval and the Vichy government trundled on, but there were Germans in Vichy now, Germans all over France. What Vichy thought of Louis Darquier was no longer important. When German military command, the embassy and the Gestapo discussed what to do with him, all agreed that he must be sacked, but decided it was 'inopportune at the moment'.

Darquier put an end to the Galien affair by repaying – most likely with Jewish money – the sixteen thousand francs he owed him. Galien retreated to the arms of Captain Sézille, whose joy at Louis' appointment had turned to rage within a month when Dannecker closed down his IEQJ and gave it to Darquier to reinvent as a more scientific propaganda instrument. Sézille was comforted by the Gestapo with a new endeavour, the Groupement des Amis Anti-Juifs (Association of Anti-Jewish Friends). There he recreated a 'veritable office of denunciation', which Galien took over when Sézille died in April 1944. Galien continued in form until the end: 'I, the undersigned Galien, declare that I was obliged to take control of anti-Jewish affairs under pressure from the SS,' he wrote in a statement for the police who arrested him after the Liberation.[37] The next day he saw things differently: 'I declare that I have never worked for the Germans . . . in addition, I never expressed any pro-German sentiments.' He had a final word for Louis Darquier too, denouncing him as 'a miserable actor, paid to strut the stage but do nothing. He works hand in glove with the Jews and is their great protector. Under his supreme administration the organisation at place des Petits-Pères has become a pro-Jewish Bastille.'[38]

Despite these unpromising circumstances, with hardly a friend to hand, Louis Darquier bounced back, his remarkable recovery guaranteed by the man chosen as Galien's successor, Joseph Antignac. A key embassy strategy in the control of the CGQJ was the appointment of reliable civil servants to key positions, and the appointment of the implacable Antignac was their most successful implementation of this policy. Antignac was a much-decorated former cavalry officer, a veteran of both wars, and like Vallat had been awarded the Légion d'honneur. He moved from being an army officer and industrialist to the PQJ, then was brought to Vichy – in the midst of Darquier's first row with Bousquet – in August 1942 to head its successor, the SEC. Until October he observed Galien restore its power as an anti-Jewish police force aligned to the Gestapo.

After his fisticuffs with Galien, Darquier brought Antignac to Paris, first as secretary to his *cabinet*, then as its chief of staff. Until his departure in June 1944 Antignac provided Darquier with the efficiency that enabled him to keep his job. Antignac was 'the man of the Final Solution of the Jewish question',[39] ending up as the last secretary-general of the CGQJ. He worked well with all the Germans, but his closest links were to the Gestapo and Röthke's Judenreferat in the avenue Foch. Antignac, dark and hefty like Vallat, was also a passionate anti-Semite and French patriot, 'the incarnation of an officer of the *ancien régime*';[40] he was a nitpicking, driven, pompous administrator, a most competent authoritarian. In the voluminous records left behind by Vichy's Commissariat for Jewish Affairs, it is usually Antignac's signature on documents, and often his voice in the terrifying dicta that issued from it.

Bousquet would never have permitted Darquier personal control of the SEC. It was Antignac, with his police and military experience, who ran the CGQJ's police force in both zones, and it was under his rule that it reached its most chilling efficiency. Notwithstanding his lack of authority over it, Louis still managed to insert into the SEC 'friends and some second-rate cronies, i.e. his henchmen, newspaper sellers etc.'. In plain clothes, with 'a pistol hanging from one side and a truncheon from the other', they would arrive at a camp, set up a table in one of the huts, then 'the internees filed past the men, who would then subject them to a minute and humiliating search. Very often they were beaten, or forced to remove their trousers . . . intimate body searches [were] suffered by the women. The search finished, cash and jewellery would be piled anyhow,' for 'the policemen were free to help themselves to banknotes and jewels'.[41]

The prodigious output of memos, reports, letters and documents which issued forth from the CGQJ were generally signed by Louis Darquier, but it was accepted that their scrupulous attention to detail demonstrated the personality of Antignac. Half-castes and the medical profession were two matters to which both men devoted personal attention. One of the sourest Darquier family resentments against Louis before the war had been his dunning of their medical connections. In his pre-war newspapers he always devoted excessive space to medical matters, particularly to analyses of Jewish blood and its evil influence. Louis liked to use his power in favour of the famous as well as the powerful, especially famous doctors. Jean-Louis Faure, the great surgeon and writer, brother of the art historian Élie Faure, intervened on behalf of his nurse Suzanne Lévy, and Louis graciously spared her: 'a Jew doctor . . . nurse to a great surgeon, professor Jean-Louis Faure. I intervene therefore, not in favour of doctor Suzanne Lévy, but in favour of professor J.L. Faure.'[42] Everywhere Darquier and Antignac looked they saw Jewish doctors. Stern letters were sent to the Secretary of State for Health about Jewish medical students, and detailed demands were sent to the Gestapo, with copious lists and carefully referenced documents which were quintessential Antignac, though either he or Darquier could have written the final paragraph of one attack: 'Without wishing to stress my point of view too often, I believe that total deportation would considerably simplify these matters . . .'[43]

Little attention was paid to Antignac by the warring factions above him. Yet it was he who resolutely ensured that the system worked. As France was about to be liberated, he bore witness to the squabbles in Darquier's rat pit, and also to the position of the CGQJ in Pétain's dreams of a New France: 'The Commissariat still has an important role to play in the National Revolution,' he told his staff. '. . . I shall personally make sure that order, confidence, probity, justice and a love for a job well done become the rules of this organisation . . . Fellow anti-Semites first, and faithful followers of the policies of the Marshal and his government second, under whose orders we are directly placed, these are the principles I wish to see us all adopt . . .'[44]

16

Death

In Marcel Ophuls' documentary *Le Chagrin et la pitié*, it is 6 May 1942 when Louis Darquier appears before Reinhard Heydrich at the Ritz Hotel in Paris. Earlier that year, on 20 January, Heydrich convened a conference in the Berlin suburb which bordered Lake Wannsee, and there, as instructed by Hitler and Goering, with his deputy Adolf Eichmann and fifteen other Nazi civil servants, he presented his plan for the extermination of the Jews. Eichmann, who had prepared the papers for the conference, and who was to run the system of liquidation decided upon, noted that the anticipated number of Jews to be killed was eleven million.

The words used for the Final Solution were always 'deportation to the east', 'expulsion', 'elimination', 'resettlement', 'migration', 'evacuation' and 'work'. The word 'extermination' was never used. The Wannsee plan was to use euphemisms to secure the necessary collaboration from civil servants and administrators of all occupied countries, the men and women who would be required to carry out Nazi orders.

Heydrich spent a week in Paris, from 5 to 11 May, personally informing the German authorities of the Wannsee decisions.[1] He moved ultimate responsibility for the Final Solution in France from the military command, the MBF, and brought in as supreme commander of all German police, intelligence and security services in France Karl-Albrecht Oberg,[2] a former fruit importer fresh from his successful oppression of Poland, a man with Hitler's moustache and Himmler's spectacles and haircut. Heydrich gave Oberg and his police 'almost full autonomy' in France.[3] This meant that the struggle for command in France between the army and the Nazi Party was over: the Gestapo were the winners and the military and the embassy had to fall in line. Helmut Knochen was promoted to become Oberg's deputy, with responsibility for all the police work associated with the Final Solution.[4]

In Paris Heydrich met his French administrators at the Ritz Hotel, and the event was filmed. Looking plumper than in his London days, Louis followed Bousquet and strode towards Heydrich in an ill-fitting suit, smiling uneasily.[5] Over thirty years later Louis insisted that he had to be cajoled into meeting Heydrich, and that the events of those May days were of no importance. But they were. Before May 1942, the exclusion measures Pétain instituted for his chosen undesirables were civic. After May 1942, for Jews and others, these measures led to death.

Heydrich then saw Darquier privately in Knochen's office, and 'drew his attention to the fact that Hitler was personally very interested in settling the Jewish question in France'. He also summoned Bousquet to a meeting with himself and Oberg, at which Bousquet was informed of the altered powers of the SS in France and was instructed to pass on the new orders to his regional *préfets* and police superintendents. Heydrich made perfectly clear to Bousquet what he required as far as the Jews of France were concerned: trains would shortly be ready and 'all Jews resident in France must be deported as soon as possible'. Bousquet made no protestations, and reported back to Laval.[6]

And so were drawn up the battle lines between Vichy and the Germans over the deportation of the Jews of France. For Vichy, the Christian-Catholic conscience could only adapt itself to the despatch of 'foreign or stateless' Jews; for the Germans and Darquier no such division was acceptable, and French Jews must go too. In the first month after Heydrich's visit Dannecker set to work with Darquier and Bousquet to fulfil his orders, and theirs.

Vichy sent most of its Jews to death at Auschwitz in Poland, but it was French concentration camps which provided Louis Darquier and René Bousquet with the Jewish bodies required, though there were never enough. During Vallat's time there were only three important round-ups of Jews. His first, between 9 and 14 May 1941, garnered nearly four thousand, most of them Poles, Czechs and Austrians, aged between eighteen and sixty: the French police, with the approval of Vichy, then bussed them to the Gare d'Austerlitz, where four waiting trains took them to Pithiviers and Beaune-la-Rolande concentration camps about eighty kilometres from Paris. Henry Coston went to see them, and rejoiced: 'I have seen Jews work . . . I have seen the sons of Israel devote themselves to something else besides speculation and the black market.'[7] There they were visited by their wives and families over the coming year. In due course all of them, the men first imprisoned, and the wives and children who visited them, were deported. When you look at the photos of visiting day – fathers, wives and children eating a picnic, looking happy to be together for a day – you know that everyone you are looking at died at Auschwitz.

The next arrests were made on 20 August 1941, largely of foreign Jews, but also including two hundred intellectuals and many lawyers: 4,078 men were sent to Drancy. The last collection in Vallat's time was in December 1941. The Germans, not the French police, managed this round-up as a reprisal, and gathered up 743 prominent French Jews, including Colette's husband Maurice Goudeket – Abetz secured his release – and René Blum, brother of Léon, who died in the Auschwitz gas chambers.[8]

On 27 March 1942, eight days after Vallat was sacked, the first train left the station of Drancy-le-Bourget, went on to Compiègne, Laôn, Rheims, Neuberg and then to Auschwitz, collecting over a thousand men. This was the only convoy not to travel in cattle trucks; they travelled to Auschwitz in third-class carriages, personally escorted by Dannecker. By September 1,008 of them were dead.[9]

At Wannsee, France was allotted the 'solution' of 865,000 Jews, 165,000 for the Occupied Zone and 700,000 for the Non-Occupied Zone, a figure which demonstrates how effective Maurras and his offspring had been in exaggerating the Jewish Peril, for the gap between the 865,000 Jews considered to be in France and the 330,000 actually there was to be a major problem for Vichy. It was in pursuit of this inflated figure that so many Jewish children – over eleven thousand Jewish children – were sent to death.[10]

The first trains promised by Heydrich were ready by June. Vichy had to find the numbers for the trains, the trains had to be filled, and they had to leave on time. Convoy number two left on 5 June, a month after Louis Darquier's appointment and two days before the yellow star made its first appearance in Paris. More trains followed on 22, 25 and 28 June: each carried about a thousand persons. The convoy of the twenty-second was the first to include women, sixty-six of them. The largest number were Polish, but there were Jews from all over Europe, from Britain to Turkey, including over five hundred French Jews. Fifteen hundred of them were still alive on 15 August 1942. When Auschwitz was liberated on 27 January 1945, 189 had survived.

In the midst of these first convoys, on 11 June, Dannecker went to Berlin for a briefing by Eichmann. He was ordered to supply Auschwitz with 100,000 Jews from both French zones as a first effort. Problems with Vichy were anticipated, but it was settled that all Jews must go, French or foreign, and that France must pay seven hundred marks per Jew. Dannecker promised fifty thousand Jews immediately, beginning on 13 July, with three trains a week. The age range was to be between sixteen and forty, male or female, and ninety per cent of them were to be fit for work.

On Dannecker's return Darquier had a meeting with him and promised several thousand unspecified Jews from the Vichy Zone, coupling this with dismal reports of the unlikelihood of any cooperation from Bousquet or Laval. The next day Bousquet met Oberg and Knochen. Bousquet learned of Darquier's interventions, and promised ten thousand Jews from the Vichy Zone. Dannecker told Eichmann that the initial supply of Jews would be forty, not fifty, thousand. As Dannecker was doing so well with the June transports Eichmann accepted this number, but only as a beginning.

In the meantime, René Bousquet, who was in the process of removing the PQJ from Darquier in Vichy, delegated police matters in Paris and in the Occupied Zone to his deputy Jean Leguay,[11] who was to arrange the round-up of thirty thousand Jews, while Bousquet set himself the task of supplying the ten thousand which he had personally promised from the Vichy Zone. Laval had been informed of the Berlin decisions, but Bousquet had not discussed the exact figures.

Since the autumn of 1941 the escalation in assassination and reprisal in France had made the German uniform synonymous with death, for the MBF's *code des ôtages* demanded the execution of between fifty and a hundred hostages for every German killed. Most of these were communist *résistants*, Bousquet's enemies being 'terrorists, communists, Jews, Gaullists and foreign agents',[12] ranked according to the amount of domestic disturbance each might cause. When sorting out French hostages for German reprisals, Bousquet made sure they were communists. Oberg wanted to control the French police, but neither Vichy nor German command could afford the inevitable public unrest if the SS were to be involved in the operation of Jewish deportations. The French police had to do the job.[13]

By 1942, the long-drawn-out siege of Tobruk had presented a propaganda victory to the Allies; in May Reinhard Heydrich was assassinated in Prague, and the first large-scale British bombing raid on Germany took place. The German reverses inspired Laval to make a show of strength. Because of the hostile reaction to be expected from the French public, he objected to the deportation of French Jews, and to French police deporting any Jew.[14] Pétain agreed. On 29 June Leguay conveyed this information to Dannecker. Laval instructed Bousquet to keep a close eye on Darquier, and Oberg summoned Laval to Paris. Dannecker had only two weeks in which to collect forty thousand Jews; he turned to Eichmann for support. Eichmann arrived in Paris on 30 June to sort matters out (it was the following day that the BBC announced the death of 700,000 Polish Jews in gas chambers). Vichy was still unhappy about French police rounding up Jews to send them to a destination that might be 'dangerous or fatal'.

Throughout this month of to-ing and fro-ing, Bousquet bargained in true Laval style.[15] He would put his French police to work in the service of Germany on condition that he maintained absolute control of the French police in both zones. The Germans expressed their worries about Bousquet's opposition to Louis Darquier. Bousquet defended his removal of Darquier's police force, but at Knochen's insistence agreed to 'place his police at the disposal of Pellepoix'.[16] All Darquier's complaints about Vichy were aired; in particular German command asked why Vichy had not given him his budget. Bousquet replied that it was 'up to Pellepoix himself . . . he believed that Pellepoix still had no plans for spending the money he was demanding'. Bousquet added that 'the French were not opposed to the arrests as such, but explained that it was "awkward" to have them carried out in Paris by the French police. This was a particular worry of the Marshal's.'[17] The threat of Hitler's personal displeasure was invoked. Bousquet moved in for the kill. The number of Jews required had now descended to thirty-two thousand – twenty-two thousand from Paris, the rest from the Vichy Zone.[18] Bousquet agreed that his police would round up the Jews for deportation 'on condition that the proposals were put forward by Pellepoix'.[19] Knochen gave in on French Jews. They were not to be troubled 'for the moment', though later Abetz recommended adding a few, little by little, to make up the necessary numbers and to habituate the population to their disappearance.

On 3 July Pétain, Laval and his council of ministers agreed the accord arranged by Bousquet. Foreign and stateless Jews in the Vichy Zone could be deported. They were just 'rubbish', to be resettled by the German government in 'a Jewish state in Eastern Europe'.[20] It was cheaper to let old Jews die naturally. In pursuit of the ten thousand promised from the Vichy Zone, Laval proposed, as a 'gesture of humanity', that they extend the age limit previously settled upon, and that children under the age of sixteen should be included in the deportations. What was decided about Jewish children in the Occupied Zone was of no interest to him.[21] This proposal endangered the fiction that these were deportations to 'labour' in the east. To send young children to the gas chambers, Dannecker had to obtain Eichmann's permission. This he applied for on 6 July.[22] Laval and Bousquet then decided that Darquier was to be placed in charge of the Franco-German action committee for the deportations, making him the scapegoat should one be necessary.

Louis first learned all of this on 4 July, a Saturday, in Knochen's office on the avenue Foch. Dannecker took the floor, most unhappy that Bousquet's men, and not Knochen's SS, should control the round-ups. But Bousquet and Knochen had their way, and a Franco-German committee was established to carry out the arrests and deportations of thirty-two thousand Jews. The day after he took away Louis' police force, Bousquet announced that the committee 'must be under the chairmanship of the Commissioner for Jewish Affairs'.

When reality attacked Louis Darquier, it always produced the same reaction: taken by surprise, he paled and looked terrified, 'appalled at accepting such a responsibility'.[23] Everyone noticed this, Dannecker in particular. Still fuming about the loss of his police force, Louis now had to recover from the shock of achieving what he had demanded for so many years – the murder of Jews, the moral and political responsibility for which Bousquet had now placed upon him.

As ever, his strategic skills rose up to save him. After an initial blast of activity, during which he issued letters and intervened in all directions while Pierre Galien, now in charge of the SEC, did the work on the ground – almost immediately he disappeared from the coalface in a puff of smoke, having used the irritation aroused by his presence to extract money from everyone to hand.

The Germans had yet to learn the true depths of Louis' disinclination to work or to spend more than an hour a day in any office. On 7 July he presided over his first meeting to arrange, as he said, 'the technical details of the deportations'.[24] Accompanied by Galien, he faced a formidable array of uniformed functionaries at Dannecker's office in the avenue Foch. Those who would do the real work were there. Amongst the French police attending was Jean François,[25] police chief of the Jewish section at the Paris Prefecture – also in charge of Paris detention camps such as Drancy – a man whose attitude 'was judged to be satisfactory from the Nazi point of view'. Another was André Tulard,[26] whose file cards, *fichiers* of Antignac-like efficiency, listed every Jew in every street from A to Z, with different-coloured cards for French and foreign Jews. Tulard was ordered to get his cards ready for use by 10 July. Dannecker, supported by his assistant Ernst Heinrichsohn, the kind of Nazi in polished leggings who relished the forthcoming procedures as much as Pierre Galien, took the minutes. They decided upon the age range – sixteen to fifty – and the physical requirements of each Jew.

On 13 July French police inspectors, assisted by female auxiliaries, armed with Tulard's cards would go through Paris arrondissement by arrondissement, arresting Jews, collecting them in various town halls, gymnasiums, schools and police stations and then transporting them to the Vélodrome d'Hiver, the winter cycling stadium of Paris in rue Nélaton, in the 15th arrondissement, near the metro Bir Hakeim.[27] Five years earlier, almost to the day, Charles Maurras' release from prison had been celebrated there, and Louis Darquier, alongside Maurras, Xavier Vallat and Léon Daudet, had heard the crowd of thirty thousand stand to acclaim him as he hailed Maurras as the leader of a France united against its Jews. The Vel' d'Hiv' was big enough to hold the quota of Jews demanded, but it was decided not to arrest Jews married to Aryans. This reduced the numbers anticipated to twenty-two thousand. They were to be divided between the camps at Drancy and Compiègne and the two camps in the Loiret, Beaune-la-Rolande and Pithiviers.

Lists of the whereabouts of house or apartment keys were to be kept by the police for easy appropriation thereafter. Children under fifteen or sixteen would be left with UGIF; animals were to be left behind – with the concierge if there was one. One convoy of a thousand Jews would go each week from each camp, thus four trains a week, to be guarded by French police under observation by a German police squad of a lieutenant and eight men.

Could the French camps cope? Drancy had limited capacity, so careful organisation was required – not a Darquier attribute, but the Germans did not yet know this, and moved to help him by issuing regulations on 8 July forbidding Jews to enter any public place, permitting them to shop only between 3 and 4 p.m. They were already forbidden to leave their homes between 8 p.m. and 6 a.m. This meant that in addition to the census of Jews already available, and the yellow star which marked them for arrest, German command made sure that the listed Jewish bodies would be at home to be collected. Louis thanked the Germans for their help.

The real worry was still the numbers. Tulard's cards revealed that there were insufficient Jews in every category, so the upper age limit of those to be arrested was raised to fifty-five for women and sixty for men, and they added back Jewish spouses of Aryans and women with children above the age of two, though not pregnant women. All were to be stateless Jews. Four thousand children between the ages of two to sixteen were anticipated, and UGIF could only care for four hundred. Dannecker sent another urgent telex to Eichmann to get his permission to deport the children, using the prevention of promiscuity as one good reason.

The day decided upon, 13 July, was the eve of Bastille Day, still a French public holiday. In the interests of a happy populace the round-ups were deferred until Thursday, 16 July, and the operation was given a pretty name: '*Vent printanier*' – Operation Spring Wind – but it is always called the '*Rafle du Vel' d'Hiv*'. Supply lists were prepared:

> . . . a) one pair of stout working shoes, 2 pairs of socks, 2 shirts, 2 undershorts, one work overall, 2 wool blankets, 2 sets of bedding (sheets and pillow cases), a bowl, a cup, a water bottle, a spoon and a pullover in addition to the necessary toiletries.
>
> b) Each Jew is to take enough food for 3 days. Only one suitcase or rucksack is allowed per person . . . [28]

As Louis Darquier was in control of UGIF, only he – though again it was Galien who actually dealt with the matter – could ensure that the trains were properly equipped. And so they were not. The CGQJ had to extract such provisions from the French Ministry of Industrial Production; correspondence between them on the matter of shoes and blankets reached unprecedented levels of mutual insult. Whatever was supplied disappeared into other pockets well before any convoy left France. Then money and cooperation had to be culled from the prominent Jews who ran UGIF. Thus it was that Jews paid for their own deportation and death. The amount of effort this required added to Louis' fury with René Bousquet. At the time he could do little to cover his back, nor did he have the temperament to do so. But Laval and Bousquet did. On 15 July Laval wrote Bousquet a protection letter for the file:

MINISTRY OF THE INTERIOR
Direction Générale de la Police Nationale
Paris, 15 July 1942
The Head of Government, Minister and Secretary of State for the Interior [Laval]
to Monsieur le Préfet de Police (Cabinet) [Bousquet]
    As you have been informed verbally, the German authorities have decided to transfer to the east those Jews resident in the Paris region and who belong to one of the following categories: Stateless, Germans, Austrians, Czechoslovakians, Polish, Russian, refugees from the Saar . . .
    As the Commissioner for Jewish Affairs [Darquier] has given his agreement for the implementation of this operation by the French police forces, I would be grateful if you would take all practical measures to this end according to the conditions set out during previous meetings to which you were summoned.
    I also confirm that the 'instructions' you submitted to me have been approved by the Commissioner for Jewish Affairs.
    Signed: for The Head of Government[29]

At 4 o'clock in the morning of 16 July 1942 the round-ups began, and went on until 1 o'clock the following day. Nine thousand French policemen and auxiliaries, working in teams, using the index cards, knocked on doors. But Parisians knew what was going on. Some Jews had been warned, and many survivors owe their lives to French policemen who did not do as they were told. In the beginning many were unafraid; it did not occur to them that French police would arrest women and children, so the men fled, and their women and children took their places. Illness made no difference: those who could not walk were taken on stretchers. No children could be left with neighbours. Children born in

France of foreign parents were legally French; this made no difference. Pregnant women were taken (some babies were born at the Vel' d'Hiv'). Twenty-four Jews were shot resisting arrest. Some raced across the roofs of Paris to escape, and over a hundred committed suicide, one a woman who threw her two babies from a fifth-floor window first, then jumped herself.

By 5 p.m. on 17 July the total came to 12,884 Jews: 4,051 children, 5,802 women and only 3,031 men. Dannecker, by now reduced to the anticipation of twenty thousand Jews, was over seven thousand Jews short, and, an even greater disaster, almost a third of his tally were children; he had gathered only 8,833 'deportable' Jewish bodies for incineration. Eichmann had not yet reached his decision as to what to do with children. Since they could not work, he was still investigating whether the gas chambers had sufficient capacity to gas them.

On 17 July began the great debate as to what to do with the children. Blood was at the root of this. Though in this instance the children had to be used to make up the numbers, more important, these children had Jewish blood in their veins. They would grow up and re-infect the sacred blood of Aryan France, Aryan Europe. Much of the dithering about the children was circumlocution around this, jiggling with Catholic or other consciences to break a taboo. The murder of children, like the eating of human flesh, is not easily done. Darquier suggested children's homes for the moment, but Leguay, François and Tulard were anxious about the numbers. The compromise over French Jews had already enraged Eichmann, and when the train of 15 July from Bordeaux had to be cancelled as only 150 stateless Jews could be found for it, he was so angry that this could never be permitted to happen again. They also realised that separating the children from their parents at the Vel' d'Hiv' would be a further public relations disaster after the scenes of hysteria in Paris of the past two days.

Until 1942, the Germans estimated that eighty per cent of the French population rejected collaboration. The round-up of the Vel' d'Hiv', during which Parisians openly reproached the French police as they went about their work, increased this percentage. After Bousquet's August round-ups in the Occupied Zone, popular hatred of the intruders became almost the biggest problem faced by the Nazis and by Vichy. So all agreed that the children should be despatched to more distant concentration camps with their parents while awaiting the decision from Eichmann as to what to do next. On 17 July fifty city buses collected the Jews. About six thousand of them, those without children, were taken straight to Drancy, soon bulging at the seams. Jews with children, over seven thousand of them – there were 4,051 children – were interned for up to six days and nights in the blistering heat of the Vel' d'Hiv'.

Nothing had been prepared for them, except policing. It was midsummer, boiling hot. The roof of the sports stadium was glass, painted blue for blackout purposes, and so an eerie blue light filled the arena. There was no water, and the few toilets there broke down almost immediately. The people were crowded together, the corners of the grounds on which they slept were their urinals. The smell was as dreadful as the heat; the thirst and hunger were followed by diarrhoea and dysentery. Some managed to kill themselves, some tried to kill their children, some went crazy and their screaming, all night long, spread panic. The Germans and Galien permitted only two doctors to enter the stadium. When UGIF begged for more medical help, Galien refused – he found the conditions 'perfectly satisfactory'.[30]

A little girl, aged five then, remembered later 'the cries of grief, of horror, of fear... that horrible odour, the tears of children'.[31] Some were there for two or three days, some were there for a week. Some died, and the really sick were taken to Drancy. Gradually these thousands were removed to the concentration camps of Pithiviers and Beaune-la-Rolande. They went from the Gare d'Austerlitz, heavily guarded so the public could not get near to help them. When they got to the two camps near Orléans there were no preparations ready for them. Many of the four thousand children died there and are buried in the local cemeteries.

The first trains left Drancy for Auschwitz on 19 July, and four more followed on 22, 24, 27 and 29 July, with over five thousand Jews, mostly those arrested on 16 and 17 July, so that in hundreds of instances Jews taken from the streets of Paris were dead within five days. By 1945 all the rest were dead except for forty-seven survivors. When the Drancy Jews had gone, it was the turn of those with children at Pithiviers and Beaune-la-Rolande. Permission to send the children had not arrived, so the French authorities decided that parents and their children over fourteen should go immediately; the younger ones would follow later. French police watched as the little ones saw their distraught parents and older brothers and sisters wrenched from them by 'rifle butts, with truncheons, with streams of icy water'.[32] Trains left the two camps on 31 July and

3, 5 and 7 August. Four convoys, four thousand people. Of these about two thousand were gassed immediately, and of those remaining, thirty-five survived.

Left behind at Pithiviers and Beaune-la-Rolande were about 3,500 children ranging in age from fifteen months to thirteen years old. After their parents were taken, there were only a few nursing mothers and Red Cross workers to look after them. The cabbage soup gave them diarrhoea; they slept on soiled layers of straw, they were filthy, they smelt. Some were too young to know how to wash themselves; some did not even know their names.

Louis Darquier did not go near the Vel' d'Hiv' or Drancy. It was clear to all that Galien was in charge. Dannecker and Galien made a fine team, for Dannecker was 'brutal and fond of drink, he was known as "the sadist" and carried out violent assaults against people who had been arrested. He personally selected Jewish internees at Drancy for the firing squad.'[33] Darquier later stated that he was in his office on 16 and 17 July, shuffling paper. Actually he, and others, saw Laval, who came to Paris for a report on Operation Spring Wind while Galien and his SEC police were on the rampage: tens of millions of francs' worth of jewels disappeared, according to directors of UGIF. Even the Germans complained that the CGQJ and Galien were 'not only highly servile but also capable of showing an over-zealous approach to their work'.[34]

By August, public and clerical outrage conveyed to Pétain and Laval over Vel' d'Hiv' led to a strong rumour that Darquier was about to be replaced because he had dealt with Jewish internments 'in too superficial a manner'.[35] Knochen and Dannecker were seriously unhappy about the numerical failure of the round-ups, Bousquet and his police were worried, and Darquier's absence was noted by all: the orchestra of Nazi objections began its crescendo at this time. Darquier had been responsible for the preparations at the Vel' d'Hiv', but left it to Galien, who prepared nothing, and did nothing, except steal. Darquier was never allowed near deportations again. After this the contribution of the CGQJ was confined to the provision – or not – of blankets and shoes.

Darquier took part in no more management meetings after July, and complained of his exclusion, blaming Laval. In future his involvement was reduced to writing and receiving letters. So many letters of his exist dated 16 and 17 July that it almost seems planned as an alibi.[36] Even the French consul-general in London received one with a little on account for Anne – £50. Another letter Louis wrote on 16 July was to the Federation of the War Amputees of France, refusing to intercede on behalf of one Victor Fajnzylberg, the father of two children aged six and four, whose wife had been arrested that morning. Fajnzylberg was 'a former soldier of the 22nd foreign (Polish) infantry regiment. He is not fully recovered from his amputation and requires specialised, daily care. He can only move with the aid of crutches ... he lives on the 5th floor ... he is now left alone with two young children.'[37] Victor Fajnzylberg died in Auschwitz, sent there on Convoy 68, on 10 February 1944.

After July Darquier also had time to address Vichy, and part of the office work he referred to is to be found in the shoal of letters he poured out to Laval. In the first, on 23 July, he adopted a guarded but threatening tone. Galien, in his mode as spy number J11, ensured that the Germans saw a copy of the letter.

... the Commissioner for Jewish Affairs was put in charge of delivering 32,000 Jews (22,000 from the Occupied zone and 10,000 from the Non Occupied zone) to the German authorities.

These Jews were to be chosen from among stateless persons and nationals from certain foreign countries.

These measures were carried out on 16 and 17 July and gave the following figures:

3,095 men
5,885 women

i.e. a total of 8,980 people from Paris and the suburbs [handwritten note in the margin by Röthke: 'and 4,000 children – total of 12,884'].

This number is well short of the planned figure ...

It should be noted that although the arrests proceeded without any particular problems on the first day, the percentage of individuals to be arrested who were absent reached 66%. Indiscreet behaviour prior to the arrests allowed a certain number of Jews to pass secretly into the Non Occupied zone.

In my meeting today with the occupying authorities I noted that they were highly dissatisfied with this situation.

The German authorities had planned a sufficient number of trains for the transportation of 32,000 Jews. It is necessary that the arrests correspond to the scheduled departure times for these trains ...

I would like to suggest that the following steps be taken:

1) All stateless Jews and those Jewish nationals of foreign countries previously designated . . . should be arrested and held ready for deportation.

2) . . . Belgian, Dutch and all foreign Jews not in possession of a recent, valid passport could also be arrested.

3) . . . it would be advisable to arrest French Jews who were naturalised after 1 January 1927 . . .

Personally, I am certain that any delay or negligence in the implementation of this evacuation plan will lead to serious consequences . . .[38]

He wrote again a week later, more plangent, more indignant, opening with the words that Laval most hated to hear: 'Following our conversation this morning . . .' A peal of complaints followed about the loss of his police force and the inadequacies of Bousquet's, ending with, 'It shall not be said that I did not warn you . . .'[39]

Laval received Darquier's views about the French police at the same moment that General Oberg concluded his first accord with René Bousquet. From now on Bousquet's French police force was to be independent, their sovereignty exchanged for French assurances of the militant maintenance of order. In other words, from now on French police would work with German officials to kill French 'enemies of the state' – the Resistance. The announcement of the Oberg–Bousquet agreement in the first week of August was the sole response Darquier received, while Laval's only reaction was to make notes about a projected 're-organisation' of the CGQJ. By 13 August, spies were informing the Gestapo that Darquier was about to be replaced.

At the same time a solemn letter of disapproval arrived at Vichy from the Catholic hierarchy. Writing on their behalf, Pétain's most faithful servant, Archbishop Suhard of Paris, protested to the Marshal about the terrible events witnessed on the Paris streets. Cardinal Gerlier wrote too, a letter 'of astonishing moderation'. The bishops did not make their protest public, however.[40]

The round-ups in the north and south coincided with a procession of statues of the Blessed Virgin Mary from all over France to Le Puy-en-Velay, whose Black Virgin was to be celebrated on 15 August, Assumption Day. Cardinal Gerlier, Monseigneur Valero Valeri, the Papal

Nuncio, Vichy ministers of state and flocks of bishops and the faithful gathered to begin what was to be a great pilgrimage of four of these Virgins throughout France over the coming years. Such a national Catholic and Vichy event prohibited more than a letter to Pétain about the Jews.

Theodor Dannecker did not trust Bousquet; he visited the Vichy camps in July to ensure that sufficient Jews would be provided, and demanded the delivery of eleven thousand in August. Bousquet promised three thousand by 10 August. All *préfets* were sent lengthy orders specifying the kinds of Jews to look out for, providing a list of a dozen more exceptions than those permitted by Darquier or the Germans. The age range to be arrested began at eighteen and ended at sixty, but Bousquet 'always considered the impact . . . on the French political situation, the difficulties of execution of them for his services, and the aggravation of the internal situation which might occur and thus automatically augment the number of *résistants*'.[41]

At first Bousquet observed the Vichy exemptions, often deciding not to deport Jews who were 'near relatives (parents, spouses, descendants) [of arrested Jews], Jewish old soldiers, foreign volunteers and POWs'.[42] Louis Darquier, maddened by these exclusions, kept the Germans informed of Bousquet's every move. This led to a crisis which forced Bousquet to remove many of the exempt categories. He had to anyway, to reach the necessary tally.[43] Bousquet's instructions were brutal: his police must 'crush all resistance'. And he was clever: he thought to investigate hiding places – convents, schools and children's homes; his police waited and watched, surrounded and pounced.

Bousquet's round-ups began on 5 August at Noé and Récédébou camps near Toulouse, but his major onslaught mostly took place between 26 and 28 August – this is when the first Jews from the Vichy synagogue would have been taken, though it was permitted to stay open until the end of 1943, thus ensuring more bodies for deportation. Bousquet used the census Vallat had prepared: 'Eliazar Davidovici of Esperaza', presumed to be Jewish because of his name, and 'One (1) Jew, thatch merchant, rue du Pont' probably disappeared on this occasion.

At first Bousquet gave Jewish parents his version of Sophie's choice:

they could leave their children under eighteen behind, or take them with them. Most left them – with neighbours, with strangers, with whoever was there, with all those who tried to help: 'Eyewitnesses will never forget the moment when these truckloads of children left the camps, with parents trying in one last gaze to fix an image to last an eternity.' The people of Béziers who watched these 'atrocious separations'[44] reacted with 'profound indignation, for despite the early hours of the morning the population witnessed heartrending scenes'.[45] When Bousquet changed the rules, after 18 August, he deported children over the age of two, and set about recalling those who had been let go before that date; he was particularly repetitive in his instructions about this.

Darquier continued to write letters. On 25 August a Monsieur Lavigne asked permission to take in care Suzanne Janowski, the daughter of Jewish friends, but born in France. She was twelve and a half, in the Lande camp; her father, a distinguished war veteran, had already been deported. Lavigne was happy to pay for her keep and education. Darquier refused.

Rounded up by French police working with the *préfets* of each department, the Jews from the Vichy Zone were sent to Drancy in cattle trains, thirty Jews to a car, with only one bucket as a lavatory. The heat of mid-August intensified the squalor and the terrible smell of the stinking straw. Their first train went to Auschwitz from Drancy on 10 August, exactly as promised by Bousquet. Of that first thousand, 760 were gassed immediately, and one man survived at the end of the war.

August 1942 was the turning point. During the war years that followed, Pétain retained the veneration of some of his people. The responsibility for the sufferings of the French themselves, and of those whose sufferings they witnessed, was distributed, as is ever the way, between God and the Devil. Laval was the Devil, the cowboy in the black shirt. Pétain was, if not God, then his Guardian Angel. There is an echo of this in the last paragraph of the famous pastoral letter sent to the churches in his diocese by the Archbishop of Toulouse, to be read out from the pulpit on Sunday, 23 August 1942. Its title was 'Human Dignity'.

My very dear Brothers,
      There is a Christian morality, a human morality, which lays down duties and recognises rights. These rights and duties stem from the

nature of man; they come from God. One can violate them . . . [but] no mortal has the power to do away with them.

Why is there no longer any right of asylum in our churches? . . .

In our diocese, moving scenes have occurred in the camps of Noé and Récédébou. The Jews are men; the Jewesses are women. The foreigners are men and women. One may not do anything one wishes to these men, to these women, to these fathers and mothers. They are part of the human race; they are our brothers, like so many others. A Christian cannot forget this.

France, beloved Fatherland; France, which bears in the consciences of all your children the tradition of respect for human dignity; chivalrous and generous France – I have no doubt that you are not responsible for these errors.

Yours devotedly, dear Brothers,

Jules Gérard Saliège[46]

Most of the priests in his diocese read out the letter, but in Cahors, Archbishop Chevrier would not permit it to be heard by his flock at the Cathédrale de St-Étienne. Two days later, when Bousquet began his massive round-ups in the Vichy Zone, four more bishops followed Saliège.[47] His message became a clandestine document, published in the underground press, passed from hand to hand, and its message 'spread like wildfire in the south-west'. Clerical unease and messages from diverse charities spread the word to America.[48]

The news of the gas chambers broadcast on the BBC on 1 July 1942 was only the beginning of the subterranean knowledge throughout the world that sending Jews and others to these camps meant they were travelling 'possibly to their deaths'.[49] The actual word 'death' was used all the time by those who were trying to save the children. It was used by their parents in the camps, in last letters home from the inmates of Drancy, and in so many other places – from pulpits, by word of mouth and in the underground newspapers, in the many reports and documents in which you read the words coupled together: 'death' and '*asphyxiés par les gaz toxiques*'.

There were heroic priests. The Jesuit Father Pierre Chaillet in Lyon, and Father Victor Dillard in Vichy – whose death in Dachau is recorded by one of the rare plaques commemorating anything in that town – are just two examples. On 31 August 1942 Père Chaillet and his fellow *résistants* refused to give up the children they had hidden because, Chaillet explained, they would be 'sent into exile and doubtless to their death'. In general, however, fewer than half the prelates in the Vichy Zone publicly objected to the deportation of the Jews, and none in the Occupied Zone.

In the camps of the south, charity workers of every religion and none had forced their way in to help in a 'veritable battle for rescue', but 'in most places the local Catholic priests felt they could not intervene without special hierarchical permission and this could not be obtained in time'.[50] Protestant consciences had been aroused for months by this time, led by the indefatigable Pastor Boegner, and their protests reached outrage during these summer months.[51] With Jewish and other charities, with French townspeople and villagers and farmers, they worked to hide and save the children in a battle royal with Bousquet and his French police. Children were snatched from railway stations, hidden in convents and seminaries, in orphanages and other Church institutions. They were 'adopted' by well-meaning French people, but many were tracked down and deported. None of them ever saw their parents again.

In Lyon, Charles Maurras greeted the deportation of the Jews with unalloyed joy. The circulation of his newspaper had halved, but his vitriol had doubled. 'The main thing is to sort out – to judge, to condemn, to execute.' For Maurras the Resistance were 'Jew-lovers'.[52] He remained Pétain's man, acquiescing in any collaboration Pétain might like to undertake, but denounced all his former acolytes – Rebatet, Brasillach, Drieu la Rochelle and thousands of others – who had become 'Paris traitors' and *collabos* with Germany. In fact he had only one true disciple left, Louis Darquier, who was interested in Germans, Hitler or fascism only if they were prepared to contribute to his welfare, or to assist him in ridding France of his imaginary monster, the Jew.

Throughout August Louis was still busy dictating letters and snapping at Vichy's heels. Bousquet was punctilious in keeping him informed of events. His deputy Jean Leguay wrote to Darquier on 3 August to tell him: 'the trains of August 19, 21, 24 and 26 will be composed of the children'.[53]

On 26 August, the day the massive round-ups began in the south, Louis was in Vichy. There he met Raymond-Raoul Lambert, in charge of UGIF in the southern zone. To this Jewish leader – and future victim – surrounded as both men were by massive Jewish arrests, Darquier complained in lofty tones about Laval and his exclusion from these Bousquet round-ups. 'What a strange regime,' wrote Lambert.[54] What a strange man, who has only his victims to listen to his complaints.

In September, according to José de Lequerica, Louis Darquier explained the correctness of the French position towards the Jews to Cardinal Gerlier.[55] This was unnecessary because although Gerlier adamantly protected Jewish children, and voiced his objection to racial hatred and persecution, his protests to Pétain always included avowals of his understanding of the 'Jewish problem' and of loyalty to Pétain, whom he was 'happy and proud' to serve.

Ambassadors in Vichy came to Pétain to make objections, muted or otherwise, and many other voices were raised too. Pétain, who received something like two thousand letters a day anyway, was sent many from Jews in the camps. One little boy wrote: 'Mama says there is nothing you can't do.' Others begged:

'Do not let them take my Mama. I am a little boy of ten, and today is my birthday. I am French and a Catholic, the parents of my mother were Jewish . . .'

'I am the mother of five children . . . my oldest fought under you at Verdun . . . my children have to wear the Yellow Star . . . have pity . . .'

'They have taken away my Mama, and I am alone and without any resource. I am fifteen years old . . .'

'My anguish . . .'

'Have pity . . .'

'I beg you . . .'

From every camp they wrote to him, for it was Laval, they believed, not Pétain, who must have arranged such terrible things. Outside the camps, his subjects wrote to him too: 'It is FRANCE which is condemned and dishonoured . . . I am ashamed to be a Frenchman, to be a Christian, to be a man . . .' They hoped for 'charity and justice', they hoped in him, their 'venerated *Maréchal*', and they hoped in France, 'eldest daughter of the Church'.[56] Donald Lowrie of the international YMCA 'appealed to Marshal Pétain in a special audience; representatives of the Quakers saw Laval. The result was nil.'

In Paris the cleverest *collabo* of them all, Robert Brasillach, wrote in *Je Suis partout*: 'We must remove the Jews in a block, and not keep the young ones.'[57] Within months the Catholic hierarchy had again fallen silent, reminded by an irritated Laval of the silence of Pope Pius XII on the matter. Any public protest against the deportation of the Jews was damaging to 'the work of the Marshal'. Vichy then offered the French Church certain concessions, and at the beginning of 1943 Pius XII sent messages. He was 'favourably impressed', he 'warmly praised the work of the Marshal', he welcomed signs of 'the fortunate renewal of religious life in France'.[58]

By the end of August, still keeping up appearances as to who was in charge, Bousquet had formally informed Darquier that 11,184 Jews had been collected, of whom 6,340 had already been sent to Drancy; the rest were about to follow, and his police were pursuing escapees. Bousquet was immensely fond of figures and of his own achievements; at the invitation of Laval, he would proudly give the Vichy council of ministers 'his description of the scene, the number of arrests' he had achieved.[59] His letter to Darquier was a rare case of inaccuracy from Bousquet: in fact his final tally from the Vichy Zone for 1942 was only 7,100.[60]

12,664 from the Occupied Zone plus 7,100 from the Vichy Zone equals 19,764, and by no means all of these came into 'deportable' categories – so the 'deportable' categories had to be changed. Thousands of French Jews had gone to Auschwitz by this time, whether Vichy liked it or not. To get more Jews of any kind, Vichy now had to accept that Jewish blood flowed through French Jews, as it did through foreign and stateless ones. First, this involved the despatch of the children. When that was done, all of them – Vichy and the Germans – turned their attention to the naturalisation laws of France. Bousquet reported that, with Pétain and Laval's agreement, he was drafting a bill which would remove citizenship from all Jews naturalised since 1932. In October Carl Theo Zeitschel from the German embassy demanded a report from Darquier on the number of Jews available in the Vichy Zone, having read in the press that they numbered 2.7 million.

Although blessed by Cardinal Suhard, only seventeen thousand Frenchmen had volunteered to work in Germany since the announcement of the Relève in June 1942. By August Fritz Sauckel had issued a decree demanding forced labour throughout the occupied territories, and on 4 September Laval had given in. But he was fighting Sauckel every inch of the way; he had no time for Jewish children or Jews, and no time for anyone who fussed about them, archbishops or cardinals or Louis Darquier. He begged the Germans to request no more from him; Jews naturalised after 1932 would follow soon, but he could no longer supply 'Jews in fixed number and at a set price "like something from a Uniprix shop"'.[61] It was this sort of response from Laval that hurled Louis Darquier into print in *Die Judenfrage* a month later.

On 20 July Eichmann had telephoned his decision that Jews unfit for work could be deported, children included, as soon as he could get sufficient transports, but that the children must be mixed with adults, so the French public would think they were being deported with their own parents. On 13 August the telegram came saying everything was ready for the children 'to roll'. On the same day the Franco-German Deportation Committee, without Darquier, held a meeting at which Leguay, Dannecker and Röthke discussed how to implement these instructions.

This was to be Dannecker's last appearance. Knochen got rid of him by reporting his sex life to Berlin. Not only did Dannecker frequent nightclubs and brothels in 'a scandalous fashion', often, it seems, with Galien, it was also implied that he ran or owned some of them.[62] The small number of Jews Dannecker offered to Berlin, instead of the fifty thousand Eichmann had first asked for, presumably made it easy for Knochen to get his way.

On 15 August the first trains set off. Small legs found it difficult to walk from the camps to the trains that took them to Drancy, or to climb up to the freight cars. French police lifted the babies and put them in. The descriptions of the departure of the children are almost as famous as the '*Marseillaise*': '. . . Jacquot, a little five-year-old of whom I was particularly fond, started shouting for me: "I want to get down, I want to stay with Mademoiselle . . ." The door of the car was shut and bolted, but Jacquot pushed his hand through a gap between the two planks and continued to call for me, moving his fingers. The adjutant . . . hit him on the hand.'[63]

Trains poured into Drancy from almost every *département*. The French authorities could not agree as to who would supply what to the camp. The result was that by the time the children got there, the conditions were so terrible that even the German officials were shocked. The inmates were skeletal, some ill to death. When the children joined them their short time at Drancy was equally piteous, and is equally notorious. They were listed by numbers, with a question mark for the children too young to know or speak their names. After days and nights in the sealed boxcars that brought them to Drancy, on arrival they were covered with insects and they smelt; they had impetigo, many were covered with sores.

Some had mementos given them by their departing parents – photos, messages, jewellery – sewn to their clothes or in their little bundles. Sometimes they lost their bundles, and searched for them in the Drancy courtyard. They lost their brothers and sisters, if they had them, and some could not speak to be able to find them. Wooden dogtags round their necks solved this sometimes, but if the children could speak, 'I'm Pierre's little brother' did not help.[64]

The bare rooms of Drancy were packed with children. Many of them were too small to navigate the stairs to the communal lavatory in the courtyard. There were buckets on the stairwells for them – always overflowing and dripping down the steps, as dysentery was added to diarrhoea. Rising and falling over this was a surge of whimpering and desperate crying. These are the children who believed they were going to some strange place to find their parents again, and they called this place 'Pitchipoi'.

The French administration and police decided the composition of each convoy and made up the lists of the Jews to go on each train: those marked 'D' were to be deported, those marked 'R' to remain. But the ill, the blind and nursing mothers went; the trains had to be filled each time. Louis Darquier's absence from all this is underlined by a letter he received from Jean Leguay at the beginning of August, outlining the systems used.

It took three days to get to Auschwitz; French police accompanied the sealed freight cars, the Germans took over at the frontier. The first of these children went to Auschwitz with adults who were not their parents on 17 August, 530 of them under the age of twelve. Sometimes sisters and brothers went together, sometimes siblings were separated to await another train. The balance of the thousand necessary in each train were foreign Jews from the Vichy Zone.

Before they left, men and women had their heads shaved, and the children did too. The day before they left Galien's men set up tables in the Drancy yard to search the bundles of the children, and took all the earrings, bracelets and brooches they found. So that the people living around Drancy would not notice, the children were woken early, to searchlights and the sound of the throbbing buses waiting for them in the yard. Shorn, many of them barefoot, the children were already beside themselves, and their sobbing meant they often could not hear as the police called out their names or numbers, the order to go. French police took some of the screaming children in their arms to the buses, and Ernst Heinrichsohn turned up at Drancy at 5 a.m. to make sure they left.

At le Bourget station the cattle trains which took them were sealed. For three days they lived in the dark, with no food, no water, and the usual bucket and straw. The seven trains that went off between 17 and 31 August took seven thousand Jews to Auschwitz, and the children made up about half this number. The youngest child sent in 1942 was Salomon Brojman, nine months old.

When Laval dined with Oberg on 2 September, his conversation about Darquier was part of his continuing attempts to get rid of him, and all the German authorities who were there or who learned about it afterwards understood it as such. When this was followed by Darquier's outburst in *Die Judenfrage* the embassy gave up on him; when he came to fisticuffs with Galien in October the SS did likewise. He had been in the job for four months, May to September 1942. Most of the 41,951 Jews sent to Auschwitz in 1942 went in those months, six and a half thousand of them Pétain's French Jews. 24,361 were gassed on arrival, the rest were put to work. In 1945, 784 men were still alive, and twenty-one women. In these four months almost half of all the Jewish deportees of France were despatched, in forty-three convoys. No trains went in October, and after a few in November they stopped for the winter.

Over six thousand children were sent to Auschwitz in 1942. A thousand of them were less than two years of age. The remainder were under seventeen. Of those, two and a half thousand were between six and twelve years of age. There are no accounts of the experiences of these children. We know that, whether aged nine months or thirteen, they had no food, no water, no air and no light on the journey to Auschwitz. As they could not be put to work, it is most probable that the children who did not die on the way were immediately exterminated, or taken, as so many children were, for medical experiments. We do know that none of the Vel' d'Hiv' children returned to France.

17

◄◦►

Having Fun

L OUIS DARQUIER WAS 'a *bon-viveur*, a bohemian, surrounded by many friends – creditors I believe – who received many favours in return', reported one of his former employees to the police after the Liberation. 'However, I don't think he was paid for any of this, despite his reputation for taking bribes. In reality, his services were probably rewarded by the bunfights he revelled in and in which his wife was very much involved. Of Irish origin, she was only too willing to display her anglophile feelings in public.'[1]

The pretence of Irish nationality was a sensible approach for Myrtle during these years. There are many glimpses of her, almost always in Paris, almost always associated with dinners in restaurants, or in the night-clubs and cafés of the city. In a few photographs of this time she is so thin she is almost unrecognisable except for the Jones mouth and her fetching hats, though her numbed expression could well have been a look of boredom. Her French remained primitive, and usually such photographs were taken at the launch of one or another of Louis' new associations, he standing under a portrait of Pétain, talking for far too long about Jews, she standing to attention, eyes glazed.

Myrtle, with her Australian and British citizenship, should have been in a Nazi concentration camp for enemy aliens, first in Besançon and then in Vittel.[2] In the early days of the war the Nazis arrested all British citizens – mostly nannies and butlers, dancers and English teachers – and a thousand British women spent the war in internment camps. At first it was hoped that Australia could be persuaded to 'move out of the orbit of Great Britain';[3] this hope soon disappeared. Everything English-owned was requisitioned, and the British embassy in Paris became a furniture depository. American women, who were not interned, had to report to the police every week – they were not allowed to own a horse, but they could own a bicycle, while English women left at liberty had to report to the police daily, and for them horses were allowed, but not bicycles.

Myrtle, neither English nor American, had other protectors besides Louis. Embassy life in Paris and Vichy, particularly that of neutral countries, was a hotbed of intrigue and subversion during the war. Franco's general staff had long been hand in glove with its German equivalent. The Spanish embassy on the avenue George V filtered mutual exchange of information and espionage activity, linking the Gestapo with French, Spanish and Italian secret police. José de Lequerica, the ambassador, a close friend of Otto Abetz and 'a notorious collaborator', often requested favours of Darquier, whom by 1943 he was addressing as 'my dear Commissioner and friend'.[4] Lequerica's military attaché in Paris for almost a decade from 1934, Barroso y Sánchez-Guerra, held just the kind of banquets Darquier most appreciated.[5]

Barroso, like Abetz, had been instructed to invite to the embassy people who were sympathetic to the Francoist cause. He was close to Franco, part of his immediate circle during the Civil War and one of his most devoted collaborators. Like Louis Darquier he was large, said to be corrupt, and was the kind of hunting-and-shooting military man much appreciated by Pétain. 'Louis always said that Barroso owed him'[6] – like Taittinger, it seems that Barroso received nuggets from Louis Darquier's CGQJ pot of gold.

For Myrtle, embassies had other uses. The Republic of Ireland had an ambassador to Occupied France, an expatriate Irishman, Count O'Kelley of Gallagh.[7] According to her family in Tasmania, O'Kelley revealed after the war that Myrtle had hidden British airmen during the Occupation. Her family also believe that she saved people from deportation and the gas chambers, but did not like to talk about it: when asked about it, her gift for fantasy seemed to fail her and she would not elaborate. There are no records of any of these events, but there are accounts of Myrtle describing such activities to others which, if true, would be equally bizarre. In such tales she took the role of Pauline, whose Perils she perhaps saw too much of in the early days of the cinema. She talked about intervening and saving people, leading them over the Alps, hiding them in apartments she did not have. She talked too of grand furniture and beautiful possessions, and also claimed to be a descendant of Inigo Jones. In fact, until early 1943 the Hôtel Fortuny remained the Darquiers' address. Myrtle was never seen at Louis' office, though her existence was well known by his staff. She was his wife in the French way, a person apart, not interested in politics – there was a daughter somewhere?[8]

'I think there were two personalities in Darquier,' said a Darquier family friend in Cahors. 'There was comedy. It was an act. He was a comedian of the boulevard. His title – you know how over the top they were about aristocratic names between the wars; his monocle from which he was never separated . . . he was a double man, he had two persons inside himself.'[9]

Louis Darquier's aim was to acquire as much money as possible – money to spend, not to hoard – with, preferably, fame and applause as an accompaniment. All this, embedded within a nationalist and aristocratic carapace, required that achievement should involve the least amount of work possible in the trade he had chosen, that of a professional anti-Semite. Myrtle was identical in this: there was her fantasy world, and her real charm and humour. Each accepted the other for different peccadilloes. Myrtle believed in Louis 'like a GOD'[10] and Louis understood Myrtle: 'Myrtle,' it was said, 'drank because the sky was blue and because it was not blue. She was an alcoholic.'[11] In addition to his womanising, Louis Darquier, like his father, had a fearful temper; he beat Myrtle, but he also told her, often, how much he loved her.

Vichy instituted *jours sans*, forbidding the selling of hard liquor on Mondays, Wednesdays and Saturdays, and of Pernod all the time, but Myrtle could always get wine. On dry days restaurants would sell it in teacups, and within walking distance of her hotel was the 'well-established wine business in the place Vendôme' of Count O'Kelley's expatriate family, 'able to provide much more than just wine'.[12] Yet Myrtle tried desperately not to drink, and not to appear drunk, because she feared Louis' anger more than anything.

Where did the money go? Louis' bar and restaurant bills were always enormous, but photographs suggest that Myrtle was not eating much black-market beefsteak or *foie gras*. Anne later said she took drugs. In public Louis repeatedly proclaimed that drug trafficking was the work of Jews, as part of their attempts to corrupt the French people, that they used 'the bindings of the Talmud to circulate cocaine . . . The Jew Lyon not only sells the drug, but also makes it. Three other Jews are his accomplices . . .'[13] Domestically, his views seem to have been otherwise.

But there was no shortage of drugs from non-Jewish sources. Louis

spoke on the radio as often as he could, and there was a drug ring associated with Radio-Mondial, the international radio station. Fernand de
Brinon, Vichy's ambassador in Paris, was said to have dealt in drugs in
his earlier days, and by 1942 'everything concerning Paris passed through
him'. Jean Cocteau, living in the Palais Royale, worried 'How will I get
my opium?' 'The answer was as usual, from someone friendly on the
staff of a restaurant in the rue Royale, who was apparently tolerated as
a supplier by the SD [the intelligence service of the SS].'[14] Doctors could
also supply drugs; not only was Jean Darquier to hand, but his wife Janot
qualified as a doctor in 1943.[15] The most likely source however was
Admiral René-Charles Platon at Vichy, a known user of cocaine.[16] If
Platon supplied Myrtle it must have been by way of Louis, because
Platon's rancorous anglophobia reached the point of hysteria after
Dunkirk, where he had been governor and commander of the French
forces.

Louis still visited Vichy. He worked for Laval, and had meetings with
him twice a month. As Darquier dealt with Jews for Vichy, Admiral
Platon, a rabid anti-Semite, dealt with secret societies and Masons; but
what connected the two men most firmly was their shared animosity for
René Bousquet and a shared admiration for Charles Maurras. Convinced
that Bousquet was a Mason, Platon pursued him, becoming a laughing
stock for this at Vichy, as well as for the gaiters and monocle he wore.
This latter resemblance to Louis Darquier was to prove fatal.

All of Germany wanted to come to Paris during the war years; it
was the prime posting. The murky grey-green uniforms of the
Wehrmacht, the chic black of the SS, the brown-gold elegance of
German diplomats and officials, were everywhere. Beautifully accoutred
German officers filled the churches on Sundays 'to show their
Catholicism [and] demonstrate that they do not persecute religions'.[17]
Beneath enormous publicity posters presenting the Russian, British and
American flags, behind which lurked an enormous caricature of a Jew
– 'The Power behind our enemies: the Jew!'[18] Parisians had to step off
the pavement to make way for any German who cared to pass.

By 1942 most of the French were scrabbling for food, for the
Germans took everything – '*ils nous prennent tout*' – and what they did
not take to Germany, they ate and drank *in situ*. When together, 'Baron
and Baroness Darquier de Pellepoix' had at their disposal all the food,
fizz and frivolities of Occupied Paris. This they could enjoy with many

old comrades. Charles Trochu became president of the Paris city council when Louis was reappointed a councillor in 1941, and Pierre Taittinger followed him. Louis was on various council committees, but rarely attended.

The most active and entertained group in Paris were the journalists and fascists of Louis' pre-war world. Nothing had changed. Some were subsidised by Laval, some by Pétain, all by one or another of the German services, and the unbridled rivalry and disputations between the Paris *collabos* were as acrimonious as ever. Céline was Shakespeare to all of them; they needed him because the *Liste Otto*, named after Abetz, banned nearly a thousand writers, including of course all Jewish writers and thinkers, and extending its disapproval to Shakespeare and Virginia Woolf.

Goebbels and Rosenberg came to Paris, and so did Goering in his white *Reichsmarschall* uniform, bejewelled and decorated, out-shopping them all and truffling out works of art for himself and Hitler. They, and now Louis, could afford the Folies-Bergère, only one of the famous cabarets and nightclubs which defied the blackout throughout the Occupation. Myrtle and Louis could stay up till five in the morning at clubs like the Lido, always full of German officers, or watch the Gypsy extravaganzas at another German favourite, the Shéhérazade, where champagne flowed through the dark nights. Maxim's, taken over by the Berlin restaurateur Otto Horcher, could get through twenty thousand bottles of champagne a month. Myrtle and Louis could go there, or to the Ritz, or to Pré Catalan near the quai St-Augustin where Picasso had his studio, or to the Café de Paris, Laval's favoured lunching place. Poets and writers and painters still frequented the Lipp and the Deux Magots; Simone de Beauvoir remained comfortably warm at the Flore.

Myrtle and Louis always lived in hotel rooms near the Champs-Élysées, whose cafés included Louis' favourite, Le Select, which was, like all those of Paris, full of Germans and French watching the midday parade of goose-stepping Nazi soldiers and whiling the hours away. The Champs-Élysées throbbed with activity. There were supper clubs and nightspots such as the Européen, a 'sumptuous rubbish bin' for *collabos*, next to dens like Le Colisée Café, notorious for black-market dealings, gigolos and gangs of wide boys.[19] The offices of Radio-Paris and Radio-City were also in the Champs-Élysées. The notorious broadcaster Jean-Hérold Paquis[20] announced every day, 'England, like Carthage, will be destroyed,' and often referred to the United States as led by 'Roosevelt and his three hundred rabbis'.[21] At numbers 31 and 33 was Organisation Todt, Albert Speer's construction office, responsible for forced, slave and paid labour, and at 52 was the Paris Propaganda Staffel which Louis Darquier used so often to issue his plans for the disposal of the Jews.

'Blindly following the Marshal', Maurice Chevalier chirped the loudest of all the French singers who performed throughout the Occupation.[22] The music halls, honkytonks and cafés of Montparnasse and Montmartre did roaring trade, and prostitutes earned a fortune from the occupying Germans, wifeless in Paris. Germans in uniform and their French companions attended 'fantastic dinner parties, with all the right French guests, Marquis So-and-so and Comte Tra-la-la'.[23] Helmut Knochen met Anatole de Monzie at the salon of the American heiress Florence Gould, whose Thursday lunches gathered every French and German of collaborative note together.

Fashion houses and couturiers, led by the horizontal collaboration of the indomitably anti-Semitic Coco Chanel, did excellent business, providing the wives and otherwise of German and collaborationist Paris with the clothes Myrtle so loved. With material rationed, much of the genius of Parisian *haute couture* was poured into the production of hats of fabulous construction, reaching from the heavens in avalanches of frills, flowers, stuffed birds or haricot beans, or, much more chic, little black netted pillboxes – most of these hats looked like feminine implements of war.

Decorated as she liked, what Myrtle remembered most about her years in Paris during the Occupation was listening to the great German musicians who came to play there. Jewish composers were of course banned – though Offenbach's 'Cancan' got away with it, in the interests of traditional French nightlife – but otherwise there was every kind of music. Wagner was sung wonderfully at the Paris Opera. There were concerts for workers, concerts in the parks and concerts by the regimental band of the Luftwaffe at Notre Dame. A Gypsy or a homosexual had more to fear from the Nazis than from Vichy during the Occupation, but it was safer to be neither. Django Reinhardt was a *Manouche*, a French Gypsy, but he saved himself by playing miraculous jazz at Porfiro Rubirosa's all-night parties and at the Moulin Rouge.

The Propaganda Staffel was a section of a much larger Nazi propaganda department, the Propaganda-Abteilung, responsible to Goebbels in Berlin. It controlled Parisian theatre, radio, cinema, art, music, literature, the press and publishing, including for the latter two the allocation of paper. Its primary aims, from the beginning, were the eradication of all traces of Jewish influence and the indoctrination of the French. To this end France was awash with posters and leaflets, tracts and brochures, plays, documentaries and newspapers explaining to the population the wonders of Nazi thought.

The Propaganda-Abteilung was attached to military command, the MBF, and it lacked finesse. Abetz and his French wife Suzanne held a more intellectually acceptable court at the embassy, but until the summer of 1942 he wrangled with Goebbels for control. Abetz won, and his Deutsche Institut (German Institute), under its director Karl Epting, became the centre for parties, lectures, exhibitions, language classes and social occasions. Through its doors and those of the embassy floated all of artistic and intellectual Paris, above all Céline, who loved music and of whom Epting was particularly fond. Darquier distanced himself a little from Céline after 1942; he was a rival prophet, rather than a hero now. But Myrtle could meet him often, because there were concerts at the German Institute more than once a week. All the masters of German music, amongst them Herbert von Karajan, Elisabeth Schwarzkopf, Walter Gieseking and Wilhelm Kempff, came to entertain and mix with the great and good of Paris.

Céline's third anti-Semitic blast, *Les Beaux draps*, was published in 1941, and Epting provided the paper to publish it and reprint its two predecessors, illustrated now with photographs of blacks, half-castes, communists and so on. Céline was fêted, better fed and wined than he had ever been, publishing articles and letters – 'Céline Tells Us' – in *Au Pilori, Je Suis partout*, everywhere. He remained impossible. He destroyed one of Abetz's dinner parties in February 1944 by insisting that Hitler was already dead and a Jew was now impersonating him.

Myrtle loved the theatre, and theatre, high and low, there was in abundance in Occupied Paris. While the Théâtre Sarah Bernhardt was forced to rename itself the Théâtre de la Cité, the Comédie-Française prospered, and most of the great actors of its company, including Jean-Louis Barrault, worked there throughout the war. Georges Courteline, a playwright Louise Darquier dined with during the First World War, had a play at the Comédie-Française during the Second, but his wife, who was Jewish, was not permitted to attend the rehearsals. Often the SEC 'set their ambushes in the corridors of the metro, at the entrances of cinemas or the exits of theatres',[24] but Cocteau, Claudel, Giraudoux, Montherlant, Anouilh and Sartre all put on plays, with varying degrees of enthusiasm, under the German occupation.

The outlook, however, was uncertain. As the defeat of Germany became more than a whisper of hope among the French population, the Paris fascists clamoured for Vichy to declare war on the Allies. When the Allies landed in French North Africa on 8 November 1942, there were 100,000 Vichy troops in Algeria, Morocco and Tunisia. Darlan, still Vichy commander-in-chief, attempted to negotiate a ceasefire, but surrendered on 11 November and went over to the Allies, only to be assassinated two weeks later. Laval had a useless meeting with Hitler a few days earlier, begging him for 'gestures' of approval and support. Hitler's reply was to invade the Vichy Zone on 11 November, and the German army moved into the villages and towns of the south. Vichy lost its empire, its fleet, which scuttled itself at Toulon, and its independence.

Laval saw Hitler again in December; with the support of Abetz, he wanted to form a single political party for Vichy, to act against the multitude of fascists and factions that made up collaborationist circles in Paris, most of whom hated him – Céline led the way, calling Laval 'a nigger and Jew'.[25] Hitler refused again, and when he did Laval turned to Joseph Darnand, a former member of Action Française, Croix-de-feu and the Cagoule. Darnand was a staunch, even a fanatical, Catholic and anti-communist. As a Cagoulard, Xavier Vallat had helped him to escape prosecution. Darnand was also a much-decorated war veteran, and was devoted to Pétain.

In January 1943, instead of forming his new political party, Laval placed Darnand in charge of the Milice,[26] a private army – blue jackets and trousers – set up to fight the growing French Resistance, and to serve as an armed guard for Pétain. To Pétain the Milice vowed: 'I swear to fight against democracy, against Gaullist insurrection and against Jewish leprosy.'[27] Henry Charbonneau edited its journal, *Combats*, and Colette wrote for it. Darnand was ruthless and violent, and so were his men, a great number of them practising Catholics, 'soldiers of Christ'. One *Milicien* leader carried around with him a Star of David made from the skin of a Jew. The Milice was in many ways a French Gestapo, and its name became as synonymous with execution and brutality as its German model. At first Pétain said of it, 'a few spectacular executions are better than riots and the breakdown of law and order'.[28]

In London, General de Gaulle had withstood the irritations of the Anglo-American alliance sufficiently to attract to his Free French movement men like Jean Moulin. Until René Bousquet displaced him, Moulin had distinguished himself by becoming, in 1937, the youngest *préfet* in France. Like Bousquet, he came from the south-west – from Béziers – but his republicanism led him swiftly into resistance, and legend. Today there is hardly a village in France that does not have a square or street named after him.[29]

By 1941 Moulin had reached London, and was recruited by de Gaulle, who parachuted him back to France in 1942 to achieve the impossible: the formation of a united French Resistance. The French who fought the Germans and Vichy, 'so different from each other ... so quick to tear each other apart'[30] were by this time a collection of disparate networks working undercover all over the country – the *Maquis* in the hills and forests, communists, Catholics, Jews, royalists, army and naval officers, socialists. Fighting alongside them were Spanish republicans, Poles, Italians, Lithuanians – and more.

Their sabotage and intelligence work for the Allies, and their propaganda, mostly through underground newspapers, had created a body of men and women whom Pétain and Laval hated as much as, if not more than, French communists. Under the codename 'Max', Moulin succeeded in his mission just as Pétain approved his Milice to destroy it. Five months later Moulin died under torture, but not before he had created a Conseil National de la Résistance (National Council of the Resistance).[31] This was the state of the French civil war in June 1943.

The year had opened with German reverses on the Eastern Front and the fall of Tripoli to the British. Then came the turning point of the war, the surrender of the German army at Stalingrad on 2 February. After this, everything changed. For the French, shortages got even worse: legal rations hardly fed half a human body. In the face of mounting German demands and increased repression from both their rulers, under the fatherhood of Pétain, life, already harsh, became horrible. In January Fritz Sauckel came to Paris again. In February Laval was required to transform the voluntary *Relève* into forced labour: the Service du Travail Obligatoire (STO), the Compulsory Labour Service, which eventually sucked almost 400,000 workers to 'serve' in Germany, or work on the Atlantic wall in France. Thousands took to the hills, to the *Maquis*, and went underground to join the Resistance. At the same time, after a gap of three months the deportations began again in February 1943. The French Church made representations to Vichy immediately: Archbishop Suhard begged Pétain that at least they should be carried out more humanely.

Most French civilians passed the war trying to avoid any contact with their German occupiers, but even in the exalted circles in which French and Germans circulated it was impossible to escape the growing unpopularity of Germany and Vichy. American films were banned in France, and the names of Jewish directors and scenes of Jewish actors were cut from existing films, but the movies remained immensely popular, and by 1945 what there was to see included many masterpieces, including Marcel Carné's ravishing *Les Enfants du paradis*.[32] Into every programme the Propaganda Staffel inserted German newsreels. By 1943 audiences were loudly booing every manufactured German triumph. The Germans reacted by ruling that films must no longer be shown in the dark. Booing under electric light proved equally popular, and soon half the cinemas in Paris were closed down.

Darquier kept his legal team at the CGQJ at work preparing new anti-Jewish decrees for presentation to Laval. Three categories obsessed him. First were those Jews who took refuge in the zone under Italian occupation – Italy refused to implement Nazi or French anti-Semitic laws. Mussolini did not have to accept Hitler's anti-Semitic laws, and did not until after his fall in 1943. When he was restored to power by the Nazis, the laws were enforced by the German police – Brunner's men did the work. Only twelve per cent of Italian Jews were deported, seven thousand out of fifty thousand living there, but it was the Italian police who protected Jews rather than Mussolini. There are many instances of furious rows between French and Italian police on the subject. Darquier's fury, of course, was more excessive.

Next came war veterans and French Jews who used Vichy's dispensations under Vallat's laws; but third, and most important, were half-Jews, both known ones and hidden ones. Only a new law and the scientific investigation of bloodlines could deal with this problem. Darquier requested the creation of a 'half-Jewish' status. He noticed that 'many half-Jews were working in the national radio broadcasting service', and considered banning mixed marriages, but knew this would never get through, the conversion of the Jews being a fixed and traditional Catholic aspiration.[33] He presented dozens of bills. Laval rejected all of them.

Louis tried another tack. Each time he was rejected he would go straight to whichever German power base he was using at the time – usually it was the Gestapo or the Judenreferat – and file a complaint. After his turmoil in the summer of 1942, first in Vichy then in Paris over the deportations, he chose the embassy. He turned for help to Zeitschel, its specialist on Jewish questions, who conferred with Dannecker; both agreed to force Vichy to give Louis support and money.[34]

Because of Bousquet, Louis knew what he had to do to reposition himself more favourably and get the money he wanted. Bousquet had told Oberg and Knochen that Louis Darquier was given no money by Vichy because he had produced no proposals. So, in the immediate aftermath of his failures of 1942, he came up with shoals of them. He turned his attention to propaganda. He would cajole the civil population, suffering in ignorance and deluded by Jewish propaganda. In 'enlightening them about the Jewish problem' he would save them, save France, and save himself.[35]

Louis' great passion was for the media, and even his numerous critics agreed that 'if he was little occupied at the Commissariat, Darquier, in another way, and at a more general level, was vastly active'.[36] What he liked best were associations and unions, floridly named little newspapers, lectures to the like-minded in halls and restaurants – preferably restaurants – surrounded by followers and henchmen who looked up to him, defended him with their fists, listened to him talking for a long time and drank with him into the night.

He decided that his new thrust would concentrate almost exclusively on FRENCH RACE and FRENCH BLOOD. It is often said of Louis Darquier that he was a French Nazi, as so many of the Paris *collabos* were. But this was not so; he would take German money, but to him Germans were uncivilised savages. He was a French hooligan, a racist *à la française*: 'The Jewish problem,' he declared, 'is not specifically a German problem . . . it faces all nations and has taken on urgent proportions in France. Germany has simply been the first country in the modern era to provide a governmental solution to the problem . . . the French government [must] do the same.'[37]

Louis set to work in a flurry of activity, and by 6 November 1942 Pétain had already approved the creation of two Chairs at the Sorbonne, one in Ethnology in the Faculty of Medicine, and one in Contemporary Jewish History in the Faculty of Letters. Within weeks Darquier came up with third and fourth inventions: a Commission Scientifique pour l'Étude des Questions de Biologie (Scientific Commission for the Study of Racial Biology) and an Institut d'Anthropo-Sociologie (Institute of Anthropo-Sociology). The institute was to be the guardian of racial purity, devoted particularly to 'the problem of mixed marriages' and 'the study, establishment and protection of the scientific bases of racial selection . . . with a view towards improving cultivation, breeding and race'. Its members – doctors, professors and lawyers – were presided over by Claude Vacher de Lapouge, the doctor-lawyer son of Georges, another nineteenth-century anti-Semitic 'racial theorist'. Robert Castille and Pierre Leroy were members, and in December Louis appointed to it his brother Jean.[38]

Although Pétain had considerable reservations about the choice of a homosexual for the post, the intellectual Abel Bonnard, 'la Gestapette', became Laval's new Minister for Education in 1942.[39] Darquier's academic chairs and anthropo-sociological arrangements came under Bonnard, 'a pathetic old queen with mascara-ed eyes' and a fuzz of white hair, a fascist and an anti-Semite, and another high-liver like Darquier. It was he who found the professors Louis required. Louis did the honours at the inaugural event of his Institute of Anthropo-Sociology at 43, rue de Monceau, in the 8th arrondissement. Talking about his work to Le Matin, he explained, 'Up till now the quality of a human being has been too often neglected in favour of quantity. It is normal to encourage and to support large families, but it is also normal and just to encourage healthy individuals rather than imbeciles and the physically handicapped.'[40]

In its few months of life, streams of anti-Semitic figures from Darquier's past came and went through the revolving doors of the institute; it had three directors within six months.[41] At the CGQJ, as Darquier had learnt from his experiences with Galien, German spies were omnipresent, everyone was watching everyone else, everyone was on the take, and everyone was reporting this to the Gestapo. Louis wanted to filter his profits away from suspicious eyes. To achieve this he created his fifth and favourite group, the Union Française pour la Défense de la Race (UFDR), French Union for the Defence of the Race. This was no more than a rebirth of his pre-war Anti-Jewish Union. He told the embassy that he wanted his new union 'to lead the masses in the struggle against the Jews'.

He had grandiose ideas about Jewish properties he could Aryanise to house each of his new associations, but particularly the UFDR, for which he had his eye on a sequestered Jewish bank in the boulevard Haussmann.[42] In fact its registered office, in December 1942, was Louis and Myrtle's room in the Hôtel Fortuny, though soon an exasperated embassy pushed it into the ground floor of 21, rue la Boétie, where the Nazis housed a miscellanea of anti-Semitic organisations.[43] More than anything else, the UFDR got Darquier out of his German-infested head-quarters, because in theory it had sections in all the CGQJ's regional offices. Off Louis would go, 'encouraging, monitoring and coordinating' his troops.[44]

Nothing about the French Union was new; Louis even used the statutes of his Club National from 1936, changing only the words 'the practice of sport' to 'the integrity of our race'.[45] The moral values of the race were also to be restored. One of his cronies later explained that Louis founded it 'to strengthen French unity by the following means: the fight against abortion, venereal disease, alcoholism, immigration policy etc. . . .'[46]

By 12 December 1942 Louis Darquier's *magnum opus*, his propaganda manifesto, was ready, and when he presented it to the German author-ities he announced his sixth and seventh innovations, a Propaganda Department and the transformation of Sézille's IEQJ into the lengthier IEQJER – the Institut d'Étude des Questions Juives et Ethno-Raciales (Institute for the Study of Jewish and Ethno-Racial Questions). Under Georges Montandon, the IEQJER would lecture the public: 'pure doctrine' for the educated Frenchmen, 'basic information for the lower classes'.[47] This, another 'organisation for scientific study',[48] rose upon the flickering shadows of Louis' Commission for the Study of Racial Biology and the Institute of Anthropo-Sociology, which by March 1943 had already been deemed 'inappropriate' by Heinz Röthke. What Louis wanted from these organisations, apart from money, was scientific authority for his racial views, 'it was his pet subject'.[49]

Once again it was to Ernst Achenbach at the embassy that Louis revealed his plans, attaching to his lengthy proposals for propaganda a request for an automobile which he could use at night and on Sundays, the better to circulate around Paris: a car was absolutely necessary if they wanted him to educate the French masses about Jews.

A Vichy law of 11 July 1942 had allocated the Commissariat a further 2.1 million francs (worth £360,000 today) for its propaganda service. Darquier's multitude of plans forced Laval to give in to German pressure, and by the end of December 1942 Louis finally got the money he had been demanding from Vichy for so many months.

The embassy was the German patron of Louis' propaganda efforts, financing up to two-thirds of the costs, though as the prospect of German defeat loomed Louis had already begun to announce publicly, again, that he refused German money. Pierre Gérard ran the propaganda department at the CGQJ in addition to the UFDR; it was Gérard, like Antignac, who did the real work.[50] One of his first tasks was to hire an assistant 'to compile reports as to how certain Jewish companies, and the Louis Dreyfus firm in particular, gained their fortunes'.[51]

The propaganda proposals Gérard wrote for Darquier covered every contingency, categorising the French public like railway carriages. There were first-class ('cultivated'), second-class ('this group does not have the same capacity for grasping complex issues as the first') and third-class persons ('the masses'). For the latter he proposed:

- fiction (crime, romance, swashbuckling stories) in which the Jew plays a pernicious role
- Amusing radio shows (Jewish jokes, funny sketches etc.)
- theme films (e.g. the Jew SÜSS)
- special newspapers adapted to the intellectual level of the masses providing information in a humorous format ('Le Canard enchaîné', 'Le Rire' etc.)

Darquier, in Gérard's prose, promised German command that each class of French person would be targeted by newspapers suitable to their intelligence. He announced hundreds of plans: a youth section, radio programmes, a radio station to be called Radio Révolution, a cinema section which would make films and documentaries, a press agency to assist anti-Jewish journalists with subsidies for press campaigns against Jews. He would hold exhibitions, arrange lectures and publish tracts, brochures and books – these were to be only '2–300 pages long . . . the style and text should be light and the works well illustrated'. He would produce posters and leaflets, and the militants who distributed these throughout the regional offices would be 'an excellent way of keeping central intelligence informed'. He proposed infiltration, too, into schools and youth clubs, 'sports societies (sailing, cycling, camping, swimming etc.) [and] student bodies, mutual benefit societies ... philosophical and religious societies'.[52]

Darquier had learnt many tricks of propaganda from Germany and fascism, of which the one he used most was repetition. His mantra ran: 'We have lost everything – our army, our navy and our colonies: all that remains is our race. It is still pure. Let us start a national revolution and together we shall help to build an eternal France in a new Europe.'

By the end of January 1943, cheques in pocket, Louis had returned to his social life, celebrating the launch of each of his new projects at dinners, lectures, *soirées* and receptions. He gave interviews and speeches, he broadcast on the radio. In the New Year, perhaps because it was all too much to pack into his room at the Hôtel Fortuny, he moved back to his old hotel, the Terminus, opposite the Gare St-Lazare.[53]

In 1942 Louis had complained that Laval would not permit him to broadcast on Vichy's radio station, Radiodiffusion Nationale, Radio-Vichy; he thought Bousquet was responsible for this. In October 1942, to counteract the profound public reaction to the July and August deportations, Vichy gave the CGQJ its own programme. Basically these broadcasts were rousing 'Thoughts for the Day'. For ten minutes, three times a week, on Mondays, Wednesdays and Fridays, just before 10 p.m. Louis addressed the French nation on the subject of 'The Jewish Question in France and Throughout the World'.

For such a large man, Louis' voice was high and squeaky, and of course untrained. He repeated himself too, in an amalgam of paragraphs from the *Protocols* and nationalist patter about French glory, French blood and the Jewish peril, much of it culled from his 1930s editorials. Most of all, his forty broadcasts ridiculed any suggestion of pity for the Jews – every tall story about their sufferings was just 'Jewish propaganda'. One listener, signing the letter 'A Christian', wrote to him: 'You say that Jews are dirty and speak no languages correctly. We are sure that you are well washed and that you speak German very well indeed.'

Louis was taken off after three months of such performances, and a professional took over. But radio was a key segment of his propaganda promises, so he was given a twice-weekly broadcast, again on Radiodiffusion Nationale, at midday on Mondays and Fridays. This was three minutes of anecdotal anti-Semitism, solemnly topped and tailed with Louis Darquier's theme song: 'We have lost everything. The only treasure left to us is our race . . .' accompanied by a gong.[54]

After the war Pierre Gérard defended Louis' performances – and his own, because he probably wrote all of the fifty or so broadcasts – by stating that 'their excessive nature was calculated deliberately to reduce their impact'. Louis appealed for denunciations on the air, and he got them; they were always followed up by Antignac and Louis, who passed on the results of their enquiries to the German authorities.

In general, however, throughout 1943 Louis Darquier was permitted to play, and play he did, interrupting this with forays in all directions aimed at capturing or recapturing favour from above. This is not to say he had no hand in the deportations which continued, for each department of the CGQJ was inevitably involved in them. The persecution of every Jewish person was the result of some aspect of its work, but mostly Darquier concerned himself with propaganda and money, and with anything to do with secret Jewish blood. As soon as Bousquet had fulfilled his August 1942 obligations as to the number of Jews deported, Darquier issued a decree instituting a provisional monthly payment of six million francs, to be withdrawn from 'Jewish fortunes'. On 27 November 1942 he replied to a query from Maurice Papon, secretary-general of the Gironde *préfecture*. Papon had deported two convoys of Jews from Bordeaux: who was to pay for this? Darquier told him to send the bill to UGIF, who paid it.

All this Louis Darquier achieved as German disillusion with him rose from a hum to a roar. After Abetz was withdrawn from Paris in disgrace on 12 November, his assistant Rudolf Schleier had taken over at the embassy; he was soon driven to distraction by Louis. The embassy was already shaken by the affair of *Die Judenfrage*, and an exceptionally shrill note was added to the memos of indignation poured out by Dr Peter Klassen, chief of its propaganda office, who provided Darquier with two-thirds of the funds his propaganda efforts required throughout 1943. 'How did we get ourselves in this situation?' Klassen would ask his fellow Germans. 'How can we get rid of him?'[55]

Knochen was the first to agree with him. After the débâcle with Galien, his SD and Gestapo had no need to rely on Louis Darquier.

They still had spies everywhere amongst the anti-Semitic underworld – Coston, Henri-Robert Petit, Galien himself, the gang of criminals known as the French Gestapo at the rue Lauriston, and hundreds of others who could provide the fervour Darquier lacked. But Knochen had chosen Darquier over Galien, and by now it was clear to him that both Pétain and Laval didn't take Louis seriously, and that 'his behaviour was often contradictory, depending on the fluctuations of his private life or his financial position'.[56]

On 12 March Darquier's response, probably when drunk, was to attack Laval in public again, and violently. The Propaganda Staffel held two or three press conferences each week. In the usual manner, Nazi officials sat at a long table and instructed the press. On this occasion Louis Darquier sat with them, and let forth in considerable detail about Vichy's recalcitrance over the new bills he wanted Laval to introduce. Darquier's livid attack on Laval, being delivered at a Propaganda Staffel press conference, seemed authorised, so his astonished audience wondered whether this was a German attack on Laval. Such was not the case. The French police, who never stopped recording Louis Darquier's activities for Bousquet's security service, noted a week later that Laval was musing over exactly how to get rid of Louis Darquier. Parisian *collabos* were also complaining that Louis was 'too assiduous in his attendance at *"les boîtes de nuit"'*. The patience of the embassy, Laval's supporters, was near its end.

In truth, Louis was not spending his money only on the pleasures of the flesh – he used it for his friends too. This is how it worked. André Chaumet, a deputy vice-president of Louis' UFDR, was also a vice-president of the Association of Anti-Jewish Journalists, the AJA, as was Henry Coston, who wrote letters to Louis these days asking for favours and humbly addressed to 'My dear Minister and friend'. Through his UFDR, Darquier gave sixty thousand francs to the AJA and twenty thousand francs to finance its press agency. Louis' friend André Chaumet received a subsidy of fifteen thousand francs and a sequestered 'Jewish' publishing house, Éditions Strauss, was placed at his disposal.[57] All these francs seem to have been spent elsewhere: 'lacklustre' was the mildest word Dr Klassen used to describe the AJA and all its works.

By March 1943 Louis Darquier had seven institutes, associations and unions in his portfolio, but none of them proved a success. The first person to go was Pierre Gérard; the Germans 'resigned' him in February

1943, and the thoroughly disillusioned Dr Klassen took over, appointing a businessman, Louis Prax – 'our man at the CGQJ' – to control Louis' 'pet subject'.[58] The demise of these endeavours – Louis watched as students booed and threw liquid gas during the lectures at the Sorbonne, and whistled and shouted 'None of this rubbish in France' – more or less coincided with Louis' now desperate launch of his IEQJER on 24 March 1943.[59]

Under a bombardment of choleric announcements from Captain Sézille, with Professor Montandon in charge, Louis gave one of his longest speeches, evoking the past, present and future of French anti-Semitism, praising himself and his adventures in the place de la Concorde on 6 February 1934, denouncing a list of his enemies, rendering homage to the Germans, and also, unctuously, to Laval. His 'I have confidence in him' was an anxious attempt to dampen down the scandal he had created by attacking Laval twelve days before. 'Our battle,' Louis cried, 'is nothing else but a fight between good and evil, between God and Satan.' Georges Montandon announced the courses at the institute, one each for onomastics, eugenics and demography, history of literature, Judaeocracy (how Jews take over a country) and ethno-racial philosophy. He then gave the first lecture himself, on the Jewish virus and its responsibility for the fall of Rome, the French Revolution and the fall of France in 1940.[60]

Louis' speech was the opening gambit in a last desperate struggle to save himself. By 6 March 1943, forty-nine thousand Jews had been deported, nothing approaching the number demanded by Eichmann. Bousquet was almost ready with his own denaturalisation law, about which he had not consulted Darquier. Dr Klassen sent a memo of despair to his boss, Rudolf Schleier:

All German services . . . have declared that it is no longer possible to keep Darquier de Pellepoix . . . the result of Darquier de Pellepoix's activity over his past year in office is nil in all areas . . . Vichy does not take Darquier seriously . . . the Aryanisation programme has come to a standstill . . . this *bon vivant* loses all interest in work when he finds himself in such a well-paid position . . . the failure of Darquier in all areas is striking, especially in the field of propaganda . . .

However, 'Darquier has declared that he considers himself to be irreplaceable.'[61]

On 14 April 1943 Darquier was removed as president of the UFDR and Alex Delpeyroux, a protégé of Fernand de Brinon and a former political journalist from *Le Jour*, replaced him. Louis had thought of Delpeyroux as his vice-president; in fact Delpeyroux, briefed by Laval that Darquier was a 'fanatic and a madman', kept Laval informed in detail of the plans of the CGQJ.[62]

Through a miraculous coup Darquier hung on, for a time, as honorary president of his UFDR. Darquier's miracle, though brief, was of such magnitude that every German commandant and French official had to bow before it and, temporarily, before him. On 10 April he announced the discovery of a hidden Jewish art collection – the Schloss Collection – of such value that every German official had to go into reverse mode, and for four months his fortunes were in a fabulous ascendant. Two days after the discovery of this treasure he began a counter-attack against Bousquet's denaturalisation proposals, but mostly, he partied. On 30 April he sent out invitations:

> On the occasion of the first anniversary of my appointment to the
> post of Commissioner for Jewish Affairs, I shall be bringing
> together my senior colleagues for a lunch on Saturday 8 May . . .
> Monsieur de Brinon [is] hosting this luncheon . . .

Dinner followed dinner, lunch followed lunch, and to these events every German official who had read and agreed with Dr Klassen's indictment of Louis Darquier had to turn up and celebrate with him. Most typical was a luxurious banquet on 29 May at l'Écu de France in rue d'Alsace to celebrate the twentieth anniversary of the foundation of the anti-Semitic newspaper *Le Pilori*, now *Au Pilori*. Gathered with German command were all the Paris *collabos*, including its literary stars – Céline, Brasillach and Rebatet amongst them.[63]

One of the few not to have to temporarily bow and scrape before Louis was Georges Oltramare, founder of *Le Pilori*, although his own programme on Radio-Paris, 'The Jews Against France', was financed by Louis. On this occasion, however, it was necessary to accept Louis Darquier as guest speaker. Oltramare later recollected:

Although I played an important role in the appointment of
Darquier de Pellepoix to the High Commission for Jewish
Questions, he knows nothing about it. As he has seduced so many
women, he likes to think that Lady Luck shines on him, that it is his
merit and his merit alone that manages to achieve miracles.

. . . Both delegates to a Congress for the reform of the League
of Nations, we quickly used the familiar 'tu' when speaking to each
other. The moment he assumed the dignity of Commissioner,
Darquier, afflicted by amnesia, asked me: 'By the way, do we use
"tu" or "vous" with each other?'

'What a question, my dear minister!' [replied Oltramare] 'Every
time I had the honour of approaching Your Excellency, I used the
third person.'

My witticism didn't offend Darquier who snorted, readjusted his
monocle and let out a jerky, whinnying laugh. Valiant, always drunk
and always broke, Darquier was as vain and self-important as a
vaunting musketeer.[64]

The waters of Louis' salvation flowed swiftly away. His Institute of
Anthropo-Sociology was subsidised with 100,000 francs a month. These
payments, already irregular, were diminished substantially after Louis had
processed the money via his UFDR. On 24 August Pétain was to seal
his doom, but well before that the Germans scented another Darquier
failure on the horizon, and closed down the institute. Next they shut
down Louis' IEQJER, and took him off the radio. Although they did
not officially dissolve the UFDR until October, its last meeting was held
in July, as 'Delpeyroux and M. Prax . . . came into conflict with Darquier
de Pellepoix for personal reasons'.

Prax was spying on Darquier and reporting his every move to Dr
Klassen at the embassy. To prevent this, in July Darquier tried to insert
his own man, Hafner, to 'paralyse' Prax.[65] Klassen, who had been told
to lay off Darquier, erupted again, issuing more and more outraged
memos about the 'startling' behaviour of the Commissioner for Jewish
Affairs and demanding his replacement.

At the same time Louis came up with a new venture, an attempt to
buy *Au Pilori*, which was up for sale in July 1943. *Au Pilori*, dismissed
by Darquier two years earlier as 'in the pay of the Germans', was now
the anti-Semitic newspaper of his dreams, with a circulation of eighty

thousand copies. After complex financial twists and turns, in the end Prax won the battle, paying 3.5 million francs plus '1,700,000 francs under the table' for *Au Pilori*, and a grateful embassy moved him from the UFDR to run it for them. Alex Delpeyroux replaced Prax as director of propaganda at the CGQJ. Louis immediately fell out with him. At this point Dr Klassen had reached a ceiling of fury.[66]

The struggle over the bone of *Au Pilori* brought down the final curtain on Louis Darquier's propaganda business affairs. His propaganda department had a monthly budget of 300,000 francs, excluding salaries. Of this Darquier paid himself 200,000 francs a month (worth £26,000 today), by transferring this sum from the CGQJ to his UFDR. This was meant to fund his institutes and so forth, but it rarely if ever did. Where did all the money go? No one came to any meetings at rue la Boétie. The proposed films were never made. There were no lectures or exhibitions, no swashbuckling novels and no infiltration of schools or sailing clubs. The only activity was the 'huge purchase' of anti-Semitic books, some distributed free to the press, but mostly sold at the UFDR's bookshop. Darquier also charged for the privilege of joining his UFDR – ten francs a head. This limited customers to almost none.[67]

He did produce one glossy twenty-four-page brochure for the UFDR, printing twenty thousand copies of it, but it was never distributed. On the front is a picture of a mother feeding five children, with the slogan 'Our greatest National Treasure IS OUR RACE!' Inside, one of the points covered – mostly written by Pierre Gérard – reads: 'madness is three times more frequent amongst Jews than Aryans'.

18

◄○►

Loot

ONE OF THE ABIDING beliefs of the apostles of *The Protocols of the Elders of Sion* is an almost mystical faith in the vastness of hidden Jewish wealth. From his exalted position as commissioner, first through the organisation inserted by Pierre Galien, then by the daily dedication of Joseph Antignac, Louis Darquier was now at the helm of a business whose principal concern was the legal and illegal appropriation of Jewish assets. This was called 'economic Aryanisation'. It occupied two-thirds of the time of the CGQJ and was 'the cornerstone of the whole system'.[1]

Louis had his eye on all this from the beginning: 'It is mainly a question of depriving Jews of their principal weapon, i.e. money,' he told the press in May 1942. 'Economic Aryanisation is achieved either by transferring Jewish property to Aryans, or purely and simply, in such cases when the first solution is not possible, the liquidation of Jewish assets. This is a huge task involving some 100 billion francs, perhaps more. In Paris alone, for example, are 3,500 apartment buildings belonging to Jews.'[2]

Darquier was interested in 'political Aryanisation' – laws, camps, deportation, exclusion – because only then could 'good economic Aryanisation' be effective. He paid considerable attention to the removal of Jews from the professions, particularly doctors and teachers, and of Jewish children from schools. But such controls were well exercised by Vichy, as they were by members of these professions, as anxious as Vichy to eliminate Jewish competition. For economic Aryanisation however, the CGQJ provided a complete service for the Vichy state, with scrupulously kept files which identified all Jewish businesses; this was easier to do from Paris, as most Jewish assets were in the Occupied Zone.

While Coston and Faÿ got on with despoiling Freemasons for Vichy, the CGQJ became, more than anything else, its money factory. This was a perfect job for Louis Darquier, as he could extract money from a stone. Keeping it was quite another matter. He could now be crucially involved in the Aryanisation of all Jewish 'industrial, commercial, real estate and trading enterprises', buildings, apartments, offices, shares and possessions – furniture, antiques and jewellery; pianos, bathtubs, basins and chandeliers if it came to that. Vichy's 'elimination' of 'all Jewish influence in the national economy' included 'hidden assets' and artistic property – libraries, decorative art, porcelain collections and, above all, some of the great painting collections of France. All that was missing was the 'agriculture, fishing and mining industries', and forestry, a consequence of the modest number of Jews working in these sectors.[3]

Louis Darquier could now strut before the 'international speculators' typified by the Lévy, Baumann and Louis-Dreyfus families, those Jews who had blighted his life. Most members of these families had fled, were in prison or concentration camps, or were dead, but strut Darquier did – to the usual degree. His approach to other people's money was always small-time: it was pickings he was after, percentages, and while he scurried about after money, spending it was his prime concern. His involvement in economic Aryanisation was spasmodic, and nearly always personal or emotional. He would spot a name he did not like, he would decide that some Aryan asset was full of lurking Jewish blood, and he would pounce.

Above, beneath and to the left and right of him, an empire of appropriation sprang up, for it was here, in the area of Jewish wealth, that the Germans and Vichy worked most closely together. Jews were to be separated from every possession and from every financial enterprise. The rules the Germans issued to Vichy were that 'both French laws and German ordinances for Aryanisation are enforced in the Occupied Zone. If a contradiction arises between them then German ordinances take precedence. In the event that German ordinances go further than French laws, then the former also take precedence. It is the duty of the Commissariat for Jewish Affairs to enforce French instructions and German ordinances.' 'To avoid creating the impression that Germans alone wish to take the place of Jews', in all instances Frenchmen were required to do this work.[4] To make sure that Frenchmen did it, they inserted German overseers into an entire floor of the CGQJ headquarters in place des Petits-Pères, the 'infestation' so loathed by Louis Darquier.

To avoid illegal appropriation, the Germans needed Vichy's agreement and its civil service, for economic Aryanisation involved the sequestration of such vast enterprises as Galeries Lafayette and Messageries Hachette, banking companies such as Rothschilds and Lazard Frères, oil, steel and insurance companies, and art collections of value beyond imagining; in fact everything into which German control could be inserted to transfer products, money and shares to the Reich.

Preliminary measures began as soon as Paris fell, and appropriation began in earnest on 18 October 1940, when the Germans issued a decree setting up provisional administrators for all Jewish concerns in the Occupied territory and requiring Jews to go to police headquarters to declare their possessions.[5] Jewish enterprises were to be handled in three ways: taken over by a non-Jew, sold, or liquidated. All such decisions were to be reported by the temporary administrator, French, to the military authority, German. Shareholdings were considered Jewish if a third of the shareholders were Jewish. This broadened opportunities. Vichy also set to work in October 1940, and matched the German decree by establishing the Service de Contrôle des Administrateurs Provisoires (SCAP) – the first move in a vicious struggle between Vichy France and Nazi Germany for control of the Jewish wealth of France.

From the very beginning Vichy asserted that Jewish property would not be touched, but from the very beginning, it was. Attention to the niceties about who was and who was not Jewish became a movable feast once property was involved. If you were Jewish or half-Jewish, or had a Jewish name, or were denounced as any of these, your property came under the eagle eye of the Vichy state.[6]

On 13 May 1942, a week after Louis Darquier's appointment as its commissioner, the CGQJ incorporated SCAP into its new Economic Aryanisation Section. Darquier did not deal with this himself. Lucien Boué had been chief secretary to both the Paris and the Seine city councils, and had lent Darquier money over the years. In return Louis placed him in charge of the Economic Aryanisation Section with a staff of over seven hundred, three-quarters of the entire personnel of the CGQJ. As Boué's deputy, briefly, Louis promoted his most loyal servant, Pierre Gérard.[7]

Fanning out beneath both of his chiefs of staff, first Galien then Antignac, the Aryanisation Section, linked on the one hand to German command, on the other to the CGQJ's own police, the SEC, became by far the largest section of Louis Darquier's empire, with many sub-sections devoted to specific areas of spoliation. For the Germans, collaborating in economic despoliation was also a weapon of propaganda, as 'approval of the fight against the Jews is given easily when they are seen to enjoy economic advantages'.[8] This meant that many levels of French society were corrupted by the sequence of events which followed appropriation. Aryanisation was a creeping plant which grew into almost every aspect of French business, professional and commercial life during the Vichy years, trailing down from the bankers, industrialists and insurance companies, the doctors, lawyers and judiciary on high, to the secretaries, employees, shopkeepers and concierges who served them.

Galien put paid German informers into various departments of the CGQJ, sold Jewish properties to his friends and mistresses at knock-down prices or placed them in appropriated apartments, and appointed others – many of them considered criminals even by avenue Foch – as provisional administrators. Thus the row between Darquier and Galien in October 1942 began through Boué, supported by the tireless Pierre Gérard, who produced a lengthy report detailing all Galien's embezzlements and misdeeds. Gérard's reward for the defeat of Galien was to be despatched immediately to an equally uncomfortable hot seat in Darquier's propaganda activities.

Because Darquier survived, so did Boué, but Galien's replacement by Antignac made no difference to the atmosphere. Aryanisation had been 'a battle to the death between Galien and Boué, with Darquier the filling in the sandwich'.[9] Antignac and Boué carried on in the same manner as before, but Antignac's efficiency and his control of the SEC ensured that Boué's incompetence, at least, was kept in modest check. If Antignac was on the take – and his staff certainly thought he was – he was much better at hiding it, and at the Liberation he was clever enough to burn as many files as he could lay his hands on.

Darquier and Boué took a much noisier approach. Behind every Aryan administrator they saw a hidden Jew, the original owner, gesticulating behind a helpless Frenchman – 'men of straw', such front men were called. But Darquier, Antignac and Boué would deal with Jews if the money was right, so whether for purposes of bribery or for spoliation, their investigations extended to 'all people with a German-sounding name' or 'with a name thought to be Jewish'.[10]

The first move of the Economic Aryanisation Section was to

appoint a provisional administrator or trustee to sell or liquidate a Jewish asset. If sold, it must be to an Aryan; if liquidated, it was to be asset-stripped by auction. Vichy insisted that 'trustees replacing removed Jewish owners will, in almost all cases, be French', and except for a hundred-odd who were Germans, they were.[11] Besides the legal profits arranged by Vichy law, the illegal profits in all this were vast, for the trustee himself, already salaried, and for the organisation and for anyone who worked there.

Every possibility could present extra income. Should the business be sold? There was money in making this decision, by taking bribes from competing bidders. The collection of profiteers and grafters who became involved in this were very often friends of Darquier and his henchmen. Apartments and commissions, buildings and garages, villas in the south of France, all were Darquier's now to distribute, and to be paid for the favour. Sometimes such 'friends' could acquire as many as a hundred trusteeships. Most favoured of all were his old colleagues from the Paris city council, of whom Pierre Taittinger proved to be perhaps the most enthusiastic. He was particularly well placed from the beginning, because his relationship with Vallat went back for decades. Taittinger replaced Trochu as president of the Paris city council in May 1943. This made matters even easier for Taittinger, and indeed for others on the city council. Trochu was of course also rewarded, as were the Comte de Castellane and many others. On 3 February 1943, in a letter carefully written before his presence was required at the Madeleine to celebrate Darquier's annual Mass for 6 February, Taittinger enquired of Darquier about some establishments in Lille. He 'would be delighted to receive their Aryanisation in the near future'. A month later they were his.[12]

Taittinger used the headed writing paper of the president of the Paris council for the requests which he fired off to both Boué and Darquier, asking for and receiving 'interesting Jewish businesses' for his brother-in-law Louis Burnouf.[13] After the receipt of one, Taittinger wrote to Darquier asking for more. Three months later Burnouf had sixteen Jewish enterprises to 'administer'. In December 1943 Taittinger again asked for more – he had a large family – managing to irritate Darquier, who sharply reminded him that by this time Burnouf was on the point of controlling twenty-seven Jewish enterprises.

Trochu also asked for more lucrative provisional administrations 'for a friend', while Taittinger continued in this mode until the Allies were at the gates of Paris. At that point Taittinger's transformation into a *résistant* was one of the most startling of the war.

There are hundreds of thousands of such examples: the papers of the Economic Aryanisation Section are an Aladdin's cave of boxes bursting with papers testifying to the enormous energy called forth by human greed. However, any analysis of the unseemly scramble after Jewish wealth is often ambiguous, always complex and often – very often – impossible to unravel. For in theory there were many Vichy controls of this empire.

Another reason Louis Darquier held on to his job by a thread was because, in the tussle between Vichy France and the Germans, he was much easier to manipulate than a more capable or principled replacement. Amidst the chaos and animosities, the Germans felt that they could control Darquier. They were right. His regime eased German acquisition of Jewish wealth in a way Vallat would never have permitted; this was also why Laval was always trying to pass Louis and the work of his CGQJ to another ministry, or to find some way of closing it down.

When Vallat left, spoliation in the north was well advanced, but in the Vichy Zone matters were far less satisfactory. SCAP and the Vichy Ministers of Industrial Production and of Finance were at loggerheads with the German authorities, slowing Aryanisation down where possible in an endless battle to keep the money out of German hands. Laval took over the CGQJ and appointed ministers to assist him who were formidable Vichy bureaucrats, generals of Aryanisation in the presence of whom Louis Darquier was no more than the lowest *poilu*.

Pierre Cathala, Laval's school friend, was his Minister of Finance from the beginning of his 1942 regime.[14] With the brilliant young technocrat Jean Bichelonne – Albert Speer's French counterpart – as his Minister for Industrial Production, from August 1942 Laval had a team that was almost a match for the Nazi forces ranged against him. He had René Bousquet in charge of French policing; in theory nothing could be sold to 'foreign hands' without the signature of the Ministry for Finance, while the Ministry of Industrial Production had to agree to all appointments of trustees to Jewish enterprises. In practice, under Darquier, such processes were often 'forgotten' as the balance of power shifted to the Germans.

But Vichy had other weapons, mostly the banks and state offices which held the Jewish money Aryanisation produced. One of them was the Administration des Domaines, the State Property Department – it was to this Vichy department that Laval wanted to transfer the CGQJ's Aryanisation Section. For *beaux arts*, at Laval's service was the Direction des Musées de France, the French Museums Administration, under his Minister of Education and Culture Abel Bonnard.

Legally, Vichy was permitted to keep the proceeds from the appropriation of Jewish assets as long as 'specific German interests were not at stake'.[15] All such proceeds were to go into a special department of the French Treasury, the Caisse des Dépôts et Consignations. This Deposit and Consignment Office received everything, ranging from the little sums taken from prisoners as they were booked into detention camps – all that was not stolen en route, that is – to Jewish securities which it 'purchased' from its own State Property Department.

Ten per cent of everything, however, went to the CGQJ, from which the administrators and 'other costs' were to be paid, a poisoned chalice from which many drank. The residue of this ten per cent was to be 'placed in a solidarity fund for destitute Jews'. In fact it was used to finance UGIF in the Occupied Zone, and thus, once again, destitute Jews paid for their own deportation. The remaining ninety per cent of the proceeds of each sale or liquidation went into a blocked account in the name of the Jewish owners. The only occasion when despoiled Jews were allowed access to their own money was when the Minister of Finance forced the CGQJ to allow them to pay their taxes. Otherwise, their own wealth could be allotted to them by the Vichy state in 'strictly limited amounts', but they had no access to the money.

Everyone else did. When the Germans wanted a billion francs as punishment for civilian resistance in December 1941, they took the money from the proceeds of French Aryanisation. As the Nazis considered some of the industries most important to their war effort to be in Jewish hands, they and Vichy potentates, together with administrators and civil servants ranging from the downright corrupt to the nitpicking bureaucrat, now began to wrangle over the bonanza.

Denunciations poured onto every official desk, but it was usually Vichy's CGQJ that set the ball rolling. This letter from the Aryanisation Section of the CGQJ could have been sent to any German or Vichy police service: 'I am writing to ask you to arrest and intern the Jew B ... of 99–101 rue L— in Paris who, contrary to ordinances now in force regulating the activity of the Jews, continues to run his business with the assistance of his daughter.'[16] Another approach, equally ubiquitous, was that adopted by de Brinon to Darquier on 16 March 1943, recommending a friend of Himmler's: 'Our friend, Baron Michel Bruyère ... is interested in purchasing a Jewish business "La Maison de la Laine Mode" whose owner is the Jew Hagenuenauer, of Besançon. This firm retails knitting wool to thirty different shops of which ten are in Paris ...'[17]

Sometimes no denunciations were needed. The Louis Dreyfus business was simply liquidated on 16 October 1942, and most of its vast trading fleet sequestered. Under Darquier, for two years the CGQJ simply took what it wanted. French trustees of Jewish property were not permitted to purchase Jewish properties, or shares in them. They often did. Bids for assets were meant to be sealed, and to be knocked down to the highest bidder. This was often, and easily, avoided. Assets were often sold to mysterious groups of crooks and 'financiers' who would pay for an incurious sale. A significant number of administrators surfaced from the criminal classes. By 1943, of twelve thousand provisional administrators in the Department of the Seine, more than fifty per cent had criminal records; some of these were administering thirty to forty former Jewish businesses.

Then, should a business be liquidated and the proceeds put into French coffers, asset stripping during liquidation could provide a rich source of income. And there was also money to be made from the Jewish owner, who might pay to have his company sold to a French person of his choice, his man of straw, to run it for him – Jewish owners were not allowed to participate in the fate of their assets, but from the shadows they often did.

Another source of money was denunciation to any German service, generally to the MBF, military command, whose hated representatives in place des Petits-Pères ensured that Germany got its share of the spoils. Jewish owners would pay to prevent such denunciations. And there was money to be made in reporting Vichy's inadequacies to the occupiers, who might pay to know if the French administration was filching money under German noses, or shielding Jewish assets.

Bribes, denunciations and extortion flowed too from the fact that the Jews of France, as anywhere else, were not a homogeneous body of victims. They fought back. Some Jews were rich, and had influence, some were crooks and had influence too. Many had French friends who helped them. Aryanising Jewish assets involved detailed and laborious work which required a certain sort of businessman or accountant, not the scoundrels Darquier liked to appoint.

And so Vichy watched the non-existent business experience of Darquier's camp followers lead to the decline or ruin of prosperous Jewish enterprises. Laval's dislike of Darquier contributed to his desire to get rid of him, but another powerful reason was the distress of every Vichy ministry over the CGQJ's Aryanisation techniques. Their attempts to protect massive French industries were doomed to failure since when money was involved Louis Darquier would pay attention to German demands or Vichy demands depending on who paid him most, and whether he was in the office on any particular day.

It was known by all and sundry that 'Darquier did not supervise letters sent in his name'.[18] Antignac signed authorisations on a massive scale in Darquier's absence, but Darquier was too busy pocketing money confiscated from Jews to make any objection. Here great names of German industry like Krupp and IG Farben, and French enterprises such as Helena Rubinstein, entered the picture. Fierce territorial rows blew up as the CGQJ permitted Rubinstein's shares to be sold to a German company, or Krupp to take over Austin, a former French Rothschild agricultural machinery company, without the approval of the Minister of Finance.

IG Farben, those masters of slave labour at Auschwitz and elsewhere, and of the German war machine, were only one example. During the years of the Occupation German business interests, hitched to war production, made full use of every opportunity to spread their wings of ownership. With Darquier at the helm, German takeovers of French assets were so constant that French industry and big business felt in no way protected. In one swindle of this kind 'a certain Darquier de Pellepoix, who speaks German fluently and who ... is a very judicious industrialist whose brother occupies an important position within the present French government' did a deal with a German company over a piping construction firm said to belong to René Darquier.[19] Louis never missed an opportunity to aim a kick at his younger brother; using his name for such deals was as good a way as any. Louis' German was as good as René's; René never called himself 'de Pellepoix', and at the time of this deal was informing his professional colleagues in no uncertain terms that the end of the war was nigh, and also firmly signing his name as 'René Darquier, Président Général du Comité Général d'Organisation des Corps Gras'. Most of Louis' ruses began in the rue la Boétie, and the Paris office of the German company in question was at number 3, very near to Louis, who at that time was busy with his UFDR at number 21. Thousands of French 'piping companies' were at the mercy of this vicious tug-of-war between the occupier and Vichy.

Aryanisation brought about day-to-day contact between the CGQJ and every German service in France, but while Boué, Galien and then Antignac carried out their duties, Darquier 'exerted himself without cost in propaganda and above all in keeping himself in the spotlight'.[20] One of his secretaries remembers: 'The little time he spent each day in his office was always taken up with numerous visits. His service directors had literally to grab him on his way in or out to ask for instructions.'[21]

Darquier had his salary from Vichy, and his German subsidies, but he seems to have kept himself in pin money in the following ways. First, there were the *Certificats de Non-Appartenance à la Race Juive*, a tremendous source of income for Louis Darquier and Georges Montandon. Then he also used the denunciations which poured into the offices of the CGQJ. These 'numerous visits' would be from supplicants denying such accusations, who would pay him to 'forget' what he had been told. The long sequence of payoffs involved in selling a sequestered house or business at a knockdown price to a 'friend' was another source. Finally, he seems to have done well out of protection. He believed that Jews had squirrelled away their assets in the Vichy Zone in order to escape controls in place in the north. Also, he loved the Midi – the more glamorous part of it, that is – and so, much of his corrupt activity took place outside Paris. That was where his income from bribery could flourish, where he kept his mistresses and where he could live off the fat of the land. The regional offices of the CGQJ became 'property brokers' in the Aryanisation game.

Alexandre Salzedo lived in Nice, and was Jewish, but as one of Pétain's 'old French Jews' and a war veteran he, and his property, should have been safe from Vallat and Darquier. They were not, so to avoid further seizures Salzedo, a careful man, placed some of his property in the hands of a woman of straw, Madame de la Paz. Salzedo was foolish, probably dishonest, and certainly a man who needed protection. His wife and one daughter were arrested and sent to Auschwitz. They did not return, and Salzedo was left in Nice with his elder daughter. After the

Liberation he accused Louis Darquier of extortion 'through the inter-mediary of his mistress in Nice, who called herself Jeanne Robin, and afterwards Jeanne Destanches. This woman came to me with a note written and signed by Darquier asking for 100,000 francs for Darquier, 100,000 francs for herself and 25,000 francs for her travel expenses . . . I know that many Jews in Nice were her victims since she used to claim – in the name of Darquier, by showing notes and letters from him – that the trusteeship procedure would be stopped.'

Darquier asked Salzedo for money on another occasion, again using 'the Robin woman'. He would stay with her at her Villa Royale in Nice, and 'spent several days in the summer of 1943, at the villa "La Brise" in St-Aigny (Alpes Maritimes) with his mistress. This despite the pres-ence of M. Robin, who seemed quite happy with this situation.' Madame Robin freely boasted of her connections, and extracted large sums of money from hapless Jews by telling 'anyone who wanted to hear it that Darquier was ready to favour Jews with large fortunes'. She also told them that Darquier 'had been appointed to the post of Commissioner for Jewish Affairs by de Monzie'.[22]

Louis Darquier's 'friends' were often clients who would pay him for favours, but among them were also those young men who had been his 'biff boys' in the days of the rue Laugier. One of them was Fernand Roirmarmier, a former member of his National Club whom Darquier placed as a clerk in the propaganda service of the CGQJ. His mission was 'to establish contacts between the Commissariat and various ministries in order to compile reports as to how certain Jewish compan-ies, and the Louis Dreyfus firm in particular, gained their fortunes'.[23]

Despite the deportations, Jews continued to apply to Vichy courts for justice. Louis enjoyed satisfying his lust for quarrelling in the courts, in a reversal of his pre-war role, when he was so often the accused himself. He made two attempts to Aryanise the property of Geneviève and René Dreyfus, first in 1942, then in 1943. For her second appeal Geneviève Dreyfus claimed 'in her capacity as a descendant of the Jew PERPIGNAN, resident of Bordeaux, to be able to rely on letters patent of the king of France Louis XVI, signed in 1776, according to which, "the Jew Perpignan, his family and descendants are entitled to acquire property . . . no ordinance or ruling of the kingdom [can] be used to prevent them from exercising these rights"'. Geneviève and René Dreyfus were thus two of Pétain's 'old French Jews', and so their property had been 'wrongfully provided with a trustee'.[24] Cases like this, which presented pretensions on behalf of any Jew, but particularly any Jew named Dreyfus, caught Louis Darquier's wandering attention and stirred him to vicious activity.

Some of Darquier's 'supplicants' were the French administrators of Jewish assets. They needed protection, and they would pay for it; there was always an illegal air to the appropriation of Jewish businesses or apartments, and what would happen should the Germans lose the war? By 1943 these wealthy purchasers of Jewish property feared they would find themselves obliged to return it. There was a three-year restriction on reselling appropriated Jewish property, and they would pay to circumvent this. Darquier produced for them an Association Française des Propriétaires de Biens Aryanisés, a French Association of Owners of Aryanised Property.

Occasionally Darquier could be moved by other things besides money. He would, for example, do anything de Monzie instructed. A month before Dr Klassen's all-out attack on Louis Darquier on 5 April 1943, Captain Sézille wrote Klassen a very long and overwrought letter, bringing to his attention Louis' scandalous protection of wealthy Jews, amongst them Claire Boas, first wife of de Monzie's friend, Henry de Jouvenel. Sometimes Darquier would extend the same expensive sympathy to other distinguished Jews, particularly doctors. An old war colleague could have some influence, and so could his family – Janot Darquier could ring Lucien Boué for inside information about forthcoming Aryanisations, and she did.[25]

After the death of her husband, Louise Darquier had returned to Neuilly. Through her sons, life was easier for her than for most women in Occupied France, who generally passed the day queuing or scrounging for food. She spent months with René's family on holiday, and returned to Cahors every year to see to her properties, rented out now, while Jean took her to visit friends in the country. Presumably Louis provided her with the necessary passes for so much activity. Nevertheless, she suffered: 'Everywhere I go I take my incurable wound with me. It is awful and now, almost six months later, I feel even more in a state of despair, I cannot get used to [Pierre] not being here and I think only of rejoining him. In November I shall be back [in Cahors]. I can't leave him alone for All Souls' Day. After that, I shall see my children as much as I can while I continue on the path to my own tomb.'[26]

In Neuilly Louise lived amidst the domestic worst of the Nazi regime; over four thousand Germans moved into the large public buildings, gracious apartments and private houses of the suburb, many of them left empty by fleeing Jews or unacceptable foreigners. Neuilly was full of Germans – kommandants, the Gestapo, Hitler Youth and the German Red Cross. Worse, for a woman like Louise Darquier, was the presence of the two most notorious criminal gangs of the Occupation. The leader of the French Gestapo of the rue Lauriston, Henri Lafont, used some of the nine hundred million francs he earned as head of a terrorist arm of the German Gestapo to hold lavish court at his townhouse in Neuilly. Then there was the Neuilly Gestapo, another gang of thieves and cutthroats, at internecine war with Lafont's gang. Louise noted, 'in Paris, if you have a lot of money, you can get by'.[27]

One of René's colleagues at Henry Lévy's Grands Moulins de Strasbourg reported that René 'was upset by his brother's attitude when he became Commissioner for Jewish Affairs, and had always remained unhappy about his brother: meetings were a rare event and such as there were, were tense'.[28] But René's job entwined him in the work of the CGQJ and the Occupation authorities. The Ministry of Production regulated the French economy through its Comités d'Organisation, COs, which grouped each trade or profession together. As president of the Organisation Committee for Fats, René Darquier worked for the Vichy state. COs were instructed to involve themselves in the appointment of administrators, to try to establish professionals in such positions rather than the friends and racketeers preferred by the CGQJ. René dealt with the staff of the CGQJ, with Pierre Gérard and Lucien Boué: he pointed out Aryanisation possibilities in his field, and recommended a friend, Major Dendoid, for a job: 'The worth of Dendoid is very well known . . . he gave extremely well documented lectures on the Jewish question.' René also intervened on behalf of Jews. On one occasion he asked the Status of Persons department to reverse its decision about a friend, Alice Maître, who had been defined as Jewish. When his request was rejected he asked Louis, who refused him.[29]

By July 1943, in the Northern Zone alone, the total amount earned from Jewish property sold was '1,289,139,035 frs, after commissions'.[30]

The statistics involved in the rape of France – the rape of Europe – by the Nazis are fluid, but estimated at about a fifth of the world's art treasures. Each year more discoveries of lost paintings, hidden libraries, great sculptures, come to the surface. At the Liberation the French republic established a restitution service immediately, and the trains which had taken the loot away were quickly set to work to bring it back again.

Decades of effort culminated in the Matteoli Commission, authorised by the French government in 1997, which produced its final report of April 2000. The conclusion of the Matteoli Report was that the looting of Jewish bank accounts and insurance policies, confiscated homes, artworks, books and furniture, the washbasins and sheets from Jewish homes, and the last possessions stripped from Jews as they entered France's detention camps or were put into trains to take them to Auschwitz, came to five billion unadjusted francs. Restitution remains a grey area, in which even the Matteoli figures are suspect. Its conclusion was that between seventy and ninety-five per cent of the loot which has been accounted for had been returned to survivors or heirs, less being achieved in the return of companies and properties.

But there remains the spoliation which Matteoli lists as unaccounted for. Post-war legislation included only French citizens. A liquidated business was not as easy to restore as a painting; there were no written records of the pillage of furniture, no procedures to replace lost profits. There were unclaimed shares, unclaimed cash, their Jewish owners deported, disappeared, dead. By 1949, in the department of the Seine, nearly three thousand estates had not been claimed. To this day looted paintings hang in hundreds of museums, galleries and private collections. One hundred and seventy-one paintings from the Schloss collection have not been recovered, though some have been seen in sales, or found in foreign museums.

During the Vichy years over eighty thousand bank accounts and six thousand strongboxes were frozen, several million books pillaged, forty thousand apartments looted. Over sixty thousand of the 100,000 paintings and *objets d'art* taken have been returned; the forty thousand remaining are lost to this day. Twelve million francs were taken from the prisoners in Drancy; the sale and liquidation of companies came to three billion francs: the figures go on, and on. A lifetime spent in the bowels of every French archive would not suffice to clarify this muddy area, or to place a figure on such losses. And all this is in addition to the two hundred million, later four hundred million, francs the Nazis charged France per day for its 'Occupation costs'.

In the immediate aftermath of defeat in 1940, under orders from Hitler, the pillage of France was allocated to military command, the MBF, while Ribbentrop authorised Abetz to seize Jewish works of art. Between them any collection belonging to a Rothschild, and the stock of many Jewish art dealers of Paris – Georges Wildenstein, Paul Rosenberg (the great pre-war art dealer, no relation to Alfred) and Alphonse Kann amongst them – was crammed into packing cases. Fifteen cases from an early cull went straight to Hitler; years later a painting from the Rosenberg collection was found on the walls of the house of Laval's daughter, Josée de Chambrun.

Hitler gave Rosenberg's ERR an extra mandate, to 'transport to Germany cultural goods which appear valuable'.[31] The ERR became Hitler's official looting agency, pillaging Jewish art collections and apartments, libraries and *objets d'art*. All German services used the cooperation of the SS to assist their confiscations, and the ERR and the Gestapo in turn used a network of French and German spies, criminals and informers in a long trail of villainy that looped throughout France – and Occupied Europe – to deliver booty to the Reich.

This moved spoliation onto a new level altogether, because while the Vichy administration concentrated on keeping Jewish wealth out of German hands, the Nazis were after both French and Jewish assets. It was pillage for the Germans, Aryanisation for the French. The Nazis stole gold, currency and foreign securities, but the greatest pillage was of works of art. Hitler, failed artist, considered France degenerate, but was spellbound by its cultural wealth, and for this reason, of all the conquered territories France was pillaged the most. Hitler's envy and *folie de grandeur* inspired a Nazi war on France, modern art and Jews. His aims were the elimination of degenerate modern art – burning and slashing were the usual methods used, plus the creation of his huge personal museum at Linz in Austria, and the fashioning of Germany as the cultural centre of the New Europe.[32]

After Hitler, Goering carved a special niche for himself by giving his personal protection to the work of Alfred Rosenberg. Through the ERR in Paris, Goering ravaged France for his own collection at Carinhall, his baronial hunting estate north of Berlin. Rosenberg could choose after that, then came German museums and universities. French museums were allowed the residue, or it was sold. Profits from sales were supposed to go to French war orphans, but well before this could even be thought of the spoils were shared between accomplices.

'Degenerate' art was not allowed into Nazi Germany, though Goering in particular ignored this. Unacceptable painters – Cézanne, Degas, Van Gogh, Manet – were exchanged for 'pure' works; those of lesser worth to Hitler – Bonnard, Vuillard, Braque, Matisse – were sold off, and the proceeds used to buy approved art for the Reich. The residue, the work of modern or Jewish artists, was destroyed. On 27 July 1943 five or six hundred paintings, amongst them works by Miró, Picabia, Valadon, Klee, Ernst, Léger, Arp, Kisling and Picasso, were burnt by the ERR in the garden of the Jeu de Paume in Paris.[33]

Throughout all this Vichy struggled, protested and lost. Vichy laws for the control of French national patrimony were as strict as those for the exclusion of Jews from la patrie, and the Reich liked a semblance of legality. Middlemen scrambled for rich commissions, but if Hitler, Goering and their lackeys paid at all, low valuations, dubious 'exchanges' and the favourable exchange rate enabled those with Reichsmarks to buy French art for pin money. Vichy was particularly indignant about the Rothschild collections, which it wished to liquidate itself. When Vichy objected to Abetz's seizures, his reply was that the Jewish owners were no longer French citizens. Thus Vichy's own laws excluding Jews had unlocked France's coffers for Nazi looting. In these circumstances the art market boomed. In 1940 the initial mountain of confiscated works of art was so vast that the Louvre could no longer accommodate it, and the small museum, the Jeu de Paume, became the new depot, stuffed also with 'clocks, statues, jewellery and furniture' – and tapestries, rugs, embroideries, church bells and pianos. More treasure was stored all over Paris and in the provinces.

Many great Jewish collections had been confided to the protection of the French Museums Administration and were hidden, mostly in châteaux in the Vichy Zone; they came under the sovereignty of the Vichy state. Only the Vichy Ministry of Culture could authorise the export of such national patrimony. The ERR, under direct orders from Hitler and Goering, acted outside this law, and by August 1941 had seized the great collections of David-Weill, Jacobson, Leven, Reichenbach, Kapferer, Erlanger, Raymond Hesse, Léonce, Bernheim and two Lévys, Roger and Simon. One of the most important Jewish collections, that belonging to the Schloss family, French Jews, was still undiscovered by March 1943. Everyone was after it, for the Schloss collection was one of the unique collections of France, consisting of the 'racially pure' Dutch and Flemish old masters so coveted by Hitler.

It was 12 March 1943 when Darquier lambasted Laval at the press conference in the Champs-Élysées; but he was not the only one in trouble at this point. The following month Hitler withdrew his favour from Alfred Rosenberg; in future his experts at Linz were to take charge of his looting arrangements. Desperate to demonstrate the irreplaceable services of his ERR, Rosenberg wanted the Schloss collection for Hitler. The man he chose to run ERR in Paris, Baron Kurt von Behr, was a *doppelgänger* for Louis Darquier. The ERR was not a military department, so Rosenberg was particularly happy that von Behr liked to wear spectacular uniforms, generally that of the German Red Cross. Von Behr had a glass eye and an English wife, and entertained in grand and lavish style.

With five offices and four warehouses, as well as the Jeu de Paume, von Behr ran his looting headquarters at 54, avenue d'Iéna – another appropriated Jewish property – in the Darquier manner. Its atmosphere was 'fraught with terrible intrigues and jealousies', exacerbated by von Behr's unremitting sexual dalliance with his female staff.[34] Like Louis Darquier, von Behr was 'large but handsome', a playboy some found charming, as ignorant about art as Darquier but a little more efficient, particularly in carrying out Rosenberg's idea that Jewish furniture should be sent to make life comfortable for Germans 'colonising' the east. It was this operation, M-Aktion (Möbel-Aktion, Furniture Project), that took the residue from great lootings, the everyday objects of Jewish life – cutlery, pots and pans, bed linen and washbasins.

By 1943, in the greediest, if not the most vicious, of all Nazi inter-service battles, the combined forces of Goering and Hitler had pushed the MBF and the embassy into the background, and the ERR had the field to themselves. All this Darquier knew in March, when his relations with every Vichy and German department were so bad that Klassen at the embassy was clamouring for his dismissal.

So it was that Rosenberg and von Behr provided his leap to salvation. When, in 1941, Dannecker had placed Captain Sézille and his Institute for the Study of Jewish Questions into 21, rue la Boétie, he had sequestered the property: it was the former gallery and home of the great art dealer Paul Rosenberg, agent of Picasso, Matisse and Braque. The IEQJ opened its doors in May of that year, since when all the professional anti-Semites of Paris had thronged to what had been Paul Rosenberg's elegant showrooms, and Darquier was often there. In June 1942 Darquier had taken over the IEQJ. His French Union for the Defence of the Race had moved into the ground floor of 21, rue la Boétie, and on 24 March 1943 he inaugurated his last desperate propaganda endeavour, the IEQJER – Institute for the Study of Jewish and Ethno-Racial Questions – there. Six days later Louis appointed a ferocious vulture of the art world, the 'expert' Jean-François Lefranc, his friend and close collaborator, as a provisional administrator at the CGQJ 'for Jewish goods of high value'.

Dannecker had made Sézille and his institute directly responsible to the ERR, and thus to von Behr. From May 1942 'Darquier de Pellepoix greatly helped the Germans in their work, particularly in plundering works of art where he worked closely with the services of Colonel von Behr;'[35] but von Behr was not Darquier's only source of information about art looting. Louis had lived in rue la Boétie for most of the last ten years. This thoroughfare was the centre of the art market of Paris, part of a triangle of streets, bordered also by the Faubourg St-Honoré and the avenue Matignon, where French art dealers did their business. In 1918 Picasso himself lived at number 23, rue la Boétie. One of the greatest galleries was at number 57, that of Georges Wildenstein, run during the Occupation by his Aryan replacement Roger Dequoy. Until January 1944 Dequoy did flourishing business acquiring works of art for the Reich, regularly visited by German agencies looking for, and getting, anything from Renoir to Rembrandt. Darquier was not the only one suspicious of these arrangements, for suspicion and intrigue pervaded everything in this triangle, and nowhere more so than in the pursuit of the Schloss collection.

As early as August 1942 Dequoy approached the Schloss family for a possible sale. There would be huge commissions for any dealer who got his hands on it. Its 333 Flemish and Dutch paintings included Petrus Christus' *Pietà*, Gossaert's *Vénus*, Rubens' *Marie de Médicis* and works by Rembrandt and Frans Hals, Brouwer, Ruisdael, van der Heyden, Bruegel, van der Neer and rare works by other masters. Rembrandt's *Jew in a Fur Bonnet* was also part of the collection.[36]

It is most unlikely that Laval knew how close the contacts were between Darquier and the ERR, preceding the war by a number of years. Alfred Rosenberg had been financing Ulrich Fleischhauer for years, and either directly or indirectly had bankrolled Louis Darquier since 1936. One of Darquier's contacts at that time was the Rosenberg spy Georg Ebert, who by 1942 was ensconced in the Paris embassy, sending back reports to Berlin about his 'double task' in Paris, infiltrating here and there on 'ideological questions'. 'I work cautiously and unobtrusively,' he wrote to Rosenberg on 22 May 1942, telling him that 'Darquier de Pellepoix and his colleagues have a strong confidence in me which stems from our encounters before 1939.'[37]

At the outbreak of war in 1939, Lucien Schloss placed his family's art collection for safekeeping in the Banque Jordaan, which hid it in the cellars of the Château de Chambon, near Tulle in the Corrèze. On 10 September 1942 Jean-François Lefranc visited Bruno Lohse at the ERR. Lohse was an art historian, chosen by Goering to work with von Behr and paid by commission. Lefranc told Lohse that the ERR were missing out on seventy per cent of Jewish works of art, which were mostly hidden in the country and under false names. For twenty-five per cent of the take, the commissioner – Louis Darquier – would disclose where they were, on the condition that paintings valuable to the French people, for example the Impressionists, were kept in France. Darquier seems to have been unaware that Impressionists were of no value to Hitler. As for himself, Lefranc demanded half the profits. To discuss the proposal of Darquier and Lefranc, von Behr took another art historian, a Dr Eggemann, to Maxim's for dinner. There Darquier was introduced, and the three men discussed the Schloss collection. On 29 September Lohse asked Goering about the proposed cooperation and payment: 'After all, these Frenchmen are traitors to their country, and a traitor wants to be paid.'[38]

On the same day that Darquier appointed his friend Lefranc as a provisional administrator, 30 March 1943, he wrote a letter of authorisation to give to the prefect of Tulle, *Préfet* Musso, informing him that Lefranc was 'one of the best-known art experts in Paris and a man of the highest worth in whom he could have complete confidence'. This view was not shared by Lucien Boué: he scented gross pillage, gross illegalities and the hand of Antignac, and 'refused to have any of it and above all to sign anything whatsoever', despite the 'lively pressure' of Antignac.[39] He would not ratify Lefranc's appointment to his department.

Nevertheless Lefranc and Darquier continued illegally, and the SEC was sent off in search of the Schloss brothers.

On 6 April Henri Schloss was picked up in Nice by Lefranc and the SEC, and forced into a car. His house in St-Jean-Cap Ferrat was searched and he was arrested. He stated he did not know the whereabouts of his brother Lucien. Unfortunately, in the midst of 'threats and interrogation' a telegram arrived from Lucien, bearing a return address.[40] Henry was taken to jail in Marseille; two days later the Germans arrested Lucien. Darquier and Lefranc now had the information they wanted, and on 10 April Darquier supplied Lefranc with a letter to *Préfet* Musso in Tulle, issuing authority to seize the collection and to transport it to Paris for 'identification and valuation'. On the same day Darquier also sent an official telegram from Vichy to Musso authorising the transport of the paintings to Paris, and sent Lefranc and Jean Armilhon, director of the CGQJ's legal department, to the Château de Chambon to oversee the transfer.

The Schloss family had been French citizens since 1871. Legally, their property should not have been confiscated. Darquier ignored this. Furthermore, property confiscated legally by the CGQJ belonged to the Vichy state. It was only in Vichy itself that the valuation and sale should be done. Sending these paintings to Paris was tantamount to handing them over to the Germans.

Lefranc made the mistake of sharing his intention of selling the paintings to Goering with one of Louis' SEC policemen, and offered him a cut. This policeman warned *Préfet* Musso. On 12 April Musso consulted Laval's Ministry of the Interior as to whether Darquier's permission held water. They said it did not. A police guard was placed around the château.

Lefranc returned to Paris; he and Darquier met von Behr and Lohse at the ERR and made some conditions. The Germans were to promise not to grab the collection once it came to Paris, the Louvre was to have first choice of its works, and German transport would be required to bring it to Paris. Lohse reported to Goering. Goering agreed to the terms but stated that German trucks could not be used.

On 13 April a tourist bus and a van (requisitioned by Organisation Todt) turned up at the Château de Chambon, and out leapt various denizens of Henri Lafont's rue Lauriston gang, dressed up in the uniforms of the French police and led by a 'French Alsatian' with a thick

German accent who turned out to be a German policeman named Hess, a friend of Bruno Lohse. All of them were armed.

Lefranc had left *in situ* at the château as his deputy a man called Jean Petit, a 'blatant profiteer' who had been sacked from the CGQJ in November 1942 for embezzlement, but whom Lefranc rehired for this 'extremely special case, for which the services of the Commissariat could not find a replacement trustee willing to assume my duties'.[41] Darquier later blamed Lefranc for this 'clumsy' appointment.

At 8.15 that evening René Bousquet, in Vichy, rang Antignac in Paris, absolutely forbidding the removal of anything from the château, and most particularly the crates containing the Schloss collection. In the morning the rue Lauriston gang struck. Taking Petit and the Schloss collection with them, and much else that had been hidden in the same cellars – for the bombproof cellars also contained 'stores of considerable value, much of it Jewish property' (Toulouse-Lautrec, Vuillard, Bonnard . . .) – the bogus French policemen hared off, pursued by the French police, who had warned headquarters. The truck was stopped by a roadblock at Masseret, on the way to Limoges. German and French officials, high and low, converged on the roadblock. One of the two SS men who turned up gave his word of honour that the truck would be delivered to the Vichy police in Limoges. But a very short distance from Masseret, the Gestapo diverted the truck first to a German villa, then next day to a German army base. At each stop French and Germans exchanged threats and insults.

Laval summoned Darquier, whether in person or on the phone is not known, but Darquier, as ever, followed their conversation with a long letter of 'explanation' on 21 April. As he and Lefranc had finalised matters with Lohse only one week before, this letter is an exceptional example of Louis Darquier's mastery of lies and fabrication. 'I immediately wrote to Lohse,' lied Darquier to Laval, 'that I intended to have brought to Paris an important collection of paintings, but that I could only do so if the Occupying authorities gave me assurances that [they] would give up all rights . . . Dr Lohse replied . . . giving his formal agreement.' Darquier lied to Laval that 'the events that arose' – the robbery by the rue Lauriston Gestapo – 'particularly surprised me'.[42] Lefranc, he assured Laval, was 'a qualified expert whose honour is above all suspicion'. He blamed the unhappy episode on an abuse of power by a subordinate, and promised Laval that the crates would be returned to the Château de Chambon.

Six days later, Darquier being 'unavailable', Antignac received orders to return the paintings to Chambon. At this point Laval intervened. On 24 April the Schloss collection arrived, was accepted by and secured at the Banque de France in Limoges. On 4 May Lefranc, still the authorised provisional administrator for the Schloss collection, arrived to value it, expressing Goering's interest in it.

By April 1943, violent criticism was raining upon Laval from every quarter. Pétain continued to plot against him; in Vichy he was surrounded by rumours and intrigues. Germany demanded a further 220,000 workers. In Paris the *collabos* flourished their uniforms and their pens, schemed and paraded angrily through the streets. Outside Paris, the Milice began their civil war with the Resistance. Defeat, and so murder, was in the air. Laval desperately needed anything that would please Hitler. On 5 April he gave Blum, Reynaud, Daladier, Mandel and Gamelin – kept imprisoned by Vichy since their trial at Riom a year before – to the Germans, who incarcerated them in Buchenwald. Laval had to borrow heavily from the Banque de France to pay the German Occupation costs, and so the Schloss collection stayed in its vaults, and became one of Laval's bargaining tools. Some estimated its worth at fifty million francs, though Darquier told Laval that one painting alone was worth that much.

Once Bousquet knew of the attempt to steal the collection, the French police became involved. Von Behr was moved away from art plunders and told to devote himself to furniture. Negotiations passed from Rosenberg's ERR – and Darquier's control – to the embassy. On 26 April Schleier sent a telegram to Dr Erhard Göpel, in charge of Hitler's Linz museum, who had been appointed to examine the Schloss collection. Schleier's chosen scenario was that Hitler should have first pick, then Goering could get the leftovers.

Darquier may have lost his twenty-five per cent, but he kept some irons in the fire. It was his CGQJ that would do the deal, whichever German got the collection. At worst, the CGQJ would still legally get ten per cent of the take. Lefranc was yet to get his commission, and it is more than probable that Darquier came to a private agreement with him. Until August he sailed on, hoping to please Laval and to provide Hitler with this 'gigantic coup for Linz'.[43] Losing out were Lohse, with his huge commission, and Goering, speechless. And so, from April through the summer of 1943, Louis Darquier partied and pontificated at one or another of his dinners, banquets or propaganda institutes, and the great paintings lay in vaults in Limoges.

While they bickered over the Schloss collection, the Germans capitulated in North Africa, Jean Moulin held the first, secret, meeting of the National Council of the Resistance in Paris, and de Gaulle arrived in Algeria to begin his last battle with Roosevelt and Churchill over the place of France in their version of a new Europe. Twelve months ahead lay D-Day and the Liberation of France. Laval needed every old master he could lay his hands on.

19

D-Day

In Neuilly Louise Darquier, like her compatriots, knew the war was not going well for the Third Reich. 'We are standing at the edge of a terrible volcano. How is it all going to end? Life is becoming very hard here. On some days there are no vegetables.'[1] After the German army took over the Vichy Zone Hitler ordered the deportation of all Jews, French and stateless, but he did not change his arrangements with Vichy. The myth of Vichy independence still held good; it remained a sovereign state. The major change was the presence of the Gestapo, but not in great numbers: Hitler's army was stretched to breaking point on the Russian front and in North Africa, and later in Italy. In France only Bousquet's police could keep order for Germany, only they could send more Jews to the death camps.

In 1942 nearly forty-two thousand Jews had been sent to death. It was obvious by this time that no one came back from deportations; there were no letters. After that December no rolling stock was available for deportations, but on 9 February 1943 the convoys began again, taking 126 children, one of them only two years old. Vichy remained recalcitrant about French Jews, and without them they could not fulfil Eichmann's requirements. Eichmann came to Paris again in February to make sure they would do so. Röthke, Dannecker's successor at the Judenreferat, stated that with Vichy 'only duress will bring results'.[2] But Bousquet's raids in February 1943 were seamlessly efficient, and by March the tally was up to forty-nine thousand, but the census told the Germans there were a further 270,000 Jews at large. They, and Louis Darquier, believed there were thousands more than this, particularly in the south.

There were two possible sources of supply. Vichy and the Nazis constantly urged Mussolini to apply French laws in the Italian zone. Mussolini would concur, but he, his police and government officials would, energetically, do nothing. By 1943 Röthke believed that fifty thousand Jews had fled to the Italian zone for safety; something between fifteen and twenty thousand Jews were certainly there, many of them in Nice. Henri Schloss was one of them, and Darquier was acting illegally when he sent his police to Nice to arrest him.

Darquier's solution was the withdrawal of citizenship from the estimated fifty thousand Jews naturalised between 1927 and 1932. His draft law specified that their wives and children should be included. He believed that with the law of 1927 (the year of his Antwerp disgrace) the international Jewish conspiracy had sent in a specific species of Jew to corrupt France, and take her into the 'Jewish war'. All these thoughts he presented time and again to Vichy, embedded in proposals for the pursuit, discovery and elimination of half-Jews, for if half-Jews were added to the quota, the trains would overflow.

Jean Armilhon, the CGQJ's legal director, prepared Darquier's 1927 denaturalisation law, and a bill about half-Jews which Darquier presented to Laval on 31 December 1942, just as German pressure had forced Laval to give him the money he had been demanding from Vichy for so many months. This bill was not even discussed at Vichy. What they assented to was the public identification of Jews in the south. The yellow star was never adopted, but in December 1942 Vichy passed a law which required all Jews – French and foreign – to have the word '*Juif*' or '*Juive*' stamped on their identity cards. This, as good a ticket to Auschwitz as any census or star, was the only proposal of Louis Darquier's ever accepted by Vichy.

From January to April 1943, Laval, procrastinating and haggling as only he could, continued to avoid Darquier and his bill. During this time Nazi persecution became indiscriminate and brutal for every dissident, not only Jews. Denunciations became rampant; a cross neighbour offended by anything, real or imaginary, could be the gateway to Drancy. Nevertheless Röthke and Knochen had to work within a restraining Vichy framework. Jewish children could still go, warily, to school, and synagogues remained open for their communities until 1944.

These exceptions, and Laval, who 'allowed things to drag on for months',[3] enraged Knochen and Röthke, and made them desperate. Life became perilous for everyone, because if the SS acted swiftly and randomly they could, and did, ignore Vichy laws. On one occasion in February 1943 the French police rounded up stateless Jews – some aged sixty and over, more than forty orphaned children, and thirty sick – to replace French Jews the Germans had targeted to go. The Germans accepted them as additions, not replacements, and sent them all to Auschwitz.

Vichy now thought Germany would lose the war, and Knochen told Eichmann's superior, Heinrich Müller in Berlin, that Vichy would 'not allow any other measures against Jews in order to show the Americans that France does not follow the instructions of the German government'.[4] As French resistance grew, so did reprisals. But culprits were becoming harder and harder to find. Ordinary citizens, the elderly and sick – Jews in their eighties and nineties and psychiatric patients – went to Auschwitz in 1943.

Bousquet began his year of reprisals by working alongside the SS to raze the old port at Marseille. This round-up produced nearly six thousand prostitutes, criminals, relief workers and Jews, French and foreign. As the desperation of the Germans grew, so Bousquet clung to his safety blanket, Vichy law: in this last year of his control, as it weakened, his tally was 17,069 Jews sent to the death chambers, of whom 1,816 were children. Only 466 were still alive in 1945. This was less than half his toll for 1942.

By March the gas chambers of Auschwitz were overloaded, so the next four convoys were taken to Sobibor. In April the first *Milicien* was killed by the Resistance, and Bousquet signed his second agreement with Oberg, extending the rights of his French police throughout France. At the same time – a quid pro quo? – Röthke demanded the deportation of eight to ten thousand Jews a week. But Bousquet could no longer always keep his troops in line. By early 1943 the sullen fury of the French population had become a dull roar of disillusion; French police were faced with fighting their fellow French now, not only *résistants* and the *Maquis* but also thousands escaping compulsory labour service, the STO. If given a quota to fill, they would fill it; they liked to arrest by list, and they would arrest foreign Jews, but French police unwillingness saved many in 1943.

Bousquet, however, had to provide Knochen with a minimum of forty thousand Jews before the end of the year. On 1 April he presented his law to the Germans, proposing denaturalising Jews who had taken French citizenship after 1 January 1932. This would provide twenty thousand Jews. Ignoring Darquier, Bousquet's draft law was sent directly to German command, in a document Laval requested to be sent to

Hitler and which 'must not be taken', Bousquet stated – seemingly unaware of how much such an attitude might please a vast number of German officials – 'as a personal attack on Darquier'.[5] Two weeks later, Darquier was removed as president of his UFDR. Louis went into vicious battle. He was at the top of his form: he had just discovered the Schloss collection.

Berlin replied on 21 May instructing Oberg to reject Bousquet's version of the new law, and to adopt Darquier's. To emphasise the point, on 1 June, on Himmler's instructions, Eichmann sent Aloïs Brunner, an SS captain armed with full powers from Himmler, to bring the French into line. Taking his orders direct from Berlin, Brunner began to edge Bousquet out. He always used his own SS men, to whom he would add ruffians from the collaborationist parties in Paris – Doriot's and Bucard's fascists, and Darquier's SEC.

Brunner's arrival came at the time when *refuseniks* from Laval's STO were swelling the ranks of the *Maquis*, although Darnand's Milice, after five months of action, was providing the Germans with ferocious support in the fight against the Resistance. The Germans began to lose confidence in Bousquet, once their favourite and most 'precious collaborator'.[6] Röthke rallied behind Darquier, demanding support for his 1927 law. There were more luncheons at l'Écu de France. The anti-Semitic and collaborationist brotherhood of Paris rallied round, their newspapers pillorying Laval.

On 6 June spy number VM200 sent the following report to German intelligence, the SD:

Re: Denaturalisation of Jews in France.
Source: Commissioner for Jewish Affairs in France, Louis Darquier de Pellepoix.

According to information from de Pellepoix, he is currently in the midst of a fierce disagreement with Laval, whom he refers to as the 'Auvergne bumpkin'. According to de Pellepoix, Laval has always tried to hinder his anti-Jewish activities. Now these two gentlemen have starkly different views concerning the planned denaturalisation of Jews in France. Laval wants to shape the law so that it is retroactive to 1932 while de Pellepoix wants to fix this date at 1927. These two dates illustrate a fundamental problem given that around 90% of naturalised Jews obtained French nationality between 1927 and 1932

... As de Pellepoix says, the law according to Laval's concept would hardly be worth the paper it was written on ... [7]

Five days later Darquier sent a long, poisonous letter to Laval, listing the flaws in the law that had been produced without him, notably its exclusion of women and children and Jewish prisoners of war. Nor did Bousquet's version ban all Jews from ever taking French nationality again. Darquier reported everything to Röthke, Röthke reported everything to Oberg, Oberg reported to Himmler. Himmler was furious; *diktats* were issued, and on 20 June Laval was forced to sign Darquier's bill, removing citizenship from all Jews naturalised since 10 August 1927, though women and children were still excluded.

Darquier had devoted ten years to this goal, the peak of his career as a professional anti-Semite. For everyone else, the summer of 1943 was a bitter time. On 21 June Gestapo chief Klaus Barbie captured Jean Moulin and other leading *résistants* at Caluire near Lyon. Within a fortnight Moulin, beaten to a living pulp of broken bone and flesh by Barbie and his Gestapo, died, having revealed nothing, on the Paris–Berlin train taking what was left of him to concentration camp. With his personal army, Aloïs Brunner began to cut a lethal swathe through the Jews of France, and on 1 July he took over control of Drancy concentration camp from the French police.

By this time – as though in fury over the murder of Moulin – that other France was rising everywhere, in the hills and mountains, in villages and towns. In Algeria, de Gaulle outmanoeuvred Roosevelt and Churchill to control the Resistance and the French government to come. And all over France grew the network of French and international charities and relief agencies, working over and underground in a massive effort to hide – to save – the children. There were Quakers, the Protestant community in the Cévennes, the YMCA, Jewish rescue organisations and the French people themselves, thousands of whom took in Jewish children. Some Catholic institutions hid Jews, as did some nuns and priests.

Most to be pitied was UGIF, which, being Vichy's Jewish agency and part of the CGQJ, had to appear, at least, to do its work in public. The implacable Antignac was its chief tormentor. UGIF was supposed to be financed from the proceeds of Aryanisation, but was always at the very bottom of the receiving end of its own money. Whatever UGIF disgorged it was impossible to satisfy Darquier, for he continually fretted

COMMISSARIAT GÉNERAL
AUX QUESTIONS JUIVES

ÉTAT FRANÇAIS

CABINET

PARIS, le **11 Juin** 1943

1, Place des Petits-Pères (2ᵉ)

+ CENtral 01-52

Cher Dr Röthke,

Je vous envoie la copie de la note que j'adresse au chef du Gouvernement avec les observations que je crois de mon devoir de faire sur le texte nouveau.

J'adresse par le même courrier au chef du Gouvernement une lettre personnelle au sujet de la serpentante procédure employée pour mettre au jour ce décret !

Croyez, je vous prie, à mes sentiments les plus distingués.

Darquier de Pellepoix

Louis kept the SS constantly informed. 11 June 1943 (© Archives du CDJC, Mémorial de la Shoah).

about some hidden pot of Jewish gold and about clandestine UGIF activities, particularly the 'shielding' of Jewish children. Antignac and Darquier and their SEC, working closely with the Gestapo, kept a close eye on every UGIF office throughout France. Informers were inserted into their offices, UGIF staffs were anyway constantly decimated by arrests, internments and deportations. Vichy was bombarded with proposals for tighter controls, new bills, additional suggestions for extracting money, to which Vichy's response was always negative.

When Laval signed his 1927 naturalisation bill, Darquier's intense gratification lasted barely more than a week. By the end of June an order came through that the bill was not to be published in the *Journal officiel.* This was the point at which the embassy, well connected to Laval and his office, closed down Darquier's Institute of Anthropo-Sociology and his IEQJER, and took him off the radio.

If Stalingrad was the turning point of the war, the Allied landing in Sicily on 9 July 1943 tolled a final bell for Vichy. In Paris Knochen, Röthke and Brunner were making preparations for massive round-ups of the newly stateless Jews, to begin as soon as Darquier's bill was promulgated. Darquier warned Knochen and Röthke of trouble ahead, and urged Röthke to hasten German authorisation of his bill – 'I have no need to point out how important it is that this bill is published as rapidly as possible.'[8]

On 19 July the Allies bombed Rome, just as Darquier was digging himself deeper and deeper into his troubles with the embassy, fighting with Klassen and creating tremendous scenes with Delpeyroux and Prax. Klassen, banquets forgotten, began to assail Schleier again. On 19 July he begged him: now that the 'more careful handling of Darquier' temporarily required by 'the Schloss affair' was no longer necessary, could he please be sacked? Darquier was no better, in fact he was more useless than ever. It was a farce to have a Commissioner for Jewish Affairs who had made such a mess of everything.[9] The 1927 bill still awaited promulgation: the round-ups were deferred until the end of July.

And so, Darquier's frustration and hatred fell upon UGIF: on André Baur, director of UGIF in the Northern Zone, and especially upon Raymond-Raoul Lambert, director in the Southern Zone, which ran its section more independently. Darquier saw to the end of both of them, though it was Antignac, as usual, who did the dirty work. On 21 July 1943 André Baur was arrested with his wife Odette and their four children.

Lambert followed in August, with his wife Simone and their four children, Lionel (fourteen), Marc (eleven), Tony (four) and the youngest, Marie-France (eighteen months old); they were deported on 7 December. The Baur family – Pierre (ten), Myriam (nine), Antoine (six) and Francine (three) – followed on 17 December. None of them survived.

The Assembly of Catholic Bishops of France met four times in 1943, but the persecution of the Jews was never discussed. However, in August Monseigneur Chappoulie, possibly acting on behalf of the bishops, warned Laval and Pétain that it was 'against natural law' to 'snatch children from their parents'.[10]

Pétain fretted about his declining popularity. While Pétain was a dictator in the mould of Salazar and Franco – traditionalist, authoritarian, Catholic – for Laval and men of his ilk a populist and nationalist fascist such as Mussolini was more admired. On 25 July Mussolini was arrested and his government fell. Foolishly, Darquier had made a two-line amendment to his bill: 'Nationality is also withdrawn from the Jewish wife of a Jew from whom French nationality is denied by the present decree, and from their children.'[11] Darquier's 'improvements' gave Laval the opportunity to withdraw his agreement. In explaining himself to Knochen, Laval accused Darquier of 'incorrect presentation' which forced him 'to bring the whole law back to the first text put forward by Bousquet'.[12]

This temporary victory for Bousquet coincided with Klassen's fusillade of complaints over Darquier's propaganda portfolio; but the embassy's fury was nothing to that of Oberg, Knochen and Röthke. In these circumstances, Darquier vanished. Different reports surface as to his whereabouts – 'he had broken his leg', 'he was in hospital at the time', he had 'broken his ankle', he was 'in a clinic' – but we also know that he stayed with Jeanne Robin in Nice and summered with her at her villa, La Brise.[13]

Meanwhile the Germans descended upon Laval to force him to change his mind, again. Over the next months a beleaguered Laval produced a flurry of excuses, but he had already turned his attention to the bargaining chip at his disposal in the vaults of the Banque de France in Limoges. Darquier had not forgotten about this either, and had put out feelers about bringing the treasures from the Château de Chambon to Paris on 2 July, in the brief interregnum between his victory and defeat by Bousquet and Laval.[14]

Darquier's disappearance – 'then in hospital'[15] – gave Laval the opportunity he wanted; by 2 August Antignac had been briefed. He was to oversee the transport of the Schloss collection to Paris; Hitler was to have his paintings. The collection arrived at the place des Petits-Pères on 11 August, 'minus several items that disappeared en route'.[16] By this time it was valued at five hundred million francs, the next day, six hundred million. Antignac, afraid of an attack – the CGQJ had 'received menaces' – arranged for police protection day and night. Fortunately the CGQJ, being the former Louis Dreyfus Bank, had a strongroom. From 13 to 23 August the collection was valued at the CGQJ. Everyone visited the basement vaults of place des Petits-Pères: the French police, Lefranc, representatives of the Louvre, Antignac, Bonnard, art experts, Lohse, the SEC, bailiffs, dealers. Their 'meetings were surrounded by secrecy and finally the collection was dispersed for a derisory price'.[17]

In the meantime, a second contingent of Germans descended upon Laval and Bousquet at Vichy on 14 August. For this meeting, Antignac accompanied Röthke. Laval repeated one of his excuses: 'his signature was not valid as a decree for denaturalisation had to be signed by the head of state'.[18] French public opinion, a hovering Catholic Church, the enemy at the gate: all this gave Pétain and Laval pause, and both baulked at denaturalising fifty thousand Jews for instant deportation.

By 23 August the Schloss collection had been divided up. The gift made no difference: Laval had provided the Louvre with first choice, and this infuriated Hitler, who retaliated by forbidding Goering any part of the proceeds. The Louvre took forty-nine paintings, Hitler 262, Lefranc twenty-two for himself. In 1950 Laval's daughter Josée was found to have one of the Schloss paintings too. Hitler's minions paid fifty million francs for his paintings. 18.9 million francs was the price set on the Louvre's paintings – never paid, and the Louvre returned the paintings in 1945. Hitler's money went into Vichy's Aryanisation bank accounts; Lefranc was 'given' his portion. Darquier's twenty-five per cent was quite a thing of the past, but the CGQJ got ten per cent.

The next day, 24 August, Marshal Pétain, while accepting 'the principle of actively reviewing the naturalisations', finally refused to sign Darquier's bill. His letter of refusal stressed that he had 'shown his willingness to work with Germany on countless other occasions'.[19] He also expressed an 'inability to understand the sending of Jews of French nationality while there were still so many other Jews in France'.[20] Röthke had already warned Laval of what the result would be, for with Brunner in France it hardly mattered whether the bill was signed or not. 'Following the Marshal's refusal, reprisals began to be taken against Jews, especially French, including the deportation of Aryan spouses.'[21] War veterans, French Jews, any Jew went now.

Nice was the first city to suffer. When Italy surrendered on 8 September this meant death for the Jews in the Italian zone. Brunner and his men moved in immediately and sealed the frontier. With Bousquet and his French police, their files and lists out of the way, Brunner savaged the south. The manhunt of trapped Jews in Nice in September 1943 was as horrific, and became as notorious, as that of the Vel' d'Hiv' the year before. Brunner was a sadist, indiscriminate and thorough. His torture headquarters were in the Excelsior Hotel; he packed its leafy courtyard with trapped Jews. Every other dwelling in Nice was searched, every hospital, bus, train and car, day and night. Brunner arrested any Jew he could find, and anyone who, to him, looked Jewish. Checking penises was his method, which meant that many Jews escaped, and many circumcised Catholics and Moslems went to Auschwitz. Yet after all this, Brunner's tally was small – 'only' 1,800 Jews went to Drancy from Nice.

One of them was the young Berlin artist Charlotte Salomon, who had painted nearly eight hundred pictures in her years of hiding on the Riviera. Brunner's men dragged her to the Excelsior on 24 September. Freighted out of Drancy on convoy number 60, she was probably killed on arrival – she was given no Auschwitz number, though her husband was. This could also mean that being young – she was twenty-six – and five months pregnant, she was used for experiments.[22]

Darquier, back in Paris in September, was voicing his despair all over the city, threatening to resign, hoping that the Germans would sack Laval and provide a new government. He had no need to resign: universal plans for his dismissal were underway, and all his propaganda institutes, associations and groups were firmly shut down by the Germans by the beginning of October.

In the interim of his brief success, Louis and Myrtle had moved to the five-star Hôtel Bristol in the Faubourg St-Honoré, where 'one ate so well'.[23] This was 'the Nazi hotel in Occupied Paris', where visiting German dignitaries lived in style. It was also home to 'important guests' upon whom the Nazis needed to keep an eye, together with a 'nest of informers, collaborators and racketeers'. In her time there Myrtle could

36. Louis Aragon, writer and poet, surrealist, communist and political activist, at the time of the Spanish Civil War, c. 1936.

37. Léon Blum, the first socialist and the first Jewish prime minister of France, at the time of his Popular Front government, c. 1936.

38. Edouard Daladier, leader of the Radical Party between the wars, and many times prime minister of France, February 1934.

39. Bernard Lecache, c. 1930. Militant journalist, founder of LICA, Ligue Internationale contre l'Antisémitisme, and its newspaper *Le Droit de Vivre*, 'The Right to Live'. Fought Louis every inch of the way, from 1936 onwards.

40. Louis' companions within the extremist fringes of French fascism, anti-Semitism and Nazi collaboration before and during the Second World War. Left to right: Jean Boissel, Louis-Ferdinand Céline, Henry Charbonneau, Henry Coston, Pierre-Antoine Cousteau. All journalists or writers, ranging from the lunatic (Boissel) to the great (Céline). The next three: Pierre Gaxotte, Henri Massis and Thierry Maulnier, elected to the Académie Française in 1953, 1961 and 1964 respectively, were all Maurrassians: nationalist and anti-Semitic writers and editors, representing the intellectual and Catholic wing of Louis', and Vichy's, supporters. Last: Bernard Fäy, a Professor of American Civilisation, murderer of Freemasons, friend of Gertrude Stein and Alice B. Toklas.

41. More of the same, with some of the Nazis they served. Clockwise: Joseph Darnand, fanatical Catholic and head of the Milice, the Gestapo-style army set up by Vichy to fight the resistance; Philip Henriot, called the 'French Goebbels', the brilliant Catholic broadcaster for Vichy France; Paul Sézille, demented anti-Semite and alcoholic; Georges Montandon, sinister doctor and scientist, who decided which Jewish attributes qualified for Auschwitz.

(*Left*) SS Hauptsturmführer Dannecker who headed Eichmann's Judenreferat, his Jewish Bureau, in Paris, 1940–42.

(*Right*) Otto Abetz, Hitler's Ambassador to Occupied France.

42. Franco and Pétain,
Montpelier, February 1941.

43. May/June 1940, just before the Fall of France. Left to right: General Maxime Weygand,
Commander-in-Chief, Paul Baudouin, Minister of Foreign Affairs, Paul Reynaud, Prime Minister,
and Marshal Pétain, then ambassador to Spain, summoned at this point, by Reynaud,
to save France.

44. Cardinal Emmanuel Célestin Suhard, Archbishop of Paris, behind Cardinal Pierre-Marie Gerlier of Lyon. With their hero, Marshal Pétain, head of state, and Pierre Laval, head of the Vichy government. Outside the Hôtel du Parc, in Vichy, November 1942, as the Germans invaded the Vichy zone and occupied all of France.

45. Military parades were a feature of Vichy life. Here the *2ème Régiment d'Infanterie Coloniale* marches past Marshal Pétain, Admiral Darlan, and Pierre Laval. Louis Darquier is immediately behind Darlan; Vichy was about to announce his appointment as Commissioner for Jewish Affairs, April 1942.

46. The men of the second Vichy government, August 1940, on the steps of Pétain's state residence in Vichy, the Pavillon de Sevigné. Second left, behind: Admiral Darlan. In front, left to right, Paul Baudouin, Pierre Laval, Marshal Pétain, General Weygand.

47. General Charles de Gaulle broadcasting on the BBC in London, his now famous Appel of 18 June 1940 – his call to the French people to fight on.

48. Jacques Doriot, the leading French fascist, holding a press conference in Paris, February 1944, on his return from the Russian front, where, in the uniform of the LVF (the Legion of French Volunteers against Bolshevism), he fought for Germany. With him, members of his fascist party, Parti Populaire Française, the PPF.

49. Léon Degrelle, devout Catholic and the leading Belgian fascist, who commanded his Légion Wallonie on the Russian front. Decorated by Hitler in February 1944, he escaped to live well in Spain until his death. With Pope John Paul II on 11 December 1991.

50. Louis' anti-Semitic propaganda. Here the *Métro* advertises one of his wartime creations for Vichy, l'Institut d'Etude des Questions Juives, the Institute for the Study of Jewish Questions, *c.* 1942–43.

51. Louis shaking hands with Reinhard Heydrich at the Ritz Hotel, watched by senior commander of the SS in Paris, Helmut Knochen, 6 May 1942. It was the BBC's subtitle on this shot, in Marcel Ophuls' *Le Chagrin et la pitié*, that first explained to me who Anne Darquier's father really was.

have encountered P.G. Wodehouse and his wife Ethel padding round the corridors – they were housed at the Bristol in September, after Wodehouse's unfortunate and jaunty broadcasts on Berlin Radio.[24]

Confined to the Bristol and protected by knowing too much, all that was left to Darquier was self-publicity. In an attempt to placate both the Germans and Vichy he indulged in an interview with the anti-Semitic news-sheet *France-révolution*, subsidised by his own UFDR. Only a man who had been hounded by debt collectors in many countries could produce the bombast of 'Fifteen Minutes with Darquier de Pellepoix':

> Darquier de Pellepoix – love him or hate him . . . he leaves no one indifferent. He has been criticised, pilloried and slandered – but he remains resolute . . .
>
> 'In my region, in Gascony,' said Darquier, adjusting his monocle '. . . half-Jews . . . I can hear the chorus of Jew-lovers: "Darquier de Pellepoix you will hang." I think I am more likely to die with a bullet in the head, but what does that matter!'
>
> With this proud, forceful declaration, the Commissioner stood up. A solid handshake and a final loyal glance back up the firm language of a man who, while never losing his good humour, continues his perilous task to save the French race.[25]

A few days later, on 2 November, as the Schloss collection was handed over at the Jeu de Paume, Darquier put a brave face on things: 'Lefranc kept the meeting lively with jokes. Darquier de Pellepoix exchanged pleasantries with Lohse.' After the festivities Lefranc was seen departing with another painting under his arm.[26] Alfred Rosenberg inspected the loot two days later, 'accompanied by his suite and seven automobiles'. Goering's agent Lohse managed to 'remove three paintings from the collection, including a Rembrandt and a work by a student of Hals', which he offered to Goering, who refused them.

Laval, hounded by so much else, nevertheless gave a moment of his time to punishing Darquier. As a man of the people, he liked to invite second-rank personnel to lunch; he found it an excellent way of discovering what was going on in the bowels of his ministries. Pétain was always summoned to give his blessing to these commissioners and secretary-generals. In November, Laval included Darquier in such a gathering at the Hôtel du Parc. 'I know your importance to the state,' said the Marshal to the gathering, 'and I follow your activities very closely. To prove how closely, I can tell you that one of you will be sacked within the next eight days.' Pétain pointed his finger at Darquier's bosom and added, 'I'm talking about you.'[27] In front of Laval and the eighteen other senior officials, this time Pétain did not call Darquier 'the torturer', but *un bourreau*, 'a butcher'.[28]

After November Darquier moved his office to Paris completely, and did not return to Vichy. He made one of his last public speeches on 23 November when the Aryan Club, replete with bar, restaurant and meeting hall for the anti-Semitic soldiers of the pen, opened in Paris. Klassen had to listen patiently while Darquier elaborated on the successes of his Aryanisation of Jewish property. At this time the Schloss collection was still in Paris. It went to Munich four days later, and just over three weeks after that, on 20 December, the German order for Darquier's dismissal was sent to Vichy.

By the end of 1943 Pétain and Laval were rearranging their positions in light of the coming German defeat. Hitler would not let Pétain sack Laval. Pétain, self-pitying, duplicitous and self-deluded, was deeply offended when the Germans banned him from issuing his thoughts on the radio. In December they gave him a keeper, a German diplomat, Cecil von Renthe-Fink, who was placed in rooms in the Hôtel du Parc. Pétain emerged from his sulk to face the final months of his reign, and nicknamed his keeper 'Rintintin'.

In Paris rumours flourished that everyone concerned with the fiasco over the denaturalisation law and the convolutions of the Schloss collection was to be sacked. Vichy buzzed with the names of the departing, Louis Darquier always among them. Darquier hoped to fend off the evil day by appointing Boué as secretary-general of the CGQJ in November. Meanwhile the raids of the SS and Brunner intensified, and neither Laval, Pétain nor Bousquet objected, nor were they consulted. On 2 December Darnand and his Milice murdered Bousquet's friend and patron Maurice Sarrault, the Radical newspaper editor of *La Dépêche du Midi*, and at the end of December came the German order that Bousquet should go. He was sacked on New Year's Eve. During his time as Vichy's police chief Bousquet had arrested and handed over sixty thousand Jews to the Germans; in 1943 alone, according to Abetz, forty thousand Gaullists, communists and anti-German persons were also arrested, many handed straight to the Gestapo.

But every murder of a communist or Gaullist, every deportation of every Jew, took place amidst the STO – the 'deportation' of French men, and now women too, to forced labour. By the Liberation nearly 700,000 French workers had been put to work in the Third Reich, to add to those already there, and to the million and a half French prisoners of war, most of them now put to work too, in German factories and farms. In France, knowing this, watching thousands more go, many resented the fact that Jews were not required for forced labour in Germany. Why were they spared?

What energy was left to a hungry people was devoted to hating Laval: on 11 November 1943, Armistice Day – not a permitted celebration during the Occupation – public bile found relief in shouting '*Mort à Laval!*' and reverting to the old national anthem, the forbidden '*Marseillaise*', as anyone who has seen the film *Casablanca* knows.

———————————— ❦ ————————————

Colonel von Behr and his ERR pillaged eight thousand pianos during the Occupation; in April 1943 over a thousand of them were still in storage in Paris, but Louis seems not to have troubled to allot one to Myrtle, who so loved to play. What Myrtle felt about mistresses like Madame Robin is not recorded, nor how she reacted to Louis' obsession with half-breeds and French blood.

Anne Darquier had only a half portion of this blood; this may account for Louis' unwillingness to send any of his newfound wealth to her. Since September 1942 the Foreign Office at Vichy had continued to receive letters from London complaining about the £50 Louis had sent for Anne, demanding the back pay he owed Elsie and the reimbursement of the Free French charities which had been supporting her. The consul insisted not only on repayment, but also an advance against future expenses. Further letters followed: Louis sent nothing. By 1943 he owed them all a great deal more, because the French charities continued to give Elsie £5 a month as well as paying for Anne's education – nine guineas a term. In an act of even more heroic generosity, the charity that paid Anne's school fees, the French Benevolent Society, described her as the daughter of an 'Officer, Free French Forces' when she enrolled in Chipping Norton Grammar School in September 1943.

CHIPPING NORTON COUNTY SCHOOL.   Admission Number....**796**....

Pupil's full Name .... DARQUIER . ANNE
(Surname first)
            Name and Address of Parent or Guardian :

Miss E. Lightfoot, Great Tew, Oxford.

Previous education of pupil :

East Ham Grammer School, September 1941 - July 1943.

Administrative County, if not Oxon :	Boro., Urban District, or Rural Parish :
	Great Tew.
Date of Birth :	
3.9.1830.	Occupation of Father :
Date of Admission :	
2.9.43	Officer, Free French Forces.
	Status of Pupil :
Date of Leaving : 21.12.43	Fee -payer / see over

Remarks :

        French Benevolent Society, 41, Fitzroy Square, W.1.
    accept responsibility for fees. Fees reduced to
    £9.9.0d per annum . (letter H(G/R) dated 21st.Oct.1943)

300/10/39

The Free French paid for Anne's education (courtesy of Mrs Brenda Morris of Chipping Norton School).

In Kidlington, life had changed. Aunty Maud had remarried. As house-keeper at the Schusters' estate at Nether Worton she had met Arthur Haynes, who worked there as a groom, or a gentleman's gentleman, reports vary. It was unanimously agreed that Arthur was a 'nice country man' and a perfect match for the ebullient Maud.

By the summer of 1943, in England, the war had entered a

different phase. The British were still hungry, but they were surviving austerity. London had withstood the Blitz, and East Ham Grammar, Anne's school at the zoo in Kidlington, went back to London. In September 1943 Maud's husband Arthur became landlord of the Falkland Arms pub in Great Tew, and Elsie and Anne moved there to live with them.[29]

At the time, Louis Darquier's propaganda department in Paris was churning out radio scripts like this:

> A reporter visits a working-class suburb. He is standing in the
> courtyard of one of the housing blocks. The text and the sound
> evoke the lack of light, the poverty and the dirty, miserable games
> which keep the children entertained.
> He exhorts people to save the race and make this plague disappear.
> Other sounds and words show that children need sunshine and
> fresh air.
> The soundtrack evokes life in the country, open fields, campfires
> at night, singing, gymnastics and a balanced life. 'That,' the reporter
> concludes, 'is youth enjoying life.'[30]

Today Great Tew, with its picture-postcard thatched cottages, its village green and pub, and its quaint names – 'Bee Bole Cottage', 'Tulip Tree Cottage', 'Hangman's Hill' – wins prizes as 'the most beautiful village in England'. Breathless journalists write articles about its preserved antique perfections, its village black magic and its ghost: a coach and horses which sporadically trots around the lanes. But until the death of the last owner of the village, in 1985, this tiny place, well off the beaten track, was almost medieval in its rural poverty and isolation. Great Tew was on the way to nowhere, and no one passed through it. There was a blacksmith, a church, a butcher and a post office and stores, the pub and a beautiful church, St Michael and All Angels. Over the centuries the village had always belonged entirely to one owner in a sequence of aristocrats, industrialists, eccentrics and rogues whose estate office ran the village, the tenants and the lower orders on behalf of the inhabitants of the manor at Tew Park.

One of these was Viscount Falkland, Secretary of State to Charles I, whose family gave its name to the island outposts of the Empire in the South Atlantic which both Argentina and Britain claim as their own, and also to the village pub, drowned in roses and wisteria. But in 1943 even Great Tew had been affected by the war. Rationing was more severe by this time, and the tiny village, like the rest of England, now lived close to the poverty level. Memories of those who lived there then bear witness to the harshness of the times, but poverty, fierce cold, hard relentless work, one egg a week, weak tea, no petrol and few cigarettes were the common lot in the war years, as normal as the sound of combat in the skies above. Everyone was subject to the sense of loss, to the absence of fathers, the delivery of telegrams, the announcements of death.

Nearby, very often, was the heartening presence of the great man himself. Oxfordshire was the home county of Winston Churchill, and it was firmly believed by the country people that they could not be bombed, because when he conquered Britain Hitler was planning to live in Blenheim Palace, where Churchill was born. Blenheim and Oxford, a stone's throw from Kidlington, were therefore quite safe, and much the same feeling was extended to Ditchley Park near Enstone, about three miles from Great Tew, where Churchill spent many weekends during the war.

When Anne went to live there, the winding lanes of Great Tew had turned into a civilian battleground. Most of the inhabitants of the village are called Clifton – each branch insisting that it is not related to the other – diluted with Keals and Paintins and many branches of Tustains. Now there were land girls and Italian prisoners of war, foreigners all, disabled children billeted in the Great House. Great Tew bulged with grumpy and unloved London families. The villagers loathed their streetwise ways, while the outsiders accused the natives of being standoffish and unwelcoming – and over-inquisitive at the same time. Anne remained a child apart, a quiet girl who kept herself to herself, mixing neither with the London children nor with the children of the village.

The Falkland Arms pub is often described as 'unspoilt'. In 1943 being unspoilt meant that it was bitterly cold and gloomy, its oak beams and low ceilings darkened to the funereal by the blackout. The public bar was simple, with flagstone floor and straight-backed chairs, while the taproom next door, with inglenook fireplace and dartboard, was the smoking and drinking room for the men of the village. Elsie, Anne, Maud and Arthur lived and ate in the tiny family room next to the public bar, and here Anne studied in what light could reach through the stone-mullioned windows. All of them slept in the cramped bedrooms upstairs. The pub, like Great Tew, was 'medieval': the privy was out the back, and water came from the tap outside the post office. There was no electricity either: the blackout and the dark winter months were survived with lamps and candles and cigarettes glowing in the night. But the inhabitants of Great Tew were occasionally better off than most: farm produce and wild animals often provided goodies city folk could only dream of.

Arthur stood behind the bar, and Maud poured the beer. Maud was a marvellous bar lady: big-bosomed, big-hearted, she would start a singsong to cheer everyone up. In those days most major towns had their own brewery, and nearby Hook Norton or Flowers provided the barrels kept in the cellar of the Falkland Arms. There was no pump for the beer, and Anne's job – down the winding cellar stairs, up the winding cellar stairs – was to fill the jugs with 'Hookie' every time someone wanted a beer.

Elsie continued to take no nonsense from anybody. Her forceful personality, her dyed ginger hair and bony presence, 'very sharp and to the point', did not prevent the people of Great Tew from sticking their beaks into her affairs. To this day they continue to believe that Anne was her illegitimate daughter: 'We all thought Elsie was mixed up with some superior man.' 'She was very well spoken,' and, to the country people, she seemed 'posh, and Anne the same'. The unanimous conclusion was that Anne's bossy nanny guarded her from village life because of her secret aristocratic connections. Anne's respite from this came from Maud and Arthur, who broadened her life and moderated Nanny Lightfoot's rigour: 'they adored Anne'.

Maud made the pub the centre of village life, a happy place. Anne had to scrub the floors and pour the beer, but she was sent up to the Big House to join the Girl Guides, and climbed the big tree, still there, outside the pub window. Her childhood friend was Beryl Clifton, the daughter of Ada and Bert at the post office, a few doors down from the pub. Anne and Beryl played at dressing up – Anne made the perfect nun.

By this time Anne had made a habit of leaving schools. At thirteen she was already ambitious, and she could not tolerate the diet of home nursing, wartime cookery and handicrafts which interspersed the basic curriculum for girls at Chipping Norton Grammar School. She hated it, and managed only one term there. The school had accepted her at a reduced rate, but there were school-dinner fees and games fees, and a bottle-green school uniform that Elsie could not afford. She felt she did not fit in. As for Elsie, the fact that the Free French were paying for Anne's upkeep was something she kept to herself.[31]

January 1944 found Anne's father more – much more – at his desk, and in a filthy temper. Otto Abetz had been sent back to Paris and the embassy to get Vichy back on track, and Louis had been officially notified that he would soon be relieved of his functions. He knew that Antignac was manoeuvring to take his place. 'I don't understand how a former officer like Antignac could let himself be led so much by the Germans,' spat Darquier. He would nag Antignac about his approach: 'You don't have to suck up to them like that.'[32]

Louis could still pull some strings. De Monzie came to see him in Paris in January 1944. Pierre Combes – later the director of the Museum of the Resistance in Cahors – had been arrested together with a dozen or so other young Cadurcien *résistants*, found bearing guns, while Combes himself had thrown into the river a sack of post destined for the local STO office. A father and son from Cahors, Henri and Jean Gayet, went to see de Monzie in Paris. The next day de Monzie took them to Louis in his office. The Gayets sat facing Louis. 'I noticed one thing,' said Jean Gayet: 'there was one master of this story, and that was de Monzie . . . For four hours, he remained standing, he gave orders and instructions to Louis. He said, "You do this, you do that, you must get in touch with Y, you must telephone Z," and Louis obeyed like a little boy . . . it was flagrant, the servitude of Darquier in face of de Monzie.' By the time they left Louis' office, Pierre Combes and his fellows were not to be shot; instead they were to be sent to prison camp in Germany. Two of them did not return.[33]

Darquier found other experiences equally unpleasant. All the staff of the CGQJ, including Louis himself, were now required to submit baptismal certificates of their four grandparents. Even worse was the propaganda witch-hunt the Germans whipped up for his departure: 'In preparation for this, two public meetings were held on 22 January and

7 February 1944 during which the Commissariat was strongly criticised. Darquier de Pellepoix, Commissioner, was obliged to submit his resignation.' 'Den of thieves', 'shameless plunder of Jewish businesses', 'scandal of the billion-franc fine' were only some of the accusations.

The story of Pierre Combes whistled through the corridors of anti-Semitic power. Jacques Lesdain of *l'Illustration*, whom the Germans favoured as Darquier's replacement (and who liked to urge *Occult Forces Behind Roosevelt* by Dr von Leers as recommended reading), publicly attacked every aspect of Darquier's scandalous behaviour, and in particular the hold de Monzie had over him and the protection he thus provided for wealthy Jews.

Meanwhile the Paris *collabos* were in final pursuit of Pétain and Laval, castigating Vichy as 'Jerusalem on the Allier'. Sézille and Galien had almost the last word: 'As for Darquier de Pellepoix,' thundered Sézille, 'he thinks only of his stomach, his women and his re-election. We helped him at the beginning, but he has betrayed us. He disgusts us. One day his punishment will come.' Two months later Sézille died, avoiding the fate of all his cronies.[34]

Newspapers began to report Darquier's arrest – 'his improbity is notorious,' stated the *Dépêche de France*.[35] When Laval dismissed him officially, on 26 February, the reason was 'irregularities over the administration of Aryanised assets'.[36] Boué was sacked with him. *Paris-soir* reported that Darquier had been arrested for malpractice at the frontier on 21 January. If this was true, he was quickly freed. The police reported the private but universal pleasure of certain political personalities and senior officials at the Hôtel de Ville; otherwise Darquier's departure was greeted with silence from all sides. After a brief interim Antignac returned to lead the CGQJ, and his zeal in persecution remained exemplary, and vigorous, to the end.[37]

Louis Darquier proved to be one of the few men to put on weight during the Second World War. Hotels like the Bristol and restaurants like Maxim's, under German favour, suffered no food restrictions. Photographs of him taken in 1944 reveal a plumper version of his 1930s self, buttons straining to cover a corpulent stomach, the round face bejowled, the hands pudgy. Anne, on the other hand was skinny, like all those children raised in poverty during the war years. She never became large, as Myrtle did after the war. Anne had enough of Louis and Pierre Darquier about her face to connect her with generations of citizens of Cahors and the Lot, but the cast of her face was her mother's; she had a Jones look about her, but nothing else of Australia at all. Her legs were slightly bowed, but her sweet face was always transformed by a charming smile. Nevertheless, like so many war children, she looked as though a large dose of vitamins at the right time could have made her taller, more robust. She was pale, with an air of indomitable fragility; she always lacked the substantial quality of her parents. For the rest, whereas her parents were noisy, years of Elsie's will had made Anne silent.

Neither Elsie nor Anne ever mentioned Myrtle, or receiving any letters from her, but about her father's family, in general terms, Anne knew a great deal more. She told her friend Beryl that she was the daughter of a French baron, and she knew that her grandfather had been, and that her uncle was, a doctor. By 1944 Elsie knew, as did everyone else in Great Tew, that Anne Darquier had a mind of her own, and that she had already determined to follow her French family and become a doctor herself.

Accounts of Anne's education after the age of thirteen are hazy, and Anne too was secretive about it: her lack of formal teaching was something else she always had to hide. What is known is that she completed what was left of her secondary education at the Green School in Chipping Norton, left as all such children did at the age of fourteen, and went to work in the Falkland Arms with Elsie, Maud and Arthur. She was now as tall as she would ever be: about the same height as her mother, five foot five, slim, with long brown hair. Although still shy, she astonished her peers with remarks such as 'You're suffering from an inferiority complex.' Another of Anne's books from childhood is an exhaustively thumbed copy of Baker and Margerison's *New Medical Dictionary* (with an Air Raid Precautions Supplement), dated 1942. Candles were often rationed, and matches hard to come by, but when she had them Anne stayed up all night to study.

Great Tew admired her for it, but were baffled by her obsession: 'We all knew women weren't doctors.' 'I have never forgotten Anne,' said Beryl Clifton, 'and to this day if I hear anyone say, "I can't, it can't be done," I tell them of a girl I once knew who through sheer guts, hard work and a refusal to give up and an undying ambition to be a doctor

– and to be this doctor had to study at Oxford University (there could be no second best) – and succeeded.'[38]

The armed forces were always a substantial presence in wartime Oxfordshire: the county was near to London and its villages and towns housed men in training, or on rest and recuperation. There were many Canadians, some Australians, and, after 1942, American soldiers too. Great Tew was surrounded by military airfields, most of them training grounds. The biggest airfield was Moreton-in-Marsh, but its satellite airfield Enstone was on the doorstep of Great Tew and the bombing station of Upper Heyford not far away. Negotiating the dark country lanes to the nearby towns of Banbury or Chipping Norton was dangerous in the blackout, and lack of petrol made public transport almost non-existent. Though the beer was diluted, the gin tasted like ether, and the whisky was dubious, these pilots made their way to the Falkland Arms. 'Every girl in the vicinity pursued the pilots,' a contemporary of Anne's remembered. Anne learned to drink with them, and gained her sexual initiation from one of these Canadian airmen.

Great Tew remained cut off, but by 1944 no one in southern England could be isolated from the troops and equipment which poured in as the United States and the Allies prepared for D-Day. American GIs and their tanks and jeeps occupied Cow Hill; they were supplied with electricity, the first time it reached the environs of Great Tew. The Oxfordshire skies buzzed with planes and gliders and with parachutists practising for the French landings. The county became a military dormitory and a vast armaments storehouse, with the grass verges on the road to Chipping Norton and Banbury stacked with bombs, shells and miscellaneous ammunition.

For Vichy, the months before D-Day were chaotic and savage. On Bousquet's departure, at German insistence Vichy appointed Joseph Darnand to the government as Secretary-General for the Maintenance of Order. Jacques Doriot's PPF fascists were fighting throughout France alongside Darnand's Milice and the Gestapo. The fanatical Catholic Philippe Henriot, de Monzie's enemy during the Stavisky affair, became Minister of Information and Propaganda in January 1944, and a few months later another fascist, Marcel Déat, became Minister of Labour and National Solidarity. As Vichy and the extremists in Paris moved together to fight the Resistance and the Allied landings they expected any day, France was alight with sabotage and hand-to-hand combat. The

Nazis kept to the towns, surrounded by *Maquis* and *résistants*; the British were increasing their arms and supply drops all over France.

Encounters could become all-out battles; in March, on the plateau of Glières in the Alps, the Gestapo and the Milice fought nearly five hundred *Maquisards*. In 1944 nothing but treachery, torture and death stopped the Resistance, and by May *résistants* and *Maquis* had gathered together as the Forces Françaises de l'Intérieur, the FFI, the final Resistance force against Germany. They were massacred, assassinated, shot in the back, tipped into pits and down wells, executed in those lonely spots you can still find everywhere in the French countryside, marked by a *stèle*. *Miliciens*, if caught, died savagely too. And nothing stopped the freight trains: after April 1944, Knochen gave up on Vichy and gave instructions that all Jews, whatever their nationality, were to go. Within the eight months left to them in 1944 another 14,833 Jews were deported: 9,902 were gassed on arrival, 1,289 were found alive a year later.

Aloïs Brunner was particularly keen on taking children, and nearly 2,500 were sent to death camps in 1944. Brunner, the SS and Vichy's Milice did the work: they raided prisons and camps, hospitals, hotels and apartments, old people's homes. Children's homes and Jewish institutions for the children of the deported became an easy target; informers made a fortune. In April 1944, at an isolated farmhouse in Izieu, near Lyon, Klaus Barbie's men 'cleaned out' forty-five children, at breakfast with their carers. 'They seemed to have become little old people,' wrote one Jewish survivor of Auschwitz who watched the children arrive. 'They did not seem to cry, but wore a fearfully resigned expression, as if they understood better than we what was going to happen.'[39] There were eleven homes for orphans run by UGIF in Paris. The Gestapo raided eight of them, and took off 258 children and their thirty adult carers. Two hundred and thirty-two of these children went on one of the last convoys to Auschwitz, on 31 July 1944. There were 1,300 people on this train; none of the children survived.

The Allies had been announcing their imminent arrival in France daily: 'Each night, each day the relentless Anglo-American bombers cut down our young in thousands, destroy our houses, set our towns on fire, destroy our cathedrals and museums,' wailed the collaborationist magazine *Le Nouvelliste de Neuilly*.[40] Allied bombing of Paris and other major French cities in March, in April, in May, increased German terror and reprisals. The population starved, died, and were advised not to eat cat.

Pétain made his only visit to Paris on 21 April, after a raid which killed or wounded over a thousand Parisians and damaged the Sacré Cœur. From the balcony of the Hôtel de Ville he addressed an ecstatic crowd, roaring for what the Hero of Verdun had represented in better times. Louis and Myrtle were still in Paris. Louis was still a city councillor, and it seems still living well at the Hôtel Bristol. Though he had not left the CGQJ with a Goya or a Rembrandt, he was still in funds. In Paris, approaching nemesis meant little to his fellow anti-Semites and fascists, whose faith in their cause never wavered. On 3 May all of them gathered for one final demonstration, to celebrate the centenary of the birth of Édouard Drumont, their prophet, fittingly held at the cemetery of Père-Lachaise. Henry Coston organised the event, and every pillar of the anti-Semitic and fascist community was present. Louis Darquier, on speaking terms with nobody, was not.

As the vast Allied armada prepared for the D-Day landings sailed from Portsmouth on 6 June 1944, Louis' activities were already under investigation. Secretaries at the CGQJ were arrested and documents seized.[41] On 1 June the police noted that Louis Darquier had applied to open an Office of Genealogy at 1, rue de Caumartin in the 9th arrondissement. Céline, much more intelligent, had already begun to go about with a pistol, and by D-Day had fled to Baden-Baden. Throughout June, in *Action française* Maurras commanded what was left of his public: 'Discipline! Obey!' stand up with the 'rare and sublime' Marshal against the 'Gaullo-Communists' descending upon *la patrie*.[42]

In the east the Russian army was advancing inexorably towards Berlin. On 6 June, 'the longest day', the supreme commander of the Allied forces General Eisenhower broadcast to the French people, and eight hours later General de Gaulle was permitted to proclaim that the final battle for his country had begun, while Pétain told his subjects to be calm and accept the 'special circumstances' the German army might have to impose.

After the beach landings in Normandy, at Capestang, in the Hérault, at Tulle, at Oradour-sur-Glane near Limoges, SS detachments massacred village populations in retaliation; women and children were burnt alive in the Oradour village church. Over six hundred *Maquisards* were bombed to death on the plateau of Vercors.

The Resistance was taking over; in the Lot, they controlled the entire department except for Cahors. Philippe Henriot now broadcast on radio twice a day; 'the French Goebbels' they called him, though he called himself the Voice of France. He was the Lord Haw-Haw of Vichy, a mesmeric performer; everyone listened to him, and mealtimes were moved so families could hear him speak. After D-Day, as the Allied armies slowly fought their way inland from the Normandy beaches, his broadcasts grew in vitriol. Anti-Semitic always, he was violent too about de Gaulle, Moscow, London, Washington and the descending 'liberators', for by 14 June both Churchill and de Gaulle had visited their troops in France.

Henriot kept a special poison for his own people, the 'communists and terrorists' of the Resistance. In this he was still faithful to his Church, for the four senior cardinals of France, however much they wavered as Pétain's 'renewal of France' turned to ashes around him, remained united to the end in their condemnation of the Resistance and of General de Gaulle. His victory, they believed, would open the gates to communism. Cardinal Gerlier's dislike of de Gaulle was compounded by his being distantly related to him.

On 28 June the Resistance invaded Henriot's apartment in Paris and shot him dead. Xavier Vallat took over his broadcasts, calling the Catholic faithful to cleave to the Marshal until the very end, by which time his voice was frantic, for in July 1944 de Gaulle had granted an audience to the Pope. Henriot was accorded a state funeral. His body lay in state at the Hôtel de Ville in Paris, and his funeral provided the last great gathering of Pétain's faithful as Cardinal Suhard celebrated his Mass for the Dead at Notre Dame, attended by officers of German command. In reprisal for Henriot's death, on 7 July the Milice lifted Georges Mandel from Santé prison, took him to the forest of Fontainebleau and executed him. There was no Mass for Mandel; he was one of Pétain's French Jews.

At his trial after the war, Pétain attributed all his worst actions to his desire to shield France and its people from the ravages of Nazi rule. Yet every town and village in France is marked by what he did. Today his name is obliterated, hidden under the thousands of rues du 18 Juin 1940 and 25 Août 1944 you can see all over France. Vichy, which denies every public sign of his presence, provides the richest trawl. A very short walk from Louis' headquarters at the Hôtel Algeria is Le Petit Casino. This became the detention centre for the Milice, where they tortured French *résistants.* When the city was liberated in 1944, the lift of the Petit Casino was found to be full of blood.

In one sense the years 1940 to 1944, for the French people, had little to do with the world war raging outside their occupied territory, but much to do with what the French did to the French, and how they ended the long civil war which had begun with the Revolution in 1789. Both Pétain and Laval were guilty men, but the passing of time has been kinder to Laval's less hypocritical chicanery. Pétain's reputation was a gift from his people: his rock-solid hypocrisy, and the terrible use he made of his people's trust, gives him the edge in villainy. France was tragically unlucky to have either, and both, of them. The Vichy France which allowed Louis Darquier full scope for his activities was essentially the product of the governance of both, but there was only one man who continued in power throughout the Vichy years, from 16 June 1940 to 17 August 1944: Marshal Pétain.

V

SOME PEOPLE

20

‹○›

The Family

LOUIS DARQUIER TOOK HIS time; he did not leave France until the Liberation, and then only when his assassination was announced. Almost every member of the Vichy government and the *collabos* of Paris left before him. The Allied armies landed between Cannes and Toulouse in August 1944, and met the D-Day troops near Dijon in September. Battle casualties were severe, northern French towns were bombed to smithereens and something approaching fifty thousand French civilians died as the Allies advanced through France.

But the French were also killing each other. After D-Day, the civil war became savage. In early August, finally, Pétain complained to Laval about the atrocities: his Milice had become 'Frenchmen delivering their own compatriots to the Gestapo'. Darnand's reply was Vichy's epitaph: 'In the course of these four years ... you encouraged me. And today, because the Americans stand at the gates of Paris, you start to tell me that I shall be the stain on the history of France? It is something which might have been thought of earlier.'[1]

Throughout France the Germans too were fighting, killing Allied soldiers and the French, shredding papers, burning files, emptying their rooms and offices, and packing their cases to depart. By 17 August street fighting had broken out in Paris; on the same day, in the lovely summer weather, Karl Epting gave a farewell party at the Deutsche Institut, and Aloïs Brunner left Drancy for the last time, taking with him fifty-one Jews, headed for Buchenwald. Some of these Jews escaped, and ten survived. One who did not was the twelve-year-old son of the director of the Rothschild Hospital, Georges-André Kohn, who was sent on to another camp for medical experiments. On 20 April 1945, with twenty other Jewish children, he was hanged in the cellar of a school in Hamburg.

By 1944 the 'system of children's control' had reached its peak: 'Every

377

day brings us new tragedies ... the manager of our Brout-Vernet home has been arrested together with his babies, one of six and the other of two years ... sent to Drancy from where there is but one way ... please continue to do your utmost ... yesterday we had to pay the boarding of four thousand kids' – desperate letters such as this reached the British Foreign Office in February 1944.[2]

The last French convoy left Clermont-Ferrand on 22 August, making the year's total fifteen thousand Jews. By the time the Nazis stopped gassing Jews in Auschwitz, on 20 November 1944, 523 men and 766 women of this convoy were left alive. Despite the efforts of so many German and French officials, the Vichy state finally deported something between seventy-five and seventy-six thousand of the 850,000 Jews they believed to be living in France, less than a quarter of the actual Jewish community. Over seventy thousand were sent to Auschwitz, and well over half of them were gassed on arrival; only 2,564 survivors returned to France.

Céline saw his great friend Georges Montandon for the last time in June. By September Céline, his wife and his cat Bébert had found sanctuary in Sigmaringen in south-west Germany. Before then, on 17 August the Germans informed Pétain that he was to be taken 'to the east'. Pétain would not go. On 20 August German troops surrounded and broke into the Hôtel du Parc, forced the Marshal's door with crowbars and escorted him downstairs. As a small crowd sang the *'Marseillaise'* he was put into a convoy of German cars and, in civilian clothes, was whisked away to an unknown destination. He told his German keeper Cecil von Renthke-Fink that matters had descended into 'farce, a slapstick comedy'; his last message to his people told them, once again, to obey, and to remember his sacrifices on their behalf.[3] Within a week the Hôtel du Parc was in use for courts martial.

Meanwhile in Paris, as politely as possible, Abetz gave Laval his marching orders, leading to what was probably their first row. Laval would not go, and nor would his ministers. On 15 August the French police joined the metro workers and, finally, went on strike. Postal workers followed; Radio-Paris (German) went off the air, the collaborationist papers ceased publication. Earlier that month Hitler had sent a new military commander to Paris, General Dietrich von Choltitz, with orders to defend the city or destroy it. The Germans left in trucks and trains, the Paris *collabos* in whatever they could lay their hands on, often together, in convoys. Doriot organised trucks, Coston hired a car. On 17 August Laval resigned his post and delegated powers to Taittinger and the Parisian *préfets*; they were to maintain order, receive the Allies and negotiate with von Choltitz.

By the beginning of September Pétain and Laval, with their respective retinues, were in Germany, installed in the chocolate-box Hohenzollern Castle of Sigmaringen, perched above the Danube. Squeezed into the town below were the wives, children, mistresses, informers, criminals and refugees from the Vichy state. Overseen by Abetz, there they all stayed, quarrelling and plotting as before, attending Mass, with Céline in medical attendance noting every malevolent moment for posterity. (This led to arguably Céline's best book, *D'un Château à l'autre*, at once incomprehensible and perfectly clear, and always hilarious.)

An army of Darquier's colleagues were at Sigmaringen: Fernand de Brinon, nominal head of government, Darnand, Déat, Jean Luchaire, Lucien Rebatet, Georges Oltramare, Marcel Bucard, Jean Bichelonne, Abel Bonnard. Nearby, Doriot hatched plots with Ribbentrop. Another selection of comrades – the remnants of the ten-thousand-strong French division of the German army, the Charlemagne Division of the Waffen SS, by this time cut to pieces on the Russian front – ended up in Berlin in April 1945, defending Hitler as he prepared to commit suicide in his bunker.

Louis Darquier remained holed up with Myrtle in the Hôtel Bristol, watching as the Hôtel de Ville – *his* town hall – passed to his enemies. On 19 August barricades went up all over Paris and squabbling *résistants* – communist and non-communist – took to the streets. Taittinger raised the *tricolore* at the town hall, but to no avail: by Sunday the twentieth the Hôtel de Ville was occupied by the Resistance. Taittinger and his fellow councillors were whisked off to imprisonment by those French they had fought for decades: 'men in armbands bearing a hammer and sickle'.[4]

Von Choltitz received the final order to destroy Paris on 23 August – he had already received nine such instructions from Berlin – but he did nothing, considering Hitler to be deranged. At the same time General Eisenhower – more sympathetic than Churchill or Roosevelt to the symbolic importance of such a move – had authorised the French General Philippe Leclerc and his 2nd Armoured Division to be the first of the liberating forces to enter Paris, followed by the US 4th Infantry.

A unit of Leclerc's forces, escorted by the Resistance, greeted by ecstatic Parisians, reached the Hôtel de Ville on the evening of 24 August. By this time de Gaulle had contrived to get his way with the Allies and to establish his authority over all the Resistance groups.

The next day, von Choltitz signed his surrender; de Gaulle arrived, and from the balcony of the town hall delivered his famous speech: 'Paris! Paris humiliated! Paris shattered! Paris martyred! But Paris liberated, liberated by itself.' Amidst scenes of wild rejoicing, to the sounds of rolling tanks, the occasional rifle-shot, accordions and harmonicas, American soldiers distributed chocolate and were showered with kisses and hugs.

Taittinger was a close friend of the Archbishop of Paris, Cardinal Suhard; on 26 August de Gaulle led a victory parade down the Champs-Élysées from the Arc de Triomphe to Notre Dame, where a thanksgiving service was held; Suhard was not permitted to attend. The rest of the cardinals and bishops got off lightly. While some of their obedient clergy were summarily executed, and the pro-Nazi chaplain Monseigneur Mayol de Lupé was imprisoned for five years, only a quarter of the Catholic hierarchy were indicted, of whom the Vatican allowed only a handful to be 'resigned'. This clemency enraged a multitude of Catholic *résistants*, amongst them those of Cahors, where the rumour that Bishop Chevrier had been arrested proved false: he survived as archbishop until 1962.[5]

Men of the cloth might be spared, but for men like Louis Darquier the Liberation was the end of their world.[6] At the CGQJ, 'Antignac held a meeting to tell us that he no longer had any reason to be there, the Allies were at the gates of Paris and he disappeared.' The CGQJ was closed and sealed in early September. Pierre Galien had continued in the service of the Gestapo until May 1944, and was arrested in September. He thought he had burnt all his files, but some were later discovered in his St-Denis tyre factory. Joseph Antignac was arrested in November; the hapless staff well before that date.[7]

French cities and towns were gradually liberated throughout the following month, and as the Resistance, including its formidable communist *cadres*, came to terms with a French government in the hands of de Gaulle, something like nine thousand collaborators were summarily executed before special courts were set up in September 1944. These illegal purges were wild and vicious, each community exercising its own rough justice in an *épuration sauvage* as the French civil war came to an end. Women thought to have copulated with Germans had their heads shorn in public for their *collaboration horizontale*, and sometimes they were paraded naked. *Miliciens* and collaborators were tortured and shot without trial.[8]

Resistance newspapers first reported Louis Darquier's arrest on 8 September, and continued to do so for some months. In Bordeaux, in Brive, his execution was announced, usually coupled with the despatch of Admiral Platon. In London on 17 October, *The Times* reported that Darquier and Platon had been shot in Limoges. The next day *The Times* retracted; the reports were 'premature'. The paper may well have been alerted to its error by the French charities which were still pursuing Louis for money for Anne. The French police remained suspicious, but at a press conference at the Ministry of Justice on 23 October, journalists reiterated that both Darquier and Platon were dead.[9] Platon was indeed executed by the Resistance on 19 August 1944; perhaps, to these men, one of Pétain's monocled officials was the same as another.

Louis' version of events tells some of the truth: 'One fine day *they* fell upon someone who resembled me in a remarkable way. This was a completely hysterical period, you know. They arrested anyone, they fired indiscriminately. Anyway, *they* took this poor chap and the crowd cried "It's Darquier! It's Darquier! Shoot him!" Just between ourselves, I have always thought that there must have been friends of mine in that crowd . . . They shot this poor unfortunate in my place . . .'[10]

Decades later, a friend of Louis Darquier in Madrid told this story: 'One day, a French doctor who knew Darquier before the war visits Madrid. There he bumps into Darquier . . . Shortly after, the doctor attends a medical conference in France . . . he joins some colleagues for dinner. One of the diners reveals that he shot Darquier. "But Darquier is alive and well," says the doctor, "and living in Madrid. I've just seen him." Some time later, tormented by the knowledge that he has killed the wrong man, the colleague puts a gun to his own head, leaving a note behind saying he couldn't live with the idea that he'd shot the wrong man.'[11]

Meanwhile, Louis' secretary Paule Fichot was interviewed on 5 September, and told her investigators he was still at the Hôtel Bristol. She also told them that Louise was in Neuilly, where she heard Louis' assassination announced on the radio; and at the Bristol, Louis and

Myrtle heard it too. Myrtle was frantic. She was 'aware of the danger but she could not convince Louis'. When they came to get him, the moment she heard the expected knock on the door, she shoved Louis out through a second exit. That is the story Myrtle told her family, but the truth was that René came to their aid, again. René Darquier had an immensely strong sense of family, of *tribu*.[12] Despite everything, he could not abandon his brother. He hid Louis in a room on the sixth floor of the house in Neuilly where Louise and René's parents-in-law had apartments.

Louis Darquier himself told more lies than usual about his escape: 'In 1944, when everything had begun to break up, I began to think of my own safety. A friend took me to Toulouse, another to Bordeaux, and a third got me into Spain.'[13] One account, reported by the Jones family, has him arriving in Spain by submarine; in another, he crossed the border in the boot of the car of a woman variously reported as Yvonne, Germaine or Giselle de Bayehache, who was 'in love with him'. When Louis used this version he said he walked across the Pyrénées: 'Do you know who helped me to get from Bordeaux to Spain over the mountains? A half-Jewish woman, who, what is more, went under her father's Jewish name . . .' ('Louis was not past having a Jewish lover').[14]

In fact René put him into the boot of his car and drove him across Paris in September 1944, to where 'people' were waiting to get him south, to the Pyrénées. These 'people' seem to have been organised by de Monzie, whom Louise Darquier had called immediately: 'he still had ministerial contacts and he said to Madame Darquier "I'll do what I can to save him." He achieved the impossible.'[15]

The Spanish ambassador to Vichy, José de Lequerica, was back in Madrid by 11 August 1944, when he was sworn in as Franco's Minister of Foreign Affairs. His Vichy office informed him of Louis Darquier's 'assassination', and seven days later Louis had his pass to Spain. 'Lequerica helped Louis because Louis had helped him.'[16]

Much about the defeat of France and its suffering during the Occupation becomes clearer when those years are viewed as a French civil war, a variant of that of its Spanish neighbour. And so, certain aspects of the Vichy state become more comprehensible when viewed from a Spanish rather than a German or Italian perspective. The archives of Spanish libraries and institutions, open since Franco died – though much culled by him – demonstrate the closest of ties between Franco and the Vichy state; they were kissing cousins, not a relationship Pétain and his fellows had with Hitler, or Mussolini.

Both Franco and Pétain came to power in reaction to democratically elected Popular Front governments in the 1930s. Pétain's Spanish connections were always strong: he had been ambassador there in 1939, when he commended the 'wise leadership of General Franco'; he used José de Lequerica as a conduit to the Germans for the armistice of 1940; de Lequerica, with de Monzie, worked on the provisions for that armistice, and it was de Lequerica who took the ceasefire offer to the Germans. Lequerica was ambassador to France throughout the war years, from 1941 until 1944 when Pétain was taken to Sigmaringen. In his Vichy villa de Lequerica was only a step away from shared strolls, dinners and lunches with Pétain at the Hôtel du Parc.

In June 1941 Cardinal Gerlier went to Madrid to reopen the French church of St-Louis des Français, which had been destroyed in the Civil War; he took Franco a personal message from Pétain. This church was to become the centre and meeting place for the French political exiles who found shelter in Madrid after the war.

———————————— ⌘ ————————————

Cordons of police and customs officers lined the Spanish border in the autumn of 1944. On the French side large bands of Spanish republican partisans roamed the frontier, and the fighting between Milice and *Maquis* was savage. The smuggling racket was well organised and indiscriminate, supporting a flourishing black market in everything, particularly escaping war criminals. By the time Louis Darquier reached the border there were roadblocks at every village. Louis was in disguise: spectacles instead of a monocle, which he hated: 'He felt as if he was wearing a bicycle over his nose.'[17] He walked over the Pyrénées and crossed over to Spain at the town of Vera de Bidasoa on the little Bidasoa River, inland from the border towns of Hendaye on the French and Irún on the Spanish sides. There he presented his papers on 30 October 1944. He was now a French citizen named Jean Estève, authorised to travel to Madrid by the Spanish Ministry of Foreign Affairs. His credentials were sufficiently elevated for him to avoid the temporary camps or cells other exiles had to endure. When he got to Madrid he was provided with 'all necessary documents to stay in Spain'.[18]

In 1945 Franco's government was floundering as the Catholic and fascist dictatorships of Europe disappeared before its eyes, and accommodation had to be arranged with the United States and the victorious democracies. For them, within months of the war's end, Nazism and fascism defeated, communism became the sole enemy, and the Soviet Union was divided from western Europe and the USA by what Churchill called an 'Iron Curtain'. Thus Nazi and other war criminals were often spared punishment as they became useful to American and Western intelligence in the Cold War – a prime example of this being Gestapo chief Klaus Barbie, the 'Butcher of Lyon'. Thousands got away, and not only to South America – the residue of Hitler's and Pétain's followers found boltholes in Australia, Switzerland, Britain, Italy, the Middle East.

But the Franco regime made Spain the chosen refuge for *Miliciens*, the Paris *collabos* – particularly its journalists – and Doriot's fascists. For most it was getting out of France that was the problem; once across the border, false documents were produced in a flash to see them safely on to Madrid, Barcelona or Cadiz. The coastal stretch between Cadiz, Barbate and Algeciras was a favoured refuge for Nazi exiles; some French war criminals went to Barcelona, but most chose Madrid.[19]

The Cold War saved Spain from punishments due, but for many years after the war it was ostracised, an isolated, backward and brutally repressive country. Within its dismal confines Louis Darquier swiftly reassembled himself, but some things – money, high living, power – had gone forever.

Franco believed all opponents of his regime to be 'the scum of Jewish-Masonic-communist conspiracy'.[20] His dictatorship was in every way unfriendly to Jews, albeit more modestly than Vichy or Nazi Germany. Otherwise Franco's Spain was the perfect spiritual home for Louis Darquier, a regime entirely free of the errors of democracy, socialism and communism. After the Civil War Franco had imprisoned or killed most of his people who believed in such things, and the rest were in exile, or silent.[21]

In early 1945 reports reached Paris that Louis was not dead but living in Madrid, where he was writing his memoirs. He was soon seen around town with a woman on his arm, a pretty, very young 'shop girl' from the

Basque country, with a strong southern accent. His new mistress, Geneviève, was only twenty-five, and had fled France to escape punishment: she was pregnant by an occupying German. On arrival in Madrid she sought help from an association for such exiles and so met Louis, as ever its founder.

The considerable émigré community of French and German war criminals who had preceded Louis to Madrid now offered him such cocktail parties, lunches and dinners as they could afford. Louis would appear, monocle in position, thunderous of speech, his girlfriend silent and timid at his side, his audience immediately stunned by his vociferous pretensions. By March 1945 the French government knew where he was.[22] Three months later a warrant was issued for his arrest, and the French ambassador in London began his attempts to return Anne to the Darquier family in Paris. In the Hotel Margerit, in Madrid's avenida de José Antonio, Louis' new mistress became pregnant again.

According to Louis' accounts, he and his 'wife' were impoverished when they first arrived in Madrid, and were reduced to selling braces in Retiro Park, but very soon he was teaching French at the Friedendorff-Norris, a German language school near the avenida. This street, renamed Gran Via today, became Louis' Spanish Champs-Élysées. He was often seen there, 'suit badly crumpled and stained, monocle glued in, with his eternal walking stick . . . passing by the luxurious terraces of the cafés of the Gran Via, which he could not afford, scornful of eye, his soul as light as his purse'.[23] In its purlieus he began again the life he knew all too well from his London years: small hotel rooms, flitting from one place to another up and down the avenida, then descending to lodgings with a sequence of Spanish landladies – he would give them French lessons in exchange for a room.

Many of the French *collabos* taught for a pittance at language schools, chief among them the École Briam, still there today. Its director then was the *Milicien* leader François Gaucher, for many years Doriot's friend and right-hand man. Gaucher's life was typical of these impoverished war criminals in the early years after the war. Life was still dangerous for them then, as one by one their death sentences were announced in France. Gaucher would not arrive at the school until 4 p.m., and then worked behind a closed door until late at night. 'He was very very retiring and few people came into contact with him at all . . . he followed the same routine, day after day.'[24] In the boiling heat of summer, teachers like

Louis would scurry from one windowless classroom to the next with scarcely a break, using pseudonyms taken from the great names of literature: Sr H.G. Wells, Sr Gustave Flaubert . . .

On 30 July 1946 the Spanish government gave Louis a passport; he became Jean Estève Roussel, born in Hirson, France, on 16 August 1899; the next day Teresa, Anne's half-sister, was born.

Meanwhile, in Paris, in November 1944 de Gaulle had set up an Haute Cour de Justice, a High Court of Justice, to try '*les grands responsables*', the men of position who had committed the crimes and offences of Vichy's 'government or pseudo government'. It took some months to track down Louis, but a warrant for his arrest was issued in June 1945.

Life was wretched for men like de Monzie after the Liberation; he was kept under investigation for treason, but never formally charged. For the people of Cahors he was the 'prototype of a collaborator, a *Vichyiste*'. He was on the point of being executed by the Resistance but the man who carried the order was killed in an ambush.[25] In Cahors de Monzie's name was linked with Louis Darquier; he was not safe in the Lot, his country house was burgled, and even in Paris, where he died in January 1947, his apartment was pillaged.[26]

In 1943 de Monzie had published a book, *La Saison des juges* – The Season of Judges – in which he argued that French statesmen had always been pulled between revenge and tolerance, between pursuit of those responsible for a national catastrophe and letting sleeping dogs lie. This expressed something of de Gaulle's position: at the Liberation his transformation of France into a nation of *résistants* and his limitation of state punishment meant that compromise tempered justice – wise at the time, but leaving France with festering wounds.

State '*épuration*' by military and civilian courts throughout France – the collaboration trials of 1945 to 1949 – did not begin with Pétain and Laval, but theirs were the most sensational cases. When the Sigmaringen fantasy came to an end as General Patton's army approached the castle, its exiles fled in all directions. In April 1945 Pétain insisted on returning to France. At his trial in July Charles Trochu appeared as a witness for his defence – startlingly transformed into a republican and Gaullist since 1940, 'the only person' at Vichy 'supporting this viewpoint'. As for the enemy whom he, Pétain, Maurras and their *confrères* had fought for so long, communists, Trochu now had 'nothing but admiration' for them.[27]

Trochu's court statements were typical: lies and bombast, obfuscation and fantasy became the order of the day, particularly evidenced by men such as General Weygand, who testified on Pétain's behalf in a diatribe that was also a ferocious defence of himself. Pétain, nearly ninety by this time, still managed to present his years of belief in, and service to, a Nazi victory as devoted protection of France. By playing 'a double game' with the Allies, he claimed, he was 'the shield' of France, its protector against the invading Hun.

Pétain and Trochu were only two of hundreds of thousands of hitherto unsuspected supporters who made themselves known to de Gaulle and the Allies at this time. The truth came from Pétain's public prosecutor: 'Hatred of the Republic stands at the beginning of the whole Pétain case.' Pétain's death sentence was commuted to exile for life on the Île d'Yeu, off France's Atlantic coast. Eighty per cent of the French public were in favour of his punishment; the remainder, to this day, clamour for the reinstatement of his reputation and the transfer of his bones to Verdun – he died on his prison island in 1951.[28]

Like Louis Darquier, Laval applied to José de Lequerica for sanctuary in Spain. In May 1944 de Lequerica claimed that history would one day recognise the greatness of his friend Laval. By July this was forgotten, and his 'friend' was surrendered to the Allies.[29] Laval's trial in October was a farce. Hatred spewed from prosecutor, judge and jury. He was barely permitted to speak or defend himself. Condemned to death, he tried to commit suicide the night before his execution by swallowing cyanide; he failed, and was carted half-dead to the firing squad.

By now Louis Darquier had a good idea of what lay in store. Most of his fellows were captured and punished in these years. In 1944 Eugène Deloncle was assassinated by the Gestapo, and Georges Montandon by the Resistance. Pierre Taittinger found himself incarcerated in the Vel' d'Hiv', complaining of the cold, of the biscuits and jam and sardines, and of the ragtag and bobtail – Negroes, Indians even – mixed up with the mayors, *préfets* and other officials who had served Vichy and Germany. Taittinger's indignant protestations when he was transferred to Drancy – used by the new government as a camp for French war criminals now – continued up to and throughout his 'ridiculous legal proceedings', his imprisonment in cell number 210 at Fresnes, and the Pooterish books he wrote about himself after his release in early 1945.[30] Inexplicably, his only punishment was prohibition from holding any public office.

Robert Brasillach was executed in Feburary 1945. In March 1945

Drieu la Rochelle killed himself. Later in the year Joseph Darnand, Jean Hérold-Paquis and Marcel Bucard were executed – Bucard went to the firing squad singing 'I am a Christian, that is my Glory'.[31]

Charles Maurras was arrested in Lyon in September 1944, two weeks after the last issue of *Action française*. Amongst his indictments were 'incitement to murder' and 'intelligence with the enemy'. During his trial, which began on 25 January 1945, he delivered a six-hour declamation of his innocence and the guilt of the republic: 'When you say, as you do, M. le Président, that in February 1944 drawing public attention to a Jew was to point him out, his family and himself, to the reprisals of the Germans, to spoliation, to concentration camps, perhaps to torture and to death, not only did I ignore these fine things, but I knew the contrary . . .'[32] When sentence was pronounced – *dégradation nationale* (loss of civic rights) and life imprisonment – Maurras declaimed that it was 'the revenge of Dreyfus'. His lifelong colleague Maurice Pujo, tried with him, was condemned to only five years in prison and released after two years.

The crimes of Vichy and its collaborators were called 'intelligence with the enemy' and 'plotting against the security of the state'.[33] Manifestation of hatred of Jews was one indictable offence, as was working in an executive position at the CGQJ. Otherwise, the imprisonment and murder of Jews and others did not become criminal offences until 1964, when French law changed to allow retroactive trial for crimes against humanity. Until then, the Nazis were allotted blame for Vichy atrocities.

The business community was lightly dealt with; writers and broadcasters, warriors of the word, received the harshest treatment. *Dégradation nationale* was only one punishment. Solitary confinement, life and other prison sentences and hard labour were alternatives. Some seven thousand men were sentenced to death; but nearly four thousand of the accused had already fled France.

Of Darquier's deputies at the CGQJ, Joseph Antignac was condemned to death in July 1949, but ill health saved him. After six months of investigations Pierre Galien fled to Turkey and was tried, *in absentia*, with Antignac. Galien was occasionally heard from again through letters to his wife in Neuilly.

The Nazi alumni from whom Louis received money from 1936 onwards – Rosenberg, Ribbentrop and Streicher – were all hanged in

Nuremberg in 1946. Goebbels, Himmler and Goering committed suicide. The Germans who worked in France were spared. Otto Abetz was condemned to twenty years' hard labour in 1949, but was released after five years. Helmut Knochen's death sentence in 1954 was commuted to twenty years' imprisonment, but he was pardoned in 1962: a retired insurance agent, he was reported as still alive in Germany in 2004, 'weary and bitter'. General Karl-Albrecht Oberg, 'the Butcher of Paris', was tried with Knochen and received the same sentence, but died three years after his release. Theodor Dannecker hanged himself in an American prison in Bavaria in December 1945. Colonel Kurt von Behr and his wife mixed cyanide with champagne in their castle in Germany. Ernst Achenbach became a deputy in Germany until 1970, when his past caught up with him. Heinz Röthke was as fortunate as Darquier: untouched, he became a lawyer in Wolfsberg in Germany, and died in 1966. Lesser German officials – Rudolf Schleier, Dr Peter Klassen – seem to have been equally ignored.[34]

Henry Charbonneau and Henry Coston were sentenced to prison and forced labour – Charbonneau for ten years, Coston for life, though he was free by 1951, and lived on, writing in the same manner and voluminously, for another fifty years. Lucien Rebatet received a death sentence in 1946, but was pardoned and freed by 1952.

Many, like Louis, escaped altogether. Marcel Déat was given refuge in a Catholic convent in Turin. Céline took shelter in Denmark; tried, convicted and amnestied in his absence, by 1951 he had returned safely to France.[35] Trials and executions continued for some years – Jean Luchaire was executed in 1946, Fernand de Brinon in 1947 – but by then furies had abated. Amnesty laws began in 1947, and by 1951 retribution had ended. Very few served their full sentence.

'We need to ensure social isolation so as to make the Jewish community what it should never have ceased to be – a foreign colony,' was a Darquier hymn tune during the Vichy years.[36] After 1944 Madrid became the Madagascar for this colony of French political refugees. In the coming years some of them lived well: the leader of the Belgian fascists, Léon Degrelle, who eventually married the former wife of Henry Charbonneau, spent years in considerable comfort on the Costa del Sol and in Málaga, honoured by Franco's government, his Catholicism permitting him to be photographed with a beaming Pope John Paul II on 11 December 1991. Léon and Jeanne Degrelle both knew Louis Darquier, but in Spain they avoided him as much as they could, despising his irregular private life from the lofty heights of their own unusual marital arrangements – Darquier was vulgar, impecunious, tiresome. Louis reciprocated by describing Belgians as belonging to a 'sub-culture'.

At lower altitudes the lesser losers mixed together: Vichy collaborators, Milice, Paris *collabos*, Nazis ranging from Gestapo to camp commandants. Gradually fear of pursuit and betrayal passed and, embittered, mutually supportive, living under a wide and changing variety of assumed names, they helped each other get work. The French exiles were additionally fortunate in that after the Civil War, French was the official second language in Spain, but the wretched state of the Spanish economy meant that though there was plenty of work, it was miserably paid. This was the greatest change for Louis: once he arrived in Spain he took up work, and never abandoned it again; work became a kind of replacement addiction for him and his fellows. They toiled in language schools, libraries, publishing houses, educational institutions, government offices; they worked as interpreters and edited language dictionaries; they broadcast to France on Radio Nacional de España about the wonders of Franco's Spain. All of them hovered around the French embassy, their fortunes there varying with the politics of the incumbent ambassador. As before, they fought over women.

Eugène Schueller's beauty empire l'Oréal became 'a factory to recycle the extreme right' into safety, in particular two murderers from the Cagoule.[37] Jacques Corrèze, Deloncle's right-hand man, ran l'Oréal's American subsidiary until the 1990s, and Jean Filliol, Deloncle's top gun, a subsidiary in Spain. François Mitterrand's brother had married Deloncle's niece, and his sister Jo was the mistress of Jean Bouvyer, Cagoulard and senior official at Darquier's CGQJ. So Mitterrand became a considerable recycler of dubious collaborators himself; he worked for l'Oréal after the war, and was working for Schueller when he fought his first election campaign in 1946.

Another early exile ushered in by José de Lequerica was Alain Laubreaux, the theatre critic of *Je Suis partout*, whom the actor Jean Marais had thrashed on behalf of his lover Jean Cocteau for Laubreaux's characteristic but atrocious review of Cocteau's play *La Machine à écrire* (*The Typewriter*) in 1943. Laubreaux was a clone of Louis Darquier, as large, but slimier and fleshier of lip, a man of epic rages and an enthusiastic *coureur de jupons* who made the mistake of approaching Louis' mistress. He and Darquier quarrelled about everything, but over Geneviève they had 'a blood row . . . and came to blows'.[38]

⁕

One French view of Britain described it as a country 'where nothing is provided for women, not even men'.[39] However, in 1945 Anne Darquier lived in encouraging times as the nation's governing classes turned their attention to the population who fought its wars. The Beveridge Plan, published in 1942, followed by the Butler Education Act in 1944, ushered in the welfare state and universal education, just a year too late for Anne to benefit or for Elsie to cease pursuing Free French charities, but in good time for Anne to find the gates of Oxford University open to children such as she.

She was even luckier to be a young girl with ambitions as Clement Attlee's Labour government was swept to power on 26 July 1945. Three months earlier, in May, Churchill had presided over the final defeat of Germany and the end of the war in Europe. Labour promised people like Elsie – though a Tory voter all her life – social security, full employment, decent health, housing and education; running water and electricity came to Great Tew village itself.

Despite the decisive achievements of the Red Army and the huge contribution of American arms and money, it was Britain which had fought against Germany from the beginning to the end. Now it was bankrupt, hungry – rationing was worse than ever, and continued until 1954 – and shedding its Empire right and left. But although every Briton was tired to death of austerity, it was not the class to which Elsie and Anne belonged which suffered from nationalisation, fierce taxation and the loss of Empire during the post-war years.

These were years of hope for Anne. Her other piece of luck was to have been given, through Elsie and Maud – 'enormous characters, both of them' – that Ealing Comedy British sense of humour exported everywhere in the Anglo-Saxon world after the war, but very much in evidence in Great Tew during it. However much Elsie kept Anne apart from *hoi polloi*, Anne learned to laugh during her childhood, and she absorbed in remembered detail the mysteries of the British class system. It was only to Elsie that Anne could unleash any rage. With everyone else she was gentle and controlled, but with Elsie she could flare up if she was upset. Elsie 'had a job to calm her down', but she could do it.[40]

From her father, if such attributes can be innate, Anne inherited remarkable single-mindedness. Since the age of fourteen she had taught herself, and when she was not working in the pub, friends remember that she 'studied all the time': 'She didn't mix with the other kids, she stayed in the pub most evenings, and didn't roister about the village as the others did.'[41] Her devotion to medicine and the hours she spent over her books were always a mystery to the inhabitants of Great Tew.

At East Ham Grammar, Anne's teachers had taken the girls on sight-seeing tours of Oxford. Anne determined on a medical degree from Oxford University. Nothing else would do. She may have looked fragile, but her perseverance was startling. One account, from a medical contemporary, tells of her getting the Chipping Norton bus to Oxford to knock on the door of every educational establishment, asking, 'Will you teach me chemistry and physics?' Those who knew her well were aware that Anne, outwardly shy and withdrawn, had a will of iron when it came to her ambition to become a doctor.

As Britain began its social revolution, everything changed for Anne too. Twelve months after Louis escaped to Spain, in October 1945, the French ambassador in London approached de Gaulle's Ministry of Foreign Affairs on behalf of the French benevolent societies, who could not continue to support Anne indefinitely: 'a member of his family [must] take charge of the infant', or she would be sent to a charitable institution in France.

At this point the French Ministry of Justice was anxious to find Louis Darquier too. Investigators were sent to interview his brother Jean, who told them that though he would take Anne if 'the worst came to the worst', 'his professional obligations, in addition to those of his wife, would oblige them to neglect the education of this child who does not speak French'.[42] He recommended that they approach the Jones family, by way of Myrtle, who was currently in London. Jean gave them her address: 35 Sussex Square, in Bayswater, near Hyde Park; they should write to her *poste restante*, Jermyn Street, Piccadilly.

And so Anne came up to London to meet her mother. After Myrtle pushed Louis out of the door in September 1944 she got away, according to her Tasmanian family, with her maid, leaving behind her beautiful clothes – possibly true – and a lifetime's collection of valued possessions. If the latter ever existed, neither the police who raided rue Laugier, nor the grim rooms of the Hôtels Fortuny or Terminus, showed any sign of them. It was February 1946 when Jean Darquier reported Myrtle's whereabouts. Her British passport would have enabled her to escape to London well before 1946, but she did not contact Anne or Elsie, perhaps one reason being that she was living under the name of Cynthia de Pelle Poix, another being that she had lost out to Elsie in their tug-of-war over Anne years before. Myrtle had always presented herself to her family in Tasmania as a darling of Parisian society. At 35 Sussex Square there were many other residents, and no sign of a maid; it was, most likely, a boarding house.

It was after this meeting at Sussex Square that Anne described Myrtle as a 'total write-off' from drink and drugs. Myrtle's state of alcoholic stupor might well have been due to Louis' disappearance, for she did not know his whereabouts until early 1947.[43] The Darquiers in Paris knew where he was, of course, but it seems that time had in no way altered their view of Myrtle.

Anne's meeting with her mother was her greatest shock, and one she buried immediately, a manner of dealing with loss which never changed. Anne looked 'amazingly like her mother'[44] – she had Myrtle's blue eyes – but she identified with her father, not with the theatrical but by this time raddled charmer whom she met at Sussex Square in 1946. Anne was fifteen then; she would say later that she met her mother only a few times in her life, and always, after this meeting, she could barely manage to mention her name.

There were, however, happier distractions. In early 1946 Maud and Elsie's niece May came back from the war to live at the Falkland Arms; she was engaged now, marriage preparations were in the air and Anne was to be bridesmaid. Then Louise Darquier invited Anne to Paris.

René Darquier had already left for Argentina. In June 1945 the resistance newspaper *Franc-tireur* attacked him for profiting from Louis' position – headlines such as '*Darquier Frères & Cie*' meant he had to go. Henry Lévy's grandson remembers: 'After the Second World War he [René] wanted my father to give him a job again in the company. This matter came up in family discussions. But with a brother like Louis Darquier de Pellepoix, my father thought it was not possible that he hadn't benefited in some way or another. So my father said no, he could not take him back.'[45]

For Louise, many of the friends who had showered her with flowers before 1944 now avoided her, and to bring the daughter of Louis Darquier de Pellepoix to Paris in 1946 was no simple matter. Louise was summoned to the British embassy in Paris. She cried all night before her interview, but when she met the consul – she thought she met Duff Cooper, the incumbent of the time, but doubtless it was a minor official – she wept all over him too: 'Monsieur, if you had a grandchild in a foreign country . . . whom you had never seen, what would you do in my place?'[46]

When Anne arrived in Paris in 1946 her French was only up to Elsie's standard, but otherwise Louise was pleased with her: 'She was different, but she did not disappoint. She smiled so nicely.' On her return to Great Tew Anne's friends found her 'quite different, very sophisticated'. And she came back a Catholic: she was baptised, she had been to Mass. The country people were astonished by her altered accent and her attendance at 'Marss' – Anne insisted on pronouncing the word in this Evelyn Waugh-esque way: 'Her head was turned a bit.' She said not a word about Myrtle, but her friend Beryl was told that Anne's parents had sent her to Britain to keep her out of 'war-torn France'. Everything else she continued to keep 'very close to her chest'.[47]

Anne took her new religion very seriously. Though there were two big Catholic churches at Banbury and Chipping Norton, and a little one at Hook Norton, nearby at Enstone was the famous Jesuit college Heythrop Hall, with its ancient library and philosopher priests. Anne met a different class of person once she came back from Paris. She had learned about ballet and theatre, and she began to mix with families whom the villagers of Great Tew called 'the upper classes' at Little Tew. Under their wing she was taken to Mass at Heythrop Hall. She was confirmed, and chose the name of Anne Marie; at Mass on Sundays there she met Polish and French servicemen – there were plenty of Catholics around Great Tew in those days.[48] She learned about music – her favourite composers were French, Delibes and Ravel – and she listened to the piano at the houses of her new friends.

At the end of 1946 Elsie and Anne returned to Kidlington and Anne signed up with Wolsey Hall correspondence college in Oxford, appointed by the War Office in 1942 to provide courses for the forces. Either knocking at doors, or her pub servicemen, led her towards it. In April 1947 Aunty Violet died of cancer, nursed at the Falkland Arms and buried in the churchyard of St Michael and All Angels at Great Tew. By the summer of that year Anne had passed her Higher School Certificate with the London External Exam Board. Mystery surrounds Anne's entrance to Oxford; she did not have the Latin matriculation qualification necessary for enrolment, and she does not seem to have taken the usual entrance examination later in 1947. Perhaps she sat it and failed, for she did not get to Oxford until 1949. But she was lucky, again. Anne was exactly the sort of person the post-war British government wanted to help. An Oxford contemporary said, 'She lied to get into Oxford, got there under false pretences . . . things were more casual then. People just believed you.'[49]

As Anne turned eighteen in September 1948, May Brice married her Sussex farmer, Gilbert Rapley, at St Michael and All Angels. In the wedding photographs Anne, usually thought of as charming but 'not quite pretty', *is* pretty in a long floral dress, with flowers in her hair. These are the happiest photos: she smiles with the gaiety that marked her as much as her charm. She had not yet met her father, but she had been back to Paris, this time to stay with Jean and Janot in the rue Jouffroy. Typically, she had now perfected her French. After this visit Anne changed her medical aspirations: she was adamant that she would enter her uncle's branch of medicine and become a neurosurgeon, but the person she talked about most was her Aunt Janot, not only a woman doctor as Anne longed to be, but also one whose recent thesis had been concerned with the medical care of employees in the workplace.

The Oxford entrance examination was Anne's only remaining problem. Her luck continued; she now had the money to pay for a university education. For Australia, the World War ended in August 1945, after the atomic bomb had been dropped on Hiroshima and Nagasaki. As soon as the first ships could sail bearing letters, Lexie Jones took charge of her granddaughter, always called 'Anne-France' by Myrtle's family. From Tasmania, Lexie put her children to work on Anne's behalf. For years the middle sister Olive, for whom Louis Darquier was 'sun, moon and stars', had been posting parcels to Myrtle and Hazel, and now she added Anne to her list. Hazel Jones, the competent one, 'half in love with Louis',[50] had worked all over the world, and was often in England. She dealt with Elsie on behalf of the Jones family; there was no love lost in this relationship either. Tasmania felt that Nanny Lightfoot was mercenary, and overprotective of Anne. The Jones family in Tasmania blamed Elsie for Anne's hatred of her parents, whilst Elsie, Maud and Arthur thought the worst of all of them, and often said so.

Anne had other offers of help too. By early 1947 the Darquier family and Myrtle knew where Louis was, and Anne was again in touch with 'Dear Daddy' from afar. Nothing of this had changed from her visit to Paris the year before, for Louise's attitude towards Louis' activities was always a mixture of private misery and public pride. Anne learned no truths about her father in Paris. With Elsie's encouragement, Anne's childhood melancholy – and fury – were still focused on Myrtle. Apart from instructing Anne in Catholicism, Louise had wanted to teach her granddaughter to sew, so she in turn could teach her own children. Anne refused, and said to Louise: '*Bonne-Maman*, I will never have children.'[51]

Anne still believed she had an aristocratic father with money and hopes. One account has it that Louis offered to pay for her medical education on the proviso that she came to live in Madrid. As Louis was penniless at this time and, unknown to the Jones family, or to Anne or Myrtle, had a new baby to support, this may well have been a lie invented by Myrtle to ease her way into Anne's heart. This she failed to do. That her medical education was paid for by Myrtle's mother, at Myrtle's request, made no difference to Anne. She found Myrtle intolerable; Oxford entrance was her Holy Grail; 1946 marks Elsie's final victory over Myrtle, and the end of Myrtle's relationship with her daughter. It is clear from the fantasies about children which peppered her conversation that Myrtle never recovered; but then, neither did Anne.

And so in 1947 Myrtle, who had once told René 'I love Louis and cannot imagine life without him',[52] left London and joined Louis in Spain. He dismissed his *foufou* – she was only a simple girl from the south-west, half his age and too 'provincial'. For Louis, Geneviève could not compete with Myrtle, whom he always called his '*Grande Dame*'. Teresa, six months old, was despatched as Anne had been. In France, Louis had very occasionally admitted that Anne was his daughter, though he could not remember the year she was born; but with Teresa he was different: she had a hundred per cent French blood. Teresa's mother wanted to put her up for adoption, but Louis would not have it; she was farmed out to live with poor families, for payment, until Louis needed her to take care of him in old age. (Teresa's memory of her childhood is identical to that of Anne: abandonment, banishment and anguish, mixed with poverty and no running water.)

Myrtle remained with Louis in Madrid for the rest of her life, as incapable of speaking Spanish as any other foreign language. Once they were together again, they set to work to get their money out of France, paying the cultural attaché at the Spanish embassy in Paris 'important sums' to smuggle it out in the diplomatic bag. It is impossible to track down exactly what monies these were, or how much Darquier extracted from the CGQJ. What evidence there is derives from a mass of allegations. It is even more impossible to know what they did with it, or exactly where it went, because no riches arrived for the couple in Madrid, and whatever Louis had amassed by the end of the war was anyway confiscated by the French state.

By the end of 1947 Louis had begun to earn his living at the Escuele Central de Idiomas (Central School of Languages), where he taught English under the name of Juan Estève, still living in one room in and around the avenida. His trial had opened in the Palais de Justice in Paris on 2 December 1947. He was tried in his absence, with Xavier Vallat, before the High Court of Justice.[53] 'In this double trial the martyrdom of all the Jews during the Occupation is brought back to life,' said *Le Matin*. Vallat attended, and called upon Catholic philosophy and precedents in his defence; he was sentenced to ten years (he only served two, some of it with Maurras as his prison companion).

Darquier's case was speedily dealt with. His character had already been thoroughly assassinated, in public and during his trial, so most of his prosecution was devoted to trying to work out what exactly could be placed at his door, granted that every secretary and official testified to his near-permanent absence from the CGQJ office. In a great many cases the conclusion was: 'Antignac is wholly responsible.' What emerged chiefly from the investigation and trial, and from numerous witnesses, was that Louis Darquier was little more than a con man. Even his loyal secretary Paule Fichot declared, 'I have heard him say, like everyone else, that money comes before principles.'[54] The indignity of acknowledging that this manipulating scoundrel had reached such a position in a French government was one of many reasons why his extradition from Spain was never requested.

On 10 December 'Darquier sans Pellepoix' was declared guilty of 'collusion with agents of a foreign power' and was sentenced to death *in absentia*, his goods were confiscated and his French citizenship withdrawn.[55] Eighteen Frenchmen were sentenced to death by the High Court of Justice, of whom only three were actually executed. Abel Bonnard was one of these condemned men who escaped his sentence.[56] With Louis Darquier he would lunch after Mass on Sundays at the Church of St-Louis des Français in Madrid.

Reports of Louis' condemnation appeared in all the newspapers in France, in *The Times* and in other British newspapers; Hazel in Europe kept in constant touch with Tasmania. There, Lexie Jones took action. Just as the will of Henry Jones had been entirely concerned with Myrtle, so the will Lexie made within months of Louis' death sentence was entirely concerned with Anne. When Henry died in 1929 he had left Lexie a millionaire at today's values, just. In 1948 circumstances were not the same, but everything she had was put into trust for Anne. None of the Jones children could touch their shares until Lexie was satisfied that Anne had been educated. Myrtle was never to have more than a life share in hers, and every clause in the will was qualified by 'other than my said daughter Myrtle Marion Ambrosine Baroness Darquier de Pellepoix'.[57]

With Lexie masterminding affairs from Tasmania, Myrtle's older brother Hector, a dentist in Toowoomba, Queensland, became Anne's guardian, and Hazel arranged matters in England. Hazel felt she was 'on excellent terms' with Anne and Elsie.[58] This was only one of the sad and strenuous delusions of the Jones family, who in the words of the youngest daughter Heather viewed Louis' post-war circumstances as the Jews wreaking revenge. Lexie, who never met Anne, and never saw Myrtle again after 1929, seems to have been the only one to have some idea of the truth. Myrtle's siblings continued to view her as a glittering European baroness whose grandeur and style illuminated the salons of cosmopolitan society.

Either Lexie or Louis paid for Anne to go to Madrid some time in 1948 or 1949. She seems not to have known about her father's deeds or death sentence before she went; or rather, the violent shock she received in Madrid implies such ignorance, for when Anne met the man she believed to be her aristocratic French father, for a little time she thought she had struck gold. How long her visit was remains unknown, nor do I know why she did not mention seeing her mother again in Madrid – it may well be that Louis had once again sent Myrtle somewhere for treatment, for he 'took her to many many doctors for her alcoholism'.[59]

In the years after the war, Louise took good care to speak about Louis only to those she trusted – usually these were women who worked for her. She excused her son by saying, 'He saved those he could; if he hadn't been there, the Germans would have taken everyone.'[60] Such comforting messages from her grandmother were comprehensively destroyed once Anne got to Madrid.

Louis Darquier never kept himself to himself for one moment, and he had only one subject: Jews, about whom he talked continuously, out loud, to his dying day. Jews were 'encrusted onto his persona'.[61] He remained combative and extravagant to the end, and the deranged words he had borrowed from the *Protocols* never changed.

In Madrid everything would have become apparent to Anne. Where were the accoutrements of baronial life? Why was Baron Darquier de Pellepoix living in a rented room? How could the loudmouth barfly and bruiser she met be related to the heroic count of her imagination? He could not. In 1949 Anne of Great Tew and Kidlington, raised on austerity, the Home Front and Churchill, and Anne of the Jesuits and Heythrop Hall, discovered exactly who she was, and what her father was responsible for. On her way to an education now, she had the skills to find out more, to find out exactly what she needed to know.

Anne mentioned not a word about this visit to her friend Beryl when she came to stay in Kidlington; all she talked about was Oxford and her arrangements to begin her medical studies. She did not talk of her parents, nor of her Tasmanian family, and Beryl felt there was some secret she was keeping: 'Anne only let you know what she wanted you to know.' If she had to contact her father at all he was no longer 'Dear Daddy', but 'Dear Louis', and from 1949 she refused, savagely, to acknowledge or forgive either of her parents. Louis never threw out the letter of bitter reproach she sent him.[62] The silence Elsie had taught her during the war years now became Anne's way of life. Dominique Jamet, a French writer, son of a journalist *collabo*, is only one of the many children who have written and spoken about what it is like to 'carry the crimes of their fathers in silence and solitude', coated in an 'invisible and ignominious stain'.[63]

For Anne, the loss of her father was not the same as her dismissal of Myrtle; Louis the baron had been her hope and her idol, and while she said nothing about Myrtle to her closest friends or those she trusted, over the coming years she would speak about her father: she hated him. Although she did not habitually blame people, she always talked of him without forgiveness, and of 'the burden of living with a father who was a devil . . . sending Jews out of France'.[64]

Anne came back with 'a deep hatred for her father', 'hatred, contempt and shame'. Talking to her half-sister Teresa today about their father, you hear the same force as Anne used when she told me: 'There are some things and some people you can never forgive.' After her visit to Madrid Anne became another of those children who tremble, and 'not only from cold in the night'.[65]

21

The Cricket Team

THE FINANCIAL GENEROSITY OF Lexie Jones towards her grand-daughter was exceptional, but careful. Anne had to get a scholarship, and she did – 'Lord Nuffield's gift to the college of a medical Scholarship of the value of £100 per annum', an open scholarship for sciences provided by the Morris motorcar millionaire. Thus fortified, in October 1949 Anne entered St Hilda's College, Oxford, to study medicine, one of the 970 women permitted to study at Oxford that year. To those initiated in the mysteries of college hierarchies St Hilda's was less illustrious than its rival women's colleges – Lady Margaret Hall and Somerville – but its rank and accommodation were more than acceptable to someone used to the Falkland Arms and Hazel Crescent.

Founded by Dorothea Beale, the famous educator of women and principal of Cheltenham Ladies' College, St Hilda's was full of Cheltenham girls, a class apart from Anne, who had not even managed a grammar school. In 1949 clothing rationing ended: this changed little, but you could now spot the difference between grammar school and Cheltenham girls, and they hardly mixed socially. Anne was a 'scholarship girl' who had told white lies about her previous education.

The Oxford University Anne entered in 1949 was still a masculine establishment. Articles in its magazine *Isis* complained that 'Oxford women were pimply, wore shapeless tweeds, pedalled furiously from lecture to lecture, drank Nescafé in their silly little chintz-curtained rooms, and became French mistresses eventually in Birmingham.'[1] There were courses women could not study, places they could not go, societies they could not join. In addition, Anne had entered a profession in which women were still a rarity.

Post-war Oxford was vigorously uncomfortable. There was no central heating – St Hilda's was 'like a refrigerator' – and clothes were so rationed that it was not so much a problem of having coupons for shoes as of finding shoes to buy. Men (in demob suits) were rationed by St Hilda's, and food by the government, to such a degree that contemporary accounts of life at the college in Anne's time seem to concentrate entirely on butter. Everything was shabby but cheerful, although Anne's gaiety seems to have evaporated within the confines of St Hilda's. Very few from her year remember her well, mostly because the science and humanities students did not mix, but also because memories of the war were still vivid in 1949, and Anne had to be careful. Her fellow students remember her as 'slight in build, quiet and rather withdrawn', 'charming', 'highly intelligent' and 'scholarly', 'a slender, slightly stooping girl with an exceptionally sweet smile'.[2] All noted that she was kind but reserved, and she was known for not going to lectures, working in laboratories and libraries all day and studying all night, and for having a permanent boyfriend.

Immediately after the war Catholicism in Oxford burst into life, and Anne always went round with a Catholic foursome, of whom her boyfriend John Varley was one. Anne could afford the fines St Hilda's charged if she came back to college after 11.15 p.m. Varley, a fellow medical student, was a dour and sardonic Scot, clever in the sense that Anne, with her difficult education, could never be. His father had a cinema in Stranraer; he was not poor. Students with steady boyfriends were almost unknown at the time, so Anne and John were remembered, also for their notorious quarrels – they were often vile to each other, but for years were never seen apart.

Varley and his friends were fond of drink – very fond – and Anne's Catholic coterie had riotous times together. Anne could be waspish about Oxford – she was particularly envious of the shooting star of her years there, Shirley Catlin, daughter of Vera Brittain, now Shirley Williams – but she had a good time. St Hilda's had its own punts and canoes. When Beryl came to visit Anne in Oxford, they went to see *Swan Lake* at the New Theatre, and punted on the river.

On her Oxford registration in October 1949, Anne stated that she was her father's only child, but then, Myrtle knew nothing about the existence of Teresa for many years. But Hazel Jones knew, and always saw Teresa on her annual visit to Myrtle in Madrid; Teresa called her 'Aunty Hazel' years before she met Myrtle. It is probable that Anne learned about her half-sister from Hazel; how the news affected her can only be deduced from the fact that she resolutely refused to see or speak to Teresa throughout her life.

In the midst of her years at Oxford, Anne abandoned her Catholicism and became a communist – of an intellectual, carpet-slipper and non-conspiratorial kind, and only temporarily. Communism and Catholicism were much in the air at Oxford, and often interchangeable. Anne's abandonment of Catholicism came after Pope Pius XII's proclamation, in 1950, that the Assumption of the Blessed Virgin was now Catholic dogma. Also in Oxford, libraries, which had always been the source of Anne's self-education, presented all the opportunities she needed to learn about her father's activities during the war. By the end of her final year she could tell the student who roomed next to her that she had 'a Nazi father', to whom, of course, communists were the Devil's Own.

While she was a medical student little changed in Anne's family life. After Anne left home, Elsie took on some of Myrtle's attributes. She lied about her age, making herself younger by some years, and, never seen without a hat, went back to work again as a 'nurse' in the children's homes of the City of Oxford. 'She liked having many jobs and names and being above herself.'³ She took to calling herself Eva Victoria – this was her upmarket name – or Lucy Lightfoot, while the children called her Aunty Lucy. 'All the children loved her . . . she had a wicked sense of humour, she was like a godmother to the kids.' But when Anne was on vacation, Elsie would leave work to look after her at Hazel Crescent. 'When she talked about her, there was no one else on earth like Anne. She was the centre of Elsie's universe.'⁴

Anne often went back to Great Tew, and was godmother to May's baby Alistair, christened at St Michael and All Angels in 1950.⁵ Iris Prissian, one of Elsie's evacuees from the early days of the war, enrolled at St Hilda's in 1950. There was also Anne's grandmother Louise and the family in Paris; she became particularly close to her aunt the doctor, Janot Darquier; but then, except for Louise, everyone was fascinated by Janot, she was an original. In those years Anne was very fond of clothes, and Janot, who practised as a gynaecologist, had some connection to Paris couturiers; Anne came back from France with the unheard-of luxury of a dress made of handkerchief point lace.

After the war the Jones family set sail from Tasmania, making many trips 'Home' in the coming years. All of them came to see Anne – in 1959 Aunt Olive took her on one of her travels – and then went on to

Madrid to see the Baron and Baroness, none of them happy about Anne's attitude to her parents. Hazel loved Anne, but was furious with her for this – she was virulent against anyone who attacked Louis. Other matters seem to have displeased them too, because Lexie, who was always adding codicils to her will, temporarily disinherited Anne at the end of 1951 and returned her portion to Myrtle. The Jones view of Louis as a fervent French patriot assailed by communism and international Jewry perhaps explains this, for in 1951 a Liberal (conservative) government tried – and failed – to ban communism in Australia.

By this time Anne knew she could not be a neurosurgeon – she disliked, and had once fainted at, the sight of blood – and she knew she was no academic. And so she turned to neurology's twin discipline, psychiatry, which attempts to explain the mysteries of the human psyche, and heal damaged souls. She told the Jones family that she wanted to become a psychiatrist because she had had such a difficult life; this decision too was viewed unhappily in Tasmania. No money or support, so generously offered by them, could give Anne anything in common with her mother's family, so enthralled by the 'aristocratic' Darquiers. Anne saw her mother as an alcoholic and worse, and her father as a war criminal. The Jones family did not find Anne easy to deal with.

Anne managed only a Third Class degree when she graduated in 1952. Her career was unaffected: she had learned that she was not going in the natural direction for her talents, and remained 'ambitious and single-minded' about her new plans. When she moved to London, where she chose to complete her training, she took a room in Nevern Square in Earl's Court, and began three years as a clinical undergraduate at St Bartholomew's Hospital in east London.

The British medical world of the early 1950s was a strange and inbred one, overwhelmingly masculine, imbued with venerable stratifications and customs as yet little changed by the National Health Service, introduced in July 1948. Doctors had fought a vicious campaign against the provision of free medical care for the British public, which they lost, and the acrimony which had greeted this 'socialist tyranny' was still very much in the air when Anne began at Bart's.

Known as 'The Mother Hospital of the Empire', Bart's is one of London's most ancient medical establishments, a teaching hospital, although women had only been permitted as students since 1947. Anne went to Bart's in 1952 accompanied by some of her Oxford coterie, but women were sparse there in these early years under its Dean, Sir 'Slasher' Tuckwell, and she was seen as a 'mousy oddity' by some of her pipe-smoking and tweedy fellow students. Photographs of Anne's year at Bart's are all of men in rugger scrums, or naked in the communal bath after a game, forty or so young men with Brylcreemed hair and side partings, peering studiously through microscopes or clustered around a skeleton. Within its often brutal and fixed culture, the pecking order of consultant physician or surgeon, registrar, house officer and lowly student was rigorously maintained, but by the end of her years there Anne had walked the wards and delivered babies, and had a grounding in medicine and surgery.

On all her student registrations Anne listed Hector Jones as her guardian. For Bart's, next to his name someone added 'Father in Spain, never sees', and next to her name, Anne Darquier de Pellepoix, is added 'known as Darquier for personal reasons'. Students at Bart's prayed for a house job at the end of their training: they would be the lowest of the low, but they would be residents. The captaincy of the Bart's cricket team automatically ensured a coveted house job, but this possibility not being open to Anne, when she graduated in December 1955 – she was now Dr Anne Darquier, BA, BM, B.Ch Oxon. – she took a bedsit in Belsize Park Gardens in north London. She was twenty-five.

Anne told her childhood friend Beryl that John Varley wanted to marry her, but that she was too obsessed with her medical studies for marriage. She also said, 'I wish I could be happy with the things other folks have, instead of this burning ambition.'[6] After two years of medical practice, including a year of neurology, she turned her attention to the world of Freud and Jung, and by the 1960s her relationship with Varley was over.

When Anne settled in London, Elsie sold Hazel Crescent and returned to Great Tew to live with Maud and Arthur. Anne didn't actually love Elsie – 'That would be too strong a word' – but she was grateful to her, and often went back to the Falkland Arms to see her 'old folk', as she called the three people who had raised her.

In February 1958 Lexie Jones died in Tasmania, and two months later Anne began her postgraduate studies for a Diploma in Psychological Medicine at the Bethlem Royal and Maudsley Hospitals in south-east London, called the 'joint hospitals' then, often called the Maudsley today.[7] Anne's intake of twelve young doctors, 'mostly shabbily dressed but several of whom were to become eminent in their fields',[8] now entered the medical subculture of psychiatry, ruled at the Maudsley by the Australian psychiatrist Sir Aubrey Lewis, an 'obsessional polymath' who ran its Institute of Psychiatry with a mixture of chivvying and criticism so fierce that one survivor admitted, 'I owe Lewis one thing, at least. Once you had suffered the experience of presenting a case at one of his Monday-morning conferences, no other public appearance . . . could hold any terrors for you.'[9]

Many of Anne's contemporaries – many indeed eminent and still practising – have talked to me about these years at the Maudsley, but about Anne they talk unhappily. Some of them followed John Varley in Anne's affections. Most of her friends and lovers were doctors or psychiatrists, who spend their lives trying to help people to live. Anne Darquier's story is a harsh subject for them; for Anne herself, the ending of her long relationship with John Varley, however tortured it was, intensified her loneliness. 'She was a friendly person, but guarded . . . REMARKABLY silent.' At the same time, 'everyone liked her . . . she was an attractive person, with abilities', and she flourished at the Maudsley, where her true gifts were put to use. One of her former pupils described the mental hospitals and observation wards in which Anne worked – Bart's, the Maudsley, all were grim, cockroaches everywhere: 'Nightingale rows of beds, both sexes, the demented with the young, all kinds of mental illnesses all mixed up together, they dressed and undressed in public – rape was common; it was appalling. When a duchess came to open a new wing instructions were given to keep certain patients out of sight.' When Anne saw a nurse pouring hot tea over a screaming, hallucinating patient, locked in the padded cells of the observation ward at the Maudsley, she told Aubrey Lewis that the place was 'pure evil'. 'To say that to Lewis took some saying, but Anne identified with the needs of people and she would not lower her standards of the way that they should be treated . . . she was very sympathetic to human distress.'[10]

Academically, she had the same problems. Her dissertation, 'Some Considerations in the Evaluation of Psychotherapy', was an essay – and an undistinguished one – rather than a piece of scientific research, and unlike all the others of her year, who offered copious thanks and acknowledgements to the professors and lecturers who had nurtured them, Anne thanked nobody. But she performed well in psychotherapy seminars, and impressed her fellows and her professors with her particular gift, an ability to see connections. She understood anguish, and she was clinically astute. She had – would still have – many friends from her years at the Maudsley.

The Maudsley nurtured psychiatrists who followed both Freud and Jung, but it was Jung, the less paternal, the dreamer, the believer in roots, culture and the unconscious, whom Anne chose to follow next, a dangerous journey for which she needed luck, and she did not get it. By 1961 she was Dr Anne Darquier, BA, BM, B.Ch Oxon., DPM. She was thirty-one, and whilst at the Maudsley had already begun her training to become a Jungian analyst. For Anne this was not a soft option; she had found the medical work for which she had an exceptional talent. By 1963 she was senior registrar at the Westminster Hospital, and had completed her analytical training at the Jungian Society of Analytical Psychology, then in Devonshire Place, near Harley Street. She was to live in this part of London for the rest of her life.

Anne's training analyst was Robert Hobson, a consultant physician at the Maudsley during her years there, who had qualified as a Jungian analyst in 1954. He was a clever and creative doctor and a famous and pioneering psychiatrist of his time, the president of the Analytical Society and a man who had met and corresponded with Jung. Hobson was a 'golden boy' who seemed arrogant to some and seductive to many. He was a northerner, with a formidable stammer and much charm, and he liked to shock his pupils by lecturing on the psychopathology of the foreskin. Views about him vary: he was seen as charismatic but flirtatious, warm but intrusive, an inspiring and generous teacher but dangerously vain. During the war Hobson had been a surgeon lieutenant on the Arctic convoys, which carried specially trained 'human torpedoes' – heroic frogmen who sat astride high-explosive warheads and guided them to their underwater target in the Arctic wastes.

Hobson should have been the piece of luck Anne needed, the man who took her apart and put her together again, which is what a training analysis should be. Through a strange conjunction of his inadequacies and Anne's savage circumstances, this did not happen, although Hobson's therapeutic belief was that 'the therapist's task was to "reach the heart of loneliness and speak to that"'.[11]

At the Maudsley it was felt that Hobson had picked Anne out. Such recognition by 'the famous man of his age' was to prove a poisened honour. But Anne left her training analysis licensed to practise, and Hobson called her 'the most brilliant Jungian of her generation'.

Louis Darquier fitted happily into Franco's Spain, protected as he was by prominent members of the government, in particular by Antonio Barroso y Sánchez-Guerra. After the war, Barroso rose higher and higher within Franco's stratosphere: by 1956 he was head of Franco's Military Household, then Minister for the Army. After his retirement in 1962 he remained a rich and powerful force in Spain, heavily involved in business and industry. In return for favours previously received, Barroso 'helped Louis all his life, always . . . he paid for hospitals, everything'.[12]

Louis' aliases varied between Destève or d'Estève or Roussel; sometimes he was Jean, sometimes Jean Étienne or Juan, sometimes Léon, but for men like Barroso, he was still Baron Darquier de Pellepoix. Despite his protection by the Francoist hierarchy – much boasted about privately – 'there was never, never any money'. Fascist Spain, puritanical and poor, was not Paris, and Louis' old life of wining, dining and gambling was over. Also, there were tens of thousands of fleeing Milice, Nazis and *fascisti* making demands on Franco's purse.

Louis worked at many jobs, much as Anne was to do. In one way he was happy, because every job he had involved using words. By 1950, 'looking ten years younger',[13] he and Myrtle were living in a room in calle Férnandez de la Hoz; nearby, unknown to Myrtle, Louis paid a cleaning lady with six children and many relatives, all living in a two-room flat with no bathroom, to take in Teresa.

Louis was working at the Ministry of Education's Central School of Languages, in the beautiful building which also houses the Falange Española.[14] He was also given work by the diplomatic office of the Ministry of Foreign Affairs, he taught French at the Ministry of Defence, and translated for the Red Cross and for Radio Nacional – Abel Bonnard and Alain Laubreaux worked in the French section there too. As a freelance translator Louis could work in French, English and German; he was considered one of the best of all the translators, if not the best, within the group of French refugees, and he translated Franco's speeches into English.

As the years progressed he began to add 'Baron' to his name, and eventually gave up all pseudonyms. He then added an apostrophe from the name of a favourite purloined ancestor, Seigneur Étienne d'Arquier d'Estève, ennobled in 1655, whose eldest son had been a Louis and whose surname Louis Darquier had used on his first arrival in Madrid. Louis and Myrtle began to call themselves Barón y Baronesa Louis d'Arquier de Pellepoix. He liked to be called 'the Baron', '*el Barón*', she '*Baronesa*' – but all the exiles in Spain used aristocratic names; it helped them get jobs. Louis also claimed to be a university graduate with a degree in science. He was wont to say that no member of the French colony was a stranger to him. This was hardly the case, but he mixed happily enough amongst the '*Maquis blanc*', as the exiled war criminals were sometimes called, 'strutting round the streets wearing his monocle, his eyebrows raised and his utterances full of disdain'.[15]

Every Sunday these outcasts would meet for Mass at St-Louis des Français, the old French church just off the avenida, in calle Tres Cruces, and afterwards would eat together at the Posada de Mar, a fashionable fish restaurant in the avenida itself. Who, if anyone, paid the bills is a puzzle, because in the 1950s Spain had not yet begun to find economic salvation in the tourist industry, and all of them worked for minimal pay.

Louis did not go to Mass, but never missed these lunches; they were the centre of his world in Madrid. He always went alone, without Myrtle, but as soon as Teresa was old enough, she was taken to see him there. Later these gatherings – *tertulias* – moved to the Café California in the street next to the church.[16] Most of the French *collabos* were accredited as foreign journalists by Franco's Ministry of Information, whether they wrote a word or not. Here they came to talk, united by hostility to de Gaulle and, after 1954, by the Algerian war. These Frenchmen of the extreme right remained passionately nationalistic, and the excesses of the French forces in Algeria during the long and losing battle to keep it quite lifted their spirits. Maurice-Yvan Sicard, Doriot's PPF national secretary, was an early refugee in Madrid, and he spoke for all of them: 'I am a patriot and all my thoughts, all my efforts converge on my country: France.'[17] From time to time they welcomed important guests – a network of friendships and influences whose names are only muttered in Madrid to this day – the Marquis de Grijalbo, de l'Encomienda, Juan Perón, Patrice Lumumba, Xavier Vallat, General Weygand. There was always someone who could pay Louis' bills.

The war exiles met in restaurants, sometimes seedy, sometimes grand.

Horcher's, opposite Retiro Park, was opened in 1943 by Otto Horcher, former manager of Maxim's in Paris and thus known to all. Horcher's private dining rooms sheltered many such an encounter, as did the International Press Club or the Edelweiss, where fifteen or so Nazi exiles would eat at the same table every Friday.[18] All this went on, year after year, until the 1980s, when one by one the old men died off.

After the Organisation de l'Armée Secrète (OAS) was formed in 1961, there were many more meetings in obscure rooms in the outer suburbs of Madrid. The OAS was a terrorist army with roots in every part of that French right which had produced Charles Maurras, Marshal Pétain and Louis Darquier. Its aim was to resist the granting of independence to Algeria. In 1962 only ten per cent of the French people voted against ratifying de Gaulle's final negotiations for Algerian self-determination; much the same percentage of the French people vote for Jean-Marie le Pen today. This terrorist organisation – which attempted the 'Day of the Jackal' assassination of de Gaulle in 1962 – provided a last, and muffled, *frisson* of excitement in Madrid for Louis' *collabo* subculture.

As Pierre Darquier had often insisted, every member of the Darquier family suffered because of Louis. In Cahors, Pierre is still spoken of as 'a good man', but 'the town is ashamed to have had Darquier as mayor',[19] and so Pierre has nothing – no street, lane or cul-de-sac, salon or school – named after him. Of Pierre Darquier, unwilling parent of his second son, *'Zéro, vaut mieux pas prononcer le nom ici'* – 'Nothing, it's better not to say his name in Cahors.'[20]

By 1945 Louise had only one son left in France, Jean, and he was childless. In the last decade of her life 'Madame Louise' was lonely, white-haired but still fine-skinned and beautiful. She turned to religion, and threw herself into good works, knitting and crocheting for babies, unmarried mothers and charity sales. She crocheted altarpieces and lace for priests' albs, and visited the sick at the cancer hospital at Villejuif, just outside Paris.

After the war Darquiers could not easily visit Cahors. At the Liberation the editor of Louise's old family newspaper was shot for collaboration, and the *Journal du Lot* was shut down. In Cahors, Louis was *'une crapule'*: *'C'est pas une gloire pour le pays, on aurait préféré qu'il soit plutôt de Castres ou Carcassone'* – 'He brought no glory to our town, we would have preferred that he came from Castres or Carcassone.'[21] But

Louise returned regularly. She would stay at the Hôtel des Ambassadeurs – demolished now – and summon safe old friends and former servants to visit her. Some greeted her with real affection, some found her capricious and affected, and the airs she put on tedious. Every day she would visit Pierre's tomb.[22]

She never ceased to grieve over Louis, but varied her comments about him according to her audience. His name never passed her lips with male family friends in Cahors, but to women she spoke of him often: 'She admired him very much,' one of them remembered. With others, Louis was her lame duck, and she wept and moaned that he was the nightmare of her life. She knew that should he be caught he would be shot, and was in a permanent state of nerves, anticipating telegrams from Spain bearing such news.

Louise rarely talked about her other sons, except to complain about their wives. One reason for this concentration on Louis was that he wrote to her from time to time to ask for money, or sent messengers from Spain on a similar mission. Louise would tell them, 'He has no money and neither have I,' but she was convinced that he 'had an excellent position with General Franco who was his adviser, and who appreciated Louis' qualities very much'. In Cahors today, distant relatives who were subjected to this kind of conversation complain, 'In my family we were not proud to be connected with the Darquier family.' One Cadurcien friend added, 'Louise defended Louis until the end, but he was a *salaud* pure and simple. There are collaborators, even celebrated ones, for whom one can find excuses, even Laval, but with Darquier there is not one ray of light.'[23]

In 1954 Louise went to Madrid for Teresa's first Holy Communion. Teresa was eight when she met her grandmother. Louise pulled her round by the shoulders and placed her in front of Louis, saying: 'Well, you can't renege on this one.' Louis never had. On one occasion, when there was no money at all, he took a tin of condensed milk to Teresa and because she 'lived so far away and he had no money, he walked all the way to give it' to her. As she grew older, he would visit her three or four times a week.

Teresa was the image of Louis, though darker of hair. About her childhood she felt, like Anne, 'rather like a car one has to garage out because it will be damaged if it stays out in the open', and she 'wished he had chosen the garage more carefully'. But Louis educated her properly, and according to Louise, who was Teresa's godmother, General Weygand was her godfather, and was present at the Communion ceremony she attended in 1954. According to Teresa herself, neither was there but Weygand's wife was her godmother, with Louise her proxy; but Louise told with pride the story of General Weygand and Teresa's christening time and time again.[24]

In 1956, just after Anne graduated from Bart's, Louise Darquier died in Neuilly, and was taken back to Cahors to be buried with Pierre. Louis seems to have made a useless attempt to return to France to see her before her death. He liked to say that he had an Oedipus complex, and there was always a photograph of Louise next to his bed. Facing it, on the other side, was the saucy photo of a younger Myrtle, in a swimsuit with her stockings half-rolled down her thighs.

Myrtle was still trying to emulate Louise, and she was never, ever, seen without a hat. After Louise's death, 'The silver went to René, the gold to Jean, and something to Anne to allow her to finish her studies.'[25] What Louis got was obviously immediately sold, or hocked, because the only family heirlooms he left behind were the odd bit of crested silver, a teapot and two or three spoons and forks.

By now Louis was balding, 'fat and tall – a large human being. Very bumptious. He didn't behave very well – he was very tiresome with young girls.' 'People were very sorry for Myrtle', who was 'depressed and drinking heavily . . . she became enormously fat'.[26] Louis had a big hole in his leg from his operations after 6 February 1934, and a finger that didn't work, about which he made unedifying and constant dirty jokes.

Assorted collections of the Jones family would visit Myrtle and Louis in Madrid. Myrtle reciprocated by sending her multitude of nieces and nephews little presents and letters and cards over the years. Louis the Baron, and Myrtle the Baroness are mentioned in all Jones family documents, but Myrtle was not in touch with her daughter, which pleased no one in Tasmania, while those who knew Myrtle and Louis in Madrid say that they 'did not think about Anne, did not talk about her'.

To the end the Jones family resolutely refused to see the exact nature of Myrtle's addictions, nor of the strange bond between her and Louis – the miserable dwellings and physical battering she endured. Louis' temper was still terrible; he still hit Myrtle. She spent her days writing letters, drinking, trying not to drink, reading novels, and 'desperate for company'. 'Her friends were her family, who visited her from Australia and to whom she wrote all this time.' She was 'a hopeless housekeeper who could not do normal things like cooking and shopping'.[27]

Myrtle drifted around the outer reaches of the British expatriate community, which, though generally very pro-Franco, mixed not at all with German or French war criminals. She, married to one, was, necessarily, an outsider. They knew of her – vaguely – at the British church of St George – 'she was Australian and there was some scandal about her ... a false passport?' She would borrow novels from the British Council library: 'She was very kind, very gentle, big, tall, a very strong woman with a large bosom,' and would bring them occasional gifts of chocolates. She tried the British embassy, but met with a cold shoulder. Louis Darquier, war criminal, was absolutely unacceptable, and Myrtle was tarred with the same brush. Eventually the Baroness was allowed entrée on the basis that no one, anywhere, could match her devotion to the British royal family. In Tasmania, the family were told that ultimately Louis was welcomed there too.[28]

By the 1960s brighter men than Franco had begun to prise his hands from total control of the Spanish economy, and the starvation wages earned by the populace – and Louis Darquier – enabled the country to turn its face towards tourism. Whenever Franco appeared in public, his subjects were still required to give the fascist salute, and they had to drape their windows with Spanish flags as he passed by. Policemen were still everywhere, but tourism added another government department to Louis' portfolio – he became translator at the Ministry of Information and Tourism. Translating pamphlets on Spanish *paradors* alternated with other government jobs and work for publishing houses in Madrid and Barcelona.

By now he was earning more, and he could afford to ride again – 'Baron Darquier ... tall, very elegant, monocle, extremely polite but distant', often came to collect his work from the ministry 'in his riding clothes, with a whip under his arm'. Myrtle, brought up on a horse, was incapable of doing the same, but Louis could now afford to take her out to dinner every Wednesday. They had a daily, 'the only person Myrtle had to talk to', and at last a piano.[29]

At this time, based on the similarity of their names, Louis was investigating his connections to Joan of Arc, while Myrtle would talk of her descent from Inigo Jones. Louis still dabbled in his pet subjects; it was said that his connections got him special permission to work at the

National Library of Madrid on secret Masonic documents for a book about Freemasonry, which he never finished.

As was the custom in Franco's Spain, in 1965, for his twenty years of service to the Spanish state, and after the same number of years in assorted rooms and lodgings, Louis was given, for minimal rental, an apartment in Madrid. He was sixty-seven and Myrtle seventy-one: this was their first home, a very modest apartment, jerrybuilt – 'anyone could have lived there', and did; their tower block was surrounded by many others, constructed for a similar purpose. Their apartment on the ninth floor had a terrace and, at last, more than one bedroom, but their furniture was 'rubbish', the place 'a tip', with 'photos everywhere'.³⁰ And they were near the insalubrious Manzanares River, which at that time smelled to heaven in the summer and was infested with mosquitoes. This was the apartment the Jones family were so happy to visit, and here Myrtle lived until 1970, her kitchen lined with photographs of the British royal family.

Louis' contribution to Spain's welfare was modest too. What brought him this reward was translating *The Red Book of Gibraltar* for Fernando Maria Castiella, Franco's hardline Foreign Minister from 1957 to 1969. Louis would proudly point out the silver tray given him by Castiella as a token of recognition. In 1963 Castiella formally demanded the return of Gibraltar from Britain, and the *Red Book*, which details the Spanish claims, was written after the British prime minister Harold Wilson told the House of Commons in 1964 that 'Franco was a fascist . . . and the shit hit the fan. After that things were very difficult for years about Gibraltar.'³¹

Life improved greatly for Myrtle after 1963, when Australia sent its first consul-general to Spain, then opened an embassy in 1968. Myrtle would 'come to the embassy with the slightest problem, and constantly told stories about rescuing children in wartime, of crossing the Pyrénées with them. She was very sentimental, soft . . . she was certainly an alcoholic . . . she never mentioned Anne, not once.' One of the Australian officials, John Booth, was repeatedly invited by Myrtle to visit them at home, but he was officially warned: 'You don't want to accept invitations of this kind.' All the same, he felt so sorry for them that he went three or four times, sometimes for dinner. When Louis and Myrtle talked about themselves, they said not a word about politics – they were aristocratic refugees 'in trouble'. On one occasion Louis took Booth into his study, and 'there was a photograph of eight men marching down some street, dressed in raincoats and jackboots'. Louis did all the cooking, wearing a tall white chef's hat on his large head, monocle screwed in, looking ridiculous. Though Booth found Louis charming – and a very good cook – and met Myrtle's sister Olive, he knew Myrtle best: 'a sad woman. Desperate for friends . . . always something wrong with her . . . little illnesses, problems . . . She was an amazing royalist.' Booth thought she was a baroness, because she constantly referred to it.[32]

Throughout his life in Spain, Louis' anti-Semitic ravings did not cease; he would explain how after the First World War Jews had taken control of the grain cartels and set France on the road to ruin. Franco's full name was Francisco Franco Bahamonde, and his wife was originally Carmen Polo y Martinez Valdes. Louis would insist that both of them were Jewish: 'Bahamonde is a Jewish name, and so is Polo.' At Sunday lunches his fellow exiles would tease him: 'You see a Jew in your soup.' 'I see a Jew in my soup because there IS a Jew in my soup.' His favourite hobbies were genealogical study into his purloined Darquier ancestors and reading encyclopaedias of French history. Otherwise he spent his spare time inveigling himself and Myrtle into as many embassy parties as possible.

Both of them needed embassy life, because while Louis' Spanish was adequate, Myrtle's remained 'disastrous'; she would make her daily laugh when she asked for a cockroach – *cucaracha* – to stir her coffee, instead of a teaspoon, *cucharadita*. Although it was later strenuously denied by the French diplomatic service, Louis claimed he was a welcome guest at the French embassy in Madrid, received every 14 July by the ambassador. Mostly this was not the case, but when Baron Barbara de Labelotterie de Boisséson took over as ambassador in 1964, life became much easier for the French exiles. 'All the old *collabos* were there' every year to see Boisséson weep as he paid homage to Pétain on Bastille Day.[33]

Teresa was a grown girl when she first met Myrtle. Sometimes Louis took his daughter on holiday, pretending to Myrtle that he was alone; on other occasions he would take them both, and farm Teresa out some-where. He would visit her in the mornings; the rest of the day he would spend with Myrtle in their hotel. Did Myrtle know? Perhaps. When they finally met – which they did only three or four times – Teresa liked Myrtle. 'She was a very sweet lady. Alcoholic. Always drunk.' Louis' favourite holiday spot was the beautiful port of Santander in the north, on the Cantabrian coast, where he liked to be photographed exposing his hefty body, biceps clenched in the pose of Hercules.

Louis remained Myrtle's hero, and in his limited way Louis was good to her. He tried to cure her alcoholism and to protect her from the insults that came her way, the people who would not know them, the places where they were never invited. Louis became almost entirely bald, and Myrtle even larger. She could do nothing for herself, and needed constant looking after, but she still had 'a lovely sense of humour', and this kept them together. Louis remained a womaniser and a loudmouth, always telling the same stories – 'He repeated himself like garlic.' So did Myrtle; everyone heard her tales about rescuing children. One of Louis' most unchanging repetitions was to tell Myrtle how much he loved her. Once Myrtle said to Teresa, 'Oh God, how I love that man.'

After 1944 René Darquier came back from Argentina occasionally, but he never saw Louis again, while Louis, if he mentioned René at all, despised him because he was 'in trade'. The French medical profession was purged at the Liberation, but publicly Jean Darquier, though compromised, was never brought to justice. However, he did not progress in his career: 'To carry the name of Darquier in those days was not easy . . . people did not want to know Darquiers.'[34] Jean settled in St-Tropez, and in the sixties both he and René separated from their wives. In Jean's case he acquired a young female companion, which did not disturb Janot, who seems to have shared his St-Tropez villa until the end, and who paid for the upkeep on the Darquier tomb in Cahors until her own death in 1997.

René Darquier died in 1967, contemplating his orange groves in Agadir. He was only sixty-six, but though the one who suffered the most, in later life he was the most fortunate of the Darquier brothers. On rare occasions Jean was visited by the police in search of 'the wanted party', but always denied any specific knowledge of Louis' whereabouts and activities, though he knew he was in Madrid.[35] Louis, on the other hand, said that Jean visited him every year. Janot kept in touch with Louis. She had always liked him, and wanted René's children, two of whom had married Jews, to visit him. None of them ever did.

After René's death came others, more worrying for Louis. Many of his colony were living in wretched circumstances as they got older; in 1968 Alain Laubreaux, exactly Louis' age, died in Madrid, and so did Abel Bonnard, a closer compatriot. For Louis, however, 1968 marked the end of his death sentence, which expired in March of that year. In twenty-one years no French government had made any serious attempt to find him; now extradition was no longer possible. But his exile for life remained: he could never return to France. Shortly after his amnesty, Louis asked the French embassy for authorisation to return to France for 'family reasons'. Although Labelotterie was ambassador in 1968, there was no reply.

Myrtle still had her British passport; she could leave Spain. Every year she went to Gibraltar to see her English doctor and dentist, and she could cross the border to France to go shopping or to meet the travelling Joneses in Paris. On one rare occasion she went with Teresa. They crossed the border at Irún/Hendaye; Louis left them at Irún station, with tears in his eyes. Returning from Hendaye, Teresa watched Myrtle walking down the platform ahead of her, peeing as she went, oblivious to this habitual result of her drinking. At the same time, when visiting Joneses saw Myrtle in Madrid, they only noticed that she still managed to be the cynosure of all eyes.

Mostly Myrtle drank wine, but she drank anything she could lay her hands on, like most alcoholics; she drank cognac if offered, and was seen to finish off a bottle of Mirabelle in one sitting. Opposite the tower block in the quiet street where they lived is a handful of small shops. There is a dry-cleaner's where Louis is remembered as a Frenchman who always wore a small French flag in his buttonhole, and a little further down an off-licence, all too familiar to Myrtle; she was, on the very worst occasions, seen in the neighbourhood very drunk.

By the end of the decade Louis had started his own translation service from home, which was why, in April 1969, Myrtle signed a contract to translate into French a catalogue for the museum of Santa Cruz. She was seventy-five, and had little French and no Spanish.[36] When she fell ill, Louis could not cope at all. Her sister Hazel, living in Beirut at the time, was summoned to look after her, and on 18 June 1970 Myrtle died of a heart attack in the Red Cross Hospital in Madrid. Eight days before, her first and possibly only husband, Roy Workman, died in Northampton.[37] Louis finally discovered that Myrtle was older than he.

Myrtle was buried the following day, in the British Cemetery in Madrid. John Booth, of the Australian embassy, went to the service at St-Louis des Français, and was intrigued by the people there: 'Darquier had very few friends to carry Myrtle to her grave.' One who did so noticed how exceptionally heavy Myrtle was, while Booth noticed that the few mourners were 'elderly mostly and strange-looking'.[38]

I was sent to see Anne Darquier in 1963. I was twenty-five years old, and Anne only eight years older. By this time she was very successful. Besides being senior registrar at the Westminster Hospital she held teaching and clinical research posts at the Middlesex and Hammersmith Hospitals, and at Bart's. As a doctor she was on a fast track, and she began earning money before any of her medical fellows. She was always absolutely frank about money: she loved having it. Friends floated in and out of her various flats around Harley Street, and she was known for her extravagance with taxis, if not much else. Later she became a consultant to the students at King's College, London, and she had also begun a private practice.

When others talk about Anne's particular skills as a therapist, always they mention her singular empathy: this was her great gift, something which came from her own experience of pain. There was a sense of instant comprehension about her, which made it particularly easy for a foreigner such as me to talk to her. She was down-to-earth, and her gentle, often smiling charm was balanced by the steely mind and determination she had demonstrated even as a child. With her patients she listened, she sympathised, she understood, but above all she was honest and direct, never given to psychobabble of any kind; and with me at least, she laughed a lot. Raised by Elsie and Maud, Anne was good at laughing, and she had an excellent sense of injustice. This was marked in her: she had that acute British awareness of class divisions; she did not like them.

Generally Anne was silent about her family, and she kept herself to herself. As I had never known a psychiatrist before I met Anne, and knew nothing of Freud, Jung, or any principles of analytic behaviour, the stories she told me about her own life seemed perfectly normal to me – and still do. Yet in talking to me about herself, however little, she broke a strict professional rule. For ninety-nine per cent of our time together over seven years, Anne looked after me and concentrated on changing my life, which she did. But Anne was not the kind of therapist who did not give her opinions. She told you what she thought, she told me something about her past – not much, but enough – although she should not have done so. For the rest, I liked hearing the little she told me; we sometimes laughed about our various furies, we never laughed about dysfunctional families, and never about childhood anguish. We discussed our political opinions, and shared a black-and-whiteness about injustice which was certainly naïve, but was comforting at the time. Anne's method of therapy was not maternal, nor was it *de haut en bas*.

Outside the hospitals and doctors' rooms in which Anne passed most of her adult life, the men she chose and who chose her were the usual *mélange* that awaits any woman who remains unmarried at thirty-five. I was told, 'Her men were all alcoholics or rejecters in one way or another'; but rejecters and alcoholics can also be lovely men. She still supported her 'old folk' financially and visited Great Tew, or May Rapley in Sussex, bearing cream cakes. May, Gilbert and her godson Alistair always returned to the Falkland Arms for holidays, or came up to London to see her. She took Alistair out to restaurants, opera and theatre, embarrassed him by shouting '*Olé!*' and clapping to Spanish dancing, hoped for a university career for him, and was very much the favourite aunt of a favoured nephew.

Elsie and Maud grieved that Anne had not married John Varley, who had sometimes driven her to Great Tew and had met with their approval. When Maud died in 1964, Arthur and Elsie left the Falkland Arms, and three years later Arthur died too. Anne had loved Maud and Arthur, but then everyone loved them. With Elsie it was different; she was more of a prickle pot, but the bond remained. Later Anne bought a car, an Austin 1100. Shortsighted, unable to drive, she offered it to Alistair, and said, 'I want you to take me up to see Nanny.'

Carl Jung wrote: 'Only the wounded physician heals.' That would be the diagnosis for Anne: she was a wounded healer, who could heal others but could not heal herself. By the late 1960s she was on the treadmill of a high flyer. She had substantial hospital and other commitments, and a thriving private practice. She worked unsparingly, at the call of her patients night and day, at home and abroad. She would even make midnight appointments to see undergraduates who needed her at King's College. Anne never became proficient in the requirements of academe: she left behind no written body of work. What is remembered is her singular concentration upon her patients; in the public wards at the Maudsley it required extra effort to take over from her, because the patients had become so dependent upon her intense care.

She worked too hard, and had perhaps become too successful. One colleague, who disliked her, told me, 'She gave far too much, she wasn't professional,' and added – shades of Myrtle – 'Anne lived with and by fantasies.' 'She would make a pass – not necessarily sexual – at anyone with power.' 'She only wanted to make money; she'd help anyone with status.' Of this litany the attribute I recognise is that she gave too much; the rest, true or not, used to be par for the course for any successful working woman.

By 1968 Anne had grown into a way of life in which her silence about her own past, the black hole of despair she kept to herself, were both aspects of her personality she used to bring force to her healing of others. By then, if she still loved clothes, you would not have known it to look at her, and her apartment was ruthlessly functional and un-titivated. It was clear that whatever she had learned late in life about self-indulgence or fripperies had quite slipped away. She lived through her work, her colleagues and her friends, who were numerous, and the patients whose lives she changed. She was sociable, but within limits; she disliked sharing the family Christmases of her friends, and began to have increased difficulty in sleeping. She took pills for that, and often looked exhausted. Swinging London of the sixties, all around her and making life brighter for so many, made little difference to her, although she was only in her thirties.

When Anne's half-sister Teresa was twenty-one she came to London as an au pair. Teresa wanted to meet Anne and talk to her; they shared 'not having a mother . . . the most painful thing in the world' – but when she rang, Anne 'put the phone down on her, saying she wanted nothing to do with her family'. They never met.

In 1968 Teresa married a British journalist and went to live in Oxford. She lived there for some years, and her children were born there, so that both Louis Darquier's daughters knew the town well. Anne was often nearby, visiting Elsie at Woodstock, though by 1968, when she became a senior lecturer at Bart's, her workload had become 'appalling'.

When psychiatrists become ill, when they know they are not coping as they should, there is an accepted routine which must be adhered to. In the last year of her life, Anne knew she was existing on alcohol and pills. She had learned to drink in the Falkland Arms as a young girl, with her Canadian Air Force boyfriends during the war, and with her Oxford friends thereafter. Her mother was an alcoholic; Anne was not, but she knew how to use drink to ease stress. Like many doctors, she had easy access to drugs to lessen every kind of pain, and she was prescribing for herself, always a dangerous thing for a doctor: 'Anne knew she must look for help.'

In the first instance she turned to the doctor with whom she underwent her full training analysis, Robert Hobson, and asked to be taken on again. He refused her, for reasons which were probably obscure even to him, but some of which he later revealed, if unwittingly. Such a refusal can be accepted practice. What is usually done under these circumstances is to transfer the doctor in need of help to another practitioner. This Hobson did not do. Anne went for help to another doctor, one with whom some of her contemporaries felt she was in love. So did he, and he rejected her too. By the summer of 1970 Anne Darquier was barely surviving, and the two members of her profession she had turned to for help had refused her.

Anne heard of Myrtle's death in late August. There is no explanation for this two-month delay, except perhaps the state of Anne's relations with Tasmania as well as with Madrid at this time. When I saw her on Friday, 4 September, the day after her fortieth birthday, Anne was distraught; she looked as though she had been weeping uncontrollably; at one point she had to leave the room. She had no alternative but to tell me she was in trouble, and she told me little enough. She had been to see her family – I knew she hated anything to do with them – and she was very angry. Did she visit Louis? I don't know, but it was on that occasion that she told me: 'There are some things and some people you can never forgive.' I remember well how disturbed I was, but it did not occur to me then that a psychiatrist should not show such feelings to a patient. Now I realise that she would never have done so had she not been almost past help.

A few days later, on 7 September, I rang the doorbell of her flat as usual – we had arranged to meet at 8 a.m. – but there was no response. Later that day she was found dead on the floor in her bathroom. PC Champion, the policeman called to the scene, recorded that she was 'lying on her left side between the back of the W.C. facing the wall. Near her right hand there was a glass. In the bedroom and lounge, in almost every drawer, there were tablets, loose and in bottles . . . the flat was not very tidy. She was wearing a night-dress and a watch.'[39]

It was not suicide, though there are slow ways of trying to kill yourself not given that label. She may have died as the result of a fall; one friend thought she had banged her head against the bath: she 'was in the habit of taking something to help her sleep, along with a glass of whisky, and there was a gash on her head'. The coroner agreed. Anne's death was labelled accidental, but the amount and the mixture of barbiturates and alcohol in her body were poisonous.[40]

In her apartment, after her death, there was a cheque from Louis for £5,000, never cashed, 'a small inheritance from her mother' – probably Myrtle's legacy from Lexie, Anne's now that Myrtle was dead. Louis said that he saw Anne again after her visit to Spain in the late 1940s, others think not. But perhaps she had flown to Madrid to see her father when she heard of Myrtle's death? Whoever she visited at the end of August 1970, within less than two weeks she was dead.

22

◄○►

Dinosaurs

THIS WAS NOT THE end. Anne died without a will, and Louis inherited her worldly goods: £16,552.6s.od, after tax. Elsie was devastated, all the more so because she was not family; the funeral arrangements passed into the hands of strangers. She and May went to Bow Street police station to find out what had happened to Anne. Elsie wanted some small memento, but the police officer said, 'You're not kin. I can't do anything.' Elsie knew what could be expected of Louis: 'He'll know she's died, he'll find out, and he'll come after her money, he always does.'[1] Anne was cremated at Golders Green crematorium on 15 September 1970, and her ashes were scattered over Section 1A of the Garden of Remembrance. There was no service, but many people I have met subsequently were there, and so was I. Her coffin, placed in front of the curtains, awaiting descent to incineration, was labelled 'Anne Darquier de Pellepoix'.

This was the first time I saw her name written thus, and it would not have been had Teresa not been living in Oxford. The police had contacted Louis in Spain; Teresa was the nearest relative as far as the authorities were concerned. Four years earlier Louis had devoted strenuous efforts to legitimising his second daughter; he 'wanted her to have his name'. He called upon all his Francoist protectors to arrange it, so that he could bestow upon Teresa as many aristocratic appurtenances as he could translate into Spanish. This he did. His detailed researches proved, he said, that he was descended from a cadet branch of the Dukes of Gascony, so he added that too.

The husband of one of Anne's patients paid for her funeral, but Teresa made the arrangements, and so she buried her half-sister with the name she never used, Anne Darquier de Pellepoix, and it was the strange addition of 'de Pellepoix' which struck me at the time, and caught my eye again when I saw Louis shaking hands with Reinhard Heydrich in Marcel Ophuls' film *Le Chagrin et la pitié* a year or so later.

Teresa was seven months pregnant at the time of Anne's death; all she ever knew of her half-sister was what she saw when she visited her flat to clear up her affairs. Robert Hobson drove her to the crematorium, and according to Teresa complained about Anne all the way there: she 'thought he was awful'. Hobson's state of mind is understandable, as he had been called by the police to identify the body, and was the only witness at the inquest on 11 September. 'I have known her as a friend and fellow doctor for about thirteen years,' he told the court. 'Recently we have been working together on various cases. She had been suffering from depressed periods for some months. She was informed of her mother's death two weeks before she died.'[2]

Hobson and Anne's friends had been profoundly shocked by the state of Anne's flat. She had always been neat and tidy, but when she died it was a mess: clothes, dirty glasses, papers and pills all over the place, the flat of someone who had gone to pieces. She had probably had no sleep for weeks, for the drugs she mixed with alcohol were for severe and intractable insomnia.

Louis lived on. He buried Myrtle in the British Cemetery in Madrid, but wasted no more time or money on her after that. Her grave is a bare patch of earth in a charming cemetery full of the miscellanea of expatriate life. For Myrtle there is no tomb, no tombstone, nothing. You find her by consulting the cemetery register, where she is listed under almost all her names – Jones, Myrtle Morrison, Baronese d'Arquier de Pellapois (sic), Australian – lying in the block of earth number VIII, JI, and that is all. All around her are ornate and loving tombs; she is quite overshadowed by Jewish graves with Hebrew names and inscriptions in Yiddish and Spanish – Moses, Franckel, Mansberger, and many named Levy – put up by the descendants of these Jews who fled from Hitler and actually did escape over the Pyrénées. Stranger still, none of the Jones family who visited Madrid after Myrtle's death asked to see her unmarked patch of earth, or ordered even the smallest cross for their baroness sister.

Myrtle Jones married under a false name, then married again, probably bigamously. She spent her life with a man whose clamorous existence required her to abandon her daughter, but the Jones family heroically accepted her explanations and did what they could to fill the breach. She married a man who hated Jews, communists and Freemasons, though her father Harry Jones was a Mason, and her brother Vernon was Grand Master of the Grand Lodge of Tasmania. Yet Louis was fond of the Jones family, and they thought the world of him. In some ways, their aspirations were similar. This is demonstrated by remarks made when Vernon Jones was appointed headmaster of Launceston Church Grammar School. There were those in Tasmania who were 'shocked and upset' because they 'wanted the son of a gentleman for headmaster and he did not fit into that category'.[3]

The upward climb of the Jones family and their insistence upon respectability is as marked as the worm of incorrigibility which continues through the family to this day. Olive Jones married an accountant, Tom Room, who, appointed mayor of Launceston in 1975, raised her to the position of lady mayoress. In 1989, after the longest criminal trial in Tasmanian legal history, Myrtle's nephew, Olive's flamboyant son Colin Room, an accountant and investment adviser – 'handsome, sophisticated' with 'an easy charm', 'born into the Launceston Establishment' – was convicted on 193 charges of forgery and stealing nearly A$2 million from his clients. Colin Room equalled his aunt as a fabulist: 'He used aliases' (five in all), explaining, 'I invented those things to assist my clients.'[4]

To Myrtle's siblings, her life was a tremendous success. 'In their eyes, Myrtle is a much-loved sister who travelled overseas, married an Englishman, then a Frenchman and then had a child. She had an interesting life, met some wonderful people, had a handsome husband who absolutely adored her, who could possibly be interested in that?'[5]

Louis said he was upset by Anne's death, though one of Myrtle's pall-bearers commented, 'Nobody, it seems, survives Darquier.' But when Myrtle died, 'his mood changed completely, he became sad, taciturn'.[6] He was almost as domestically incapable as Myrtle, and he and the flat became equally decrepit. In 1972 he made another tentative attempt through an intermediary at the Red Cross to return to France, to visit 'his sick brother', asking for sympathetic consideration because of the loss of a wife and daughter in such a short period of time. He received no reply.

Marcel Ophuls' documentary *Le Chagrin et la pitié* was released into cinemas in March 1971. Its genius was not in any condemnation of French collaboration during the Vichy years, but in its realistic portrait of what that collaboration had actually consisted of. Still a remarkable documentary, its account of the German Occupation and French collaboration – or otherwise – in one French provincial town broke a taboo. Some of the stories it revealed were shameful, some heroic, but for the first time, men who had belonged to Louis' world of the ultra-right – most of them at that time languishing in Madrid or Buenos Aires – were not excluded. *Le Chagrin et la pitié* reminded the French people of what had actually happened. It said, 'This is what we did, this is what we were.' It broke box office records in France, but was not permitted to be shown on television until 1981.

This was unimportant, because the film began an intense national debate in France about its 'Dark Years', which thereafter never ceased. In Britain I saw it by chance on the BBC in 1972, with English subtitles. Louis Darquier could have seen the same broadcast, because in that year he came to stay with Teresa and her family in Rayner's Lane, Harrow. No longer a French citizen, he could only come on a special Spanish passport, for one visit only. British officials came to the house to interrogate him, but at the age of seventy-five he was evidently considered harmless.

Louis was not happy in England, 'stuck in a little suburban house in Harrow where he knew no one and had nothing'. He was not interested in grandchildren, who would anyway have only fifty per cent French blood. He returned to his tower block in Madrid, and in 1976, using £3,000 of Anne's money, bought the apartment outright, the first home he had ever owned.[7]

Louis was beginning to outlive everyone. Jean, his favourite brother, was the next to go. Interviewed in the 1960s, Jean remained as unrepentant as Louis, complaining about the 'Jewish occupation' of St-Tropez. There he died in 1975, and was brought to Cahors to be buried in the family tomb. An old friend attempted to have him buried with some honour, and was rebuffed. Jean, he was told, was '*un salaud et un collabo*', a shit and a collaborator.[8]

Franco also died in 1975, and within a year the structure of Louis' life collapsed. The one country in which his vision of the world had flourished so thoroughly for so long changed abruptly and entirely. Franco's Spain was swiftly dismantled: by 1977 the country was a democracy, with an elected parliament, a legal Communist Party, and all those liberal attributes of life that were anathema to Louis Darquier. He was still doing some work for the Ministry of Tourism, but he was nearly eighty and in such a bad way that when he was threatened with a public ward, Teresa and her husband returned to look after him. This was the first time in her life she actually lived for any length of time with her father.

The signs of life Louis had made after his amnesty were probably a mistake. In France, news that he was living openly in Spain provoked protests from LICA (now LICRA) and Jewish institutions. 'Someone, a French voice, phoned to abuse me,' Louis recounted later. '"Bastard. We're coming to get you." I was afraid. Not only for me. For my family. I immediately called upon my military friends to ask for their special protection. They immediately gave it.[9]

The first book published in France which detailed the actions and responsibilities of Darquier, Bousquet, Galien, Antignac and hundreds of others inside and outside the CGQJ, *Le Commissariat Général aux Questions Juives*, by Joseph Billig, was published in three volumes in France between 1955 and 1960, but almost no one took any notice of it. The truths it exposed about Bousquet were ignored for over twenty years. But historians read it, and Louis' name appeared occasionally in many books and newspapers over the years. Because of this he developed a new tic, another bugbear, garnered from the voracious reading of French books and media – all the Madrid exiles avidly followed French affairs.

On 8 May 1967 an article appeared in *l'Express* about the Vel' d'Hiv' round-up, and Louis' part in it, with no mention of Bousquet or his deputy Leguay.[10] In 1972 a second article appeared, more detailed, more condemnatory: Vallat was mentioned with Darquier, but still no Bousquet, no Leguay. *l'Express*, the first French US-style news magazine, was founded in 1953 by Françoise Giroud and Jean-Jacques Servan-Schreiber; in Madrid Louis would hiss with rage about *l'Express*'s coverage of his wartime activities. He said he had prevented the deportation of Servan-Schreiber's mother: 'I saved her life.'[11]

His attempts to return to France were always reported in French newspapers; sometimes they called him 'Antoine', but whenever his name was mentioned his crimes were referred to, and the adjectives used about him were always worse than derogatory. In Madrid, he would furiously deny that he had anything to do with the round-up of Jews or their deaths in Auschwitz, and 'got very angry when he was accused of things he said he hadn't done . . . very angry indeed'. *He* hadn't gassed anyone – he said this always – his signature could not be found on any documents. He also said, again and again, that the Jews were sent to labour camps; no Jews were gassed at Auschwitz, the ovens were used to get rid of lice.[12]

In 1972, after its second description of his wartime activities, Louis gave an interview to the Madrid correspondent of *Le Monde*: 'Pure invention . . . absolute lies. It is not true that I took part in the expulsion of foreign Jews from France . . .'[13] Despised or ignored, over thirty years of this had made him an even angrier man. 'I WAS NOT A NAZI!' he would yell, 'I WAS A NATIONAL SOCIALIST!'

'He loved France, he didn't think France condemned him for what he had done, he thought it was the fault of the people in power in France, not his France.'[14] He saw himself as wronged, ignoring, to take only one instance, his conversation with the UGIF leader he sent to his death, Raymond-Raoul Lambert, to whom in 1942 he had vented his frustration about Laval and Bousquet's refusal to allow him to participate in the deportations, or his speech in the 1930s which concluded with the words: 'The Jewish question must be solved urgently. Either the Jews must be expelled, or they must be massacred.'[15]

Louis was particularly scornful when his 'Australian career' was referred to. He would spot any regurgitated lie which appeared in newspaper articles about his past, and use it to dismiss everything written about him as vicious inventions; he seems to have forgotten that he had fabricated these lies himself.

Worst of all, he, the man who had wanted to expel every Jew from France, was repeatedly refused permission to return there himself. And so, in the wake of Franco's death and the disappearance of all he believed in, Louis Darquier decided to tell the world, by way of the investigative journalist Philippe Ganier-Raymond,[16] in *l'Express* magazine, that he still existed, that he had done nothing wrong, and what he had done, he did not regret.

The interview he gave, published in 1978, triggered *l'affaire Darquier*, a tempest of outrage in France, a national scandal. Afterwards Ganier-Raymond was much attacked over the ethics of the interview. There are various versions as to how he managed it, but many people still alive to tell the truth of it.

Ganier-Raymond covered Franco's death in Madrid. In the same year, 1975, he published a book about French anti-Semitism during the Occupation, a selection of writings of the time; the book opened with one of Louis Darquier's anti-Semitic tracts, and included others. In Madrid Ganier-Raymond found Darquier's name in the phone book, and 'couldn't believe his eyes'. He rang Louis, who answered the phone; Ganier-Raymond abused him thoroughly, and hung up – it must have been after this call that Louis demanded, and got, protection from his 'military friends'.[17] When he got back to Paris, Ganier-Raymond called Serge Klarsfeld, the French attorney who, with his German wife Beate, has brought so many Nazi war criminals to justice. Klarsfeld was discouraging: 'In your place, I would do nothing at all, France shouldn't be rushed into something like this.'[18] Before *l'affaire Darquier* it was German war criminals who were pursued, never the French.

Ganier-Raymond was one of those investigative journalists who smoke two cigarettes at once; bohemian, disordered, politically passionate, he was obsessed with the French holocaust. The next time he went to Madrid, three years later, on a story for *Paris-Match*, he asked a fellow Frenchman, Jean Michel Bamberger, to arrange an interview with Louis Darquier. Bamberger was a freelance journalist familiar with right-wing circles in Madrid; everyone thought he worked for French intelligence. At first Louis said no, then Bamberger used one of his contacts and, on the basis that he was to be interviewed by a French historian – Ganier-Raymond had already published five books – Louis agreed. Bamberger admitted that it was a contact of Jeanne Degrelle who acted as intermediary; Ganier-Raymond said it was a former member of the Waffen SS: there were dozens of such men in Madrid.[19]

The interview in Louis' apartment took about two hours. Naturally Louis did not realise that Ganier-Raymond was the man who had threatened him on the phone a few years earlier; but the interview was sufficiently acrimonious for him to howl that he had been trapped by an Israeli spy. Ganier-Raymond took with him Juana Biarnés, a photographer on *Pueblo* magazine in Madrid (and now Bamberger's wife). He did not tell Louis he was a journalist, nor that he had a tape recorder. Juana Biarnés spoke French badly at the time, and did not follow the entire conversation. Louis did not want any photos taken, so the camera was hidden in Juana's photographer's bag. Ganier-Raymond hid his tape recorder in the fan, and took notes discreetly on small pieces of paper.

In the hurricane which followed publication, all these facts were held against Ganier-Raymond, and were used to cast doubt on the authenticity of the interview; he was accused of spreading anti-Semitic propaganda, and was interrogated by the police. Ganier-Raymond's response was to insist that Darquier 'was not senile, and was happy to see me and talk to me'. What those who questioned the interview ignored was that 'for all his life Louis would have done ANYTHING to be famous'. His boasting was as notorious in Madrid as it had been in Paris: this interview was his last boast, almost a conversation about himself, as he loudly told Ganier-Raymond: 'Jews are always ready to do anything to get themselves talked about, to make themselves interesting, to complain.'[20]

At the age of eighty-one, Louis was almost bedridden. He drove Teresa mad with his talking and his opinions, to such a degree that they gave each other ten minutes by the clock to talk in turn. Through this, Teresa knew 'what he was really like'. He would refuse to get up, or exercise, so for the interview he lay on the wicker chair in his room. He could speak, as ever, but often he would not make much sense. It was August 1978, blazing hot in Madrid, and there was no air conditioning, but there was a fan and it was whirring. Louis expressed himself badly, dribbled a bit, but every word he said was authentic and no effort for him, for however senile he might have been, he had said it all and written it all thousands of times before.

'In Auschwitz They Only Gassed Lice', Philippe Ganier-Raymond's interview, was published in *l'Express* in Paris in the issue of 28 October–4 November 1978 (see Appendix I). It covers sixteen pages, is well illustrated and includes a photograph of the aged Darquier lying in his chair, bellowing to camera. In France few people had thought of Louis Darquier for thirty years. Yet here he was, alive and unrepentant, telling the French nation of men and deeds they wanted to forget. As usual, Louis mixed shameless lies – yes, he had slapped Léon Blum, and was proud of it – with his emphatic version of the truth: 'I was not responsible . . . I wanted the children to be taken into care . . . I had nothing to do with the Vel' d'Hiv' round-up as you call it.' Mostly he told Ganier-Raymond that everything said to have happened to the Jewish people during the war was

A Jewish invention, of course. Jews are like that: they're ready to do anything to get publicity . . . Jews have only one idea in their heads: to wreak havoc everywhere. And why? You know perfectly well: to make Jerusalem the capital of the world . . . When the Marshal put me in charge of the Commission for Jewish Affairs, I determined on one fixed end. A humanitarian end, please note: to make the situation of French Jews as comfortable as possible . . .

Here we go again with Jewish propaganda! . . . Jewish propaganda has always been based on lies. Always . . . Always . . . I don't remember anything about this story of the yellow star . . . another example of your Jewish propaganda . . .

Auschwitz . . . Auschwitz . . . You know there have been too many stories about Auschwitz! It's time to begin to face up to what really happened there . . . satanic Jewish propaganda which has spread and encouraged this myth . . . The Final Solution is an invention, pure and simple. Do you know anyone who has ever seen what they call a gas chamber?

Finally, Ganier-Raymond asked Louis if he had any regrets or remorse. Louis replied: 'Regrets for what? I don't understand your question.'

This interview produced the only worthwhile result of Louis Darquier's life: it triggered the process by which France joined Germany as the only major belligerent of the Second World War to try its own citizens for crimes against humanity. A stupefied French nation rediscovered a Frenchman whose existence questioned all comforting interpretations of their Vichy past, and de Gaulle's myth of 'un seul peuple' united in resistance to Germany. A Frenchman whose anti-Semitism was of a violence they hardly knew existed, or, if they did, thought had disappeared forever.

Louis' words broke another taboo, and led to an eruption of shamed and painful remembrance which expressed itself first in – almost unbelievably – condemnation of those who carried the message. Ganier-Raymond was hauled over the coals, and the authenticity of his tapes questioned. Because Darquier's speech was impaired and the tape recorder was hidden in the fan, the whirring made the tapes almost inaudible. *l'Express* was accused of promoting anti-Semitism, of providing Louis Darquier with a soapbox and of irresponsible journalism for publishing the interview without condemnation and explanatory texts. To all this, the only possible response was the one the magazine used at the time: '*l'Express* is stupefied that a section of public opinion and commentators could confuse or pretend to confuse the publication of a document on French anti-Semitism under the Occupation with anti-Semitic propaganda itself. This proves that French society is not yet sufficiently mature to come to terms with its past and to examine it critically.' It also demonstrated, added *l'Express*, that France did not want to acknowledge that there was a French Nazism, or that anti-Semitism was not merely an importation.

Ganier-Raymond was accused of lying to get the interview, by pretending he was researching a book that was already published; he was accused of provoking Louis, and of transcribing his words incorrectly. Some of this was true, but not all of it. In the media coverage of *l'affaire*, the occasional presence of a young woman with Louis was often noted. Some reporters said that this was Darquier's wife, some his maid, others that she was a young woman with a very new baby. In fact it was Teresa, her identity protected by Ganier-Raymond, who also changed the location of the interview from Madrid to Estremadura for the same reason.

Until 1978 Teresa had no clear idea of her father's past, though she knew there were things that did not tally; and after two years of living in close contact with him, she knew what she thought of him: he was 'mad, completely cuckoo . . . closer to a beast than a human being'. Later, Ganier-Raymond told *Le Monde* that Teresa was the 'sworn enemy' of her father. Throughout the interview she came and went from his room, and 'asked almost as many questions as Ganier-Raymond'.[21] The day after the August interview, Teresa and Ganier-Raymond compared notes; they confirmed that Darquier had said, five times, that in Auschwitz they only gassed lice. At this meeting with Teresa, Ganier-Raymond settled on the final version of the text.[22] Teresa had listened to her father talking like this for years, and this was also what Anne heard, when she visited Louis in Madrid in 1948 or 1949.

L'Express protested that it wanted to illuminate 'the mentality of a dinosaur'. It was referring to Louis, but it could have used the words in another sense. Unwittingly, Louis Darquier gave the French a new opportunity for ethical soul-searching: after *Le Chagrin et la pitié, l'affaire Darquier* was a second watershed. Despite the fact that he was now a little too doddery to fully enjoy it, Louis Darquier had made himself the centre of an affair of state. Articles, television and radio programmes and letters from the public poured into the public arena: 'Why drag this nonentity out of his obscurity?' 'I am outraged.' 'When will the French grow up?' 'I knew nothing about this man before . . . our history books do not mention him . . . though I have heard about those Nazis who spend happy hours in South America, I have never read such a vivid document as this . . .'[23]

Throughout France there were public meetings of protestation; indignant journalists and writers objected to the soiling of their trade with the derisory outpourings of an 'old imbecile, under the pretext that he was a dirty bastard'.[24] In Paris, Ganier-Raymond received death threats and *l'Express* installed security doors in his flat. Valérie Giscard d'Estaing, president of France at the time, warned about lack of balance in any discussion of Nazism and anti-Semitism; Simone Weil, Minister of Health, herself a survivor of three years in Auschwitz, regretted the banality of Darquier and what she considered to be the ambiguity of *l'Express*'s approach; in the National Assembly members of all parties called for Louis' extradition.

French communists abused political personalities, and vice versa; philosophers opined about the meaning of it all; the Church lectured against racial hatred. In *l'Express* Louis had said: '. . . until the recent past I always maintained the best relations with the French ambassador in Madrid. We saw each other often. I sometimes went to their receptions.' Louis de Guéringaud, then Minister of Foreign Affairs, denied that Darquier had ever frequented the French embassy or consulate in Madrid, although Jeanne Degrelle affirmed as recently as 1999 that she and her husband Léon were invited to celebrations organised by the French embassy in Madrid on 14 July every year.[25] Prime Minister Raymond Barre warned all television and radio channels about 'vigilance in the presentation of history', and a TV programme about Pétain was cancelled. Giscard's Minister of Justice, Alain Peyrefitte, stated that a demand for Darquier's extradition from Spain would have been possible after his sentence had been passed, but because of *'une bizarrerie'* – a peculiarity – this had never been done.

Louis Darquier's death sentence expired in 1968, but French law incorporated crimes against humanity in 1964: the interview supplied more than sufficient grounds for opening a new case. The Ministry of Justice instructed the Paris public prosecutor to institute proceedings against Louis for 'war crimes and collaboration, provocation towards discrimination and racial hatred, racial defamation and racist abuse'. A police investigation began almost immediately. The examining magistrate, Émile Cabié, interviewed Ganier-Raymond several times, and other journalists too; he listened to the tapes – barely audible, but you could hear the voice of a rambling old man, and also, very clearly, the words 'In Auschwitz they only gassed lice.' In her sheltered housing in Woodstock, Elsie could have read in any English newspaper articles such as 'How a War Criminal Shocked France'.[26]

The French police arrived in Madrid – Cabié had ordered a medical evaluation of Louis – and their investigation led to disconcerting enquiries among his friends there, all of whom reported in Louis' favour. They were not the only ones to have an uncomfortable time of it in November 1978. All the Spanish newspapers covered the affair – in Madrid, Teresa was hiding behind her door, besieged by journalists. There were many people trying to protect her: François Gaucher even slipped out of his École Briam late at night to advise her. On 5 November the *Sunday Times* in London reported that Louis was now living on his estate in Spain, and that 'a member of his staff [this would have been Teresa] said "He is very ill, quite deaf and his doctors give him three months to live."' Louis' speech had miraculously disappeared. Both Louis Darquier's daughters exhibited a preference for self-destruction, rather than patricide.

The investigating police reported doubts about the tapes and the capacity of Darquier to express himself; the judicial inquiry concluded that Louis was very ill, near death, and that extradition was out of the question. The tempest did not so much subside as blow into many nooks and crannies, to explode in a series of law cases over the next twenty years.

More immediate was the dagger Louis plunged into the back of his old enemy René Bousquet, for revenge on whom he had waited for over thirty years. 'The Vel' d'Hiv' round-up,' Louis said to Ganier-Raymond, 'it's funny that you want to talk to me about that. It was Bousquet who organised the Vel' d'Hiv' round-up. From A to Z. Bousquet was the chief of police. It was he who did everything. And you know how Bousquet ended up? He only got five years of national indignity. He had helped the Resistance! What a farce! And he ended up the director of the Bank of Indochina. Oh, he wangled things very well, Bousquet! Whatever, it was he who organised everything.'

And so *l'affaire Darquier* led to *l'affaire Bousquet*. En route, other French war criminals were brought to trial as an exorcism of French evil spirits began, not without constant delays, prevarications, stallings and much anger. 'Thanks to the interview with Darquier in *l'Express*,' said Serge Klarsfeld, 'I was able to attack Leguay, and then Touvier, Barbie, Bousquet, Papon – only Aloïs Brunner is left.'[27]

Jean Leguay, Bousquet's police deputy in the Occupied Zone, was the first Frenchman to be arraigned for crimes against humanity; Klarsfeld brought an end to Leguay's successful career in cosmetics (at Nina Ricci) when he filed a complaint on behalf of the Association des Fils et Filles de Déportés Juifs de France – Sons and Daughters of the Deported Jews of France – only a week after the *l'Express* interview. Leguay died of cancer, untried, in 1989; unusually, when the case was closed, he was pronounced guilty.

The *Milicien* Paul Touvier was the first Frenchman to be convicted of crimes against humanity. In 1946 Touvier had been, like Louis Darquier, sentenced to death *in absentia*. Aided and protected by the Catholic hierarchy, for many years a fugitive hidden in convents and monasteries, he was sentenced to life imprisonment in 1994, and died in prison two years later. Lyon's Gestapo chief, Klaus Barbie, under whose direction Touvier worked, was sentenced for life in July 1987, and died in prison in 1991.

Of all of them, Maurice Papon was the most unfortunate, his gravest mistake being to continue in public life after the war. As chief of police in Paris in 1961, the violent repression of an Algerian demonstration was laid at his door – two hundred died, sixty of their bodies found floating in the Seine – and Papon was actually Budget Minister in Raymond Barre's government in 1978 when Louis Darquier fingered Bousquet.

There were hundreds if not thousands of French officials, civil servants and police, most of them, if alive, now in old people's homes, who had done even worse than Papon. But it was he who provided the longest and most flamboyant of all these French trials, for Papon was a *haut fonctionnaire*, a senior civil servant, and a quintessential example of a Vichy functionary, amoral, unquestioning, arrogant. His trial was the nearest a new generation could get to the sins of their fathers. Papon's trial was stalled by friends in high places for sixteen years, and only began two years after François Mitterrand stood down as president of France. Papon was eighty-seven. He was finally condemned to ten years' criminal detention in 1998 for the deportation of Jews from Bordeaux – his corre-spondence with Darquier only one clear piece of evidence of his activ-ities. It was all too late, particularly for the old men and women who clustered round the trial courtroom wearing yellow badges (not yellow stars). In 2002, Papon was released.

Klarsfeld did not get Aloïs Brunner, although the decision was taken to try him for crimes against humanity. If alive, Brunner is still securely hidden in Damascus.[28] René Bousquet, protected by influential friends, amongst them President Mitterrand, had, like so many others, flourished after the Liberation. A few days after D-Day in June 1944 he was taken into custody and sent to Germany with his family, where they stayed in modest comfort until the end of the war. This permitted him to qualify himself as one of the 'deported'. Arrested at the Liberation, he spent three years in Fresnes prison, from 1945 to 1 July 1948, and was with Laval the night before his execution.

Bousquet was brought before the High Court of Justice in June 1949, when he was acquitted. At his trial he repeatedly blamed Dannecker and Darquier for the July 1942 round-ups and Vel' d'Hiv'. He insisted that dealing with Jews was outside his bailiwick, that there was a specific office for that – the CGQJ, run by Louis Darquier. Bousquet's instruc-tions had always been to dampen the ardour of Darquier, to watch him closely; the proposal for the transfer of Jews from the Vichy to the Occupied Zone had been entirely Darquier's; it was Darquier who had sent copies of his, Bousquet's, correspondence with Laval to the Germans. As to the Vel' d'Hiv', Darquier coordinated it; he, Bousquet, was merely an observer. Forty years later, Bousquet could still use the Vichy argument that French Jews (he would admit that foreign Jews suffered) were protected under his regime, quite oblivious of the impli-cation of such remarks.

In 1949 Bousquet was sentenced to five years of *dégradation nationale*, which was immediately suspended in recognition of his putative 'acts in favour of the Resistance'. The judgement came from the High Court, and therefore no appeal was possible. Bousquet proceeded into his bril-liant career with the Banque de l'Indochine and the *Dépêche du Midi*. He held many directorships and led a most comfortable life. In 1955 every-thing for which Bousquet was responsible was published in Joseph Billig's book, but on he went. His Légion d'honneur was restored to him, and he stood in the legislative elections of 1958 as an anti-Gaullist Radical.

In 1965, as Louis Darquier was moving into his tower block in Madrid, Bousquet was helping to finance François Mitterrand in the presidential elections, opposing de Gaulle.

Bousquet, who arranged so imperturbably the deaths of so many, who could do everything better than Louis Darquier and who was, above all, a better liar, was finally brought to book by Louis' rantings. Louis' revenge turned into fifteen years of misery for Bousquet; not as long as Louis' exile in Spain, and perhaps insufficient acknowledgement of the crimes of this meticulous functionary, but more than Klarsfeld or anyone else had achieved. After the interview Bousquet resigned from the Banque de l'Indochine almost immediately, but it took ten years before Klarsfeld could assemble new facts and documentation which had not been presented at the High Court trial of 1949. By September 1989 these were in place, but two years of judicial procrastination and state protection meant that Bousquet was not indicted for crimes against humanity until March 1991.

In his last defence, presented in August 1992, Bousquet once again denied culpability and passed all responsibility to the Germans and to Louis Darquier. Except for Pétain and Laval, who were not accused of these crimes, Bousquet would have been the first French collaborator responsible for the French holocaust to come to trial. As this was about to begin, on 3 June 1993, Bousquet was shot by an unhinged publicity-seeker who rang the bell of Bousquet's front door pretending to be an agent of the Ministry of the Interior. It took four shots to kill him. The deranged assassin stated that he was happy to have executed justice and to have rid the world of a 'piece of garbage'. Bousquet was eighty-four years old. François Mitterrand's protection of and friendship for him – there is a famous photograph of Bousquet dining with the Mitterrands in 1974, and Mitterrand also avowed his friendship for Bousquet on television in September 1994 – has encouraged the view that it was Mitterrand who had Bousquet shot before he could come to trial and make uncomfortable revelations.

Louis Darquier's statements about the gas chambers and the murder of Jews were not the birth of Negationism, as the denial of the Holocaust is called. Paul Rassinier opened the subject for the French with his book *The Lies of Ulysses*, published in 1950, and Louis' old anti-Semitic comrades, particularly Céline, had been saying the same for years. The day after the *l'Express* interview was published, Robert Faurisson, a university professor in Lyon and a seasoned warrior in the war against the Holocaust, wrote to *Le Monde*. His letter of 1 November 1978 expressed the hope that Darquier's words would enable a large public to discover that 'the so-called massacres in gas chambers and so-called genocide, were one and the same lie'. Negationism exploded again in *l'affaire Faurisson*, and has never gone away.

Louis did not live to enjoy these events, but he soldiered on happily for another two years, and was on holiday when he died in his bed on 29 August 1980. Teresa, as ever, was looking after him in the small spa town of Carratraca in the Sierra de Málaga, replete with oleanders, orange and lemon trees, and white houses with tumbling geraniums.

Above the town is the cemetery; there are no tombs, only niches; it is a very pretty cemetery. Louis has no tombstone because his daughter wanted no one to know where he was, but she gave him a funeral. The entire community of Carratraca came out for it – though no one knew at all whose funeral they were attending – and, in a moment of what Teresa called 'divine justice', communists carried him to his resting place, niche number 121 at the cemetery. When it was over, they all sat down in the village square and drank whisky. Teresa kept Louis' death quiet, and it was not publicly known until 1983, the year written on his civic documents in Cahors as his date of death, the town's last word on its least favourite son.

In 1998 the niches at the cemetery above Carratraca were decaying. When rebuilt, new numbers were allotted; there is no niche number 121 now, and Louis Darquier's bones were given no new number. There is an annual fee for a niche; if unpaid the corpse is removed, put into a black plastic bag, numbered, and stored in a warehouse near the small chapel next to the cemetery. If the plastic bag is not claimed, in time it is destroyed. When asked to check for bag no. 121, it was missing.

In England Elsie lived on, never without her floppy old felt hat, which she wore in and outside the house, her photograph of Anne always displayed on the mantel. She fell to skin and bone in old age, still saw the funny side of things when possible, expected traffic to stop for her, and vigorously shook her stick at all comers. She died just after her ninetieth birthday, in 1983, and is buried with Arthur and all her sisters in Great Tew churchyard. She left behind a little trinket box of treasures: three ashtrays, a nappy pin, a thimble, a small metal mouse and the photograph of Anne, with four of her childhood books. Elsie's life savings, all £2,000 of them, she bequeathed to the National Children's Home.

Anne's greatest suffering came from the silence in which she lived, suffering which she could ease only by contemplating the pain of others. When she tried to deal with it, her inner demons led her to place her trust in a man who treated her in adult life as her father had as a child. At the time of her death, Robert Hobson wrote a poem about her – 'In Memoriam' – in which he calls her a

psycho

therapist.

The space between the words makes his meaning clear.

In 1985 Hobson published a book about his work, *Forms of Feeling: The Heart of Psychotherapy*. He aspired to be a psychiatrist who was also an artist/scientist; he was a pioneer of what is called the 'conversational model' of psychotherapy. Hobson loved to use words, yet he could write: 'I hope to respond to my unique client by sharing in an ongoing act of creation, expressing and shaping immediate experience in the making and remaking of a verbal and non-verbal language of feeling.' He once told an interviewer: 'Charismatic leaders can leave a trail of destruction.'[29] In *Forms of Feeling* he fictionalised his patients, never an acceptable practice then, but today there is a code of ethics prohibiting, and a system of investigation for, offences such as this.

Hobson's reaction to Anne's suicide probably encompassed many emotions, extraordinary guilt being one, grief another. He wrote that the last section of his book, which he headed 'The Heart of a Psychotherapist', was 'an intimate statement', which it is, but it is also a thinly disguised portrait of Anne, and reveals a formidable lack of self-knowledge, injured vanity and a – probably unconscious – desire for the last word, for revenge.

'The Heart of Darkness' is the title of the chapter in which he recounts his relationship with her in considerable detail; he renames Anne 'Sue'. Anne had been dead for fifteen years. Presumably he thought no one would notice; who was left to remember Anne Darquier? But her friends noticed, and so did I.

'Sue's story is one of loneliness, guilt, destruction, and meaninglessness. It is also a story of courage and love,' Hobson wrote. After briefly reporting Anne's childhood and her 'girlhood fantasies about her absent parents', he is accurate about Louis, 'an idealised aristocratic father', and Myrtle, 'a loathed alcoholic mother'; and accuses Elsie of child abuse, 'terrible deprivation . . . squalid filth . . . sexually perverted nanny'. He goes on to describe, in perfectly identifiable terms, the years of analysis Anne Darquier underwent in his care. He notes the 'disillusionment of seeing her idealised father as a cruel monster', and how 'with sensitivity and courage she helped, in an amazing way, very many difficult patients'.

Elsie was two years dead when Hobson accused 'Sue's sadistic nanny' of child abuse. No one who knew Elsie believes this: 'No way, they were just not that kind of people. Elsie was not like that'; 'Elsie loved Anne as her daughter'; 'I wouldn't say she worshipped her, but she loved her, was proud to be associated with her; she was devastated when Anne died.'[30] The Jones family certainly thought Nanny Lightfoot was capable of anything, and did not believe she should look after children. But as they thought of Louis and Myrtle as characters in an aristocratic love story, their views are at best questionable. Hobson coupled this irresponsibility, and the assumption that people of Elsie's class would not have access to the kind of book he was writing, with a serious betrayal of Anne's trust. He tells how Sue/Anne pointed a loaded revolver at him, flung herself down the stairs of his house, smashed every milk bottle outside the houses of the street where he lived, hurled a table at his head, ripped the buttons off his 'lime-green waistcoat with delicately coloured buttons'.

'Sue was brilliant and she was ruthless. And she certainly had charm,' Hobson writes. '. . . She died suddenly. Since she had no available relatives I was asked to identify the body. The Coroner's verdict was "accidental death". I knew it was suicide.' And: 'We might consider the effects of abandonment in infancy, and to what extent damage is irreparable.' His account throbs with his sense of failure and regret, but also with unusual self-absorption: 'Here, I am concerned with how Sue, and many other patients, have compelled me to acknowledge the hidden regions of my own heart . . . I came to see once more how, despite a long training analysis, I had only a passing and causal acquaintance with myself. I was faced with meaninglessness and with the essential loneliness which lies at the heart of psychotherapy and of all personal relationships.'[31]

The words are his, but Anne's fatal dependence on narcissistic dinosaurs was the legacy of Louis and Myrtle Darquier.

When I rang the doorbell of flat number 38, 59 Weymouth Street on 7 September 1970, at 8 a.m. as usual, Anne Darquier was upstairs, dead on the bathroom floor. Although she was courting oblivion, it is unlikely that Anne was courting death. Hers was one of those silent suicides, in which stopping the pain, rather than the ending of life, is the point. How I know this, and whether I am right about it, hardly matters. What I am more certain of is that people who commit suicide are not alone: they are addressing someone.

Postscript

━━━━━━━━━━━━━◄○►━━━━━━━━━━━━━

I HAVE NEVER BEEN ABLE to think of Anne's story simply as a tragedy. When I began my research I felt a great sense of injustice on her behalf, but as the years went by I came to feel not so much less sympathy for her, as regret, for her sake, that she lived in a *milieu* and at a time when silence was the only way she could live with her story and survive. Sometimes I wanted to rise up and retrospectively shake her. She was so clever, so astute. She had such ambition for the happiness of those she cared for. She could heal others – there are many besides myself living well because of her – but she could not heal herself. And, the child of gamblers, she had wretched luck.

After the Second World War each country produced myths about its victory or defeat. In Britain and America, the Russian and Eastern European experience was obliterated for decades during the Cold War. General de Gaulle too orchestrated a mythology, probably necessary at the time, about the role of France after its defeat by Germany in June 1940, in which his *vraie France* was entirely and always opposed to the German occupiers, obscuring the minuscule size of the Resistance and of his own Free French forces, ignoring Vichy, its deeds and its initial popularity, such as it was.

It is now many decades since the French have rejected this Gaullist myth; their self-scrutiny of the Dark Years is unmatched by most Western countries. An ocean of books has been published – accusatory, analytical, anecdotal and revelatory – telling the truth about France's role of collaboration with the Nazis during the war. Historians and academics have minutely chronicled French collaboration, and worse. Though the Vatican remains the great unpunished, and Catholic fascism is still glossed over, the Catholic hierarchy have acknowledged guilt, and once François Mitterrand was dead, Jacques Chirac, when president of France, apologised too.

There was a bit of Louis Darquier in all French collaborators and Paris *collabos*. There were many political thugs. Certain French banks made a great deal more money out of the war than Louis Darquier. Pétain was more than his match as a womaniser, and the list of raving anti-Semites stretches into infinity. With hardly an exception, all these men were marked by the First World War. It is perhaps only as a braggart and a *boulevardier* that Louis Darquier was their superior. The most distinguished historians continue to label Darquier as a Nazi and to index him under his assumed title. If remembered, he is known as the French Eichmann; but he was not, not at all. He was the natural inheritor of generations of anti-republican attacks by the old order, of ideas borrowed from strangely revered French intellectuals such as Charles Maurras, of centuries of Catholic anti-Semitism and nationalist myth-making.

But he was not a clever man; he was a mountebank and a chancer who stretched the charity, tolerance and patience of those few who loved him, and irritated to breaking point the many who hated him, yet still survived to do it all again. Funded by the Nazi Party from 1936, he used French fascism and anti-Semitism to make his way in the world and to aggrandise his small self.

Louis Darquier's rightful place was in the rue Laugier, addressing the minuscule number of his fellow misfits, and repairing to the bar as soon as his posturings were over. Immersed in the abracadabra of his trade as an anti-Semite, his hold upon reality was always as inadequate as his intelligence. Yoked in mutual self-deception with Myrtle, the Baron and Baroness, twin children – wicked children – played games, murderous games, pulling wings off butterflies, dispensing cruelty like liquorice water. Left to himself, Louis Darquier would have destroyed only his own children and any adult – except his adoring acolyte Myrtle – foolish enough to dabble in his fantasy world. But, the only professional anti-Semite with a public appointment, put to dirty work by his betters, thousands, besides Anne, died because of him.

He could have achieved nothing without the Vichy state and the Nazis, who used him for their own purposes. Here was a man – a con man, but they turned a blind eye to that for as long as they could – who openly called for the massacre of Jews, the appropriation of their property and the pursuit, and hopefully the elimination, of any 'half-caste' with Jewish blood. Primo Levi rightly called Louis Darquier a 'cowardly and foolish man'. Above and around Darquier were the real criminals, the Pétains and Weygands, the Bousquets and Vallats, the cardinals and clergy, the judges and lawyers, the industrialists and businessmen

Académiciens and intellectuals, writers and journalists and functionaries who put his babbling mouth to work for their own ends.

Vichy decorated its murderous activities in the purple prose of the Church and the state. That is why Louis Darquier was so scorned and so hated by his Vichy *confrères*. Looking at him, hearing him speak, pontificating from his CGQJ, they stared their own inhumanity in the face. Louis Darquier formed no part of the way the men of Vichy saw their relationship with Nazi Germany or their relationship with the French people they governed. He was ridiculous, he was their fall guy, but he was also the dark essence of the *l'Etat français*.

Louis Darquier distinguished himself in another way. No one remembered him. Many of his contemporaries, from both sides of the political chasm that divided France, wrote their memoirs. Granted that all of them disliked him to a man; none of them recollect the meetings, lectures or marches they shared with him, nor, during the Occupation, the correspondence, parties and dinners, records of which exist in exhausting detail. Otto Abetz spoke for hundreds of them when he said, during his time in Cherche Midi prison after the Liberation: 'I must have seen Darquier de Pellepoix at least once during official visits. But I have no exact memory of the event.'[1]

The French forget Vichy, Australians forget the Aborigines, the English forget the Irish, Unionists forget the Catholics of Northern Ireland, the United States forgot Chile and forgets Guantánamo. Everyone forgot East Timor and Rwanda. As I wrote this book, people constantly asked me how I could bear to write about such a villain and about such terrible things. In fact, horrors from the past did not deter me. What caused me anguish as I tracked down Louis Darquier was to live so closely to the helpless terror of the Jews of France, and to see what the Jews of Israel were passing on to the Palestinian people. Like the rest of humanity, the Jews of Israel 'forget' the Palestinians. Everyone forgets, every nation forgets.

Remembering has to do with justice, and as there is no justice, acknowledgement has to do. I hope this book will be some kind of testament to a debt and a friendship I've carried with me for forty years, and in a more oblique way to children and others who are powerless, who live in silence.

Appendix I

In Auschwitz They Only Gassed Lice

An interview with Darquier de Pellepoix, former Commissioner for Jewish Affairs in the Vichy Government, by Philippe Ganier-Raymond (*l'Express*, 28 October–4 November 1978)

'Six million dead Jews? An invention, pure and simple! A Jewish invention!'
A small shopkeeper from Cahors, with a monocle and an assumed title, is one of those most responsible for the deportation of seventy-five thousand Jews from France. To this day, he regrets nothing. For Louis Darquier de Pellepoix, Commissioner for Jewish Affairs from May 1942 to February 1944, is not a phantom from the past. He lives in a village on the borders of Estremadura and Andalusia. Just as the trial of one of the Gestapo chiefs in France, Kurt Lischka,[*] is about to begin in Frankfurt, Darquier, meticulous organiser of the round-up of the Vel' d'Hiv' in 1942, explains himself in an interview with Philippe Ganier-Raymond. You will need to read it more than once.

L'Express: Sir, it is barely thirty-six years since you handed over seventy-five thousand men, women and children to the Germans. You are the French Eichmann.

---

[*] Lischka was one of Knochen's principal deputies and chief of German police in Paris. The German courts sentenced him to ten years' imprisonment in 1980.

Louis Darquier: Where did you get those figures?

LE: Everyone knows them. They are official. You can see them in this document too. (I show him, open at the right page, Serge Klarsfeld's *Mémorial de la déportation des Juifs de France* – Chronicle of the Deportation of the Jews of France).

LD: Just as I guessed. A Jewish document. Here we go again with Jewish propaganda! Of course, you can show me nothing but Jewish documents. And why? Because no others exist.

LE: Is that so? There are hundreds, thousands of others, ones that do not come from Jewish organisations. That said, perhaps you would admit that Jews might be interested in the disappearance of six million of their own people.

LD: That figure is an invention, pure and simple. A Jewish invention, of course. Jews are like that: they're ready to do anything to get publicity.

LE: Do you really believe what you've just said? Could you repeat it?

LD: Oh, I see. You're intoxicated like the rest of them. You're all blind . . . You don't want to face up to the fact that Jews have only one idea in their heads: to wreak havoc everywhere. And why? You know perfectly well: to make Jerusalem the capital of the world. Even today you only need to open any newspaper to realise it. You have come here to accuse me, but . . .

LE: No. I'm not a prosecutor. And I'm not a Nazi-hunter. I have come to see you to try to understand what goes on in a mind like yours after thirty-six years. That's all I'm after.

LD: You are an agent of Tel Aviv.

LE: An agent of Tel Aviv, should he be interested in you, would not waste time asking you these questions.

LD: Anyway, you're the one who is wasting time. I've nothing to tell you.

LE: You've still got it wrong. You have already taught me something essential: you are a rather unique case. You don't say: 'I had my orders. I carried them out.' Your position doesn't seem to have changed one iota since 1942.

LD: You think the Jewish question dates from 1942! No, the Jewish question has been a problem for a thousand years . . . Since the Middle Ages, the West and Christianity have fought against the creeping stranglehold of the Jews. The yellow star – we didn't invent it. If it proved necessary as far back as the twelfth century to make Jews eat pork, it was for a good reason. As for our recent history, it was entirely governed by the search for a solution to the Jewish problem.

Look, here is a question: Have you ever wondered why we had to wait so long for the application of the Balfour Declaration? Have you counted the wars, counted the deaths that have got us to the position we are in today: the settling of the Jews on disputed territory? When the Marshal put me in charge of the Commission for Jewish Affairs, I determined on one fixed end. A humanitarian end, please note: to make the situation of French Jews as comfortable as possible.

LE: You're not serious. Who do you hope will believe that?

LD: I forgot that you are one of those unhappy victims of Jewish propaganda. And Jewish propaganda has always been based on lies. Always ... Always ... I tell you again, that during the months when I was minister, I spent most of my time trying to protect Jews from trouble. I'm talking of French Jews, that goes without saying. I'll take an example. Between ourselves, do you think it was necessary to deport the Debré family?

LE: No. Absolutely not. Neither the Debrés, nor anyone else ...

LD: The father Debré was half-Jewish, that is well known. What is more, these people had a record of service. They were Jews who had chosen France. To deport them would have been profoundly unjust. I've cited that case, but there were many others. Generally speaking, I wanted to keep French Jews out of it.

LE: It is certainly true that in the month of February 1943, you proposed to the Vichy government a certain number of measures which the Germans themselves had not even dreamt of.

Declaration of Louis Darquier de Pellepoix to *Le Petit Parisien*,
1 February 1943.

I propose to the government:

1. To institute the obligatory wearing of the yellow star in the Non-Occupied Zone.

2. To prohibit Jews, without any exception, access to, and the exercise of, public office. Whatever the intellectual worth of, and the services rendered by, any individual Jew, he is nonetheless Jewish and by that very fact brings into govern-

447

*ment organisations where he has a position not only a natural resistance to
Aryanisation, but also an attitude that in the long term profoundly alters the
effectiveness of our French administration.*

*3. The withdrawal of French nationality from all Jews who acquired it after
1927 . . .*

LD: I don't remember anything about this story of the yellow star in
the free zone. It must be another example of your Jewish propaganda . . .

LE: Absolutely not. It is there in black and white in *Le Petit Parisien* of
1 February 1943.

LD: Perhaps . . . perhaps . . . In any event it was a mistake. Because you
know, contrary to what has been so often said, the yellow star was
not popular.

LE: And was the denaturalisation of the Jews an error?

LD: That, oh no! That was definitely my responsibility . . .

LE: Your predecessor at the commission, Xavier Vallat, otherwise
considered too soft by the German authorities, had fixed upon 1932
as the final date for naturalisation; before that date – in principle
– no one could be affected by the racial laws.[*] You put it back to
1927.

LD: But of course. There had to be more!

LE: More deported Jews, is that it?

LD: Of course. We had to get rid of those foreigners, those wogs, at
any price, and of the thousands of stateless persons who were the
source of all our problems. They wanted the war. They led us into
it. It was vital to get rid of them. As quickly as possible, as far away
as possible. I fixed upon that as my second aim when I took up
my responsibilities: to send all those people back to their own
country to do the damage there that they had tried to do to our
country!

LE: What do you mean, their own country? In 1942, Jews did not have
a fatherland.

LD: I mean – over there, I don't know where, in Poland. The idea was

---

[*] This was a purely formal law: in practice, from the month of March 1941, the French
police arrested Jews who had been French since 1897, to hand them over to the
Germans! (PG-R)

to give them land somewhere over there. Then they would no longer be stateless people! That is what I wanted: the end of the wandering Jew. So that at last, after two thousand years, those people would no longer be foreigners wherever they were.

LE: This is stupefying. You are not far short of telling me that Auschwitz is in line with the Balfour Declaration!

LD: Auschwitz . . . Auschwitz . . . You know, there have been too many stories about Auschwitz! It's time to begin to face up to what really happened there.

LE: A million dead. Amongst them, innumerable children. All gassed.

LD: No, no, no . . . You'll never make me believe that. Here we are again with the satanic Jewish propaganda which has spread and encouraged this myth. I tell you again, Jews are always ready to do anything to get themselves talked about, to make themselves interesting, to complain. I'll tell you exactly what happened at Auschwitz. They used gas. Yes. That's true. But they gassed the lice.

LE: What are you trying to say?

LD: I am saying that when the Jews arrived at the camp, they were made to take their clothes off, as is normal, before being taken to shower. During that time, their clothes were disinfected. After the war, the Jews circulated photographs everywhere, showing piles of dirty linen in shreds. And they wailed . . . 'Look,' they said, 'there are the clothes of our brothers who have been exterminated.' That was a lie, absolutely. But what do you expect; the Jews are like that. They just have to tell lies.

LE: I was right in saying that you are a one-off. Even Eichmann did not deny the existence of the Final Solution. You do. Nonetheless, you were well aware of it.

Internal memo from the Central Security Office of the Reich 1VB4, 11 June 1942.

A conference took place attended by, besides the undersigned SS Hauptsturmführer Dannecker, those responsible for the Jewish sections in Brussels and La Haye.

Object: This summer, military reasons prevent the departure of German Jews to the zone of operation in the east. And so the Reichsführer SS has ordered the transfer of the largest number of Jews from south-west Europe or the Occupied regions in the west, to the concentration camp of Auschwitz. The essential

*condition is that Jews, of both sexes, must be between sixteen and forty years
of age. These convoys can include 10 per cent of Jews unfit for work.*

*Decision: It has been agreed that fifteen thousand Jews will be deported from the
Low Countries, ten thousand from Belgium and 100,000 from France, including
the Non-Occupied Zone.*

LE: You don't find that this simple text, which automatically landed in
your office, is a barely veiled implication of the Final Solution?

LD: No. I repeat. The Final Solution is an invention, pure and simple.
Do you know anyone who has ever seen what they call a gas chamber?

LE: The millions of survivors of Auschwitz. Not to mention the Allied
Commissions of Inquiry after the war, and all the visitors to the
museum at Auschwitz. Myself, amongst others.

LD: Your gas chamber was invented after the event. You won't get me
to change my mind.

LE: That's true. You won't change your mind. Now, these photos. You've
already seen them?

(I try to make him look at photographs showing the bodies of women
and children that have just come out of the gas chamber. He turns
away.)

LD: I don't even want to look at them. They're fakes. You know, I'm
very well informed. I know that after the war the Jews invented thousands of lies, and as I told you before, they have intoxicated the
whole world with their fabrications. You are only one of their millions
of victims.

LE: Good. Now, could you tell me where these people come from? (I
turn over the pages of Klarsfeld's book in front of him, a kind of
directory of the deportations.) What became of the one thousand
deportees of the convoy no. 33 – I take this example from among
others – who left the station at Drancy on 11 September 1942? What
became of Daniel Belchatowski, ten years old, Solange Grinsztein,
two years old, Raymond Hubermann, seven years old?

LD: How do you think I know? It wasn't my job to know what happened
to Jews *afterwards*. My work was exclusively administrative. I was a
senior French civil servant. I always made sure that the Jewish
problem in France should be resolved by the French. And, believe
me, it wasn't easy. You had always to navigate between Pierre Laval
and that raving idiot Dannecker. Between those two, it was almost

impossible to do one's job well. If I had to do it again, I tell you straight, I would refuse.

LE: Your reply raises several questions. Here is the first: what exactly do you mean by doing one's job well?

LD: To separate the wheat from the chaff. To protect French Jews, as I have already said. Apart from that, I shall surprise you. Do you know that I had many Jewish friends? Later, they thought it better to cut me dead. That's life. I don't hold it against them. All the more so because some of them helped me; I'll tell you about that later. To return to your question, to do my job well consisted in preventing the Germans from interfering in Jewish affairs. If they had done so it would have been a catastrophe.

The Marshal and President Laval took a fortunate decision in giving M Darquier de Pellepoix the Commission for Jewish Affairs . . . There are those who sometimes say that our struggle against the Jews is only a pale copy of German racism. Fools! Don't they know that a true, pure Frenchman, and Darquier is one such, has nothing to learn from anyone in this respect.

André Chaumet, vice-president of the Association of Anti-Jewish Journalists.

LE: Second question. Pierre Laval. What were your relations with him?

LD: Very cordial.

LE: Nevertheless, he had you arrested on 26 February 1944, for 'irregularities in the administration of sequestered estates'.

LD: No! Not at all! Where did you get hold of that? Laval never had me arrested. We had words sometimes, that is true, but Laval was a splendid fellow, he did his job very well. They tell many stories about Laval. One recent account was that he was a Portuguese Jew. What a lie! He was ugly, that's true. Good Lord, that man was ugly! But he wasn't Jewish for a minute. He had the ugly head of the typical Auvergnat, that's the truth of it. Besides, I often called him 'ugly old Auvergnat', and he wasn't offended by it. It was the same with Pétain. They say everywhere that Pétain opposed my actions, that he hated me. But, first, it was he who nominated me to the commissariat, and secondly, he never disapproved of me. Each time I went to see him, as soon as he saw me in the distance he would call out: 'Look, here comes my torturer!' But that was a joke. What's more, he laughed. And that did not prevent him from shaking my hand. As for Laval, he was a good man, very hard-working, very competent. Unfortunately, one must be frank, he knew nothing about the Jewish question.

LE: We'll get to details soon. Dannecker . . .

LD: He was mentally ill. I never stopped having trouble with him.

LE: What kind of trouble?

LD: Well, he couldn't help himself: every time he saw a German Jew on a list, he did everything he could to save him from deportation! Never did stateless Jews have a better ally.

Telegram from Dannecker to Berlin, 6 July 1942, summarising his discussion with Eichmann of 1 July on the subject of future round-ups:

For the moment there is no question of arresting any but expatriate and foreign Jews. In a second phase, we will get on to Jews naturalised in France since 1919 or 1927.

LE: On the contrary, it seems to me that you got on very well with Dannecker. All the documents prove it.

LD: Absolutely not. The Germans never stopped putting a spoke in my wheels.

LE: Well, what is the significance of this note of 29 May 1943, sent by Röthke, Dannecker's successor, to Knochen: 'Several times, Darquier has asked us to apply his draft legislation, because for a long time now he has lost all hope of the French government accepting even one of them.'

LD: That's another lie! A lie made up after the event by the Jews! Oh, these Jews! They're priceless! They'll do anything to invent a scape-goat. They have made me into a character out of a novel. They want to blame me for absolutely everything! I, who helped them so much! But they've not succeeded. Besides, it would have been very difficult to get me, because I've died twice.

LE: How is that?

LD: I'll tell you . . . In 1944, when everything had begun to break up, I began to think of my own safety. A friend took me to Toulouse, another to Bordeaux, and a third got me into Spain. And then, the Liberation arrived. One fine day *they* fell upon someone who resem-bled me in a remarkable way. This was a completely hysterical period, you know. They arrested anyone, they fired indiscriminately. Anyway, *they* took this poor chap, and the crowd cried, 'It's Darquier! It's Darquier! Shoot him!' Just between ourselves, I have always thought that there must have been friends of mine in that crowd. To continue – in brief. They shot this poor unfortunate in my place. Then, some years went by. They discovered that I was well and truly living. Then they condemned me to death in my absence on 10 December 1947. They could not do otherwise. (He laughs a little.) Since then, let me tell you, *they* have left me in blissful peace.

LE: They never asked for your extradition?

LD: Never. What on earth are you thinking of? I would add that until the recent past I always maintained the best relations with the French ambassador in Madrid. We saw each other often. I sometimes went to their receptions.

On 27 August 1978, the spokesman for the Minister of Justice told me: 'In fact, Louis Darquier de Pellepoix was condemned to death in absentia on 10 December 1947 for collaboration with the enemy. Under the statute of limitations his punishment lapsed in 1968. Only the ban on living in France is maintained for life.'

LE: If I've got it right, the originator of the Vel' d'Hiv' round-up of July 1942 has not been brought to book for crimes against humanity.

LD: First, I had nothing to do with the Vel' d'Hiv' round-up, as you call it. It was decided upon much earlier. I had been commissioner for only a few weeks. I knew nothing.

LE: What is terrible about you is that you never stop telling outrageous lies, so that whoever begins to ask you for simple information is obliged to turn into an accuser. You had not been commissioner for only a few weeks. You had been at the head of anti-Jewish repression since the month of May. More than two months! And you had already taken decisions which surprised even the Germans!

LD: The Vel' d'Hiv' round-up, it's funny that you want to talk to me about that. It was Bousquet who organised the Vel' d'Hiv' round-up. From A to Z. Bousquet was the chief of police. It was he who did everything. And you know how Bousquet ended up? He only got five years of national indignity. He had helped the Resistance! What a farce! And he ended up the director of the Bank of Indochina. Oh, he wangled things very well, Bousquet! Whatever, it was he who organised everything.

LE: Forgive me for talking to you like a policeman. What did you do on the days of 16 and 17 July 1942?

LD: What's so special about 16 and 17 July 1942?

LE: The Vel' d'Hiv' round-up. Thousands of men, women and children were crammed into the Vélodrome d'Hiver before being sent to Auschwitz.

LD: It will be easy for you to understand that I do not remember precisely what I was doing on those days. But, in all probability, I went to my office to get on with current business. Always, always, administrative work.

LE: You did not go to the Vel' d'Hiv' to see what was going on?

LD: Certainly not! Why would I go there? I repeat that it was Bousquet who was in charge of all that.

Minutes of a conference in the avenue Foch, 4 July 1942.
Present were: Standartenführer Dr Knochen, SS
Hauptsturmführer Dannecker, SS Obersturmführer Schmidt.
French representatives: Bousquet, Secretary of State for the
Police, Darquier de Pellepoix, French Commissioner for Jewish
Affairs.

...A commission must be set up by the French including a representative of Jewish Affairs, a representative of the Secretary of State for the Police ... Bousquet stated immediately that the management of the Commission must be in the hands of the Commissariat for Jewish Affairs ... It must be noted that at this point Darquier de Pellepoix almost gave the impression of being appalled at the idea of accepting such a responsibility.

LD: Oh well! Someone had to do the work. If it hadn't been me, it would have been someone else. A German perhaps.

LE: You belonged to the Germans. It was they who put you in the job.

LD: Another fairy tale. It was the Marshal who appointed me. In full knowledge of the reason. He knew very well that only I – as well as a few others – was capable of achieving success in the anti-Jewish struggle within the context of French law.

LE: That did not ever stop you from going to complain to the Germans when the Vichy government were too timorous and rejected your proposals.

LD: Lies! Lies! Monstrous lies! You have no right to say such a thing! You are free to be deluded by Jewish propaganda, but at a certain point...

LE: But you certainly wrote this: 'I do not believe, in my soul and conscience, that the French state will be able to carry through this national revolution. What is necessary, and my French heart compels me to demand of you, Germans, that you take over the governance of France, and then let us act for ourselves.' You can search the archives of all of Occupied Europe, and not find another example of such servility towards the Nazis. You were begging for a Gauleiter!

LD: Quite the contrary. I was putting them off the scent. In making a pretence of following them, of anticipating their wishes, I was keeping in my hands (in French hands) the reins of the anti-Jewish struggle. Laval did not understand this strategy at all. He always put his foot in it as far as this was concerned...

LE: Let us return to the Vel' d'Hiv' round-up.

LD: If you wish. But I have truly nothing more to add.

LE: Yes. The children. I have a document here. A Gestapo note. Annotated by Dannecker.

LD: That fool!

LE: This note is the German translation of your report after the round-up in the Vel' d'Hiv'. You complain that only 8,980 persons were arrested. And Dannecker has written in the margin: 'This proves Darquier's industry very well.' And then further down he adds: 'More than four thousand children.' Sir, what became of those children?

LD: This was not I... I was not responsible... It was Laval. I'm tired out telling you that he understood nothing about the Jewish question. You know what Laval did? When we talked to him about a mass deportation, he said: 'Above all, do not separate the children from their mothers.' It was he who insisted that the children should be deported with their parents. A stupidity. I wanted the children to be taken into care.

LE: Perfectly true.

Urgent telegram from Dannecker to Berlin (addressee unknown)
summarising Laval's position, 6 July 1942.

The negotiations with the French government have concluded today with the following results: President Laval has proposed that with the deportation of Jewish families from the Occupied Zone, it should include children aged less than sixteen years old.

The question of Jewish children remaining in the Occupied Zone does not interest him. I beg you to take a decision urgently and tell me, by telegram, whether children under sixteen years of age can also be deported, beginning with the fifteenth Jewish convoy . . .

LD: There, you see: it wasn't me.

LE: I notice that you don't contest this document. And this?

> First meeting of the Organising Committee for the round-ups.
> Present at this meeting: Dannecker, Heinrichsohn, Darquier de
> Pellepoix, etc., 8 July 1942.

In opening the meeting, Darquier de Pellepoix noted that the Occupation authorities had declared themselves ready to rid the French state of the Jews, and that they were meeting to discuss the practical arrangements for the deportation . . . Under discussion was the arrest of about twenty-eight thousand Jews in Paris . . . The inspectors of the Anti-Jewish Police and women auxiliaries are to bring their cards classified by arrondissement . . . The Jews will then be assembled in the different town halls and taken to the rallying point (Vel' d'Hiv').

LD: Well, on paper I was responsible for what took place. But, in reality it was Bousquet who managed everything. With his filthy police force! I did not want the anti-Jewish police! I wanted a French police force, who would have understood their responsibilities, you know what I mean? But there was nothing I could do!

LE: You maintain that you had nothing to do with the Vel' d'Hiv' round-up?

LD: Absolutely. I was only a civil servant. I was very far removed from the day-to-day practicalities. And I was too busy saving good Jews, the French Jews . . .

> Letter from Darquier de Pellepoix to Laval, 23 July 1942.

. . . The Commissariat for Jewish Affairs has been charged with placing at the disposal of the German authorities thirty-two thousand Jews and Jewesses (twenty-two thousand from the Occupied Zone and ten thousand from the Non-Occupied Zone) . . . Action was taken on 16 and 17 July and yielded the following figures: 3,095 men, and 5,885 women.

... The conversations I have had today with the Occupying authorities leave me no alternative but to tell you that they are not at all pleased. The number of trains the German authorities prepared for this job corresponded to the transport of thirty-two thousand Jews.

... May I propose the following supplementary procedures:

1. The arrest of all stateless Jews.

2. The arrest of all Belgian Jews and Dutch Jews and all foreign Jews without a recent passport.

If, after the application of these measures, the anticipated figure is still not reached, it would be worthwhile envisaging fulfilling the requirements by having recourse to Jews and Jewesses whose French naturalisation is dated after 1 January 1927.

LE: You were obsessed with the year 1927. It's the year that appears on all your statements. Why?

LD: Because it was the years between 1927 and 1936 that produced the great onslaught of stateless persons, people who came from everywhere and nowhere. People who wanted to destroy us. People who wanted us to wage war on their behalf. Who, above all, did not want us to prepare for war. People who wanted our defeat, who wanted our ruin. You are too young: you don't know what it was like before the war.

LE: I know one thing, anyway: in 1935, a year before the Popular Front, a man like you was elected to the city council in the 17th arrondissement. And on a single platform. Anti-Semitism.

LD: False. I was elected on a na-tio-na-list programme! That is entirely different. And more important, the word anti-Semitic is inaccurate ...

LE: God knows how often you have used it!

LD: Possibly! But it was a mistake. After all, the Arabs are Semites too. Do not confuse things. But I would like you to know, dear sir, that in 1935, after the Stavisky affair and all the rest of it, to be a nationalist implied that one was anti-Semitic. Because of corruption and because of this Jewish hold over all means of expression. At that time there was only one press free of Jewish influence: the right-wing media! And, I'll say it again, the Jews wanted the war. I fought in '14, I had what is called 'a very good war'. I had no intention of doing that again. And, then, to be defeated! Besides, a Jew – this will give you pleasure – Georges Mandel himself, wrote in the thirties: 'It is the democracies that declare wars.' For a Jew ...

LE: . . . Whom your friends in the Milice assassinated . . .

LD: It's much more complicated than that . . . For a Jew to come to the point of avowing a thing like that, it has to be true. Don't you think so? So, the Jews wanted the war. I did not want it. And then, if you wanted a war, you need to prepare for it seriously. But the Jews, under the cloak of pacifism, refused to do precisely that. That is why I was anti-Jew.

LE: How did this come about? From where?

LD: I must tell you: I am from Cahors. In Cahors we have never liked Jews. It is like that. An ancient tradition. It goes back to the Middle Ages. But I repeat that I was not elected on an anti-Jewish platform. A national movement existed. This movement elected me, doubtless because of my performance on 6 February 1934. Look at this. (He raises his trouser leg and shows me a hole in his right calf.) I did not get that in the trenches. I got it on 6 February. The Parisians knew that I had fought for my principles. Physically. That must have impressed them.

Meeting of the Paris city council, June 1936. M. Darquier de Pellepoix, addressing M. Georges Hirsch:

As I make a distinction between Jews, I will make one now in telling you that you are a dirty little Jew . . . the most racist people in the world are the Jews . . . Until we are rid of those people, the national survival of the country is in grave danger . . .

LE: Admit it, for the Nazis, you were the man of their dreams. From 1936, you clamoured aloud in Paris for measures – denaturalisation, amongst others – which they did not even dare impose themselves in 1942.

LD: Once again, you have no idea of the atmosphere of the country in the thirties. Jews were everywhere. They controlled everything. When I slapped Léon Blum – yes, I publicly slapped Léon Blum, and I do not regret it – it was a natural gesture, a gesture that many other Frenchmen dreamed of making. At that time you could not love your country, or wish for peace, without coming up against Jews. It was impossible! But I must say that even the French are a funny bunch. They have an allergic reaction to demographic changes. When there are too many Jews, when they feel themselves surrounded, put upon by the Jews, they begin to shout: 'Out with the Jews!' Eventually, they take to the streets. But kill fifty Jews and you have an outcry. I tell you that the French in general are only moderately anti-Semitic.

LE: It's still a fact that these moderate anti-Semites elected you over-whelmingly. In 1935. You, a person who had declared in the Salle Wagram, at a meeting on 11 March 1937: 'The Jewish question must be solved urgently. Either the Jews must be expelled, or they must be massacred.' It seems to me that even at Nuremberg at that time, they used words in a more guarded way.

LD: It was a way of talking. As for me, I have never wished the death of anyone.

LE: Not even the death of the Jews you sent to Auschwitz?

LD: I wanted to get them the hell out of the place, the rest I didn't care about. Wasn't my problem.

LE: I think that you were meticulous in pursuit of persecution in a way which was quite unusual. Also, on 9 September 1942 you wrote the following internal memo:

The Commissioner has noticed that in the correspondence of certain depart-ments, Jews are referred to as 'Israélites'. The use of this term is due to Jewish influence which, by banishing the word 'Jew' has managed to achieve, finally, the first principle of Jewish defence, which is to pretend that the Jewish problem is only a religious problem. At the Commissariat for Jewish Affairs, a Jew must be called a Jew, and you must not write 'Monsieur Lévy' or 'Monsieur Dreyfus', but 'the Jew Lévy' and 'the Jew Dreyfus' . . .
Signed: Darquier de Pellepoix
Notified to all Vichy departments.

LD: What's the problem? Aren't Jews a race? Isn't it true that they hide behind the pretence of religion to perpetrate their crimes all over the world? Honestly, I cannot see what you can object to in that memo. It is perfectly anodyne. There is no trace there of any of the persecution you suggest.

LE: Those who talked about race in 1942, in France, as a description of an individual or a people, made themselves accomplices to genocide. No?

LD: But, once again, there was no genocide, for Heaven's sake! Get that idea out of your head.

LE: Do you know that in Germany they are about to begin the trial of Kurt Lischka? I am reliably informed that the Frankfurt tribunal would be happy to have your testimony.

LD: You're talking about Lischka? Who is this man?

LE: Well, the chief of the Gestapo in Paris between 1940 and 1943.

LD: I see, a minor German civil servant. I must have met him two or three times. But this is definitely something that you cannot seem to understand: I knew very few Germans.

LE: That is exactly what is terrifying. Your decisions were not dictated directly by Berlin. You know what Knochen told the examining magistrate on 4 January 1947, just before his trial?

LD: Knochen was not mad like Dannecker. I wish to make that clear.

LE: Knochen said: 'After the arrival of Darquier de Pellepoix, the Commission for Jewish Affairs demonstrated an excess of zeal, anticipating our wishes, and sometimes going well beyond what we wanted.'

LD: But of course. Put yourself in his place a little. He is about to be tried, he'll say anything to save his own skin. That's normal. That's human . . .

LE: And then, at that famous meeting between Heydrich, Bousquet and you, in May 1942, on the very day of your nomination, what did you talk about, you and Heydrich?

LD: At first, I did not want to meet the man. But Knochen insisted, and I ended up by agreeing, since he said that after all it was better to know exactly what kind of person Heydrich was. And so I went. We shook hands. We exchanged a few words. We saw each other for five minutes, in all and once and for all.

LE: You did not talk, that day, about the measures you were to take in the weeks and months to come?

LD: No. I have no idea of what he might well have said to Bousquet and what Bousquet said to him, but as to what concerns my own conversation with Heydrich, I assure you that it was perfectly anodyne.

LE: To continue: Bousquet and you received *carte blanche* from the Germans to bring the repression of the Jews to a successful conclusion: the arrests, the round-ups. They must really have had confidence in you! And, finally, the Germans even helped you to get to Spain . . .

LD: That's not true. It was the French who saved me. But when you come to that period, I'll surprise you. Do you know who helped me to get from Bordeaux to Spain over the mountains? A half-Jewish woman, who, what is more, went under her father's Jewish name. I saw her again, later on, in Barcelona; we remained close until her death. That astonishes you, no? And, earlier, a minute ago, I told you they left me happily alone. And do you know whom this is thanks to? To Jews, for the most part. Good French Jews, whom I helped in difficult times. Between ourselves, a certain Worms. I will say no more . . .

LE: And so, contrary to what is often said about it, far from making a fortune from Jews' assets, you permitted certain rich families to keep their wealth? You sent the furriers of the 11th arrondissement to Auschwitz, and you protected the big capitalists of the 16th? At bottom, that's logical . . .

LD: I refuse to answer those kind of questions. I remind you that my punishment is prescribed.

LE: So, you arrive in Spain . . .

LD: Yes, at the beginning, my wife and I were as poor as Job. I have read, I don't know where, that I started a braces business. That is false. I did sell braces, that is true, but as a street vendor in the gardens of the Retiro in Madrid. But, happily, that poverty did not last for long. I had good friends in Spain, from the period of the Civil War. Soldiers. They helped me. They set me back on my feet. They protected me.

LE: What soldiers?

LD: You would not know them. I have a horror of informing, dear sir. (Note: The protector of Darquier was General Barroso y Sánchez-Guerra.) I became the official translator for the Diplomatic Office. It was I who translated the official speeches of Franco's ministers. I also translated *The Red Book of Gibraltar*. Later, I was able to open a small language school.

LE: And during all this time you were even in the Madrid phone book under your own name, no? You had better luck than Laval. The Spanish extradited him.

LD: Not at all. If he had remained in Madrid, perfectly quietly, as I did, nothing would have happened to him. But one fine day his wife said: 'Let's go back. You've done nothing. They won't dare touch you.' And he went back, to please his wife. You know what followed. They shot him, the poor old thing. Poor ugly old Auvergnat . . .

LE: In thirty-four years, no one came to see you, no one tried to stop you, no one threatened you?

LD: Not a soul . . . Oh yes . . . Three years ago, someone, a French voice, phoned to abuse me. 'Bastard. We're coming to get you.' I was afraid. Not only for me. For my family. I immediately called upon my military friends to ask for their special protection. They immediately gave it. Since then, nothing!

LE: And do you sometimes have regrets? Remorse?

LD: Regrets for what? I don't understand your question.

Interview conducted by Philippe Ganier-Raymond.
© *l'Express*/Philippe Ganier-Raymond/Novembre 1978.
Translation by Carmen Callil.

Appendix II

◄O►

'The Snows of Sigmaringen'
by Louis Aragon

ROM THE PROSECUTOR'S SPEECH at Darquier's trial at the High Court of Justice on 9 December 1947: 'After the Liberation, the poet Louis Aragon composed a ballad about the writers and notable political men of the collaboration. It is Darquier that he chose as its most representative type and it is Darquier's name which recurs like a *leitmotif* at the end of each stanza of the poem ... Gentlemen, I have not reminded you of these verses casually, but because they demonstrate something about that period. Darquier seems like the expression of it, like the symbol and synthesis of all collaborators.'

Louis Aragon, poet, novelist, essayist, one of the founders of Surrealism, political activist and communist, was born on 3 October 1897, two months before Louis Darquier. He was the illegitimate son of a Parisienne and the *préfet* Louis Andrieux, an anticlerical republican and a notable of the Radical Party, like Pierre Darquier. For years Aragon's mother, Marguerite, passed as his sister or his aunt. Aragon lived and went to school in Neuilly. When the First World War broke out he was studying medicine at the medical faculty of the University of Paris, as Jean Darquier was to do. Aragon fought as Louis did, late in the war, in 1917, and for a short time, but won the Croix de Guerre for gallantry. The horrors of the Great War were the same for both of them.

Louis Aragon, lyrical idealist, and Louis Darquier, unruly rascal, were both twenty-two when they were demobbed, and Aragon's family home in Neuilly was only one street away from the Darquier apartment. In May 1919 his squadron leader wrote up Louis Darquier's military record: 'Can and should do very well, on condition that he is well guided, as he is still young and has an influenceable character.'

Louis Aragon became a communist in 1927, and remained dedicated to the Party for most of his life, through the years of Stalin, the purges and the Hungarian uprising.[1] In 1933, under the influence of Action Française, Louis Darquier took the opposite direction. Throughout the Occupation Aragon was always a *résistant*, and his poems and writings of those years are his finest; they came to be symbolic of that underground France which was not Vichy. During the war his mother Marguerite took refuge in Cahors; she died there in March 1942, three weeks before Pierre Darquier, and is buried in the Cahors cemetery as he is. Aragon was in Cahors when she died, attended her funeral and engraved a poem – a beautiful poem – on her tombstone. It is still there, in the same cemetery as the abandoned Darquier tombs. In October 1944, as Louis Darquier crossed over to Spain, Aragon and his fellow writers and *résistants* were honoured by de Gaulle at a ceremony in Paris.

When I asked about Louis Aragon's mother in Cahors, one old woman said that Aragon must have been a Jew: 'All people with the names of a town in France are Jewish. She must have been Jewish otherwise she would not have needed to hide.'

As Louis Darquier married Myrtle Jones and sailed to Australia in 1928, Louis Aragon met Elsa Triolet, the writer and sister-in-law of the Russian poet and dramatist Vladimir Mayakovsky. He married her a decade later; she died two days before Myrtle Darquier, on 16 June 1970. Aragon died in 1982.

The poem was published in *Les Lettres françaises*, no. 43, 17 February 1945, while Pétain and company were still in Sigmaringen.

> *Où est ma cinquième colonne*
> *Seigneur Bergery m'abandonne*
> *J'ai ni Morand ni Chardonne*
> *J'ai vu mourir mon Bichelonne*
> *Où sont mes sbires d'autrefois*
> *C'est déjà la fin de la farce*
> *Où ma garde s'est-elle éparse*
> *Ma cour de nervis et de garces*
> *Où sont dispersés mes comparses*
> *Où est Darquier de Pellepoix*

Qui noircira mes paperasses
Hélas Massis Hélas Maurras
Tous mes beaux encriers s'encrassent
Drieu n'a pas laissé de traces
Ajalbert a fui dans les bois
Céline est caché sous les cendres
Lesdain si doux Béraud si tendre
Laubreaux toujours prêt à se vendre
Où sont-ils Va-t-on me les rendre
Où est Darquier de Pellepoix

Quoi la combine n'est plus bonne
Paul Chack Platon Chiappe Carbone
Bony le colonel Labonne
Philippe Henriot Plus personne
Où est Bonnard ma fleur des pois
Où sont Taittinger Renaitour
Ô Lagardelle Ô mes amours
Quand donc reviendront les beaux jours
Et de Montoire et d'Oradour
Où est Darquier de Pellepoix

Qu'Hitler qui me juge et me voit
Réponde à ce vieillard sans voix
Jusqu'ici fidèle à sa voie
Dans les fourgons de ses convois
Qui vers la honte s'échelonnent
J'ai mis ma confiance en toi
Où sont-ils mes tireurs des toits
Mes panthères et mes putois
Tous mes Darquier de Pellepoix
Où est ma cinquième colonne

'Les Neiges de Sigmaringen' by Louis Aragon
(*L'Oeuvre Poétique: Tome IV, 1942–1952. Quelques Poèmes Inédits.*
Livre Club Diderot)

Where is my fifth column?
Noble Bergery has abandoned me
I am without both Morand and Chardonne
I have seen Bichelonne die
Where are my henchmen of yesteryear?
It's already the end of the farce.
Where has my guard dispersed?
My court of bully boys and bitches
Where have my stooges disappeared?
Where is Darquier de Pellepoix?

Who will write my wretched papers?
Alas Massis Alas Maurras
All my lovely inkwells are clogging up
Drieu has vanished without a trace
Ajalbert has fled to the woods
Céline is hidden under the ashes
Gentle Lesdain affectionate Béraud
Laubreaux ever ready to name his price
Where are they, will they ever be returned to me?
Where is Darquier de Pellepoix?

What, is the game really up?
Paul Chack, Platon, Chiappe, Carbone,
Bony, Colonel Labonne,
Philippe Henriot have all gone
Where is Bonnard, the best of the bunch?
Where are Taittinger, Renaitour
And Lagardelle? Oh my beloved ones
When will the good old days return?
The days of Montoire and Oradour
Where is Darquier de Pellepoix?

Let Hitler be my witness and my judge
And answer this silenced old man
Who has kept his pledge
In the trucks of the convoys
Heading away to shame

I placed my trust in you
Where are my rooftop snipers?
My panthers and howling cats
All my Darquier de Pellepoix
Where is my fifth column?

Translation by David Holland © Carmen Callil

Appendix III

◄◊►

Louis Darquier's
Baronial Inventions

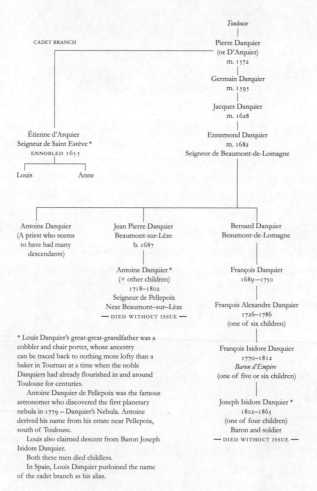

Toulouse

CADET BRANCH

Pierre Darquier
(or D'Arquier)
m. 1572

Germain Darquier
m. 1595

Jacques Darquier
m. 1628

Étienne d'Arquier
Seigneur de Saint Estève *
ENNOBLED 1655

Ennemond Darquier
m. 1682
Seigneur de Beaumont-de-Lomagne

Louis   Anne

Antoine Darquier
(A priest who seems
to have had many
descendants)

Jean Pierre Darquier
Beaumont-sur-Lèze
b. 1687

Bernard Darquier
Beaumont-de-Lomagne

Antoine Darquier *
(+ other children)
1718–1802
Seigneur de Pellepoix
Near Beaumont–sur–Lèze
— DIED WITHOUT ISSUE —

François Darquier
1689—1750

François Alexandre Darquier
1726–1786
(one of six children)

François Isidore Darquier
1770–1812
Baron d'Empire
(one of five or six children)

Joseph Isidore Darquier *
1802–1863
(one of four children)
Baron and soldier
— DIED WITHOUT ISSUE —

* Louis Darquier's great-great-grandfather was a
cobbler and chair porter, whose ancestry
can be traced back to nothing more lofty than a
baker in Tournan at a time when the noble
Darquiers had already flourished in and around
Toulouse for centuries.

Antoine Darquier de Pellepoix was the famous
astronomer who discovered the first planetary
nebula in 1779 – Darquier's Nebula. Antoine
derived his name from his estate near Pellepoix,
south of Toulouse.

Louis also claimed descent from Baron Joseph
Isidore Darquier.

Both these men died childless.

In Spain, Louis Darquier purloined the name
of the cadet branch as his alias.

The Toulouse Nobility

TRAWLING THROUGH HUNDREDS OF old documents of the French state and the French Church was all that was required to trace Louis Darquier's real ancestors, who in the end turned out to be much the same as those of Myrtle Jones.

The noble Darquier *seigneurs* came from Toulouse, and were ennobled for their role as magistrates in that city. The first aristocratic Darquier Louis claimed as his own, the great astronomer Antoine Darquier (1718–1802), died unmarried at eighty-four, a wonderful age for the time, and left everything to his twin sister and her son. Everything included his family estate at Beaumont-sur-Lèze to the south of Toulouse, in which commune is situated the modest Domaine of Pellepoix. It was sensible of Louis Darquier to use the title of de Pellepoix, because no other Darquiers except the astronomer seem ever to have done so.

The family seat of the Darquiers was in Beaumont de Lomagne in the Tarn-et-Garonne, many miles distant from Antoine's seat at Pellepoix. The astronomer's grandfather Ennemond Darquier of Beaumont-de-Lomagne was ennobled in the seventeenth century, and acquired the small château of Pellepoix at that time. It is possible that some ancestor of Louis' real great-great-grandfather Antoine, the baker of Tournan, could have been the grandchild or great-grandchild of a by-blow of Ennemond, but at that point we are in the realm of Adam and Eve, and all of us are aristocrats.

Antoine Darquier de Pellepoix, the astronomer, was the first cousin thrice, or even four times, removed of the Darquier baron who was Louis' second choice as a distinguished ancestor. Baron François Isidore Darquier, great-great-grandson of Ennemond, as a baron d'empire was not an aristocrat of the *ancien régime*. He became a commander of the Imperial Guard, fought and died in the Peninsular Wars in 1812, and was ennobled by Napoleon for his efforts. His son Joseph Isidore Darquier was born in Phalsbourg in the Moselle, far from the Lot, in 1802. He became in turn an excellent soldier, and the second Baron Darquier, and was much decorated and honoured throughout his military career. Like Antoine the astronomer he remained unmarried, and he died on 20 March 1863.

Bernard Avril, Louis Darquier's real great-great-grandfather, born in Martel in 1761, was one of seven children of a wealthy Martel merchant who destined his second son for the priesthood. When Bernard became a priest he did so in revolutionary times, and presumably adapted his

habits to political circumstances. Certainly the new French republic carefully recorded his arrangements with his common-law wife, the four children they had between 1796 and 1804, and their respective marriages
and descendants. Father Bernard Avril lived and died with the spinster
Marie Anne Fazillot, sometimes misspelt Fagillaud, Fagilles, Fazille,
Fazilhot, Fazillaud – she could not write – and their four living children
were all, necessarily, illegitimate, but legally acknowledged by their father
the priest. A decade later, after Father Bernard and his Marie Anne had
died within a year of each other in the same house in Martel, Marie
Anne bequeathed her children only a hat and coat-stand worth forty
francs – all she had in the world; the same inheritance their daughter
Marguerite was to pass on, in her turn, to her son the tax collector.

Pierre Darquier was doubly related to Father Bernard Avril, because
Eugénie's great-grandmother was Elizabeth Avril, sister to the priest.
Jean Joseph Darquier, the gendarme and true husband of Marguerite
Avril, died on 3 March 1841, leaving behind an affecting testament to
his wife Marguerite, who was to outlive him until 1 February 1865. It is
therefore possible that Marguerite of the small town of Martel in the
Lot encountered Baron Joseph Isidore and had an illegitimate child by
him after her husband's death, but Baron Joseph Isidore spent most of
his life, minutely chronicled in his military records, in French barracks
nowhere near the Lot, or at war abroad. Joseph Isidore is a bachelor in
every official file; there is no mention of wives or children in any documents relating to him, only to a niece in Toulouse.

In his military file in Vincennes Joseph Isidore is listed as a bachelor; thus, if he ever married, the military authorities of this distinguished
soldier and baron knew nothing of it, which makes it certain that he
died a bachelor. Even if he broke the habit of a lifetime and took up
with Marguerite Avril after the death of her husband, Baron Joseph
Isidore Darquier was not related to Louis Darquier, whose great-grandfather was Marguerite's husband the gendarme.

These tortuous threads had to be unravelled because in the municipal library of Toulouse the genealogical expert who traced the Darquier
family for me found *La France moderne, Haute-Garonne et Ariège: dictionnaire
généalogique des familles nobles et bourgeoises*, written by Jules Villain, published
in two volumes from 1911 to 1913. There is also a copy of this edition
of the book in the diocesan library in Cahors. In the Toulouse library
copy someone has circled the marriage of Baron Joseph Isidore Darquier

to Marguerite Avril. In the academic year of 1914–15, which began a month after the outbreak of the First World War, Louis Darquier began his studies at the University of Toulouse. The faculty where he studied is only three streets away from rue Darquier, named after, and housing the home of, Antoine the astronomer at number 8, suitably adorned today with a plaque. One can but speculate that Louis Darquier took up the astronomer as his ancestor at this point, that he investigated putative aristocratic Darquiers in the library, found Villain's book and circled the fictitious marriage of his great-grandmother to the unfortunate Baron Joseph Isidore, so adding a second name to his pretensions.

The well-named Villain made a mistake, or perhaps he was paid to do so. In 1913 Pierre Darquier was made a chevalier of the Légion d'honneur for his work as mayor of Cahors, and was also elected as a councillor of the Lot. It is possible that Pierre paid Villain to publish false information about his grandmother, obliterating his policeman grandfather and replacing him with Baron Joseph Isidore, in an attempt to get rid of his ancestral priest.

A distant relative of Louis Darquier in Cahors disclosed that her grandfather, a close friend of Pierre Darquier, had given false family information to a noted *Lotois* genealogist of the time, for 'At the end of the nineteenth century, genealogy became a disease . . . people did everything to discover a noble ancestor: they paid genealogists to find a noble with the same name as themselves . . . and they suppressed ancestry that did not suit them.' Someone in the Darquier family – Louise? – Eugénie? – was sufficiently infected with the genealogical virus to hang a print of Antoine Darquier the astronomer in the family home, and to have to hand the family crest of the noble Darquiers. It is not altogether impossible that Louise favoured such things, and paid Villain to make his mischief and obliterate her husband's true descent from his priestly ancestor. However, though the ascent of Pierre and Louise Darquier to the highest ranks of Cahors society was only recent, both of them were heard to disown Louis' assumed baronetcy of Pellepoix with vigour.

What is more likely is that it was Eugénie, the widow of Jean Darquier the tax collector – who lived long after him – who paid to falsify Villain's records. Louis Darquier's grandparents were the first to acquire bourgeois wealth: Jean was the grandson of the priest, and Eugénie his great-great-niece. What was acceptable for the poor and provincial in the eighteenth century was out of the question for bourgeois French Catholics at the end of the nineteenth.

Later, in Spain, Louis added a third string to his bow with a cadet branch, Ennemond Darquier of Beaumont-de-Lomagne. This was Étienne d'Arquier, Seigneur of Saint-Estève, ennobled in 1655, whose eldest son was named Louis, and whose youngest daughter was named Anne.

To complicate matters already complex, not only did Villain marry Baron Joseph Isidore Darquier to Marguerite Avril, he also gave them a son called Pierre, born on 18 October 1839 in Martel. At that time Marguerite's real husband, the gendarme, was still alive, she had a year-old baby, Henri, and had already given birth to her other three sons: Jean, Louis' grandfather; Guillaume the shoemaker; and the soldier Pierre, born in Martel in 1829, not 1839. Louis would have done well to use this real great-uncle Pierre for his aristocratic assumptions, because he actually could have provided his great-nephew with something to boast about.

This Pierre Darquier, Jean the tax collector's brother, godfather and uncle to Louis' father, was born on 18 October 1829 to Marguerite and her policeman, and his godmother was his grandmother, Marie Anne Fazillot, common-law wife of the priest. He entered the army as an ordinary soldier, but rose through the ranks to corporal, sergeant major, lieutenant and captain, and led his men in distinguished campaigns in Rome, Mexico and in the Franco-Prussian war. He was much decorated and became an officer of the Légion d'honneur, a higher grade than the chevalier achieved by his nephew and godson Pierre, and his military service was far more adventurous than that of Baron Joseph Isidore Darquier. Pierre Darquier the distinguished soldier died only six months before his godson married Louise Laytou.

'The great recipe for success is to work, and to work always,' was a noted saying of the great man of Cahors, Léon Gambetta. Unless his work was with words, writing them, bellowing them, translating them, crowding them onto his bulletins and newspapers, Louis Darquier was allergic to work for most of his life. Reading one erroneous genealogical tome is light work; he did not bother to trace his real ancestors, worthy or otherwise, but purloined the baron, the astronomer instead and the seigneur.

Acknowledgements

THE RESEARCH FOR THIS book has taken me many years. I began knowing almost nothing and by the time I had finished I had travelled the world and had learned, perhaps, more than I cared to know. In that way, working on this project has been exactly like starting the book publishing company I founded in the 1970s, Virago Press. I began on my own, but within a year or two I was surrounded by remarkable young people who took on the project with a passion equal to mine. This time, again, many have helped me, but there is one person without whom this book could not have been written, a young French researcher, Sylvie Deroche.

In a sense I am something of a child of the French, as well as the British Empire – one pair of my grandparents emigrated to Australia from the Lebanon in the 1881. I was brought up hearing French spoken. I remember my parents wearing the cross of Lorraine during the Second World War. Although my childhood was quintessentially Australian, nothing French seemed foreign to me. That said, the complexities of this period of French history, and access to so many institutions, libraries and government departments, could not have been so easily achieved without French assistance. This Sylvie Deroche provided. But more than that, during our years on the trail, she mounted guard, and sustained me with almost daily support, amusement, and information. We became Sherlock Holmes and Doctor Watson – on occasion alternating roles. In our pursuit – sometimes together, often apart – we spent days and weeks in European archives; we interviewed hundreds of citizens and subjects of France, Spain and Belgium. My heartfelt gratitude goes first to her.

A younger generation of the Darquier family talked to me at length and over many years. I am especially grateful for the patience and tolerance extended to me by Anne's half-sister in Spain. The co-operation of René's children, two of whom talked to and corresponded with me (I was unable to meet the third), was equally indispensable. I am deeply grateful to them for the information they gave me, the errors they

corrected, for reading the final manuscript with forbearance and understanding, and for their kindness throughout.

May Brice, with whom Anne Darquier spent so many of her younger
years, had one son, Alistair Rapley, Anne's godson. As the great-nephew
also of Elsie and Maud Lightfoot, he provided me with invaluable information and with tireless support. Alistair Rapley opened up his family
files to me and often accompanied me on research and interview trips
to Great Tew and Oxfordshire. In London, many of Anne's friends,
doctors and otherwise – those who studied with her and those who
worked with her and some of her pupils and patients – allowed me to
talk to them about Anne time and again. Amongst those doctors my
greatest debt is to Griffith Edwards and Mary Coghlan who continued
to help me as the years rolled by, and who read and commented on my
final manuscript.

I had other exceptional pieces of good fortune. In Cahors, a woman
overheard me asking about the Darquier family when I was in the *Archives
Diocésaines*. This was Paulette Aupoix. She approached me, told me she
was distantly related to the Darquiers and gave me family letters and
photographs going back to the eighteenth century. I am greatly in debt
to her and to Simone Reste, who had worked for Louise Darquier over
many years. Both these women of the Lot aided me in more ways than
I can enumerate. I am indebted to Jacques Marques of Cahors for expert
genealogical research and to the enthusiastic research assistance of Pierre
Wolf. I benefited in particular from an exchange of ideas and from the
information supplied by Laurent Joly, French historian of Vichy France
and author of a biography of Xavier Vallat and a study of Darquier de
Pellepoix and French anti-Semitism.

In Australia, when I went to the house where Myrtle was born, the
beautiful Freshwater Point which slopes down to the Tamar River, a
Jones relation followed me down to the river bank and told me I was
asking about his family. Myrtle was an inveterate letter writer, and kept
in touch with her Tasmanian family throughout her life. Myrtle's
remaining sisters held many of the secrets about Myrtle and Louis' life
in Tasmania and in Europe, in the correspondence she kept up with
them and all her family there. This correspondence was not made available to me. Anyone who lives in these decades of tabloid journalism will
be sympathetic to the position of Anne's elderly Tasmanian relatives,
and I am. I am grateful therefore to the younger generation of Joneses,

who knew little or nothing about their great-aunt's story, for what information they felt they could give me.

In Great Tew and Oxfordshire, Robin Denniston – once publisher of Oxford University Press, and my landlord at one point in my Virago years – turned out to be the Vicar of St Michael and All Angels, the very beautiful local church in Great Tew. He put me in touch with many of the old people in Great Tew who remembered Anne and Elsie. I owe a great debt to him, to his late wife Rosa and to the people of Great Tew and Kidlington who so willingly helped me.

My most persistent debt is to my friends, for so many years of moral support and encouragement. Suzanne Lowry, Paris Correspondent for the *Daily Telegraph* in the 1990s, introduced me to Sylvie Deroche. David Malouf first told me to write this story; Robert Skidelsky read my work at a very early stage, set me on the correct narrative path and gave me constant, and much needed, encouragement. Antony Beevor gave me splendid advice at the beginning of my task and both Margaret Atwood, Edmund White and the late Ian Ousby helped me in the early days. Towards the end, Jenny Uglow heroically read and honed my vast manuscript. I am especially beholden to those friends who read, and commented on, my work-in-progress: Susannah Clapp, Peter Conrad, Polly Devlin, Philippa Harrison, James Herrick, Suzanne Lowry, Hilary McPhee, Diana Melly, Frances Stonor Saunders. Many faithful friends read my first efforts and helped me continuously on my way: Hanan Al Shaykh, Louis Baum, Liz Calder, Christine Carswell, Frances Coady, Kate Griffin, John Hayes, Michael Holroyd, Helena Kennedy, Craig Raine, Gail Rebuck, Deborah Rogers, Gus Skidelsky, Harriet Spicer, Colm Tóibín, Marina Warner. Their friendship, company and interest and that of Julian Barnes, Margaret Drabble, Caroline Conran, Anna Coote, Nell Dunn, Peter Eyre, Jeff Fisher, Lennie Goodings, Pat Kavanagh, Nick Lander, Sonny and Gita Mehta, Kate Metcalfe, Lynn Nesbit, Deirdre O'Day, Dan Oestreicher, Jancis Robinson, Michael Siefert and Don Watson lightened my days.

In France, I owe a considerable debt to the inhabitants of Caunes Minervois in the Aude, where I wrote much of this book, and in particular to years of French happiness with Simone and James Herrick, Christopher Hope and Ingrid Hudson, much of it fuelled by a continual supply of good meals provided by Frédéric Guiraud at the Hotel d'Alibert.

In London Karin Syrett, Delfina de Freitas, Jenny Ledger, Jimmy, Ian and Richard Carter and his team, Stanley Rosenthal, Damian Corr, Gregory Micallef, Dr Diane Watson, Louise and Charles Voyantzis, Sophi Stewart, Graham Smith, Keith Butt, Tessa Brown, Deborah and Louis made my daily life possible. Deborah Rogers was always there for me at the best and worst of times as were Liz Calder, Gail Rebuck and Philippa Harrison. The unfailing friendship, commiseration and common sense of Diana Melly requires a special tribute, as does the constant infusion of energetic brilliance from Frances Stonor Saunders.

In Australia, my friend Hilary McPhee has been a generous and enthusiastic reader from the beginning, as has her brother, Peter McPhee, Professor of History and Deputy Vice-Chancellor at the University of Melbourne. He opened many doors for me and, like Robert Skidelsky, was an important historical guide for all my researches. I am also grateful to Dr Julie Evans for early research assistance, to Mimi Corrigan and above all to the indefatigable Lucille V. Andel. Particular thanks to Charles 'Chips' Sowerwine, Professor in the Department of History at the University of Melbourne, who read my finished manuscript with expert knowledge and understanding and gave me excellent advice on finer points, and to my old friend Christine Downer, then at the State Library of Victoria. My Australian family, Julian, Sue and Adrian Callil, were always there for me, my brother Julian in particular with essential counsel on the minutiae of Australian financial matters.

In London, Helena Ivins helped me more than I can say. Her early researches into Anne's life sent me correctly on my way, and her work and support in Spain, and as a friend and research companion, I gratefully acknowledge as I do the work of Judy Collingwood, Joshua White, Becky Swift and Peter Bennett. Thanks to Selina Hastings for disciplinary advice, to Patrick Marnham for his help with the airfields of Enstone, to Robert McCrum for the peregrinations of P. G. Wodehouse, to Peter Kessler for information about Theodor Dannecker and his family, to Roy Foster for the writings of Hubert Butler. Exceptional Spanish research, advice and knowledge was provided by Gerard Howson whose remarkable book *Arms for Spain* is a model of historical investigation and revelation. Special thanks are due to Cristina Rivas whose enthusiasm for the project and detailed research work into many mysterious Spanish archives was of inestimable help, as was Klemens Rothig's similar effort in Germany.

I am grateful to all my publishers: to Peter Straus, then of Picador, who first commissioned this book, to Sonny Mehta of Knopf who understood it immediately, and to Michael Fishwick, Robert Lacey, Caroline Michel and the team at HarperCollins, London who first edited it. A special thank you goes to my publisher Dan Franklin at Jonathan Cape and to my wise and tireless editor, Ellah Allfrey; to Alex Milner, Christian Lewis, David Parrish and Suzanne Dean, to all the Cape team in particular and the staff of Random House in general.

I would like to express my gratitude to all those who agreed to be interviewed, sometimes more than once, and to the librarians and staff in the libraries and institutions of so many countries who provided important information and assistance over the years. All these names and organisations are listed on page 591, but a mere list cannot express my obligation to them all. Amongst so many, special acknowledgement is due to the *CDJC*, the *Centre de Documentation Juive Contemporaine* in Paris (now renamed *Mémorial de la Shoah, Musée, Centre de Documentation Juive Contemporaine*). Its exceptional repositories continually enabled me to unravel the inner workings of persons often hidden from history.

All those entering these byways owe an especial acknowledgement of the work of the historian Joseph Billig, whose truths about the Vichy years were first published in 1955. In the near decade during which I worked on this book, when I told people what I was writing about, so often I received a response about the need for a book such as this: a book which might require the French to face up to their past, something which might wake them up from their wilful amnesia about the Vichy years. I did not really begin intensive research into the life of Louis Darquier until the 1990s and by then, not only had the French faced up to their collaboration with Nazi Germany, notably in their treatment of their Jewish population, but more, I was swamped by the number of books, articles and research sources open to them, and to me. Much of this is due to the great historians of this period, not all of them French of course, but many were, and are. Their works are listed within the bibliography on page 578 but I would like to express a particular debt to the following historians who were my daily companions in my work, as was Dr Simon Kitson's excellent website at Birmingham University: *http://artsweb.bham.ac.uk/vichy/*

Jacques Adler

Philippe Burrin

Robert F. Byrnes
Joachim Fest
Bertram M. Gordon
W. D. Halls
Stanley Hoffman
Julian Jackson
Laurent Joly
Tony Judt
H. R. Kedward
Serge Klarsfeld
Pierre Laborie
Michael Marrus
Ernst Nolte
Denis Peschanski
Henry Rousso
Robert Soucy
John F. Sweets
Pierre-André Taguieff
Edward R. Tannenbaum

Special thanks to David-Paul Holland who remained at my beck and call over difficult translations for so many years. The majority of original translations in this book are by him, or myself. Most Spanish translations are by Helena Ivins or Cristina Rivas. Some German translations are by Klemens Rothig. Some French translations are by Sylvie Deroche, Rebecca Palmer or Simon Pleasance.

My agent Gill Coleridge of Rogers Coleridge and White has been a crucial tower of strength, efficiency and understanding throughout, and to her, and Lucy Luck and others at that agency, I am truly grateful.

Carmen Callil
London
December 2005

Notes

◄O►

The notes for each chapter are preceded by a list of individuals who provided the author with information used in that chapter, original documents and published material quoted, consulted or referred to; this should be read in conjunction with the list of abbreviations below. Complete details of interviews, correspondence, and of archives and other primary sources consulted by the author may be found in the list of sources at the end of the Bibliography.

ABBREVIATIONS

AAPA: Staasbibliothek, Berlin. Political Archives of the German Foreign Ministry. Bonn AAPA, Akten zur Deutschen Auswärtigen Politik, 1918–1945. Aus dem Archiv des Auswärtigen Amts

AGA: Archivo General de la Administración, Alcalá de Henares, Paseo Aquadores, 2, 28804, Alcalá de Henares, Madrid

AGA (a): Ministerio de Educaciòn y Ciencia, Relaciones de Personal de Idiomas. Antiguas Plantillas 1960/70 93352, Ref. 3/91

AGA (b): Ministerio de Cultura No. IDD 49.23, Signatura 54.401

AGA (f): AE (Asuntos Exteriores) No. IDD 97, Signatura 11.619 and 11.649

AMAE: Archivo del Ministerio de Asuntos Exteriores, Departamentos Ministeriales, Madrid, Fondo 1.2.1.2

AMAE (a): Archivo del Consulado de España en Hendaya, Embajada de España en Francia 1939–44

AMAE (b): Politica: Información y Negociaiones, R-2295

AMAE (c): Información Politica Interior de Francia 1943–44, R-1179

AMAE (d): Salida de Alemania para España de periodistas franceses, R-2167

AMAE (e): Segunda Guerra Mundial, Francia: Immigrantes Clandestinos de Francia, R-2182

AMAE (f): Judios en Francia, R-1715

AN: Archives Nationales, Paris

AN 3W142: Dossier d'Instruction de Louis Darquier, at the Archives Nationales, Paris

AN 3W142-KNO: Dossier d'Instruction de Louis Darquier. Statement of
 Helmut Knochen, 4 January 1947
AN 3W147 and AN 3W156: Berlin Archives at the Archives Nationales, Paris
APP: Archives de la Préfecture de Police, Paris
APP GA D9: Louis Darquier's file, Archives de la Préfecture de Police, Paris
APP GA R4: Rassemblement Antijuif de France file, Archives de la Préfecture
 de Police, Paris
BCRA: Bureau Central de Renseignements et d'Action (Free French Centre for
 Intelligence and Action), London
BMO: Bulletin Municipal Officiel, Bibliothèque de la Mairie de Paris
BNF: Bibliothèque Nationale de France
CAC: Centre des Archives Contemporaines, Fontainebleau, France
CDJC: Centre de Documentation Juive Contemporaine, Paris, now renamed
 Mémorial de la Shoah Centre de Documentation Juive Contemporaine
INA: Institut National de l'Audiovisuel, Direction d'Archives Phonothèques,
 Paris
PAF: Correspondence between family members of Paulette Aupoix and the
 Darquier family
RG: Renseignements Généraux
SHAT: Service Historique de l'Armée de Terre, Vincennes
SRD: Simone Reste: Correspondence and interviews with the author, 1999–2006;
 Souvenirs de Vichy 1940–1945. An account of the Vichy years in St-Paul-de-
 Loubressac, written for the author by Simone Reste, June 2001.
Tasmania J: The information in these notes comes from correspondence and
 telephone conversations with members of the Jones family.
TNA: PRO: The National Archives, Public Record Office, Kew

PROLOGUE

SOURCES: AN 3W142; CDJC DLV1–132. PUBLICATIONS: Klarsfeld, *French Children
of the Holocaust*

1 **Adolf Eichmann** (1906–62): Austrian Nazi whose office organised everything
   to do with the Final Solution, ranging from gassing techniques to death camps
   to train timetables. By August 1944 he could acknowledge to Himmler that his
   achievement was the death of six million Jews: four million in the death camps,
   two million in mobile units. He escaped to Argentina in 1946, was abducted
   to Israel in 1960 and tried in 1961. Eichmann was executed for crimes against
   the Jewish people and crimes against humanity.

CHAPTER I

The Priest's Children

INTERVIEWS AND CORRESPONDENCE: Madame Andrieu, Paulette Aupoix, Colette Calmon, Pierre Combes, Philippe Deladerrière, Alain Dubrulle, Jean Gayet, Pierre Gayet, Yvonne Lacaze, Père Lucien Lachièze-Rey, Pierre Orliac, Pierre Pouzergues, Simone Reste. SOURCES: PAF; SRD; Rapport du Commissaire de police de Cahors au Préfet du Lot, 23 May 1910; Rapports mensuels du Préfet du Lot au ministre de l'intérieur en vue des élections législatives de 1910; Table de décès de Cahors 3Q 16.4; TNA: PRO FO 371/31939–2300, Z3005; TNA: PRO FO 892/163. PUBLICATIONS: Abbellan, *Contribution à l'étude de la société Lotoise sous la IIIème République*; Arnal, *Ambivalent Alliance*; Binion, *Defeated Leaders*; Joly, *Darquier de Pellepoix et l'antisémitisme français*; Nolte, *Three Faces of Fascism*; Tannenbaum, *The Action Française*

1 Philippe Deladerrière, December 1998.

2 In 1907 the grocery shop was first rented, then sold, to the Bertrand family, whose shop it is today.

3 Contract of marriage between Jean Joseph Darquier and Marguerite Avril, 24 February 1827.

4 Charcot treated hysteria through hypnosis. He was a great influence on Freud. Louis' brother Jean took up neurology, and after Anne met Jean in 1946, she took up psychiatry.

5 Louise Darquier: SRD. Pierre Orliac, January 1999; Jean Gayet, November 1999. Pierre Gayet/Colette Calmon: Pierre Gayet, January 2000. All interviews say the same thing about Pierre Darquier's womanising – and the same about the two elder Darquier boys too.

6 Paulette Aupoix, January 1999 and February 2000.

7 Binion, p. 8.

8 Louis himself was never much interested in the Dreyfus case, and was criticised by Charles Maurras for this.

9 Philippe Deladerrière, December 1998.

10 SRD.

11 Mme Andrieu, January 2000.

12 Paulette Aupoix, April 2000.

13 **Anatole de Monzie** (1876–1947); PRO FO 892/163. Biography of de Monzie.

14 PRO FO 371/319 39 – Z3005.

15 SRD.

16 Pierre Orliac, January 1999.

17 Pierre Combes, January 2000.

18 Louis Darquier, *La France enchaînée*, no. 7, 4–18 June 1938. Article entitled

'Peut-on se dire National et ne pas être antijuif', quoted by Joly, *Darquier de Pellepoix*, p. 51.

19 *L'Express*, 4 November 1978.

20 Arnal, p. 38, note 18.

21 Père Lachièze-Rey, January 1999.

22 Paulette Aupoix, January 1999.

23 Abbellan, p. 239; *La Défense*, 18 May 1920.

24 Tannenbaum, p. 52.

25 **Édouard Drumont** (1844–1917): Deputy for Algiers 1898–1902. He was hailed by all anti-Semites before, during and after the Vichy years as the source of French anti-Semitic theory and principle. An illustrated edition of *La France Juive*, published in 1887, contained 'three illustrations of ritual murder, one of Huguenot atrocities, and three of Jewish and Masonic responsibility for anti-clericalism. The closing illustration depicted the pious Drumont, prayer beads in hand, saying a devout Our Father and Hail Mary for France.' 'Everything comes from the Jew, everything returns to the Jew,' was Drumont's classic exposition of the Jew as the persecutor of Catholics and the French Catholic Church, for which service the book was much praised in Catholic papers such as *La Croix*. Jews became the scapegoat, a position they shared with Freemasons, considered responsible for the separation of Church and state in France in 1905, and so perpetrators of the anticlerical hostility of republican France towards the French Catholic Church. In Drumont many strands of French anti-Semitism converged, for Drumont and his most important disciples often called upon a conservative version of socialism as part of their mass appeal. His widow lived on until the Occupation to honour his followers with her presence at anti-Semitic events. In 1963 a group of his literary followers – Maurice Bardèche, Xavier Vallat, Henry Coston – his 'friends' – gathered to celebrate his work, particularly his thoughts on *The Protocols of the Elders of Sion*. A support group seemingly still defends his memory in Paris today.

26 **Alphonse Daudet** (1840–97): found Drumont a publisher and persuaded a friend to review *La France Juive* in *Figaro*, after which controversy began. The publisher was Marpon et Flammarion. Drumont had to pay for the first print run himself; by 1886, after the review, it had sold 100,000 copies.

27 **The Marquis de Morès** (1858–96): After reading Drumont's *La France Juive*, he founded the Ligue Antisémitique Nationale de France with Drumont. Morès fell out with Drumont, as Darquier was to fall out with Maurras. The history of French anti-Semitism is more complex and more peopled than this brief description of its exponents; these are the ones who influenced Louis Darquier most.

28 A truer translation of *métèques* might be 'wogs'.

29 Arnal, p. 68, note 9.

30 One of Maurras' joys during the German occupation was that Jewish street

names were changed; in coming years Louis was to spend a great deal of time endeavouring to change the names of various Paris streets to rue Drumont.

31 **Maurice Pujo** (1872–1955): Journalist and co-founder of Action Française, at Maurras' side for decades, including their trial together and their imprisonment. Released in 1947, he ran the post-war reincarnation of Action Française, Restauration Nationale, and its paper, *Aspects de la France*, until his death.

32 Nolte, p. 131.

33 'As we might expect, the reports of the provincial police show a great many names with a particule and, in the Gironde for instance, seven out of ten section presidents were titled. But not all the titles carried the same weight, and after clashes between royalists and communists occurred in the little Berrichon town of Blanc (Indre) in August 1926, a letter in *L'Oeuvre* (3 September), signed Marie de Comines, denounced the assumed nobility of Action Française supporters, whose members had enriched themselves at the expense of the native aristocracy, sometimes by buying up Church and emigrants' land in Revolutionary times' (AN F713200ff; AN F713203, 7 July 1931).

34 **Antoine Darquier de Pellepoix** (1718–1802): Darquier's astronomical observations between 1748 and 1773, *Observations Astronomiques faites à Toulouse*, were published in 1777. While searching for the comet of 1779 he discovered the Ring Nebula (M57) in January 1779. Nebulae are the dying remains of stars, 'a curiosity of the heavens'. Stars die, and as they do so they become more and more unstable, and the strong stellar winds leave behind a black hole, a nebula, extremely hot, radiating energy. Darquier's Nebula has a dark hole in its centre, and is 'a very dull nebula, but perfectly outlined' (see www.klima-luft.de/steinicke/ngcic/persons/darquier.htm).

CHAPTER 2

The Convicts' Kin

INTERVIEWS AND CORRESPONDENCE: Pierre Gayet, Jenny Gill, Paul McFarlane, Beryl Stevenson. SOURCES: Olive Jones, 'Morning Coffee Talk,' Queen Victoria Museum and Art Gallery Community History Department, Launceston, 27 February 1991. PUBLICATIONS: Abbellan, *Contribution à l'étude de la société Lotoise sous la IIIème République*; Alméras, *Je suis le bouc*; Arnal, *Ambivalent Alliance*; Binion, *Defeated Leaders*; Boisjoslin, *A Travers les rues de Cahors*; Byrnes, *Antisemitism in Modern France*, vol. 1; Louis Darquier, *'Peut-on se dire National et ne pas être antijuif?'*, *La France enchaînée*, no. 7, 4–18 June 1938; *La Défense*, 18 May 1920; *l'Express*, 4 November 1978; Cornwell, *Hitler's Pope*; Crémieux-Brilhac, *Les Français de l'an 40*; Downer, *All the Rage: 150 Years of Posters, State Library in Victoria News*, June–August 2001; Guy, *The Cyclopedia of*

Tasmania: An Epitome of Progress; Halls, *Politics, Society and Christianity in Vichy France*; Jolly, *Dictionnaire des parlementaires français*; Joly, *Darquier de Pellepoix et l'antisémitisme français*; Laborie, *Résistants, vichyssois et autres*; Lartigaut, *Histoire du Quercy*; Molinié, *Enfance à Cahors*; Nolte, *Three Faces of Fascism*; Planté, *Un Grand seigneur de la politique*; Tannenbaum, *1900*; Tannenbaum, *The Action Française*; Weber, *Action Française*; Weber, *France, Fin de Siècle*

1 Pierre Gayet, February 2000.
2 Guy, p. 388.
3 Australia's second penal colony, on Norfolk Island, was established in 1789.
4 Guy, p. 402.
5 Downer, p. 2.
6 Britton Jones's criminal record continued: 30 November 1825 – Harbouring a convict to tipple in his house, fined sixteen shillings; 22 November 1826 – Riding in his cart without reins, fined twenty shillings; 29 December 1827 – Riding in his cart on the Highway without reins, fined twenty shillings; 29 December 1827 – Swearing two profane Oaths in the Police Office, fined four shillings; 8 January 1832 – Obstructing the Chief District Constable in the execution of his duty, reprimand; 17 March 1831 – Committing a Breach of the Peace by assisting in rescuing a prisoner from the Constable, fined £5 and sureties to keep the peace for six months.
7 Hector Jones, 'The Jones Family', revised by Vernon Jones, 1960 and 1971, Launceston Reference Library, Local Studies Library. Hector refers to this portrait in his documents and there seems to be some portrait in Launceston which Britton Jones senior painted, but no research could connect any of this to George III.
8 The Free Church of Scotland was formed after the Great Disruption of 1843, when Evangelicals split from the established Church of Scotland.
9 The Morrison family were respected members of the Kirk. Most of them are now buried in an isolated cemetery at Winkleigh, north of Launceston.
10 Olive Room, 'Morning Coffee Talk,' 27 February 1991.
11 *ibid.*

CHAPTER 3

Soldier's Heart

SOURCES: Archives Departmentale: Confidential report on Action Française, 29 March 1911, intercepted by Paris police; Archives Municipales de Neuilly: census of 1921; Australian War Memorial statistics; Louise Darquier's wartime correspondence; Lycée Gambetta list of decorations of past pupils; AN 3W142, Dossier militaire de Louis Darquier; CDJC LXII-11; SHAT JMO 49 RAC; SHAT JMO 3CR 26N876; SHAT, Dossier militaire de Pierre Darquier, no. 149923; Will Jones War Record: a) National Archives of Australia, Canberra, World War I Personnel Records Service, Access and Information Service, and b) Australian War Memorial Research Centre, Canberra: William Robert Jones, No. 8911. PUBLICATIONS: Abbellan, *Contribution à l'étude de la société Lotoise sous la IIIème République*; Atkin, *Pétain*; Atkinson, *The Europeans in Australia*, vol. 1; Audoin-Rouzeau, *Men at War 1914–1918*; Bean, *Anzac to Amiens*; Bean, *The Australian Imperial Force in France*; Becker, *The Great War and the French People*; Burton, *The Australian Army Medical Services in the War of 1914–1918*; *La Défense*, 17 June 1923; Grant, *A Dictionary of Military History*; Hamilton, *The Appeal of Fascism*; *l'Histoire*, no. 107, January 1988; Horner, *The Gunners*; Keegan, *The First World War*; Lottman, *Pétain, Hero or Traitor?*; *Marianne*, 9–15 November 1998; Weber, *Action Française*; Weber, *The Nationalist Revival in France*

1 Monseigneur, later Cardinal Baudrillart. Weber, *The Nationalist Revival in France*, p. 144.
2 Pierre's military file is excessively complimentary; Jean Gayet said 'he had not been very courageous at the front'.
3 Quoted by Becker, p. 170.
4 French casualty figures from Keegan, p. 146.
5 Louise Darquier: PAF, 1916.
6 AN 3W142, Louis Darquier military file.
7 Alec Raws, Victorian 23 battalion (see www.users.netconnect.com.-au/~ianmac/Pozières.html).
8 SHAT, Pierre Darquier military file no. 149923.
9 AN 3W142, Louis Darquier military file.
10 Burton, p. 99ff.
11 Horner, p. 161.
12 October 1917 was the second time in a year that Australia had been convulsed by its government's attempts to bring in conscription. Each time, the Australians who thought of themselves as British were defeated by those who did not.
13 Atkins, p. 23, quoting Fayolle.
14 *Fourragère*: honorary insignia, worn on the left shoulder, awarded to military units (and automatically awarded to all members of the decorated unit).
15 Horner, p. 168.
16 Louis Darquier is not mentioned amongst the wounded, nor is he listed amongst the wounded for the month of April 1918.
17 Louise Darquier, PAF.
18 AN 3W142. The letter is in his military file.
19 *ibid.*
20 *ibid.*
21 National Archives of Australia. World War I Personnel Records Service.

Dossier: no. 8911 Jones, W. R. Findings of the Court of Inquiry, 9 June 1919: Inquiring into the death of 8911 Sapper William Robert Jones of Second Australian Divisional Signal Company.

22 AN 3W142, Louis Darquier military file.

23 **Henri-Philippe Pétain** (1856–1951): born in a village in Pas-de-Calais, that part of northern France which most resembles England. Of peasant stock and Catholic education, the army cemented these early conservative and rural influences. After a long and undistinguished military career, Pétain's life and reputation were revolutionised by the First World War, which offered him rapid promotion. Three-quarters of the French army served at Verdun, and thus he was the hero of almost all the eight million French soldiers who survived the war. Constantly seen as a symbol of national unity, as a republican marshal, as a leader in waiting, behind his carefully maintained public persona he remained an ambitious man, always pessimistic, suspicious and vain, hostile to a parliamentary government and its politicians, to Bolsheviks, socialists and Freemasons, and wedded to military tactics which were to be disastrous for France in the decades which followed the war. Between 1920 and 1939, Pétain remained a key military figure and adviser, sat on or headed a multitude of military committees and posts, and was omnipresent in the formulation of French military policy. He became ambassador to Spain in March 1939, after which he fulfilled H.G. Wells's most apt description of his strange personality as 'an artlessly sincere megalomaniac'. Pétain maintained a life of constant womanising before and after his marriage in 1920, at the age of sixty-four, to the divorcée Eugénie Hardon; she remained loyal to him until his death in exile, senile and suffering from hallucinations, at the age of ninety-five. The *Association pour Défendre La Mémoire du Maréchal Pétain*, whose honorary chairman until 1965 was Maxime Weygand, continues to campaign for Pétain's rehabilitation.

24 **Maxime Weygand** (1867–1965): Not French, but a wiry and dapper Belgian who looked like 'an aged jockey'. A vigorous Catholic, Weygand matched every opinion Pétain kept carefully to himself with outspoken dabbling in most of the right-wing movements of the post-war period. Said to be the illegitimate son of, perhaps, Leopold II, King of Belgium, or of the king's sister Carlotta, wife of Emperor Maximilian of Mexico, or possibly of others, he shared Louis Darquier's violent anti-Semitism – and like Darquier lived in an aura of ancestral mysteries, real or imagined. He also shared an inability to take orders, a passion for giving them and considerable indulgence in intemperate behaviour. Weygand was anti-Dreyfus, deeply influenced by Charles Maurras, close to la Roque and Croix-de-feu, he was a hero of Taittinger's and rumoured to be an honorary member of Jeunesses Patriotes. As an army man who more than dabbled in politics, in 1936 Weygand was devastated by the election of the Popular Front in general, and hysterical about Léon Blum, the Jew, in particular.

52. Louis Darquier on his appointment as Commissioner for Jewish Affairs
for the Vichy government, May 1942.

53. Xavier Vallat, Vichy's first Commissioner for Jewish Affairs, at
his desk at the Paris headquarters of the Commissariat,
which were in Louis Louis-Dreyfus' appropriated
bank, Place des Petits-Pères, Paris, 1941.

54. Joseph Antignac, Louis' chief of staff in the Commissariat, the real power behind
the throne during and after Louis' tenure.

55. Monseigneur Mayol de Lupé, chaplain of the LVF, who liked to end Mass with the cry 'Heil Hitler!' At an LVF demonstration at the Paris sports stadium, the Vélodrome d'Hiver, April 1944.

56. René Bousquet, Vichy's Secretary-General for the Police, the zealous and efficient civil servant who organised the Jewish deportations to Auschwitz. With him, outside the Hôtel du Parc in Vichy, are the SS General in France, Karl-Albrecht Oberg, SS chief Helmut Knochen and his deputy, Herbert-Martin Hagen.

57. François Mitterrand, President of France 1981–95, connected through his family and his own activities to extremists and men of Vichy and protector of many after the Liberation, when he worked himself for L'Oréal. Friend and defender of René Bousquet, here seen dining with him in 1974.

58. The Schloss Collection, one of the most important private art collections in France, shown here before the war in the Long Gallery of the Adolphe Schloss residence, 38, Avenue Henri-Martin, Paris. Hidden at the Occupation, Louis masterminded its discovery, sale and disbursement to Hitler and an assortment of other German and French raptors.

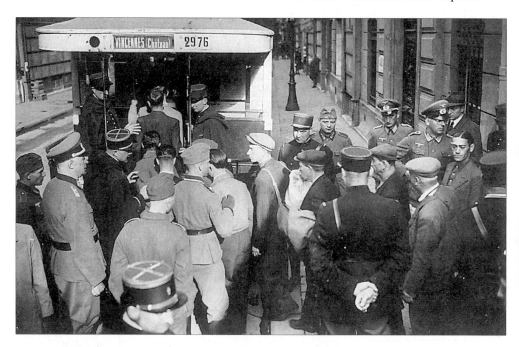

59. René Bousquet ensured that his French police force worked closely with their German counterparts to collect and transport Jews to the death camps. Here Nazi and French services oversee Jewish arrests.

60. Jewish men, women and children in Drancy concentration camp in Paris, 3 December 1942, a photograph taken by a German, Wagner, who worked in the Propaganda office in Paris.

61. Jewish women and children at Drancy on the same day: here you can see more clearly the yellow star Louis ensured that they wear.

62. The Nazis enabled Louis and Myrtle, on the far right of this picture, to wine and dine as they liked to do. Louis, paid by both Vichy and the Nazis, gave and attended sumptuous celebrations during his tenure as Commissioner for Jewish Affairs.

63. Louis launches yet another of his anti-Semitic ventures: this time it is his Institute of Anthropo-Sociology in Paris, December 1942. A thinner Myrtle stands looking dazed.

64. Great Tew, Oxfordshire, showing the Falkland Arms pub where Anne Darquier lived during the war, and to which she often returned after it.

65. The wedding of May Brice to Gilbert Rapley, September 1948, with Anne as bridesmaid. She is eighteen. Maud Lightfoot Haynes (Aunty Maud) is on the far left. Next to Anne is the rest of the Lightfoot family, Arthur Haynes, Annie (Lightfoot) Lewis (mother of May), Aunty Violet, Newton and Elsie Lightfoot.

66. Elsie Lightfoot in 1961.

67. Anne aged twelve.

68. Louis in Madrid, walking down the Gran Via, some time in the 1960s, when his worst years as an exile were over and he was working for many of Franco's government departments as a translator.

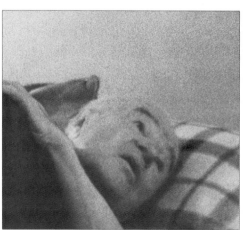

69. Louis Darquier photographed by Juana Biarnés, the photographer who accompanied Philippe Ganier-Raymond to interview Louis for *l'Express* in 1978. Louis was not dying, but liked to keep to his bed or wicker chair.

70. 59 Weymouth Street, London W1, where Anne died, in flat number 38, on 7 September 1970, four days after her fortieth birthday.

In June 1939 he claimed, 'The French army is greater than it has ever been in its history.' In May 1940 Weygand lasted for less than a month as Allied commander-in-chief, during which time he relentlessly bewailed the military position he was brought in to rectify, opining that France should never have declared war in the first place. After the fall of France, loyal to Pétain, he reconstituted the French army in North Africa, was arrested by the Germans in 1942 and kept prisoner until 1945.When he was freed in 1945 he was immediately re-arrested. Weygand was finally cleared of charges of treason in 1948 and lived on to join almost every reactionary movement of the post-war period. He published his most unreliable memoirs, *Recalled to Service*, in 1950, which justify, lengthily, his military inadequacies.

25 **General Noël-Marie-Joseph-Édouard de Curières de Castelnau** (1851–1944): Aristocrat and soldier. In 1924 this devout Catholic, dedicated anti-communist and First World War general formed the Fédèration Nationale Catholique. By 1925 it numbered two million supporters throughout France, and voiced its thoughts in extremist Catholic newspapers, the most important of which was the daily paper of the Assumptionist order, *La Croix*. 'If Hitler rises against communism and manifests an intention to suppress it, or at least to vigorously fight it, such a project can only meet with general approval,' wrote *La Croix* in 1933. The FNC was the favourite child of the Vatican, and many Catholics of the FNC were members of Action Française until 1926, when it came under papal interdiction. This was a tremendous blow for practising Catholics of the AF, 'an agonising drama, sometimes a real calvary'. Many of them moved en bloc to the FNC, though the two movements still worked closely together. From both came the devotion, so strong in Pétain and his men of Vichy, to the sacred soil of France, *la patrie*, the Fatherland, and both were to spawn yet more nationalist splinter groups, which called themselves leagues, formed to fight against the republic.

CHAPTER 4

Scandal and Caprice

INTERVIEWS AND CORRESPONDENCE: Colette Calmon, Michael de Bertadano, Jean Gayet, Pierre Gayet, Bertrand Leary, Jean Lindoerfer, Pierre Orliac, Teresa. SOURCES: Darquier family correspondence; CDJC LXII; CDJC XXXV-2; Olive Jones, 'Morning Coffee Talk', Queen Victoria Museum and Art Gallery Community History Department, Launceston, 27 February 1991; PAF; TNA: PRO FO 892/163. PUBLICATIONS: Cobb, *Promenades*; *La Croix*, 14 February 1933; *Les Dernières nouvelles de Strasbourg*, 7 April 1937; Field, *British and French Writers of the First World War*; Gee, *Keeping up with the Joneses*; Goodfellow, *Between the Swastika and the Cross of Lorraine*; Gordon, 'Fascism, the Neo-Right and Gastronomy'; Gun, *Pétain, Laval, de Gaulle*; Hamilton, *The Appeal of Fascism*; Joly, *Darquier de Pellepoix et l'antisémitisme français*; *Journal d'Alsace et de Lorraine*, 9 April 1937; Laborie, *Quercy Recherche*, May–June 1979; *Launceston Examiner*, Harry Jones obituary, 11 February 1929; Planté, *Un Grand seigneur de la politique*; Soucy, *French Fascism*, vol. 2; *The Stage*, 10 May 1923; *Sydney Mail*, 1 August 1923; Thurman: *Secrets of the Flesh*; *The Times*, 4 May 1923; Weber, *Action Française*; Williamson, *The British in Germany 1918–1930*

1 Louise Darquier, PAF.
2 **Henry de Jouvenel** (1876–1935): Politician and journalist. Deputy 1906, senator 1921, delegate to the League of Nations 1922 and 1924, Minister of Public Instruction 1924, High Commissioner to Syria 1925–26, ambassador to Italy 1933. De Monzie's oldest and dearest friend.
3 De Jouvenel's other wives were: Claire Boas, daughter of Alfred Boas, Radical, Freemason, wealthy industrialist; Germaine-Sarah Herment, whom he married in 1933. She was the widow of Charles Louis-Dreyfus, brother and partner of King Two Louis. Germaine-Sarah's colossal Louis-Dreyfus fortune was added to when her daughter with Charles, Arlette Louis-Dreyfus, married Henry de Jouvenel's second son (by his mistress Isabelle de Cominges), Renaud. All Jouvenels were influential. In 1914 Henry's brother Robert published a famous attack on parliamentarians (such as de Monzie) in his *République des camarades*. The title of his book was often used to describe the Third Republic itself, when it was not being called epithets much worse.
4 His admirers were by no means all of the right: others, initially at least, were Jacques Maritain, André Malraux, Apollinaire and Georges Bernanos.
5 Worth an average of ten to twelve billion francs each year, the largest agricultural sector in France, providing a living for twenty million farmers and peasants.
6 Henry Lévy's partner in the Grands Moulins de Strasbourg was Achille Baumann. Except for Ernest Vilgrain, who was younger, all these wheat barons were of Pierre Darquier's age and generation, and all of them were Jewish. Quarrels and uproar mark every relationship in this closed and powerful world. Vilgrain fought with King Two Louis, Achille Baumann fell out with his brother Lucien, who formed his own milling company. Secretly, while in government, Vilgrain bought out Lucien Baumann's company.
7 The Coopérative d'Approvisionnement, de Transport et de Crédit (CATC), operated as a purchasing cooperative for the company Ernest Vilgrain bought from Achille's brother Lucien Baumann, La Société des Grands Moulins Réunis, which he renamed La Société d'Entreprise Meunière. This incorporated nine firms and a total of thirteen mills. The Under-Secretariat of Supplies existed until 1921, and Vilgrain benefited by being the state's grain supplier. He was later denounced for the huge profits he made from this racket, particularly by using his Australian contacts.

8 When he took over as Under-Secretary of State, Vilgrain cut out the Louis Dreyfus Company – he had now moved into the same lucrative business for himself. King Two Louis accused Vilgrain of using his position to profiteer, and Vilgrain counter-attacked in a series of newspaper exposés. War broke out between Vilgrain and King Two Louis in 1921.

9 'Different services' was Louis Darquier's euphemism for office boy in one of the portentous CVs he produced in 1942 for his Vichy appointment.

10 Adam Lindsay Gordon, *Ye Wearie Wayfayer, hys ballad in Eight Fyttes, Fytte VII* (from his collection *Sea Spray and Smoke Drift*, 1867).

11 **P. L. Travers** (1899–1996): interviewed by Jane Cornwall, *Qantas: The Australian Way Magazine*, July 1999.

12 Photographs of Myrtle and Roy were given to the Gilbert and Sullivan Museum in London. The museum says it has boxes and boxes of unarchived material which are inaccessible.

13 Charles Workman was born in Bootle, Lancashire, of a musical family, with no ties at all to the Northern Irish Lord Workman-Macnaghten his son Roy later claimed as his uncle. In 1898, Charles Workman married Totie Adams, a soprano in the company. Totie was also known as Bessel Adams – though her real name was Caroline. She came from Belfast, they married there, and there James Roy was born in 1902.

14 Gilbert v. Workman, High Court of Justice, Chancery Division, 18 January 1910, reported in *The Times*, 19 January 1910.

15 One of the properties Harry Jones bought in 1920, run by a younger Jones brother, Norman, was also called Weymouth.

16 Louis to René, probably June 1927.

17 Myrtle to René, undated, 1932.

18 Louise Darquier, PAF, 1924.

19 Jean Lindoerfer, October 2000.

20 Information about Louis' career in the wheat business comes from: Stadsbibliotheek, Antwerp, Annexe au Moniteur Belge – Recueil spécial des Actes, procès – verbaux et documents relatifs aux sociétés commerciales année 1925. This one is 'acte 1488, enregistré à Anvers le 3 février 1925'.

21 PRO FO 892/163.

22 All quotes from 'Enclosure no. 2 to Despatch no. 1602 of August 10, 1942, from American Consulate General, Algiers, Algeria' in Gun, pp. 263–4.

23 Louis Darquier to Urbain Gayet, father of Pierre and Jean, 26 January 1926, given to Sylvie Deroche by Jean Gayet.

24 *Les Dernières nouvelles de Strasbourg*, 7 April 1937; *Journal d'Alsace et de Lorraine*, 9 April 1937.

25 CDJC XXXV-2. See also Joly, *Darquier de Pellepoix*, p. 54.

26 Gun, pp. 263–4.

27 Louis to René, probably June 1927.

28 *ibid.*

29 The brief facts of the Macnaghten/Workman link are: Francis Macnaghten
(1763–1843) of Bushmills, Co. Antrim, a judge of the Supreme Court of
Madras, assumed the additional surname of Workman by royal licence in 1809
and was created a baronet in 1836. It is suggested that the name Workman
came from his cousin Caroline's father Meredyth Workman of Co. Armagh.
The children of Francis Macnaghten, a baronet, demonstrate no link to Charles
Workman, actor from Bootle. On the female line, Roy's mother Caroline
Josephine Bessel Adams (as her birth was registered), or Caroline Josephine
Russell Adams (at her marriage), or Totie for the London Savoy Theatre, came
from a very humble background. Her father was a baker. Charles Workman,
father of C.H. Workman, appears in the 1851 census as an ironworks labourer.

CHAPTER 5

Baby

INTERVIEWS AND CORRESPONDENCE: Paulette Aupoix, Colette Calmon, Jean Gayet,
Pierre Gayet, Mrs Margaret Gilson, Danny Puddefoot, Alistair Rapley, Simone
Reste, Tasmania J., Teresa. SOURCES: Darquier family correspondence; APP GA
D9, 25 April 1935; Archives Municipales de Paris, PER 242: Le Conseil Municipal,
nos édiles, Annuaire illustré municipal et administratif de la ville de Paris et du
département de la Seine (44ème année), 1935–1941; Archives Municipales de Paris,
file D3M2/3, Conseillers municipaux de Paris. Election leaflet, 5 May 1935; CDJC
LXII-II. PUBLICATIONS: Breese, *Hutch*; *Daily Telegraph*, 19 April 1928; Grove, *Laurie
Lee*; *Launceston Examiner*, 11 February 1929; Newby, *The Last Grain Race; Melbourne
Argus*, July–December 1928 index; Rees, *Biographical Dictionary of the Extreme Right
Since 1900*; Stevenson and Cook, *Britain in the Depression*

1 Louise Darquier, PAF, 1924.
2 The *Daily Telegraph*, 19 April 1928.
3 Paulette Aupoix, July 2000.
4 Louise Darquier, PAF.
5 'Johnny One Note', from *Babes in Arms*, lyrics by Lorenz Hart, music by Richard
Rodgers (see www.fortunecity.com/tinpan/newbonham/6/johnny.htm for full
lyrics, all of which are apposite).
6 A member of the Darquier family.
7 Jean Gayet, November 1999.
8 I have sought evidence for this divorce in all Australian states and in Britain.
In France, as she was never registered as Darquier's wife on his state documents, there are no official records of Myrtle at all. Finding details of her

Australian passport proved impossible, as some records of the time are sketchy.

9 CDJC LXII-11.

10 Archives de Paris PER 242: Le Conseil Municipal, nos édiles, Annuaire illustré municipal et administratif de la ville de Paris et du département de la Seine (44ème année) – 1935–41.

11 Rees, p. 77.

12 Teresa.

13 Tasmania J. Hazel Jones studied Arts and Education at Melbourne University from 1926 to 1929. She was a resident at Trinity, now called Janet Clarke Hall. Her departure for England was noted in the college magazine, *Fleur de Lys* (ironically the emblem of Action Française) in 1936. Hazel worked for the British government, for UNRA (United Nations Relief and Rehabilitation Agency), for the Shell Oil Company and the Red Cross, in West India (*sic*), Morocco, central Africa, China, Singapore and the Lebanon.

14 In Australia Louis Darquier was a trader, according to his passport, delivered by the French Consulate in Sydney in 1929.

15 Archives Municipales de Paris, file D3M2/3, Conseillers municipaux de Paris Election leaflet, 5 May 1935.

16 The *Argus*, Melbourne, July–December, Index 1928.

17 Harry Jones left assets worth £17,474.8s.6d. – just under 1 million Australian dollars today.

18 Lady Mountbatten had a jewelled penis sheath made especially for Hutch.

19 Louis to René, telegram, 15 April 1930.

20 Louis to René, probably April 1930.

21 There is no trace of any change of name for Louis Darquier in the *London Gazette* or Deed Poll records; in any case, between 1916 and 1971 aliens were not allowed to change their names.

22 Lloyds Bank could find no trace of Mr Robinson in their records.

23 *Evening Standard*, 17 April 1930. £100 would be about £4,800 today. The law they offended reads as follows: 'Leave shall not be given to an alien to land in the United Kingdom unless he complies with the following conditions, that is to say: - he is in a position to support himself and his dependants . . .' Louis could not pay the hotel bill at Brown's.

24 Treen Cottage no longer exists, but it was near the corner of Straight Road and Church Street in old Windsor.

25 Laurie Lee on country life in the 1930s, quoted in Grove, p. 14.

26 Alistair Rapley and Danny Puddefoot, a friend of May Brice, September 1999.

27 Myrtle to René, undated, 1931.

28 Newby.

29 'At one time I may have caused difficulty to him' – Myrtle to René, September 1931. 'I do not want to have grave difficulties before having been able, again

to discuss the question with you – without being, like the last time handicapped by a weakness (which you would have found excusable if you had put up with what I put up with for the previous six months)' – Louis to René, 1931. Their joint 'difficulty' most probably means alcohol.

30 Myrtle to René, 11 January 1933.
31 Myrtle to René, undated, 1931.
32 *ibid.*
33 Louis to Jean Ostermeyer, undated, July 1931.
34 Jean Ostermeyer to René, July 1931.
35 Myrtle to René, undated, probably 1931.
36 Louis to René, undated, probably 1931.
37 Myrtle to René, undated, probably 1931.
38 Louis to Jean Ostermeyer, undated, July 1931.
39 Myrtle to René, undated, probably 1931.
40 *ibid.*, 6 January 1932.
41 *ibid.*, undated, probably 1931.
42 Louis to René, undated 1931.
43 Myrtle to René, undated, probably 1931.
44 Louis to René, undated, probably 1931.

CHAPTER 6

Shreds and Patches

INTERVIEWS AND CORRESPONDENCE: Bill Coy, Julia Keal, Danny Puddefoot, Alistair Rapley, Teresa. SOURCES: Darquier family correspondence; APP GA D9, police report, 25 April 1935. PUBLICATIONS: Crémieux-Brilhac, *Les Français de l'an 40*; Planté, *Un Grand seigneur de la politique*; Stevenson and Cook, *Britain in the Depression*

1 Myrtle to René, 29 September 1931.
2 The trajectory of Louis and Myrtle's darting trips to Paris is hard to ascertain. This account is based on an analysis of their letters, but also some speculation.
3 Louis to René, undated, probably 1931.
4 Myrtle to René, 29 September 1931.
5 *ibid.*
6 I would like to think this 'Major Lawrence' was T.E. Lawrence, particularly as a cottage is mentioned, but I have been unable to track down this major.
7 Myrtle to René, 29 September 1931.
8 Louis to René, undated, probably 1931.
9 *ibid.*
10 *ibid.*, 14 January 1931.

11 Alistair Rapley, September 1999.

12 Myrtle to René, 3 April 1933.

13 Alistair Rapley, September 1999; Julia Keal, May 2000.

14 Danny Puddefoot, November 1999.

15 Myrtle to René, undated, probably 1932.

16 Louis to René, 10 February 1932.

17 Louis to René, undated, probably 1931.

18 Myrtle to René, undated, 1931 and 1932.

19 *ibid.*, 29 September 1931.

20 It is impossible to verify who this 'Comte de Castellane' was; there appear to have been three Comtes de Castellane around at this time. Marquis Boniface de Castellane, son of Boni de Castellane, a diplomat, was French *chargé d'affaires* in London in 1940. His famous father was a wealthy supporter of Charles Maurras. However, it could be, and probably was, the Comte de Castellane with whom Louis later served on the Paris city council.

21 Myrtle to René, undated, probably 1932.

22 Myrtle spelt Ramy as 'Rami': Ramy is always coupled with de Monzie's name, at his parties, his offices, in their letters, as his housekeeper and the woman he loved. Everyone I met in Cahors mentioned it. De Monzie's sole legatee was his secretary, Madame Debrand, which intimates that Ramy Debrand was the woman with whom he shared his life. She seems, anyway, to have been a different kind of *governante* from the two housekeepers he had, one in each of his Lotois demesnes. Ramy seems to have been with de Monzie from 1914, when he dedicated his book *Les Réformes maritimes* to her: '*A Notre-Dame de Ramy, protectrice impérieuse . . .*'

23 All quotes in this paragraph from Myrtle to René, 4 January 1932.

24 Louis to René, August 1932.

25 Louis to René, 10 February 1932.

26 Handwritten letter of debt to René, 29 August 1932:

> Monsieur René Darquier
>
> My dear René
>
> I owe you in all the sum of 126,000 francs (one hundred and twenty six thousand French francs) that I will return in whole or in parts, at your demand as soon as that will be possible for me. This acknowledgement annuls all precedents.
>
> (signed) Sandra Darquier, Louis Darquier

27 Louis to René, August 1932.

28 Myrtle to René: 9 October 1931; 4 January 1932; 1 January 1933. The horses were across the road on Danny Puddefoot's uncle's farm.

29 Louis to René, undated, probably 1931; 29 August 1932; undated, probably end 1932.

30 As a candidate of the Anti-Waste League, Sir James Erskine stood for 'the true

blue policy of 100% Toryism and no tinkering with Socialism' (*The Times*, 6 March 1931). Duff Cooper, a pro-Baldwin Conservative, won the seat after a tremendous row with the Westminster Conservative Association. See *The Times*, February–March 1931, for the turmoil over the St George's Division election of March 1931. Two nationalist press lords, Beaverbrook and Rothermere, had launched the United Empire Party in 1930 to get rid of the leader of the party – Baldwin at that time – and replace him with one who would do as they instructed. Rothermere was eventually to support Mosley's Blackshirts, Hitler, Munich etc.

31 Louis to René, undated, probably Decmber 1932.
32 All this from an exceptionally long letter, Myrtle to René, 11 January 1933.
33 Myrtle to René, 11 February 1933.
34 *ibid.*, 16 February 1933.
35 *ibid.*, 23 March 1933.
36 All quotations from Janot Darquier: her letter to René, 28 March 1933.
37 Myrtle to René, undated, April 1933.
38 *ibid.*, 13 September 1933.
39 Coy, July 2001.
40 Myrtle to René, 11 January 1933.

CHAPTER 7

The Street

INTERVIEWS AND CORRESPONDENCE: Paulette Aupoix, Jeanne Degrelle, Pierre Gayet, Audrey Kirby, Yvonne Lacaze, Pierre Orliac, Danny Puddefoot, Pierre Pujo, Teresa. SOURCES: Darquier family correspondence; AN 3W142; APP: Commission d'Enquête du 6 Février 34, Audition de M. Pierre Gérard; APP GA D9: Dossier Darquier, 25 April 1935; APP GA R4: Rassemblement anti-juif de France, 14 April 1938 and 30 May 1938; Archives Municipales de Paris, D3M2/3, Conseillers Municipaux de Paris: Dossier Darquier, election leaflet, May 1935; CDJC LXII-II; TNA: PRO FO 371/31941–Z3005–3004/81/17. PUBLICATIONS: Agulhon, *The French République 1879–1992*; Albert, *Histoire générale de la presse française*; Anderson, *Conservative Politics in France*; Beloff, *The Sixth of February*; Billig, *Le Commissariat Général aux Questions Juives (1941–1944)*; Charbonneau, *Les Mémoires de Porthos*; Coston, *Partis, journaux et hommes politiques d'hier et d'aujourd'hui*; *Le Crapouillot*, new series 77, summer 1984; Eatwell, *Fascism*; Gordon, *Historical Dictionary of World War II*; Halls, *Politics, Society and Christianity in Vichy France*; Hamilton, *The Appeal of Fascism*; Jackson: *The Popular Front in France: Defending Democracy 1934–38*; Joly, 'Darquier de Pellepoix: "Champion" des antisémites français'; Joly, *Darquier de Pellepoix et l'antisémitisme français*; Kingston, *Anti-Semitism in France During the 1930s*; Larkin, *France since the Popular Front*

Government; Launceston Examiner, 4 December 1984; Marrus and Paxton, *Vichy France and the Jews*; Pélissier, *6 Février 1934*; Planté, *Un Grand seigneur de la politique*; Soucy, *French Fascism: The First Wave, 1924–1933*; Soucy, *French Fascism: The Second Wave, 1933–1939*; *The Times*, 9 December 1942; Weber, *Action Française*; Werth, *France in Ferment*; Werth, *The Twilight of France*; http://members.aol.com/thidal/-anthinea.html; www.taittinger.com/prix/main/maingenese.htm

1 Louis to René, dated 1934, probably 20 February.

2 The decade following the Great War was the heyday of the young men of Action Française – the Camelots du Roi – who prepared for the return of a French king by attacking the Republic with every means to hand. They policed Action Française meetings and disrupted those of almost everyone else, using force to prevent theatre performances or lectures on subjects or with attitudes unacceptable to their faith. Splattering their enemies with coal tar and printers' ink, wrecking offices, orchestrating riots, they added the Bolshevik Menace to their list of targets and attacked Jews, Germans, Republicans, Freemasons, foreigners and communists, accusing those they assaulted of representing all these things.

3 Jean became Chef de Clinique à la Faculté de Médecine de Paris – head of the neurology clinic at La Salpêtrière; later his stationery from the rue Jouffroy was headed 'Former Head of the Faculty'. Another doctor who arranged a similar banquet in Bordeaux was Pierre Mauriac, the brother of François Mauriac.

4 Pierre Gayet, January 2000 and Yvonne Lacaze, January 1999: 'Jean shared the ideas of his brother Louis.'

5 The Lambert Law of 1927 reduced the period of residence in France necessary for naturalisation from ten to three years. This gave the French state, which was suffering from the losses of the First World War, more men for the armed services. Between 1923 and 1926, 112,337 immigrants became French citizens; 269,872 between 1927 and 1930.

6 Marrus and Paxton (p. 36) give Jewish refugee intakes as follows: USA 190,000; Palestine 120,000; Great Britain 65,000; France 55,000. Maurras exaggerated this figure by three or four times.

7 **Édouard Daladier** (1884–1970): Premier of France from 1938 to 1940. During the Occupation, after the fiasco of the trial at Riom, he was handed over to the Germans and was kept prisoner until 1945. He continued as a deputy after the war.

8 Louis to René, 14 November 1933.

9 Pierre Pujo, December 2000.

10 **Henri Charbonneau** (1913–82): Ebullient member of the Camelots du Roi and Action Française, of the Cagoule and, after the fall of France, of the MSR established by Deloncle in 1940 and funded by Eugène Schueller. In 1944 he

married Jeanne Brevet, the niece of Joseph Darnand, and they had four children. At the Liberation, he took refuge in Sigmaringen then in Switzerland, was arrested in 1945 and sentenced to ten years' hard labour. On his release he took up journalism again.

Léon Degrelle (1906–94): Son of a brewer in the Ardennes, a brilliant orator, devout Catholic and founder of the Belgian fascist party, the Rexists, in 1931, originally as a wing of the ruling Catholic Party. Financed by Mussolini. In August 1941 he formed and then commanded the Flemish and Walloon troops which fought for Germany on the Russian front. His Légion Wallonie was transferred to the Waffen SS and Degrelle was decorated by Hitler in February 1944. Sentenced to death at the Liberation, he crash-landed an aeroplane into San Sebastian in 1945, where considerable efforts by Franco's staff protected him from extradition to Belgium, which clamoured for his return. Degrelle was another of those fascists who knew Louis Darquier – on 2 October 1936 he was turned away at the frontier en route to speak at Louis' National Club – but he avoided him in Spain after the war.

Jeanne Brevet Charbonneau Degrelle (dates unknown): In Spain in 1962 Jeanne Charbonneau met Léon Degrelle, whom she married, and with whom she lived until his death in 1994. The researcher and journalist Sylvie Deroche interviewed Jeanne Degrelle in Madrid in 1999. Like Action Française, Mme Degrelle considered Louis Darquier beneath her: she and Degrelle regarded Louis' private life as unacceptable. So did her first husband, Henri Charbonneau, inasmuch as he does not mention Louis Darquier at all in his vivid and unreconstructed autobiography, *Les Mémoires de Porthos*.

11 The only exception to AF's anti-parliamentary stance was Léon Daudet's election as a deputy from 1924 to 1929, the first and last AF parliamentarian.

12 **François Coty** (1874–1934): Perfume and cosmetics manufacturer, secretive millionaire and endless source of wealth for the far right between the wars. He was the founder of the fascist party Solidarité Française and owner of the populist *Ami du peuple* and *Figaro* newspapers.

Croix-de-feu was also funded by the aristocrat Joseph-Jean-Mathieu-Jérôme, 4th Duca Pozzo di Borgo, who became vice-president of the league. He was director of the Anti-Marxist Institute of Paris; pro-Hitler and Mussolini.

François de la Roque (1885–1946): Wounded and decorated First World War veteran. Croix-de-feu was launched in 1928 and la Roque joined the following year, becoming its president in 1931. In 1936 he converted it into a political party, the Parti Social Français (PSF), renamed Progrès Social Français in 1940. It was authoritarian, anti-democratic, paramilitary, anti-communist and anti-Masonic. La Roque was resented by all other parties of the extreme right for his more conciliatory position towards the Republic, and his concentration on discipline rather than demagoguery. During the Occupation he was anti-German and anti-Nazi, but pro-Pétain, pro-Vichy and anti-Gaullist. His position was always ambiguous, which led to his arrest and deportation by the Germans in 1943, and, despite two years in captivity and wartime resistance services, his re-arrest at the Liberation. He died before trial.

13 **Pierre-Charles Taittinger** (1887–1965), Jeunesses Patriotes was founded initially under the patronage – and funding – of General de Castelnau of the FNC and other patriotic and Catholic movements, as a reaction to the Cartel des Gauches government of that year.

See website of Taittinger, http://www.taittinger.com/prix/main/maingenese.htm.

14 Soucy, vol. 1, p. 211

15 Soucy, vol. 1, p. 49, ref. *La Liberté*, 1 January 1926.

16 I have found it impossible to get the membership lists of these leagues, whose activities and archives, should they exist, are shrouded in mystery. Jackson (p. 72) says Croix-de-feu's membership was 300,000 in 1935; Soucy (vol. 2, p. 36) says nearly a million. Beloff gives the following figures for 1934:

Action Française: 60,000 adherents, of which 8,300 in Paris

Solidarité Française: 180,000, of which 80,000 in Paris

Jeunesses Patriotes: 90,000, of which 6,400 in Paris

Croix-de-feu: 50,000, of which 18,000 in Paris (Soucy says 100,000, of which 21,000 in Paris).

In 1934 the four big leagues totalled 370,000 members. Later, Croix-de-feu became by far the largest. As to Darquier, there is considerable documentary proof of the dates given for his trajectory.

17 **Eugène Schueller** (1881–1957): Of Alsacian origin, Schueller studied chemistry, invented a new form of hair colouring, founded l'Oréal and, with Henri de Rothschild, Monsavon. A supporter of Eugène Deloncle and the Cagoule, he was co-founder with him of the MSR in 1940, and a close friend of Henri Charbonneau. After Deloncle's eviction from the MSR in 1942, Schueller kept a low profile. His record was investigated at the Liberation, but he was not brought to trial. He went on to protect, through his worldwide beauty empire, many French war criminals after the war, in Spain, the USA and South America.

18 Wealthy men like this might have been members of what were known at the time as the 'two hundred families'. In fact this figure referred to the largest shareholders of the Banque de France. These 'two hundred' had voting rights, and so were seen as the dictators of French financial policies. In the parlance of the time they came to stand for the powerful and exclusive financial elite of the country.

19 Werth, p. 90ff.

20 **Philippe Henriot** (1889–1944): Politician, broadcaster, Catholic militant, anti-Semite, anti-communist, anti-*résistant*, anti-republican and, after the British attack on the French fleet at Mers-el-Kebir in 1940, anglophobe. He was pro-Pétain. He broadcast against the BBC and the Allies from 1942 to

1944, exhorting Frenchmen to volunteer for work in Germany. In 1943 he joined Darnand's Milice. He was Minister of Information and Propaganda from January 1944 until his assassination on 28 June 1944. His state funeral, held on 30 June at Notre Dame, was attended by cardinals, seven weeks before the Liberation of Paris and the mass at Notre Dame which celebrated it.

21 **Jean Chiappe** (1878–1940): In 1935, the year of Darquier's election, Chiappe became president of the Paris City Council, in 1936 a deputy. Pétain designated him High Commissioner for the Levant in 1940 but he was killed in an aeroplane, brought down, it is said, by a British plane. His brother **Angelo Chiappe** (1889–1945), a préfet and member of the Milice, was sentenced to death and executed in January 1945.

22 *Action française*, 6 February 1934, quoted by Werth, p. 144.

23 Those involved in the rioting included Coty's Solidarité Française, Taittinger's Jeunesses Patriotes, Maurras' Action Française and its Camelots, and some elements of the French left.

24 It seems that la Roque was paid by the government of the time not to take direct action. This accusation came from la Roque's former deputy Pozzo di Borgo, a typical dénouement in the relationships of these league leaders. **André Tardieu** (1876–1945), former premier, later gave evidence that he had often received la Roque in his apartment in Paris and given him money from secret funds.

25 Weber (p. 336) says Darquier marched with Jeunesses Patriotes from the town hall to join Action Française on the Concorde. If that is the case, then he was one of fifty men wounded at the Pont de Solférino. APP GA D9: Dossier Darquier, 25 April 1935: '*Ligueur d'Action Française, il a été blessé le 6 février d'une balle dans la cuisse.*' Others, including Louis himself, all say he was on the Concorde with Action Française.

26 All Louis' words are from: Louis to René, 1934, probably end of February.

27 Doumergue's government brought in an amendment to French naturalisation laws: recent citizens had to wait ten years before they were permitted to practise law or to hold public office. In 1935 this was extended to the medical profession, and led on to Vichy's laws.

28 All Louis words are from: Louis to René, 29 March 1934.

29 Louis to René, 3 June 1934.

30 **Marshal Louis-Hubert Lyautey** (1854–1934): Marshal of France, renowned military leader, and administrator of Morocco from 1912.

31 Louis to René, 3 June 1934.

32 Janot Darquier to René, undated 1934.

33 Louis to René, 8 August 1934.

CHAPTER 8

Fame

INTERVIEWS AND CORRESPONDENCE: John Booth, Mary Coghlan, Jeanne Degrelle. SOURCES: Darquier family correspondence; AN 3W142: Rapport de la police municipale du 8ème arrondissement, 24 May 1936; AN 72 AJ 592: Fonds Vaniakoff; AN AJ38 6305: Dossier Paule Fichot; AN F7 12963, 3 November 1934, 10 December 1934; AN F7 12964, 14 March 1936; AN F7 12965; APP GA D9, 27 August 1934, 25 April 1935, 13 June 1942; Archives Municipales de Paris, D3M2/3, Dossier Darquier: municipal election leaflet, 5 May 1935; Archives Municipales de Paris, PER 242; Archives Municipales de Strasbourg; BMO, 6 July 1935, 17 January, 4, 5 and 6 June 1936, etc.; BNF JO-77305; CAC 880509, art. 15, investigatory file (*dossier d'instruction*) of the Cagoule: telegram of 1 June 1936; INA 1939/40. PUBLICATIONS: *Action française*, 29 January, 2 February, 15 November and 6 December 1935, 19 February 1936; Albert, *Histoire générale de la presse française*, vol. 2; Anderson, *Conservative Politics in France*; Arnal, *Ambivalent Alliance*; Augé, *Paris Années 30*; Billig, *Le Commissariat Général aux Questions Juives (1941–1944)*; *Le Canard enchaîné*, 8 July 1936; Charbonneau, *Les Mémoires de Porthos*; Combes, *Le Conseil municipal*; Crémieux-Brilhac, BBC Radio, 1 July 1942.; *La Défense*, 27 May 1934; Dubief, *Le Déclin de la IIIème République, 1929–1938*; Philippe Ganier-Raymond, interview with Louis Darquier, *l'Express*, 28 October 1978; Godechot, *Les Constitutions de la France depuis 1789*; *l'Humanité*, 6 June 1936; *l'Intransigeant*, 6 March 1936; Jackson, *France: The Dark Years 1940–1944*; Joly, 'Darquier de Pellepoix: "Champion" des antisémites français'; Joly, *Darquier de Pellepoix et l'antisémitisme français*; *Le Jour*, 1 February 1935, 19 February 1936; Kaplan, *The Collaborator*; Kingston, *Anti-Semitism in France During the 1930s*; Laborie, *Quercy Recherche*, May–June 1979, nos 29–30; Lacouture, *Léon Blum*; Larkin, *France Since the Popular Front*; *Libre parole*, February 1934; Martin, *A History of the Schools of Kidlington*; *Le Matin*, 22 December 1942; *Paris Soir*, 5 and 10 March 1936; Paxton, *French Peasant Fascism*; Péan, *Une Jeunesse française*; Randa, *Dictionnaire commenté de la collaboration française*; Soucy, *French Fascism: The First Wave 1924–1933*; Soucy, *French Fascism: The Second Wave 1933–1939*; Sternhell, *Neither Right nor Left*; Taguieff (ed.), *L'Antisémitisme de plume 1940–1944*; Thornton-Smith, *Echoes and Resonances of Action Française*; *La Tribune Juive*, 'Les amis parisiens de M. Hitler', 27 March 1936; Venner, *Histoire de la collaboration*; Vitoux, *Céline*; BNF: *Le Voltaire*, 1936 and 1937, in particular 1, 8 and 22 February, 25 April and 20 June 1936, and 23 October 1937; Weber, *Action Française*; www.academie-fran-caise.fr/immortels; http://www.phdn.org/negation/rassinier/coston.html

1 **Léon Bailby** (1867–1954). *l'Intransigeant* was the largest French evening newspaper until 1930. Nationalist and jingoistic, it was noted for its sport and literary coverage. When Louis Louis-Dreyfus bought into it in 1931, he said, 'Bailby

sold me a watch, but prevented me from finding out the time.' In 1932 they fell out and Bailby went off to start *Le Jour*.

2 *Le Gringoire* (1929–44): Conservative, anti-communist, nationalist, Catholic – the most successful weekly newspaper of the far right, selling about 200,000 copies a week. Its most famous polemicist was **Henri Béraud** (1885-1958): condemned to death in 1944 but pardoned by de Gaulle.

Candide (1924–44): Violent and polemical, this right-wing weekly was run by the Action Française historian Jacques Bainville, and then by Pierre Gaxotte. Its circulation was more than 500,000 copies in 1937.

Pierre Gaxotte (1895–1982): Maurrassian. After Jacques Bainville, he was the historian of AF, and was for a time Maurras' secretary. Elected to the Académie Française in 1953, there he was 'received' by General Weygand and joined a large number of former AF intellectuals.

Je suis partout ('I am everywhere', in other words, 'I spy'): Right-wing, pro-fascist periodical, founded by Arthème Fayard in November 1930 and published by him until 1936. Very AF. Editors were Pierre Gaxotte and Robert Brasillach. Shut down in 1944.

3 Louis to René, 15 August 1934.

4 *ibid*.

5 Association document in letter, Louis to René, September 1935.
The programme continued:

2. To organise support of all kinds for the members of the Association.

3. To commemorate the tragic events of 6 February by appropriate ceremonies, to propagate the spirit of sacrifice and patriotism and to participate in all efforts made to re-establish public cleanliness and national honour.

We will realise this programme with energy and perseverance, under the spiritual sign of bloody sacrifice, for the health and grandeur of France.

6 **Pierre-Étienne Flandin** (1889–1958): Conservative politician and deputy, leader of the Alliance Démocratique; prime minister 1934–35, then for eight weeks Pétain's chief Minister in 1940. He was pro-Munich and an arch-appeaser of Germany. Escaped to Algeria, sentenced to five years' of *dégradation nationale*, immediately suspended, but, like all Pétain's former ministers, he remained prohibited from standing for political office.

7 Achille Liénart, Cardinal of Lille, Arnal, p. 158.

8 **François Mitterrand** (1916–96): President of France 1981–95. He worked for the Vichy state until 1943, when he joined the Resistance.

9 On the wall of Louis' Madrid apartment 'there was a photograph of eight men marching down some street, dressed in raincoats and jackboots' (John Booth, former head of immigration at the Australian embassy in Madrid).

10 Louis to René, 8 August 1934.

11 **Charles Trochu** (1898–?): a descendant of the Napoleonic General Kléber, and a grandson of General Trochu, military governor of Paris during the siege

of 1870–71. Born in Chile, he was wont to emphasise that 'His family comes from old Breton stock. On his maternal side he belongs to one of the oldest families in the French Basque country . . .' Paris city councillor and its president from December 1941 to May 1943. At the centre of so much anti-republican activity for over twenty years, Trochu seems to have escaped punishment and to have disappeared from public life after the Liberation, except for a reference to his standing for Parliament in 1951.

12 *Le Jour*, 1 Feburary 1935, *Action française*, 29 January 1935 and 2 February 1935. See Joly, *Darquier de Pellepoix*, p. 56–8.

13 The *Miss Hobart* crash was on 19 October 1934. Colin, also a dentist, was listed as killed with his wife.

14 Correspondence and letters of debt between Louis and René Darquier, 1 April 1935; 29 April 1935; 1 May 1935. Correspondence between René Darquier and G. Habault of Banque Cotonnière, 30 April 1935; 1 May 1935; 4 May 1935.

15 Myrtle to René, 22 May 1936.

16 Although glossed over in his political leaflet, in the information later published by the city council his academic credentials were changed to: 'Bachelor of Science, he obtained his PCN and his first *certificat de licence* at the Faculty of Toulouse.' This is false – he failed. He also lied about the year he enlisted in the army, making himself a heroic year younger, and told them he spent the year of 1927 in Australia managing an agricultural and breeding business.

17 In the first round, Louis won 1,520 votes of the 7,932 votes available. According to the Third Republic constitution, the Seine département had a vote to elect five senators.

18 **Henri Massis** (1886–1970): Authoritarian Catholic and colleague of Jacques Maritain, literary critic, philosopher and journalist, disciple and follower of Maurras. The website of the Académie Française (see www.academie-francaise.fr) states that he did not write for *Action française*, but in fact Massis was responsible for the 'Literary Chat' section of the paper. With Alfred de Tarde he wrote a study of French youth, *Les jeunes gens d'aujourd'hui* in 1913, under the name of Agathon, and with Jacques Bainville he founded *La Revue universelle* in 1920. Massis exerted considerable influence on younger intellectuals such as Thierry Maulnier. He was a supporter of Franco, Salazar, Mussolini and Pétain, for whom he drafted many speeches. He was also a member of the National Council of Vichy. Untouched after the Liberation, he was elected to the Académie Française in 1960.

19 Paule Meslier, then Fichot, began work for Louis Darquier on 7 February 1936 and worked for him till 2 September 1939, then joined him at the CGQJ.

20 There were fifty-six right-wing councillors, thirty-four from the left.

21 Lacouture, *Léon Blum*, p. 223.

22 *Action française*, 15 November 1935.

23 *Action française*, 6 December 1935; Joly, *Darquier de Pellepoix*, p. 61.
24 Dubief, Chapter 3: 'La crise sociale'.
25 Joly, *Darquier de Pellepoix*, p. 69; Coston in *Libre Parole*, 3 June 1937.
26 Coston is quoted in Busi, 'In the Lair of the Fascist Beast', *Midstream*, vol. XIX, no. 2, February 1973, p. 22 (see www.phdn.org/negation/rassinier/coston.html).
27 Joly, *Darquier de Pellepoix*, p. 70, Ganier-Raymond, *l'Express*, 28 October 1978.
28 *Le Jour*, 19 February 1936 – AN 72 AJ 592 Fonds Vaniakoff.

    Jean Filliol (1909–?): Led a notorious Parisian section of the Camelots and the Action Française attack on 6 February 1934, then became hit man of Eugène Deloncle's Cagoule. Amongst others, he assassinated the Rosselli brothers at Mussolini's request. Fled to Italy, then to Spain in 1937. Returned to France in 1939 and joined the MSR. He quarrelled with Deloncle, and spent fifteen months in prison camp at the order of Laval, but was freed by Darnand in 1944 so he could join the Milice. Fled with other Milice to Germany at the end of summer 1944. He was condemned to three death sentences *in absentia* in 1948. Like Darquier, he was by then in Spain where he remained working for L'Oréal. Never brought to justice.

29 **Thierry Maulnier** (real name Jacques Talagrand, 1909–88): Writer, journalist, school friend of Robert Brasillach and member of Action Française. Nationalist and anti-Semitic editor in the 1930s, a leader, with Jean-Pierre Maxence, of the *jeune droite*; wrote for *Action française* and *Je suis partout* during the Occupation, and also edited two volumes of poetry with Dominique Aury (the author, under the pseudonym of Pauline Réage, of *The Story of O*). Later blanked out this past; elected to the Académie Française in 1964. His activities in Darquier's company were ignored or forgotten in France during the Darquier *affaire* of 1978, when Maulnier was still very much alive.

    Robert Castille (dates unknown): Leader of Les Étudiants d'Action Française, secretary and fellow advocate of Xavier Vallat, in particular working with Vallat for the Cagoule. Defended Pierre Gérard in court in 1939. He worked as legal adviser in Vallat's CGQJ, and is said to have betrayed him by providing the SD with information about his private life, presumably because the SD at the time were investigating Castille as a supposed Freemason. Also closely connected with François Mitterrand's family friend Jean Bouvyer, a relationship maintained in the years after the war. Punishment for collaboration, if any, unknown.

    Jean-Pierre Maxence (real name Pierre Godmé, 1906–56): Diligent member of Solidarité Française. Anti-Semite, Action Française, then a dissident. With Thierry Maulnier, a leading Catholic intellectual of the right, and like him a contributor to the dash of 'spiritual renewal' Louis Darquier often invoked in his fascist speeches. With Maulnier, Maxence published an anti-Semitic and fascist review, *l'Insurgé*, at the end of the 1930s. In 1940 he was in the same German prison camp as Darquier.

30 Vigilance Meeting, 28 March 1936, AN F7 12965.

31 **Henri de Kérillis** (1889–1958): Much-decorated First World War veteran aviator. Journalist, traveller, deputy for Neuilly, elected in May 1936. Formed a propaganda centre for National Republicans. In 1938 he founded *L'Époque*, a unique anti-Nazi paper of the right, as 'an important instrument of Catholic information'. Others involved included de Castelnau, and one of its backers seems to have been the Louis Dreyfus bank. Forcefully anti-Nazi and anti-Munich, de Kérillis became famous for his articles exposing the Ribbentrop/Abetz scandal of which Louis Darquier was a beneficiary, naming de Brinon, Déat, *Je suis partout* and *le Matin* as recipients of Nazi largesse. Hostile to the left and to Action Française, and later to de Gaulle. He was the sole conservative to vote against Munich in the Chamber of Deputies. In 1940 he fled to the USA, where he remained until his death.

32 Georges Oltramare in Randa, p. 117.

33 Some of the funders of these leagues were: Gabriel le Roy Ladurie of the Worms Bank, close to Action Française; François de Wendel and his subordinate Pierre Pucheu with funds from the Comité des Forges (the Steel Trust) – both had been members of Croix-de-feu. Taittinger was supported by the Worms Bank and the Banque de Paris et des Pays Bas, and other Jewish businessmen. La Roque was also funded by the government itself, under Tardieu, by the Banque de France, by Ernest Mercier, industrialist and founder of Redressement Français and by many many other big companies and businessmen. The Rothschild Bank, when it funded Doriot's Fascist League in the 1930s, seems to have ignored the fact that Rothschilds were favoured whipping boys of both left and right, and in particular of Édouard Drumont.

34 *La Tribune Juive*, 27 March 1936, 'Les amis parisiens de M. Hitler' in AN 72 AJ 592, Fonds Vaniakoff.

35 De Gaulle signed the ordinance granting women the right to vote on 5 October 1944. They first voted in the elections of 1945.

36 The Socialists won 146 seats, Communists 72, Radicals 116. This was the Popular Front.

37 Laborie, p.11; *La Défense*, 27 May 1934.

38 Kingston, p. 8; AN 3W142. Rapport de la police municipale du 8ème arrondissement, 24 May 1936 and Joly, *Darquier de Pellepoix*, p. 74.

39 The Paris Council (Conseil de Paris) combined the city council of Paris and the general council of the Seine.

40 1918 is a particularly early date. Most of those of Darquier's ilk chose the naturalisation law of 1927.

41 Coston's instructions were given to the Jeunesses Anti-Juives movement he had founded in 1930.

42 For impotence, sexual organs, Dreyfus etc. see BMO: 6 June 1935, 17 January
    1936, 5 June 1936 et al. See also BMO, 4 June 1936 and 6 June 1936.
43 *L'Humanité*, 6 June 1936; Augé, p. 656.

CHAPTER 9

Pot of Gold

INTERVIEWS AND CORRESPONDENCE: Jeanne Degrelle, Auguste Mudry. SOURCES:
Darquier family correspondence; AN 3W142, Georges Hirsch statement; AN 72
AJ 592: Fonds Vaniakoff; AN AG/3(2) 326 (BCRA); APP BA 1896, police note,
14 June 1936; APP GA D9, 5 November 1936, 30 January 1937, 12 June 1942; APP
GA R4, 14 April 1938 and 30 May 1938; Archives du Bas Rhin, Strasbourg, 98AL698
BMO, 23 June 1936; US National Archives and Records Administration (NARA):
Records of the US Office of Strategic Services COI/OSS Central Files 1942–1946,
box no. 502, file no. 3, 22 September 1944, p. 14, declassified; BNF JO-77305;
CDJC CI: 'The Jewish War'; CDJC CXLII-152; CDJC CCXIV-78; CDJC
CCCXXIX-22; CDJC CCCLXXIX-3; Bundesarchiv, Berlin; AAPA; Thüringisches
Hauptstaatsarchiv: Weimar Amt zum Schutz des Volkseigentums Nr. LK 2787,
Ulrich Fleischhauer, 11 August 1947; Stadtarchiv Erfurt; Stadtarchiv Ludwigsburg,
EL 904/2, EL 904/5; TNA: PRO FO 371/31941–Z3005; TNA: PRO FO 892/163:
Fernand de Brinon; TNA: PRO: note on Abetz. PUBLICATIONS: *Action française*, 4
August 1936; Agulhon, *The French Republic 1879–1992*; Bankwitz, *Maxime Weygand and
Civil-Military Relations in Modern France*; Ben-Itto, *Die Protokolle der Weisen von Zion*;
Bollmus, *Das Amt Rosenberg und seine Gegner*; Brechtken, *Madagaskar für die Juden*;
Bulletin du Club National, 17 and 24 April 1937; Burrin, *France Under the Germans*;
Byrnes, *Antisemitism in Modern France*, vol. 1; Cohn, *Warrant for Genocide*; *Le Crapouillot*,
no. 23, 1953; Crémieux-Brilhac, BBC Radio, 16 May 1942; Crémieux-Brilhac, *Les
Français de l'an 40*; Eatwell, *Fascism*; *La France enchaînée*, October 1938; Frank, 'Holocaust
– Das Brandopfer in Niemandsland', *Zeitschrift zwischen den Kulturen*, Heft 3 und 4, Berlin,
1987; Guérin, *La Résistance*; Heiber, *Walter Frank und sein Reichsinstitut für Geschichte
des neuen Deutschlands*; 'How Popular was Streicher? His Friendship with Hitler',
Wiener Library Bulletin, no. 5–6, 1957; Jackson, *France: The Dark Years*; Jackson, *Popular
Front*; Joly, *Darquier de Pellepoix et l'antisémitisme français*; *Journal de la Résistance*, 16 May
1942; *Les Amis de Rassinier*, © by Gilles Karmasyn 1999, www.phdn.org/nega-
tion/rassinier/coston.html; Kingston, *Anti-Semitism in France during the 1930s*; Laloum,
La France antisémite de Darquier de Pellepoix; Larkin, *France Since the Popular Front*; *Libre
parole*, 22 November 1936; Marrus and Paxton, *Vichy France and the Jews*; *l'Oeuvre*,
15 October 1937; Planté, *Un Grand seigneur de la politique*; Randa, *Dictionnaire commenté
de la collaboration française*; Sternhell, *Neither Right nor Left*; Taguieff (ed.),
L'Antisémitisme de plume 1940–1944; Tannenbaum, *The Action Française*; Thornton-

Smith, *Echoes and Resonances of Action Française*; BNF: *Le Voltaire*, 27 June 1936 and 4 December 1937; *Weltdienst*, newsletter no. 16/17, 1938; *Weltdienst*, World Service, no. V1/10, 15 May 1939; Zucotti, *The Holocaust, the French and the Jews*

1 The ONT, Ordo Novi Templi, published the *Ostara*, full of Hitler babble, which was closed down in 1921. It was followed by the Pan-Aryan Anti-Jewish Union of France, founded in 1923–24 by George de Pottere and Edwin I. Cooper. The Pan-Aryan Anti-Jewish Union of France is supposed to have survived. The ONT still has headquarters in Vienna. *Ostara* has its own website. The Illuminati believed in worldwide conspiracy, imminent takeover by Antichrist/Jew/Communist/Mason, a new world order, etc. The British mystic Nesta Webster (1876–1960) was a vociferous believer.

2 The *Protocols* were published in Britain by Eyre & Spottiswoode, who were also publishers of the Bible.

3 When *The Times* proved that *The Protocols of the Elders of Sion* was a forgery (August 1921), Bainville maintained that this was of no consequence: 'What does that prove about the Bolsheviks and the Jews? Absolutely nothing!'

4 Cohn, p. 84.

5 **Ulrich Fleischhauer** (1876–196?): First World War veteran, a regimental commander. Seriously wounded and pensioned off. He became a choleric pacifist and monomaniacal anti-Semite. He launched his Weltdienst as a roneoed bulletin, published fortnightly, in three, then eight, and later in nineteen languages. Fleischhauer was obsessed with the *Protocols* and the World Jewish Conspiracy, and worked for the despatch of all Jews to a distant land. Often in bad odour with more fastidious Nazis. By 1938 – at a time when he cared about such things – Hitler was advised that Fleischhauer was placing Germany in embarrassing positions abroad, as he was the kind of 'anti-Semite who pretends to see a threatening Jew behind every street corner of the world and who tries to deal with the matter in a psychosis of fear and secretiveness'. Fleischhauer had worked with de Pottere – see note 1 – and also helped found the Pan-Aryan Anti-Jewish Union, an international anti-Semitic organisation whose annual congresses, held in secret, he chaired. He held congresses for the Weltdienst in Erfurt from 1936 to 1938; attendance ranged from sixty to seventy delegates from up to twenty-five countries. From 1945–46 he was in American internment camps and hospitals for 'denazification'. Released, in 1947 he made a written statement denying that he was a Nazi, a reactionary or a fanatical anti-Semite.

6 **Louis T. Weichardt** (1894–1985): leader-in-chief of the South African National Party (Greyshirts). As to agents, a Swiss journal said there were thirty thousand of them, but Brechtken (p. 60) thinks this highly exaggerated.

7 **Julius Streicher** (1885–1946): Gauleiter of Franconia, early follower of Hitler, co-author of the Nuremberg racial laws, officer of the SA, the paramilitary

police of the Nazi Party. His nympholepsy exhibited itself in accusing women of sexual offences with Jews, but pardoning them for favours permitted himself. He was a close friend of the Mitford sisters.

8 Quoted by © Randall Bytwerk: www.calvin.edu/academic/cas/faculty/-streich3.htm.

9 These comrades were Pierre Clémenti, Marcel Bucard, Jean Boissel and the aptly named Serpeille de Gobineau, grandson of the nineteenth-century French racial determinist prophet, and perhaps one of the most objectionable denizens of the French Nazi pond.

10 *Weltdienst*, World Service, no.V1/10, 15 May 1939.

11 Sylvie Deroche was refused access to the file which contains the correspondence between Louis Darquier and Emilie Vasticar in 1936 by the Ministry of the Interior, on the grounds that this book is not a university thesis. French academics can thus have access to it (CAC 880509, art. 15, investigatory file ((*dossier d'instruction*)) of the Cagoule). The correspondence seems to have been about propaganda, meetings, but not money. As to Henry Coston, he wrote politely to Sylvie Deroche on 23 August 2000 saying that he could not give us the information we wanted: 'I am nearly ninety years old and I am very busy finalising my "Dictionary of French Politics"' – a new edition of it, making something like his two hundredth publication.

12 BMO, 23 June 1936, sitting of 17 June 1936.

13 According to Hirsch, Louis Louis-Dreyfus paid some eighty million francs for Bailby's *l'Intransigeant*, and this money funded *Le Jour*. Bailby remained on the board of *l'Intransigeant* after the sale until Louis-Dreyfus showed him the door. The intimation here is that Louis Darquier was undertaking this attack on Jews under the influence of Bailby's enmity with Louis Louis-Dreyfus. AN 3W142 Georges Hirsch statement.

14 Marrus and Paxton, p. 39; Jackson, p. 106.

15 Jackson, p. 250.

16 The Louis-Dreyfus family had moved partially to Switzerland earlier; after the defeat of 1870 they moved to Marseille and Paris.

17 France's population was nearing forty-two million as the Second World War began. There were nearly three quarters of a million Italians in France, and by 1939 over four hundred thousand refugees from the Spanish Civil War.

18 Louis' salary for 1937 was 41,473 francs (worth approximately £14,000 today). Net of his pension and overheads he had twenty thousand francs a year to live on (£6,800 today), support himself and Myrtle in the style to which both were accustomed, Anne perhaps, and the rental of two houses, with all the activities, publications and meetings both entailed.

19 Joly, *Darquier de Pellepoix*, p. 81.

20 APP GA D9, 5 November 1936.
    From a final receipt from an employee paid by Myrtle in March 1937, it looks

as though the club closed in that month; so it lasted ten months, a long time for one of Louis Darquier's endeavours. Auguste Mudry (interview, November 1999), a former Director of Aryanisation at the CGQJ, says the club did not belong to Darquier: 'The sports club belonged to Henri Becquerel, he gave bodybuilding classes there, and physical education from 7 to 8 in the evenings. There were all kinds of fellows there, of all ages, from eighteen to forty. There were also hot showers, with jets. He rented the top floor, the sixth – of this building in the rue Laugier, and the cloakrooms and the bar were in the basement. After the courses, we would go and drink a lemon juice – there was a lift to go to the sixth floor.' However Louis paid the rent, the police had him marked as the leasor, and there is no reason to believe Mudry's version, particularly in the light of his recollections of his days at the CGQJ, quite at odds with those of the police who interrogated him at the Liberation: 'It was at these times that I met Darquier – two or three times – he had the offices of his Club National above.' (He [Mudry] said he'd never set foot in these offices, but later said that they were small). 'But Darquier didn't do any physical culture.' It is hard to choose between Darquier and Mudry as witnesses.

21 Some of the money to publish the *Bulletin*, and to pay the rent, may have come from Pozzo di Borgo, who had now fallen out with la Roque, and who was in the midst of planning a more revolutionary attack on the republic.

22 'Biff boys' was Oswald Mosley's name for his British version of the same kind of young men. Later, in prison camp in 1940, one of Louis' fellow prisoners implied that he had his own 'biff boys'. When the inmates of the prison camp turned upon him 'he no longer had his thugs from the funfair to protect him'. Crémieux-Brilhac: BBC, 16 May 1942.

23 This brochure (AN72 AJ 592: Fonds Vaniakoff) in which the membership rules are outlined was issued in October 1936. Strangely enough, Louis Darquier, as president, only used his real name, but this may well have been for legal reasons, because he was about to go to court, and also about to receive René's bailiffs.

24 Taguieff, p. 397; *Action française*, 4 August 1936.

25 **Robert Brasillach** (1909–45): A Maurrassian, a novelist and one of the most important men of letters on the French right. Like Lucien Rebatet, a collaborationist – pro-Nazi. Editor-in-chief of *Je Suis partout*, a prose murderer. Condemned to death and executed by firing squad in 1945.
Georges Blond (1906–89): Married Germaine Garrigue of St-Paul-de-Loubressac, whose parents were very close friends of the Darquier family. Blond was a ship's captain turned journalist and writer, colleague and partisan of Brasillach; he was put on the index for collaboration (one of his works was a selection of the choice words of Hitler). After the war he wrote quantities of novels and books about the sea and those who sail on it.

26 Tannenbaum, p. 224. These hundred deputies wanted heavier sanctions against Italy for its war on Ethiopia.

27 The elders of anti-Semitism, men born in the 1860s, were all editors or journalists. As well as Lucien Pemjean, the lieutenant of the Marquis de Morès, there was **Urbain Gohier** (1862–1951), professional anti-Semite, journalist, editor and writer, who published the first French edition of the *Protocols* in 1920. A noted polemicist, financed by Coty, and a hounder of Maurras and Daudet, he was nearly eighty when France fell, but continued his vituperative journalism throughout the Occupation. He was convicted after the Liberation but his age spared him imprisonment. **Jean Drault** (1866–1951) was another professional anti-Semite and journalist. Drumont's closest disciple, he also wrote successful humorous books for children. Associated with Coston and Boissel, a vicious collaborationist during the Occupation, he edited *La France au travail* until in 1943 the Germans gave him the editorship of the pinnacle of anti-Semitic publications, *Au Pilori*. Arrested in August 1944, he was imprisoned at Drancy, sentenced to seven years' imprisonment, and freed in 1949.

Joining these fathers of anti-Semitism were those born a decade later, men such as the fanatic and alcoholic **Paul Sézille** (1879–1944), another wounded and decorated First World War veteran, the mystic Hitlerian **Alphonse de Chateaubriant** (1877–1951) and the demented anglophobe Paul Chack (1876–1945). Louis Darquier's generation came next. All of them were veterans of the trenches, bearing wounds and honours in varying degrees. Louis was easily the most unscathed physically, but shared their eccentricities, rages, conspiracy theories and paranoia. Louis' continued subservience to Charles Maurras managed to alienate all of them:

Jean Boissel (1891–1951): Severely disabled First World War veteran, he lost his right eye and wore an eye patch like Vallat. Professional anti-Semite, fascist, journalist. A prolific founder of minuscule parties, papers and groups, his prose was even more poisonous than Darquier's. Visited Germany, appearing with Streicher at a Nuremberg rally, and met Hitler in 1935. Subsidised by the Nazis in the Darquier manner; he was often in prison or in court. Participated in the foundation of the LVF in 1941. A refugee in Sigmaringen, he was arrested and condemned to death in 1946, but the sentence was commuted to life with hard labour. He died in prison.

Marcel Bucard (1895–1946): First World War veteran, with honours, journalist and failed politician. Founder of the Francistes, the 'Paris Blueshirts' (not to be confused with Coston's group of the same name), his newspaper *Le Franciste,* and his political party after June 1936, was the Parti Unitaire Français. Originally financed by François Coty. No Jews or Freemasons were allowed. A neighbour of Darquier's in the Ternes, he was funded by the Nazis, but was an advocate of Mussolini's approach and, again like Darquier, was financially questionable and often in court. A Catholic in the Vallat mould, he was also a speaker for the FNC and a member of Croix-de-feu. Arrested in 1944, he was sentenced to death and executed by firing squad.

Henri-Robert Petit (or Henri, or Henry-Robert) (1899–1985): Professional anti-Semite. Son of a royalist, joined Croix-de-feu, then Henry Coston on *Libre parole* in 1935. Founded the Centre for Information and Propaganda with Coston, and was also secretary-general of the International Anti-Communist League. Fell out with Coston over purloining his archives and library, and moved over to work with Darquier in 1937. In 1938 he fell out with Darquier, who accused him of stealing money. After various other checks, all of a similar nature, he went to Erfurt to work for the Weltdienst. His life during the Occupation was equally marked by accusations of swindling and successive rows, though he managed to maintain a correspondence with Céline. He was in close contact with the propaganda departments of the German occupiers, and it seems he was a member of the French Gestapo. Condemned after the war, *in absentia*, to twenty years' hard labour and *dégradation nationale*, he was granted amnesty in 1959 and remained in France, adding investigations into astrology, druidic rituals and esotericism to his *oeuvre*, though his anti-Semitism continued in the post-war neo-Nazi organisation FANE: he was condemned several times for incitement to racial hatred. Typical of his published works is *Rothschild, King of Israel and the Americans*, published in France in 1941.

After Louis' generation came the Young Turks (*Jeunes Turcs*), born too late to fight in the First World War, but often fatherless because of it. Henry Coston was their most indefatigable representative, whilst Pierre Clémenti, who reduced Coston's Francistes to ruin and absconded with Coston's wife, was the most criminal. Most of them were former followers of Maurras, la Roque or Coty, but had by the mid-1930s chosen new leaders:

Pierre Clémenti (1910–82): Professional anti-Semite, fascist, journalist, took over Coston's Francistes in August 1934. A suspected arms trafficker, failed politician and client of Fleischhauer, he was often at war with Coston. He joined the LVF and fought on the Russian front. Disputed again with other collaborationists on his return, including Christian de la Mazière, a notable performer in *Le Chagrin et la pitié*. Throughout he was an informer for the Germans. Sentenced to death in 1948, he was reprieved, and freed after five years to repeat the same performances over Algeria.

Henry Coston (sometimes Henri) (1910–2001): Coston said he came across the works of Édouard Drumont in his uncle's attic, and so joined Action Française at the age of sixteen. With fellow anti-Semite and journalist Jacques Ploncard d'Assac he rescued and reissued Drumont's *Libre parole* in 1928. In May 1930 he founded his Anti-Jewish Youth. In 1933 he formed his own fascist party, the Francistes, not to be confused with Marcel Bucard's party of the same name. The similarity of his approach to Hitler's caused a rift with Maurras. The Nazis financed Coston as early as 1934; in 1935 he stood as an anti-Semitic

'France for the French' candidate for the Paris city council as Drumont and Morès had before him, and like them both, but unlike Darquier, he failed. His CDP (Centre de Documentation et de Propagande), and *Libre parole* poured out tracts, brochures, reviews, books, badges, stamps and stickers. Some of his tracts were notorious for printing an anti-Semitic text on the other side of a hundred-franc note. The names of his organisations, offices and publishing houses changed again and again, but the impetus was always the same. Coston wrote literally hundreds, possibly thousands, of books and pamphlets. By the time Louis met him, in 1934–35, he had already published *Parliament Under the Orders of Freemasonry* (1931), *The Masonic Cartel Against France* (1932), *The General Directory of French Freemasonry, The Lodges and Their Principal Leaders* (1933), *Celebrated Freemasons, Nationalist Words* and *The Mysteries of Freemasonry* (1934). The following year his works included *The Jewish Conspiracy* and *Jews and Freemasons Unmasked*. Coston left Paris in August 1944, after destroying nearly all his papers. Arrested in Austria in 1946, he was sentenced in 1947 to hard labour for life, confiscation of his assets and *dégradation nationale*. He spent five years in prison, was released for ill health in April 1951 and granted amnesty in 1959. He never ceased to write and to publish voluminously, using every outlet and form available, and also the services of his wife, so that he became an invaluable archivist and chronicler of the far right in France. His major work was his five-volume *Dictionnaire de la politique française*, a prodigious work, recording with malice and bias the underbelly of French history in the twentieth century.

28 Louis Darquier in his preface to the *Protocols*.

29 Jean to René, undated, probably October 1936.

30 *Le Voltaire*, 27 June 1936; BNF JO-77305.

31 AAPA: 24 February 1937 Herr Feihl, head of the press office at the German embassy in Paris, gives a full account of Castille's visit and Darquier's request for money (Feihl to the German Foreign Ministry, with footnote by Ambassador Welczek, 18 February 1937). Castille showed Welczek a letter from 'Baron Darquier de Pellepoix'. Another approach seems to have been made later when Louis planned to visit Dr Bohle, Secretary of State at the Ministry of Foreign Affairs, and head of the AO, the foreign organisation of the Nazi party. Police reports of Louis' Anti-Jewish Union of France meetings state that they were very ill-attended at this point, and as to lawyers, I have traced only three. Welczek also told the ministry that because of 'divisions between the right and the Popular Front, new, radical right-wing parties are being founded and their representatives come to the German embassy asking for money or material support'. He mentioned Bucard, and Renaud of Solidarité Française, and requests for funding from other newly formed extreme right-wing political parties.

32 **Elizabeth Büttner** (dates unknown): Women are not easily found without

knowing the name of husband, maiden name or date of birth. On Elizabeth Büttner's chequebook there was an address in Berlin, Uhlandastr. 167/8 Berlin-Charlottenberg, now occupied by a company called Frankenstein. This turned out to be Frankenstein, H., publishing director, head of the Prämien Reklame GmbH (Bonus Advertising Ltd.), registered at Uhlandstrasse 167/168. The caretaker there refused to talk, and we could not find any records of old tenancies. Postbank, the legal successor of Postscheckamt Berlin, where Elizabeth Büttner had her bank account, confirmed her address and stated that she cancelled the account on 8 April 1940, but cannot explain how she was not listed at the given address, while Frankenstein was. Many other avenues were pursued, with no result. Elizabeth Büttner, according to *l'Humanité*, had, like Abetz, been expelled from Britain before the war. Today there are over six hundred Büttners in Berlin. I tracked down a Eugen Walter Büttner, an SS leader in Freiberg, a sadistic commander of various concentration camps – he had three daughters. There was also a Walter Büttner in Ribbentrop's Foreign Office, of whom 'Missie' Vassiltchikov gives a good account – inasmuch as she hated him – in her *Berlin Diaries*. This Büttner, born in 1908, was obviously a Nazi. The Landesarchiv in Berlin confirmed that there was a Walter Büttner married to an Elizabeth Büttner, whose maiden name was Glintzer, but this also proved a dead end.

The file for Louis' trial before the Haute Cour de Justice in 1947 refers to counterfoils from a chequebook. These were taken during a search of his premises at rue Laugier in 1939; they were given back to him in 1942 when he requested the return of his seized property after his appointment to the CGQJ, then seized again when investigating officers from the Haute Cour searched Gérard's home on 12 February 1945. 'It seems obvious that these items were gathered up along with my personal effects,' said Gérard. When asked about this in 1945, and again in 1947, Gérard said that when Darquier got back his property in 1942 he was 'also given items that did not belong to him', and denied all knowledge of Elizabeth Büttner. The chequebook belonged to Büttner, resident in Berlin, and the counterfoils detail payments made to several leaders of French extreme right-wing parties (Coston, Bucard, Clémenti, de Gobineau) and two payments made to Darquier de Pellepoix: one of 2,500 Reichsmarks on 4 January 1937, and another of 3,000 Reichsmarks on 25 August 1938. The bank concerned is only referred to by the initials BIC or BIG – possibly the Banque Internationale de Commerce in Paris.

33 **Jean Luchaire** (1901–46): Journalist and editor. A member of the Radical Party and supporter of the Popular Front. Like de Monzie he was pro-European, pro-peace and pro-Munich. His *Une Generation réaliste*, published in 1928, summed up the views of those too young to have fought in the war, Henry de Jouvenel's son Bertrand being one such. During the Occupation he launched *Les Nouveaux temps*, a leftish, collaborationist daily. Luchaire belonged to the

Abetz/Laval camp, like Déat, though without the latter's principles. He was utterly venal, and took money from anyone for anything. He also had much in common with a man like de Monzie, politically and as a *bon viveur*; he was, however, more honest and self-knowing. After the Liberation he fled with others to Sigmaringen, where with de Brinon and Darnand he was part of a trio of government in exile. Escaped to Italy, arrested there in 1945, condemned to death and shot. His daughter Corinne was a well-known actress of the time.

Fernand de Brinon (1885–1947): First World War veteran. Lawyer and journalist. Rabid anti-Semite and advocate of Hitler: 'Hitler has always detested the shedding of blood.' Some sources say he was the son of a marquis. Others suggest that like Louis Darquier, he 'borrowed' his title of Comte. Served under Pétain in the trenches. Worked for a Greek millionaire who was an occasional importer of cocaine. Married the actress Jeanne or Yvonne Ducas, lost her, and his money on racehorses, then married Lisette Franck, a wealthy Jewish woman; through her he worked for the Jewish bank Lazard Frères. Friend of Ribbentrop. First French journalist to interview Hitler (*Le Matin* and *l'Illustration*, December 1933). Laval's secretary in September 1940 before becoming *chargé de mission* in Paris, i.e. Vichy ambassador in the Occupied Zone, at the Hôtel Matignon where Laval spent his time in Paris. To de Brinon's rooms there came thousands of French supplicants, which made him one of the most hated of all French collaborators. From April 1942 he was also in Laval's Vichy cabinet. Lisette de Brinon spent most of the war safe in the countryside, which was just as well, as de Brinon was given to complaints about 'Yids' and 'Youpins' at his numerous dinner parties, even in her presence. During the Occupation he formed a trio of power with Abetz and Laval. Formed Groupe Collaboration, successor to the pre-war Comité France–Allemagne, and was president of the LVF committee. In Sigmaringen he headed its government in exile. Arrested in Bavaria in 1945, tried in 1947, sentenced to death and executed by firing squad.

Pierre Drieu la Rochelle (1893–1945): First World War veteran. Fascist intellectual, poet, novelist, essayist and editor of *La Nouvelle revue française* during the Occupation. Friend of Abetz and for a time a follower of Doriot. Committed suicide in March 1945.

Monseigneur Jean Mayol de Lupé (1873–1955): See Chapter 20, n. 5.

34 This Foreign Office document (TNA: PRO FO 371/31941–Z3005), written by the Foreign Research Press Office at Balliol College in 1942, is not entirely trustworthy, as it couples Baroness von Einem with Elizabeth Büttner as one of Abetz's espionage assistants. If this refers to Elizabeth von Arnim, the author of *Elizabeth and her German Garden*, then I find it very unlikely. It could however be a reference to another member of the German family into which Elizabeth von Arnim married. As Professor Achim von Arnim, SA Gruppenführer, was president of Abetz's German branch of this organisation, this is probably the case.

35 If the money did not come from Abetz, it may still have come from

Ribbentrop's office through the multitude of Nazi conduits – Fleischhauer, Streicher – available to support men like Louis Darquier before the war. The list of names implies Fleischhauer's contacts.

36 No. 53, 24 April 1937, Bulletin du Club National AN 26 AS/6.

37 The vice-presidents of the Comité Antijuif de France were Jean Boissel and Philippe Poirson of the Union Anti-Maçonnique de France (Anti-Masonic Union of France), founded in 1895 and revived in March 1935 by a Parisian deputy and war veteran, **Dr Georges Cousin** (1886–?), who also founded the parliamentary party group devoted to fighting Masonry, of which Xavier Vallat and Jean Ybarnégaray were members. Darquier met Poirson in 1934, when he was working for *le Jour*.

38 Bulletin du Club National no. 53, 24 April 1937.

39 CDJC CC XIV-78.

40 *La France enchaînée*, October 1938 quoted by Crémieux-Brilhac: BBC, 1 July 1942 and also in CDJC CCXIV-78.

CHAPTER 10

On the Rampage

INTERVIEWS AND CORRESPONDENCE: Jean-Louis Crémieux-Brilhac, Danny Puddefoot, Alistair Rapley, Pat Smalley, Tasmania J., Teresa. SOURCES: Darquier family correspondence; AN 26 AS/6; AN 3W142; AN 72 AJ 592: Fonds Vaniakoff; AN AG/3(2)326 (BCRA); AN F7 14781: confidential note of the Sûreté Nationale; AN F7 14781: dossier of Charles Roze, secretary to Darquier de Pellepoix; APP GA D9, 25 February, 25 November 1935, 5 November 1936, 31 December 1938, 6 January 1939; APP GA R4, 14 April and 30 May 1938; Archives Départementales du Bas-Rhin, Strasbourg, 98 AL698: Fonds Valot; Bibliothèque de Paris, *Bottin Mondain*; BMO, 5, 7 and 14 April, 30 November 1937; BNF FRBNF-31370526; BNF JO-77305; CAC 880509, art. 15, investigatory file (dossier d'instruction); CDJC CCCLXXIX-3, March 1937; CDJC CCXIV-78; TNA: PRO FO 892/163. PUBLICATIONS: *L'Alntijuif*, 22 May, 3 and 26 June, 17 July, July–August (Special Propaganda Edition), 25 October, 30 November, 4 and 18 December 1937; Ben-Itto, *Die Protokolle der Weisen von Zion*; *Biographisches Handbuch der deutschsprachigen Emigration nach 1933*; Bollmus, *Das Amt Rosenberg und Seine Gegner*; Brechtken, *Madagaskar für die Juden*; Bulletin du Centre de Documentation et de Vigilance, no. 59; Byrnes, *Antisemitism in Modern France*, vol. 1; Cohn, *Warrant for Genocide*; *Le Crapouillot*; *Le Droit de vivre*, 5 February and 16 April 1938; Dubard, '*En buvant un verre avec Céline*', *la France enchaînée*, 15 December 1938; *l'Excelsior*, 5 March and 5 May 1938; *La France enchaînée*, 19 April 1938 and 3 August 1939; Gordon, *Collaborationism in France*; Halls, *Politics, Society and Christianity in Vichy France*; *l'Histoire*, no. 15, October 1992; Hoffman, *Change and Tradition*; Jackson, *The Popular Front in*

France; Joly, 'Darquier de Pellepuix: "Champion"', *Darquier de Pellepoix et l'antisémitisme français*; Kaplan, *Relevé des sources et citations dans Bagatelles pour un massacre*; Princess Karadja, *King Solomon: A Mystic Drama*, www.sacred-texts.com; Kingston, *Anti-Semitism in France during the 1930s*; McCarthy, *Céline*; Marrus and Paxton, *Vichy France and the Jews*; Paxton, *Vichy France*; Randa, *Dictionnaire commenté de la collaboration française*; *Le Réveil du peuple*, 15 March 1936; Taguieff (ed.), *L'Antisémitisme de plume*; Vitoux, *Céline*; BNF: *Le Voltaire*, 25 April 1936; Weber, *Action Française*

1 BMO, 30 November 1937.

2 Tasmania J.

3 *ibid.*

4 Taguieff, p. 398.

5 APP GA R4, 14 April 1938.

6 Tasmania J.

7 Neither Danny Puddefoot nor Alistair Rapley believe Elsie could speak French, but Pat Smalley, a neighbour in Hazel Crescent, is certain of it. Elsie worked for other members of the upper classes before she came upon the Darquiers: this may be how she learned it.

8 'In order to mark the foundation of the Anti-Jewish Union of France with a gesture of solidarity and to make more efficient the battle that we are leading to create a France for the French, we have decided to combine the Bulletin of the National Club and the Bulletin of the Centre for Information and Propaganda in a single publication . . . *l'Antijuif*.' *L'Antijuif*, 20 May 1937.

9 Joly, *Darquier de Pellepoix*, pp. 109–110 quoting *l'Antijuif* of 3 June 1937.

10 Brechtken, pp. 50, 69,70.

11 There were various predecessors of *l'Antijuif*, including the newspaper of Father E.A. Chabauty in 1881 and that of Jules Guérin, disciple of Drumont, during the Dreyfus case.

12 Joly, *Darquier de Pellepoix*, p. 127.

13 **Bernard Lecache** (1895–1968): First World War veteran, joined the Communist Party, wrote for *l'Humanité* but left both. In 1927, horrified by the pogroms in the Ukraine, founded the Ligue Internationale contre l'Antisémitisme (LICA) and the newspaper *Le Droit de vivre* (*The Right to Live*). An anti-fascist and lifelong militant, he remained president of LICA (now LICRA, the added 'R' being for 'Racisme') until his death.

14 Five Nazi organisations were funding men like Louis Darquier in these years:
   i. The German Foreign Office. Louis applied to them by way of Ambassador Welczek in January/ February 1937. Another approach seems to have been made later when Louis planned to visit Dr Bohle, Secretary of State at the Ministry of Foreign Affairs and head of the AO, the foreign organisation of the Nazi Party. See extract from a note sent by the Interior Ministry on 9 July 1938 in Goebbels' note below.

ii. The Ribbentrop Bureau, established in 1934, until Ribbentrop himself became Foreign Minister in 1938. Ribbentrop had much more money at his disposal than Rosenberg. Louis received money from Abetz/Büttner or Fleischhauer/Büttner; reports differ. Sources: a) in Louis Darquier's trial dossier AN 3W142; b) CAC 880509, art. 15, investigatory file (*dossier d'instruction*) of the Cagoule for the correspondence between Louis Darquier and Emilie Vasticar; c) Crémieux-Brilhac used information from **Manfred Simon** (1898–?) in his BBC '*Ici Londres*' programmes in 1942 – AN AG/3(2)326 (BCRA). Simon was a German-Jewish industrialist and expert on international law; emigrant to France, pacifist, philanthropist, contributor to educational and Jewish causes. A lawyer and economist with a doctorate of law from the Sorbonne; an anti-Nazi, he had good contacts with German resistance groups and those in exile. He fed important intelligence to the French Resistance and British government, and to de Gaulle and the Free French in London. Simon reported that it was Fleischhauer, not Abetz, who funded Darquier. Sources for Simon: interview with Crémieux-Brilhac, 8 October 1998; *Biographisches Handbuch der deutschsprachigen Emigration nach 1933*, which gives the following sources: Institut für Zeitgeschichte and Privatarchiv Hanns G. Reissner, Princetown, USA; also CV written by his sister, Sofie van Neyenhoff-Simon, at Institut für Zeitgeschichte, München. First Büttner cheque: 4 January 1937. For Manfred Simon's thesis: BNF FRBNF-31370526.

iii. Rosenberg's Foreign Office of the Nazi Party. Rosenberg funded Fleischhauer, who funded Louis Darquier, Coston et al., but we are in a more unfathomable area here, and it may well be that the Büttner connection was by way of Rosenberg and not Abetz, though the British Foreign Office was certain of the Abetz connection. See Bollmus, pp. 121–2 and throughout. See also extract from a note sent by the Interior Ministry on 9 July 1938 in Goebbels note below. During the Vichy years Rosenberg's other activity, the Einsatzstab Reichsleiter Rosenberg (ERR) in Paris, was the official state agency for looting Jewish possessions, so Louis Darquier had much to do with this office then. Grau (see below) worked there. Coston met Fleischhauer and Streicher in 1934; Louis connected with Coston in 1935.

iv. Goebbels' Ministry of Propaganda. The Ministry of Propaganda provided thirty thousand Reichsmarks for Fleischhauer for the Berne trial (Brechtken, pp. 57–8). For Fleischhauer's Nazi funding see also Marrus and Paxton, p. 284. Their sources are: AA: Pol. II, 'Innere Politik: Parlamant-und Parteiwesen, Frankreich 5, 1936–40 (T-120/753/269596–604); Report of 1 July 1939 (APP: 37022–B). However, it was impossible to find the report of 1 July 1939 in the archives at the Préfecture de Paris. The filing system at the archives has been changed, and ref 37022–B cannot be traced. But

Robert Paxton, the great historian of Vichy France, saw this document, and there is a later report from the Renseignements Généraux, dated 31 December 1938, in Darquier's file. This report mentions a note of 29 December 1937 from the Interior Ministry to the Foreign Ministry. It says: 'Darquier de Pellepoix is in regular contact with the Internationale Antisémite . . . The latter receives orders from Mr Julien Strasser [sic: police misspelling for Julius Streicher], the leading anti-Semitic theoretician of the Third Reich, and is supported by Germans and Italians.' APP GA D9, 31 December 1938. Date of contact: 1937.

The organisation the police called the Internationale Antisémite de Genève could be the Alliance Anti-Israélite Universelle (World Anti-Israelite Alliance), founded in August 1886 in Bucharest. Jacques de Biez, failed French playwright and disciple of Drumont, helped found it, and its inspiration came from Biez, Drumont and Paul de Lagarde, the nineteenth-century German equivalent to Drumont who proposed such ideas as 'Blood and Soil', the 'Master Race' and 'German living space in the East'. Hitler used all of these ideas. I have been unable to find out anything about Otto Grutzner. The Alliance spread all over Europe in the Twenties and Thirties and became a counter-movement to the Communist International.

Another extract from a note sent by the Interior Ministry on 9 July 1938 mentions: 'It is to be noted that Darquier de Pellepoix will soon visit Nuremberg where he is to meet Messrs Alfred Rosenberg and Fleischhauer. We believe he will then go to Berlin for a meeting with leaders of the Nazi party, particularly Dr Bohle, Secretary of State at the Ministry of Foreign Affairs, and head of the AO, the Foreign organisation of the Nazi Party.' However, there is no proof that Louis Darquier made this visit.

iv. Himmler and his SS. Louis received money directly from them later; in the Thirties Fleischhauer was in direct contact with the SS. See: a) Brechtken, pp. 54–5, and Sicherheitsdienst, SS reference file Cooperation with other offices/Fleischhauer-Finke BArch.R 58/988, BL. 3, and also BL 26,90.286; b) Ben-Itto, p. 134; c) Marrus and Paxton, p. 45, outlines Coston and Darquier's funding, to which their notes refer.

In addition, the involvement of:

vi. Rudolf Hess, Hitler's deputy, Walter Frank's Reich Institute for the History of the New Germany and Wilhlem Grau's Frankfurt Institute for Research on the Jewish Question are often mentioned as funding agents in these years.

vii. The police report of July 1939 states that another source was the publisher Deutscher Fichte-bund of Hamburg, with the French anti-Semite most active in this connection being Serpeille de Gobineau. This report calls Darquier a '*Fourrier d'Hitler*', Hitler's Harbinger. This may well be the money Louis received in June 1939. 'After establishing contact with the prefecture of the Rhône on 30 June 1939, the funds serving to finance *La France enchaînée* were to be transferred into France by the intermediary of agents residing in Belgium and by the secretary of Darquier de Pellepoix, a man called Roze,' (Joly, *Darquier de Pellepoix*, p. 113. Joly's source is AN F7 14781, dossier of Charles Roze, secretary to Darquier de Pellepoix.) Nothing can be discovered about this Charles Roze.

viii. Jean-Louis Crémieux-Brilhac believed Louis was funded directly by Fleischhauer (BBC Radio, '*Ici Londres*', AN AG/3(2)326 (BCRA), transcript of broadcast by Crémieux-Brilhac on 16 May 1942. There are many errors of fact in his résumé of Darquier's relationships with the Nazis, what they funded and what they did not: for instance, Crémieux-Brilhac asserts that they paid for Louis' election to the city council. 'He [Louis Darquier] handled the French distribution of the periodical the *World Service*. This *World Service* was one of the publications issued by the "L'Internationale Antisémite", whose headquarters were in Erfurt, under the directorship of Colonel Fleischhauer. Each month, Darquier de Pellepoix, who was already a purveyor of betrayal before becoming a profiteer of defeat, received payments from Germany in the form of international money orders stamped in Erfurt. It was therefore the money from Colonel Fleischhauer, that is to say from Hitler, that was used to finance his anti-Semitic newspaper *La France enchaînée*, which was run by Darquier and which was nothing less than the French edition of the German paper *Der Stürmer* published in Nuremberg. It was therefore the money from Colonel Fleischhauer, that is to say from Hitler, that financed Darquier's electoral funds and allowed him to recruit a whole crowd of thugs from a sideshow at a funfair to work as his security police during public meetings . . .' The gist is right, but it is unlikely that Fleischhauer was doing much more than disbursing the money both Rosenberg and Goebbels gave him – as, probably, did other Nazi anti-Semitic organisations too.

15 *L'Antijuif* (first issue 3 June 1937, last issue 22 January 1938) seems to have appeared about every three weeks. All quotes from *l'Antijuif* nos. 4 and 5, 17 July 1937; no.3, 26 June 1937; no.10, 25 October 1937; and July–August 1937, A Special Propaganda Edition.

16 Christian Polemon, 'Hitler Creature of Israel, etc.': 'The Jewish race has always been tightly allied to the German race by a close, almost fraternal bond, and Yiddish is based on the German language . . .' *Action française*, 17 November 1938.

17 *L'Antijuif*, Special Propaganda Edition July–August 1937.

18 CDJC XIV-78, quoting *La France Réelle*, 5 August 1937.

19 CDJC CCXIV-78 RG report 3.9.1937; Also in PRO Fo 892/163.

20 Princess Karadja, p. 130–131 (see also www.sacred-texts.com).

21 *L'Antijuif*, Special Propaganda Edition, July–August 1937.

22 The presiding magistrate, a M. Roux, asked Pierre Gérard how the Jews managed to stop French people having children. Gérard replied that he had shown how in his newspaper article. Tribunal Correctionnel (Magistrates' Court) de la Seine, 12ème chambre, 26 July 1939.

23 *L'Antijuif*, no. 1, 3 June 1937.

24 Joly, *Darquier de Pellepoix,* p. 108, and *l'Antijuif*, October 1937.

25 The Cagoule was the popular name for the Organisation Secrète d'Action Révolutionnaire Nationale (OSARN).

26 Pétain was a reactionary, not a revolutionary; but his aide Loustanau-Lacau instigated an anti-communist network in the army, called the Réseaux Corvignolles. Weygand and Pétain were connected with the Cagoule through the army and the Corvignolles, which had a lot to do with Pétain and which later surfaced in Algérie Française.

27 **Eugène Deloncle** (1890–1944): Distinguished First World War veteran, broke with Action Française to found the Cagoule. A right-wing revolutionary, he led the Mouvement Social Révolutionnaire (MSR) in 1940 and was co-founder, with Marcel Déat, of the collaborationist political party the RNP (see note on Déat, Chapter 12, n. 33) and was also involved in the creation of the LVF. Deloncle was an anti-Semite who blew up synagogues in Paris with the SS, but he fell out with them, as with others, and was shot by the Gestapo in January 1944.

28 'Henry Charbonneau, a Camelot who had gone over to the more effective activities of the Cagoule' – by becoming Deloncle's secretary while he was in the Santé prison. 'The Comité National [de Vigilance des Jeunes Français Mobilisables] held a huge meeting in the Magic City Music Hall, at which four thousand determined young Frenchmen heard the professional anti-Semite Darquier de Pellepoix announce that he, for one, would not fight at the bidding of international plutocracy. No one could count on *them* for a Masonic and Soviet war, the organisers announced amid general enthusiasm' (Weber, *Action Française*, p. 293). Pozzo di Borgo was another Cagoule member. In addition Fleischhauer had fallen out with de Pottere in 1936, but the following year the latter turned up in Switzerland as an agent of the Weltdienst, and seems to have inserted funds into the Cagoule.

29 Jean Boissel and Jean Drault also attended Fleischhauer's Congress in Erfurt in September 1937 and met Streicher and Eichmann; Emilie Vasticar was fed the calumny that Louis and his club were 'friendly to Jews'.

30 Registered Letter

Paris, 5 November 1938

Monsieur Darquier de Pellepoix

12 rue Laugier Paris

Monsieur,

Following the visit made on your behalf by messieurs Rémondy and X . . . we believe that a meeting to discuss the amount of your rent would be a waste of time for all parties since we cannot envisage reducing this amount in any way.

Furthermore, we regret to have to inform you that we can no longer tolerate the constant late payment of your rent as has been the case during the past 15 months. Therefore we ask you to pay in full before the 20th of the present month, the amount that was due on 15th October. Our professional situations do not allow us to engage in these incessant and futile requests.

We remain, Sir, yours etc.

The heirs of Ballagny

31 The banker was Pozzo di Borgo.

32 APP GA D9D9, 31 December 1938.

33 November 1938, Joly, "Champion", p. 47. His source: AN F7 14781 Confidential note of the *Sûreté Nationale* (the C.I.D.).

34 *L'Antijuif*, no. 11, 30 November 1937, no. 12, 4 December 1937 and no. 13, 18 December 1937.

35 **Pierre-Antoine Cousteau** (1906–58): Anti-Semite, collaborationist, political journalist, noted polemicist in *Je Suis partout*, and author of *l'Amerique juive*. Joined the Milice in 1944, then fled to Germany for whom he broadcast to France. Sentenced to death in 1946, commuted to life imprisonment in 1947, released in 1955, to some degree due to the good offices of his oceanographer brother.

    Alain Laubreaux (1898–1968): From French New Guinea, he became a radical journalist in Toulouse. Notorious theatre critic of *Je Suis partout*, but more, wrote the 'Echos' column devoted to denunciations and informing. Also a novelist and a broadcaster for Radio-Vichy. Member of Doriot's PPF. He denounced the existentialist Robert Desnos, and sent him to his death. Larger than life, as quarrelsome and violent as Darquier, of whom he was in many ways a more intelligent version. Fled to Germany, then Spain. Tried in absentia in 1947 and sentenced to death. He lived untouched in Madrid where he worked for Radio Nacional. He is Daxiat in François Truffaut's film *Le Dernier métro*.

36 Vitoux, p. 319.

37 Taguieff (ed.), p. 153.

    Lucien Rebatet (1903–72): Member of AF, film and music critic for *Action française*, enthusiastic anti-Semite and one of the most important writers for *Je suis partout* from 1932 to 1944. The most notorious and celebrated fascist and collaborationist writer of the war. After the war he fled to Germany, then Austria. Arrested and condemned to death in 1946, he was pardoned and freed in 1952, and continued his literary career until his death.

38 McCarthy, pp. 149 and 152, quoting Céline's *Bagatelles*.

39 Vitoux p. 319 quoting Céline's *Bagatelles*

40 *La France enchaînée*, no. 18, 15 December 1938, *En buvant un verre avec Céline* by Robert Dubard.

41 If we are to believe his tax return for March 1938 – and, of course, there is no reason to do so – Louis' taxable income was 20,473 francs (worth £6,800 today). Obviously, he declared none of his German monies on this return.

42 Jean to René, undated, probably October 1936.

43 Archives départementales du Bas-Rhin, 98 AL698 Fonds Valot, 25 November 1937, Prefect of the Department of the Bas-Rhin to Ministry of the Interior.

44 Prefect of the Haut-Rhin to Ministry of the Interior. Archives Départementales du Bas-Rhin, Strasbourg, 98 AL698, Fonds Valot, Archives de la Direction Générale d'Alsace-Lorraine, 98AL698, Sémitisme et Antisémitisme (1926–40). This letter, one of many, is undated, but must be after March 1938, as it refers to the tract of that date. Louis himself called the Nazis 'generous donors' who enabled him to publish three thousand copies of *La France enchaînée* in Strasbourg. When advising the furniture salesman from Lyon who wanted advice as to how to get money from German sources for anti-Semitic activities, Louis also told him to continue contact with the German Consul there.

45 Archives Départementales du Bas-Rhin, Strasbourg, as above. Letter of 19 September 1938.

46 *ibid.*, letter of 23 April 1938, leaflet distributed in the market of the old station of Strasbourg on 23 March 1938.

47 On 5 February and 16 April 1938 *Le Droit de vivre* accused Louis of being in the pay of Germany. On 22 April in *La France enchaînée* Louis wrote of him: '*Lecache est un individu ignoble, il accomplit dans l'humanité une abominable besogne et déverse sur les officiers des poubelles d'excréments . . . cet excrément de ghetto . . . ce pourceau circoncis*'. ('Lecache is a vile individual, one of those human beings who carries out his repellent deeds and showers his betters with bucket loads of excrement . . . that excrement from the ghetto . . . that circumcised swine'.) On 5 May 1938 Lecache's men invaded one of Louis' meetings – five people were injured, and there were seven arrests.

48 Company declaration, authorised 2 March 1938. Louis said he published it himself, on the first and fifteenth of each month, but it was actually printed by *Action française*. It began with only two pages, went up to four or five, and then to six pages after issue no. 8.

49 AN 3W142/288 et AN 72 AJ 592, Fonds Vaniakoff.

50 Councillor Hirschovitz, of the St-Gervais quarter, is not to be confused with Georges Hirsch, Louis' previous opponent. AN 3W142. This episode was not recorded in the BMO.

51 BMO, 5 April 1938.

52 *La France enchaînée*, no. 3, 19 April 1938.

CHAPTER 11

War

INTERVIEWS AND CORRESPONDENCE: Bill Coy, Jean Gayet, Yvonne Lacaze, Auguste Mudry, Pierre Orliac, Alistair Rapley, Simone Reste, Pat Smalley. SOURCES: AMAE (b), no. 392; AN 3W142; AN 72 AJ 592: Fonds Vaniakoff; APP dossier 79/501/882–B; APP GA D9, 28 November, 14 and 31 December 1938, 4 and 7 January 1939, 28 February 1940, 7 May and 13 June 1942; APP GA R4: draft of 14 April 1938 and later version of 30 May 1938; BMO, 21 December 1938; CAC 880509: art. 15, investigative file of the Cagoule; CDJC 6600; CDJC LXII-11; CDJC LXXIV-13; CDJC XCV-31, 75; CDJC XCVI-57; CDJC CXLIV-424; TNA: PRO FO 371/31941–Z3005. PUBLICATIONS: *Action française*, 1 October and 17 November 1938, 1–15 April 1939; *l'Antijuif*, May, June, August and November 1937; Bankwitz, *Maxime Weygand and Civil–Military Relations in Modern France*; Billig, *Le Commissariat Général aux Questions Juives (1941–1944)*; Crémieux-Brilhac, BBC Radio, 16 May 1942; Crémieux-Brilhac, BBC radio broadcasts 1 May 1942, 1 July 1942; Crémieux-Brilhac, *Les Français de l'an 40*; de Monzie, *Ci-devant*; *La France enchaînée*, 15–31 December, 15–30 November 1938, 1–15 and 15–30 April, 15–31 May, 1–15 June 1939; Gee, *Keeping up with the Joneses*; Horne, *To Lose a Battle*; Jackson, *The Popular Front in France*; Jardin, *Vichy Boyhood*; Joly, 'Darquier de Pellepoix: "Champion" des Antisémites Français'; Joly, *Darquier de Pellepoix et l'antisémitisme français*; *Les Amis de Rassinier*, © by Gilles Karmasyn 1999, http://www.phdn.org/negation/rassinier/coston.html; *Keesing's Contemporary Archives*, 12–19 June 1948; Kingston, *Anti-Semitism in France during the 1930s*; Koestler, *The Scum of the Earth*; Laloum, *La France antisémite de Darquier de Pellepoix*; Larkin, *France Since the Popular Front*; Laubreaux, *Ecrit pendant la guerre*; Lottman, *Pétain*; Lukacs, *The Duel*; Marrus and Paxton, *Vichy France and the Jews*; Mazet, *Céline et Montandon*, www.louis-ferdinandceline.free.fr; Ousby, *Occupation*; Paxton, *Vichy France*; Peschanski, *La France des camps*; Pryce-Jones, *Paris in the Third Reich*; Saint-Paulien, *Histoire de la collaboration*; Soucy, *French Fascism: The Second Wave 1933–1939*; Taguieff (ed.), *L'Antisémitisme de plume*; Taylor, *The Strategy of Terror*, *The Times*, 20 June 1939; Warner, *Pierre Laval and the Eclipse of France*; Weber, *Action Française*; 'What the Taxpayers are Paying for', *l'Ordre*, 25 October 1938; Waygand, *Recalled to Service*

1 *L'Antijuif*, May, June and August 1937.
2 Telegram from Robert Dubard to Emilie Vasticar, Fleischhauer's secretary, 26 April 1938: '*Le combat mené par Darquier est commencé, espoir que des " moyens" viendront bientôt.*' ('Darquier's battle has commenced, let us hope that the "means" will come soon.')
3 Tasmania J.
4 *La France enchaînée*, no. 26, 15-30 April 1939.
5 *Action française*, 1 October 1938.

6 Larkin, p. 71.

7 **Pierre Auguste Galien** (1898–1978) lived at 26, rue du Château, Neuilly. Super Gom was at 110, rue du Landy at la plaine St-Denis. Pierre Galien, in the histories of Vichy, is often called Joseph, and his name is often spelled as Gallien. Vague as such histories are about Darquier, they are vaguer still about his germanophile deputy. At the Liberation he was arrested on 1 September 1944, then moved from jail to hospital prison in December on the assumption that he had a brain tumour; but this may have been no more than a rumour based on the testimony of Galien's personal doctor, Maurice Tussau, who said of him, 'From a mental point of view, he is a sick man.' Time was kind to Galien, as it was to so many of Darquier's war cronies. He was released on parole in April 1945 and did not attend his trial in July 1949. He died in his bed in a nursing home in Lyon in March 1978.

8 Some Germans certainly thought Galien was the 'principal financier' of *La France enchaînée*.

9 APP GA R4: draft of 14 April 1938 and later version of 30 May 1938:

10 APP GA D9, 48 5830, report of 14 December 1938.

11 *Action française* reported Louis' outburst in the council chamber the next day, 16 November 1938. The BMO censored his comment to M. Hirschovitz; *Action française* did not.

12 Police reports: APPGA/D9 dossier Darquier. The first report dated 6 June 1938, is almost solely concerned with Louis Darquier; the second, more detailed report, 'La Propagande anti-juive' is July 1939 AP dossier 79/501/882–B and is reprinted *in toto* in Kingston, p. 7.

13 **Marcel Jouhandeau** (1888–1979). Prolific and much-quoted French writer. Doctors were omnipresent. *La France enchaînée* ran a medical column written by Dr Fernand Querrioux, a good friend of Louis-Ferdinand Céline and the most envenomed adversary of Jewish doctors and their 'invasion' of the medical profession, while Dr Georges Rémondy, a nose specialist, became the Union's treasurer and wrote a 'Doctor's Corner' column for the newspaper, producing an 'harmonious' anti-Semitism attuned to the French spirit, not 'racism in the vulgar sense of Hitlerian doctrine'. The rest of his news team were Pierre Gérard, joined by other men of affairs and a token representative of the working class, and by anti-Semitic writers old – Urbain Gohier, Jean Drault, the cartoonist Ralph Soupault – and new – a recent anti-Semitic notable, Laurent Viguier, and Léon de Poncins, whose talents and insights closely echoed those of Princess Karadja.

14 Letter of Montandon to Professor Hans F.K. Günther, 23 October 1938. CDJC XCV-31 (Billig, p.109).

15 Georges Francoul, a lawyer, was the new vice-president of the Union. Louis put him to immediate use as his defence counsel and as the flagellator of Jewish lawyers in *La France enchaînée*. The anti-Masonic journalist Philippe Poirson remained as his secretary-general.

16 Source for all this: Joly, "Champion", p. 53.

17 *'Le Conseil Municipal tient séance matin et soir et boycotte M. Darquier. Dès qu'il parait à la tribune, le préfet de la Seine et le représentant du préfet de police quittent ostensiblement la salle des séances'* ('The City Council sat in the morning and the evening and boycotted M. Darquier. As soon as he stood up to speak, the préfet of the Seine, and the representative of the préfet of police, conspicuously left the meeting room') *Justice*, 12 July 1939, AN 72 AJ592: Fonds Vaniakoff.

18 Joly, "Champion", p. 61, quoting BMO, 21 December 1938.

19 Taylor, p. 58. He was particularly fond of pastis.

20 *La France enchaînée*, no. 16, 15-30 November 1938, quoted in Joly, *Darquier de Pellepoix*, p.112, *La France enchaînée*, no. 25, 1–15 April 1939.

21 *L'Antijuif*, November 1937

22 *'Perroquet d'Hitler, au point d'insulter le noble Président Roosevelt'* ('Darquier is so much Hitler's parrot that he is now insulting the noble President Roosevelt') *Presse Municipale*, 23 April 1939.

23 *La France enchaînée*, no. 29, 1–15 June 1939.

24 Louis Darquier and all the French extremists in the pay of the Nazis were dealt with similarly. Coston's house was searched and his archives seized, Pemjean and Poirson came next, then Pierre Gérard and even his mother's home. The police found Büttner's chequebooks when they searched Gerard's home on 12 February 1945, but Manfred Simon knew of them as early as 1942.

25 De Monzie, *Ci-devant*, p. 123.

26 Darquier and Gérard were charged for articles written in *La France enchaînée*. Louis' article was entitled *'Le Défi insensé'* ('The Insane Challenge'), 15 May 1939; Gérard's was on the unsatisfactory French birth rate, 1–15 June 1939.

27 *The Times*, 20 June 1939.

28 Jardin, p. 72.

José Félix de Lequerica y Erquicia (1890–1963): Of a rich industrialist family in Bilbao. Educated as a lawyer, completed his doctorate at the London School of Economics and in Paris. Initially a right-wing monarchist and Basque separatist, he became mayor of Bilbao in 1938 and joined the Falange during the Civil War. Appointed ambassador to France in March 1939, and then to Vichy from 1940 to August 1944. A convinced Catholic anti-Semite, pro-German, friend of Abetz and Laval, but also sympathetic to French fascists such as Doriot. A *bon vivant* and like Anatole de Monzie in many other ways – intelligent, noted as a conversationalist, physically grossly unattractive but an incorrigible womanchaser. Minister of Foreign Affairs from August 1944 to 1945. Infamous as a collaborator with Germany, for his ruthless delivery of Spanish refugees to the Gestapo and for his responsibility for the return to Spain – to execution – of prominent Spanish Republicans. From 1945 to 1951 he kept his head down in the diplomatic service in Madrid, but he rose again when appointed ambassador to the United States from 1951 to 1954, and from 1956 as Spain's representative at the United Nations. In these latter incarnations he claimed that he had gone to great lengths to save French Sephardic Jews. Documents prove the contrary. Pétain gave the Légion d'honneur to de Lequerica on 29 January 1943.

29 The Duke of Windsor left Paris at dawn twelve days later. AMAE (b) no. 392, Lequerica letter, Paris, 12 May 1939.

30 De Monzie, *Ci-devant*, and PRO FO 371/31939/- Z 3005. Pétain's appointment: 2 March 1939.

31 Kérillis' famous article '*La Trahison déchaînée*' ('Unbridled Treason') named names throughout the Abetz scandal in July 1939 until January 1940. Abetz was expelled at the end of July 1939.

32 Saint-Paulien, p. 41.

33 *La France enchaînée*, no. 25, 1–15 April 1939.

34 Tribunal Correctionnel de la Seine 12ème chamber, 26 July 1939, Louis Darquier's deposition. AN 72 AJ 592: Fonds Vaniakoff.

35 *La France enchaînée*, 15-31 July.

36 *La France enchaînée* ceases publication - APP GA D9, 7 May 1942.

37 Some 465,000 Spanish refugees crossed into France after Franco's victory.

38 Koestler, p. 39.

39 Tasmania J.

40 Louis joined the 10th anti-tank battery of the 66th Artillery Regiment in General Huntziger's 2nd French Army. **General Charles-Léon Huntziger** (1880–1941) was Minister of War from 6 September 1940 until 11 August 1941. Anglophobe and anti-German, he died in a plane crash on 12 November 1941.

41 Laubreaux, p. 37 (see note 833).

42 The trial was reported in *Paris soir*, 4 October 1939. Prison sentences were suspended for general mobilisation.

43 According to a letter dated 15 September 1941 from the Comité d'Assistance aux Familles des Soldats Français in London, which gave Louis' address as: Lieutenant Darquier de Pellepoix – Batterie antichard [sic] – 66ème R.A.D.I.N.A. – Secteur postal 513. His first appeal against his prison sentence came to court in December, and he was still attending council meetings in January 1940 and treating himself to an elegant room at the Hôtel Castille in the rue Cambon.

44 APP GA D9, 28 February 1940 and Joly, *Darquier de Pellepoix*, p. 133.

45 AN 3W142, 12 January 1940.

46 **Paul Reynaud** (1878–1966): Conservative politician of the centre-right Alliance Démocratique party until he resigned after Munich. Fervently anti-communist, an anglophile and anti-Munich, supporter of de Gaulle before the war, though not of his presidential approach to politics after it. Many times a minister in the early 1930s. Daladier and Reynaud disliked each other, and de Monzie disliked them both. Reynaud was arrested, tried at Riom, then passed by Vichy to the Germans and imprisoned throughout the rest of the war. He testified against Pétain at the latter's trial, where he had a vigorous argument with

Weygand. After the war he was a member of the Chamber of Deputies until 1962, and held office in two governments during that time.

47 The Prissians brought the war to the Lightfoot doorstep; their father was killed on the train back to London after delivering his wife and their new baby Sandra to visit Mildred and Iris at Hazel Crescent. Pat Smalley, May 2001.

48 The Maginot Line was formulated by Pétain in 1927, constructed throughout the 1930s as an impregnable defence of French borders, except for the northern Belgian frontier, because Pétain considered its Ardennes forest as either impenetrable or easily defended. Between them Pétain and Weygand had been responsible for French military policy throughout the inter-war years, Pétain as Chief of the General Staff until 1931, when Weygand took over until 1935.

49 **General Maurice Gamelin** (1872–1958): Distinguished soldier and aide to General Joseph Joffre in the First World War. Replaced Weygand as commander of the General Staff in 1935. In early 1940 Reynaud made many attempts to replace Gamelin, Daladier's Supreme Commander of French land forces. Outraged by his failures, Reynaud condemned Gamelin as 'all right as a priest or a bishop', but no 'leader of men'; but he could not afford a breach with Daladier, and until this point Gamelin remained. Finally sacked on 17 May 1940, arrested on Pétain's order in September, tried at Riom (with Reynaud amongst others), then deported to Germany in 1943. Liberated in 1945.

50 *Keesing's Contemporary Archives*, 12–19 July 1948.

51 This is Churchill's famous speech: 'We shall fight on the beaches, we shall fight on the landing grounds, we shall fight in the fields and in the streets, we shall fight in the hills; we shall never surrender . . .' Still marvellous to read, decades later.

52 Billig, p. 84, quoting CDJC LXXIV-13, pp.3–5.

53 At Pétain's trial in July–August 1945 he was accused of many treacheries, and of being on 'intimate terms with the Fascist Cagoulard organisation; of having desired to set up in France a regime analogous to that of General Franco in Spain; of having, while Ambassador in Madrid (1939) got in touch with Hitler'. Historians differ as to the extent of Pétain's subterranean activities. Many of the leather-jacketed, metal-helmeted men of his personal bodyguard at Vichy came from the Cagoulards.

54 Horne, p. 659.

55 Lukacs, p. 140.

56 De Lequerica belonged to the right-wing Spanish political group, 'Accion Espanola'. Bankwitz (p. 322) states: 'The Germans had been aware of Weygand's and Pétain's armistice theses at least since 6 June, and were kept closely informed of the struggle within the Reynaud cabinet from this date to its collapse on 16 June.'

57 Pryce-Jones, p. 89.

58 Koestler, quoted by Horne, p. 653.

59 Weygand, pp. 229–230.

60 *Les Amis de Rassinier* © Gilles Karmasyn 1999. See http://www.phdn.org/-negation/rassinier/coston.html.

CHAPTER 12

Work, Family, Fatherland

INTERVIEWS AND CORRESPONDENCE: Pierre Combes, Bill Coy, Audrey Kirby, Yvonne Lacaze, Père Lucien Lachièze-Rey, Danny Puddefoot, Simone Reste, Pat Smalley. SOURCES: Darquier family correspondence; AMAE (b) no. 10; AN 3W142; AN 72 AJ 292: Testimony of M. Françoise Eugène Jean Pierre Lalin, Lieutenant of the 607 régiment infanterie de pionniers, 31 March 1956; AN AG/3(2) 326(BCRA); APP GA D9, 20 January and 6 February 1941, 7 May and 13 June 1942; Archives Municipales de Neuilly, 3D19/22, Réorganisation des corps municipaux; CDJC DLVI-132, Mme Laurens; CDJC LXXV-105; Préfecture de Police, Paris, no. 1093517, 28 July 1941; SRD, Tasmania J., TNA: PRO FO 371/31990 61288; TNA: PRO FO 892/163. PUBLICATIONS:Agulhon, *The French Republic 1879–1992*; Atkin, *Pétain*; Bankwitz, *Maxime Weygand and Civil-Military Relations in Modern France*; Billig, *Le Commissariat Général aux Questions Juives (1941–1944)*; Burrin, *France Under the Germans*; Crémieux-Brilhac, *Ici Londres 1940–1944*; de Gaulle, 'Appeal to the French People', BBC Radio, 18 June 1940; *De Gaulle*: TV documentary written, produced and directed by Sue Williams. WGBH Educational Foundation and LNK Images, 1990; *l'Eclaireur* (Nice), 14 January and 12 August 1943; Felstiner, *To Paint Her Life*; Gildea, *Marianne in Chains*; Gordon, *Collaborationism in France During the Second World War*; Halls, *Politics, Society and Christianity in Vichy France*; Jackson, *France: The Dark Years 1940–1944*; Jardin, *Vichy Boyhood*; Joly, *Darquier de Pellepoix et l'antisémitisme français*; Langer, *Our Vichy Gamble*; Larkin, *France Since the Popular Front*; Lartigaut (ed.), *Histoire du Quercy*; Lottman, *Pétain*; Malcolm, 'Gertrude Stein's War', *New Yorker*, 2 June 2003; Marrus and Paxton, *Vichy France and the Jews*; *New York Times*, 28 August 1944, 6 December 1946; Ousby, *Occupation*; Paxton, *Vichy France*; *Le Petit Marseillais*, 9 February 1941; Planté, *Un Grand seigneur de la politique*; Pryce-Jones, *Paris in the Third Reich*; Ragache, *La Vie quotidienne des écrivains et des artistes sous l'Occupation*; Taguieff (ed.), *L'Antisémitisme de plume*; Tournoux, *Pétain and de Gaulle*; Warner, *Laval*; Weber, *Action Française*; Werth, *The Twilight of France*; White, *The BBC at War*; Zucotti, *The Holocaust, the French and the Jews*; http://www.masonicinfo.com/fay.htm

1 De Gaulle 'Appeal to the French People', BBC, 18 June 1940. Agulhon, p. 258.

2 Around four million people fled. This chaos produced no agreement about the number of refugees involved and many historians believe that as many as six, eight or even ten million people took to the roads in this exodus.

3 St-Paul-de-Loubressac was formerly known as St-Paul-la-Bouffie.

4 Tasmania J.

5 The other sections: i) Northern sections were sliced off as a *Zone rattachée* and joined up with Belgium under German command; ii) Below it a forbidden zone which included Calais and, later stretched down the Atlantic and Channel coasts; iii) Alsace-Lorraine was taken into the Reich and separated from the rest of France by iv) fifteen *départements* given different administration as a *Zone réservée*.

6 For a brief period the two major partitions were called the *Zone Occupée* (*ZoneO*) and the *Zone Libre*, the Occupied Zone and the Free Zone, but the Germans correctly dismissed any concept of freedom that Pétain's zone might fancy with a decree in December 1940 that it should be called the *Zone Non-Occupée* (*Zone NonO*).

7 Planté, p. 307.

8 Fifty-seven per cent of socialist deputies and fifty-eight per cent of Radical deputies voted for Pétain.

9 *De Gaulle*, TV documentary written, produced and directed by Sue Williams.

10 Pétain's *Quatre Années*, p. 49 in Bankwitz, p. 316.

11 Larkin, p. 92; *Pater Noster* by Georges Gérard, Larkin, p. 83.

12 **Pierre Laval** (1883–1945) was a class above Pétain in his origins – he was the son of the innkeeper and postmaster-proprietor of the small village of Châteldon, near Vichy.

13 Warner, p. 152 and Lottman, p. 152.

14 Quoted by Burrin, p. 61.

15 Langer, p. 116.

16 BBC, *Les Français parlent aux français*, 16 May 1942, in *Ici Londres 1940–1944*. Jean-Louis Crémieux-Brilhac gave two broadcasts about Louis Darquier. For 14 May 1942, see AN AG/3(2) 326(BCRA) and AN 3W142; for 1 July 1942, see Crémieux-Brilhac's *Ici Londres*. See also White, p. 33ff.

17 The Militärbefehlshaber in Frankreich controlled France through the Armistice Commission in Weisbaden: see chart of German Command, p. 213. The first military Commander-in-Chief was Otto von Stülpnagel who was replaced in February 1942 by his cousin Karl Heinrich von Stülpnagel. Otto was the harsher of the two, prone to the shooting of hostages whenever his men were attacked 'by men in the pay of Anglo-Saxons, the Jews and the Bolsheviks', as he put it.

18 Ousby, p. 54. Goebbels came to Paris in July 1940. See also Pryce-Jones, p. 88.

19 Billig, p. 23.

20 Abetz's French henchmen, among them Jean Luchaire and Fernand de Brinon, arranged this encounter on 19 July 1940. The third go-between was Jean Fontenoy, a morphine addict who could also have been of help to Myrtle.

21 He may have been staying in rue Laugier, as one document implies. This, however, is most unlikely, as he had not paid the rent for years and it had been

occupied by German troops. The police were often wildly inaccurate in their reports about Darquier.

22 Paxton, p. 249.

23 **Marcel Déat** (1894–1955): Decorated First World War veteran. A professor of philosophy and former socialist deputy and political journalist who wrote the famous article in 1939 as Poland was about to be abandoned: 'Must One Die for Danzig?' in *l'Oeuvre*, 4 May 1939. Déat's collaborationist Rassemblement National Populaire (RNP), which he ran with Deloncle until 1941, and Doriot's PPF were the only political parties permitted by the Nazis. He joined the Vichy government as Minister of Labour and National Solidarity in March 1944. Fled to Sigmaringen in 1944, then to Italy to escape the death sentence handed down *in absentia* in 1945. Given refuge in a Catholic convent in Turin until his death.

24 Gordon, p. 338, quoting Paxton, pp. 352–7.

25 Occupation newspapers: Pre-war newspapers such as *Le Matin* reappeared – its editor liked to add '*Heil Hitler*' to his copy. *Vogue* was permitted to continue on the condition that it had no 'Jewish capital or attachments'. Henri-Robert Petit started up his *Le Pilori* again, but was swiftly removed for embezzlement and for his suggestion that Laval was a Jew. The paper flourished however, renamed *Au Pilori* and achieving under Jean Lestandi an anti-Semitic frenzy in a class of its own. *Au Pilori* was the French *Der Stürmer,* producing cartoons of outstanding obscenity and providing a comfortable journalistic home for all professional anti-Semitic writers, from Coston to Drault.

New intellectual journals were created, and the best of those already in existence were appropriated and turned to the Nazi cause. The most renowned of such papers, the *Nouvelle revue française,* fell into the hands of that high-flying collaborationist Pierre Drieu la Rochelle, a fervent anti-Semite dressed in the uniform of 1920s Oxford. In 1941 Brasillach returned from prison camp to turn *Je suis partout* into the most successful weekly of the time. New newspapers and journals were created. Abetz placed his favourite, Jean Luchaire, as head of the Paris Press Corporation and funded his daily evening newspaper *Les nouveaux temps.*

Some papers of the extreme right moved to the Vichy Zone – *Candide*, *Gringoire*. Some writers, such as Colette, were happy to work within the *milieu* of German censorship; others kept their heads down. In 1941 de Monzie, deprived of his immense portfolio of committees and appointments, was sidelined in the Lot. When he published *Ci-devant,* his sour diary of the last days of the Third Republic, he was happy to let it be serialised in the pro-fascist slander sheet *Gringoire*.

26 **Bernard Faÿ** (1895–1978): Professor of American Civilisation, Collège de France; director, Bibliothèque Nationale, from 1941. He ran Vichy's Commission Judeo-Maçonnique. Faÿ was linked to the Gestapo; listed amongst

his crimes at his trial after the war was the creation of 170,000 files on Freemasons, of which sixty thousand were investigated. He was arrested by French partisans in August 1944, and sentenced to life imprisonment at hard labour. Faÿ was aided by Gertrude Stein and Alice B. Toklas, who also helped to finance his escape to Switzerland in October 1951. Pardoned in 1953.

Vichy set up Faÿ at 16, rue Cadet, the former headquarters of Freemasonry, Coston was at 8, rue Puteaux.

27 Paxton, p. 69, 24 October 1940; Burrin, p. 65.

28 The reparation payments were lowered to 300,000 francs a day; after the Germans occupied all of France in November 1942, they went up to half a million francs a day. In order to eat, each subject needed a *Carte d'alimentation*, a ration card, and tickets, coloured stamps issued by the town hall, with which each person had to register. Then registration was required with a butcher, a baker, for whom there were bread tickets, and so on. It was forbidden to sell certain foods on specific days of the week: meat, sugar and alcohol for instance.

In 1939 Daladier passed a decree, the *Code de la Famille*, which included all the usual incentives for large families. The decline in the French birth rate had been a running sore to the Third Republic. The laws of this period included affirmation that husbands remained head of the family, and their right to forbid their wives to work.

29 Vichy set about increasing the birth rate almost immediately. In October 1940 a law was passed requiring married women to cease working in the public sector. This changed as the war began to require women's work, but management of women continued in other ways. There were over three hundred youth centres for girls, and just as physical education became mandatory for boys, school instruction in managing the home became so for girls. Women under Vichy, like women in Nazi Germany, were valuable to the state primarily as mothers of the next generation. For both Church and Vichy restoring the family as the central force of a Christian state was a key tenet. Vichy authorised financial rewards for the birth of children. Fathers of a family of more than five children were given additional civic rights. Being childless had employment disadvantages for men. French women, who would not have the right to vote until 1944, were not likewise rewarded, unless, as mothers, they stayed at home and had no outside employment. In that case they received a special allowance. Increased rations were given to pregnant women, and abortion was severely repressed. Twenty years' hard labour was the punishment for an abortion, and sometimes death.

30 Pétain had an affair with Eugénie Hardon while she was married; she divorced in 1914 and they married in 1920, in a civil ceremony only. By 1929 she had obtained a Catholic annulment, and Pétain could have performed the religious ceremony any time after that. He did this in March 1941.

31 SRD.

32 Gildea, p. 57–8.

33 '*Le système D*': D stands for *débrouille*, which with its verbal form *débrouiller* means literally 'untangle' or 'get out of a tangle'; *débrouillez-vous* basically means that it is your own problem, and that you should not expect any help in dealing with it.

34 Tasmania J.

35 The first hotel Louis went to, the Hôtel Castille at 37, rue Cambon, on 2 December 1940, was elegant enough to suggest that someone was paying for him there. Then followed the Hôtel Richepanse at 14, rue Richepanse and 1, rue d'Isly (the family of former CGQJ Director of Aryanisation Auguste Mudry lived at no. 8). 'Enquiries at different addresses have revealed that Darquier left the Hôtels Fortuny and Richepanse without paying his bills. The hoteliers have not lodged a complaint' (AN 3W142). In September 1945, when the Justice Ministry began their investigations into Darquier's past, the address they gave for one of his passing abodes during this period was avenue Bonnet, stating that he was staying with a 'family member' there. Charles Trochu lived at 6, avenue Colonel-Bonnet.

36 **Jean-François Darlan** (1881–1942): Darlan took over as deputy head of government on 9 February 1941, and lasted until 17 April 1942. Zealous for the French Empire, he negotiated the Protocols of Paris, signed on 28 May 1941, which granted access to the naval bases of the French empire to Germany. During his fourteen months in power he was Vice President of the Council of Ministers and Minister of Foreign Affairs, the Interior, Information and Defence.

37 In a letter of 1 March 1941 to Carl Theo Zeitschel, Abetz listed other men he had paid as alternatives: Bucard, Boissel, Clémenti, de Gobineau.

38 Citation: 'On 12 June 1940 at Le Cadran (Montagne de Rheims) [Darquier] covered the army from the very first contact, changed his battery's position and was the last to stay in position with a machine gun until his artillery pieces were out of range. On 14 June at Connantre, when leading his battery's automobile column, his vehicle was hit by machine-gun fire. One of the occupants was killed and [Darquier] carried out the necessary repairs under fire without losing a single vehicle. On 15 June he led two combats – one at Voué and the other at Bréviandes – during which he took command of two isolated infantry detachments and defended the territory on foot to the point of exhaustion.' Signed by Huntziger, 15 July 1941.

39 After their marriage in London in 1928, Louis should have gone to a French consulate with all the necessary documents for the marriage to be recognised in France (Transcription d'un Acte de Mariage), then the marriage and all relevant details should have been entered in the Register of Civil Status at the Mairie of Cahors. Louis' death was added to his civil status (wrongly dated 1983), but never a marriage.

40 *Ailes* = wings, so for pilots at Enstone.

41 Pat Smalley, January 1999. She lived opposite 98 Hazel Crescent from 1939.

42 Louis' request for decorations is in his military file, dated 26 September 1941 (date uncertain), together with the response of the Secretary of State for War to the Comité d'Assistance aux Familles de Soldats Français, dated 14 October 1941, and General Huntziger's own confirmatory letter of 20 October, stating that Louis was still a prisoner of war.

43 Louis was also reappointed to the Administrative Committee of the Council of the Seine. Between 1939 and 1943 he served on the 11th Committee of the General Council in 1939 (technical control of works); 8th Committee of the General Council in 1939 (*beaux arts*, miscellaneous matters); 6th Committee of the Municipal Council in 1939 (water, sewerage, navigation and hygiene); 7th Committee of the Municipal Council in 1939 (*métropolitain*); 3rd Temporary Committee of the Municipal Council in 1943 (public works, urbanism, architecture, transport); 2nd Committee of the Departmental Council in 1943 (health, hygiene, work, family, economic and social life, POWs). 'From the information gathered, it seems that the concerned party played a negligible role on these committees and was only rarely present' (AN 3W142).

44 Bishop Paul Chevrier: Chevrier was counterbalanced by a Monseigneur Araguay, mentioned with praise by many Cadurciens for his courage and opposition to the Germans. See also Chapter 20, n. 5.

45 Pierre Combes, 12 January 2000.

46 ANW3142 and CDJC LXXV-105.

47 Burrin, p. 133.

48 Langer, p. 117.

49 *ibid.*, p. 219.

CHAPTER 13

Tormenting Men

SOURCES: AMAE (b) no. 435, 7 September 1942; AN 3W142; AN 3W147, Archives de Berlin: Abetz to Foreign Office in Berlin, Paris, 13 December 1940; AN 3W356, Archives de Berlin, bordereau 3459, 4 September 1942; APP GA D9, 18 December 1941; CDJC LXXV-59 and 70; CDJC XCV-135 and 135a; CDJC CII-55; TNA: PRO FO 892/163; TNA: PRO GFM 33–2062. PUBLICATIONS: *Action française*, 8 April 1944; Billig, *Le Commissariat Général aux Questions Juives (1941–1944)*; Burrin, *France Under the Germans*; Calef, *Drancy 1941*; Charbonneau, *Les Mémoires de Porthos*; *Daily Herald*, 16 December 1940; *l'Express*, 1978; Fest, *The Face of the Third Reich*; Gildea, *Marianne in Chains*; Gordon, *Collaborationism in France During the Second World War*; Guérin, *La Résistance*; Halls,

Politics, Society and Christianity in Vichy France; Hilberg, *La Destruction des Juifs d'Europe*; Hoover Institution, *France During the German Occupation*; Jackson, Julian: *France: The Dark Years*; Jardin, *Vichy Boyhood*; Joly, 'Darquier de Pellepoix "Champion" des Antisémites Français'; Joly, *Darquier de Pellepoix et l'antisémitisme français*; Judt, 'Betrayal in France', *New York Review of Books*, 12 August 1993; Koestler, *The Scum of the Earth*; Lacroix-Riz, *Industriels et banquiers français sous l'Occupation*; Laloum, Jean: *La France antisémite de Darquier de Pellepoix*; Lerner, 'A Michelin noir', www.commentarymagazine.com/ Summaries/ V101I5P51–1.htm; Marrus and Paxton, *Vichy France and the Jews*; Modiano, *The Search Warrant*; *New York Times*, 16 September 1944, 26 February and 8 March 1947; Nossiter, *The Algeria Hotel*; Ousby, *Occupation*; Overy, *The Penguin Historical Atlas of the Third Reich*; Paxton, *Vichy France*; Peschanski, http://histoire-sociale.univ-paris1.fr/12.TheseConclusion.pdf; *Le Point*, February 2000; Pryce-Jones, *Paris in the Third Reich*; de Rochebrune and Hazera, *Les Patrons sous l'Occupation, vol. 2, Pétainisme, intrigues, spoliations*; Taguieff (ed.), *L'Antisémitisme de plume*; *US Foreign Relations*, 1941, vol. 11; Vallat, *Le Nez de Cléopâtre*; Weber, *Action Française*; Weisberg, *Vichy Law and the Holocaust in France*; Wistrich, 'Pope Pius XII and the Holocaust', *Times Literary Supplement*, 3 May 2002; Zucotti, *The Holocaust, the French and the Jews*

1 Zucotti, p. 44.
2 Fifteen thousand people lost their citizenship between 1940 and 1944, of whom six thousand were Jews. Foreign work units were Groupements de Travailleurs Étrangers (GTEs).
3 'For all administrative measures that it will be called upon to take, the Military Administration will pass through, on principle, the channels of the French authorities . . . Direct intervention is required only if measures prove to be inefficient' (CDJC LXXV-70).
4 Jardin, p. 63.
5 SS – first Standartenführer, then Obersturmbannführer, Helmut Knochen commanded the Gestapo and SD. Many thousands of people were recruited by the Gestapo and by the Abwehr – the intelligence service of the army: concierges, hairdressers, criminals; the world of denouncers, informers and spies was dense and tangled, and remains so.
6 On 12 August 1940 the Germans formed the Judenreferat, or police branch for Jewish affairs.
7 Hoover Institution, pp. 639, 640 and 644.
8 **Raphaël Alibert** (1887–1963): Vichy Minister of Justice from June 1940 to January 1941. He went into hiding at the end of the war and was sentenced to death *in absentia* by the French High Court of Justice at Paris on 7 March 1947. Lived in exile in Belgium; granted amnesty in 1959.
9 **Pastor Marc Boegner** (1881–1970): President of the Reformed Church of

France, leading and most outspoken French Protestant and critic of Vichy and its treatment of the Jews. Later President of the World Council of Churches.

10 *Action française*, 8 April 1944.

11 Weber, p. 471.

12 By February 1941 Déat had formed the Rassemblement National Populaire and had attached himself to the embassy. His paper, *l'Oeuvre*, which he edited, was funded handsomely by Abetz.

13 Between four and five thousand communists were arrested by summer 1941 despite the Nazi–Soviet alliance.

14 Later the camp had sixty toilets, or rather *trous d'aisance*, public holes in the ground.

15 Of seventy-four all-Jewish convoys to the death camps, two left from Compiègne, six from Pithviers, two from Beaune, one from Angers, one from Lyon, and sixty-two from Drancy.

16 Goering's extermination instructions would have passed thus: Heydrich–Eichmann–Dannecker.

17 Billig, p. 46.

18 Schleier was only a few years younger than Darquier, a committed Nazi, a solid presence, belted, booted and decorated in the accepted Nazi mode. He loved parties and receptions and proper French respect. It was Schleier and his embassy who had to agree and to help implement the plans for propaganda Louis presented. See also chapter 20, n. 34.

19 Billig, p. 76.

20 **Xavier Vallat** (1891–1972): Vallat was actually born in Vaucluse; his father came from the Ardèche and he always chose it as his *pays*. His first job at Vichy was as Secretary-General for Veterans' Affairs, and he transformed Pétain's cherished ex-servicemen into a Légion Française des Combattants (LFC, Legion of Veterans). These blue-shirted devotees were Pétain's replacement for the political parties he blamed for ruining France, and became his strongest organisation in the field for the implementation of his National Revolution. Vallat was personally selected for the Légion by his fellow Catholic General Weygand, and was as hostile to Germany as Weygand himself. This awkward sentiment meant that his new appointment lasted only twelve months. The LFC became the Service d'Ordre Légionnaire (SOL), and later the Milice.

21 Taguieff, p. 25.

22 Marrus and Paxton, p. 89.

23 Hoover, p. 626. In a twenty-thousand-word essay of justification which Vallat wrote in prison, after the war.

24 At first Vallat fiddled with Alibert's *statut*, but Alibert was dismissed as Vichy Minister of Justice for participating in the palace revolution behind Pétain's dismissal of Laval in December 1940.

Joseph Barthélemy (1874–1945): Succeeded Alibert as French Minister of

Justice from January 1941 until March 1943. His father was Professor of Science at Toulouse University and mayor of Toulouse. Close friend of Cardinal Gerlier. Defeatist, but anti-German, he supported Pétain and the National Revolution, inspired new divorce, and all post-Alibert anti-Semitic laws. Arrested by the French authorities in September 1944 and indicted by the French High Court of Justice, he died of tongue cancer at Toulouse before he came to trial.

25 US Foreign Relations 1941, volume 11, p. 508. Vichy, 16 June 1941.

26 CDJC CII-55 quoting the Security Service. Billig, p. 160.

27 The efficiency of these technocrats was corporatist, a third way, it was felt, between Marxism and liberalism, in which each profession organised itself in a social order of professions and trades. In Vichy, these autocrats instigated a mixture of state control and corporatism under a new system of Comités d'organisation (COs). As is ever the case, order took precedence over any syndicalist ideas of workers' control of industry, or any system independent of the state with which some of these Vichy men had previously toyed. Trade unions were cancelled and these committees came to be controlled by big business, keyed in to working in the service of Germany.

28 Weber, *Action Française,* p. 460ff.

29 CDJC XVII-13(58), 19 July 1941.

30 Between ten and twenty thousand communists were imprisoned. It is very hard to get correct figures; sources give conflicting numbers.

31 Pryce-Jones, p. 50–1.

32 www.historyplace.com/worldwar2/timeline/order1.htm.
    The formation of the Police aux Questions Juives was not published in the *Journal official* as it should have been.

33 The PJQ destroyed their own files, so their activities are hard to pinpoint.

34 Weisberg, p. 197.

35 In July 1933 Pius XII masterminded and signed the Concordat, of which Hitler, Chancellor of Germany since January of that year, stated, in wording agreed by Pacelli, 'that it gave sufficient guarantee that the Reich members of the Roman Catholic confession will from now on put themselves without reservation at the service of the new National Socialist state'. Another papal error was the support he gave to the terrifying murderers, 'the Ustasi', in Yugoslavia.

36 Gildea, p. 207.

37 PRO FO/892/163, *Daily Herald,* 16 December 1940.

38 Suhard said more to José de Lequerica: 'The Cardinal [Suhard] told him [Benoist-Méchin, then Secretary of State] without much prevarication although in naturally guarded terms, that he and all his clergy would be prepared to take a much more favourable attitude to the policies of the Vichy government and its relations with Germany if they had an assurance that the National Socialists, victors in the war, would not persecute the Church.' Suhard assured Benoist-

Méchin that no Church dogma prevented 'precautions' against the 'corrosive influence' of Jews (AMAE (b) no. 435, 7 September 1942.

39 Weisberg, p. 425.

40 The cardinals who voiced this view were Tardini and Montini of the Vatican State Department, in August and September 1941. Montini became Pope Paul VI in 1963. Pétain applied for papal approval of his anti-Semitic laws by way of his ambassador to the Vatican, Léon Bérard, whose report in the autumn of 1941 conveyed qualified approval. Lequerica wrote to the Ministry of Foreign Affairs in Madrid recording his discussions with Berard, Pétain's ambassador to the Vatican, who had come to Vichy to explain 'the attitude of the Church towards the measures taken by France on matters of race. According to him, the Vatican places no obstacle . . . ' AMAE, Lequerica, 1 September 1942 to Ministry of Foreign Affairs in Madrid.

Vallat sent out a press release on 11 October: 'There was nothing in the laws passed to protect France from Jewish influence in opposition to Catholic doctrine.' This was not entirely true, one instance of wool-pulling being that the Catholic Church firmly believed in Christaining Jews, and was not averse to marriages between Jews and Christians for that purpose. A Jewish convert was a Catholic, not a Jew. But papal inaction and failure to concern itself about the true nature of Vichy's attack on Jews enabled the Vichy regime to do as it wished. Much the same procedure, had, of course, occurred with Franco.

41 Taguieff, p. 188.

42 Louis certainly knew he was going to replace Vallat by 28 January 1942 – see Schleier to Zeitschel of that date (TNA: PRO GFM 33–2062).

43 AN 3W142.

44 9 November 1941, law instituting UGIF, l'Union Générale des Israélites de France.

45 AN 3W142.

46 Memo, 29 March 1942, probably from Zeitschel, to Abetz, Schleier, Achenbach and others that Darlan had agreed to sack Vallat immediately.

CHAPTER 14

Rats

INTERVIEWS AND CORRESPONDENCE: Colette Calmon, Jean Gayet, Pierre Gayet, Auguste Mudry, Yvonne Lacaze, Bertrand Leary, Simone Reste, Pat Smalley. SOURCES: Darquier family correspondence; AN 3W142; AN 3W147; AN 3W353, 18 May 1942; AN AJ38 3, André Cantel to Louis Darquier; APP GA D9, 12 March, 8 June and 8 October 1942; CDJC XLI-40, 30 June 1942; CDJC XLIX-42; CDJC

XLIXa-5; CDJC XXIX-130, 9 May 1942; CDJC XXXV-2, 35, 44, 48; CDJC LXII-11: undated biography of Louis Darquier entitled 'Note Concernant Darquier de Pellepoix.; CDJC LXXIV-4, 12 and 13; CDJC XCVI-5; CDJC CVI-103, 107; CDJCXXXV-44N; CDJC CCCXXIX-22; TNA: PRO FO 892/13; TNA: PRO FO 892/163; TNA: PRO GFM 33/2052, Schleier to Zeitschel, 28 January 1942; SRD; TNA: PRO GFM 33/2062, memo to Achenbach, 3 March 1942, unsigned but probably from Zeitschel. PUBLICATIONS: Billig, *Le Commissariat Général aux Questions Juives*; Burrin, *France Under the Germans;* Cazaux, *René Bousquet;* André Chaumet, in *Cahiers jaunes,* May–June 1941; Cointet, *Vichy; Le Crapouillot;* Crémieux-Brilhac, BBC Radio, 16 May and 1 July 1942; *Daily Herald,* 12 May 1942; *Daily Telegraph,* 15 May 1942; Débordes, *Vichy: Capitale à l'heure allemande; Les Dernières nouvelles de Strasbourg,* 7 April 1937; *l'Express,* 14–20 February 1972; Froment, *René Bousquet;* Gildea, *Marianne in Chains;* Halls, *Politics, Society and Christianity in Vichy France;* Hoover Institution, *France During the German Occupation;* Jackson, *France: The Dark Years;* Jardin, *Vichy Boyhood;* Joly, *Darquier de Pellepoix et l'antisémitisme français; Journal d'Alsace et de Lorraine,* 7 April 1937; *Journal du Lot,* 8 April 1942; Klarsfeld, *French Children of the Holocaust;* Lambert, *Carnet d'un témoin; Libération,* 'Le dossier Bousquet', 13 July 1993; *Manchester Guardian,* 23 July 1941; Marrus and Paxton, *Vichy France and the Jews; New York Times,* 28 July 1947; Nossiter, *The Algeria Hotel;* Julia Pascal, 'Vichy's Shame', *Guardian Weekend,* 11 May 2002; Paxton, *Vichy France;* van Pragg, *Daughter of France;* Taguieff (ed.), *L'Antisémitisme de plume; The Times,* 6 April 1942; Vulliez, *Vichy*

1   Klassen, cited by Joly, *Darquier de Pellepoix,* p. 142. Billig, p. 129; Myrtle moved to the Hôtel Fortuny on 16 October 1941.
    All comings and goings were observed by the Service des Garnis, the police who kept watch over the hotels of Paris and who knew their habits of old.

2   Billig, p. 73.

3   Billig, p. 115. Vallat complained about Darquier's appointment to Raymond-Raoul Lambert, in charge of UGIF in the south, on 27 March 1942.

4   **Georges Mandel** (1885–1944): Half-Jewish journalist and politician and an opponent of Munich and of Nazism. He was one of the deputies who left France on the *Massilia* to start a free government in Morocco. Arrested and imprisoned by Pétain; sent to Buchenwald with Blum and Reynaud, returned to France in July 1944 and imprisoned in the Santé. Executed by the Milice as revenge for the Resistance execution of Philippe Henriot.
    Léon Blum (1872–1950): Arrested by Vichy in September 1940, he was accused of weakening France and causing the defeat, and condemned before trial to life imprisonment. After three years in prison he was delivered to the Germans and, as a bargaining chip, was kept in special confinement for two years at Buchenwald concentration camp. Liberated in May 1945. After the war he remained leader of the Socialist Party and editor of its newspaper *Le Populaire,*

served as special ambassador to the USA in 1946, and again as premier – for two months – in 1946–47.

Blum and Daladier explained very clearly Pétain's personal responsibility, as army chief, for the 'unpreparedness of France', not to mention the uselessness of the Maginot Line.

5 PRO FO 371/319 392 3005.

6 AN 3W142. Laure was about to lose this job when he received this letter, signed by 'Schoeffer', but he remained close to Pétain and published his authorised biography, *Pétain*, in 1942.

7 *Journal du Lot*, 8 April 1942.

8 CDJC document LXII-11. Filed as 'Biographical note in French and various reports (various documents from Germany) about the calumnies propagated by the Jews against Darquier.'

9 Henry Lévy, the 'Miller King', had held every position and done every good deed that Strasbourg and France could have required of him. Shortly before he died, this 'perfect philanthropist' told Léon Blum that he had one dream to fulfil before his death. Already a chevalier of the Légion d'honneur, he wanted to be made a commandeur. Blum told him that, in the political climate of the time, it was not possible to nominate a Jew.

10 COs, Organisation Committees, were run by a chairman and a small committee, all under the Vichy Minister for Industrial Production, **Jean Bichelonne** (1904–44), prime exponent of Franco–German economic integration, involved in both the spoliations of the Jews and the STO. By August 1942, therefore, René Darquier came under this brilliant mathematician who worked so closely with Albert Speer. In 1944 Bichelonne was despatched to Sigmaringen with the rest of the Vichy government. He died in Germany in mysterious circumstances after a minor operation.

11 CDJC LX11–11 and Leary, 9 October 2000 regarding René's post war application.

12 Billig, p. 130; Vichy confirmed Louis' post on 8 May 1942.

13 Hoover Institution, p. 656. Darlan had removed the responsibility for the CGQJ from himself to the Ministry of the Interior in September 1941.

14 **René Bousquet** (1909–93): His trajectory was slightly more complicated than Louis'; he failed once, tried again, but left the university before completion; however, he seems to have been given some sort of degree by Toulouse University. He began his political career in 1931 as private secretary to the deputy Pierre Cathala, and was Vichy chief of police in the Ministry of the Interior from 18 April 1942 to 30 December 1943. The number of Jews deported during his reign was 57,908, of whom 1,228 were still surviving in 1945 (Klarsfeld, *French Children*, pp. 418–19). I have been unable to discover accurate figures of the many thousands of communists and others whose deaths he arranged.

15 AN 3W142-KNO.

16 Billig, p. 113; CDJC CVI - 103. 9 September 1942.

17 Louis Dreyfus & Co. is to this day the only international grain trade enterprise in family hands. King Two Louis' son Jean Louis-Dreyfus took over in 1940 and ran the company until 2003.

18 CDJC XXXV-2.

19 There are hundreds of letters like this. See CDJC XXXV.

20 Joly, *Darquier de Pellepoix*, p. 144, citing AN AJ38 3, letter of André Cantel to Louis Darquier.

21 Taguieff, p. 404, André Chaumet in *Cahiers jaunes*, May-June 1941.

22 Taguieff, p. 398, source: CDJC CCCXXIX-22.

23 CDJC X19-30.

24 Letter written by Dr Achterberg, director of the Weltdienst. It was taken over entirely by Rosenberg's foreign policy office of the Nazi Party in Frankfurt in 1939, and Fleischhauer was replaced by August Schirmer. By 1941 he was living in his cellar in Erfurt, running a tiny rump of his old empire.

25 CDJC XXXV-44, Étienne Genevois of Lyon to Louis Darquier, 27 May 1942.

26 SRD; Yvonne Lacaze, January 2000.

27 PRO FO892/13.

28 *Daily Herald*, 12 May 1942; PRO FO 892/163; the *Manchester Guardian*; 23 July 1941 and the *Daily Telegraph* of 15 May 1942.

29 Consul Général de France to Vichy Foreign Office, 7 May 1941. In September and November the benevolent societies continued to give Nanny Lightfoot funds for Anne, even though the Vichy military bureaucracy had finally realised that Louis Darquier was no longer a prisoner. They had their revenge; Louis never became a chevalier de la Légion d'honneur.

30 S.E. van Praag, *Daughter of France* (1945).

31 Laval also had private rooms at the Majestic, but he eschewed Vichy high life and liked to return to his small château in Châteldon, driving the twenty-three kilometres each night in a blacked-out, bullet-proof car. Outside the Parc stood Pétain's personal guard, bayonets fixed, facing the elegant Parc des Sources with its covered walkways, tall plane trees, casinos and hotels.

32 Débordes, p. 64.

33 Nossiter, p. 125.

34 Crémieux-Brilhac: BBC, 16 May 1942.

35 Urbain Gohier to Louis Darquier, 17 July 1942; CDJCXXV-48.

36 Vuillez, pp. 168–173. Wanda Laparra Vuillez was correspondent for the Swiss news agency Universum Press.

37 Today, nothing in Vichy looks seedier than the old Hôtel Algeria at 22, boulevard Carnot, on the corner of rue Roovère. With letters missing from its scruffy sign, its walls and doors are spattered with graffiti which include the sign of the FN, the Front National, the party run by Darquier's political descendant Jean-Marie le Pen. Today Robert Faurisson, the first and boldest of the

negationists – those who deny the Holocaust, as did Louis Darquier – lives only a boundary throw from the Algeria.

38 There was another deportation on 25 February 1943. The plaque was put up by Serge Klarsfeld on 26 August 1992, despite the protests of residents (today both the Parc and the Majestic are private apartments); it was removed to a modest position inside the hotel after it had been daubed with blood or the swastika on several occasions. This is not surprising, as Pétain's former rooms have been purchased by the Association pour la Défence de la Mémoire du Maréchal Pétain, which has made it a private shrine.

There is a plaque inside the opera house in the casino honouring the eighty deputies who did not vote for Pétain in that room on 10 July 1940, and another outside a Maison de Retraite to Father Victor Dillard, deported to death in Dachau. That is more or less it.

39 Nossiter, pp. 186 and 190.

40 CDJCLXI-78. Billig, p. 51.

41 Crémieux-Brilhac: BBC, 16 May 1942.

42 On 15 July 1942, according to Billig (p. 243), Darquier promised the head of the Sicherheitspolizei (Dannecker of the Judenreferat) to supply him with 'several thousand Jews from the Non-Occupied Zone'. According to Cazaux (p. 186), Darquier, without having previously consulted the government, specified to Dannecker, 'that we could count on putting at the disposal of the Germans several thousands of Jews from the Non-Occupied Zone, with a view to their evacuation'.

43 Crémieux-Brilhac: BBC, 1 July 1942.

44 Bousquet to Darquier, 18 June 1942, telling him of the suppression of the PQJ, to take effect on 1 July. On 5 July it was finalised. Darquier retaliated by starting an Anti-Jewish Brigade of his own, but as it was attached to the remnants of Deloncle's paramilitary MSR, and they were warring bitterly amongst themselves, the brigade had no time to take on Jews as well.

45 CDJCXLI-40 30.6.1942

46 On 23 May 1942. CDJC XXV-35.

47 L'Express, 14–20 February 1972.

48 CDJC XXV-48, Louis Darquier to Urbain Gohier, 13 July 1942.

49 CDJC XLIX-42.

50 AN 3W142, Dr Klassen to Schleier.

51 'Die Judenfrage', in Politik-Recht-Kultur und Wirtschaft, Herausgegeben von der Antijudischen Aktion, no. 18, Jahrgang VI, Berlin, 15 September 1942. It is probable that Darquier wrote the article in German.

52 Klassen AN 3W147, Archive de Berlin, telegram of 5 December 1942.

53 Georg Ebert, Rosenberg's agent at the Embassy, 20 May 1942. Billig, p. 231.

54 22 June 1942, quoted by Burrin, p. 151, in a slightly different translation.

55 L'Express, 14–20 February 1972.

CHAPTER 15

The Rat Pit

INTERVIEWS AND CORRESPONDENCE: Henri Fernet, Pierre Gayet, Auguste Mudry.
SOURCES: AN 3W142; AN 3W147; CDJC LXI-122; CDJC XIb-474; CDJC LXXV-105; CDJC XCIV-57, 64; CDJC XCVI-5, 57, 72, 89; CDJC CVI-75; CDJC CXLIV; CDJC CXCIII-135, 1 June 1942; 203; TNA: PRO FO 371/31941 Z4579. PUBLICATIONS: Billig, *Le Commissariat Général aux Questions Juives*; Burrin, *France Under the Germans*; Halls, *Politics, Society and Christianity in Vichy France*; Hoffman et al., *France: Change and Tradition*; Jackson, *France: The Dark Years*; Joly, *Darquier de Pellepoix et l'antisémitisme français*; *Libération*, 'Le dossier Bousquet', 13 July 1993; Marrus and Paxton, *Vichy France and the Jews*; Maspero, *Cat's Grin*; Mondiano, *The Search Warrant*; Ousby, *Occupation*; Péan, *Une Jeunesse française*; Pryce-Jones, *Paris in the Third Reich*; Zucotti, *The Holocaust, the French and the Jews*

1 Abetz also knew de Monzie, and protected fascists such as Bucard. In general the Reich thought of him as far too sympathetic to the French.

2 CDJC XCIV-57.

3 AN 3W142.

4 Jalby, former police officer, 14 September 1946: 'He [Galien] pushed Dannecker to get Darquier de Pellepoix appointed as Commissioner-General. With his plan complete, he became Darquier's chief of staff.' Knochen (4 November 1947) says Galien was appointed by the Germans. Both Dannecker and Abetz also claimed responsibility for Darquier's appointment (AN 3W142).

5 Louis Darquier merged the Status of Persons section with the Legal Affairs section run by Armilhon.

6 **Roland Lécuyer** (1913–66): Louis Darquier's wartime bodyguard, is said to have escaped to North Africa, first to Abidjan then to Dakar, where he died.

7 Billig, pp. 126, 149.

8 CDJC XCVI – 57, p. 4a; Billig, p. 120.

9 Billig, p. 131.

10 AN 3W142-KNO.

11 Billig, p. 80.

12 AN 3W142.

13 31 July 1942. *Libération*, 13 July 1993.

14 AN 3W142, Marie-Jeanne Costemale, secretary, 19 August 1946.

15 AN 3W142, Paule Fichot, 5 September 1944.

16 *ibid.*

17 **Jean Bouvyer** (1917–?): Bouvyer's parents and François Mitterrand's parents were very close friends, and remained so throughout the years. Antoinette Bouvyer, Jean's mother, was godmother to Mitterrand's son Christophe. Jean

Bouvyer became the lover of Mitterrand's sister Marie-Josèphe de Corlieu (Josette), who had made an unhappy marriage. The Marquise, or Jo, as she was known, was a portrait painter and lived at 17, rue de la Paix. Bouvyer was a constant guest there. After the Liberation, Bouvyer was tried and condemned to death *in absentia*, but was protected by François Mitterrand, who averred that Bouvyer had assisted him in his resistance work in making forged ID papers. Bouvyer found exile in Paraguay then Brazil. His activities and connections with the Mitterrand family are amply documented in Pierre Péan's *Une Jeunesse française: François Mitterrand, 1934–1947*.

18 AN 3W142 letters of 1942.

19 Pierre Gayet, November 1999.

20 Henri Fernet, former Waffen SS, Division Charlemagne, September 1999.

21 CDJC X16-474. Billig, p. 134.

22 AN W3142. Boxhorn, 27 April 1943; Dehesdain, 12 March 1943.

23 AN W3142. Report from the police judiciaire (CID) concerning the operations of the CGQJ signed by Lafarge, 10 February 1945.

24 There are numerous reports of noisy altercations in the Paris office in place des Petits-Pères. These began with Pierre Gérard, who lasted as assistant director of the Aryanisation section for the briefest time; he quarrelled with Galien and produced a detailed and damning report, pages long, on Galien's embezzlements and misdeeds. 'Paule Fichot said that Darquier found out that Galien was keeping secret personnel and aryanisation files, doubtless destined either for the Gestapo or for blackmail after the war. Darquier objected to the obvious German influence Galien exerted and inserted throughout the office' (CDJC XCVI-57, 10 October 1946). Galien retaliated by telling the Gestapo that they quarrelled over Darquier's malpractice and that which he tolerated from his staff, and he instructed the Gestapo to sack Darquier (CDJC XCVI-72, Auguste Valence, 29 November 1946).

25 The money involved in all Louis Darquier's compassion relies for evidence on the vast number of times he was accused of taking it, and the verbal evidence of his employees, but, obviously, no records exist of exactly what he received. What is recorded is that, as far as running the CGQJ was concerned, Louis Darquier 'knew how to do nothing, he couldn't manage anything, and he knew nothing about any of it' (Auguste Mudry).

26 AN 3W142.

27 The Synarchie (Synarchy): pro-fascist and infamously influential at Vichy during Darlan's time. Doing what de Monzie told him was one incentive in helping men such as Hippolyte Worms, but another would be the secret mumbo jumbo and mysteries in which Synarchists liked to indulge. The strong Anglo-Saxon connections of the Worms Bank and its associates were an added incentive, for despite his recent Anglophobia, these were the kind of men Louis Darquier had longed to encounter during his disastrous London years.

Hippolyte Worms (1889–?): Grandson of the founder of the Worms Bank, which dealt in arms, coal, naval construction and banking, and had tentacles in many other affairs. In 1939 the British government used Hippolyte as Chief of Anglo-French Maritime Transport; de Monzie had set up such an arrangement when he was Minister for the Merchant Marine in 1917, and reappointed him in 1939. Other Worms family members who could have been assisted were Édouard, Pierre, Marc and Philippe. Pierre Worms was murdered after a denunciation by Charles Maurras.

28 AN 3W142, Marie-Jeanne Costemale-Lacoste, secretary, 19 August 1946.

29 Marie-Eléonore Mathieu, CGQJ translator, CDJC XCVI-64 and -57.

30 All the above quotes from AN 3W142-KNO.

31 AN 3W142, note 118, regarding the Hospital Rothschild and the Jewess Asson, 12 October 1942.

32 Other nations were permitted to take Jews back to the countries from which they came, but only Switzerland made any use of this possibility, and then not for long. A few other countries took back Jews who were valuable from 'an industrial or financial point of view'.

33 Quoted by Pryce-Jones, p. 63; *Les Décombres* (The Ruins). Ousby, p. 101.

34 **Jacques Doriot** ('*Le Grand Jacques*', 1898–1945): First World War veteran and prominent French communist who in 1934 veered violently to the right and in 1936 founded the PPF. The leading French fascist, a born leader, a skilful if tedious orator, he courted the Gestapo and the MBF and, hostile to Laval, bowed low before the Marshal and the Church. A dominant force in the founding of the LVF, he took the uniform himself and fought on the Eastern Front. Fled France with two thousand of his followers in August 1944 to Germany, where Hitler supported him as an alternative to Pétain and company at Sigmaringen. He was killed when his car was strafed by Allied bombers in February 1945.

35 By December the embassy had interviewed Darquier twice about his *Judenfrage* article.

36 Burrin, p. 165.

37 AN 3W142.

38 Billig, p. 119; CDJC CXCIII-203, p. 11.

39 Billig, p. 121.

40 Marie-Eléonore Mathieu, CGQJ translator, CDJC XCVI-64.

41 The description of the searching of the internees is from Modiano, *The Search Warrant* pp. 60–1, citing 'an extract from an official report drawn up in November 1943 by a manager from Pithiviers tax office'.

42 AN 3W142, note 122, letter to von Behr in favour of Susanne Lévy, 9 September 1943.

43 AN 3W142.

44 CDJC LXI – 122; Billig, p. 124.

CHAPTER 16

Death

SOURCES: AMAE (b), 15 September 1942; AN AJ 38/3; AN 3W142; AN 3W353; CDJC XXXV-48; CDJC XXVb-55, 112, 128; CDJC XXVI-40; CDJC XLIX-13, 42; CDJC XCVI-15; CDJC CV-61; CDJC CXI-41, 55; CDJC CXCIV-25, 92; CDJC CCXVIII-72; TNA: PRO FO 371/32056. PUBLICATIONS: *l'Antijuif*, 17 July 1937; Billig, *Le Commissariat Général aux Questions Juives*; Burrin, *France Under the Germans*; Cazaux, *René Bousquet*; Coston, 'I Have Seen Jews Work', *La France au travail*, 18 May 1941; Eichmann Trial Judgement, 100 Cable T/443; *l'Express*, 14–20 February 1972, 28 October–4 November 1978; Halls, *Politics, Society and Christianity in Vichy France*; Jackson, *France: The Dark Years*; Joly, *Darquier de Pellepoix et l'antisémitisme français*; Judt, 'Betrayal in France', *New York Review of Books*, 12 August 1993; Klarsfeld, *Le Calendrier de la persécution des Juifs en France*; Klarsfeld, *French Children of the Holocaust*; Laborie, *Résistants, vichyssois et autres*; Laloum, *La France antisémite de Darquier de Pellepoix*; Lambert, *Carnet d'un témoin*; Lévy and Tillard, *La Grande rafle du Vel' d'Hiv*; Marrus and Paxton, *Vichy France and the Jews*; Ousby, *Occupation*; *Le Monde*, 10 November 1994; Pryce-Jones, *Paris in the Third Reich*; Sabbagh (ed.), *Lettres de Drancy*; Taguieff (ed.), *L'Antisémitisme de plume*; Weber, *Action Française*; Zucotti, *The Holocaust, the French and the Jews*

1 Heydrich's visit to Paris was one of his last displays of power. He was also Reich Protector of what was left of Czechoslovakia. Two weeks later, in Prague, he was shot by two Czech exiles trained by the SOE in London, and a week later he was dead. Czechoslovakia paid mightily for this: Nazi reprisals included the liquidation of 936 people in Prague, 395 in Brno, and all the inhabitants of Lidice. In Heydrich's honour the construction of the extermination camps Belzec, Sobibor and Treblinka, the planning and coordination of deportations there, the installation and application of gas chambers, the incineration of bodies, and the transport of Jewish valuables and belongings from dead Jews to German storage was named 'Operation Reinhard'. These extermination camps in Poland were added to that of Auschwitz, also transformed into an extermination camp in 1942.

2 SS-Brigadeführer and Generalmajor der Polizei Karl-Albrecht Oberg, the head of the German security and police services from May 1942, was not responsible to the MBF, but to the Nazi Party; this was crucial.

3 Billig, p. 23.

4 Knochen had two deputies, Herbert-Martin Hagen and Kurt Lischka. In Paris, Eichmann's Judenreferat, run by first Dannecker, then Röthke, was directly responsible to Oberg.

5 *La Mémoire courte*, a film by Henri and Francine Torrent. Bousquet went first,

then Georges Hilaire, Secretary-General of the Ministry of the Interior, then Darquier.

6 Earlier Heydrich had conveyed his orders to Fernand de Brinon, Pétain's ambassador in Paris, and instructed him to inform Laval.

7 Coston, 'I have seen Jews work', *La France au Travail*, 18 May 1941; Taguieff, p. 569.

8 These prominent Jews were taken to a concentration camp in Compiègne, where they shared their prison with over three thousand French communists and Russian prisoners of war.

9 The list for the convoy of 27 March 1942 has never been found, but the number of deportees has been estimated at 1,112.

10 French Jews: In 1939, 195,000 were French citizens and the remaining 135,000 foreign Jews. Sixty per cent of them were citizens of France; under Vichy twenty per cent of these Jews were exterminated. The immigrant Jews who had sought refuge in France between 1880 and 1939, mostly in Louis' lifetime, made up the other forty per cent; only fifty-five per cent of them survived Vichy.

11 **Jean Leguay** (1909–89): After the Liberation, despite his role in Jewish deportations as René Bousquet's police deputy in the Occupied Zone, although suspended from government office, he was permitted to leave for the United States, where he became a leading executive of Nina Ricci and Warner Lambert Pharmaceuticals. He returned to live in France until the Darquier Affair brought him to light. Indicted in 1979.

12 Jackson, p. 229.

13 Laval, occupied with other worries, was nevertheless perfectly aware of the military setbacks that were plaguing the Germans in the east and North Africa. Until the end of 1942 the Germans had little more than thirty thousand men at their disposal to control France, and Knochen and Oberg no more than three thousand German police. Bousquet commanded a French police force of about 100,000 men.

14 The Germans wanted to include forty per cent of French Jews in the deportations.

15 On 2 July Bousquet met the German SS chiefs in Paris, Oberg and Knochen, Hagen and Lishcka among others.

16 Klarsfeld, *French Children*, p. 34.

17 CDJC XXVI-40 and Billig, p. 245.

18 The target for Paris was later reduced to twenty thousand.

19 Billig, p. 245.

20 Klarsfeld, *Le Calendrier*, p. 261, quoting Laval: 'rubbish that the Germans themselves had disposed of'.

21 Intervention of Laval at the Conseil des Ministres: '*Dans une intention d'humanité, le chef du gouvernement a obtenu – contrairement aux premières propositions allemandes – que les enfants, y compris ceux de moins de seize ans, soient autorisés à accompagner leurs*

parents' (CDJC XLIX-35); and 'President Laval suggested that Jewish children under the age of sixteen should be included in the deportation of Jewish families from the Unoccupied Zone. The question of Jewish children remaining in the Occupied Zone was of no interest to him' (CDJC XXVI-46RF, 1233).

22 'Therefore, I request urgent notification by telegram of your decision as to whether children under the age of sixteen should be deported after the first fifteen convoys have left France. In conclusion, I would add that for the moment, the operation has only concerned stateless and foreign Jews. During the second phase we shall deal with Jews naturalised in France after 1919 or 1927' (Billig, p. 247).

23 Joly, *Darquier de Pellepoix*, p. 148, quoting Dannecker.

24 Billig, p. 250.

25 **Jean François** (dates unknown): Police Commissioner, in charge of Jewish Affairs at the Paris Prefecture de Police. At the Liberation the purge commission ordered his dismissal without pension, without result. Never brought to justice.

26 **André Tulard** (1899–1967): Never brought to trial.

27 The Vélodrome d'Hiver opened in 1910; by 1931 it was a Palais des Sports with a capacity of twenty thousand.

28 Billig, p. 251; CDJC XXVb – 55.

29 AN 3W142.

30 Marie Jeanne Costemale-Lacoste, 19 June 1946, CDJC XCVI- 15.

31 Zucotti, p. 111.

32 *ibid*, p. 112.

33 AN 3W142, Statement by Kurt Schendell.

34 AN 3W142.

35 CDJC XXVb-128.

36 See CDJC XXXV-48, correspondence between Louis Darquier and Urbain Gohier, on the inadequacy of the situation and the difficulties of Darquier at Vichy. Gohier wrote his first letter on 9 June 1942, Louis wrote his first reply on 13 July.

37 CDJC CXC IV-92.

38 CDJC XXXVb-92, Billig, p. 253.

39 Darquier to Laval, 31 July 1942, CDJC CXI-41/CXCIV-25.

40 The ACA, the Assemblée des Cardinaux et Archevèques, met quarterly. The persecution of the Jews was not mentioned in October 1942, at any of its meetings in 1943, nor at its last meeting before the Liberation in February 1944. In October 1942, from his prison in Le Portalet, Paul Reynaud wrote to Gerlier, accusing all the cardinals of the Church of massive betrayals, and ended: 'by making common cause with Pétain and Laval, you have worked mightily towards the divorce of the Church from all the healthy elements in the nation' (Halls, p. 76).

41 ANW 3142-KNO.

42 Cazaux, p. 190.

43 'Bousquet told Daladier, in prison, that Laval and he wanted to use their energetic pursuit of the children as a bargaining tool in other negotiations.' Bousquet permitted seventeen kinds of exemptions; on 18 August he withdrew eleven of them (Klarsfeld, *French Children*, p. 52, and Cazaux, pp.193–4).
Donald Lowrie to YMCA August 1942; sent to British Government confidentially by Save the Children Fund in November 1942. PRO FO 371/32056.

44 Between five and eight thousand children said goodbye to their parents and never saw them again. Klarsfeld: *French Children*, p. 44; Marrus and Paxton, p. 266 and Zucotti, p. 124.

45 The Prefect of the Hérault department, quoted by Marrus and Paxton, p. 256.

46 Laborie, p. 235.
Bishop Jules-Gérard Saliège (1870–1956): Archbishop of Toulouse. See also Chapter 20, n. 5.

47 Pierre-Marie Théas of Montauban, bishop of Bousquet's native town, was one of those who followed Saliège.

48 Among these messages was a clandestine tract of six pages, published in 1942, detailing almost everything that happened to the Jews in these July and August round-ups: 'It is three months since thousands of Jewish children, after having been separated from their parents and suffering horrors in the camps of Pithiviers and Drancy, were deported to the east. And then, not a word' (CDJC XLIX-13).

49 The BBC continued to refer to mass murders. On 2 July the *New York Times* published a report of the gassing. The Vatican and its cardinals knew. Whether they believed it, of course, is another matter. The Germans went to great lengths to deny it too, using all kinds of proof, model camps and so forth.

50 Donald Lowrie to YMCA August 1942; sent to British Government confidentially by Save the Children Fund November 1942. PRO FO 371/32056.
Some of the relief agencies: CIMADE (Comité intermouvements auprès des évacués): A Protestant group of five youth movements. Pastor Boegner, the French Protestant leader, presided over it and was a prime mover against Vichy's Jewish laws. He and Cardinal Gerlier, to whose diocese the anti-Nazi Jesuit Père Chaillet belonged, agreed that joint effort should be made to rescue the children. This became l'Amitié Chrétienne, which produced vast quantities of the false documents which so irritated Louis Darquier and Georges Montandon. Dr Donald Lowrie, an American, of the International YMCA, took a leading role in relief, as did the World Council of Churches. Jewish relief agencies and charities abounded, and there was UGIF in both zones to supply what it could. Some of the hundreds of charities involved in trying to save the Jews and others of France were Quakers, the Red Cross, Secours Suisse, Oeuvre de Secours aux Enfants (OSE, a Jewish children's relief agency) and the Salvation

Army. Jewish relief funds tried to get the children to America. The US government offered a thousand visas, later raised to five thousand. Laval agreed, as long as there was no publicity. Bousquet gave only five hundred exit visas; his firmness on the matter meant that delays took the matter up to November. Operation Torch brought an end to it. About 350 children finally got to the USA. The French Resistance, the World Jewish Congress and the Save the Children Fund also helped in different ways: the reports of the underground press of the former, in the CDJC and of the latter two in the TNA: PRO tell more than anyone can easily bear to know.

51 At Vichy, René Gillouin, a Protestant close to Pétain, continually protested. Admiral Platon, also a Protestant, did the opposite and refused Boegner's pleas for intervention.

52 Weber, *Action Française*, p. 471.

53 Pryce-Jones, interview with Jean Leguay, p. 232.

54 Lambert, pp. 186–7.

55 Lequerica to Ministry of Foreign Affairs, Madrid: 'I await his [Darquier's] conversation with curiosity . . . since even though they may have been some unpleasant excesses of violence in its execution, a mere eleven thousand people have been placed in camps . . .' (AMAE (b), 15 September 1942). There is a lot more like this in Lequerica's correspondence.

56 These letters are from, in order, *Coeurs Vaillants*, 21 April 1942 (*Coeurs Vaillants* is a Catholic journal for children); anonymous, 18 July 1942; Jeanne L., 24 August 1942; B.I., 24 August 1942; Françoise D., 30 August 1942. All are reprinted, with many more, in Sabbagh (ed.).

57 September 1942, Jackson, p. 203.

58 Marrus and Paxton, p. 278 and Halls, p. 80.

59 Barthélémy: *Carnets*, quoted in *Le Monde*, 10 November 1994.

60 The plaque in Vichy commemorates 6,500 Jews.

61 CDJC XLIX-42.

62 Dannecker, however, managed to meet his future wife in Paris, and got engaged there.

63 Zucotti, p. 114.

64 Klarsfeld, *French Children*, p.48.

CHAPTER 17

Having Fun

INTERVIEWS AND CORRESPONDENCE: Jean Gayet, Auguste Mudry, Teresa. SOURCES: Darquier family correspondence; AGA; AMAE (b), 9 and 13 June 1939, 13 March 1941; AMAE (f) Exp. 21; AN AJ 38/3; AN AJ38/3V, 20 May 1943; AN 3W142; AN

3W147; AN 3W155; APP GA D9, 12 January and 12 March 1943; CDJC VI-176; CDJC XIV-80; CDJC XXVI-40; CDJC LXI-104; CDJC LXXIV-13; CDJC LXXV-105; CDJC XCV-80; CDJC XCVI-12, 72; CDJC CIX-97; CDJC CXVIII-162; CDJC CXXXIX–6; CDJC CCXIV-82; CDJC CCXVI-9; TNA: PRO FO 371/28228 Z6543; TNA: PRO FO 371/49587 Z3523; TNA: PRO FO 892/163. PUBLICATIONS: Beevor and Cooper, *Paris After the Liberation*; Billig, *Le Commissariat Général aux Questions Juives*; Burrin, *France Under the Germans*; Cointet, *Vichy*; Bernadette Dubourg, '*Le Procès Papon, compte rendu d'audience du 23 janvier 1998*', www.sudouest.com/papon/procedure/page17.htm; *La France enchaînée*, 1–15 June 1939; Gordon, *Collaborationism in France During the Second World War*; Gordon, *Fascism, the Neo-Right and Gastronomy*; Halls, *Politics, Society and Christianity in Vichy France*; *History Today*, October 2001; Hoover Institution, *France During the German Occupation*; Howson, *Arms for Spain*; Jackson, *France: The Dark Years*; Jardin, *Vichy Boyhood*; Joly, *Darquier de Pellepoix et l'antisémitisme français*; *Journal officiel*, 23 and 24 November, 13–24 December 1942; Jucker, *Curfew in Paris*; Kernan, *Report on France*; Lacroix-Riz, *Industriels et banquiers français sous l'Occupation*; Laloum, *La France antisémite de Darquier de Pellepoix*; *Libération*, 13 July 1993; *Mail on Sunday*, 16 January 2000; Marnham, *The Death of Jean Moulin*; *Le Matin*, 22 December 1942; Mengin, *No Laurels for de Gaulle*; Modiano, *The Search Warrant*; Patterson, 'Ireland, Vichy and Post-Liberation France'; Paxton, *Vichy France*; Pryce-Jones, *Paris in the Third Reich*; Randa, *Dictionnaire commenté de la collaboration française*; Rearick, *The French in Love and War*; Sana, *El Franquismo sin Mitos*; Taguieff (ed.), *L'Antisémitisme de plume*; Templewood, *Ambassador on Special Mission*; Wellers, *Un Juif sous Vichy*; Woodhead, *War Paint*

1 CDJC XCVI –72, Auguste Valence.
2 Vittel is another French spa town which admits little about its Vichy years. This camp was controlled by the Nazis, and its grand hotels housed Americans and Canadians too, then came Polish Jews, who were deported. Five hundred of these women were exchanged for German prisoners of war, the rest were liberated in September 1944.
3 Jucker, p. 155.
4 Letter to Darquier from de Lequerica, 26 February 1943, marked personal – '*Mon cher Commissaire et Ami*' – about a former colleague of Lequerica's, apparently of Jewish origin: 'Spain is a country which in my opinion has never been unaware of what they call today, racial questions. On the contrary . . .' This was the affair of Gattegno Botto.
5 **Antonio Barroso y Sánchez-Guerra** (1893–1982): Close to Franco, like him born in Galicia in north-west Spain. He was a monarchist and a lifelong military man. Graduated from the Ecole Supérieure de Guerre in France, was appointed military attaché in Paris on 1 May 1934 and remained there until July 1936. At the outbreak of the Civil War he made public attempts to send arms to Franco's forces, which caused a furore in France. Returned to Spain and served as chief of operations at Franco's headquarters. In 1941 he returned

to Paris, where he performed similar services for Franco until his recall to Spain, and he became a brigadier general in 1943. During the war Barroso's banquets included immensely cordial occasions with Nazis – on 11 March 1941 General von Runstedt, von Stulpnagel, Abetz and Schleier attended. The Spanish embassy was at 25, avenue George V, the attaché's office next door at no. 27.

Governorships of Seville and Gibraltar preceded Barroso's appointments as Franco's chief of the Military Household, and then Minister for the Army. After retirement in 1962 he continued to sit in the Cortes, and was an ubiquitous presence as a consultant to leading Spanish industries, and a very rich man. He was often accused of making a good deal of money from his various positions over the years, and of the kind of corruption which included doing well out of Louis Darquier's pot of gold when he was in Paris. 'Franco never placed any obstacles in the way of corruption since a corrupt minister or general was always a vulnerable minister or general' (Howson).

6 Teresa.
7 O'Kelley was Irish Minister in Paris 1932–35, and returned to Paris in a consular capacity. It was he who safeguarded the James Joyce correspondence given to him after Joyce's death in 1941 by Paul Léon, Joyce's secretary, friend and adviser.
8 Auguste Mudry said of Myrtle: 'I never met her. I don't know if she came to the CGQJ. But it was a large building. I don't think she was very interested in politics. I was told she spoke French badly. I knew they had a daughter.'
9 Jean Gayet, November 1999.
10 Myrtle to René, undated, 1932.
11 Teresa.
12 Beevor and Cooper, p. 177.
13 *La France enchaînée*, no. 29, 1–15 June 1939.
14 Sources: Kernan, p. 37; Simone Mittre, secretary to de Brinon, interviewed in Pryce-Jones, p. 215.
15 Janot Darquier qualified on 30 June 1943.
16 **Admiral René-Charles Platon** (1886–1944): First World War naval veteran. Passionate advocate and defender of the French Empire; a true Gascon who boasted like one. He held opinions akin to those of General Weygand, except that he was a rigid Protestant of the extreme right. Darlan's Secretary of State for the Colonies 1940–42 and under Laval in charge of Vichy's anti-Masonic activities. Reprimanded by Darlan for displaying a large, signed portrait of Maurras in his cabin; also close to Doriot's PPF. Fell out with Laval in 1943, removed from office, executed by the Resistance in October 1944.
17 Lequerica to Madrid FO 25.11.41 AMAE (b). Lequerica also reported an improvement in relations between the Vatican and the Reich.
18 Wellers, p. 75. There were many different versions of such posters.

19 Members of these gangs were also called *zazous*.

20 **Jean-Hérold Paquis** (1912–45): Journalist and anti-Semite, member of Doriot's PPF. Famous broadcaster, daily, on Radio-Paris. Fled to Germany, then Switzerland. Handed over to France, he was tried, sentenced to death and executed.

21 Wellers, p. 77.

22 Maurice Chevalier in 1940: 'I blindly follow the Marshal and I believe that everything that can bring about collaboration between the French and German peoples must be undertaken' (Rearick, p. 258). After the war Chevalier would admit only to singing for French prisoners of war in Germany; in fact he sang on German-controlled Radio-Paris, and performed for Germans and collaborators.

23 Ursula Rüdt von Collenberg (frau Nottebohm, interviewed in Pryce-Jones, p. 244).

24 Modiano, p. 56.

25 *ibid.*

26 Milice: Created in 1943 under Pierre Laval, transforming the Service d'Ordre Légionnaire (SOL) into a national police force. Its leader was **Joseph Darnand** (1897–1945): Uncle of Jeanne Brevet-Charbonneau-Degrelle. Son of a railway worker, war hero, member of Action Française, then Croix-de-feu, then Cagoule, then PPF. As a Cagoulard he was arrested in July 1938. Defended by Robert Castille and Xavier Vallat, he was imprisoned for only four months. He directed Pétain's Legion Française des Combattants in the Alpes Maritimes, moved to Vichy in January 1942, became a member of the committee for the LVF, then formed the Milice. In August 1943 he joined the Waffen SS and swore allegiance to Hitler. Secretary of State for Law and Order in the Vichy government from late 1943, he was in control of all French police services. He joined Pétain and company in Sigmaringen, used the Catholic network to flee to Italy but was arrested and returned to France. Condemned to death by the High Court of Justice, he was executed by firing squad in October 1945.

27 Beevor and Cooper, p. 15.

28 Pryce-Jones, p. 180.

29 Moulin was twenty-six when he became a *Préfet*, Bousquet was twenty-four.

30 De Gaulle quoted by Marnham.

31 The Conseil National de la Résistance was confirmed on 10 May 1943, and its first meeting was held in Paris on 27 May 1943. By 3 June Moulin had set up the Comité Français de la Libération Nationale, under de Gaulle in London, the final form of the Resistance as we know it, and de Gaulle legalised the Communist Party, a crucial move towards unity. Three weeks later Moulin was arrested by Klaus Barbie and his Gestapo and tortured to death. Barbie, 'The Butcher of Lyon', was finally sentenced by the French courts to life imprisonment in 1987 for the torture and death of over twenty thousand people.

32 Marcel Carné shot *Les Enfants du paradis* in Paris between 16 August and 9 November 1943; it was first shown in Paris in March 1945.

33 CDJC LXXV-105.

34 'To support Darquier's moves' in '. . . the question of giving full powers to Darquier de Pellepoix, in accordance with the promulgated laws and also to provide him immediately with the funds he has been promised': note from the German embassy in Paris to the head of the Sicherheitspolizei (SS) and SD in France 27 June 1942 (CDJC VI-176, and cited by Bousquet in his letter to the president of the Court of Criminal Appeal, 1992).

35 Billig, p. 331; CXXXIX–6.

36 AN 3W142.

37 *ibid.*

38 CDJC CCXVI-9 1942. Institute of Anthropo-Sociology. Decreed by Darquier on 10 November 1942. Inaugurated 22 December 1942. Taguieff, p. 299; *Journal Officiel* 23 and 24 November 1942. Added Jean Darquier with Roger de Vilmorin, 4 December 1942; J.O.298 13 December 1942 - 24 December 1942. German authorisation, 4 December 1942, Prefecture of Police authorisation 14 December 1942. AN 3W142.

39 **Abel Bonnard** (1883–1968): Minister of Education from April 1942 to August 1944. Vichy did not persecute homosexuals: there is no provision for homosexuality in the Code Napoléon, so it has never been banned in France. Bonnard was ex-Action Française – he did not share Maurras' anti-German sentiments – and a true and active collaborationist, advocating close ties between France and Germany, the hounding of communists and the purging of teachers. He was a member of the Académie Française, like many of these fascists.

40 CDJC CCXIV-82; *Le Matin*, 22 December 1942.

41 Claude Vacher de Lapouge, was replaced by René Martial on 25 January 1943, who was replaced by Estripeaut on 1 June 1943.

42 For the union Louis requested the former headquarters of the Saul Amar bank, then in liquidation (Darquier to Klassen, dated 2 December 1942). For his IEQJER he asked for 32, rue la Boétie, 'belonging to a Jew in flight' (letter 4 November 1942).

43 After rue de l'Arcade the union's headquarters were first 7, rue d'Armaillé, then rue la Boétie. Thus it had three addresses in three months. There are so many references to Louis' 'agitated private life' in 1943 that it is likely rue d'Armaillé was either another hotel room or the room of a mistress briefly passed through on the way to the Hôtel Terminus.

Darquier was president of his UFDR, Pierre Gérard its secretary-general, and it was to be 'completely independent' of the CGQJ, in a clever duplicity of effort, a strategy Darquier copied from the Germans. In this way his CGQJ paid him twice, once inside place des Petits-Pères as commissioner, and once outside at his UFDR. In fact, Laval and the embassy, who financed it, inserted spies from its very beginning.

44 CDJC CXVIII-162.

45 Joly, *Darquier de Pellepoix*, p. 156.

46 AN 3W142, Lecomte, treasurer.

47 CDJC CXCIII-162.

48 19 January 1943 to the Commandant du Grand-Paris CDJC LXI—104. Billig, p. 331.

49 AN 3W142, Francequeville.

50 **Pierre Gérard** (1915–?): Met Louis Darquier in 1934 when he was working on *Le Jour*, and worked for him until 1944. He was arrested in 1945, and his testimony demonstrated the experience of years of training in fabrication: 'I was young and easily led at this time and joined this movement believing that Jews had too much influence in France. But with age, I have understood that Darquier de Pellepoix exaggerated things,' was one of his statements to the police. He was condemned to *dégradation nationale* for life in July 1949; his subsequent history is unknown.

51 AN 3W142, Fernand Roirmarmier, 21 February 1945.

52 CDJC CXCIII-162.

53 Louis may or may not have been with Myrtle, but in any case he did not pay his bill. This time, his Vichy position meant that the hotel did not complain.

54 Joly, *Daquier de Pellepoix*, pp. 152–7; CDJC XXVII-40, 4 July 1942. Based in Vichy and Marseille, Radiodiffusion Nationale was basically the national station for the Vichy Zone. Some of Darquier's radio programmes are available from INA. He began on 4 October 1942 and continued until January 1943. There were fifty or so broadcasts in that time. The pessimistic opening and closing words were changed to the more optimistic, 'The only national wealth left to us now is our race.' Race and intermarriage and half-Jews, polluted blood in one form or another as opposed to the purity of the French version, were the general theme. Specific topics were 'Time for a Laugh' – songs, jokes, caricatures 'designed to ridicule Jews and show, by means of amusing and precise examples, their dishonest ways in business, their scorn of the Aryan etc.', interspersed with 'News from France', e.g. 'Five Jewish doctors, Salomon, Isaac, Reinach, Blum and Moch had set up an undercover clinic in a private house in Neuilly where they were carrying out abortions,' and news from abroad: 'News from Rio' announced: 'The Jew Jacob Maranes has been asked to form a government.'

55 AN 3W142-KNO, see also AN3W147, Archives de Berlin.

56 AN 3W142-KNO.

57 *ibid.* Letter from Coston to Darquier, 20 May 1943, asking for advertisements from the CGQJ in his Bulletin.

58 Founded in 1941, the AJA's first president was Jacques Ménard, editor-in-chief of *Le Matin*; it numbered between fifty and a hundred journalists. Coston, who was in charge of propaganda, was amongst the members who met to hear Darquier as guest speaker on 7 October 1942, when he said: 'I am delighted to see that anti-Jewish journalism now has an office; before, its office was a prison cell. To attack the Jews before the war was dangerous, as I well know, because it earned me five months in prison ... What revenge it is for me to sit ... in the chair of the Jew Louis Louis-Dreyfus and to occupy his house ...' ANAJ38/3V.

André Chaumet (dates unknown): professional anti-Semite, fascist, journalist. Connected to the Weltdienst from 1935; during the Occupation he was funded by both the German embassy and the Propaganda Staffel. He was a member of Doriot's PPF and the driving force behind the Centre for Anti-Bolshevik Studies. Chaumet took on Sézille's *Cahiers jaunes*, and transformed it into a new weekly, *Revivre*, in March 1943. Darquier gave Delpeyroux 100,000 francs to launch his newspaper *France révolution* for the UFDR. Punishment after the war, if any, unknown.

59 Pierre Gérard had never been forgiven for bringing to light Galien's misdemeanours, and the Germans 'resigned' him as secretary-general of the UFDR in February 1943. The thoroughly disillusioned Dr Klassen took over. He appointed a businessman, Louis Prax, as administrator of the UFDR, who also took over Gérard's other job as director of propaganda at the CGQJ. 'Our man at the CGQJ', Klassen called him, and a repeat of the Galien–Darquier relationship began. To Montandon's disgust a rival he considered a buffoon, Dr René Martial, gave the opening lecture for the Chair of Ethnology. Martial had just published, with Flammarion, *Half-Castes: A New Study of Migration, the Mixture of Races, Crossbreeding, the Reimmersion of the French Race and the Revision of the Family Code*. His lectures were to be about 'The Anthropology of Race', on the theme of 'The Cranium and its Laws'. Trembling with rage and fright after the students' reaction, Martial fled, accompanied by a loud student rendition of 'The Marseillaise'. For a brief period he continued his lectures elsewhere, guarded by Louis Darquier, but nothing more was heard of them by March 1943.

Even less popular was the idea of learning anti-Semitism at the Sorbonne. On 15 December, in his inaugural lecture in the Michelet theatre, Professor Henry Labroue told his students that Jews had '*une odeur particulière*', and that Jesus Christ was not a Jew. The level – 'a very convex nose, fleshy lips ... eyes a bit damp and rheumy' – was below anything already feared by the Faculty of Letters at the Sorbonne, who ostracised him and his lectures. Darquier watched students boo the Professor – 'scum', 'bandit', 'bastard' – and throw liquid gas. Labroue had to slink out of a side entrance, and the police chased students through the streets of the Latin Quarter – not what the Germans wanted to see. Labroue was meant to lecture twice a week. From January to May 1942, an average of two to three students turned up each time. By May, protected by the police and carrying a gun himself, he was lecturing to nobody, and the Chair was cancelled. Darquier rewarded his failure with a Jewish house on the Côte d'Azur.

Henri Labroue (1880–1964): First World War veteran. Academic, lawyer and politician who suddenly veered from the liberal centre to extreme collaboration and fanatical anti-Semitism after the fall of France. Supported by Abetz and the embassy staff and, despite his failure at the Sorbonne, always in demand to lend professorial gravitas to anti-Semitic occasions throughout the Occupation. Fled to the Pyrénées and was arrested in 1945, at which point the Sorbonne changed his Chair of the History of Judaism into a Chair of the History of Christianity. Sentenced in 1948 to twenty years' imprisonment, pardoned in 1951. Lived in Nice until his death.

60 APP GA D9, 25 March 1943 and Wellers p. 76.

61 5 April 1943, AN 3W147, Archives de Berlin.

62 Delpeyroux quoted in Hoover Institution, p. 652. Utterly mendacious statement. AN AJ38/3.

63 Professor Labroue presided over all of collaborationist Paris and its German patrons: Coston and Montandon, Laubreaux and many more; in the absence of Abetz, Schleier attended, so did Achenbach; the Italian consul general, Orlandini, came too. All the fascist literati were there – Brasillach, Rebatet, Céline and Cousteau.

64 Randa, p. 117.

Georges Oltramare (1896–1960): Swiss journalist, vocal anti-Semite, fascist of the Mussolini variety. Accompanied Abetz to Paris in 1940 and became first editor of *La France au travail*, then, under the pseudonym of Charles Dieudonné, broadcast 'Les Juifs contre la France'on Radio-Paris. Escaped to Sigmaringen, was arrested and finally tried in 1947, condemned to three years' imprisonment in Switzerland, and in France to death *in absentia*, in 1950. Escaped to Spain, then to Egypt where he continued his anti-Semitic broadcasts from Cairo, but died in Paris. His memoirs are entitled *Les Souvenirs nous vengent*.

65 AN 3W142, Inspector Jansen's report on the UFDR.
It is very likely that this was the Hafner, or Haffner, a director of the SEC, i.e. the CGQJ's police service, who was said to have close contacts with the Milice, and whom Antignac had sacked. Hafner accused Antignac of stealing money. At this time Antignac put in the previously sacked Petit, the one who was to become involved in the Schloss affair with Lefranc.

66 To get an inside footing, Darquier ordered Gérard to write for *Au Pilori*. Gérard denied this after the war, despite the production of letters proving his connections, which, he told his investigators, were 'mistaken': *Au Pilori* had sent him cheques in payment for his offerings 'in error'. To buy *Au Pilori*,

Delpeyroux, president of the UFDR, was instructed to inform Prax that Darquier was withdrawing the CGQJ's subsidy to the UFDR – that is, the 200,000 francs Louis paid himself, before Prax was inserted by the Germans to make it difficult for him to do so. The embassy was also informed that as French money was withdrawn, no further subsidies from the embassy could be accepted either. In other words, Louis was planning to give up his UFDR, and hoped to add to his role as commissioner that of newspaper magnate. Klassen fulminated that Darquier was trying to use his funds to 'snatch *Au Pilori* out of our hands' (see Taguieff). Its owner (with Robert Pierret) was Jean Lestandi, from a wealthy banking family, an anti-Semite, associated with Abetz and de Brinon before the war in the Comité France-Allemagne and le Grand Pavois. Louis never had a chance of getting *Au Pilori* away from the embassy. Lestandi was also assured of a post as 'technical adviser', for which he would be paid ten per cent of the money earned from the sale of the paper, that is between thirty-five and forty thousand francs a month.

67 Pierre Gérard halved the propaganda department's budget in his 1945 statement to the police, a masterpiece of fabrications and understatement. When Darquier asked him for premises on the boulevard Haussman, he told Achenbach that the UFDR had nine hundred members who had formerly been members of his Anti-Jewish Union. He provided no proof as to how he tracked this number down after four years.

Gérard titivated one of his earlier pamphlets into a thick booklet, *The Jew: What he is. What he Wants . . . What he has Done*. Over five thousand copies were printed for the UFDR in July 1943.

CHAPTER 18

Loot

INTERVIEWS AND CORRESPONDENCE: Darquier family, Pierre Gayet, Jean Lindoerfer, Auguste Mudry. SOURCES: PAF, September 1942; AN AJ 38; AN 3W142; AN 3W147; AN 3W355; APP GA D9; BNF 4–V-14644.; CDJC XXVIII-217; CDCJ XXXIV-1; CDJC LXXV-105, 219; CDJC XCVI-57, 63, 80, 84, 88 (Antignac Affairs Schloss dossier); CDJC CVI-128, appendix 1; CDJC CXXXIX-6; CDJC CXVI-17; CDJC CXCIII-187. PUBLICATIONS: Billig, *Le Commissariat Général aux Questions Juives*; *Le Crapouillot*, no. 23, 1953; Rachel Ehrenfeld, 'Bursting Taittinger's Bubble', *Pakistan Today*, 9 January 2004; Feliciano, *The Lost Museum*; Lacroix-Riz, *Industriels et banquiers français sous l'Occupation*; Marrus and Paxton, *Vichy France and the Jews*; Matteoli, *Mission d'étude sur la spoliation des Juifs de France* (The Matteoli Commission), 17 April 2000; Nicholas, *The Rape of Europa*;

Ousby, *Occupation*; Petropolous, *The Faustian Bargain*; Pryce-Jones, *Paris in the Third Reich*; Rousso, *L'Aryanisation économique*; *The Week*, 11 March 2000; Warner, *Pierre Laval and the Eclipse of France*; Weisberg, *Times Literary Supplement*, 21 May 2004; Zucotti, *The Holocaust, the French and the Jews*; www.ambafrance-us.org/news/statmnts/1998/wchea/schlosse.asp

1 Billig, p. 10.
2 CDJC LXXV-105. Probably a Propaganda Arbeitlung press conference.
3 Billig, p. 174; Summary of the work of the study mission on the spoliations of the Jews in France: 'The Matteoli Commission', 17 April 2000.
4 Billig, p. 321; CDJC CXCIII-187, Dr Blanke of the MBF to Darquier 4 December 1943; Pryce-Jones, p. 83.
5 The German military decree of May 1940 enabled them to appoint trustees to vacant businesses. Then came their first Jewish ordinance in September 1940, and their second on 3 October.
6 Both the Vichy Ministries of Finance and of Industrial Production were involved in SCAP, which ran Aryanisation from October 1940 until March 1941, and was thus the precursor to the CGQJ in this work.

   The first director of SCAP was a former director of the Bank of France, Pierre-Eugène Fournier. On 14 February 1941 he instructed his French trustees: 'The definition of Jew is given in the ordinance of 27 September 1940. You will note that these texts speak mainly in terms of religion. However, this term should not be taken in its narrowest sense. In reality, religion is not the only criterion in the interpretation applied by the Occupation authorities and race is actually more important. I have seen questions raised by people who can prove that they themselves, as well as their parents and grandparents, have been baptised but they still want to know if they can be sure that they belong to a non-Jewish race. Enquiries in this area are clearly quite delicate and only crop up rarely but I would like to stress that religion alone is not always a sufficient criterion' (Billig, p. 29).
7 The staff of the Economic Aryanisation section increased from 425 in June 1941 to 766 in October 1941, and then to 942 in November 1942. From October 1942 there were the additional 102 agents from the SEC. These were the theoretical figures, at any rate.
8 AN 3W142-KNO; Billig, p. 50.
9 Mudry, November 1999.
10 AN 3W142. Darquier wrote to Pétain refuting such an accusation.
11 Billig, p. 37; CDCJ XXXIV-1.
12 Lacroix-Riz, p. 478 quoting AN AJ 38.
13 Taittinger also acquired the famous 1930s art deco beach-front house Hôtel Martinez in Cannes when it was Aryanised. It is said still to be owned by the holding company he founded, Société du Louvre. See also Ehrenfeld.

14 **Pierre Cathala** (1888–1947): Lawyer and Minister of Finance on Laval's accession to power. Parliamentary deputy, under-secretary to Laval and Minister of Agriculture in the 1930s. Pro-German and anti-communist. He was in Pétain's first government, then Under-Secretary for Information. Close to Bousquet and Laval: together these three made Darquier's life miserable. Cathala died of a heart attack in Paris while awaiting trial.

15 Marrus and Paxton, p. 101.

16 Billig, p. 132. Written by Boué's second in command, Elid Caris, who, like Galien, was an SD informer. He wrote this letter to the Prefect of Police on 23 September 1942.

17 AN AJ 38/3ix.

18 AN 3W142.

19 Lacroix-Riz, pp. 381–3; René Darquier's address to his associates is in *Corps gras, savons revue technique et professionnelle*, 1 July 1943.

20 CDJC XCVI–80.

21 Billig, p. 114; CDJC XCVI-57, p. 4a.

22 AN 3W142.

23 *ibid.*

24 *ibid.*

25 AN AJ 38 330, 27 February 1943.

26 PAF.

27 PAF and Pryce-Jones, p. 150.

28 Jean Lindoerfer, October 2000; PAF and Pierre Gayet, January 2000.

29 AN AJ 38 164; AN AJ 38 180; AN AJ 38 330.

30 Billig, p. 327; MBF report 21 July 1943, CDJC LXXV - 219.

31 Rosenberg was to pursue Masonic and Jewish properties specifically, but anyone could be called either of those if the art appealed to Hitler. The ERR's record, by August 1944, was 71,619 dwellings raided, 1,079,373 cubic meters of goods shipped off in 29,436 trains.

32 Acceptable art ranged from van Dyck's *Portrait of a Lady* to Vermeer's *Astronomer*, from Boucher's *Madame de Pompadour* to the van Eyck Ghent altarpiece. Paintings by Titian, Velasquez, Raphael, Rubens, Watteau, Ingres, Goya, Gainsborough, Fragonard, Cranach – an endless and awe-inspiring list of great names, were crated up and went off in trains. Returning on the same trains came Germans bearing lists: dealers, private citizens, Nazi officials, the Reichsbank and museum curators on a spending spree, slavishly served by French and German art dealers, by fraudsters, Swiss banks and international con men.

33 Some French artists, of course, collaborated – the sculptor Aristide Maillol, the painters Dunoyer de Segonzac, Cocteau, Derain, Vlaminck, Kees van Dongen – and their work remained untouched.

34 Nicholas, p. 134.

35 AN 3W142.

36 Nicholas, pp. 160, 172; Rembrandt and Hals were queried later; ANW1342; Feliciano, p. 60.

37 CDJC CXXXIX-6, George Ebert to Rosenberg.

38 Antignac dossier, CDJC XCVI-88; AN W3142; Feliciano, p. 112; Interrogation of Bruno Lohse, investigation into Lefranc, and CIR Bruno, National Archives, Washington. Lohse to Miss Limberger, Secretary to Goering, 29 September 1942.

Jean-François Lefranc (dates unkown): French art dealer in Paris, worked closely with the Germans and was responsible for the liquidation of other collections besides the Schloss. Arrested in 1945 and condemned by the Court of Justice of the Seine. Later fate unkown.

Bruno Lohse (1911–9?): Art historian and dealer, arrested by the American Art Looting Investigation Unit at the end of the war. Tried before the Military Tribunal in Paris in 1945, but later resumed his career as an art dealer in Munich.

39 CDJC XCVI-63, Costemale-Lacoste and XCVI-84; CDJCXCVI-80.

40 It is possible that this telegram was sent to warn Henri, because the informer who first revealed that the collection was in the Corrèze, stricken by remorse, tried, anonymously, to warn the family there.

41 In AN 3W142 there is an undated statement about Antignac taking Petit back into the Economic Aryanisation section as its general secretary with 'exorbitant remuneration', which caused the 'unhappy staff' to stop work.

42 Lynn Nicholas, in *The Rape of Europa*, maintains that Laval actually instructed Darquier to find the collection for him. I cannot relate this to Darquier's September 1942 arrangements with Lefranc, Lohse and von Behr. Darquier may have been playing a triple game – getting the paintings for his own cut, for Goering and for Laval, but generally speaking such complexities were well beyond him.

43 AN 3W147, Schleier telegram, 26 April 1943.

CHAPTER 19

D-Day

INTERVIEWS AND CORRESPONDENCE: Pierre Combes, Beryl Coombes (Clifton), Jean Gayet, Julia Keal, Alistair Rapley. SOURCES: PAF; AN 3W142; AN 3W356; APP GA D9; CDJC XXVI-19; CDJC XXVII-4–35, 49; CDJC XCVI-21, 66, 71, 75, 80, 83, 88; CDJC CIII-162; CDJC CXLIV-424; CDJC CXCIII-203; CDJC CCXIV-III. PUBLICATIONS: *Action française*, 8 and 30 June 1944; *Au Pilori*, 20 April 1944; Barthélemy, *Mémoires*; Billig, *Le Commissariat Général aux Questions Juives*; Cointet, *Vichy*; Feliciano, *The Lost Museum*; Felstiner, *To Paint her Life*; Gordon (ed.), *Historical Dictionary of World War II*; Gordon, *Collaborationism in France During the*

Second World War; Halls, *Politics, Society and Christianity in Vichy France*; Hoover Institution, *France During the German Occupation*; Jackson, *France: The Dark Years*; Joly, *Darquier de Pellepoix et l'antisémitisme français*; Klarsfeld, *Le Calendrier de la persécution des Juifs en France*; Laloum, *La France antisémite de Darquier de Pellepoix*; McCrum, *Wodehouse*; Marrus and Paxton, *Vichy France and the Jews*; Mengin, *No Laurels for de Gaulle*; *Le Monde*, 7 November 1995; Nicholas, *The Rape of Europa*; Nossiter, *The Algeria Hotel*; *Paris-Soir*, 29 March 1944; Pryce-Jones, *Paris in the Third Reich*; Randa, *Dictionnaire commenté de la collaboration française*; Salomon, *Life? or Theatre?*: Sergeant, *Give me Ten Seconds*; Taguieff (ed.), *L'Antisémitisme de plume*; Varney, *Great Tew*; Zucotti, *The Holocaust, the French and the Jews*; www.diplomatie.gouv.fr/archives/dossiers/schloss/sommaire.html

1 PAF.
2 Billig, p. 265.
3 AN 3W142, Antignac, 4–5 November, 1944.
4 CDJC 1-38, Knochen to Müller, 12 February 1943.
5 CDJC XXVII 4–34.
6 Schleier, in Randa, p. 65.
7 CDJC XXVII–12.
8 Billig, p. 268.
9 AN 3W356, Klassen to Schleier, 19 July 1943.
10 Halls, p. 135.
11 CDJC XXVII-34.
12 CDJC XXVII-35, Billig, p. 268 for Darquier's improvements: see Röthke's document on the four bills, CDJC XXVII-34.
13 AN 3W142; Antignac and Paule Fichot; Paule Fichot in CDJC XCVI-66; Antignac in Hoover, p. 649.
14 Darquier to Schleier, 2 July 1943. In this letter it appears that there were also collections belonging to the 'Jews Bonn, Hauser and others'. Darquier asks for Schleier's assurance that the Germans won't touch the paintings while they are in Paris, but will permit them to be returned to Vichy once they have been valued, etc. The reason for this deceitful letter would be twofold: first, to keep the embassy's hands off ERR loot; and second because Darquier was in the midst of the *Au Pilori* row with Klassen, and Schleier was in daily receipt of memos begging that Darquier be sacked. It was probably written at Laval's instruction: he was always keen on official file copies to cover all dubious activities.
15 Antignac, Hoover, p. 649.
16 AN 3W142.
17 AN W3142; CDJC XCVI-80. Several representatives of different administrations viewed the collection. A delegation from the headquarters of the security police services of Paris, Jean-François Lefranc, Postma, expert on Flemish

painting, René Huyghe and Germain Bazin, Louvre curators, bailiffs, functionaries from the SEC and the CGQJ.

18 AN 3W142, Antignac.
19 CDJC XXVII-33.
20 Klarsfeld, *Le Calendrier*, p. 74.
21 AN 3W142, Antignac.
22 Felstiner and Salomon.
23 Florence Gould the American hostess, Nicholas, p. 175.
24 McCrum, p. 340ff.
25 AN 3W142 3, 1 October 1943.
26 Rose Valland to Jaujard, Director of the Louvre, original document in the archives of the Office of the Museums of France. *Archives diplomatiques* www.diplomatie.gouv.fr/archives/dossiers/schloss/sommaire.html.
27 Barthélemy, p. 70.
28 Antignac, CDJC XCVI-21.
29 In those days you had to be employed as a 'gentleman's servant' to be allowed to run the pub; his work for the Schusters qualified Arthur for this opportunity.
30 CDJC CIII-162.
31 For Great Tew: Alistair Rapley, Julia Keal; Beryl Coombes (Clifton). See also Sergeant and Varney.
32 AN 3W142.
33 Jean Gayet, 22 November 1999. Pierre Combes later said that three or four died.
34 CDJC CXCIII and CDJC CXLIV-424, Taguieff, p. 406ff, p. 442ff.
Jacques Bouly de Lesdain (dates unknown): extremist, political editor of *l'Illustration*, convenor of two exhibitions on the new European Order at the Grand Palais in 1941 and 1942.
35 '*Dépêche de France*' may well be a misquote for the Sarrault brothers' *Dépêche du Midi*.
36 *Paris-Soir*, 29 March 1944; CDJC XCVI-83.
37 Charles Paty du Clam took over from Louis. He was the undistinguished descendant of the commandant who had arrested Alfred Dreyfus in 1894. He fled in disgust, and Antignac, who had left in a snit, returned as secretary-general, appointed by Laval, and saw the CGQJ through to the end.
38 Beryl Coombes (Clifton).
39 Zucotti, pp. 161, 196, 198 and 200, and Marrus and Paxton, p. 334.
40 *Le Nouvelliste de Neuilly,* 10 June 1944.
41 Marie-Rose Gounel was arrested on 20 May 1944 by Vichy, and interviewed by the police after the war on 16 November 1946.
42 Charles Maurras, *Action française,* 8 June 1944, 30 June 1944.

CHAPTER 20

The Family

INTERVIEWS AND CORRESPONDENCE: Maud de Belleroche, Michael de Bertadano, Pierre Combes, Bill Coy, Jeanne Degrelle, Henri Fernet, Jean Gayet, Jean-Louis Huberti (real name Alain Baudroux), Eanswythe Hunter, Violet Kench, Yvonne Lacaze, Père Lucien Lachièze-Rey, Bertrand Leary, Brian Nield, Pierre Orliac, Alistair Rapley, Simone Reste, Teresa, Mrs Jim Tustain. SOURCES: Darquier family correspondence; SRD; AGA, 18 May 1947; AGA (f); AMAE (b); AMAE (c); AMAE (d); AMAE (e); AN 3W142; APP GA D9, 15 October 1944; BNF Document 8–TH Paris – 17823: Jeanne (Janot) Darquier, '*Contribution à l'étude de la Médecine du Travail. Thèse pour le Doctorat en Médecine*', 30 June 1943; CDJC LXXIV-11; CDJC XCVI-12; CDJC CXCIII-203; TNA: PRO FO371/42755: The Deportation of the Children; TNA: PRO 892/163. PUBLICATIONS: Chalon, *Portrait of a Seductress*; Combat, 25 January 1945; Louis Darquier, *l'Express*, 28 October–4 November 1978; *Droit et liberté*; *Franc-tireur*, 21 October 1944, 16 June 1945; *France libre*, 21 October 1944; *France-revolution*, 'Fifteen Minutes with Louis Darquier,' 31 October 1943; Gordon, *Collaborationism in France During the Second World War*; Gun, 'Les Enfants au nom maudit', *Historia*, no. 241, December 1966; Halls, *Politics, Society and Christianity in Vichy France*; *Histoire*, no. 159, October 1992; Howson, *Arms for Spain*; *Keesing's Contemporary Archives*; Klarsfeld, *Le Calendrier de la Persécution des Juifs en France*; Klarsfeld, *French Children of the Holocaust*; Laurier, *Il Reste le drapeau noir et les copains*; Bernard Lecache, *Le Droit de vivre*, December 1947; Laborie, *Résistants, vichyssois et autres*; Lottman, *The Purge*; *Le Monde*, March 2000; Nossiter, *The Algeria Hotel*; *Le Nouvel observateur*, March 2000; Novick, *The Resistance versus Vichy*; the *Observer*, 5 March 1998; *l'Opinion*, March 2000; Ousby, *Occupation*; Paxton, *New York Review of Books*, 16 December 1999; Péan, *Une Jeunesse française*; Paul Preston, *Times Literary Supplement*, 29 June 2001; *Le Procès de Charles Maurras et de Maurice Pujo*; *Le Procès de Maréchal Pétain*; Pryce-Jones, *Paris in the Third Reich*; Randa, *Dictionnaire commenté de la collaboration française*; Taittinger, *Et Paris ne fut pas détruit*; Venner, *Histoire de la Collaboration*; Warner, *Pierre Laval and the Eclipse of France*; Weber, *Action Française*; *The Week*, 2 December 2000

1 Pryce-Jones, p. 187.
2 PRO FO371/42755, The Deportation of the Children; Klarsfeld: *Le Calendrier* and *French Children of the Holocaust*.
3 All material for final days from Archivo general de la administración, Alcalá de Henares, Madrid: *Compte Rendu de l'Arrestation du Maréchal Pétain* ; Lottman; Pryce-Jones.
4 Lottman, p. 79.
5 Georges Bidault, a Catholic and head of the Conseil National de la Résistance,

was de Gaulle's post-war Foreign Minister and also drew up a blacklist noting collaborating clerics whose resignations – nothing more – should be required. Only seven bishops in all were removed.

Cardinal Henri-Marie Alfred Baudrillart: (1859–1942): Auxiliary Archbishop of Paris 1921–1942, elevated to cardinal in 1935. Rector of the Catholic Institute of Paris. Dedicated anti-communist and, amongst the cardinals, the leading collaborationist; he also associated with fascist groups and was patron of the LVF.

Bishop Paul Chevrier (1886–1968): Bishop of Cahors 1941–62. His resignation was mooted, but that is all. Never brought to justice.

Cardinal Pierre-Marie Gerlier (1880–1965): Archbishop of Lyons 1937–65 and Primate of the Gauls. Gerlier was defined as particularly at fault. Never brought to justice.

Cardinal Achille Liénart (1884–1973): Bishop of Lille 1928–68. Liénart, whose attitude to Vichy and the Nazis was sometimes less enthusiastic than that of his fellow cardinals, was not singled out for special mention though he continued to defend Pétain after the war and led a campaign to free him from imprisonment. Never brought to justice.

Cardinal Emmanuel Célestin Suhard (1874–1949): Archbishop of Paris during the Occupation. Named as particularly blameworthy. Never brought to justice.

Monseigneur Jean Mayol de Lupé (1873–1955): Friend of Abetz, much-decorated chaplain in the First World War. With Cardinal Suhard's approval, became chaplain to the LVF and accompanied the troops to the east. Praised His Holiness the Pope and Our Führer Adolf Hitler in the same breath. He was astonished by German defeat, and the Archbishop of Munich could not protect him. Extradited to France and sentenced in 1947 to twenty years' hard labour. Freed in 1951.

Bishop Jules-Géraud Saliège (1870–1956): Archbishop of Toulouse 1928–56. Georges Bidault also drew up a white list of clerics such as Archbishop Saliège who had not collaborated. Saliège was elevated to cardinal in 1946.

6 Taittinger wrote a number of mendacious accounts of his experiences, in which he never refers to Louis Darquier.

7 **Joseph Adrien Antignac** (1895–?): In August 1944, Antignac gave the order to destroy the CGQJ's archives. He was arrested on 6 November 1944; in July 1945 he was transferred from Fresnes prison to a series of Paris clinics. By November 1945 he was allowed house arrest and could move around Paris at will. On 4 July 1949, in front of the court, Antignac stated that he knew nothing of what happened to the Jews during the Occupation. He said: 'I was not an anti-Semite. I accepted the job at the CGQJ as I would have accepted a job at the "Provisions ministry".' Before being interrogated by the court, Antignac read a preliminary statement in which he said he did not

want to pay for the mistakes made by the man in charge of the CGQJ (Louis Darquier), who had not had the courage to face justice. Antignac was condemned to death and to *dégradation nationale* on 9 July 1949, after five hours of deliberations. He had tuberculosis. His sentence was commuted to forced labour in perpetuity. On his birth certificate there is no mention of his death, though his four marriages are recorded. His last marriage was in 1952. He was thus out of jail by 1952 or earlier, and he probably died under another identity.

8 There is considerable argument about the actual number executed during the Occupation. Courts were both military and civilian: 160,287 cases were tried, forty-five per cent of defendants were acquitted, twenty-five per cent sentenced to prison, twenty-five per cent to *dégradation nationale*; 7,017 were condemned to death, of which 1,500 were executed. Ordnances of 1944 introduced a new crime, *l'indignité nationale*, for which the punishment, *dégradation nationale*, ranging from five years to life, was essentially civic. The person thus sentenced lost the right to vote, became ineligible for public service, or was dismissed from it, lost army rank and the right to bear decorations, was excluded from business directorships, banks, press, radio, and all professional associations, institutes and organisations, all legal and judicial matters, teaching, journalism, and was forbidden to keep or carry arms.

9 On 23 October 1944: 'Following the mention of the death of Darquier and Platon at the last press conference at the Ministry of Justice, it was stated in certain journalistic circles that Darquier had been killed while resisting arrest and that Platon had been shot without trial . . . Whatever, it was believed that the two men were dead' (APP GA D9).

10 *L'Express*, 28 October–4 November 1978.

11 Michael de Bertadano, March 2002.

12 René Darquier has passed his sense of family on to his three children, who are exceptionally close to each other.

13 *L'Express*, 28 October–4 November 1978.

14 *ibid.*, and Teresa.

15 SRD.

16 Teresa.

17 *ibid.*

18 2 November 1944, Ministry of Foreign Affairs Madrid: AMAE R-2182, Exp.12–15 *Immigrantes Clandestinos*.

19 After the defeat of Hitler, Franco's government transferred all German assets, in a variety of ways, to men of straw and others, which provided German war criminals with more lavish possibilities than anything on offer to the Vichy exiles – hence Horcher's restaurant (see also Chapter 21, n. 18).

20 Paul Preston quoting Franco, *The Times Literary Supplement*, 29 June 2001.

21 In 1944, 190,000 Spanish Republicans were executed or died in prison. Torture

led to many suicides in prison. Other figures: 200,000 executed 450,000 in exile, 300,000 imprisoned.

22 On 12 March 1945 the Minister of Foreign Affairs wrote to M Gibert, president of the pre-trial investigatory tribunal of the High Court of Justice, informing him that according to information from the French ambassador in Madrid, for the last four or five months Darquier had been living under a false name in that city. Two days later the preliminary investigation began. The warrant for his arrest was issued on 2 June 1945.

Maud de Belleroche described Geneviève as a pretty little shop girl with a tremendous southern accent who spoke French very incorrectly.

Maud de Belleroche (1920–?): Sexual rampager, writer (her books are filed under 'Erotic' in French libraries) and actress. A woman of considerable vigour on many fronts, she gives a vivid portrait of these political exiles in *Le Ballet des crabes* and *l'Ordinatrice*. Among her husbands/*amours* was Georges Guilbaud, a member of Doriot's PPF and active in Tunis, who passed through Sigmaringen then took refuge in Spain with Maud, his wife (?) of the time. They went on to Argentina, Maud only briefly, returning to France and many other activities. An example of her prose and her ideas: 'Not for me to rise up against the nobility of the holocaust. Sexuality and suffering, spirituality and mortification are indissolubly linked in the common weft of higher pleasure, with death as a watermark.'

23 Mathieu Laurier, Randa p. 114. Name changed to Gran Via in 1983. The hotel Magerit is no. 76 – it is the Coliseum Cinema today.

Mathieu Laurier (1919–80): Former member of Jeunesses Patriotes, the Cagoule, then Clémenti's Parti Français National-Communiste, then the LVF, and an editor of *Au Pilori*.

24 Brian Nield, Director of Briam School, September 1999 and Jean-Louis Huberti (real name Alain Baudroux), former journalist in Madrid, September 1999.

François Gaucher (1910–90): Lawyer, secretary-general of the Parti Néo-Socialiste, a socialist turned fascist and an intellectual; member of the central committee of the PPF, served on the Eastern Front with the LVF in 1943. He was then chief of the Milice in the Northern Zone. Condemned to death *in absentia*. After the war, as well as running the École Briam in Madrid, he published two volumes of reflections on the fate and ideology of French fascism. Never brought to justice.

25 Pierre Combes, January 1999.

26 De Monzie was seventy-one. His funeral was held on 11 January 1947. Ramy Debrand was his sole legatee; she left everything to her niece Mme Fournié.

27 *Le Procès du Maréchal Pétain*, p. 483ff.

28 According to contemporary polls, 40.5 per cent felt Pétain should receive the death penalty, 40.5 per cent punishment short of death.

29 Laval was kept under supervision in Spain, and then returned to Austria, where the US forces turned him over to France.

30 Taittinger was released on 25 February 1945. He was fined 600,000 francs and prohibited from holding any public position. His business affairs, most notably the Taittinger champagne empire, suffered not at all.

31 Venner, p. 558.

32 *Le procès de Charles Maurras et de Maurice Pujo*, pp. 470, 506; Weber, *Action Française*, p. 472. 'Ignore' in the original should have been translated as 'not know about.'

33 Warner, p. 409.

34 **Alfred Rosenberg** (1893–1946): Director of Hitler's Office for Foreign Policy, edited its official journal, wrote voluminously. Famous for his book on racial theory, *The Myth of the Twentieth Century*. Reich Minister of the Eastern Occupied Territories 1941–45.

Joachim von Ribbentrop (1893–1946): Wounded and decorated First World War veteran, salesman, Nazi from 1932. Hitler's Minister of Foreign Affairs 1938–1945. Inadequate ambassador to Britain in 1936; arranged the Nazi–Soviet pact of 1939.

Otto Abetz (1903–58): After his release from prison in 1954, spent considerable effort attempting to rehabilitate his reputation and rewrite his history. Burnt to death in a car accident on the autobahn outside Düsseldorf.

Carl Theo Zeitschel (1893–1945): Staunch Nazi and Abetz's specialist on Jewish affairs at the embassy. Condemned to forced labour in perpetuity by the French courts in 1954, but he was already dead, killed in the Berlin bombardment of 1945.

Helmut Knochen (1910–?): Arrested with Oberg in 1944. Sentenced by British Military Tribunal to life imprisonment in 1946, then to death by hanging in 1947. Extradited to France, he was sentenced to death for war crimes in 1954. Released in 1962. Said to have worked in insurance in Offenbach, then to be in retirement in Baden-Baden.

Karl-Albrecht Oberg (1897–1965): Condemned to death in Germany, extradited to France in October 1946. Condemned to death by the French courts October 1954. Commuted to twenty years' forced labour in 1958. Pardoned in 1962.

Theodor Dannecker (1913–45): After Paris, Dannecker served in Bulgaria, Hungary and Italy. Arrested by the Americans, he hanged himself in the American prison at Bad Tölz in Bavaria.

Ernst Heinrichsohn (1921–?): Dannecker's assistant. After the war he was elected mayor of Burgstadt. Brought to trial by the West German government in 1979, sentenced to six years' imprisonment.

Ernst Achenbach (1909–91): As a corporate and defence lawyer, after the war Achenbach worked tirelessly in pursuit of amnesties for his Nazi colleagues – in particular for Otto Abetz. Deputy in the German Bundestag 1957–76. His nomination as German representative at the EEC in 1970 was annulled when the campaigner Beate Klarsfeld made public the dossier of his involvement in the deportation of the Jews. Otherwise never brought to justice.

Heinz Röthke (1913–66): Theological student, lawyer and civil servant. Ferocious anti-Semite who disliked any contact with Jews, and seldom visited Drancy but enthusiastically organised and – with Brunner – oversaw deportations until the end of the war. His extradition was never requested by the French government. Never brought to justice.

Rudolf Schleier (1899–1959): First World War veteran, tradesman from Hamburg, a Nazi from 1933. Promoted from Consul General at the embassy to Plenipotentiary Minister during Abetz's absence from Paris in 1943. Released from internment in Dachau by administrative error in December 1947. Re-arrested November 1948, extradited to France and tried as a war criminal, but by 1951 he was a free man living in northern Germany, helping his old boss Otto Abetz and making an application to visit the UK.

Dr Peter Klassen (dates unknown): His department in the Information Office of the embassy was called the Politisches Lektoren. He was specifically concerned with anti-Jewish and anti-Masonic propaganda, working closely with the IEQJ. As he was also responsible for ensuring that German control was seen to be discreet, and that instructions for Jewish and Masonic persecution should be carried out only by the French, he found the inadequacy of Darquier particularly painful. With others from the embassy, he followed Pétain and company to Sigmaringen, and then seems to have disappeared from public view.

35 **Louis-Ferdinand Céline** (Henri-Louis Destouches, 1894–1961): After his return to France he carried on, as ever, from his house in Meudon.

36 *France-Revolution,* 'Fifteen Minutes with Louis Darquier', 31 October 1943.

37 Serge Klarsfeld quoted in the *Observer,* 5 March 1998.

38 Laubreaux was not the only source of conflict: fascist journalist **Maurice-Yvan Sicard** (1910–2000) had coruscated Darquier in public at a meeting of the Salle Wagram on 22 January 1944. Sicard joined Doriot's PPF in 1936, was editor of its newspapers and a member of Doriot's *bureau politique,* and finally his political deputy. Like so many of Doriot's men, he fled to Spain. Condemned *in absentia* to hard labour in perpetuity, in 1957 he gave himself up and was granted amnesty. In Spain, under the pseudonym of Saint-Paulien, he transformed himself into an art historian and novelist.

39 Natalie Barney, Chalon.

40 Bill Coy, July 2001.

41 Beryl Coombes (Clifton), April 1999.

42 AN 3W142 – letter of 5 January 1946 from French Ministry of Foreign Affairs to French Ministry of Justice, France.

43 The investigatory team for the High Court knew where Louis was in March

1945; Jean Darquier and Louise, until then 'in one of her states' (Lacaze), by February 1946 if not before.

44 Teresa.

45 Bertrand Leary: Chief executive of Les Grands Moulins de Strasbourg, is the grandson of Henry Lévy and the son of Jean Lévy/Leary who fled to the USA and changed the family name there. After the war Jean Lévy reacquired the mills from the man of straw who had been handling them (not without cost). After leaving Argentina, René Darquier was in Manila for the Worms Bank shortly before his death, in 1958–59.

46 SRD.

47 Beryl Coombes (Clifton), April 1999.

48 Heythrop Hall moved to become part of London University in 1970; its records are unavailable, so I am unsure whether Anne was baptised at Heythrop or Oxford.

49 A medical contemporary and friend of Anne Darquier.

50 Tasmania J; Teresa.

51 SRD.

52 Myrtle to René, 11 January 1933.

53 Vallat was sentenced to ten years in prison in December 1947, but was freed in December 1949. He wrote for *Aspects of France* – as *Action française* was renamed in 1947 – and ran the paper from 1962 to 1966, wrote his memoirs, and died in 1972.

54 LXXIV-11, Paule Fichot, 9 December 1947.

55 AN 3W142 and Bernard Lecache in *Le Droit de vivre*, December 1947.

56 Others in Spain at this time were: Général Eugène Bridoux, Laval's Minister of War (sentenced to death *in absentia*), Maurice Gabolde, Vichy's last Minister of Justice (sentenced to death *in absentia*). Different courts sentenced to death *in absentia* Alain Laubreaux and Georges Oltramare – who arrived in Spain in 1950.

57 Lexie's will, 5 May 1948.

58 Tasmania J.

59 Teresa.

60 Pierre Orliac, January 1999.

61 Henri Fernet, September 1999.

62 Teresa.

63 Dominique Jamet: Son of Claude Jamet, professor, journalist and intellectual, a socialist and pacifist and *collabo*. His son Dominique is also a journalist and is the author of *Le Petit Parisien* (Flammarion, 2000).

64 A medical contemporary and friend of Anne Darquier.

65 Gun, '*Les Enfants au nom maudit*', p. 47ff. A great number of those I interviewed who knew Anne, spoke to me about her hatred for her father. These quotes are culled from half a dozen of them.

CHAPTER 21

The Cricket Team

INTERVIEWS AND CORRESPONDENCE: Consuelo Alvarado, Paulette Aupoix, John Booth, Colette Calmon, Bernard Charles, Maria Clark, Pierre Combes, Beryl Coombes (Clifton), Bill Coy, Michael de Bertadano, Anne-Marie Fiel, Elaine Fraser, Colin Gale, Pierre Gayet, Jean-Louis Huberti, Jean Ibbitson, Yvonne Lacaze, María de Carmen Mansilla, Hilda Moorhouse, Pierre Orliac, Alistair Rapley, Simone Reste, Isobel Rhodes, John Rigge, Natalie Rothstein, Teresa. SOURCES: SRD; AGA (a), 24 October 1963; AGA (b); AMAE, ref. P571–37890; AN 3W142; Ayuntamiento de Madrid Area de Culture, Archivo de Villa; CDJC CCXXIII-76. PUBLICATIONS: Charroux, *Ici Paris Hebdo*, undated; *Dictionnaire de la Noblesse*; *l'Humanité*, 6 November 1978; *Isis*, 9 September 1949; Frank Margison, obituary of Robert Hobson, *Guardian*, 29 November 1999; Randa, *Dictionnaire commenté de la collaboration française*; Anthony Stevens, obituary of Anthony Storr, *Guardian*, 20 March 2001.

1 In *Isis*, 9 September 1949, Godfrey Smith complained about such views as aired by Robert Robinson. Robinson was editor of *Isis* in 1950; Smith was president of the Oxford Union in 1950.

2 Comments from Anne's contemporaries at St Hilda's, in letters to me, 1997: Natalie Rothstein, Elaine Fraser, Hilda Moorhouse, Isobel Rhodes.

3 Bill Coy and Alistair Rapley, October, 1999.

4 Bill Coy, October 1999; July 2001.

5 The vicar at the time was the Rev. E.N.C. Sergeant, father of the political journalist John Sergeant – see his memoir *Give Me Ten Seconds*.

6 Beryl Coombes (Clifton), April 1999.

7 Colin Gale, Archivist of the Bethlem Royal Hospital, November 2004. In 1958 they were two hospitals – there still are – the Bethlem is in Beckenham, the Maudsley in Denmark Hill, both South East London, today part of an even bigger and more complicated Trust.

8 Medical contemporary and friend of Anne Darquier.

9 Anthony Storr, Obituary by Anthony Stevens, the *Guardian*, 20 March 2001.

10 Medical contemporaries and friends of Anne Darquier.

11 Frank Margison, Obituary for Robert Hobson the *Guardian*, 29 November 11 1999.

12 Teresa.

13 Mathieu Laurier, Randa, p. 115.

14 The Central School is part of the Universidad Complutense de Madrid. Louis worked for the Foreign Office from 1 January 1951 to 1 January 1964, and for the Ministry of Information and Tourism from 24 October 1963 to the end of 1976.

15 Mathieu Laurier, *Randa* , p.114.
16 The French church moved to calle de Lagasca in 1972. The Café California closed down in the 1960s. Posada is the Cafetaria Nebraska today.
17 Charroux.
18 Otto's son Gustav followed Otto, and Horcher's is still run by the family.
19 Bernard Charles, Mayor of Cahors, January 1999.
20 Pierre Orliac, January 1999.
21 *ibid.*
22 Louise died on 13 March 1956. She was seventy-nine.
23 Paulette Aupoix, April 2000; Pierre Gayet, January 2000; SRD.
24 Teresa; SRD.
25 SRD.
26 Maria Clark, who taught with Louis Darquier in Madrid, November 1999.
27 Teresa; Michael de Bertadano; Maria Clark.
28 Mrs Jean Ibbetson, Church librarian, September 1999; Consuelo Alvarado, assistant at the British Council, September 1999.
29 María de Carmen Mansilla, September 1999; Michael de Bertadano, March 2002.
30 Teresa.
31 Commander John Rigge, Madrid, September 1999. *The Red Book of Gibraltar* was published in 1965 by the Spanish Ministry of Foreign Affairs. Its French and possibly British versions were translated by Louis Darquier.
   Fernando Castiella y Maiz (1907–76): Lawyer, active Falangist, politician and Spanish diplomat. Minister of Foreign Affairs in 1956.
32 John Booth, January 2001.
33 Jean-Louis Huberti, 12 September 1999; *l'Humanité*, 6 November 1978.
34 SRD.
35 'The police at St Tropez paid a visit at 4 p.m. to the house of Jean Darquier, former doctor, in retreat living at Villa Maya, the Carles quarter. Jean Darquier told them: "My brother Louis, the object of your researches, left France at the Liberation. The last news I heard of him, two years ago, was that he was in Madrid, with no settled address. He earned his living by giving French and English lessons. I have no idea at all if he is still there, and I have no other news of any kind" ' (AN 3W142, 8 May 1963).
36 Louis liked to call his translation service a language school, and when he signed the contracts with the Ministry of Tourism, or when poor Myrtle did, he gave a fictitious address.
37 Roy Workman was probably living in lodgings in Northampton. He had continued his career – he was singing in *The Student Prince* at Luna Park in Melbourne in 1961.
38 De Bertadano was one of Myrtle's pallbearers.
39 Coroner's report, 11 September 1970.
40 Teresa; Alistair Rapley; medical contemporaries and friends of Anne Darquier.

CHAPTER 22

Dinosaurs

INTERVIEWS AND CORRESPONDENCE: Jean-Michel Bamberger, Bill Coy, Maud de Belleroche, Michael de Bertadano, Jeanne Degrelle, Anne-Marie Fiel, Natalie Ganier-Raymond, Jean-Louis Huberti, Serge Klarsfeld, María de Carmen Mansilla, Pierre Orliac, Alistair Rapley, Teresa. SOURCES: TNA: PRO FO 892/163. PUBLICATIONS : Agence France Presse, cables February 1983, 16 November 1994; Jacques Derogy, 'Le Juif à la Vichyssoise', *l'Express*, 8–14 May 1967; Jean Dutourd, *France-Soir*, 8 November 1978; *l'Express*, 14 February 1972, 28 October–4 November and 4–11 November 1978; Ganier-Raymond, interview in *Le Monde*, 17 November 1978; Ganier-Raymond, *Le Quotidien de Paris*, February 1983; Jon Henley, Paul Webster, Arnold Kemp, *Observer*, 5 April 1998; Hobson, *Forms of Feeling*, *Launceston Sunday Examiner*, 4 December 1984, 20 August 1989; Ivan Levaï, *Journal du Dimanche*, 12 November 1978; *La Lumière*, 22 May 1939; *Le Monde*, 18 and 20 February 1972, 31 October, 1, 4 and 9 November 1978; *Newsday*, 6 September 1993; *Observer*, 5 November 1978; Paxton, *New York Review of Books*, 16 December 1999; Perrault, *L'Orchestre rouge*; Stein and Stein, *Psychotherapy in Practice*; *Sunday Times*, 5 November 1978; *The Times*, 31 October, 2 and 4 November 1978

1 Alistair Rapley, 19 November 1999 and 23 April 2001.
2 Hobson, Coroner's Report, 11 September 1970. Anne's cleaner found her body. She called the porter, who called the police. Coroner's report, 11 September 1970.
3 Launceston acquaintance.
4 *Launceston Sunday Examiner*, 20 August 1989.
5 Tasmania J.
6 Michael de Bertadano, March 2002.
María de Carmen Mansilla, September 1999.
7 Louis bought the apartment on 19 February 1976 for 340,760 pesetas – £2,870 at the 1976 exchange rate. This was very cheap at the time.
8 Pierre Orliac, 4 January 1999.
9 *L'Express*, 28 October–4 November 1978.
10 Jacques Derogy's article 'Le Juif à la Vichyssoise' (*l'Express*, 8–14 May 1967) referred to a book by Claude Lévy and Paul Tillard, *Betrayal at the Vél' d'Hiv*, possibly one source for Ganier-Raymond's interest in finding Darquier. See also *l'Express*, 14 February 1972.
11 Michael de Bertadano, March 2002.
12 *ibid.*
13 *Le Monde*, 20 February 1972.
14 Michael de Bertadano, March 2002.

15 Salle Wagram, March 1937.

16 **Philippe Ganier-Raymond** (?–1995): Journalist and historian, author of *Une Certaine France: L'Antisémistisme 40–44*, published in 1975. Céline's widow Lucette took action against it for its use of extracts and lampoons of Céline's writings. The book was seized and reissued in an expurgated edition, another reason for Ganier-Raymond's determined pursuit of Darquier. His daughter Natalie says his interest in French anti-Semitism had begun with the disappearance of Jewish children from his school. It is possible that Henry Charbonneau was Jean-Michel Bamberger's intermediary, and that it was Charbonneau who persuaded Darquier to allow Ganier-Raymond to interview him. Bamberger was unwilling to reveal the name of the intermediary in 1999, as his children are still alive, but implied a connection to the Degrelle family. Charbonneau died in 1982.

17 Ganier-Raymond, *Le Quotidien de Paris*, undated, February 1983.

18 Anne-Marie Fiel, September 1999.

19 Ganier-Raymond, *Le Quotidien de Paris*, undated, February 1983.

20 Jean-Michel Bamberger, September 1999; Ganier-Raymond interview in *Le Monde*, 17 November 1978; Ivan Levaï, journalist and friend of Ganier-Raymond, *Journal du Dimanche*, 12 November 1978 and *l'Express*, 28 October – 4 November 1978.

21 *L'Express* 28 October–4 November 1978.

22 Levaï, *Journal du Dimanche*, 12 November 1978.

23 Letters to *l'Express*, published 4–11 November 1978.

24 Jean Dutourd, author of *Au Bon Beurre* ('The Best Butter'), *France-Soir*, 8 November 1978.

25 Jeanne Degrelle, September 1999. *Le Monde*, 4 November; 31 October and 1 November 1978.

26 The *Observer*, 5 November 1978; there were also articles in *The Times*: 31 October; 2 and 4 November 1978; the *Guardian*, the *Sunday Times*: 5 November 1978 – to name only a some of the coverage.

27 Serge Klarsfeld, November 1999.

    Maurice Papon (1910–): The quintessential Vichy functionary, a good republican and radical socialist who as préfet in Bordeaux had particular responsibility for Jewish affairs. Punctilious in the exercise of his duties, he oversaw the deportation of nine hundred political prisoners and 1,560 Jews – 223 of them children – to Drancy and Auschwitz, and his achievements in the Aryanisation of Jewish assets were also considerable. Seamlessly transformed into a Gaullist at the Liberation, he held a series of distinguished appointments, and was elected as a Gaullist deputy in 1968, 1973 and 1981. In that year, *Le Canard enchaîné* finally exposed him. Jewish families of the Bordeaux deportees, supported by the work of Serge and Beate Klarsfeld, finally brought an indictment for crimes against humanity in 1983. After fourteen years of tortuous delays his trial began in 1997.

28 **Aloïs Brunner** (1912–?): A very small, dark and insignificant-looking Aryan, but the most practised and most vicious Nazi, the master exponent of the Final Solution. Worked for the CIA after the war before he took refuge in Damascus, where it is said that he lived under protection in the Meridian Hotel. Never brought to justice.

29 Hobson, p. xiii; Stein and Stein, p. 204.

30 Alistair Rapley and Bill Coy, July 2001.

31 Hobson, from Chapter 16, 'The Heart of Darkness'.

POSTSCRIPT

SOURCES: AN 3W142

1AN 3W142.

APPENDIX II

'The Snows of Sigmaringen' by Louis Aragon

Sources: CDJC LXXIV-13

1 The French Communist Party was founded in 1920.
  The personalities referred to in the poem are referenced elsewhere in these notes. Those not noted previously follow:

2 **Gaston Bergery** (1892–1974): iconoclastic nationalist; was Vichy ambassador to Moscow, then to Ankara.

3 **Paul Morand** (1888–1976): poet and novelist, diplomat for Vichy; collaborationist; wrote for Henri Charbonneau's Milice journal, *Combats*.

4 **Jacques Chardonne** (1884–1968): novelist, literary collaborator, said 'Hitler is our Providence'.

5 **Jean Ajalbert** (1863–1947): writer and member of the Academie Goncourt. Accused of pro-German propaganda, he was imprisoned at the Liberation and struck off by the *Société des gens de lettres*.

6 **Paul Carbone** (dates unknown): Corsican gang leader centred in Marseilles. He was an auxiliary to the *Gestapo* during the occupation.

7 **Pierre Bony**(*sic*) **Bonny** (1895-1944): With Henri Laffont one of the principal bosses of the French Gestapo in the Rue Lauriston. At the Liberation, condemned to death and executed.

8 **Colonel Roger Labonne** (1881–1966): Commanding Officer of the LVF.

9 **Jean-Michel Renaitour** (1896– ?): prolific writer forgotten today.

10 **Hubert Lagardelle** (1874–1958): French syndicalist who moved to the right and served Vichy as Laval's Minister of Works.

Louis Darquier's Baronial Inventions

SOURCES: AN LO6620, dossier 57, Darquier, Joseph Isidore; correspondence with member of Darquier family; SHAT, Dossier Militaire de Joseph Isidore Darquier, no. 17919. PUBLICATIONS : Villain, *La France moderne, Haute-Garonne et Ariège: Dictionnaire généalogique des familles nobles et bourgeoises*

Bibliography and Sources

◀◉▶

Books and Selected Journals and Magazines

Abbellan, Christian: *Contribution à l'étude de la société Lotoise sous la IIIème République.* Archives Départementales du Lot, Cahors: unpublished thesis, March 1971

Adler, Jacques: *The Jews of Paris and the Final Solution: Communal Response and Internal Conflicts, 1940–1944.* New York: Oxford University Press 1987

Agulhon, Maurice: *The French Republic 1879–1992.* Translated by Antonia Nevill. Oxford: Basil Blackwell 1993, 1995 (French edition: *La République.* Paris: Hachette 1990)

Albert, Pierre: *Histoire générale de la presse française: Vol. 2, 1871–1940.* Paris: Presses Universitaires de France 1972

Alexander, Alison: *Blue, Black and White: The History of Launceston Church Grammar School 1946–1996.* Launceston: Launceston Church Grammar School 1996

Alméras, Philippe: *Je suis le bouc: Céline et l'antisémitisme.* Paris: Denoël 2000

Amor, John: *A History of Oxford Road, Kidlington: A Guided Tour.* Oxford: Kidlington and District Historical Society. Occasional Series No.7, 1996

Anderson, Malcolm M.: *Conservative Politics in France.* London: George Allen & Unwin 1974

Arco, Manuel del: *Los 90 Ministros de Franco.* Barcelona: Dopesa 1971

Armour, Peter J.: *The French Radical Party in the 1930s.* Stanford, California: Stanford University Press 1964

Arnal, Oscar L.: *Ambivalent Alliance: The Catholic Church and the Action Française 1899–1939.* Pittsburgh: University of Pittsburgh Press 1985

Atkin, Nicholas: *Pétain.* Harlow, Essex: Addison, Wesley, Longman 1998

Atkinson, Alan: *The Europeans in Australia, A History: Vol. 1, The Beginning.* Melbourne: Oxford University Press 1997

Audoin-Rouzeau, Stéphane: *Men at War 1914–1918: National Sentiment and Trench Journalism in France During the First World War.* Oxford: Berg 1992

Augé, Marc: *Paris années 30.* Paris: Éditions Hazan 1996

Ayton, Ivy Eileen: *The Tanner's Daughter: Carrick 1888–1963.* No publication details, privately printed

Baker, A.D. and Margerison, F.M.: *New Medical Dictionary with an Air Raid Precautions Supplement.* London: Universal Text Books Ltd 1942

Bankwitz, Philip Charles Farwell: *Maxime Weygand and Civil–Military Relations in Modern France.* Cambridge, Massachusetts: Harvard University Press 1967

Barthelémy, Joseph: *Mémoires*. Paris: Pygmalion-Gérard Watelet 1989

Bean, C.E.W.: *The Australian Imperial Force in France: Official History of Australia in the War of 1914–1918: Vol. 5*. Sydney: Angus & Robertson 1941

Bean, C.E.W.: *Anzac to Amiens*. Australia: Penguin 1993

Beaumont, J. (ed.): *Australia's War 1914–18*. St Leonards, Australia: Allen & Unwin 1995

Becker, Jean-Jacques: *The Great War and the French People*. Translated from the French by Arnold Pomerans. Providence, RI: Berg 1993

Beevor, Antony and Cooper, Artemis: *Paris After the Liberation 1944–49*. London: Hamish Hamilton 1994

Beloff, Max: *The Sixth of February*. St Anthony's Papers No.5. London: Chatto & Windus 1959

Ben-Itto, Hadassa: *Die Protokolle der Weisen von Zion Anatomie einer Fälschung*. Berlin: Aufbau Verlag 1998 ('The Lie that Wouldn't Die': not yet published in English)

Billig, Joseph: *Le Commissariat Général aux Questions Juives (1941–1944)*. 3 vols. Paris: Éditions du Centre 1955–1960. Translated privately for the author by David-Paul Holland

Binion, Rudolph: *Defeated Leaders: The Political Fate of Caillaux, Jouvenel and Tardieu*. New York: Columbia University Press 1960

Birnbaum, Pierre: *Anti-Semitism in France. A Political History from Léon Blum to the Present*. Oxford: Basil Blackwell Ltd 1992

Boisjoslin, Jean de: *A Travers les Rues de Cahors: Les Monuments de la ville, les consuls, les maires et les évêques*. Bayac: Éditions du Roc de Bourzac 1993

Boisjoslin, Jean de: *A Travers les Rues de Cahors: Répertoire historique et alphabétique des voies de cette ville*. Bayac: Éditions du Roc de Bourzac 1993

Bollmus, Reinhard: *Das Amt Rosenberg und seine Gegner. Studien zum Machtkampf im Nationalsozialistischen Herrschaftssystem*. Stuttgart: Oldenbourg 1970

Bories, Patrick, Malot, Philippe and Héritier, Jacques: *Vichy mémoire*. Saint-Étienne: Edi Loire Aspect Éditions 1994

Brechtken, Magnus: *Madagaskar für die Juden: Antisemitische Idee und Politische Praxis 1885–1945*. Munchen: Oldenbourg 1997

Breese, Charlotte: *Hutch*. London: Bloomsbury 1999

Brendon, Piers: *The Dark Valley: A Panorama of the 1930s*. London: Jonathan Cape 2000

Burns, Michael: *Dreyfus: A Family Affair 1789–1945*. London: Chatto & Windus 1993

Burrin, Philippe: *France Under the Germans: Collaboration and Compromise*. Translated from the French by Janet Lloyd. New York: The New Press 1996

Burton, Col. A.G.: *The Australian Army Medical Services in the War of 1914–1918*. Canberra: Australian War Memorial 1943

Butler, Hubert: *The Children of Drancy*. Mullingar: The Lilliput Press 1988

Byrnes, Robert F.: *Antisemitism in Modern France: Vol. 1, The Prologue to the Dreyfus Affair*. New Brunswick, New Jersey: Rutgers University Press 1950

Calder, Angus: *The People's War: Britain 1939–45*. London: Jonathan Cape 1969

Calder, Angus: *The Myth of the Blitz*. London: Jonathan Cape 1991

Calef, Noel Nissim: *Drancy 1941, Camp de Represailles, Drancy la Faim, edite et presenté par Serge Klarsfeld*. Paris: FFDJF 1991

Calmon, Colette: *Mon Père, Elie Calmon*. Mercuès, France: l'Imprimerie Publi-Offset 1995

Caron, Vicki: *Between France and Germany: The Jews of Alsace-Lorraine 1871–1918*. Stanford, California: Stanford University Press 1988

Carret, J.: *Le Marché du blé, sa réglementation en France*. Besançon: Jacques et Demontrond 1934

Cassou, Jean (under the direction of): *Le Pillage par les Allemands des ouevres d'art et des bibliothèques appartenant à des Juifs en France: Recueil de documents*. CDJC Serie. Documents, No 4. Paris: Éditions du Centre 1947

Caute, David: *Communism and the French Intellectuals 1914–1960*. London: Andre Deutsch 1964

The Cavalry School, United States Army: *Cavalry Combat*. Harrisburg: The United States Cavalry Association 1937

Cazaux, Yves: *René Bousquet: Face à l'acharnement*. Paris: Jean Picollec 1985

Chalon, Jean: *Portrait of a Seductress: The World of Natalie Barney*. New York: Crown 1979

Charbonneau, Henry: *Les Mémoires de Porthos*. Paris: Les Éditions du Clan 1967

Clark, Manning: *History of Australia*. Abridged by Michael Cathcart. London: Chatto & Windus 1994

Cobb, Richard: *Promenades: A Historical Appreciation of Modern French Literature*. Oxford: Oxford University Press 1980

Cobb, Richard: *French and Germans, Germans and French: A Personal Interpretation of France Under Two Occupations, 1914–1918/1940–1944*. Hanover and London: Brandeis University Press 1983

Cohn, Norman: *Warrant for Genocide: The Myth of the Jewish World Conspiracy and the Protocols of the Elders of Zion*. London: Serif 1996

Cointet, Michèle: *Vichy: Capitale 1940–1944*. Paris: Librairie Académique Perrin 1993

Combarieu, L.: *Le Dictionnaire des Communes du Lot*. Cahors: A Laytou 1881, reprinted Mercuès France: l'Imprimerie Publi-Offset 1994

Combes, Édouard: *Le Conseil Municipal, nos édiles annuaire illustré municipal et administratif de la ville de Paris et du département de la Seine (44ème année) – 1935–1941*. Paris: Publications du Journal Municipal la Cité 1941

Communauté des Radios Publiques de Langue Française: *La Guerre des ondes: Histoire des radios de langue française pendant la Deuxième Guerre Mondiale*. Paris: Armand Colin Éditeur et al. 1985

Conan, Éric and Rousso, Henry: *Vichy: An Ever-Present Past*. Hanover: Dartmouth College, University of New England Press 1998

Cornwell, John: *Hitler's Pope: The Secret History of Pius XII*. London: Penguin 1999

'Corps Gras, savons', *Revue technique et professionnelle éditée par les presses documentaires sous le patronage du Comité Général d'Organisation des Corps Gras*, No. 1: Juillet 1943. BNF, réf. 4–V–14644

Coston, Henry: *Partis, journaux et hommes politiques d'hier et d'aujourd'hui*. Paris: Lectures Françaises, numéro spécial 1960

Le Crapouillot, Paris. Nouvelle Série No.77, September–October 1984

Crémieux-Brilhac, Jean-Louis: *Ici Londres, 1940–1944: Les Voix de la liberté*. 4 vols. 1975

Crémieux-Brilhac, Jean-Louis: *Les Français de l'an 40*. Paris: Gallimard 1990

Curtis, Michael: *Verdict on Vichy: Power and Prejudice in the Vichy France Regime*. London: Weidenfeld & Nicolson 2002

Daix, Pierre: *Aragon: Une vie à changer*. Paris: Éditions du Seuil 1975

Darquier, Louis: *l'Antijuif*. BNF Micr D-100096

Darquier, Louis: *Bulletin du Club National*. AN série 26 AS/6

Darquier, Louis: *La France enchaînée*. Institut d'Histoire du Temps Présent, Numéro de notice: 04511028X

de Belleroche, Maud: *L'Ordinatrice: Mémoires d'une femme de quarante ans*. Paris: Le Jeune Parque 1968

de Belleroche, Maud: *Le ballet des crabes*. Paris: Éditions Filipacchi 1975

de Monzie, Anatole: *Ci-devant*. Paris: Flammarion 1941

de Monzie, Anatole: *Mémoires de la Tribune*. Paris. Éditions Corréa 1942

de Rochebrune, Renaud and Hazera, Jean-Claude: *Les Patrons sous l'Occupation: Vol. 2, Pétainisme, intrigues, spoliations*. Paris: Éditions Odile Jacob 1995, Collection Opus 1997

Débordes, Jean: *Vichy, Capitale à l'heure allemande: Au temps de Pétain et de François Mitterrand*. Paris: Éditions Godefroy de Bouillon 1998

Dennis, Peter et al.: *The Oxford Companion to Australian Military History*. Melbourne: Oxford University Press 1995

Downer, Christine et al.: *All the Rage: 150 Years of Posters, State Library of Victoria 1850–2000*. State Library of Victoria 2001

Dubief, Henri: *Le Déclin de la IIIe République 1929–1938*. Paris: Seuil 1976

Dutourd, Jean: *The Best Butter: An Extravagant Novel*. Translated from the French by Robin Chancellor. New York: Simon & Schuster 1955 (French edition: *Au Bon Beurre, ou dix ans de la vie d'un crémier*. Paris: Gallimard 1952)

Dwyer, Jaqueline: *Flanders in Australia: A Personal History of Wool and War*. NSW: Kangaroo Press 1998

Eatwell, Roger: *Fascism: A History*. London: Chatto & Windus 1995

Ellis, Jack D.: *The Physician-Legislators of France: Medicine and Politics in the Early Third Republic, 1870–1914*. Cambridge: Cambridge University Press 1990

Feliciano, Hector: *The Lost Museum: The Nazi Conspiracy to Steal the World's Greatest Works of Art*. New York: Basic Books 1997

Felstiner, Mary Lowenthal: *To Paint her Life: Charlotte Salomon in the Nazi Era*. Berkeley: University of California Press 1997

Ferguson, Niall: *The Pity of War*. London: Penguin 1999

Ferro, Marc: *Questions sur la IIe Guerre Mondiale*. Florence: Casterman–Giunti Gruppo Editoriale 1993

Fest, Joachim: *The Face of the Third Reich*. London: Penguin 1983

Field, Frank: *Three French Writers and the Great War: Studies in the Rise of Communism and Fascism*. Cambridge: Cambridge University Press 1975

Field, Frank: *British and French Writers of the First World War: Comparative Studies in Cultural History*. Cambridge: Cambridge University Press 1991

Fishman, Sarah et al.: *France at War: Vichy and the Historians*. Oxford: Berg 2000

Flanner, Janet: *Paris was Yesterday 1925–39*. New York: Viking Press 1972

Flanner, Janet: *Janet Flanner's World: Uncollected Writings 1932–1975*. Edited by Irving Drutman. New York: Harcourt Brace Jovanovich 1979

Forster, Colin: *France and Botany Bay: The Lure of a Penal Colony*. Melbourne: Melbourne University Press 1996

Friedlander, Saul: *Pius XII and the Third Reich: A Documentation*. Translated from the French and German by Charles Fullman. New York: Alfred A. Knopf 1966

Froment, Pascale: *René Bousquet*. Paris: Stock 1994

Galtier-Boissière, Jean: *Mon journal pendant l'Occupation*. Paris: Éditions du Jeune Parque 1944

Ganier-Raymond, Philippe: *Une Certaine France: L'Antisemitisme 40–44* Paris: Balland 1975

Gee, June: *Keeping up with the Joneses: The Story of a Tasmanian Family*. Launceston: Michael and Pauline Brewer, The Mary Fisher Bookshop 1981

Gildea, Robert: *Marianne in Chains: In Search of the German Occupation 1940–1945*. London: Macmillan 2002

Godechot, Jacques: *Les Constitutions de la France depuis 1789*. Paris: Flammarion 1970

Golsan, Richard J.: *Memory, the Holocaust and French Justice: The Bousquet and Touvier Affairs*. New Hampshire: University Press of New England 1996

Goodfellow, Samuel Huston: *Between the Swastika and the Cross of Lorraine: Fascisms in Interwar France*. DeKalb, Illinois: University of Illinois Press 1999

Gordon, Bertram M.: *Collaborationism in France During the Second World War*. Ithaca and London: Cornell University Press 1980

Gordon, Bertram M.: 'Fascism, the Neo-Right and Gastronomy'. Oxford Food Symposium on Food and Cookery 1987: *Taste Proceedings*. London: Prospect Books 1988, pp.82 ff

Gordon, Bertram M. (ed.): *Historical Dictionary of World War II France: The Occupation, Vichy, and the Resistance 1938–1946*. London: The Aldwych Press 1998

Graham, Martin: *Oxfordshire at War*. Stroud, Glos: Sutton Publishing Ltd 1994

Graham, Martin: *Oxfordshire at School*. Stroud, Glos: Sutton Publishing Ltd 1996

Grant, Ian: *A Dictionary of Military History*. Sydney: Random House 1992

Grove, Valerie: *Laurie Lee: The Well-Loved Stranger*. London: Penguin 2000

Grynberg, Anne: *Les Camps de la honte: Les Internés juifs des camps français 1939–1944*. Paris: La Découverte 1999

Guérin Alain: *La Résistance. Chronique illustrée 1930–1950: Vol. 2, Victoire du crime.* 5 vols. Paris: Éditions Livre Club Diderot 1972

Gun, Nerin E.: *Les Enfants au nom maudit*. Paris: *Historia*, No. 241, December 1966

Gun, Nerin E.: *Pétain, Laval, de Gaulle: Les Secrets des archives Américaines*. Paris: Albin Michel 1979

Guy, The Hon. J. Allan, MHR et al.: *The Cyclopedia of Tasmania: An Epitome of Progress: Vol. 2, Business Men and Commercial Interests*. Hobart: Maitland & Krone 1900

Halioua, Bruno: *Blouses blanches, étoiles jaunes*. Paris: Éditions Liana Levi 2000

Halls, W.D.: *Politics, Society and Christianity in Vichy France*. Oxford: Berg 1995

Hamilton, Alastair: *The Appeal of Fascism: A Study of Intellectuals and Fascism, 1919–1945*. London: Anthony Blond 1971

Hauner, Milan: *Hitler: A Chronology of his Life and Time*. London: Macmillan Press 1983

Hayes, Peter: *Industry and Ideology: IG Farben in the Nazi Era*. Cambridge: Cambridge University Press 1987

Heiber, Helmut: *Walter Frank und sein Reichsinstitut für Geschichte des Neuen Deutschlands*. Stuttgart: Deutsche Verlags-Anstalt 1966

Hennessy, Peter: *Never Again: Britain 1945–1951*. London: Vintage 1993

Hilberg, Raul: *La Destruction des Juifs de l'Europe*. Paris: Fayard 1985

Hobson, Robert: *Forms of Feeling: The Heart of Psychotherapy*. London: Tavistock 1985

Hoffman, Stanley et al.: *France: Change and Tradition*. London: Gollancz 1963 (published in the USA as *In Search of France*. Harvard University Press 1963 and Harper Torchbooks 1965)

Holmes, Richard: *Fatal Avenue: A Traveller's History of the Battlefields of Northern France and Flanders, 1346–1945*. London: Jonathan Cape 1992

Hoover Institution: *France During the German Occupation, 1940–1944: A Collection of 292 Statements on the Government of Maréchal Pétain and Pierre Laval*. Translated Philip W. Whitcomb. 3 vols. Stanford, California: Stanford University Press 1958–59 (French edition: *La Vie de la France sous l'Occupation (1940–1944)*. Paris: Plon 1957)

Horne, Alastair: *To Lose a Battle: France 1940*. London: Macmillan Papermac 1990

Horner, D. M.: *The Gunners: A History of Australian Artillery*. Sydney: Allen & Unwin 1995

Howson, Gerald: *Arms for Spain: The Untold Story of the Spanish Civil War*. London: John Murray 1998

Hughes, Robert: *The Fatal Shore: A History of the Transportation of Convicts to Australia 1787–1868*. London: Pan Books 1988

Hunt, Susan and Carter, Paul: *Terre Napoléon: Australia Through French Eyes 1800–1804*. Sydney: Historic Houses Trust 1999

Jackson, Julian: *The Popular Front in France: Defending Democracy 1934–38*. Cambridge: Cambridge University Press 1988

Jackson, Julian: *France: The Dark Years 1940–1944*. Oxford: Oxford University Press 2001

Jardin, Pascal: *Vichy Boyhood: An Inside View of the Pétain Regime*. London: Faber & Faber 1975

Jolly, Jean: *Dictionnaire des parlementaires français: Notices biographiques sur les ministres, sénateurs et députés français de 1889 à 1940*. Paris: Presses Universitaires de France 1960

Joly, Laurent: *Xavier Vallat: Du nationalisme chrétien à l'antisémitisme d'état 1891–1972*. Paris: Bernard Grasset 2001

Joly, Laurent: 'Darquier de Pellepoix: "Champion" des antisémites français (1936–1939)'. Essay in *Revue d'Histoire de la Shoah, Le Monde Juif*, No. 173, Septembre–Décembre 2001, *Une Passion sans fin: Entre Dreyfus et Vichy: Aspects de l'antisémitisme français*, pp.35–61

Joly, Laurent: *Darquier de Pellepoix et l'antisémitisme français*. Paris: Berg International Éditeurs 2002

Jucker, Ninetta: *Curfew in Paris: A Record of the German Occupation*. London: The Hogarth Press 1960

Judt, Tony: 'Betrayal in France'. *New York Review of Books*, 12 August 1993

Judt, Tony: *The Burden of Responsibility: Blum, Camus, Aron and the French Twentieth Century*. Chicago: University of Chicago Press 1998

Kaplan, Alice: 'Reproductions of Banality: Fascism, Literature and French Intellectual Life'. *Theory and History of Literature*, Vol. 36. Minneapolis: University of Minnesota Press 1986

Kaplan, Alice: *Relevé des sources et citations dans* Bagatelles pour un massacre. Tusson: Du Lérot 1987

Kaplan, Alice: *French Lessons: A Memoir*. Chicago and London: University of Chicago Press 1993

Kaplan, Alice: *The Collaborator: The Trial and Execution of Robert Brasillach*. Chicago: University of Chicago Press 2000

Kedward, H.R.: *Occupied France: Collaboration and Resistance 1940–1944*. Oxford: Blackwell 1985

Keegan, John: *The Face of Battle: A Study of Agincourt, Waterloo and the Somme*. London: Pimlico 1998

Keegan, John: *The First World War*. London: Pimlico 1999

Keesing's Contemporary Archives: *Weekly Diary of Important World Events, Vol. 7: 1948–1950*. Bristol: Keesing's Publications 1950

Kernan, Thomas: *Report on France*. London: John Lane The Bodley Head 1942

Kershaw, Ian: *Hitler: 1889–1936 Hubris*. London: Allen Lane The Penguin Press 1998

Kershaw, Ian: *Hitler: 1936–1945 Nemesis*. London: Allen Lane The Penguin Press 2000

Kingston, Paul J.: *Anti-Semitism in France During the 1930s: Organisation, Personalities and Propaganda*. Hull: University of Hull Press 1983

Kirkpatrick, Peter: *The Sea Coast of Bohemia: Literary Life in Sydney's Roaring Twenties*. Australia: University of Queensland Press 1992

Klarsfeld, Serge: *Vichy Auschwitz: Le Rôle de Vichy dans la Solution Finale de la Question Juive en France 1943–1944*. Paris: Fayard 1985

Klarsfeld, Serge: *Le Calendrier de la persécution des Juifs en France 1940–1944*. Paris: S. Klarsfeld 1993

Klarsfeld, Serge: *French Children of the Holocaust: A Memorial*. Edited by Susan Cohen, Howard M. Epstein, Serge Klarsfeld. Translated by Glorianne Depondt and Howard M. Epstein. New York: New York University Press 1996

Knightley, Philip: *Australia: A Biography of a Nation*. London: Jonathan Cape 2000

Koestler, Arthur: *Scum of the Earth*. London: Collins/Hamish Hamilton 1955

Laborie, Pierre: 'Mentalités et opinion publique dans le Lot à la fin de la Troisième République, Parts 1 & 2'. Cahors: *Quercy Recherche*: Mai–Juin 1979, Nos. 28–29 and 29–30

Laborie, Pierre: *Résistants, vichyssois et autres: L'Évolution de l'opinion et des comportements dans le Lot de 1939 à 1944*. Paris: Éditions du CNRS 1980

Lacouture Jean: *Mitterrand: Une histoire de Français: Vol. 1, Les Risques de l'escalade; Vol. 2, Les Vertiges du sommet*. Paris: Seuil 1998

Lacouture, Jean: *Léon Blum*. Translated by George Holoch. New York: Holmes & Meier 1982

Lacroix-Riz, Annie: *Industriels et banquiers français sous l'Occupation: La Collaboration économique avec le Reich et Vichy*. Paris: Armand Colin 1999

Laloum, Jean: *La France antisémite de Darquier de Pellepoix*. Paris: Éditions Syros 1979

Lambauer, Barbara: *Otto Abetz et les Français ou l'envers de la collaboration*. Paris: Fayard 2001

Lambert, Barnard: *Bousquet, Papon, Touvier: Dossiers d'accusation*. Paris: Éditions de la Fédération Nationale des Déportés et Internés Résistants et Patriotes. Paris: nd

Lambert, Raymond-Raoul: *Carnet d'un témoin*. Paris. Fayard 1984

Langer, William L.: *Our Vichy Gamble*. New York: Alfred A Knopf 1947

Laqueur, Walter and Mosse, George L.: 'International Fascism 1920–1945'. *Journal of Contemporary History, 1*. New York: Harper Torchbooks 1966

Larkin, Maurice: *France Since the Popular Front: Government and People*. Oxford: Clarendon Press 1997

Lartigaut, Jean (ed.): *Histoire du Quercy*. Toulouse: Éditions Privat 1993

Laubreaux, Alain: *Écrit pendant la guerre*. Paris: Éditions du Centre d'Études de l'Agence Inter-France 1944

Laurier, Mathieu: *Il Reste le drapeau noir et les copains*. Monte-Carlo: Regain 1953

Levi, Primo: *The Drowned and the Saved*. London: Abacus 1989

Lévy, Claude and Tillard, Paul: *Betrayal at the Vel' d'Hiv'*. New York: Hill & Wang 1967 (French edition: *La Grande rafle du Vel' d'Hiv'*. Paris: Robert Laffont 1967)

Lottman, Herbert R.: *Pétain: Hero or Traitor? The Untold Story*. New York: William Morrow & Co., Inc. 1985

Lottman, Herbert R.: *The Purge: The Purification of French Collaborators After World War II*. New York: William Morrow & Co., Inc. 1986

Lukacs, John: *The Duel: Hitler vs. Churchill 10 May–31 July 1940*. London: The Bodley Head 1990

McCarthy, Patrick: *Céline*. London: Allen Lane 1975

McCrum, Robert: *Wodehouse: A Life*. London: Viking 2004

Mackinnon, Lachlan: *The Lives of Elsa Triolet*. London: Chatto & Windus 1992

Marnham, Patrick: *The Death of Jean Moulin: Biography of a Ghost*. London: John Murray 2000

Marrus, Michael and Paxton, Robert: *Vichy France and the Jews*. 2nd edition. Stanford, California: Stanford University Press 1995

Martin, Reg C. (revised by John Amor): *A History of Church Street Kidlington*. Oxford: Kidlington and District Historical Society. Occasional Series No.2. Second edition 1993

Martin, Reg C.: *A History of the Schools of Kidlington*. Kidlington, Oxon: Kidlington and District Historical Society, Occasional Series No.5, nd

Maspero, François: *Cat's Grin*. Translated from the French by Nancy Amphoux. New York: Alfred A. Knopf 1986 (French edition: *Le Sourire du chat*. Paris: Éditions du Seuil 1984)

Matteoli, Jean (présidée par): *Mission d'étude sur la spoliation des Juifs de France* (The Matteoli Commission). Paris: La Documentation Française 2000

Maurras, Charles: *Le Corps médical français et la Restauration Nationale. Discours aux médecins d'Action Française*. Paris: Presses de Guillemot et de Lamothe pour 'Les Amis des Beaux Livres', 20 April 1933

Mengin, Robert: *No Laurels for de Gaulle: A Personal Appraisal of the London Years*. London: Michael Joseph 1967

Modiano, Patrick: *Missing Person*. Translated from the French by Daniel Weissbort. London: Jonathan Cape 1980 (French edition: *Rue des boutiques obscures*. Paris: Gallimard 1978)

Modiano, Patrick: *The Search Warrant*. Translated from the French by Joanna Kilmartin. London: The Harvill Press 1997. (French edition: *Dora Bruder*. Paris: Gallimard 1997)

Molinié, Joseph: *Enfance à Cahors*. Cahors: Librairie P. Lagarde 1965

Morel, Roland and Vaysse, Jean: *Le Lot politique et administratif depuis 1800*. Cahors: Archives Départementales du Lot, 2e édition 1998

Mosse, George L.: *The Fascist Revolution. Toward a General Theory of Fascism*. New York: Howard Fertig, Inc. 1999

Mosse, George L.: *Fallen Soldiers. Reshaping the memory of the World Wars*. New York: Oxford University Press. 1990

Nicholas, Lynn H.: *The Rape of Europa: The Fate of Europe's Treasures in the Third Reich and the Second World War*. London: Vintage 1995

Nisbet, Anne-Marie and Blackman, Maurice: *The French–Australian Cultural*

Connection. Papers from a Symposium Held at the University of New South Wales, 16–17 September 1983. Sydney: University of New South Wales 1984

Nobécourt, Jacques: *Le Colonel de La Roque 1885–1946: Ou les pièges du nationalisme chrétien.* Paris: Fayard 1996

Nolte, Ernst: *Three Faces of Fascism: Action Francaise, Italian Fascism, National Socialism.* Translated from the German by Leila Vennewitz. New York: Mentor Books 1969 (German edition: *Der Faschismus in seiner Epoche: Die Action Francaise, der Italienische Faschismus, der Nationalsozialismus.* Munich: R. Piper Verlag 1963)

Nossiter, Adam: *The Algeria Hotel: France, Memory and the Second World War.* London: Methuen 2001

Novick, Peter: *The Resistance versus Vichy: The Purge of Collaborators in Liberated France.* London: Chatto & Windus 1968

Ory, Pascal: *Les Collaborateurs 1940–1945.* Paris: Editions du Sevil 1980

Ousby, Ian: *Occupation: The Ordeal of France 1940–44.* London: John Murray 1997

Overy, Richard: *The Penguin Historical Atlas of the Third Reich.* London: Penguin 1996

Patterson, Robert: 'Ireland, Vichy and Post-Liberation France, 1938–1950'. *Irish Foreign Policy 1919–1966: From Independence to Internationalism,* Kennedy and Skelly (eds), pp.96–115

Paul, Elliot: *The Last Time I Saw Paris.* New York: Random House 1942 and Bantam Press 1945

Paxton, Robert O.: *Vichy France: Old Guard and New Order 1940–1944.* New York: Columbia University Press 1972. Morningside Edition 1982

Paxton, Robert O.: *French Peasant Fascism: Henry Dorgères' Greenshirts and the Crises of French Agriculture 1929–1939.* New York: Oxford University Press 1997

Paxton, Robert: 'The Trial of Maurice Papon'. *New York Review of Books,* 16 December 1999

Péan, Pierre: *Une Jeunesse française: François Mitterand, 1934–1947.* Paris: Fayard 1994

Pélissier, Pierre: *6 février 1934.* Paris: Perrin 2000

Perrault, Gilles: *L'Orchestre Rouge.* Paris: Fayard 1967

Peschanski, Denis: *La France des camps: L'Internment, 1938–46:* Paris: Gallimard 2002

Petropoulos, Jonathan: *The Faustian Bargain: The Art World in Nazi Germany.* London: Allen Lane The Penguin Press 2000

Piketty, Caroline, Dubois, Christophe and Launay, Fabrice: *Guide des recherches dans les archives des spoliations et des restitutions. Mission d'étude sur la spoliation des Juifs de France.* Paris: La Documentation Française 2000

Planté, Louis: *Un Grand seigneur de la politique: Anatole de Monzie (1876–1947).* Paris: Raymond Clavreuil 1955

Poznanski, Renée: *Les Juifs en France pendant la Seconde Guerre Mondiale.* Paris: Hachette 1997

Preston, Paul: *Franco: A Biography.* London: HarperCollins Fontana Press 1995

Le Procès de Maréchal Petain: Compte rendu sténographique. Paris: Éditions Albin Michel 1945

Pryce-Jones, David: *Paris in the Third Reich: A History of the German Occupation, 1940–1944*. London: Collins 1981

Ragache, Gilles and Ragache, Jean-Robert: *La Vie quotidienne des écrivains et des artistes sous l'Occupation 1940/1944*. Paris: Hachette 1988

Randa, Philippe: *Dictionnaire commenté de la collaboration française*. Paris: Jean Picollec 1997

Rayner, Margaret E.: *The Centenary History of St Hilda's College Oxford*. Didcot: Lindsay Ross Publishing 1993

Rearick, Charles: *The French in Love and War: Popular Culture in the Era of Two World Wars*. London: Yale University Press 1997

Rees, Philip (ed.): *Biographical Dictionary of the Extreme Right Since 1900*. Hemel Hempstead: Harvester/Wheatsheaf 1990

Richebois, Véronique, quoting Philip Brooks and his TV programme *Mes chers antipodes*: 'Ma Fichue Tasmanie'. *TéléObs, Le Nouvel Observateur*, 3 September 2000

Rousso, Henry: 'YOD : Les Juifs de France et d'Algérie pendant la Seconde Guerre Mondiale. *L'Aryanisation économique: Vichy, l'occupant et la spoliation des Juifs*, Nos 15–16, 1982, pp.51–79

Rousso, Henry: *The Vichy Syndrome: History and Memory in France Since 1944*. Cambridge, Massachusetts: Harvard University Press 1991

Sabbagh, Antoine (ed.): *Lettres de Drancy*. Paris: Tallandier 2002

Saint-Bonnet, G.: *Vichy Capitale: Ce que j'ai vu et entendu*. Paris: Éditions Mont-Louis Clermont-Ferrand 1941

Saint-Paulien (Maurice-Yvan Sicard): *Histoire de la collaboration*. Mayenne: l'Esprit Nouveau 1964

Saña, Heleno: *El Franquismo sin Mitos: Conversaciones con Ramón Serrano Suñer*. Barcelona: Ediciones Grijalbo 1982

Salomon, Charlotte: *Life? or Theatre?*. London: Royal Academy of the Arts 1988.

Sergeant, John: *Give Me Ten Seconds*. London: Pan Books 2001

Service d'Information des Crimes de Guerre – Documents pour Servir à l'Histoire de la Guerre: *Camps de concentration: Crimes contre la personne humaine*. Fontenay-Aux-Roses: Office Français d'Édition 1945

Skidelsky, Robert: *Oswald Mosley*. London: Macmillan 1975

Skidelsky, Robert: *John Maynard Keynes, 1883–1946: Economist, Philosopher, Statesman*. London: Macmillan 2003

Soucy, Robert: *French Fascism: The First Wave 1924–1933*. New Haven and London: Yale University Press 1986

Soucy, Robert: *French Fascism: The Second Wave 1933–1939*. New Haven and London: Yale University Press 1995

Stein, Samuel M. and Stein, Jennifer: *Psychotherapy in Practice: A Life in the Mind*. Oxford: Butterworth-Heinemann 2000

Sternhell, Zeev: *Neither Right nor Left: Fascist Ideology in France*. Translated by David Maisel. Princeton University Press 1986 (French edition: *Ni droite, ni gauche: L'Idéologie fasciste en France*. Paris: Éditions du Seuil 1983)

Stevenson, Beryl: *Water Under the Bridge: A Story of Carrick*. Carrick: Beryl Stevenson 1995

Stevenson, John and Cook, Chris: *Britain in the Depression: Society and Politics 1929–39*. Harlow, Essex: Longman Group Ltd 1994

Stuer, Anny P.L.: *The French in Australia*. Immigration Monograph series 2. Canberra: Department of Demography, Institute of Advanced Studies, The Australian National University 1982

Sutton, Michael: *Nationalism, Positivism and Catholicism: The Politics of Charles Maurras and French Catholics 1890–1914*. Cambridge: Cambridge University Press 1982

Sweets, John F.: *Choices in Vichy France: The French Under Nazi Occupation*. Oxford: Oxford University Press 1986

Taguieff, Pierre-André (ed.): *L'Antisémitisme de plume 1940–1944: Études et documents*. Paris: Berg International Éditeurs 1999

Taittinger, Pierre: *Ce que le pays doit savoir: Les Leçons d'une défaite*. Angoulême: S.A. Imprimerie Charentaise 1941

Taittinger, Pierre: . . . *et PARIS ne fut pas détruit*. Paris: l'Elan 'Témoignages Contemporains' 1948

Tannenbaum, Edward R.: *The Action Française: Die-Hard Reactionaries in Twentieth-Century France*. New York and London: John Wiley & Sons 1962

Tannenbaum, Edward R.: *1900: The Generation Before the Great War*. New York: Anchor Press Doubleday 1977

Taylor, Edmond: *The Strategy of Terror: Europe's Inner Front*. Boston: Houghton Mifflin Co. 1940

Templewood, Lord (Sir Samuel Hoare): *Ambassador on Special Mission*. London: Collins 1946

Thornton–Smith, Colin: 'Echoes and Resonances of Action Française: Anti-Semitism in Early Issues of the *Australian Catholic Worker*'. *Journal of the Australian Jewish Historical Society*. Victoria: Vol. 11, November 1991

Thurman, Judith: *Secrets of the Flesh: A Life of Colette*. London: Bloomsbury 1999

Tournoux, Jean-Raymond: *Pétain and de Gaulle*. Translated from the French by Oliver Coburn. London: Heinemann 1966

'Une passion sans fin entre Dreyfus et Vichy: Aspects de l'antisémitisme français'. *Revue d'Histoire de la Shoah, Le Monde Juif*, No. 173, Septembre–Décembre 2001

United States Department of State: *Foreign Relations: Diplomatic Papers, 1941: Vol. 2, Europe*. Washington DC: US GPO 1959

Vallat, Xavier: *Le Nez de Cléopâtre: Souvenirs d'un homme du droite 1918–1945*. Paris: Éditions les Quatre Fils Aymon 1957

Van Praag, S.E.: *Daughter of France*. Translated from the French by Enid York. London: William Heinemann Ltd 1945

Varney, Michael: *Great Tew: Living in the Past*. Bexhill-on-Sea: Michael A. Varney 1991

Venner, Dominique: *Histoire de la collaboration. Suivi des dictionnaires des acteurs, partis et journaux*. Paris: Éditions Pygmalion/Gérard Watelet 2000

Verheyde, Philippe: *Les Mauvais comptes de Vichy: L'Aryanisation des entreprises Juives*. Paris: Perrin 1999

Villain, Jules: *La France moderne, Haute-Garonne et Ariège: dictionnaire généalogique des familles nobles et bourgeoises*. 2 vols. Montpellier: 1911–13

Vitoux, Frédéric: *Céline: A Biography*. Translated from the French by Jesse Browner. New York: Marlowe & Co. 1994

Le Voltaire, BNF JO-77305

Vulliez, Wanda: *Vichy: La Fin d'une époque*. Paris: Éditions France-Empire 1997

Warner, Geoffrey: *Pierre Laval and the Eclipse of France*. London: Eyre & Spottiswoode 1968

Weber, Eugen: *Action Française: Royalism and Reaction in Twentieth-Century France*. Stanford, California: Stanford University Press 1962

Weber, Eugen: *The Nationalist Revival in France, 1905–14*. Berkeley and Los Angeles: University of California Press 1968

Weber, Eugen: *France Fin de Siècle*. Cambridge, Massachusetts: The Belknap Press of Harvard University Press 1986

Weber, Eugen: *The Hollow Years: France in the 1930s*. London: Sinclair Stevenson 1995

Weisberg, Richard H.: *Vichy Law and the Holocaust in France*. Amsterdam: Harwood Academic Publishers 1996

Wellers, Georges: 'Le Cas Darquier de Pellepoix'. *Revue d'Histoire de la Shoah, Le Monde Juif*, No. 92, Octobre–Décembre 1978, pp.162–7

Wellers, Georges: *Un Juif sous Vichy*. Paris: Éditions Tiresias 1991

Werth, Alexander: *France in Ferment*. London: Jarrolds 1934

Werth, Alexander: *The Last days of Paris: A Journalist's Diary*. London: Hamish Hamilton 1940

Werth, Alexander: *The Twilight of France: A Journalist's Chronicle 1933–1940*. London: Hamish Hamilton 1942

Weygand, General Maxime: *Recalled to Service*. Translated from the French by E.W. Dickens. London: William Heinemann Ltd 1952 (French edition: *Rappelé au service*, Vol 3 of *Mémoires*. Paris: Flammarion 1950–57)

Whitaker, Arthur P.: *Spain and the Defense of the West: Ally and Liability*. New York: Harper & Brothers 1961

White, Antonia: *The BBC at War*. Wembley: British Broadcasting Corporation 1941

Williamson, David G.: *The British in Germany 1918–1930: The Reluctant Occupiers*. New York and Oxford: Berg 1991

Winock, Michel: *Nationalism, Anti-Semitism and Fascism in France*. Translated by Jane Marie Todd. Stanford, California: Stanford University Press 1998

Wistrich, Robert S.: 'Pope Pius XII and the Holocaust'. *The Times Literary Supplement*, 3 May 2002

Wohl, Robert: *The Generation of 1914*. London: Weidenfeld & Nicolson 1980

Yvert, Benoit: *Dictionnaire des ministres (1789–1989)*. Paris: Perrin 1990

Zucotti, Susan: *The Holocaust, the French and the Jews*. New York: Basic Books 1993

Archives and Libraries

FRANCE

Paris and environs
Archives de la Préfecture de Police (APP)
Archives Municipales de Neuilly-sur-Seine
Archives Municipales de Paris
Archives Nationales (AN)
Bibliothèque de la Mairie de Paris
Bibliothèque Nationale de France (BNF)
Centre de Documentation Juive Contemporaine (CDJC)
Centre des Archives Contemporaines (CAC), Fontainebleau
Institut National de l'Audiovisuel (INA) – Phonothèque
Mairie de Neuilly
Service Historique de l'Armée de Terre (SHAT), Vincennes

Provinces
Archives Départementales de la Haute-Garonne, Toulouse
Archives Départementales du Tarn et Garonne, Montauban
Archives Départementales du Bas-Rhin, Strasbourg
Archives Départementales du Lot, Cahors
Archives Diocésaines de Cahors
Archives Municipales, Strasbourg
Archives Municipales, Toulouse
Bibliothèque Municipale de Cahors
Bibliothèque Municipale de Strasbourg
Lycée Gambetta, Cahors
Mairie de Cahors
Médiathèque Valéry Larbaud, Vichy
Musée de la Résistance de la Déportation et de la Libération du Lot, Cahors

AUSTRALIA

Tasmania
Archives Office of Tasmania, Hobart,
Launceston Church Grammar School, Mowbray Heights, Launceston
Launceston Library

Queen Victoria Museum and Art Gallery, Launceston Community History
   Department
The Supreme Court, Hobart, Tasmania Probate Registry
Westbury Historical Society

Victoria
Australian Wheat Board, Melbourne
Baillieu Library, University of Melbourne
Institute for the Study of French–Australian Relations, Melbourne
Melba Conservatorium, Melbourne
Performing Arts Museum, Victorian Arts Centre, Melbourne
Public Record Office, Melbourne
State Library of Victoria, Melbourne

ACT
Australian War Memorial, Canberra
French embassy, Canberra
National Archives of Australia, Canberra
National Library of Australia, Canberra

NSW
French Consulate, Sydney
State Library of NSW, Sydney

Registries of Births, Deaths and Marriages, Tasmania, Victoria, NSW, Queensland,
   South Australia, Canberra

BRITAIN

British Library, London
Centre for Oxfordshire Studies, Oxford
D'Oyly Carte Opera Company, London
Education Department, Oxfordshire County Council, Oxford
Family Records Centre, London
General Register Office, Births, Marriages and Deaths, London
Kidlington Library
London Library
London Metropolitan Archives
London School of Economics Library
The National Archives, Public Record Office, Kew
Newspaper Library, Colindale

Oxford County Record Office
Probate Service, Principal Registry Family Division, London
Registrar General, Belfast
St Hilda's Archive, St Hilda's College, Oxford
Theatre Museum, London
Wiener Library, London
Windsor Registry Office

SPAIN

AGA : Archivo General de la Administración, Alcalá de Henares, Paseo Aquadores, 2, 28804, Alcalá de Henares (Madrid)
AGA (a): Ministerio de Educaciòn y Ciencia, Relaciones de Personal de Idiomas. Antiguas Plantillas 1960/70 93352, Ref: 3/91
AGA (b): Ministerio de Cultura No. IDD 49.23, Signatura 54.401
AGA (c): Ministerio de Educaciòn y Ciencia Relaciones de Personal de Idiomas. Antiguas Plantillas 1960/70 93352, Ref. 3/91
AGA (d): Ministerio de Cultura No. IDD 49.23, Signatura 54.401
AGA (e): Ministerio de Cultura No. IDD 49.24, Signatura 873–877 and 47615
AGA (f): AE (Asuntos Exteriores) No. IDD 97, Signatura 11.619 and 11.649
AGA (g): AE (Asuntos Exteriores) No. IDD 97, Signatura 11.631
AMAE: Archivo del Ministerio de Asuntos Exteriores. Departamentos Ministeriales, Madrid, Fondo 1.2.1.2
AMAE (a): Archivo del Consulado de España en Hendaya, Embajada de España en Francia 1939–44
AMAE (b): Politica: Información y Negociaciones, R 2295
AMAE (c): Información Politica Interior de Francia 1943–44, R-1179
AMAE (d): Salida de Alemania para España de periodistas franceses, R-2167
AMAE (e): Segunda Guerra Mundial, Francia: Immigrantes Clandestinos de Francia, R-2182
AMAE (f): Judios en Francia, R-1715

Archivo de la Villa, Madrid
Archivo Histórico Nacional, Madrid
Ayuntamiento de Carratraca, Andalucia
Ayuntamiento de Madrid, Area de Cultura, Archivo de Villa
Biblioteca Nacional, Madrid
Club Internacional de Prensa, Madrid
Instituto Nacional de Estadistica, Madrid
Institute of Spanish Studies Library, LSE, London
Ministerio de Cultura y Educación

Radio Nacional de España, Madrid
Registero Civil Único, Madrid
Registro de la Propiedad, Madrid

GERMANY

Bundesarchiv, Berlin, Stiftung Archiv der Parteien und Massenorganisationen der
    DDR im Bundesarchiv. Bibliotek
Institut für Zeitgeschichte, Munchen
Landesarchiv, Berlin
Staatsarchiv, Ludwigsburg
Staatsbibliothek, Berlin
Staatsbibliothek, Ludwigsburg
Stadtarchiv, Erfurt
Stadtbibliotek, Potsdam
Technische Universitt, Berlin, Zentrum fr Antisemitismusforschung. Bibliotek
Thüringgisches Hauptstaatsarchiv, Weimar

USA

NARA, US National Archives and Records Administration: Records of the US
    Office of Strategic Services COI/OSS Central Files 1942–1946

BELGIUM

Stadsbibliotheek, Antwerp

Interviews and Private Sources

FRANCE

Letters of Louis and Myrtle Darquier to René Darquier: given to me by members
of the René Darquier family
    Family letters of the Arteil, Constanty, Vayssade and Darquier families
1880–1954: given to me by Mme Paulette Aupoix, Darquier family friend
    Simone Reste, former employee of Louise Darquier: her own account of
1937–44 and of the Darquier family

Interviews, in person or by telephone, were conducted by myself, by Sylvie Deroche, and by Pierre Wolf

Cahors

Albert Atlan, prison guard, representative of the Jewish community at the Museum of the Resistance, Cahors; Paulette Aupoix, Darquier family friend; René Bergougnoux, Maison Diocésaine des Œuvres, Cahors; Jacques Bertrand, shopkeeper; Nicole Bousquet, bibliothécaire; Colette Calmon, daughter of Elie Calmon, former Deputy for the Lot, with Pierre Gayet and alone; Bernard Charles, Deputy Mayor of Cahors; Pierre Combes, Director of the Museum of the Resistance, Cahors, former resistant; Philippe Deladerrière, Secretary of the Society of Studies for the Lot; Alain Dubrulle, Principal du Collège Gambetta, président de l'Amicale des Anciens de Gambetta; Pierre Gayet, son of Darquier family friend; Pierre Laborie, École des Hautes Études en Sciences Sociales; Yvonne Lacaze, Darquier family friend, former lawyer and magistrate; Père Lucien Lachièze-Rey; Alexandre Marciel, Mairie de Cahors; Pierre Orliac, doctor; Pierre Pouzergues, horticulturalist; Hélène Raimondeau; Simone Reste, former employee of Louise Darquier.

Paris

M. Michel Blum, Philippe Ganier-Raymond's lawyer; Jean-Louis Crémieux-Brilhac; Maud de Belleroche; Anne-Marie Fiel, companion of Philippe Ganier-Raymond; Henri Fernet, former member of the Waffen SS Division Charlemagne; Nathalie Ganier-Raymond, daughter of Philippe Ganier-Raymond; Jean Gayet, son of family friend, brother of Pierre; Serge Klarsfeld, lawyer and author, with his wife Beate responsible for bringing to trial many Nazi and Vichy war criminals; Bertrand Leary, grandson of Henry Lèvy; Auguste Mudry, former employee of the CGQJ; Pierre Pujo; Emile Cabié, formerly Examining Magistrate, in charge of the Darquier affair in 1978

Other

Mme Andrieu, Narbonne, daughter of Georges Maury, Darquier family friend; Serge Déjean, Château de Pellepoix, Beaumont-sur-Lèze; Jean Michel Fabre, *La Dépêche du Midi*; Pierre Gérard, former Director of the Archives Départementales, Toulouse; Jean Lindoerfer, former employee of Les Grands Moulins de Strasbourg; Alain Roux, proprietor of Château, Domaine de Pellepoix; Henri Thamier, former Deputy and resistant

Australia

Some information came from correspondence and phone conversations with members of the Jones family in Launceston and Toowoomba, and from extracts from notes made by Heather Jones Murdoch in 1981 on 'The lives of Louis and Myrtle (San) D'Arquier', sent to me by a younger member of the Jones family

Beryl Stevenson of Carrick provided me with letters and documents concerning the Jones family in Carrick

Interviews, in person or by telephone, were conducted by myself, by Julie Evans, and by Lucille Andel

M. Ivan Barko, Sydney; Jacqueline Dwyer, author, Sydney; Michael Cathcart, Lecturer, the Australian Centre, University of Melbourne; Diane Dunbar, Queen Victoria Museum and Art Gallery, Launceston; Paulette Flipo, Melbourne; French Department, University of Melbourne; Jenny Gill, Archivist, Launceston Church Grammar School; Doug Hunter, military historian, NSW; Paul McFarlane, Director of College Development, Scotch Oakburn College; Mr Stewart Morrison and Gwen Scott, Westbury Historical Society, Tasmania; Elizabeth Richards, military historian, NSW; staff at the Australian War Memorial, Canberra; Colin Thornton Smith, formerly French Department, University of Melbourne; Beryl Stevenson, Carrick

Spain

Interviews, email correspondence and phone conversations with Teresa, daughter of Louis Darquier

Interviews, in person or by telephone, were done by myself, by Cristina Rivas, by Sylvie Deroche, and by Helena Ivins

Consuelo Alvarado, British Council in Madrid; Emilia Angulo, former employee, French embassy; Eileen Ashcroft, librarian, British embassy; Jean-Michel Bamberger, journalist, and Juana (Biarnés) Bamberger, photographer; Antonio Marquina Barrio; Anne Bateson, Press Club of Madrid; John Booth, former head of immigration at the Australian embassy in Madrid; Diana Burr, secretary to the British Ambassador in Madrid; Bill Christian; Mrs Maria Clark, formerly of the Escuele Central de Idiomas, Madrid; David Codling, Director, Arts and Literature, the British Council, Madrid; Louis de Bérard, French consulate, Madrid; Michael de Bertadano, colleague of Louis Darquier in Madrid; Jeanne Degrelle, first married to Henry Charbonneau, now widow of Léon Degrelle; Carmen de la Guardia, Departamento de Historia Contemporanea, Cantoblanco, Autonoma University of Madrid; Damaso de Lario, diplomat, Madrid; Professor Juan Avilés Farré, Universidad Nacional de Educación a Distancia, Madrid; Nigel Glendinning; Miguel Guerrero, Secretario de Juzgado, Carratraca; Father Raymond Hodson, Church of St George; Gerald Howson, historian; Jean-Louis Huberti (Alain Baudroux), former correspondent of *France-Inter* in Madrid; Jean Ibbitson MBE, Church librarian, Church of St George; Michael Jacobs; Père Michel Lewkowicz, Église Saint-Louis des Français; María del Carmen Mansilla, Subsecretaria General Técnica, Ministry of Information and Tourism; Cristina Gonzales Martin, directrice, Archives Ministerio de Asuntos Exterios, Madrid; Brian Nield, Director, École Briam; Francisco Perez, caretaker, British Cemetery, Madrid; Catherine Portera, formerly of French embassy, Madrid; Paul Preston; Commander John Rigge, former naval attaché, and Mrs Pat Rigge, Madrid; Casimir Tilco, translator for Radio Nacional and Ministry of Foreign Affairs, Madrid; Peter Torry, British Embassy, Madrid; Georges Tourlet, French journalist, Madrid; Jane Walker, *Guardian* correspondent; Daniel Wickham, British Embassy, Madrid

BRITAIN

Elsie Lightfoot's documents and Brice-Lightfoot family albums and information: given to me by Alistair Rapley, great-nephew of Elsie Lightfoot, son of May Brice and Anne Darquier's godson

Interviews, in person or by telephone, were done by myself, or by Helena Ivins

Great Tew
Tony Clifton; The Revd Robin Denniston, formerly Vicar of St Michael and All Angels, and Rosa Denniston; Julia Keal; Violet Kench; Danny Puddefoot, friend of May Brice; Mary Tustain; Michael Varney

Oxfordshire
Elizabeth Boardman, Archivist, St Hilda's College, Oxford; Peter Buckman, Little Tew; Beryl Coombes, née Beryl Clifton of Great Tew, childhood friend of Anne Darquier; Bill Coy, former director of a City of Oxford children's home; Gertie Eley, Enstone; Elaine Fraser, Jennifer Jowsey, Dr Ruth Klemperer, Hilda Moorhouse, Janet Purvis, Isobel Rhodes and Natalie Rothstein, Naomi Roberts, Muriel Watson, contemporaries of Anne Darquier at St Hilda's College, Oxford – correspondence; Margaret Gilson, Old Windsor; Richard Graydon, Chipping Norton School; Eanswythe Hunter, Little Tew; Elizabeth Llewellyn-Smith, Principal, St Hilda's College, Oxford; Patrick Marnham, Church Enstone; Brenda Morris, Chipping Norton School; Mrs Mary Phipps, Kidlington Historical Society; Gerry Tyack, Wellington Aviation Museum, Moreton in Marsh; Fred Wright, formerly of Cotuit Hall, a City of Oxford children's home

Kidlington

John Amor, Kidlington Historical Society; Ron Carver, former student of East Ham Grammar School; Christine Causby, Secretary, Gosford Hill School; Elizabeth Harrington, Kidlington Historical Society; Audrey Kirby, former student of East Ham Grammar School; Pat Smalley, former student of East Ham Grammar School

London

Keith Austin, Archivist, University of London Archive; Dr A.C.S. Bloomer; Jeremy Bugler; Dr Mary Coghlan; Dr Peter Dally; Dr Jack Dominion; Monseigneur Walter Drumm, formerly Catholic chaplain, Oxford; Griffith Edwards; Michael Field; Dr Hugh Freeman; Colin Gale, Archivist of the Bethlem Royal Hospital; Frank Gentry, Newnham History Society; Eva Hamburger; Dr C.W.H. Havard; Julia Hobsbawm; Dr Helen Hudson, formerly Dean of Women Students, King's College, London; Dr Maurice Lipsedge; Mary Havard Miller; Maureen O'Neill; David Pryce-Jones; Marion Rea, Archivist, St Bartholomew's Hospital; Professor Linford Rees; Professor Adrian Smith, Principal, Queen Mary, University of London; Kate Straus; Dr Benjamin Ward; Dr Diane Watson; Dr Peter Whatmore; David Williamson, author

GERMANY

Interviews conducted by Klemens Rothig

Hadassa Ben-Itto, author; Magnus Brechtken, historian

Index

◄O►

Abetz, Otto 151, *213*; 'reconciliation' work in Paris 151–2; expelled for subversive activities 184, 186; appointed German ambassador 206; finances newspapers 528*n*25, 533*n*12; lists LD as pre-war sympathiser 206; authorised to seize Jewish works of art 340, 341; relationship with Laval 206; and Paris *collabos* 208; and Pétain's arrest of Laval 215–16; and deportation of Jews 230, 286; finances *Le Juif et la France* exhibition 238; reports to Berlin on Catholic collaboration 239; and LD's appointment to head CGQJ 216, 243, 265; in touch with de Monzie 245; and hostility between Laval and LD 263, 264; entertains LD at embassy 266; secures release of Colette's husband 284; friendship with Lequerica 306; and *Liste Otto* 309; his German Institute becomes artistic and cultural centre 311; supports Laval 312; summoned back to Berlin 278; back in Paris 366; entertained by Céline 311; dismisses Laval 378; oversees detainees at Sigmaringen 379; on LD 444; postwar 565*n*34
Abetz, Suzanne (*née* de Bruycker) 151, 311
Abyssinia, Italian invasion of 102, 125, 133
Achenbach, Dr Ernst *213*, 264, 317–18, 389, 554*n*63, 555*n*67, 565–6*n*34
Action Française: and Catholic Church 16, 18–19, 103, 154; and Maurras 18, 19–20, 98–9, 103, 154; influence on LD 19, 20, 102; and Camelots 32–3; and World War I leaders 45; at height of power 51; active in Alsace 53; anti-immigrants 101; membership (1934) 497*n*16; LD as member 102, 103, 104–5, 112, 113; and dissident groups 103–4; and Stavisky scandal 106, 107; directors visit LD in hospital 112; works with Front National 117; stages funeral for Bainville 129; dissolved by government 129; members form Vigilance Committee 131; and LD 147, 148, 180; and Cagoulards 165; postwar name change 102–3

Action française (newspaper) 130; Maurras' articles and influence 18–19, 102, 148; in World War I 45; read by intellectuals 51; Daudet's articles 102, 174; and Stavisky scandal 106, 107; lists LD as 'Our Wounded' 111; and LD's new association 113, 117, 118; celebrates LD's election as councillor 124; survives the dissolution of Action Française 129; publicises LD's speeches and activities 130, 134, 147, 154, 161; peddles idea that Hitler is a Jew 162; and Munich Agreement 174; backs LD in Lecache case 176; Maurras continues publication during Occupation 225–6, 371, 388; Maulnier writes for 502*n*29
Adams, Caroline 'Totie' Bessel 57, 58, 489*n*13, 490*n*20
AF *see* Action Française
Affiches Rouges (death notices) 219–20
Agobardus, Bishop of Lyon 130
Ajalbert, Jean 572*n*5
Algerian War of Independence (1954–62) 409, 410
Alibert, Raphaël 225, 232, 532*n*8, 533*n*24
Alsace-Lorraine 51, 53; map 54
Anglo-American Aryan Protection League 163
Anouilh, Jean 312
Antignac, Joseph 562–3*n*7; personality 279, 280; succeeds Galien at CGQJ 279–81, 326, 397; and Bouvyer 271; accused of stealing 554*n*65; and LD's broadcasts 320; and Aryanisation Section 328, 334, 335; controls SEC 329; and theft of Schloss collection 344, 347, 357; and decimation of UGIF staff 355; usurps LD as head of CGQJ 366, 367; arrested 380; saved from execution by ill health 388; exposed in Billig's book 427
Anti-Jewish Union 157–8, 159, 164, 165, 166, 169–70, 172, 176, 177–8, 179, 231, 241
Antijuif, l' (newspaper) 157–8, 158, 159, 161–4, 171
Apollinaire, Guillaume 488*n*4
Aragon, Elsa (*née* Triolet) 464
Aragon, Louis 125, 463–4; 'The Snows of Sigmaringen' 464–7

Club 145–6 (*see entries*); publishes *Bulletin*
146–7, 152–3; and Maurras 147, 148, 149,
154; instructed by de Monzie to act less
wildly 150; attacks Romanian barman
151, 165; receives further cheques from
Germany 151, 152, 153–4, 155, 163,
165–6; trains dog to chase Jews 156;
launches Anti-Jewish Union and *l'Antijuif*
157 (*see entries*); clashes with Lecache
159–60, 170; celebrates Maurras' release
from prison 161; has links with La
Cagoule 164–5; expelled from
Switzerland 165; relationship with Céline
167–9; opens Anti-Jewish Union office
in Strasbourg 169–70; launches *La France
enchaînée* 171 (*see entry*); meets Galien 175;
causes *tumulte* at council meeting 171–2;
invited to meet Rosenberg and Bohle
173; meets George VI and Queen
Elizabeth 173–4; court case against
Lecache 176, 183; his union now most
important anti-Semitic organisation
176–8; denounced as homosexual 177;
breaks with Maurras 177; earns his
German keep 180–1; prosecuted under
Marchandeau Law 181, 182–3, 184–6,
187; in restaurant brawl 187

1939–42
joins up 187–8; cited for bravery
190–91; as prisoner-of-war in Poland
191, 198, 203–4; released 204–5, 206;
back in France 206–7, 209–10, 214–15;
as candidate for Commissioner of
CGQJ 216; receives decorations
216–17, 218; Elsie Lightfoot fails to
track down 217–18; obtains fictitious
post in CGQJ 219, 221; and Dannecker
225; declines to set up *Le Juif et la
France* exhibition 238; refuses to attend
Céline's *Au Pilori* meeting 241; invites
Montandon to join his Union 241;
collaborates with Sézille 241; writes
article for IEQJ publication 241;
replaces Vallat as head of CGQJ 243,
244–5, 246, 247–8, 249, 264–5; takes
revenge on René 247; publicity, praise
and denunciations 250–53; further
demands that he pay for Anne's keep
253, 361; in Vichy 249, 254, 255, 256–7,
258; attacked in BBC broadcast 255–6,
257, 260, 263; filmed with Heydrich
283; pesters Laval for the means to
accomplish his mission 258–9, 261;

takes over Paris office of CGQJ
249–50, 266–7, 272; and 'Aryanisation'
programme 267, 272–4; accepts bribes
from rich Jews 276; instigates Star of
David 268–9; opens new CGQJ offices
269; loses police force to Bousquet 261,
263, 270; and SEC 270, 275; and deportations of Jews 259, 260, 284, 286,
287–8, 303, 304; and Vel' d'Hiv' round-
up 289–93; found to be grossly inadequate 263, 264–5, 304; revenges himself
in *Die Judenfrage* 264; clashes with
Galien 276–7, 278; saved by Antignac
279–81; involvement reduced to writing
and receiving letters 293–5, 297, 299;
and Bousquet's round-ups 296,
299–300, 301

1942–80
lives the good life in Paris 305, 307–9;
uses Propaganda Staffel to issue plans
for disposal of Jews 310; distances
himself from Céline 311; prepares new
anti-Jewish decrees 314–16; creates
Union Française pour la Défense de la
Race 316–17 (*see entry*); outlines propaganda proposals 317–19; allowed to
give radio broadcasts 319–20, 363; and
further deportations 320; and
'economic Aryanisation' 326–30, 331,
333–7; attacks Laval at press conference 321, 342; drafts denaturalisation
bill 350, 352–3, 355–6, 357; removed as
president of UFDR 320–23, 352; and
Schloss collection 323, 343–8, 352, 356,
359; and closure of his institutes 324,
358; attempts to buy *Au Pilori* 324–5;
vanishes 356–7; housed at Nazi hotel
358–9; gives interview 359; Laval engi-
neers his punishment 359–60; makes
speech at opening of Aryan Club 360;
forced to submit resignation from
CGQJ 366–7; and Liberation of Paris
377, 379, 380, 381–2; escape to Spain
382, 383–4; and life in Madrid 384–5,
386, 387, 389–90, 391, 397, 399, 408;
and birth of second daughter 385, 386
(*see* Teresa); sentenced to death *in
absentia* 397, 398; meeting with Anne
398–400; meetings with other exiles
409–10; receives visitors 411, 412;
employed by Ministry of Information
and Tourism 413–14, 427; translates
Castiella's *Red Book of Gibraltar* 414;